WITH WINGS AS EAGLES

THE EIGHTH AIR FORCE IN WORLD WAR II

PHILIP KAPLAN

Skyhorse Publishing
New York

Skyhorse Publishing books may be purchased in bulk at special discounts for sales promotion, corporate gifts, fund-raising, or educational purposes. Special editions can also be created to specifications. For details, contact the Special Sales Department, Skyhorse Publishing, 307 West 36th Street, 11th Floor, New York, NY 10018 or info@skyhorsepublishing.com.

Visit our website at www.skyhorsepublishing.com.

Page 284 is an extension of this copyright page.

10 9 8 7 6 5 4 3 2

Library of Congress Cataloging-in-Publication Data is available on file.

Cover design by Rain Saukas
Cover photo: Author's collection

Print ISBN: 978-1-5107-0510-4
Ebook ISBN: 978-1-5107-0515-9

Printed in China

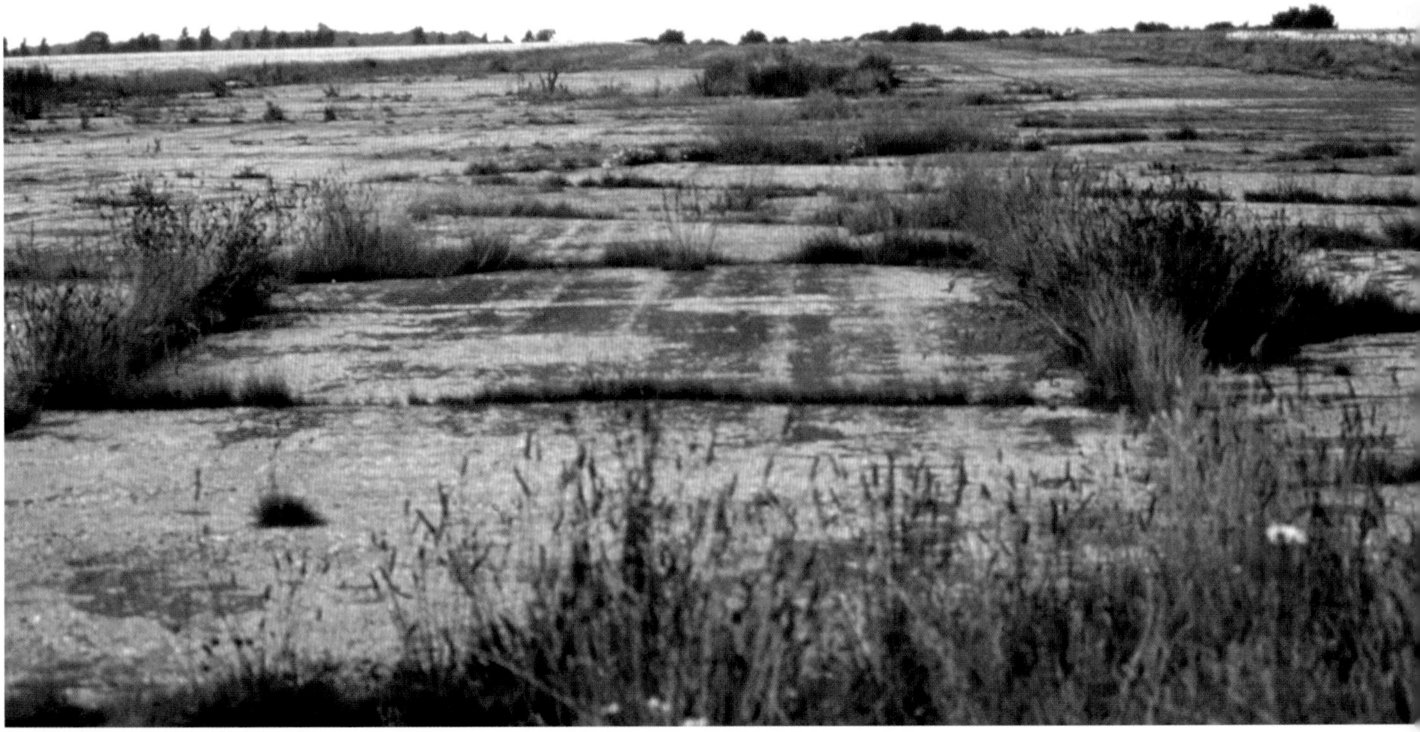

CONTENTS

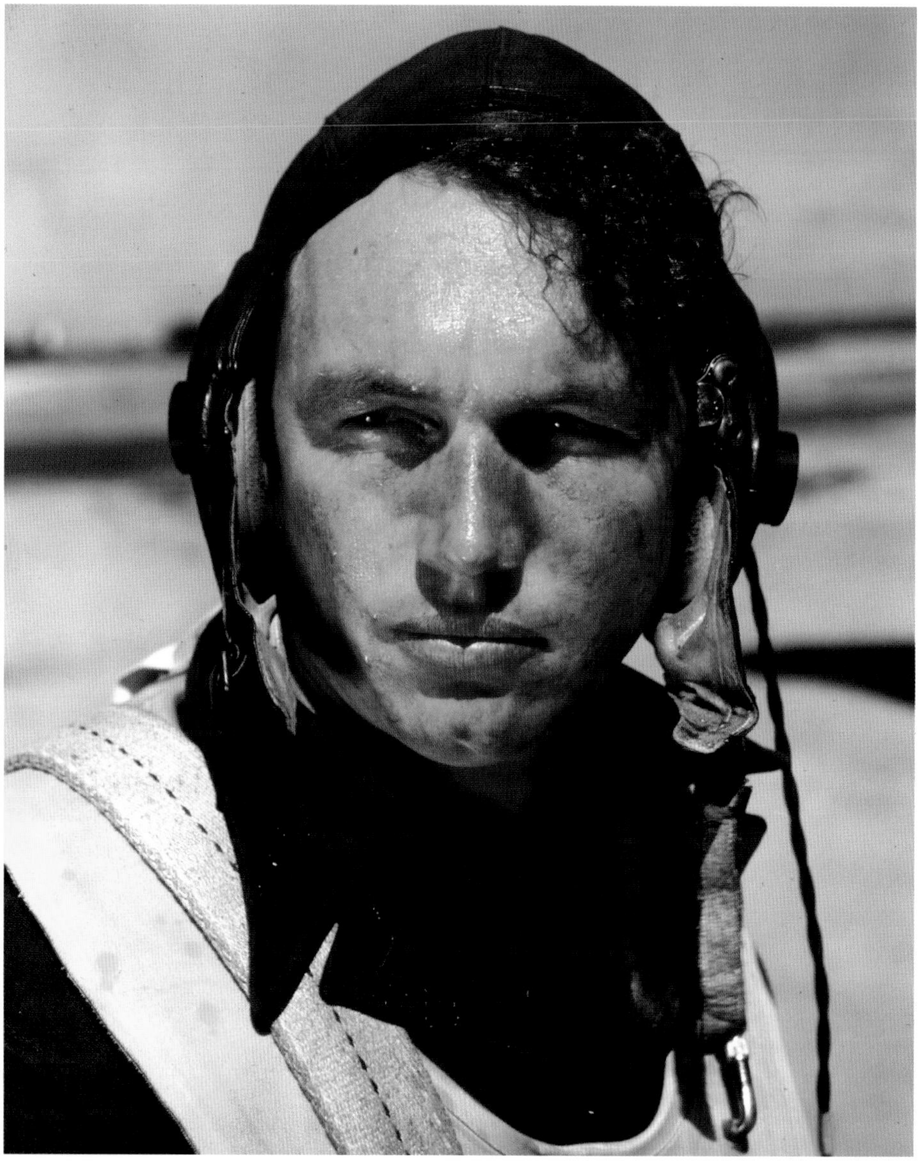

. . . they that wait upon the Lord shall renew their strength; they shall mount up with wings as eagles . . .
—Isaiah 40:31

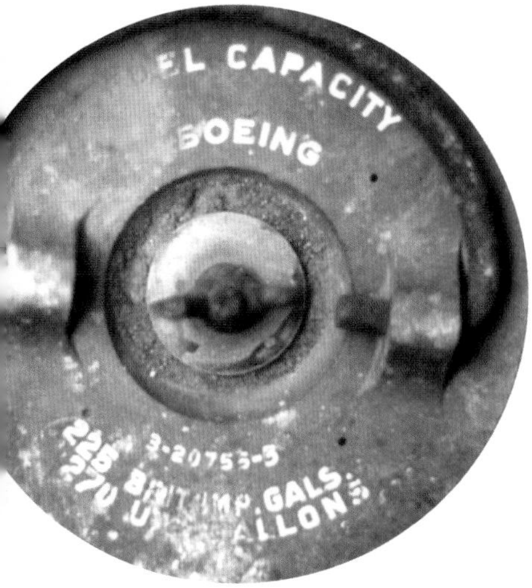

EL CAPACITY
BOEING

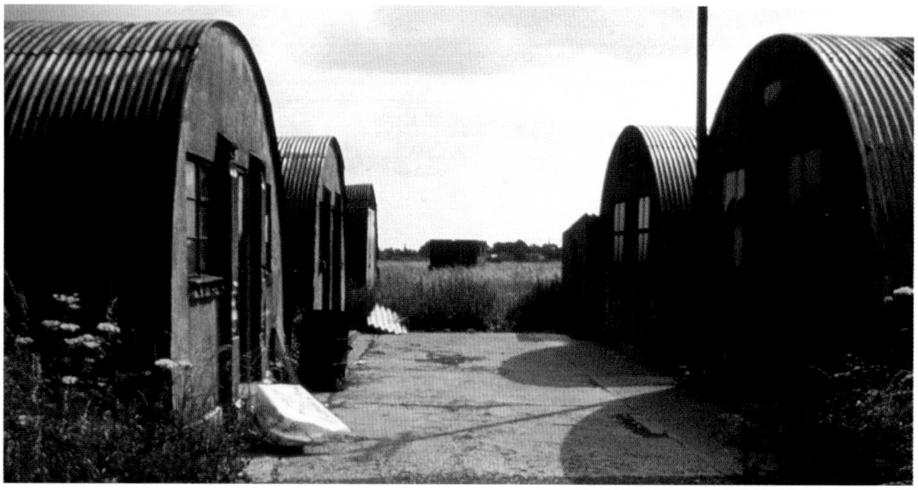

EAKER'S AMATEURS

"Somebody said that it couldn't be done, but he with a chuckle replied, that 'maybe' it couldn't, but he would be one who wouldn't say so till he'd tried. So he buckled right in with the trace of a grin on his face. If he worried he hid it. He started to sing as he tackled the thing that couldn't be done, and he did it."
—from Edgar Albert Guest's poem, "It Couldn't Be Done"

"We are coming, Father Abraham, three hundred thousand more."
—J.S. Gibbons

IT WOULD BECOME the most intensive, concentrated and effective air assault in history.

The American and British Chiefs of Staff met after the 7th December 1941 Japanese attack on US naval and air facilities and battleships at Pearl Harbor, Hawaii, an attack which brought the United States into the Second World War. Four days after that attack, Germany, an ally of Japan, had declared war on the U.S. When the Allied military leaders then conferred they had two goals in mind: To achieve air superiority over the German Air Force in order to prepare for an Allied invasion of the European continent; and to destroy Germany's war-making capacity.

The British Royal Air Force had been gradually building its own capability for taking the war to Germany and German targets in Continental Europe through a major strategic bombing effort. Having been at war with Germany since September 1939, the British government and the RAF welcomed the entry and participation of the Americans in the European air war. The RAF particularly relished the prospect of U.S. heavy bombers joining with their own aircraft in the raids they were conducting on an ever-increasing scale.

To that end the Americans set about to establish a new air force in the United Kingdom. It would ultimately become the largest and most powerful military air organization ever, and would, with the RAF, carry out a massive combined bombing offensive of almost unimaginable proportions against the German enemy.

Early in 1942 the vanguard of nearly 350,000 American Army Air Force men of widely differing backgrounds began arriving in England, where the population had already been enduring the dangers and deprivation of war for more than two years. These Yanks, as the British referred to them, came determined to do their part in the high-altitude bombing of German targets in Europe, but they had been trained to do so by daylight and not at night as the British did. Earlier in the war the RAF had tried daylight bombing and had declared it impossible. Thus, the policy battle lines were drawn between these two old allies. In time, however, the argument was settled and the Americans won the chance to prove their case for daylight precision bombing—which they did—but only at an enormous cost in lives and equipment. It would be a period of great danger for them, and death for many. It was also a time of endless fatigue, boredom, true comradeship, and the excitement of radically new experiences and emotions. For most it was destined to be the one great adventure of their lives. Those who flew the demanding, dramatic, and frequently spectacular bombing missions of the American Army Air Force from English airfields during World War Two had an utterly unique experience, incomparable to any before or since.

With four distinct U.S. Army Air Forces established and operating, the new UK-based outfit was to be the Fifth U.S.A.A.F., but within days of the new organization's designation, it was redesignated the Eighth, as the Fifth and two additional air forces had been planned for other assignments. By late March 1942, at the suggestion of Major General Carl Spaatz, commanding general-designate of the Eighth, his new organization was committed to be the nucleus of the American offensive air operations from the United Kingdom.

The Eighth Air Force would be assigned the most challenging, demanding, and dangerous job of those given to all American air forces in that war—the high-altitude daylight precision bombing campaign against Nazi Germany. Would the attacks of the Eighth, together with those of the RAF by night, sufficiently weaken German war production to reduce the cost in lives of the eventual Allied invasion of Europe? Could the Eighth be equipped and brought up to required strength quickly without unduly hampering USAAF operations in other war theatres? Could the bombing campaign of the Eighth be conducted within the parameters of acceptable losses? The young, inexperienced American air force in England had no answers to these questions. No one knew if high-altitude precision bombing of the German targets by day could be carried out successfully amid enemy flak and fighter defenses and the prevailing weather conditions in northwestern Europe. RAF leadership was politely sceptical and few in the high command of the Eighth were more than guardedly optimistic. But we are getting ahead of our story.

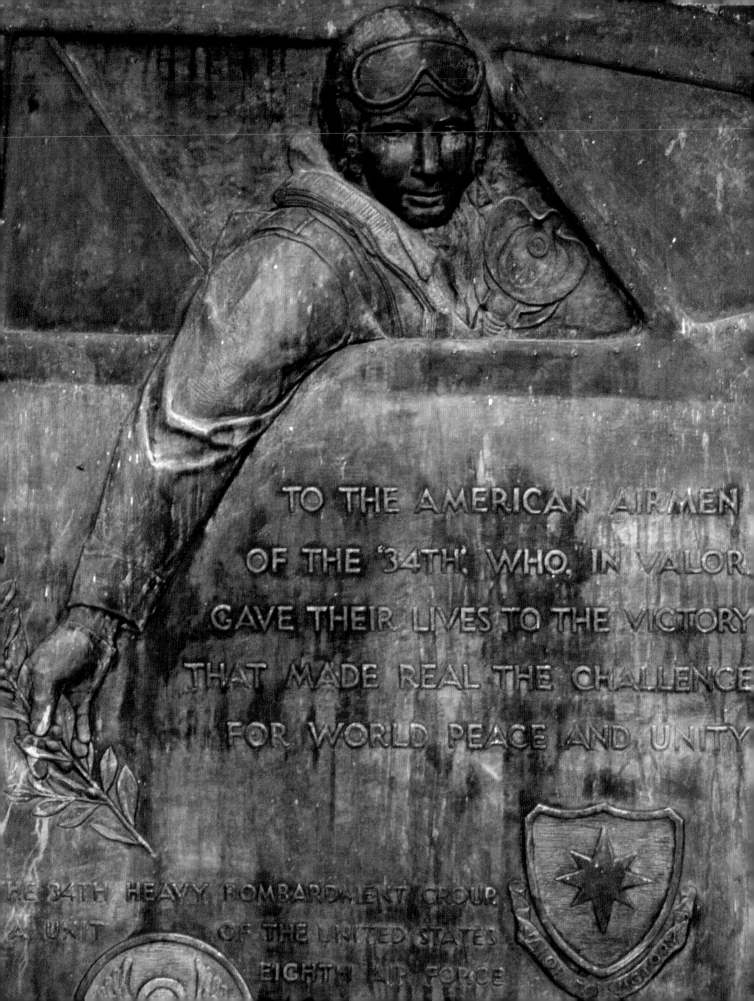

TO THE AMERICAN AIRMEN
OF THE '34TH' WHO, IN VALOR
GAVE THEIR LIVES TO THE VICTORY
THAT MADE REAL THE CHALLENGE
FOR WORLD PEACE AND UNITY

THE 34TH HEAVY BOMBARDMENT GROUP
A UNIT   OF THE UNITED STATES
EIGHTH AIR FORCE

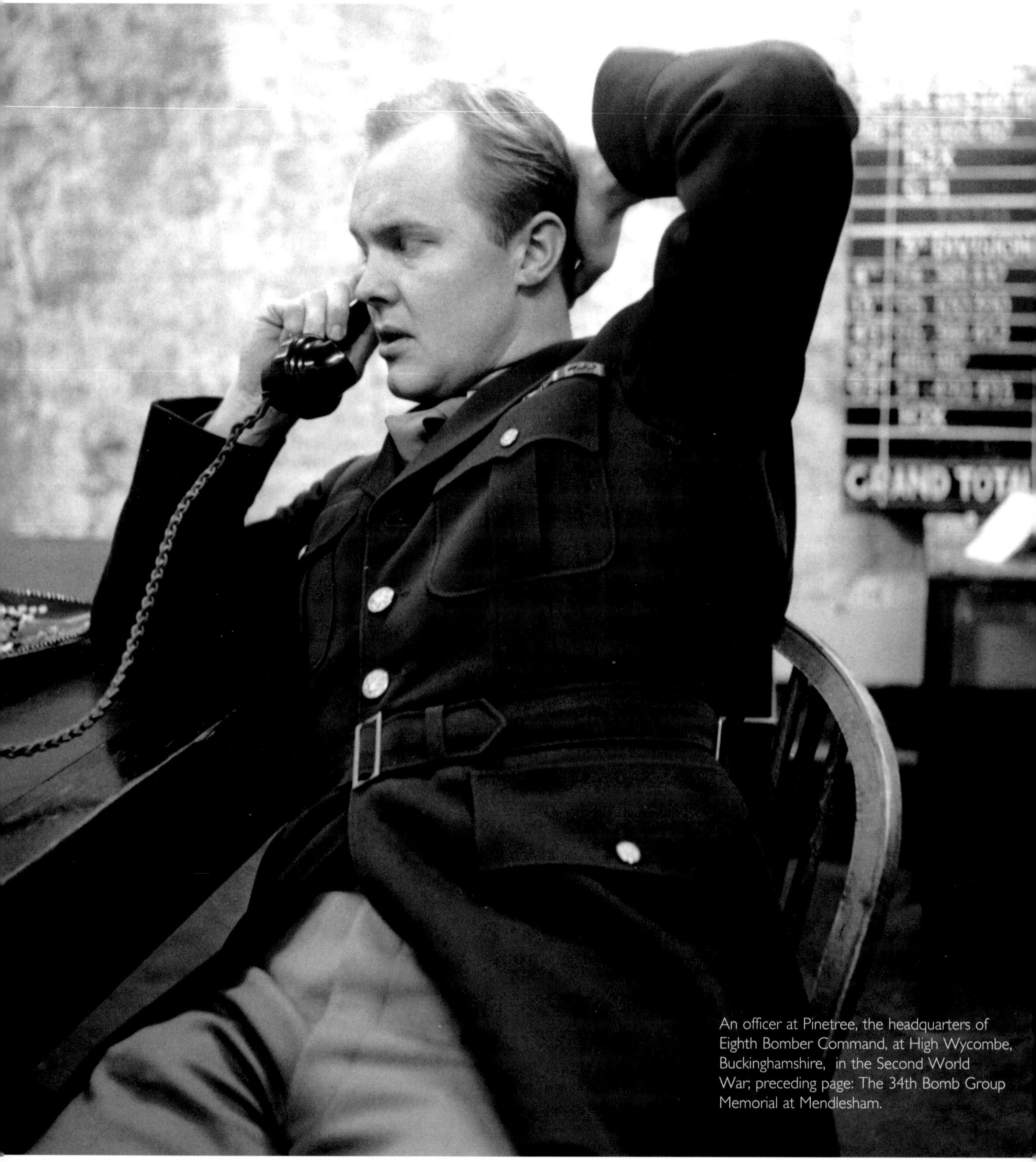

An officer at Pinetree, the headquarters of Eighth Bomber Command, at High Wycombe, Buckinghamshire, in the Second World War; preceding page: The 34th Bomb Group Memorial at Mendlesham.

20th February 1942 dawned gray and unpromising and would remain that way. Allied flights from Lisbon to Britain in those days meant risking interception by long-ranging German patrol aircraft operating over the Bay of Biscay from French bases. One such flight arriving that day at RAF Hendon, a Douglas DC-3/Dakota, carried an American air force officer who initially would be responsible for arranging the reception of the new combat flying units of the Eighth, a man who for many weeks had been studying the methods, means, procedures, and quirks of the RAF bombing operations against German targets. Brigadier General Ira C. Eaker was among America's foremost proponents of the USAAF version of strategic bombardment as a primary war-winning approach. General Eaker arrived in England at a point when war actions were mostly grim and depressing for the Allies. In addition to their surprising Pacific advances on and after their Pearl Harbor raid, the Japanese had invaded and taken Singapore, attacked and sunk the British battleships HMS *Prince of Wales* and HMS *Repulse*, and taken Bataan from the Americans; there was also the retreat of Allied armies across Libya, German panzer tanks nearing Stalingrad, and the massive Allied shipping losses on the Atlantic to Hitler's hunting U-boats. Yet another recent defeat of sorts was the "Channel Dash" escape of the German warships *Scharnhorst, Gneisenau,* and *Prinz Eugen* from their vulnerable anchorages in the harbor at Brest to a safer port in Germany. The British critics of air power were demanding an explanation for the failure of the RAF and the Fleet Air Arm to prevent that escape. Defending the poor results of that air power was proving a challenge for its champions in London.

A few positive signs were starting to appear, though. One was the arrival in the UK of General Eaker, charged with setting up a headquarters and laying the groundwork for the new Eighth Air Force, and the appointment of the no-nonsense Air Chief Marshal Arthur T. Harris to head up RAF Bomber Command.

Two months after Ira Eaker took up his new post two truly audacious bombing raids took place within hours of each other—one British, the other American. At that stage of the war, Harris's Bomber Command had only two squadrons that were then equipped with the Avro Lancaster

heavy bomber. He decided to try out his new Lancasters in a daring daylight operation deep into German territory. He mounted a small mission utilizing both Lanc squadrons, assigning them to fly a raid on the M.A.N. plant at Augsburg in Bavaria, where the bulk of diesel engines were manufactured for Germany's U-boat force. It was to be, at best, a bold, low-level, high-risk daylight venture that Harris believed had a good chance of success, a far better one than if it had been flown by the Stirlings, Manchesters, and Wellingtons that equipped most of his command. But the mission, flown in two elements of six aircraft each,

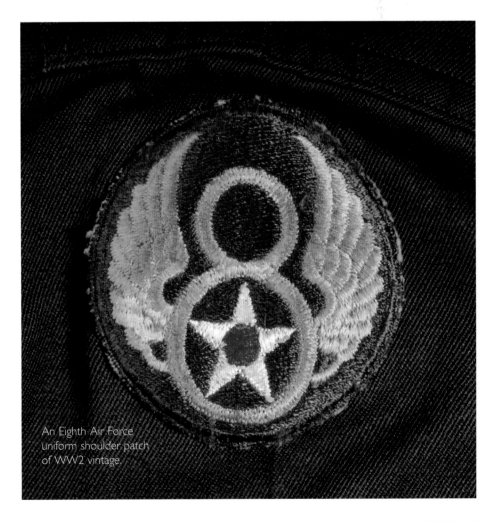

An Eighth Air Force uniform shoulder patch of WW2 vintage.

would depend heavily on an essential element of surprise. Due to a catastrophic navigational miscalculation the first group of six Lancasters happened to cross right over an enemy fighter airfield as they roared over France at low altitude. Me 109 fighters rose quickly to give chase to the lumbering Lancs and four of the big bombers were promptly shot down. A fifth heavy was hit and brought down by flak over Augsburg and two from the second group of six were also downed by target-area flak. Of the five Lancasters that managed to return to base in England that spring evening, two were heavily damaged. In the raid itself, the diesel engine factory was badly damaged by thirteen 1,000-pound bombs and Harris was able to point with pride to the undoubted heroism of its second group leader, Acting Squadron Leader John Nettleton, who was awarded Britain's highest decoration for gallantry on the mission, the Victoria Cross. One effect of the raid clearly demonstrated to Harris and the Air Ministry a fatal lack of firepower then available on the Lancaster, whose eight .303 machine-guns had been no match for the cannon-armed Messerschmitt fighters.

On the other side of the world, just a few hundred miles off the coast of Japan, Colonel Jimmy Doolittle took off from the aircraft carrier *Hornet* to lead sixteen B-25 Mitchell medium bombers on a strike at military targets in Tokyo and elsewhere on the island of Honshu. It was as bold and risky as the Augsburg attack that Harris had staged. It actually did little damage to Japan's war effort, but succeeded in showing the Japanese people that they were vulnerable to American air attack, which certainly damaged enemy morale.

Ira Eaker knew that the RAF crews

and commanders were extremely leary of the American daylight bombing concept, having suffered bitter losses in their own experience with such operations. Still, they accepted the determination of the Yanks to try their own daylight bombing experiment and would offer and provide the Americans every sort of assistance they could in the effort.

Arriving in England with Eaker that miserable winter day were six other USAAF officers who would assist him in getting the Eighth up and running. The men were Lieutenant Colonel Frank A. Armstrong Jr., who would later be the inspiration for the lead character of General Frank Savage in the book and motion picture *Twelve O'Clock High* by Beirne Lay Jr. and Sy Bartlett, both veterans of the air war against Germany; Major Peter Beasley; Captain Fred Castle, who would command the 94th Bomb Group and be killed while leading the 4th Combat Bomb Wing on a raid to attack German airfields, Christmas Eve 1944; Captain Beirne Lay Jr. the aforesaid co-author of *Twelve O'Clock High* and the first commander of the 487th Bomb Group at Lavenham, Suffolk; Lieutenants Harris Hull and William Cowart Jr. These seven were sometimes referred to as "Eaker's Amateurs."

Wycombe Abbey, a girl's school in High Wycombe, Buckinghamshire, was requisitioned in March 1942 to provide the Headquarters for the Eighth U.S. Army Air Force in England. Ira Eaker and his little advance party of officers were moved into Daws Hill Lodge, an appropriated country mansion on the property. It was handily located near the Headquarters of RAF Bomber Command. During the course of the war a substantial underground bunker was built beneath

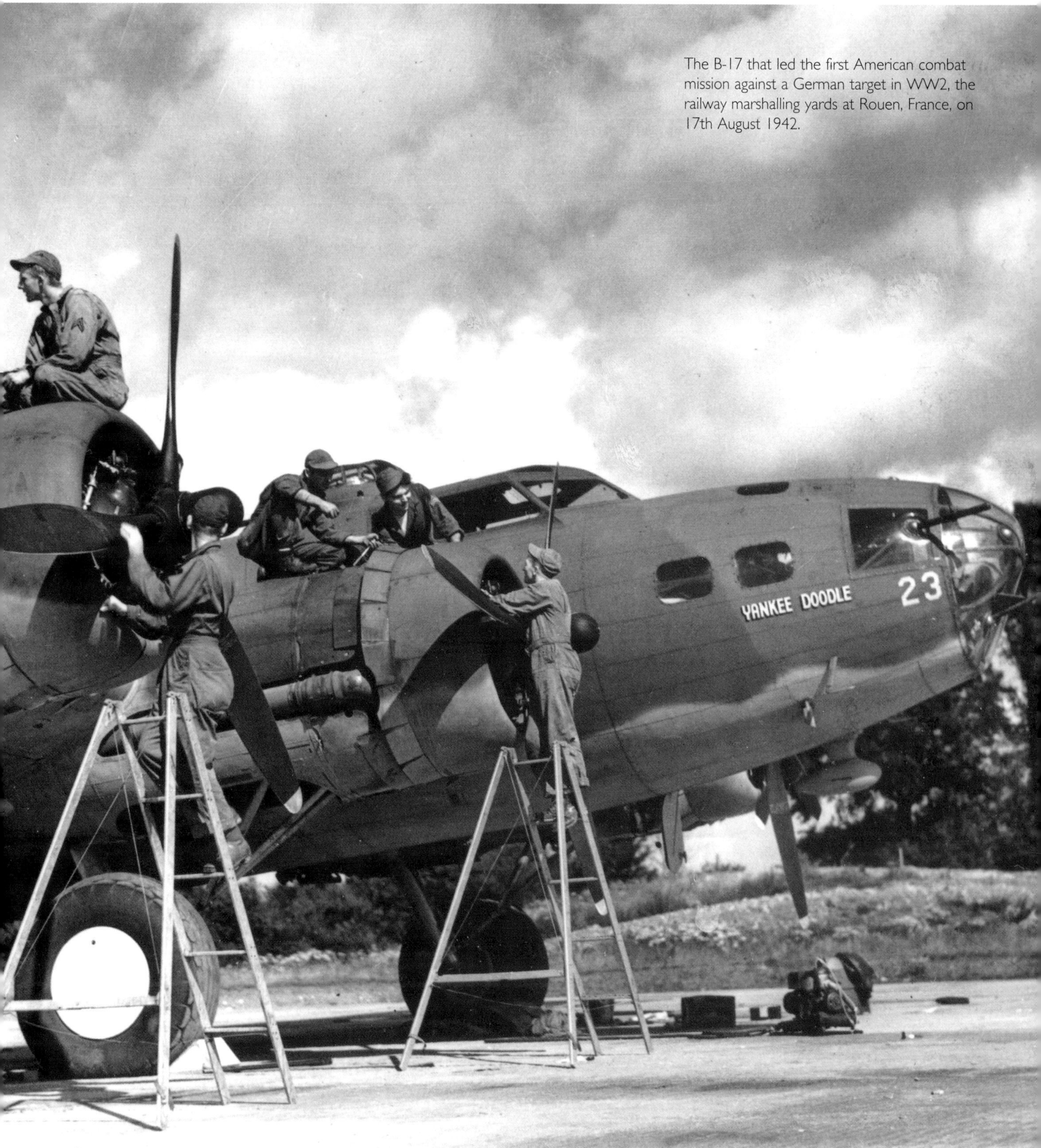
YANKEE DOODLE
23

The B-17 that led the first American combat mission against a German target in WW2, the railway marshalling yards at Rouen, France, on 17th August 1942.

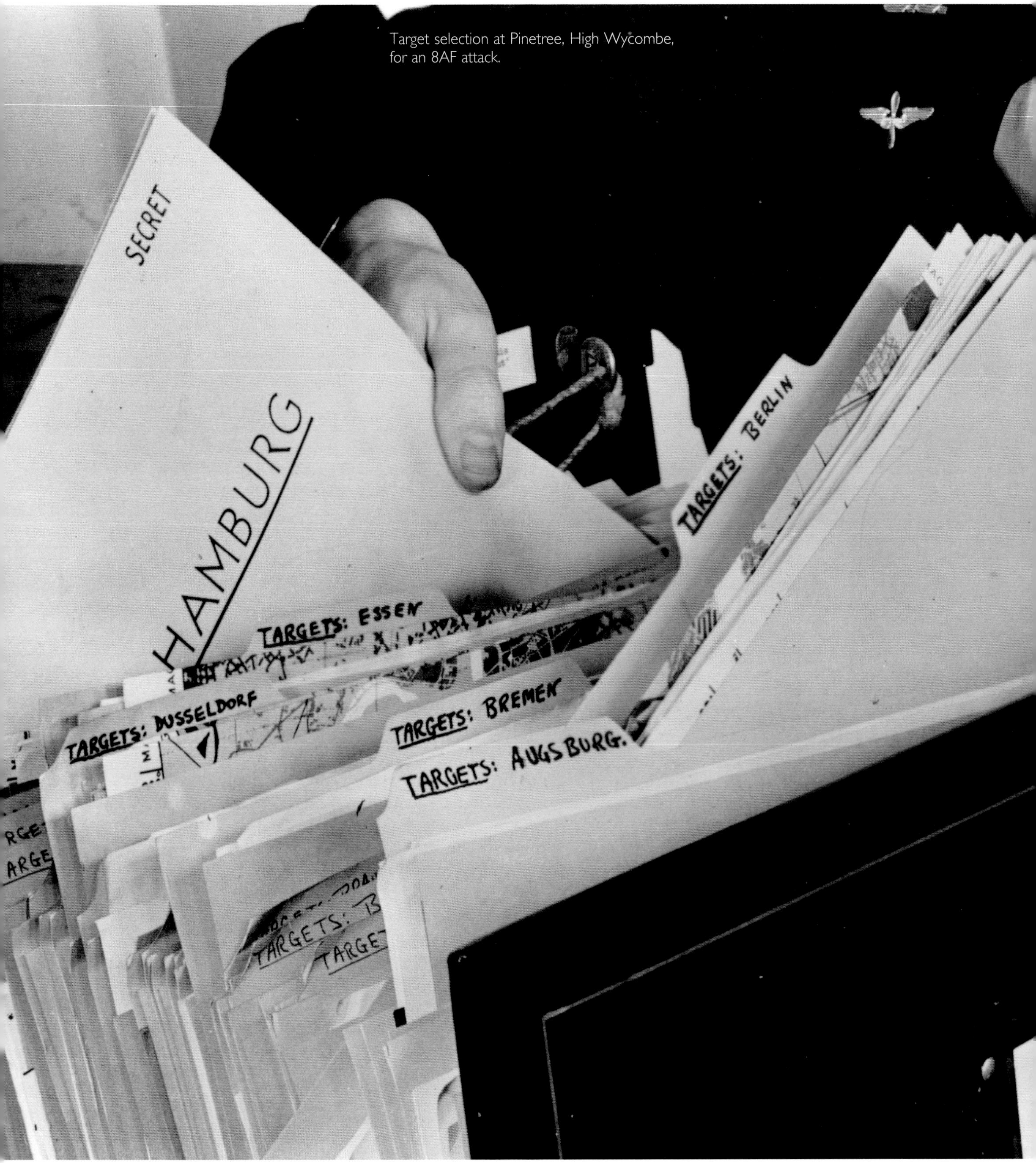
SECRET
HAMBURG
TARGETS: ESSEN
TARGETS: DUSSELDORF
TARGETS: BREMEN
TARGETS: AUGSBURG.
TARGETS: BERLIN

Target selection at Pinetree, High Wycombe, for an 8AF attack.

Roundabout Hill, below Daws Hill, and a large Nissen-hutted encampment was established south and east of Daws Hill and on the lower parkland near the Abbey. After the war, the school was returned to Wycombe Abbey and the girls reoccupied it in May 1946. However, the British Air Ministry retained the camp and the underground bunker. In October 2013 the bunker received a Grade II protected status listing from English Heritage. With occupation by the small group of newly-arrived Eighth Air Force officers, a joke was soon circulating about a small sign discovered in each of the former student rooms. It read Ring For Mistress.

Less than a month before the Eaker party was billeted in Daws Hill Lodge, the fledgling Eighth Air Force had been activated at Hunter Field, Savannah, Georgia.

Over the course of the war it would reach a peak personnel operating strength of 200,000 officers and men and was capable of dispatching more than 2,000 heavy bombers and 1,000 escorting fighters on a single bombing raid.

At peak strength it numbered more than forty heavy bomb groups, fifteen fighter groups, and two photo/ reconnaissance groups, all operating from bases in the UK. At that strength a typical mission flown by the Eighth consisted of 1,400 heavy bombers escorted by 800 fighters, consuming 3,500,000 gallons of aviation gasoline, expending 250,000 rounds of .50 caliber ammunition, destroying twenty-five German aircraft in the air and on the ground for the loss of four U.S. fighters and five bombers, and dropping 3,300 tons of bombs on enemy targets of which on visual missions, 40 percent fell within 1,000 feet of assigned mean points of impact and

75 percent within 2,000 feet. This huge force had a powerful impact on the enemy war effort, but the Americans paid a heavy price for it. They suffered 46,456 casualties with more than 26,000 killed in action. Its personnel were awarded seventeen Medals of Honor, 220 Distinguished Service Crosses, 850 Silver Stars, 7,000 Purple Hearts, 46,000 Distinguished Flying Crosses, and 442,000 Air Medals. Eighth Fighter Command produced 261 pilots who became aces, having been credited with shooting down five or more enemy aircraft.

A typical damage assessment report from photographs taken by Eighth Air Force photo aircraft after the attack reads as follows: "Very severe damage is seen in both the north and east marshalling yards. In the N. M/Y, both semi-round houses are severely damaged, one turntable is wrecked, many tracks obliterated in the center of the yard, all through-running lines out, the large transshipment shed [is] burning, large numbers of locomotives, wagons, and cars derailed, damaged, and destroyed. In the E. M/Y, the locomotive depot is severely damaged, all through lines out, and all sidings unserviceable. The passenger stations in both marshalling yards are severely damaged." (From K report covering attack on Falkenburg M/Y, 19 April 1945.)

Arthur "Bomber" Harris and Ira Eaker had worked together in Washington during 1941 when Harris had been on assignment there. They had become friends and it was as a friend that Eaker went to see his English neighbor to ask for his advice and assistance. They were friends despite their differing views on how to bomb the enemy. Eaker believed in precision daylight bombing by well-armed aircraft flying in tight, well-designed formations at relatively high altitude. Harris, on the other hand, normally sent his heavies out individually by night. He expected to make up for the attendant loss of bombing accuracy through sheer weight of numbers.

Harris went to work on his friend Ira, trying to persuade him to "come in with us on the night offensive," as well as making an attempt at humor by suggesting that Eaker's reluctance to accept his invitation might be due to the possibility that the Americans could only navigate in daylight. Then Harris read the seriousness and determination in Eaker to get on with the American experiment and he helped by providing the Americans with air bases in the English Midlands and East Anglia, having already provided the general with a headquarters for the Eighth Bomber Command at Daws Hill Lodge and one for Eighth Fighter Command at Bushey Hall near Watford. Finally, he gave his friend access to the proven British system of control and communications. An American record of that reception of the Eighth Air Force by the Royal Air Force: "With its Fighter Command guarding the skies by day, the Bomber Command striking the enemy by night, and Coastal Command sweeping the sea-lanes, the RAF might have taken a condescending attitude towards the advance guard of Americans whose plans were so large and whose means were apparently so small. The RAF took no such attitude.

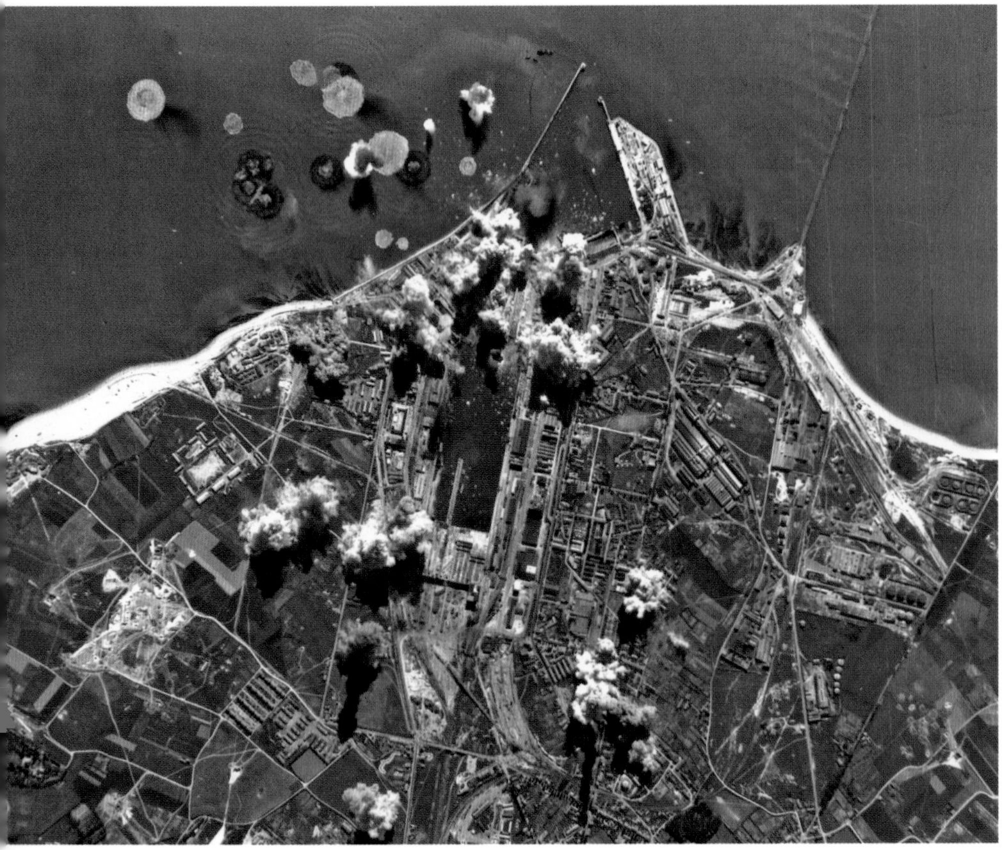

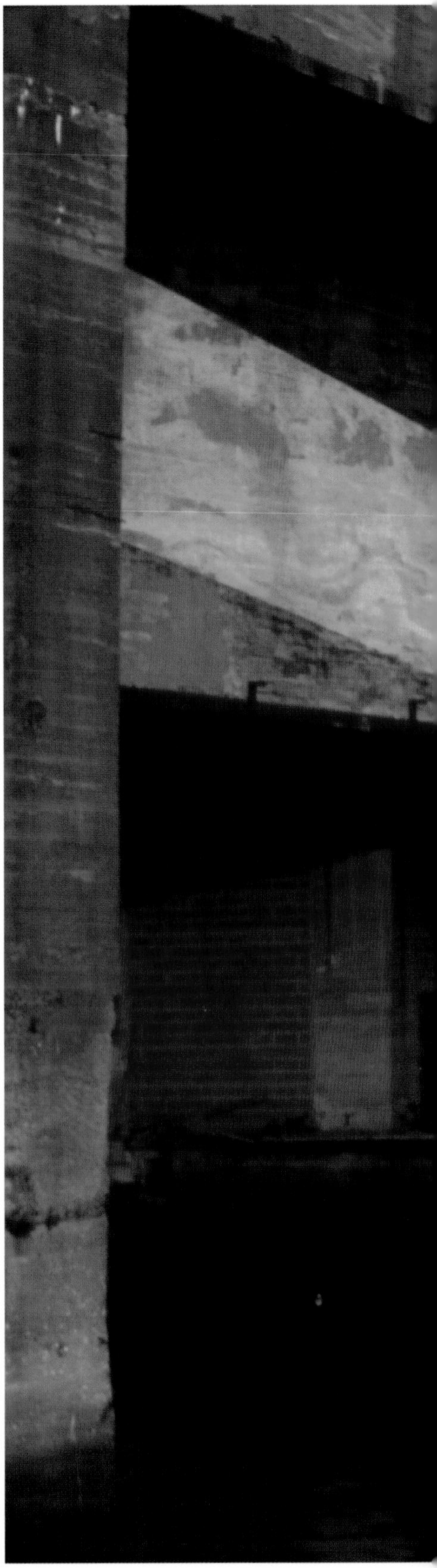

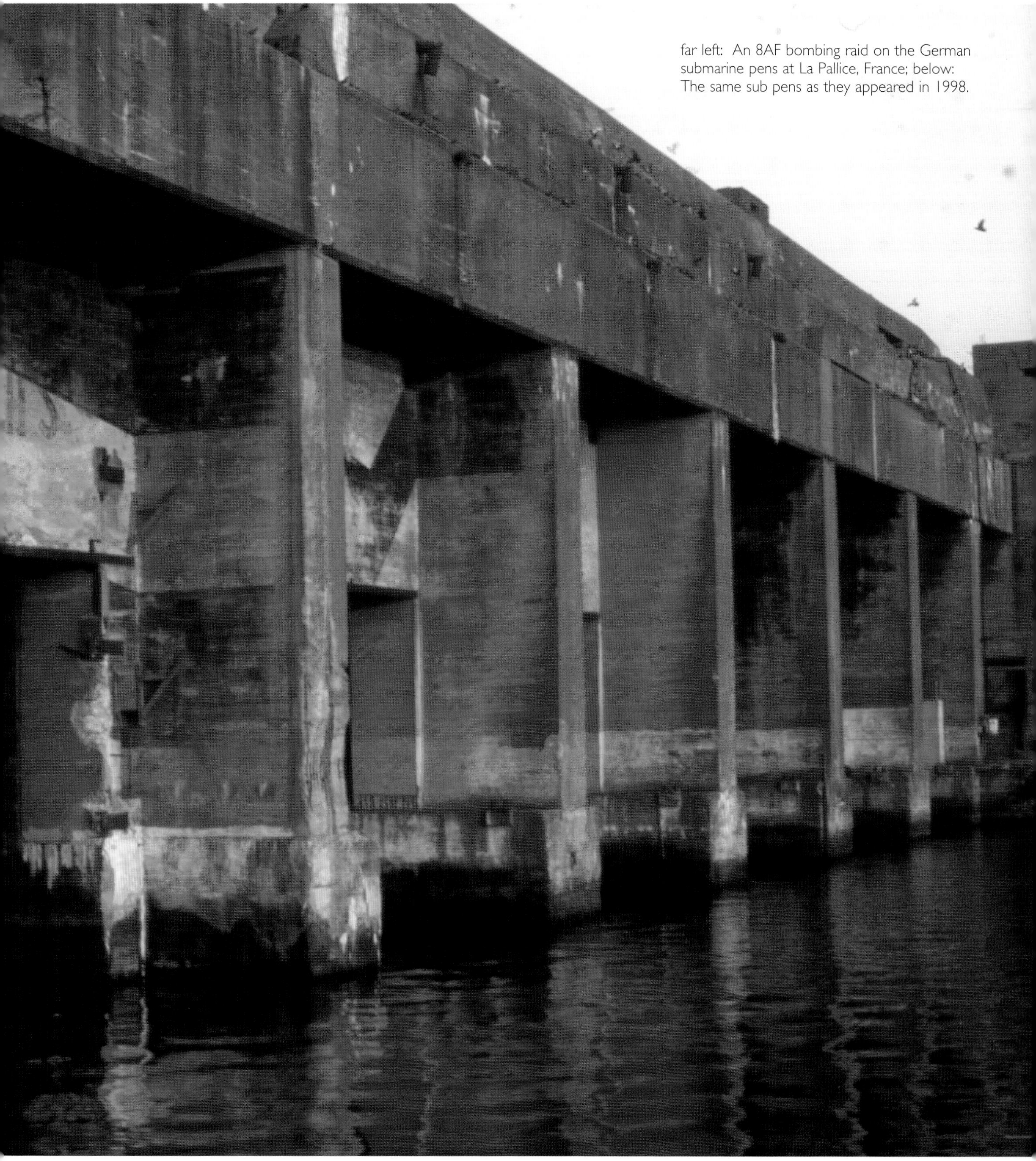

far left: An 8AF bombing raid on the German submarine pens at La Pallice, France; below: The same sub pens as they appeared in 1998.

From the start their generous and sympathetic interest were the keys that unlocked many problems. 'Tell us what you want,' they said. 'If we have it, it is yours.' They might have added, 'Whether or not we need it ourselves.'" Nearly everywhere the Americans went in the UK, they were warmly greeted and made welcome. At a dinner in his honor, Ira Eaker stood to make a speech which was short and to the point: "We won't do much talking until we've done more flying. We hope that when we leave, you'll be glad we came. Thank you."

After several months of education, preparation, hard work and practice, the Yanks of the new Eighth Air Force were finally ready (they believed) for their first one, their first combat mission of the war. It was mid-afternoon, 17th August 1942, and twelve Boeing B-17Es of the 97th Bomb Group crawled along the perimeter track of the airfield at Grafton Underwood in Northamptonshire. They took off at thirty-second intervals and climbed into a bright blue cloudless sky. Ira Eaker was not about to miss this one. He was aboard *Yankee Doodle*, in the lead of the second element of six airplanes. The target for the day was to be the railway marshalling yard at Rouen, the city where 500 years before, Joan of Arc died for the liberty of France. At the controls of *Yankee Doodle* that afternoon was Major Paul Tibbetts who, three years later, would be pilot and aircraft commander of *Enola Gay*, the B-29 that dropped the first atom bomb over Hiroshima, leading to the end of war days later.

The B-17s of Grafton Underwood released a total of eighteen tons of bombs on their target from an altitude of 22,500 feet. The raid was deemed

successful. General Eaker described it afterwards for the press: "Shortly after we turned back towards the Channel we began to get the action we had anticipated. Coming fast out of the earth pattern below us I spied three Focke-Wulf 190 fighter planes. As the first zoomed towards our Flying Fortresses, it was not yet evident to me whether he was attacking our lead plane or our No. 2 plane, directly astern of us and to starboard.

"As he opened fire I realized he was aiming at No. 2. His tracers seemed to burst wide of its left wing. After a few bursts at extreme range—perhaps 1,000 yards—he rolled over on his back and went into a dive. The other two 190s attacked the rear plane of our flight. They opened fire from below; then an instant later they too pulled away at a considerable distance. I could see the bottom turret gunner of the attacked Fortress firing at them but I could not be certain that his bullets were taking effect though the tracers

seemed very close.

"When the last of the three 190s broke off combat, I moved to the other side of the waist gunners' station and observed at least a dozen puffs from exploding shells. They were deadly accurate as to altitude but several hundred yards to port. Meanwhile there was fighter activity overhead and to our rear. The RAF wing covering our withdrawal had climbed above us and passed somewhat astern as we left the target area.

"Now they ran into some 35-40 enemy fighters which evidently had been reluctant to engage our Fortresses at close quarters. I can understand why. They had never seen our new B-17s before and the sight of the big guns bristling from every angle probably gave the Nazis ample reason to be wary."

Later that evening, Eaker received a message from Arthur Harris: "Yankee Doodle certainly went to town, and can stick yet another well-earned feather in his cap."

left: Brigadier General Ira C. Eaker, the first commander of the Eighth Air Force in Britain; right: The German city of Hamburg under 8AF attack. The targets were dockyards, oil storage facilities, and the Blöhm und Voss shipyards where U-boats were under construction.

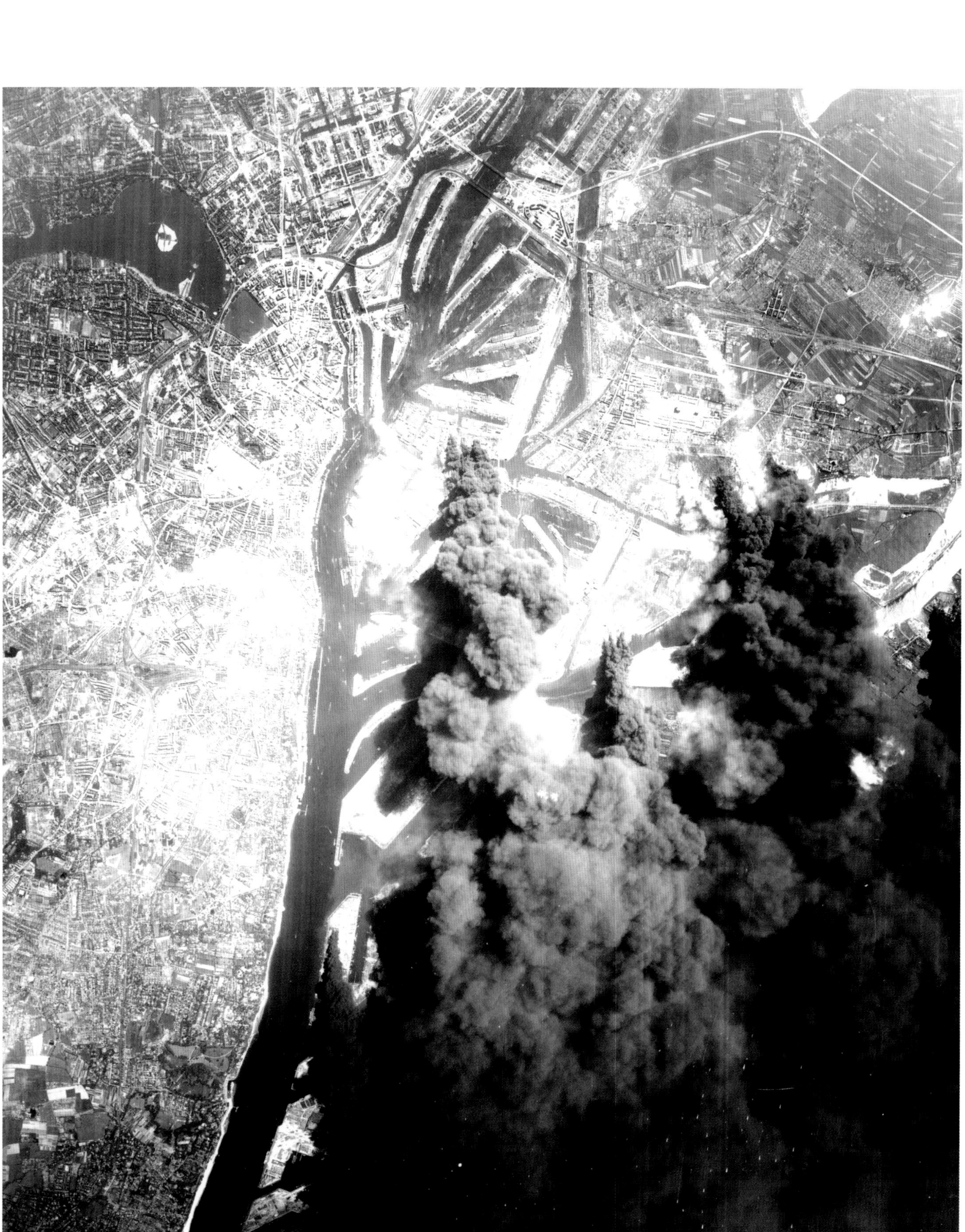

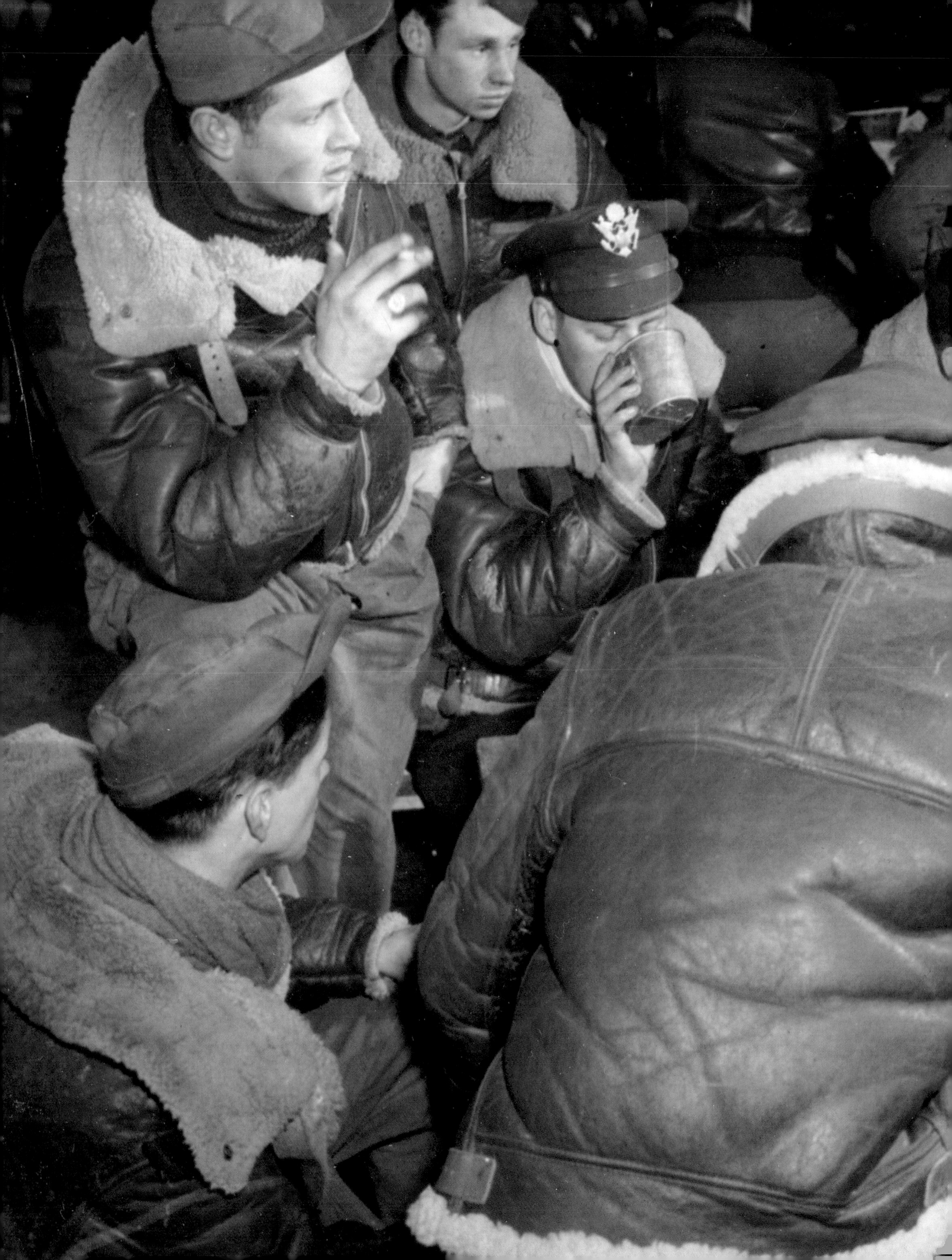

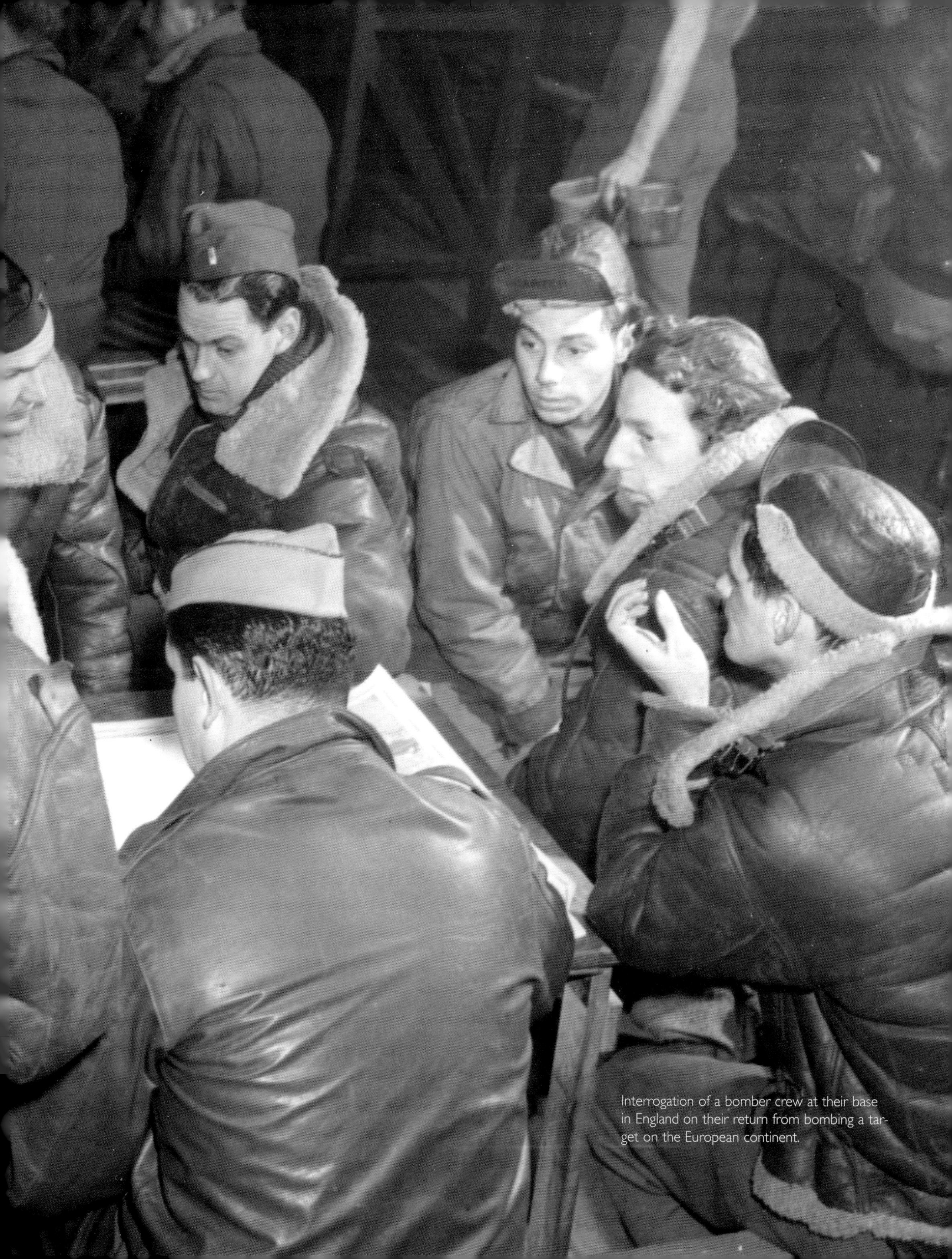

Interrogation of a bomber crew at their base in England on their return from bombing a target on the European continent.

WORKING TOGETHER

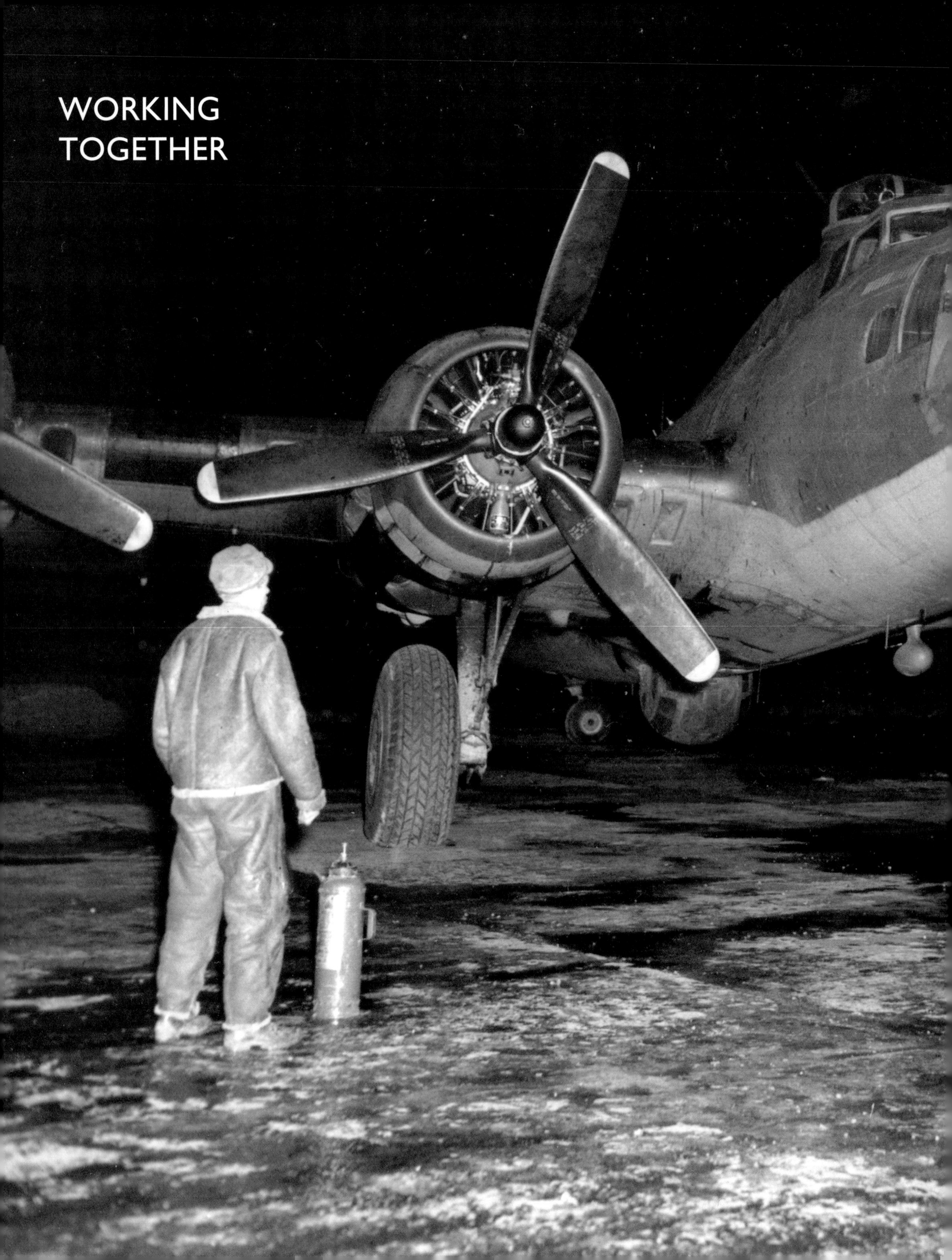

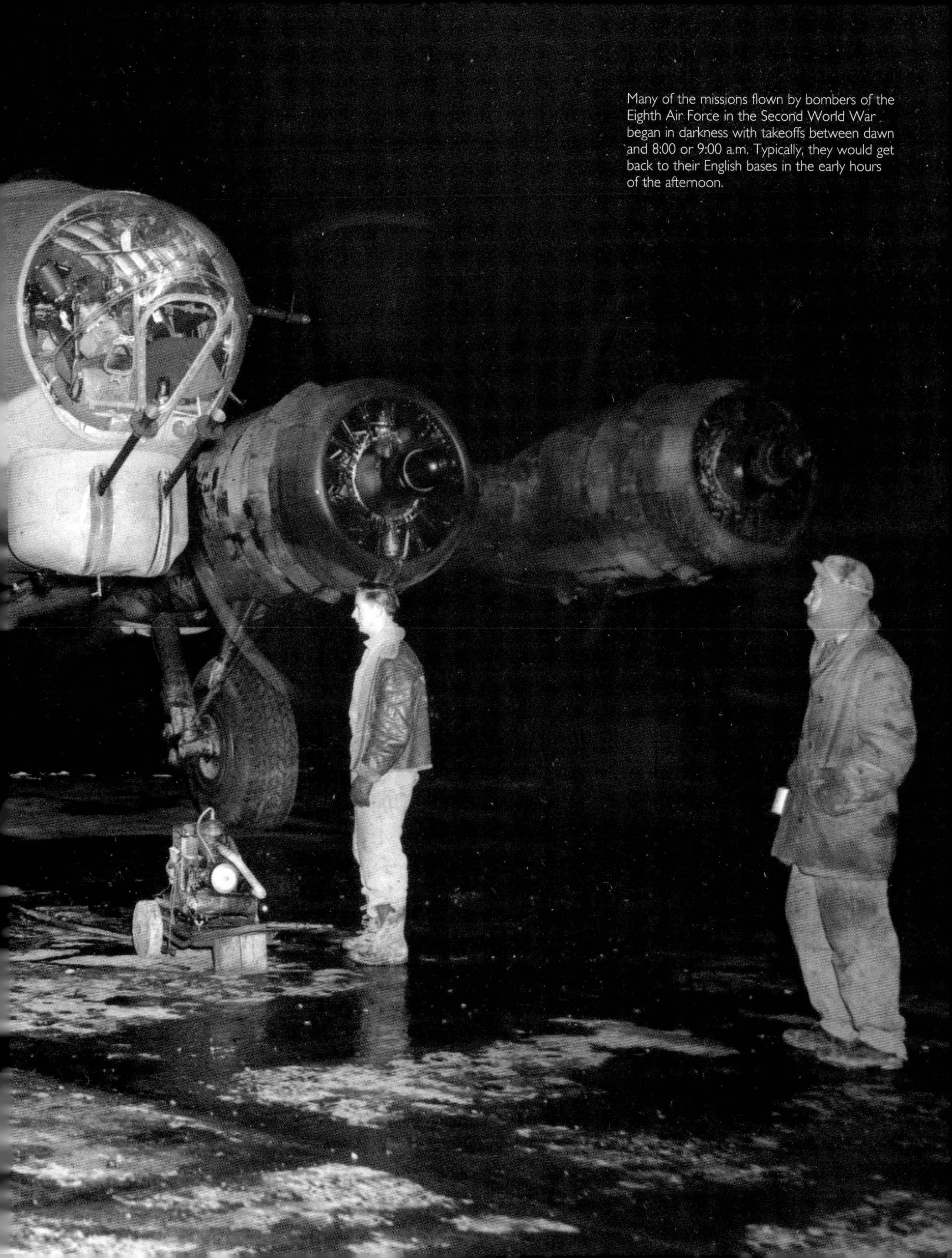

Many of the missions flown by bombers of the Eighth Air Force in the Second World War began in darkness with takeoffs between dawn and 8:00 or 9:00 a.m. Typically, they would get back to their English bases in the early hours of the afternoon.

ANOTHER REASON why "Bomber" Harris readily agreed to support Ira Eaker's determination to fly the missions of Eighth Bomber Command by day, while his own bomber force continued to operate by night, was that when Eaker met with Prime Minister Winston Churchill to discuss the American approach to bombing the German enemy, Churchill, renowned wordsmith and no mean writer himself, was immediately taken by a phrase Eaker used in describing the combined American and British bombing campaign he envisioned. He referred to it as "Round the Clock," and the Prime Minister liked the name and the concept so much that he approved it on the spot and ordered it implemented.

Sir Archibald Sinclair, British Air Secretary: "The enemy must be attacked by day and by night, so that he may have no respite from the Allied blows, so that his defensive resources may be taxed to the utmost limit. But day and night bombing are separate though complimentary tasks. Each requires a strategic plan, a tactical execution and a supporting organization adapted to its special needs. So there has been a division of labor. To one force—the Eighth Bomber Command—has been alloted the task of day bombing. To the other force—our Bomber Command—the task of night bombing. The methods are different, but the aim is the same: to paralyze the armed forces of Germany by disrupting the war economy by which they are sustained."

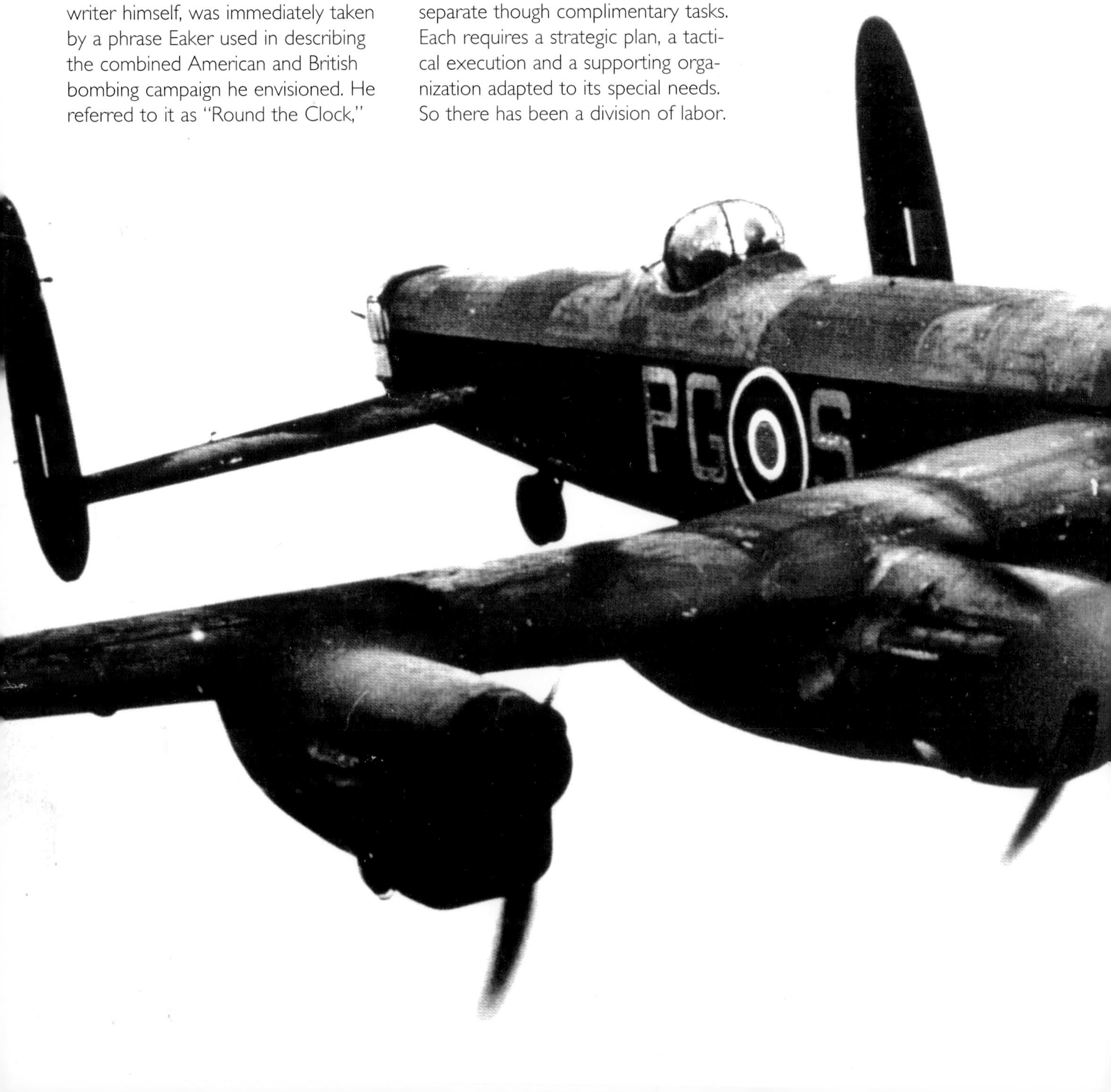

PG S

At that point, Allied bombing policy had been changed. At last, the approach by the RAF to its task was no longer limited to "military targets" or the dropping of propaganda leaflets. Spurred by the savage German bombing strikes on London, Coventry, Warsaw, and Rotterdam, the British rose to the challenge. Air Chief Marshal Harris: "They have sown the wind; now they will reap the whirlwind."

Both the German Luftwaffe and the Royal Air Force had begun their bombing activities with daylight raids, and both had suffered significant

The Avro Lancaster was in many ways the finest Royal Air Force bomber of WW2. It was operated by a crew of seven and carried by far the largest bombload of any Allied bomber in that conflict. Two examples remain airworthy in 2015; they are based in England and Canada.

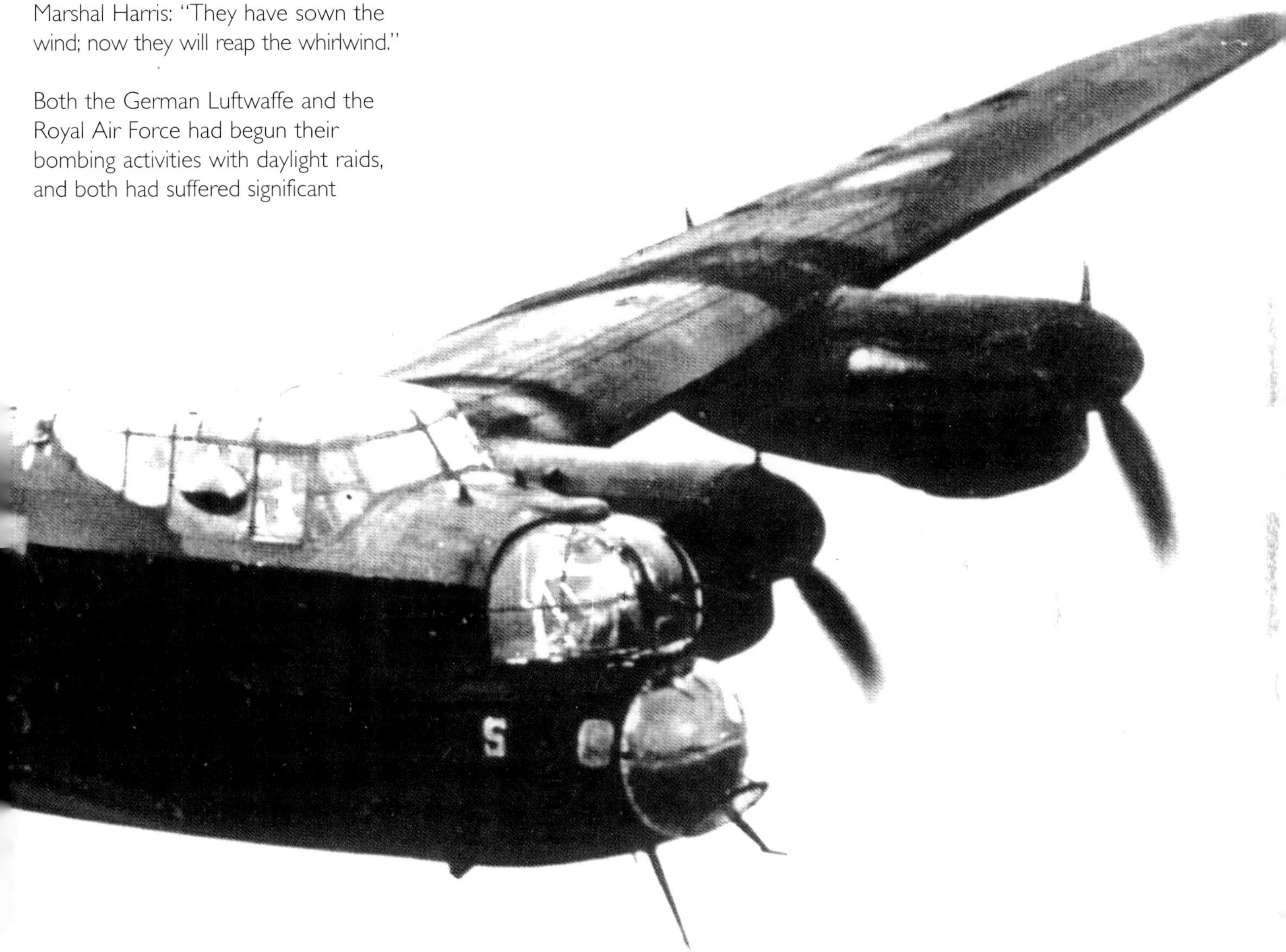

losses in the effort, to the other's air defenses. Both were then obliged to continue their campaigns as night operations. One key difference between these opponents though, was that the Germans never managed to design and develop a truly effective heavy strategic bomber. In Britain, however, aircraft manufacturers responding to requirements issued by the RAF, designed, tested, and produced three very large and largely impressive four-engined heavies in the Short Stirling, Handley-Page Halifax, and the greatest of them all, the Avro Lancaster. The other major differences between the antagonists included their methods of target location. German bomber crews were mainly dependent on finding their objectives by using visual checkpoints; rivers, estuaries, etc. When they had to bomb through overcast they flew along a radio beam sent out from transmitters in Europe. By contrast, the RAF crews had the advantage of British-developed radar navigation as well as the highly effective all-weather methods of pyrotechnic target marking.

Contrasting most significantly was the changing scale of the Allied and German bombing offensives. As Arthur Harris's new heavy bombers were operating in ever-increasing numbers and the bombing capability and capacity of Eaker's Eighth were building into those of a powerful force, their effects were being felt on the important industrial targets of Germany, whose own bomber force was declining in numbers, strength, and meaningful results. The bombing capability of the Luftwaffe was becoming less of a threat and more of a nuisance. Both sides knew that it would ultimately be the punishing work of the bombers that would win the war, but as the conflict wore on, the German aircraft makers were ordered

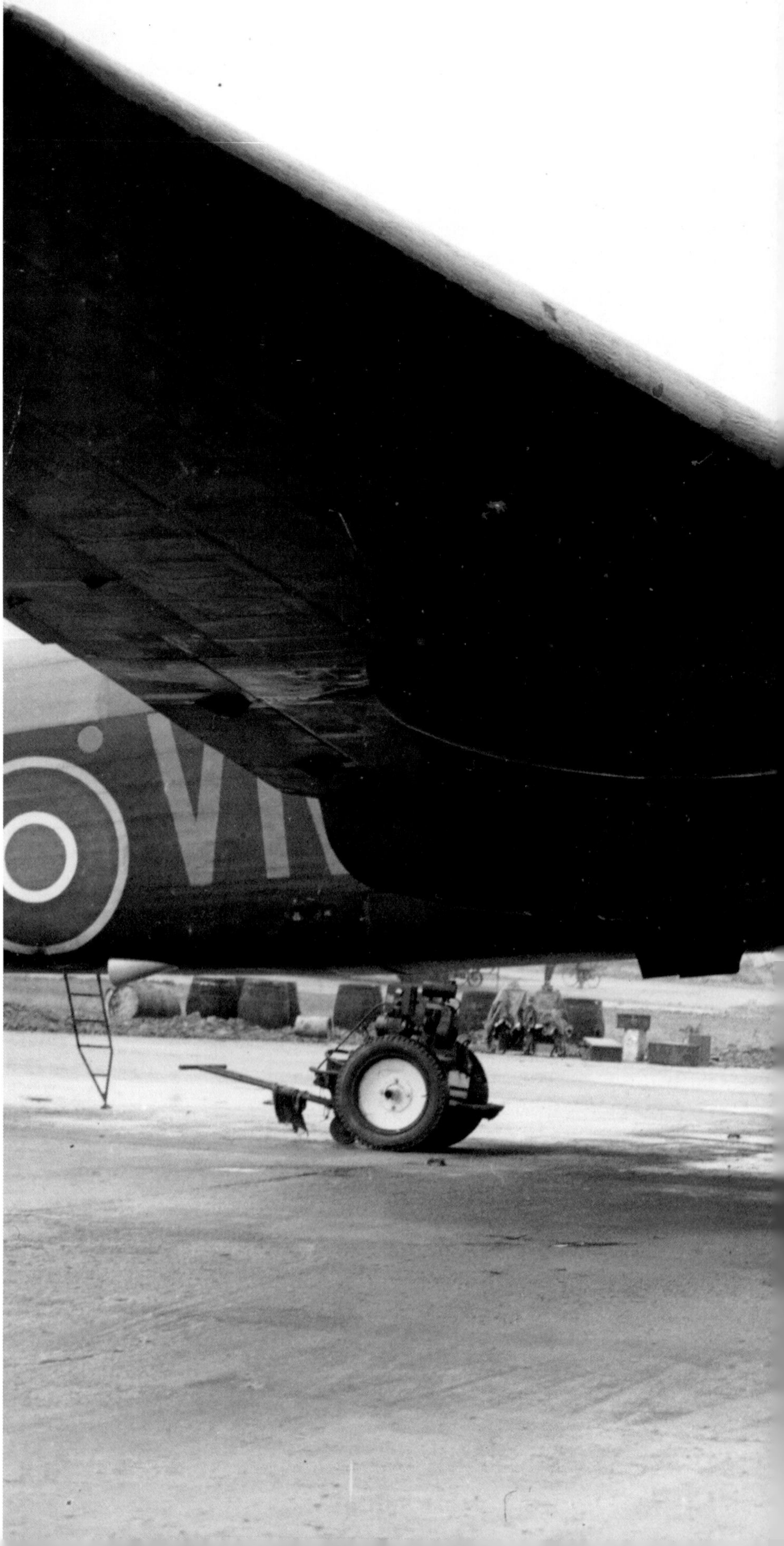

VN

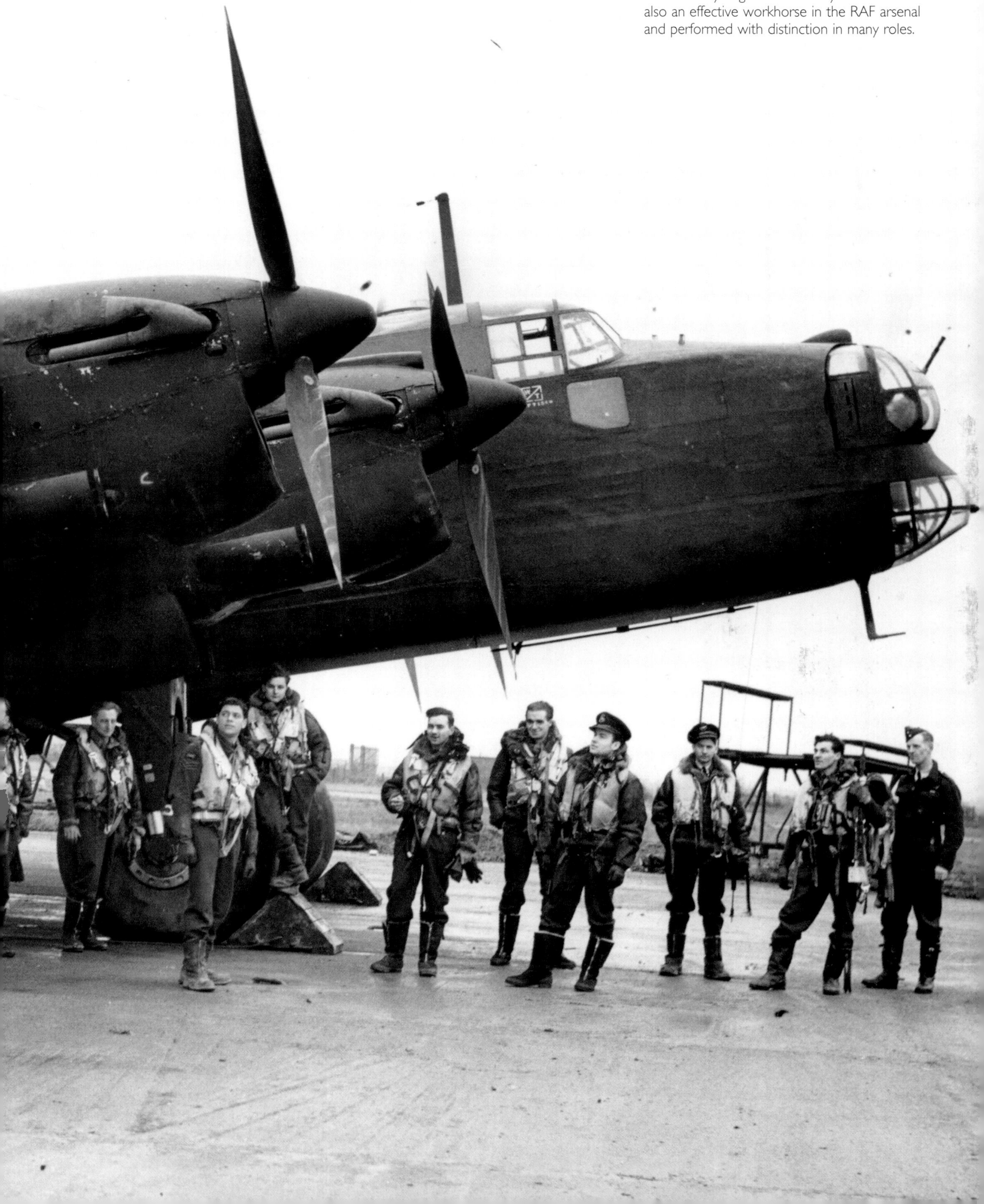

The Handley Page Halifax heavy bomber was also an effective workhorse in the RAF arsenal and performed with distinction in many roles.

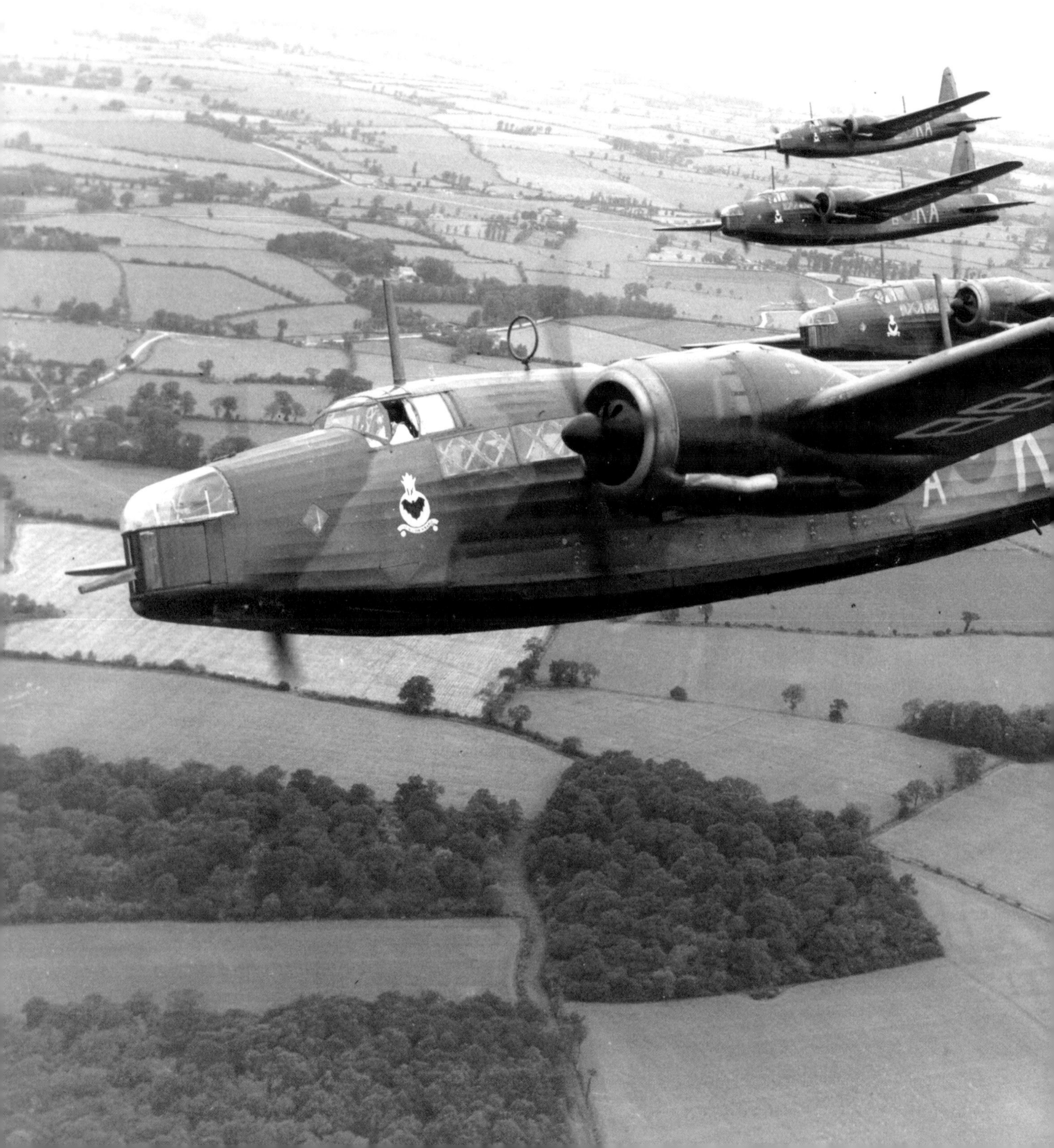

The Vickers Wellington medium bomber carried much of the bombing workload for the RAF in the early years of WW2. Designed by the innovative aircraft engineer, Barnes Wallis, the "Wimpy" utilized a unique geodesic construction method. A flight of Wellingtons is shown here in an image by the superb British wartime photographer Charles E. Brown.

to concentrate more on building fighters and less on bombers, as the leadership of the Reich was gradually backed into a defensive posture by the powerful, growing Allied bombing offensive. The part of that operation played by the B-17s and B-24s of the Eighth in their daylight raids, with the impressive accuracy of their brilliant Norden bombsights, was particularly effective in eroding Hitler's bombing campaign.

How were the day and night operations different for the crews of the Eighth and the RAF Bomber Commands? The airmen in the better-armed Fortresses and Liberators of the Eighth believed, initially, that they were ready for the fighters of the enemy and deliberately set out to take them on. Bristling with up to thirteen .50 caliber Browning machine-guns, the big bombers flew in tight, stepped-up box formations, their engines trailing silvery condensation tracks for miles behind the bomber stream, which was sometimes twenty miles long. The air crews of the RAF, on the other hand, made it an important part of their business to try to avoid running battles with German night fighters. They employed a variety of tactics and techniques to prevent such encounters and put the enemy off the scent: spoof attacks, feints, and electronic countermeasures.

There was a commonality between the day and night bomber air crews as they each approached their targets, a similar kind of reception awaiting them both. In most cases, the airmen observed a seemingly impenetrable barrier of flak blocking their path from the beginning of the bomb run all the way through to the release point and beyond. Former Lancaster pilot Jack Currie recalled, "At night it appeared as a million sparks among

The great, lumbering Short Stirling couldn't live up to its promise after the Air Ministry insisted that it have a wingspan short enough for it to fit in the doors of the RAF hangars of the 1930s. The short wing prevented it from performing well enough to match its cousins, the Lancaster and the Halifax.

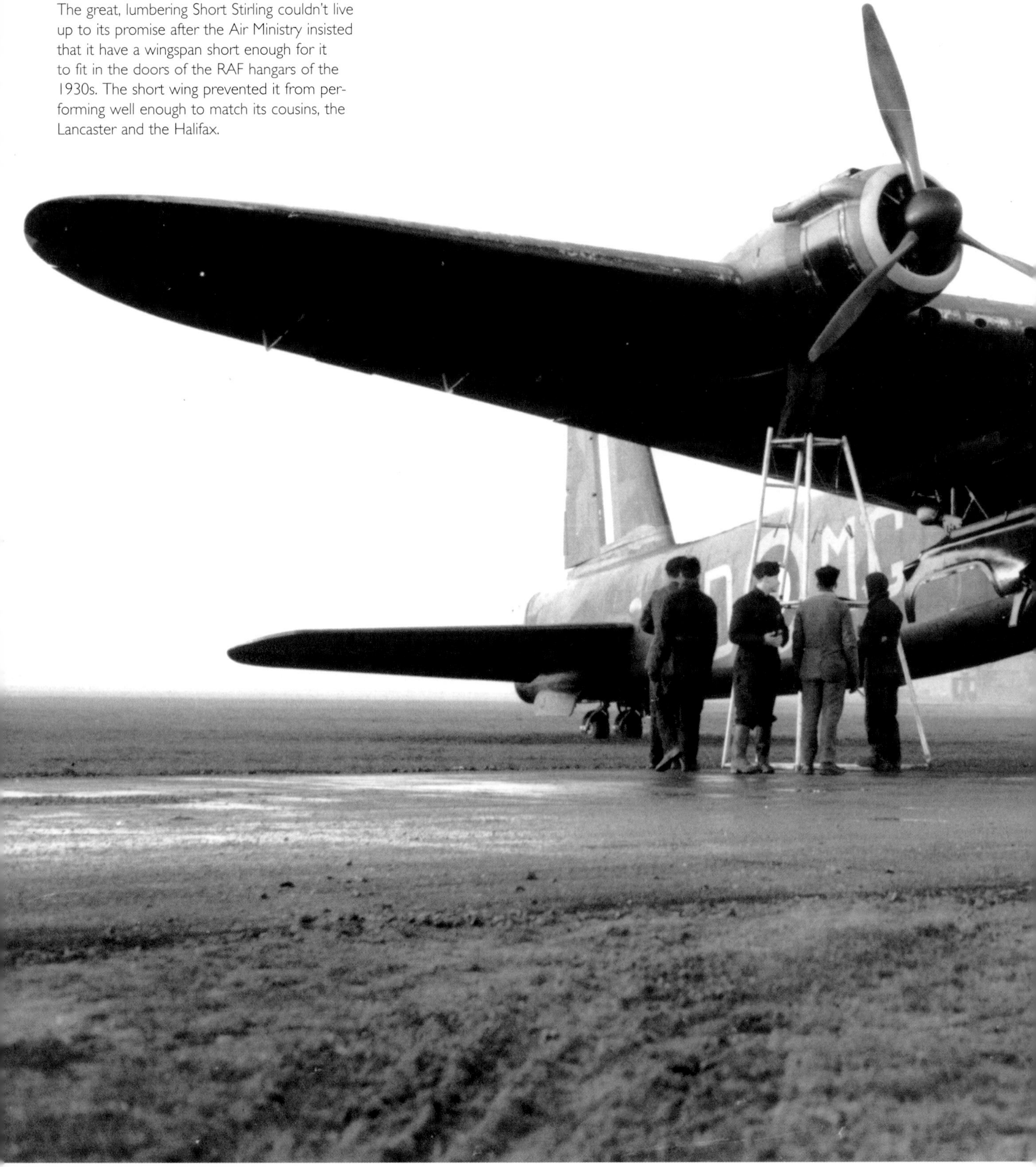

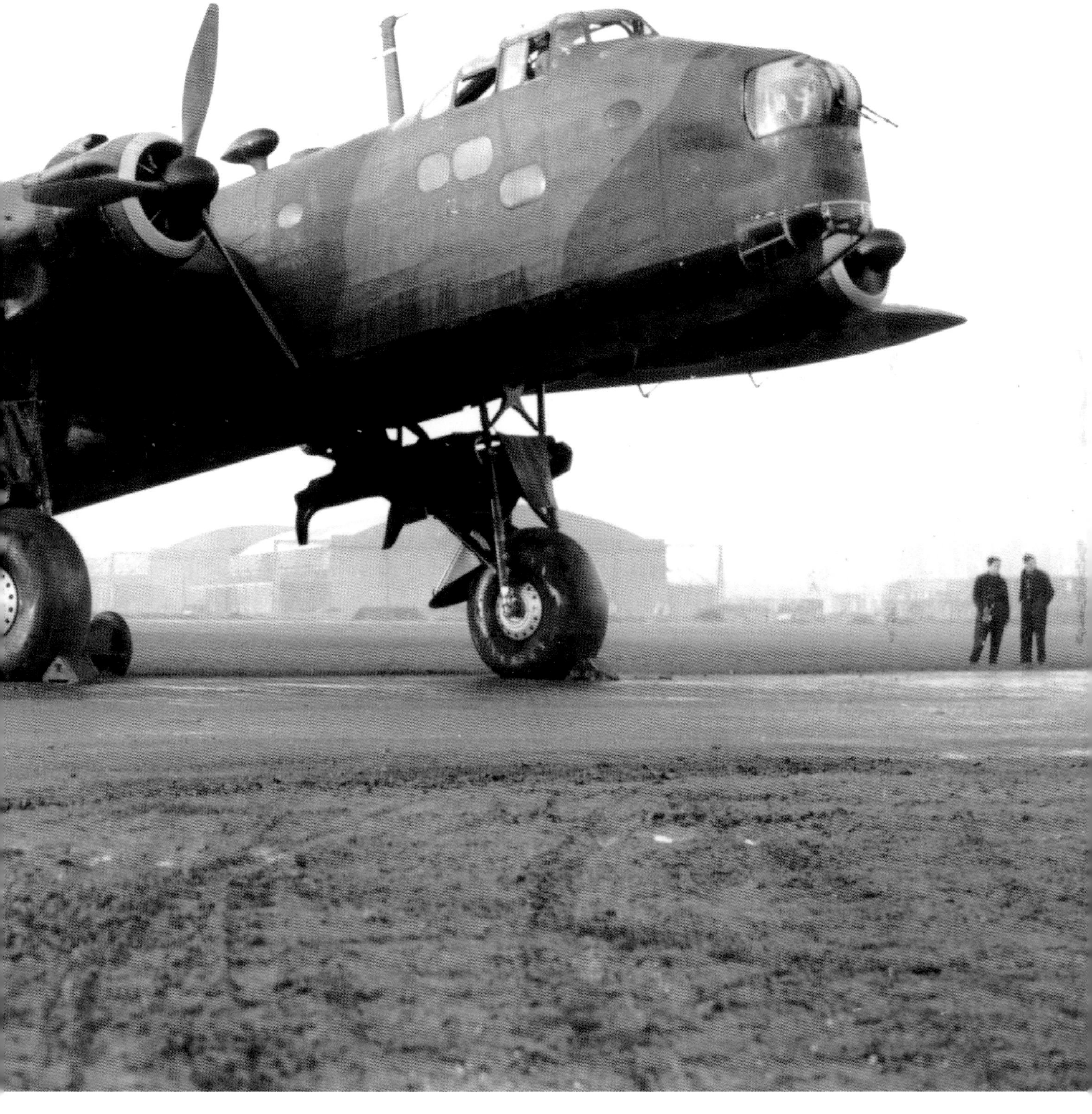

the groping searchlights; by day as a sky full of lumps of dirty cotton." They mostly had to fly through that, day or night. Many if not most felt that there was no point trying to dodge between the shell bursts because in trying to evade one they might well fly into another. And when the pilot and crew were committed to the bomb run, there was no longer any chance of such dodging even if they wanted to try it. At that point the bomb aimer—or, in the Eighth, the bombardier—the man in charge of the actual bomb release was in control. He was concentrating either on the aiming point or on the bomb bay of the lead plane.

While there were certain similar-ities in the experiences approaching and over the target, there were definite distinctions in the human side. The bomber crews of the Eighth flew in close formation and were frequently aware of their proximity to other airmen they knew. When a B-17 or B-24 was shot out of the sky by flak or a fighter, the men in the nearby bombers often had a personal interest in watching for those they might know bale out of the stricken plane. "Come on, you guys, get the hell outta there." At night, with the bomber crews of the British heavies, it was far less personal. Those who went down in a blinding flash of an exploding Lancaster could not possibly be identified by anyone in the widely-dispersed squadron aircraft with whom they had been flying. Each seven-man RAF bomber crew was quite alone in the blackness.

The great mostly-featureless flatlands of the East Anglia bulge have long been farm land and were, in the war years, largely unpopulated. With no hills to speak of and few towns of any size, it would prove ideal for locating, constructing and operating the ninety-eight RAF and USAAF bomber airfields that it would support until the end of the European war in 1945. There were so many military air bases in this eight thousand square miles of England that there was very little separation between them. Pilots and

above: The Hamburg flak tower after the 1943 Allied bombing raids on the city; right: The aftermath of an 8AF attack on the Misburg oil refinery and storage facilities.

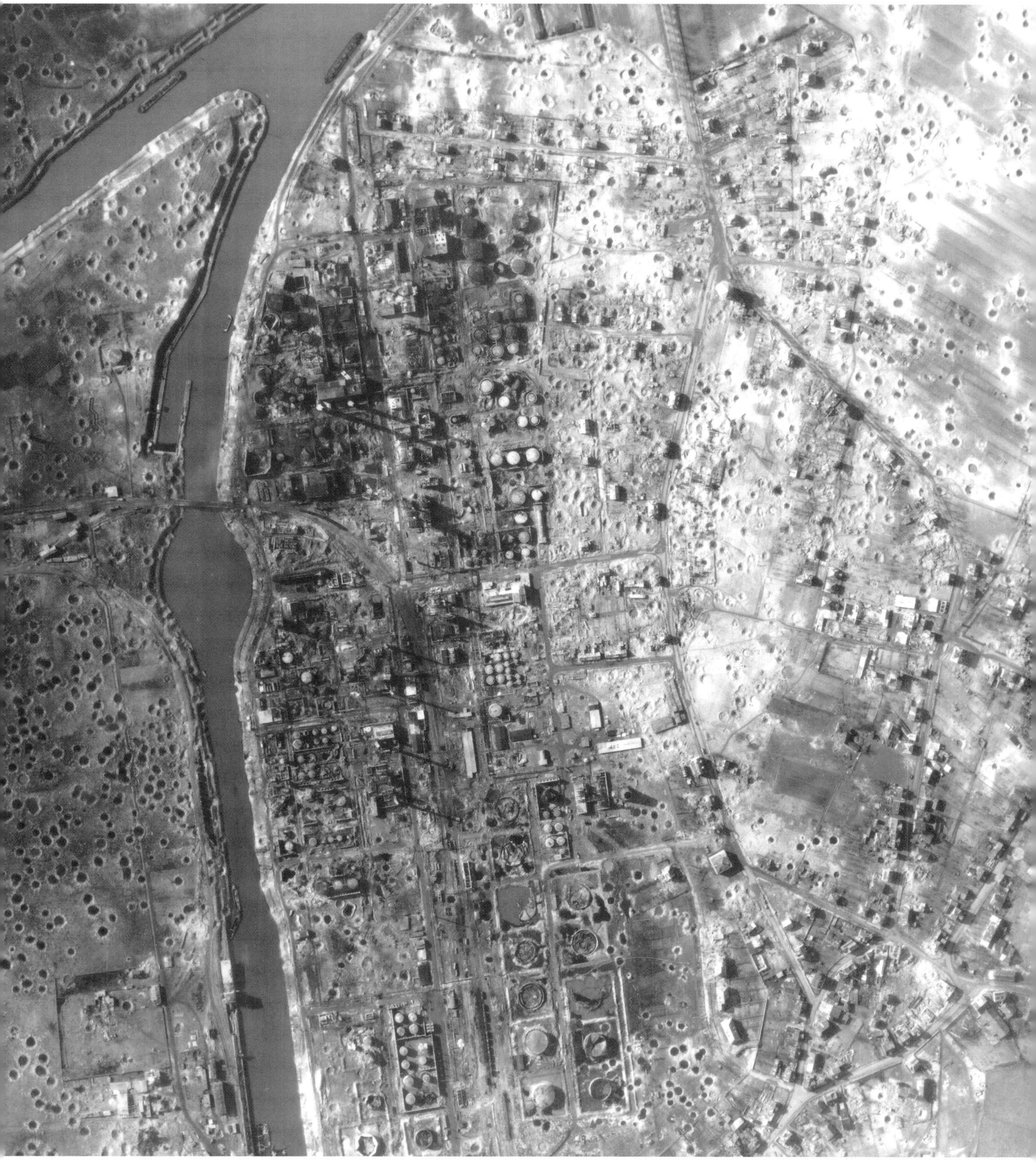

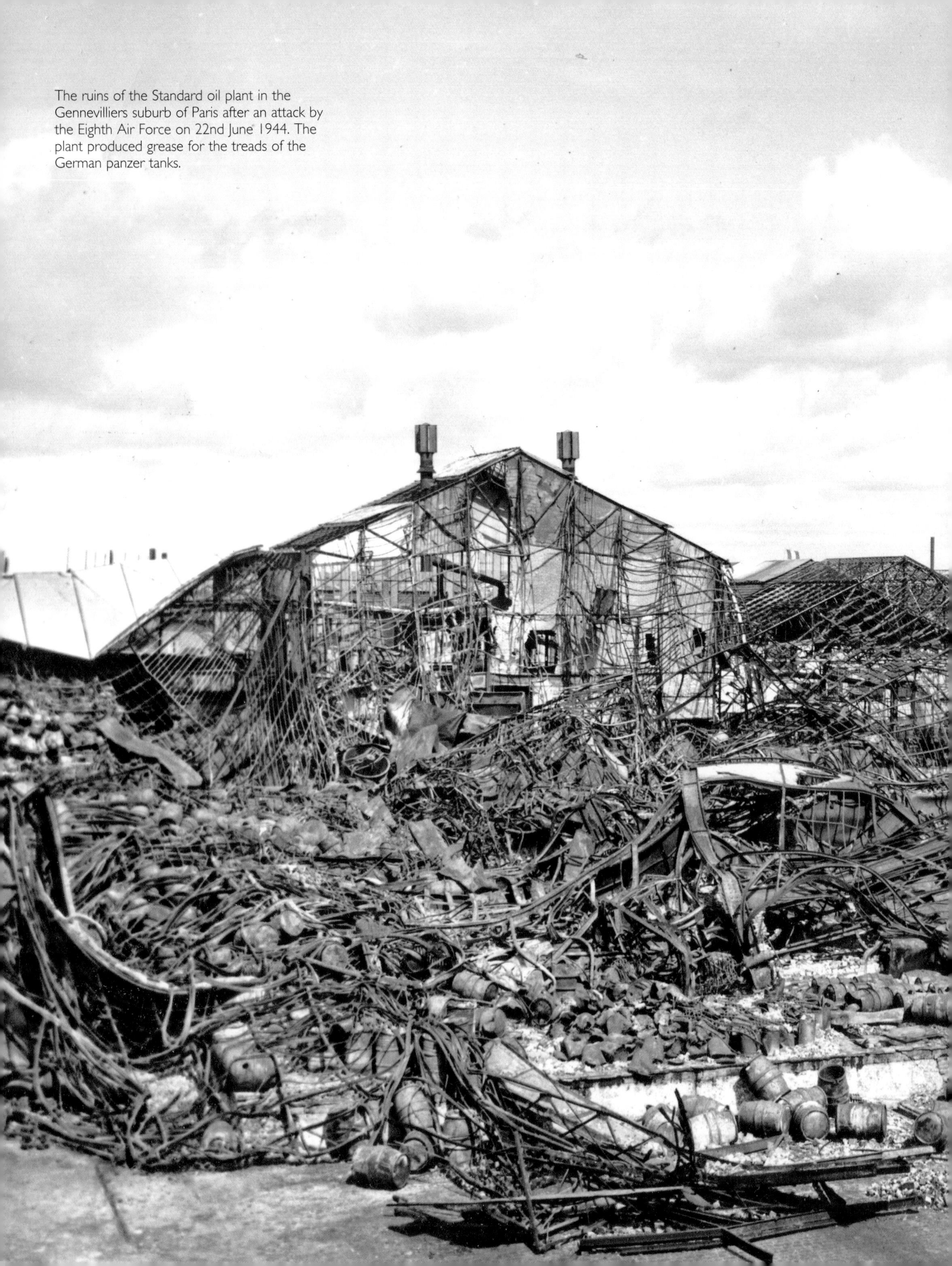

The ruins of the Standard oil plant in the Gennevilliers suburb of Paris after an attack by the Eighth Air Force on 22nd June 1944. The plant produced grease for the treads of the German panzer tanks.

navigators had to exercise exceptional caution when negotiating landing patterns and approaches.

Former RAF Lancaster pilot Jack Currie remembered that some twenty-five RAF bomber stations were occupying a stretch of Lincolnshire between the River Trent and the English coast: "On a clear night over the city of Lincoln, you could see the Drem lights of a dozen airfields. Some of them were so close together that their traffic patterns overlapped. At Scampton, for example, when a southwest wind prevailed, the pilots would fly a right-hand pattern, while their neighbors at Dunholme Lodge flew their circuits to the left." One aspect of UK wartime bomber operations was the same for both the Americans and the RAF. Whether in the dark or in daytime cloud, the protracted climb to altitude was the same for both forces; a hazardous, potentially deadly procedure with the constant prospect of midair collision awaiting them. Some such events did occur. I was told of one by the elderly porter at the Swan Hotel in Lavenham many years ago during my first visit to the charming Suffolk village that hosted the Lavenham / Alpheton airfield and the 487th Bomb Group of the Eighth Air Force in World War Two. We sat out on a low wall at the back of the hotel garden late on a summer afternoon in the 1970s and he described being almost at the same spot on a similar day in 1944 and watching the sky over the village when, in the direction of the airfield, he saw two B-24 Liberator bombers drifting toward each other until they collided at low altitude and both fell to earth fairly nearby between the field and Lavenham. He didn't know for certain, but believed that there had been no survivors of that terrible event. The memory of it, and the

vision, had remained with and haunted him all the years since. Sadly, such events were not entirely uncommon in the war years when both British and American bomber forces were operating from the many fields of England.

In another distinguishing factor between the operational methods of the American and British bomber boys, the crews of the "Mighty Eighth," so nicknamed many years after the war by the historian and author Roger A. Freeman, strove to take full advantage of the armed capability and impressive firepower of their aircraft, the B-17s and B-24s that bristled with as many as thirteen .50 caliber Browning machine-guns each. Of at least equal importance to them was their requirement to precisely concentrate their bombing pattern at the mean point of impact on their target while ensuring that none of their bombs struck another aircraft as they fell. Lancaster pilot Currie: "These were considerations of little application to the RAF night bomber crews, each of which found their own way to the target, fought individual battles with the enemy night fighters—but only if they had to—and made the bomb runs on their own."

In an effort to minimize damage to their own aircraft, RAF Bomber Command sent their bombers out in waves ten to fifteen minutes apart. Still, the three main bomber types had to fly at different altitudes due to their performance limitations, with the Lancasters above the others, the Halifaxes below them, and the Stirlings below them both. Virtually inevitable timing and navigation errors resulted in many instances where RAF heavies returned to base after their raids, having suffered bomb damage from higher-flying aircraft. These accidents occurred when large, four-engined planes suddenly appeared in the crosshairs of Lancaster bomb aimers as their aircraft crossed the target aiming points and their bombs were released. The evidence was in the photographs made from the Lancs.

The time will come, when thou will lift thine eyes to watch a long-drawn battle in the skies, while aged peasants, too amazed for words, stare at the flying fleets of wond'rous birds. England, so long mistress of the seas, where winds and waves confess her sovereignty, Her ancient triumphs yet on high shall bear, and reign, the sovereign of the conquered air.
—translated from Thomas Gray's *Luna Habitabilis*, Cambridge, 1797

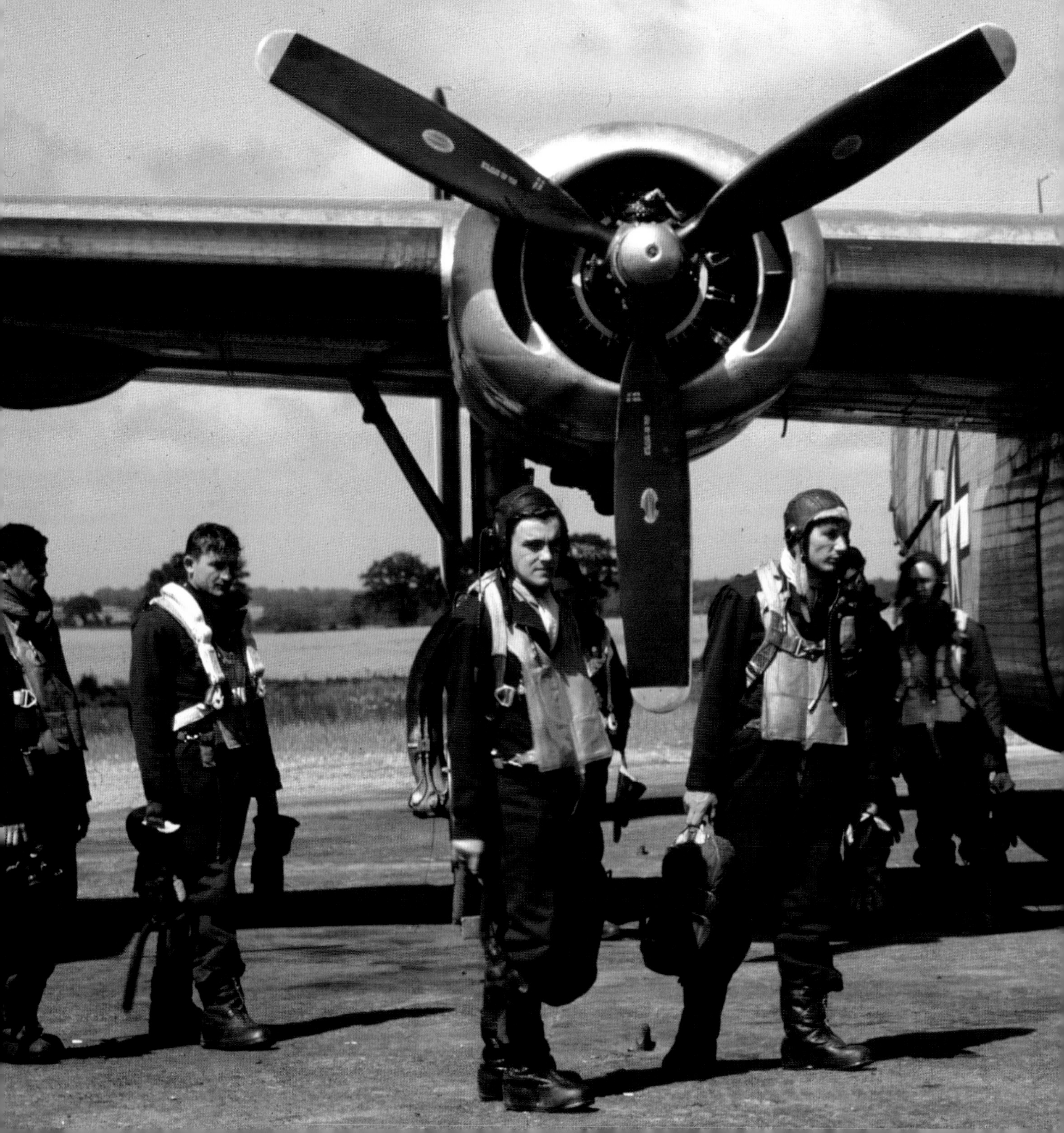

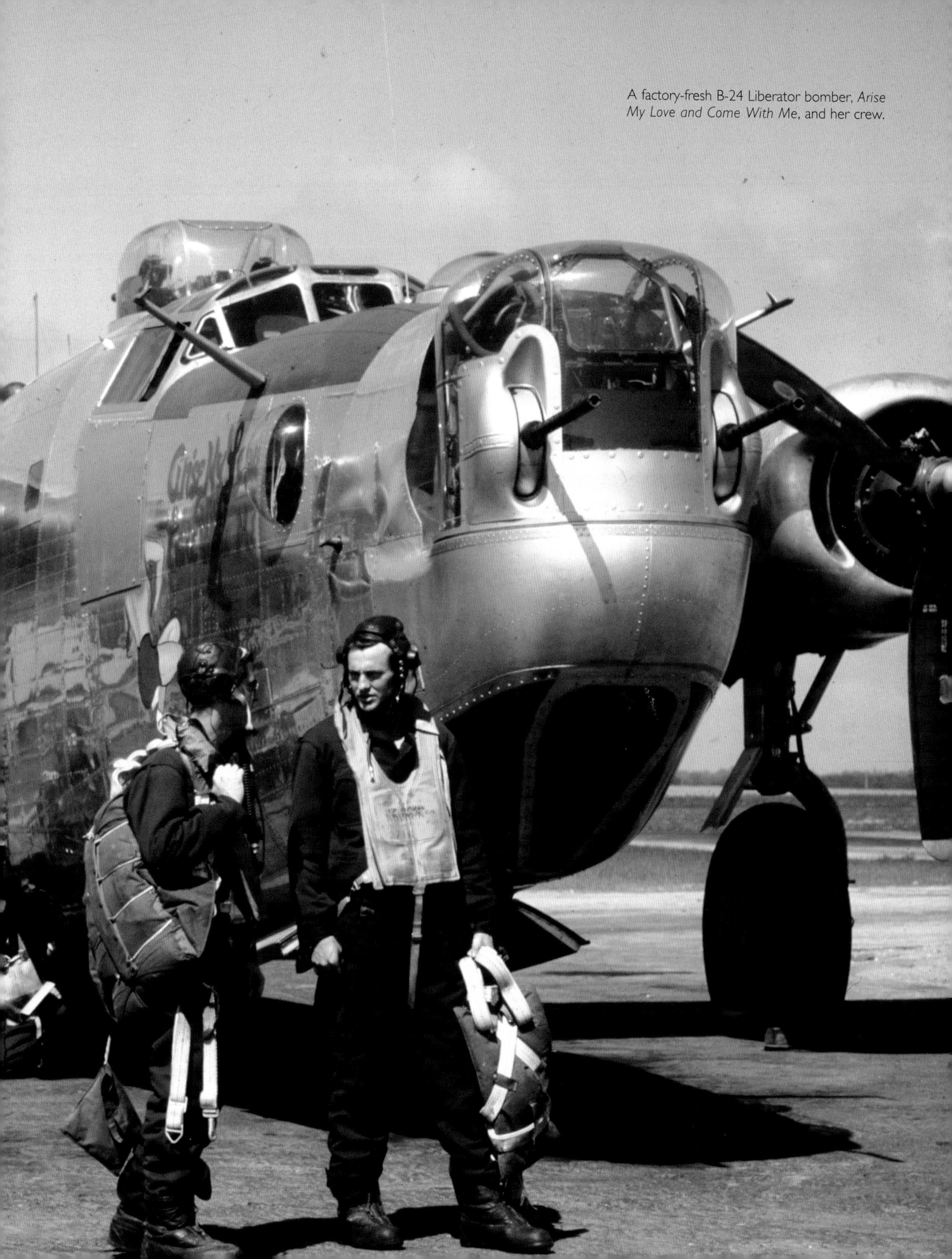

A factory-fresh B-24 Liberator bomber, *Arise My Love and Come With Me*, and her crew.

A RUDE AWAKENING

"In the officers club we had three lights, a green light, a red light, and an amber light. It would stay on the amber. It was like a traffic light behind the bar and, if the light flashed red they would close the bar down at eight o'clock. That meant we were gonna have a mission the next day. So, everybody who was scheduled to fly the next mission, whenever it was, would leave and try to get some sleep because you would have to get up at about one o'clock a.m. if you were flying the mission. It took a long time to assemble these large armadas in the air. It seemed like most of my time was spent circling round and round and round, trying to get our formation together. We tried to get over the target around noon so that we could get back and be landed before dark and also before the RAF started coming out again. Of course, in the winter time it got dark pretty early. But if that traffic light ever turned green, and it did on many occasions, there might be a mission scheduled for the next day, but bad weather or something else could scrub the mission and the light would turn green. Then, we would always have some kind of a thing where everybody would be there, the bar would stay open just as late as the people wanted, and they would break out a late breakfast and put some goodies out. When the green light was on we always had a party. You could just lie around in bed until around six o'clock the next day. On mission days, however, they just didn't tolerate you being late for briefing, so you'd get your clothes on real quick. You had to take time to shave, though, because you wore your oxygen mask real tight against your face, and the mixture of breath condensation and gunsmoke would irritate your face badly enough even if you had shaved. If I had five minutes in a chow line, I could go to sleep standing up. We carried a large fatigue factor at that time. During our tour we got one week off where we'd go to one of those hotels for rest and recuperation. I never had the slightest bit of trouble going to sleep, even when they threw rocks on the roof. You'd say a few appropriate words and go right back to sleep. To get up in the morning for a mission, an orderly would come by and touch you on the shoulder; that's all you needed. Another orderly would come to the door of our barracks. We had about fifteen or twenty men in it, and he would open the door and sing out the names of every man who was scheduled to fly that day, close the door and leave. For the breakfast on mission days, we had what we called 'combat eggs' and 'square eggs'. The combat eggs were served only at the one o'clock breakfast to the crews flying the mission. They were fresh eggs right off the griddle and very delicious. If you waited until six o'clock to eat breakfast, you would get the powdered eggs made in a very large GI pan and then cut in squares. They'd put a little cheese in there so you could tolerate them. They were always overcooked. We had some people who, whether they had to fly or not, would get up in the early morning and get those fresh eggs. The mess hall for breakfast was about a mile away from your hut and you had to walk that. The flight line was about another mile away but you could get a truck from the mess hall down to it."
—Lawrence Drew, 384BG, Grafton Underwood

IT WAS ALWAYS a rude awakening. The airman of the Eighth whose crew was on the list to participate in the mission that day was tapped, shaken, prodded, or jarred from what was more often than not a short, fitful sleep by a CQ [charge of quarters] whose job on those days was to make sure all fliers on that list were roused in time to dress, have breakfast, and arrive at the mission briefing as required. "Your name was posted on a board as being eligible to go on a raid, and you never did know it until they came through and tapped you at one o'clock in the morning, usually. You got up, took care of your ablutions and got over to the mess hall and got your fresh eggs, and by then it was about three-thirty in the morning and they took you down to the briefing room, you were briefed in the general briefing, and then they broke up and the navigators went to a special route briefing where you picked up all the weather information and all the rest of the stuff you had to have. Usually, the navigators went to the flight line and picked up the flight equipment after everybody else had been and gone, and then they'd load us on a truck and take us out to the airplanes. Takeoff would be around five or five-thirty; about three hours to get ready. One night I almost didn't get there. The driver delivered everybody and I was still there. He called my crew and found out that the plane I was supposed to be in was way on the other side of the field and it was about five or ten minutes before takeoff. The whole crew was on board when I got there. This was the one time when I actually went into the airplane through the waist door because they were running up the engines. I threw my equipment on and I lost my hat that morning. Navigators usually waited

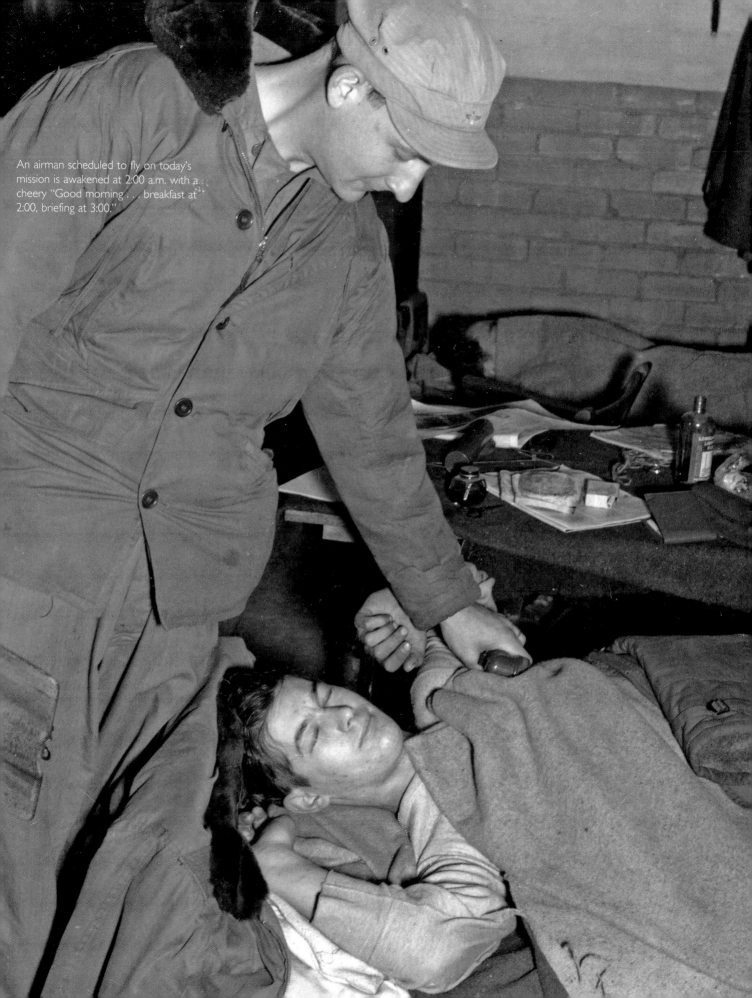

An airman scheduled to fly on today's mission is awakened at 2:00 a.m. with a cheery "Good morning . . . breakfast at 2:00, briefing at 3:00."

on the hardstand maybe ten minutes at the most. There was usually just enough time to get your gear loaded. Navigators usually did not stand the formation. Normally they'd have you stand outside where the airplane commander checked to make sure you had your gear and your parachute and the parachute was not oily. But the navigator usually didn't stand that formation because he wasn't there yet."

—W.W. Ford, 92BG, Podington

The daylight missions of the Eighth got started long before daylight. In fact, the actual preparation for a raid got going several days before it was to take place. At Eighth Bomber Command, code-named Pinetree and located in a former girl's chool at Wycombe Abbey, High Wycombe, the target for this day's raid had been selected and the various Headquarters sections—Intelligence, Personnel, Operations, and Planning, Supply—had begun the process of assembling the mission. They determined the number of bombers to be used on this target, what fighter protection was to be provided, which groups would be involved, what kind of bombs would be dropped—high explosive, incendiary, fragmentation, or a combination of these? Whether the bombers should be flown to the target by the shortest and most direct route, giving them the shortest exposure to enemy resistance, and in requiring less gasoline, allowing them to carry a heavier payload of bombs? Or should they be sent via a more lengthy route that, although longer, would distance them from at least some of the worst concentrations of flak and fighters? Were the bomb groups involved sufficiently supplied with bombs, fuel, and ammunition

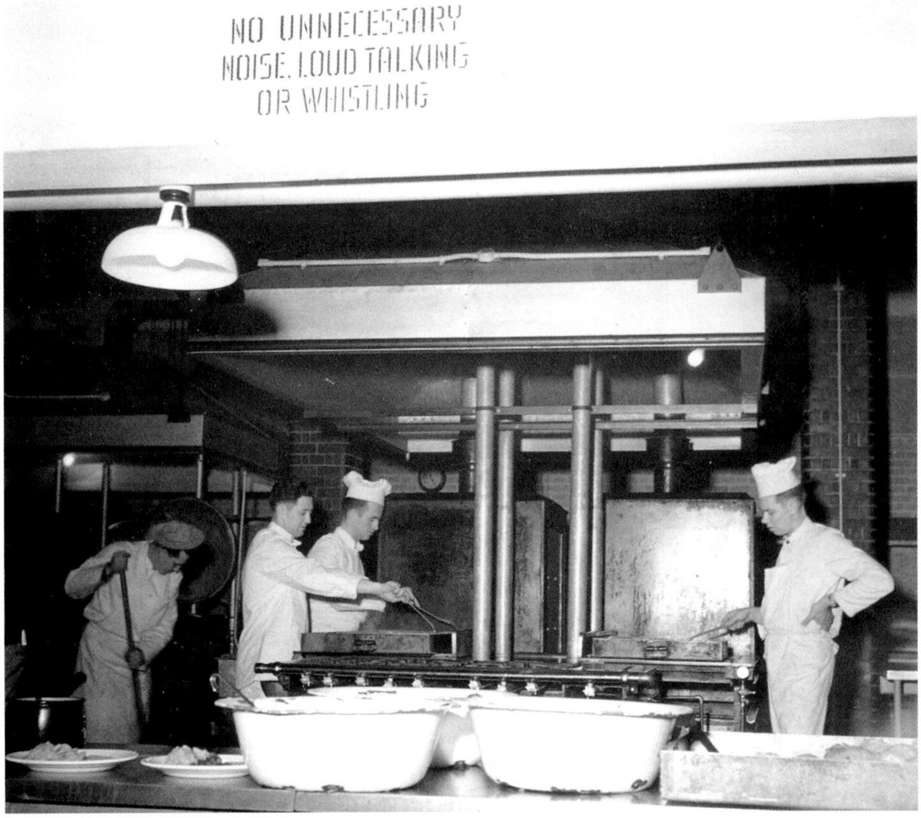
NO UNNECESSARY
NOISE. LOUD TALKING
OR WHISTLING

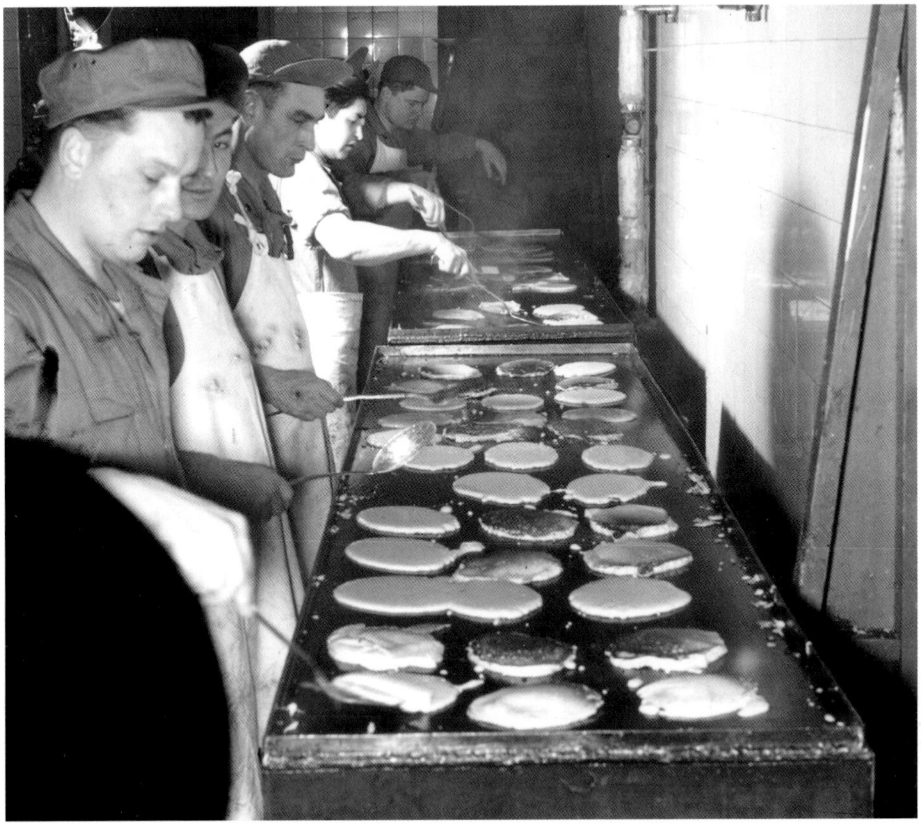

and would they need to be resupplied?

A field order came clattering from a teleprinter in group operations the evening before, alerting the group operations staff of the impending raid and providing some basic information about it. It was followed by more specific detailed instructions about the target, the aircraft required, the bombloads, the flak and fighter opposition anticipated, the navigational routes and timings, the fighter escort, and other pertinent information normally provided by the planners at Eighth Bomber Command. This field order would trigger a rash of high-priority activity in many departments across the group. Ground crewmen and maintenance stepped up the pace of their work preparing their aircraft, getting them into top condition for the demands about to be made on them. Group operations planners scrambled to prepare for their briefing presentations on the weather in England and on the Continent, the expected enemy opposition, tactics such as planned diversions etc, information about the target, and special separate breifings for navigators and bombardiers. On the many hardstands adjacent to the perimeter track, armorers had the cold, frequently miserable chore of loading the bombs aboard the B-17s or B-24s of the group, and the boxes of caliber fifty machine-gun ammunition to feed the many guns bristling from the heavy bombers. "As soon as the planes left on a mission, we would go and have breakfast and then go and sleep until about noon or

Breakfast is the first order of business on an 8AF base and for many the most important meal of the day.

so, and then have lunch. In the better weather they would then have softball games and there were a lot of movies in the afternoon. In the evening we would go back and see whether or not there was an alert. In each barracks one person was named the CQ and everyone else could sleep or play cards or whatever they wanted to do. Then, if we got a message from the top sergeant that we could start the loading, we would go to our particular planes and they would tell us what kind of bombs were supposed to be put on, whether they were fragmentation bombs, five hundred pounds, or whatever. It was usually freezing cold, but because of putting shackles on the bombs and doing other delicate work, we couldn't wear gloves. That all generally consumed from about eleven at night until about five in the morning."
—Sam Burchell, 448BG, Seething

"Those Ordnance guys were something else! They worked their tails off under the most miserable conditions, yet seemed to take delight in their labors. In my opinion, their job was more dangerous than flying combat. For example, there was an incident where, due to poor visibility from the blackout headlights, a bomb-hauling truck with about ten guys on board catapulted over an anti-aircraft pit while going about forty miles an hour. When it came to earth on the other side of the pit the only person still on it was the driver."
—Glenn Matson, 458BG, Horsham St Faith

Fuel bowsers cruised the peri track to load or top up the tanks of the big planes with as much as 2,780 gallons each, depending on how far the Forts and Libs would be going this time. The cooks in the combat mess went to work preparing the special break-

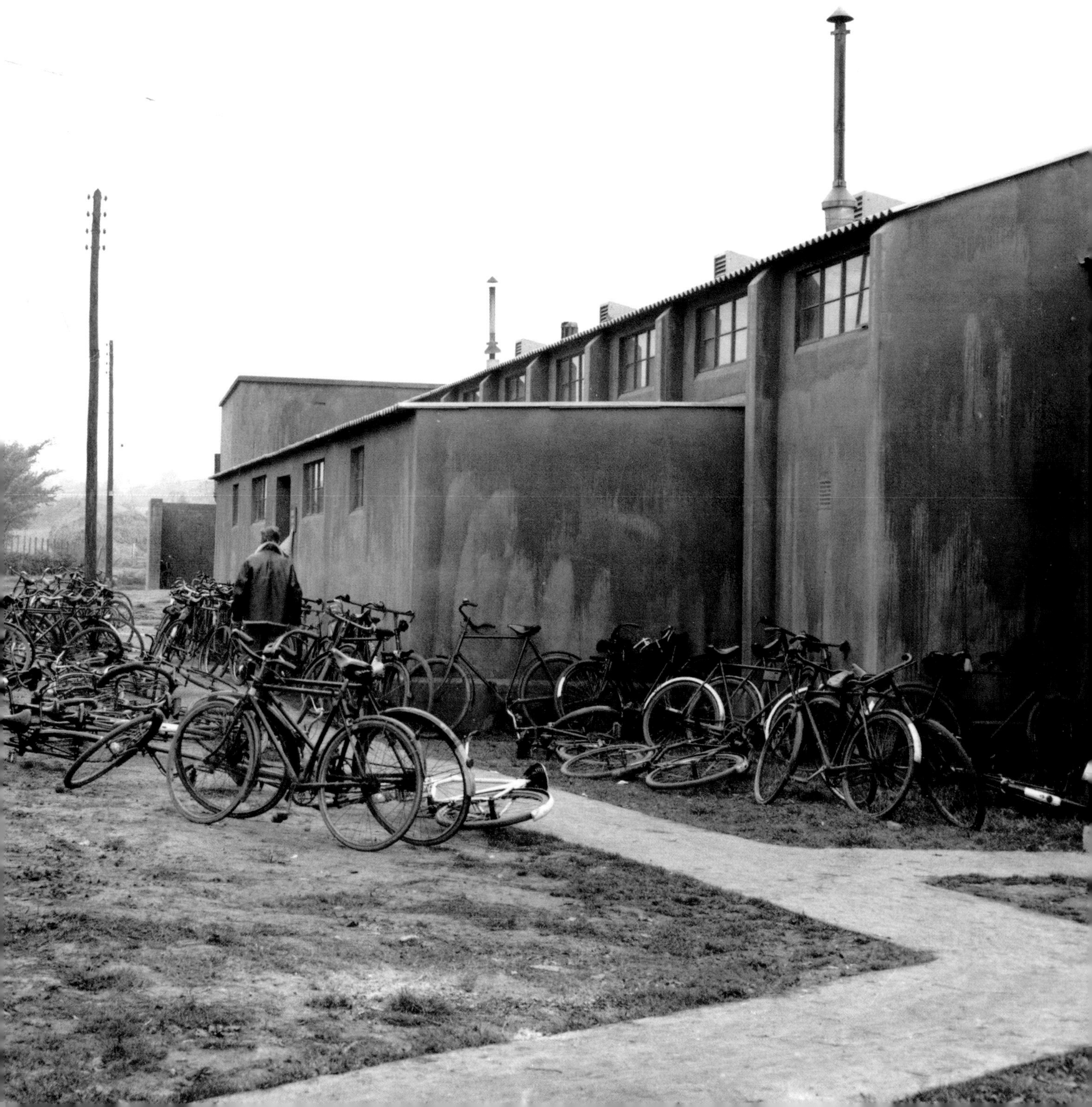

Decorating the exteriors of the various brick-built Maycrete structures on the air bases of the Eighth in WW2 England was the primary transport of the time. Distances between destinations on the fields were substantial and bikes were essential for those without access to a jeep.

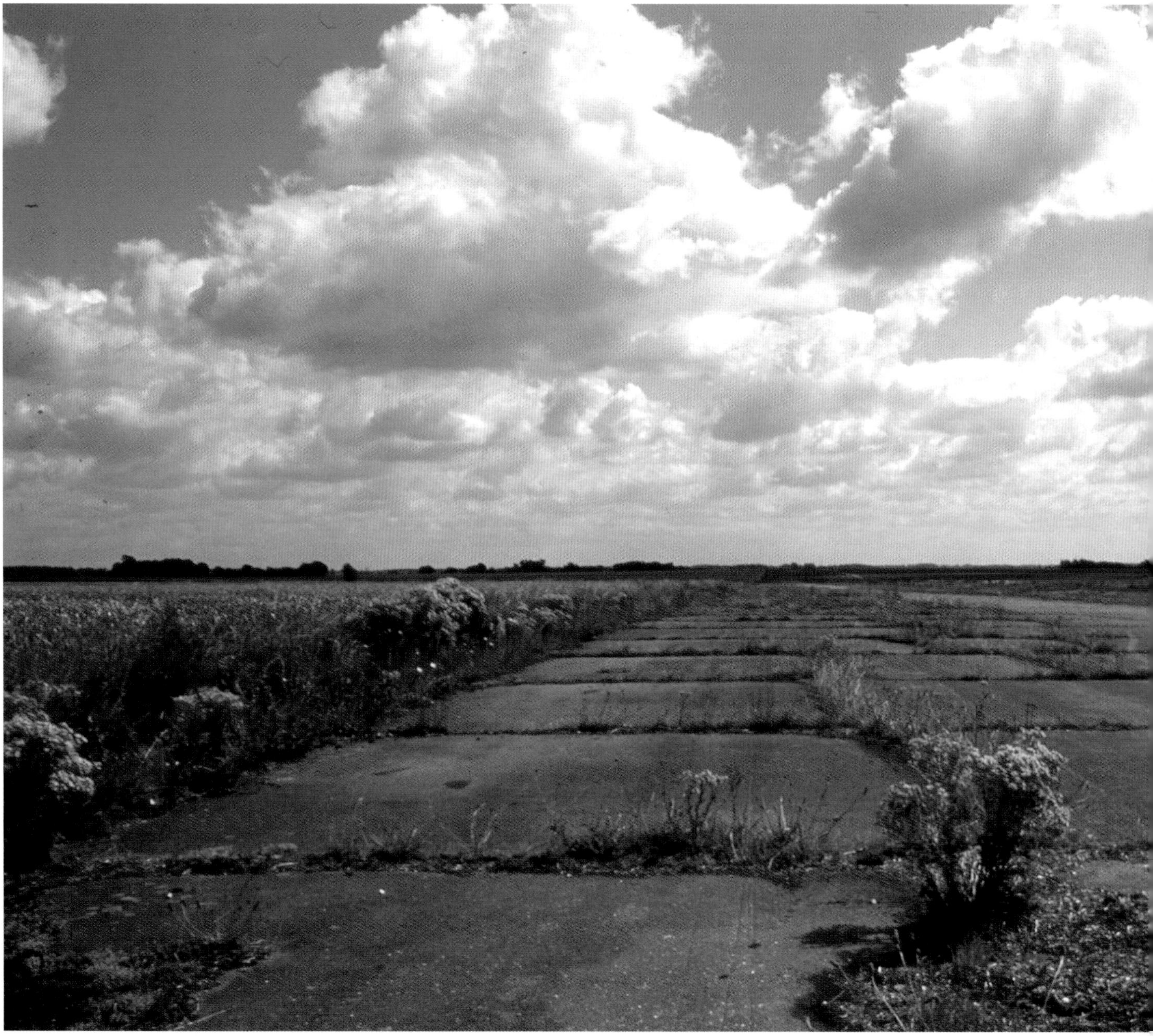

fast prescribed for those who would be spending most of their day at high altitude where certain foods of the gasier variety can lead to stomach or intestinal discomfort or worse.

The briefing was a high-security affair. Every man attending had to show his pass to be admitted. "When the briefing started they locked the doors and put guards on them. They shut those doors right on the minute that the briefing was scheduled for. In the briefing room we had a little raised platform there with a large map of Germany behind it. They'd have a cloth in front of it, some sort of roll-up type shade. We'd assemble in there not knowing where the mission was, and there was a lot of tension at that time. Of course, we'd all be hoping for a good 'milk run', a mission when we would be back in four or five hours, and then, rather dramatically they would pull up the shade and

The main runway at Lavenham, the former base of the 487th Bomb Group, as it looked in the 1990s.

then you'd see a red ribbon on the map from our base showing our flight path into the target and back. We'd generally have three targets, a primary, secondary, and tertiary. A lot of times you couldn't hit the primary and so the leader would decide to go to the secondary and if you couldn't hit any

of the three, then we had targets of opportunity. Searching around, trying to find targets you think would do some good. We had several of those. If the raid was to Berlin—we called it 'Big B'—everybody would sigh about that because it was a long mission with heavy flak. A colonel would get up there and make a little speech and let you know that the entire war hinged on how good a job you did on this one particular target. He'd sell it a little bit. Then he turned it over to the lower-ranking operations officers who'd have special briefings for the bombardiers, navigators, and pilots. From the time we went into the room until we got out was about thirty minutes. Then we'd all get out to the planes and we had to make sure they were serviced properly and do a preflight on them, get your bombs loaded, get your ammunition stowed, get the guns checked out. While you were in those special briefings, the gunners were checking out their guns and installing them in the planes; they were removed after every mission. Kind of a busy time. You'd get the crew aboard and sit. You had a schedule that showed which plane you were supposed to follow out, and when that plane comes by you leave your hardstand and follow behind him. Many's the time we'd sit and sit and sit, perhaps for an hour, waiting on the weather man. The weather man was reluctant to scrub the mission, but he didn't want to authorize the takeoff. If the mission was scrubbed, they would fire the flares from the operations building and that was all the signal we'd need, so we'd get down and unload the airplane. Eventually, we'd get a green flare and that would tell us to start our engines and taxi out. Some missions would be delayed an hour or so. You couldn't delay them too long

because you'd get into this conflict with the RAF; you'd be getting back in too late."
—Lawrence Drew, 384BG, Grafton Underwood

After the briefing, the air crews went to the ready room to pick up their equipment for the flight: helmets, oxygen masks, parachutes and harnesses, Mae West life jackets, pistols, escape kits, and more. "When you knew you were gonna go on a raid the next day, you didn't sleep that well. You went to bed around eleven o'clock, you were gonna get up three or four hours later, and the deepest sleep you'd get was right five minutes before they'd call you. You were so damp and cold, I wore my heavy socks, then I'd put shoes on over those, coveralls and flying boots and fur-lined jacket and your hot-shot Charlie hat, the garrison thing with the grommet taken out, into breakfast. The trucks would take you to briefing and then to the ready room. When you were a lead crew and you came back from a raid, usually the colonel met you with a staff car; he wanted to find out how good the hit was, he wanted your camera, and then you'd get on up to interrogation. But after briefing they'd take you to the ready room where you'd sit around shooting the bull, go to the john fifteen times. You'd pick up your Mae West, parachute—back or chest, most pilots and co-pilots wore chest packs, because the armor plate was only about twelve inches apart and you couldn't get through with a chute on; when you had to get out you'd pick up your chute which was right behind your seat and hook that on, on the way down sometimes . . . and you also picked up your flak suit which was like a baseball catcher's chest protector. My ground engineer on my plane, every time we changed planes we'd change the armor plating

under the seat because most of the flak would come up from underneath. It could kill you but most of the threat was castration from the flak coming from underneath the airplane. Some used flak gloves; I couldn't. I just used very thin kid gloves. I didn't use a flak helmet; just took the inner liner out of an ordinary infantry helmet. The bombardier, navigator, pilot, and co-pilot all carried a forty-five [caliber pistol]; the chief engineer had a Tommy gun and the other five men had carbines. I was against them because they told you that if you got hit and knocked down, not to give up to civilians because they's lost a mother, father, uncle, brother, sister, somebody in a bombing raid and they might pitchfork you to death. If you saw military and you were caught, give up to them. As soon as you hit the Pas de Calais coast, everything was occupied by

the Germans then. You were told that if you were shot down, roll up your parachute, bury it and stay right there because the Free French knew where you hit. You had an escape kit with Hershey bars, francs, and stuff like that and a picture taken of you in civilian clothes."

—Ray Wild, 92BG, Podington

"The equipment hut was a mess, with everyone trying to dress in the same place at the same time. I decided to wear an electric suit because I hate long johns. I put my OD's on over that, a summer flying suit over that, and a leather jacket on top. A Mae West comes last. I was sweating before I got into all my clothes, and by the time I had heaved my flak suit and parachute onto the truck I could feel sweat rolling down my knees."

—Bert Stiles, 91BG, Bassingbourn

Finally, sometimes as much as three hours after they had been awakened, the air crews arrived, by truck or jeep, at their airplanes. The sergeant gunners loaded their guns aboard the bombers while the pilots, navigator, and bombardier were busy with preflight checklists. "You'd get into the airplane and just sit after doing the preflight. Many a time we sat as long as an hour and a half, ready to go but waiting on clearance from the weather man. If then they decided to scrub the mission, they'd fire red flares from the Operations building. Wouldn't use the radio, just flares. But if they fired a green flare, that told you to start engines and be ready to taxi out."

—Lawrence Drew, 384BG, Grafton Underwood

"When your turn came to take off, you

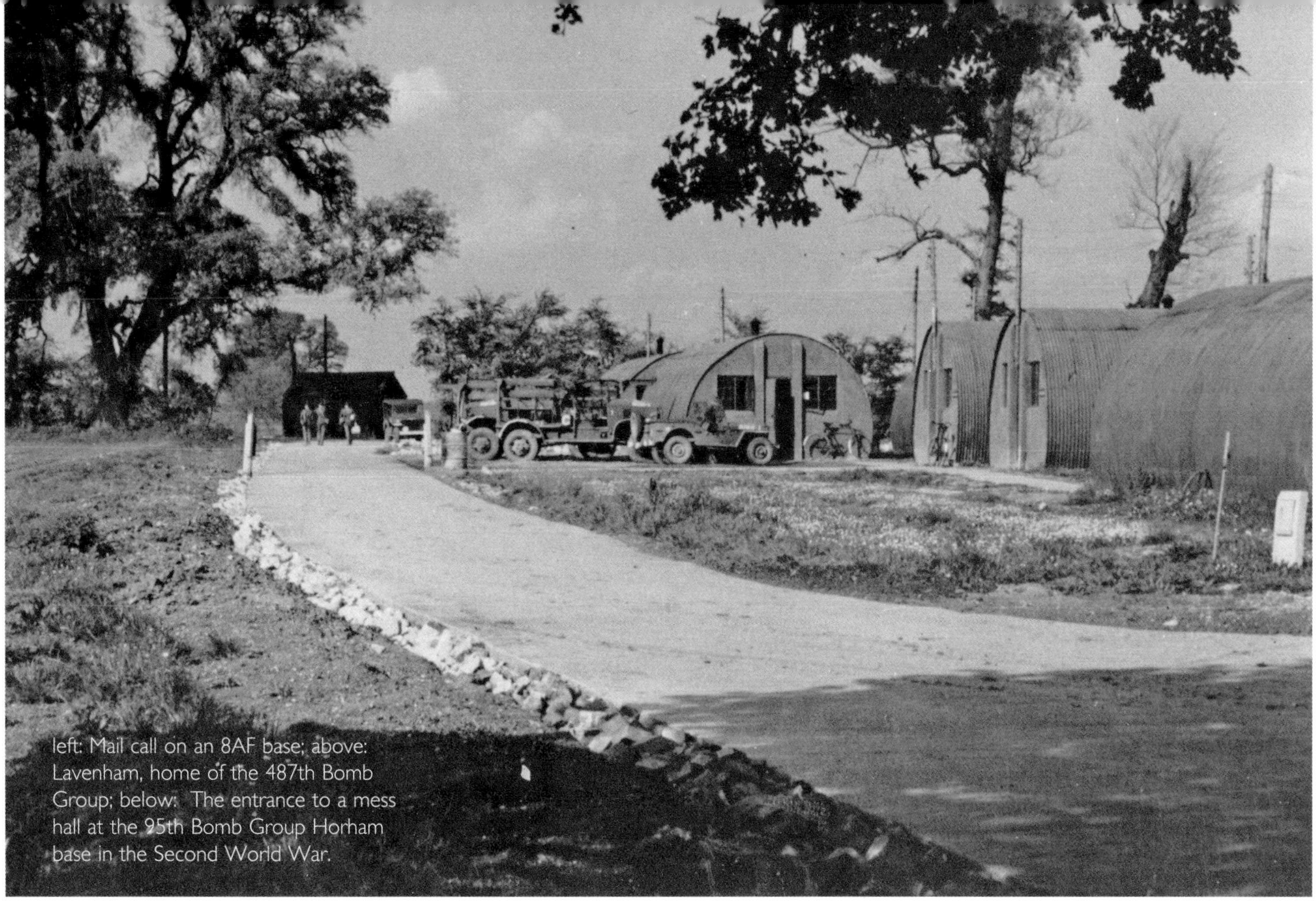

left: Mail call on an 8AF base; above: Lavenham, home of the 487th Bomb Group; below: The entrance to a mess hall at the 95th Bomb Group Horham base in the Second World War.

lined up so that one guy would take off from this side of the runway, and the next guy from the other side. That way you had a better chance of avoiding each others' prop wash."
—Ray Wild, 92BG, Podington

"We took off and climbed through dense fog, and that required the God-damndest precision. We were reversing our course and reversing again, so the danger of collision was always there, until we finally broke out of the cloud. It was a good feeling to be in the lead ship, because we were first off the ground and constantly climbing."
—Sidney Rapoport, 94BG, Rougham

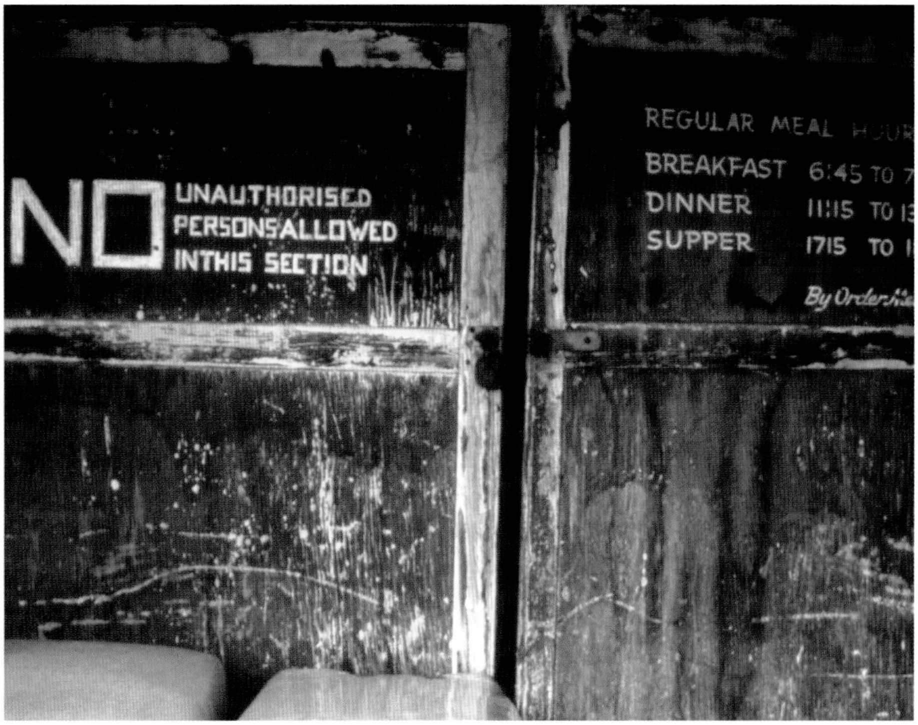
NO
UNAUTHORISED PERSONS ALLOWED IN THIS SECTION
REGULAR MEAL
BREAKFAST 6:45
DINNER 11:15
SUPPER 1715

Making do in a Nissen hut in wartime England; right: What a well-dressed B-17 gunner wore at Bassingbourn on a mission in 1944.

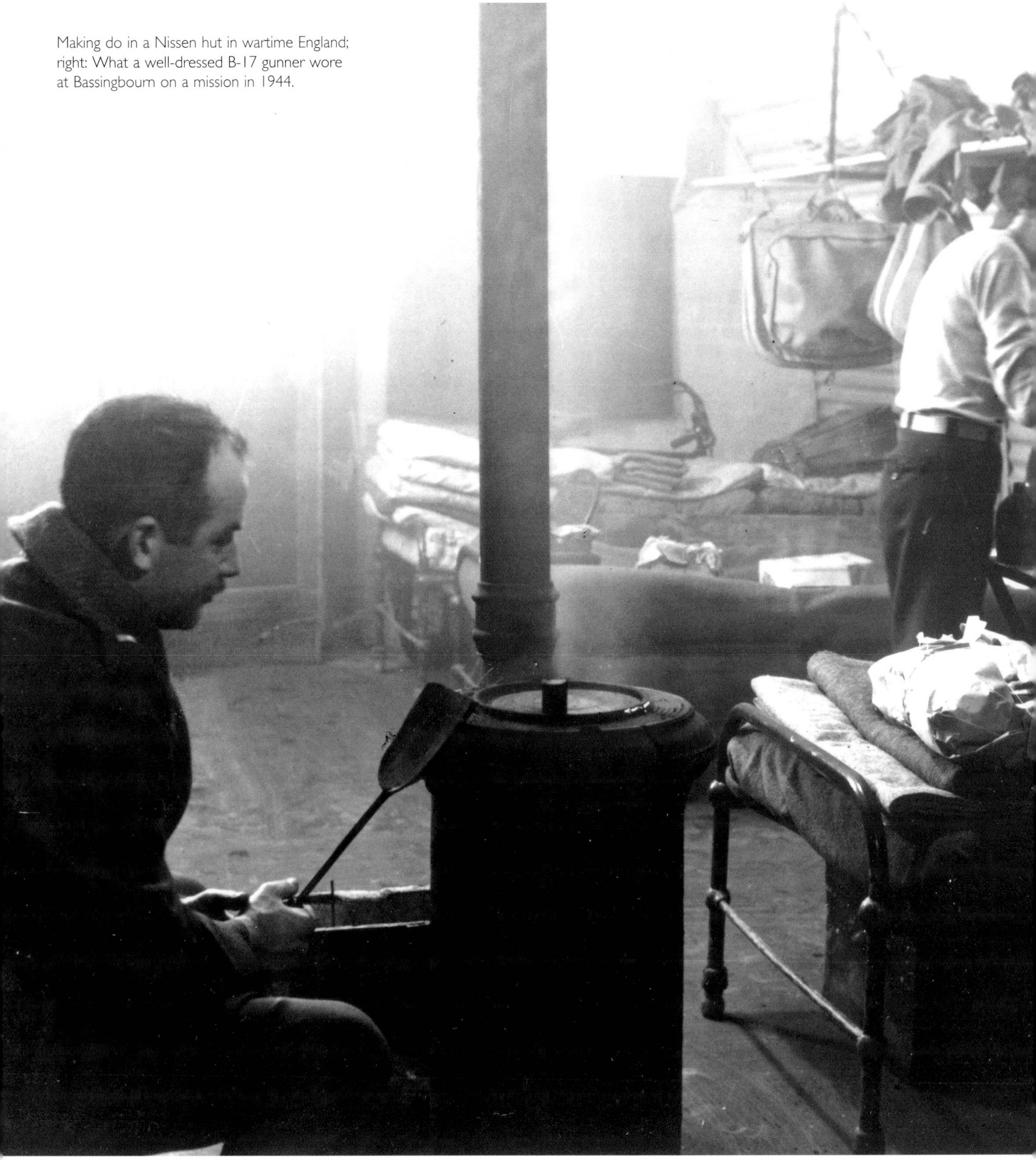

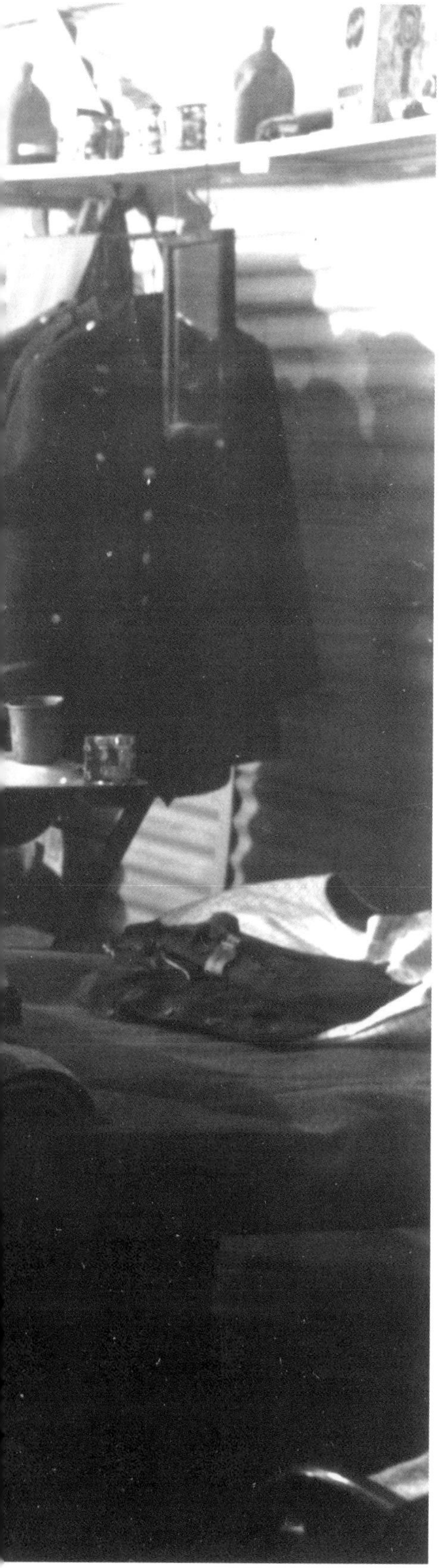

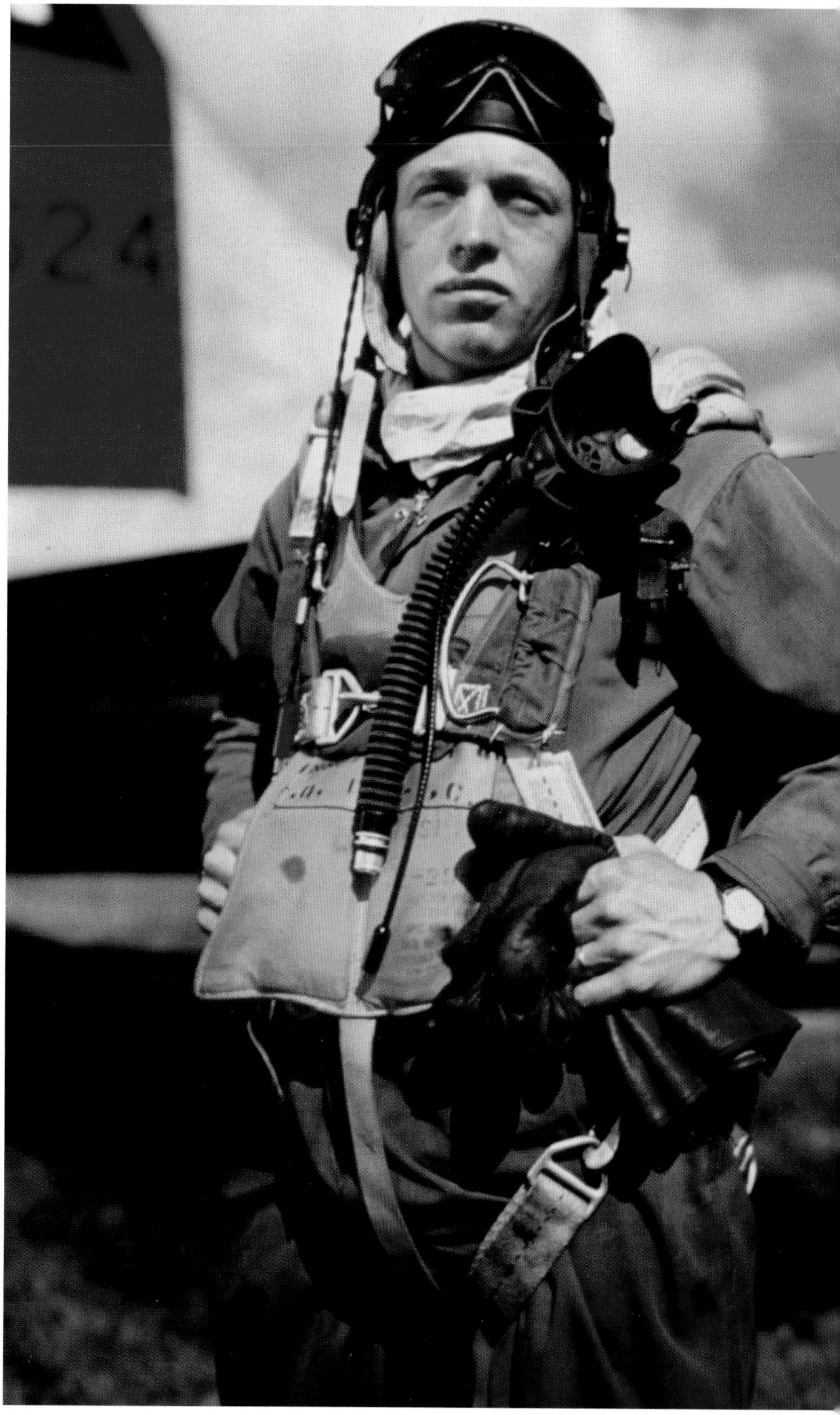

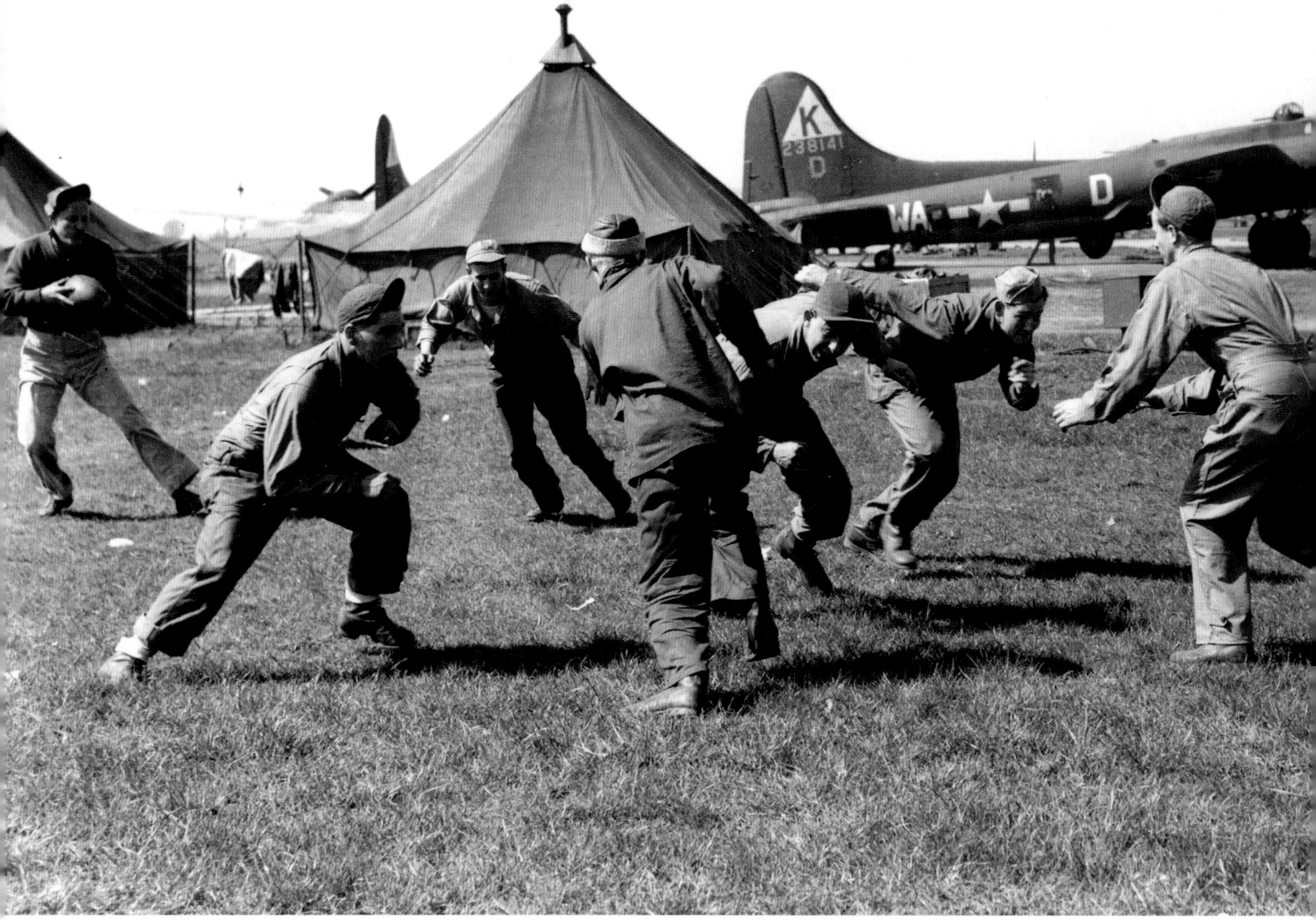
K
238141
D
WA
D

above: A pick-up game of American football on the airfield of the 379th Bomb Group at Kimbolton; top right: Popular pin-ups line the walls of this barber shop at the 381st Bomb Group's Ridgewell base; right:: Recent Hollywood movies entertained personnel of the 384th Bomb Group at Grafton Underwood in 1944; far right: Bomber air crew enjoying a Red Cross show staged for them at Kimbolton in January 1944.

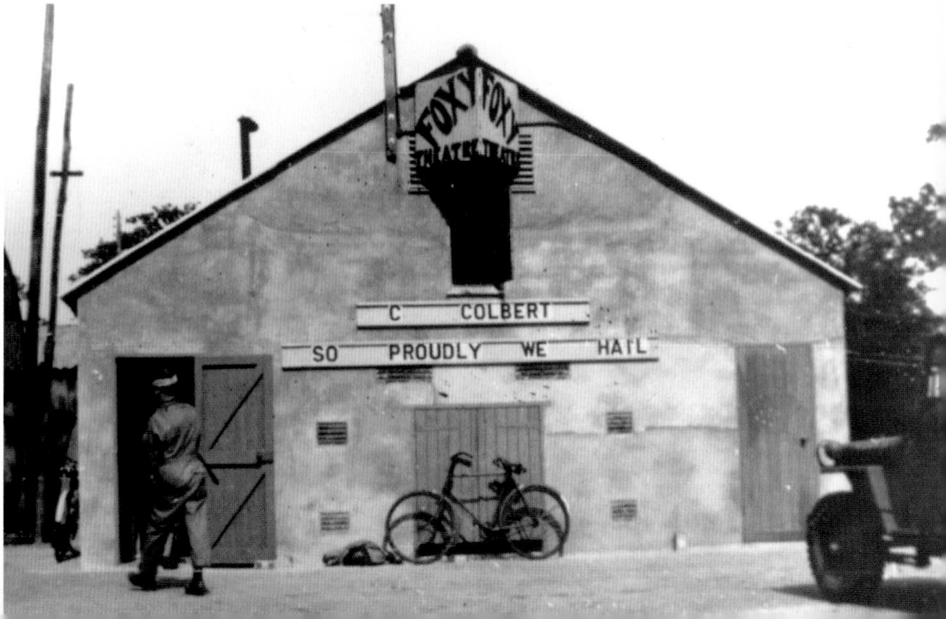
FOXY FOXY
THEATRE THEATRE
C COLBERT
SO PROUDLY WE HAIL

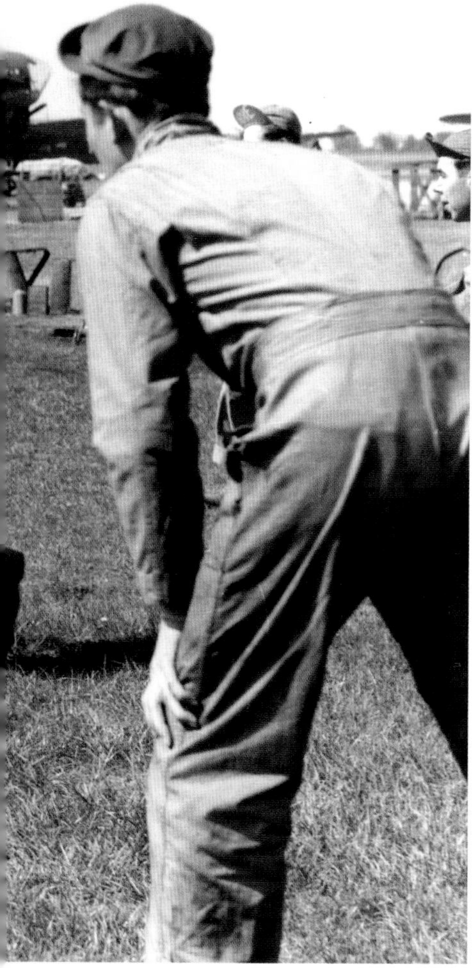

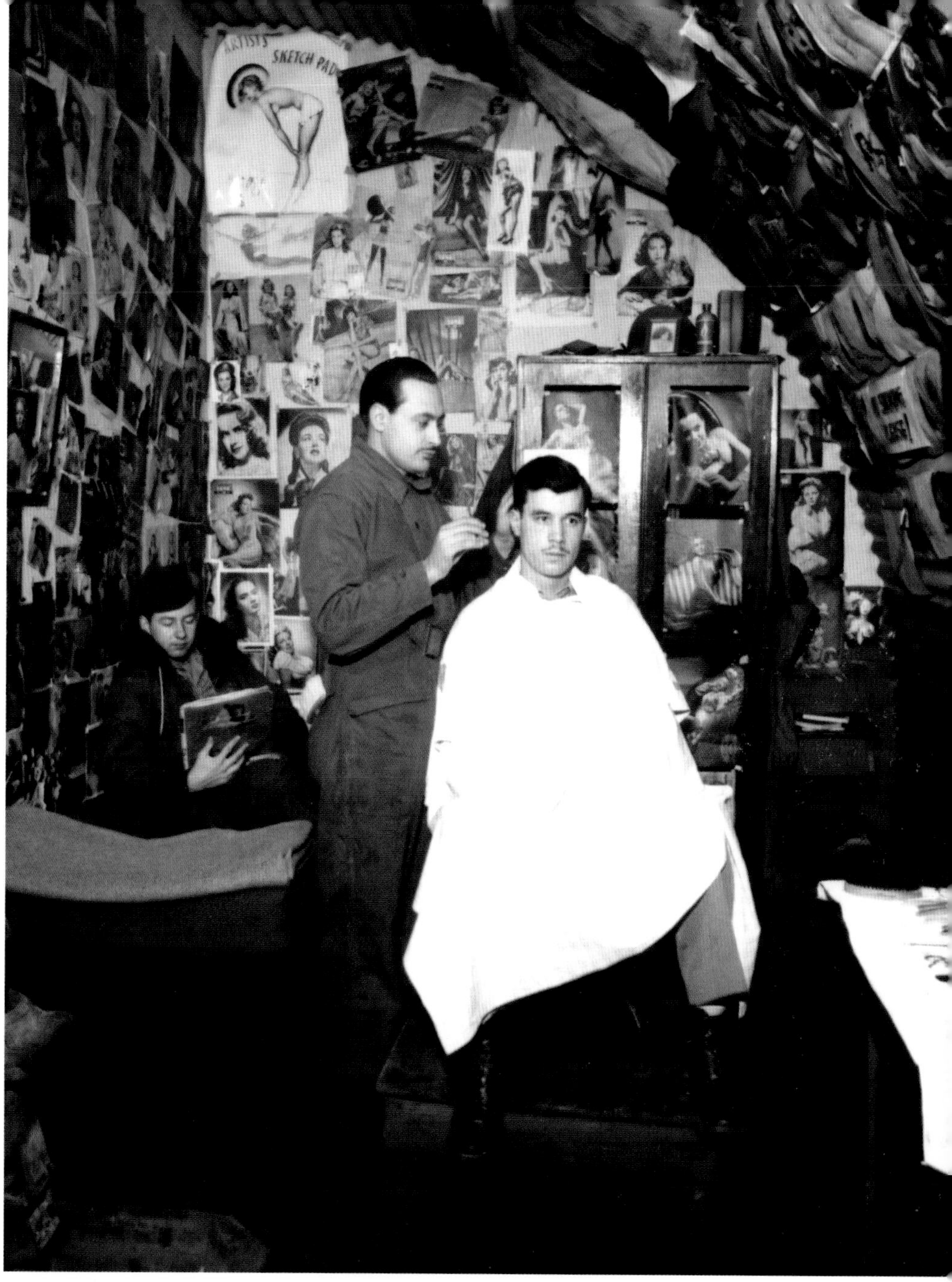
ARTIST'S
SKETCH PAD

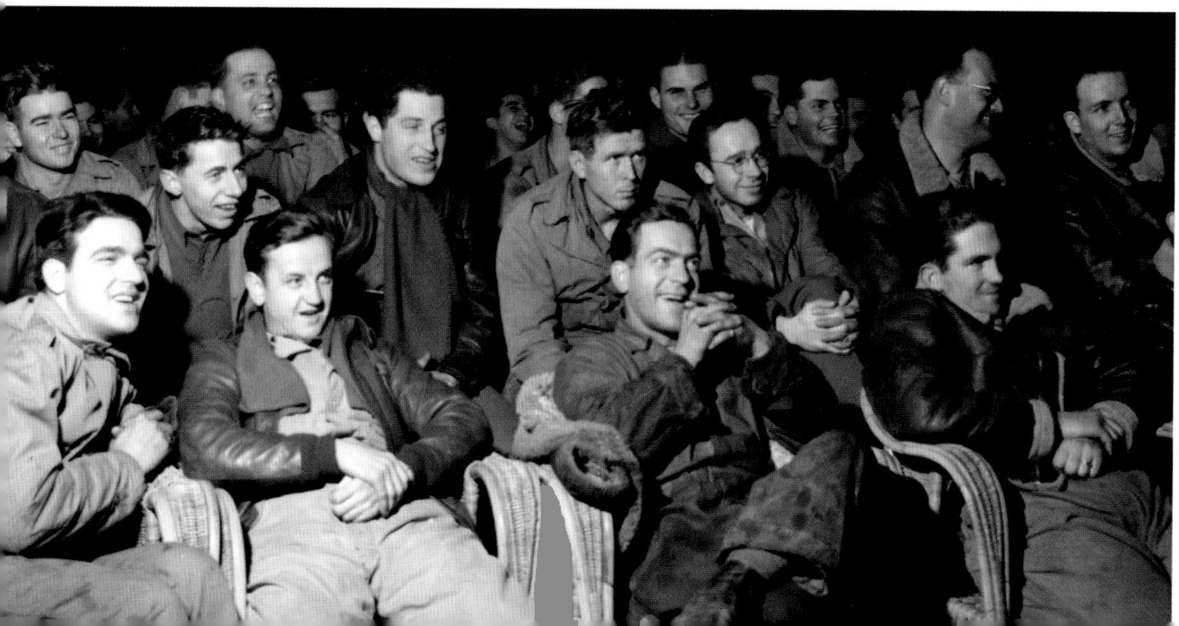

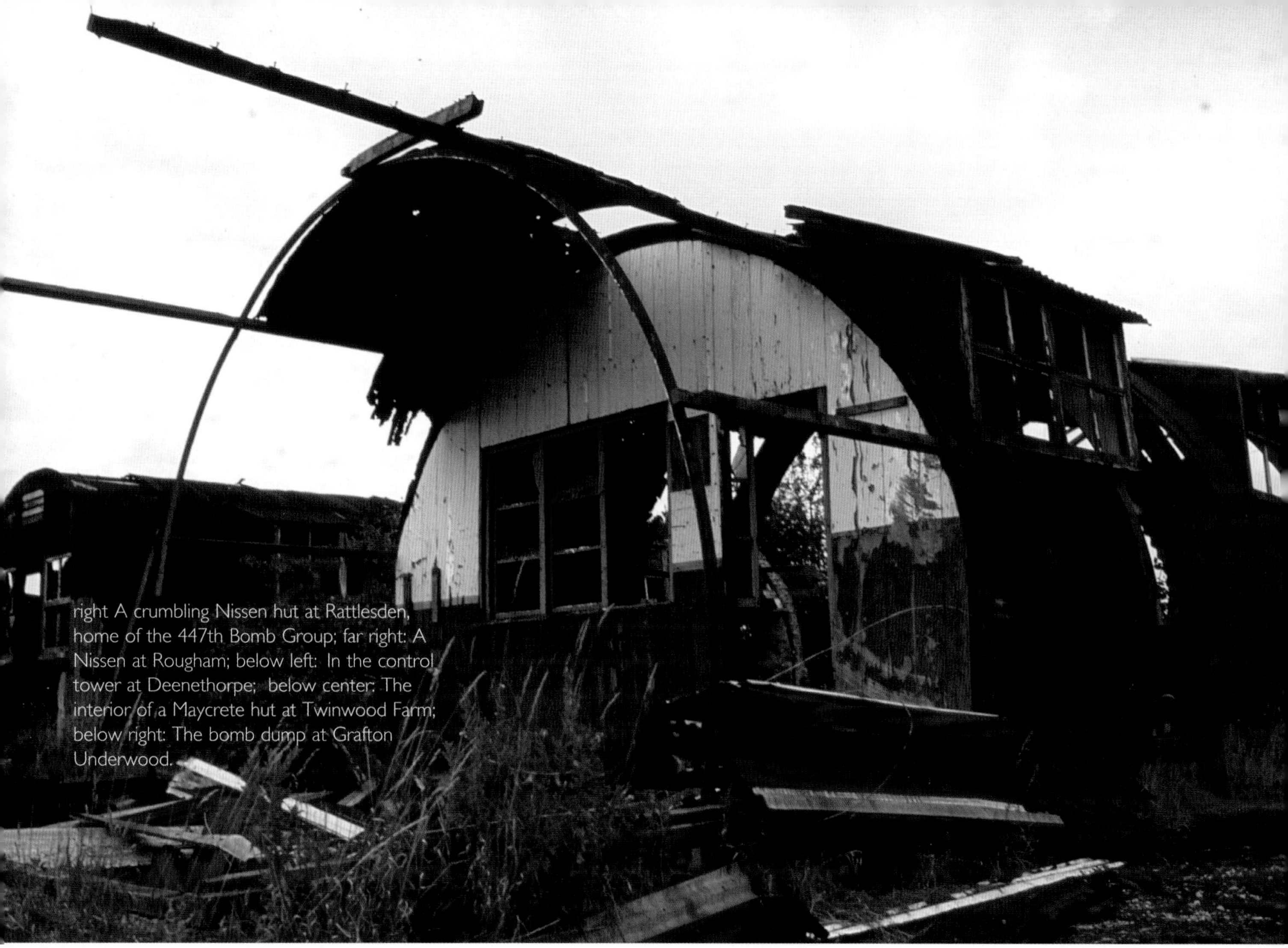

right A crumbling Nissen hut at Rattlesden, home of the 447th Bomb Group; far right: A Nissen at Rougham; below left: In the control tower at Deenethorpe; below center: The interior of a Maycrete hut at Twinwood Farm; below right: The bomb dump at Grafton Underwood.

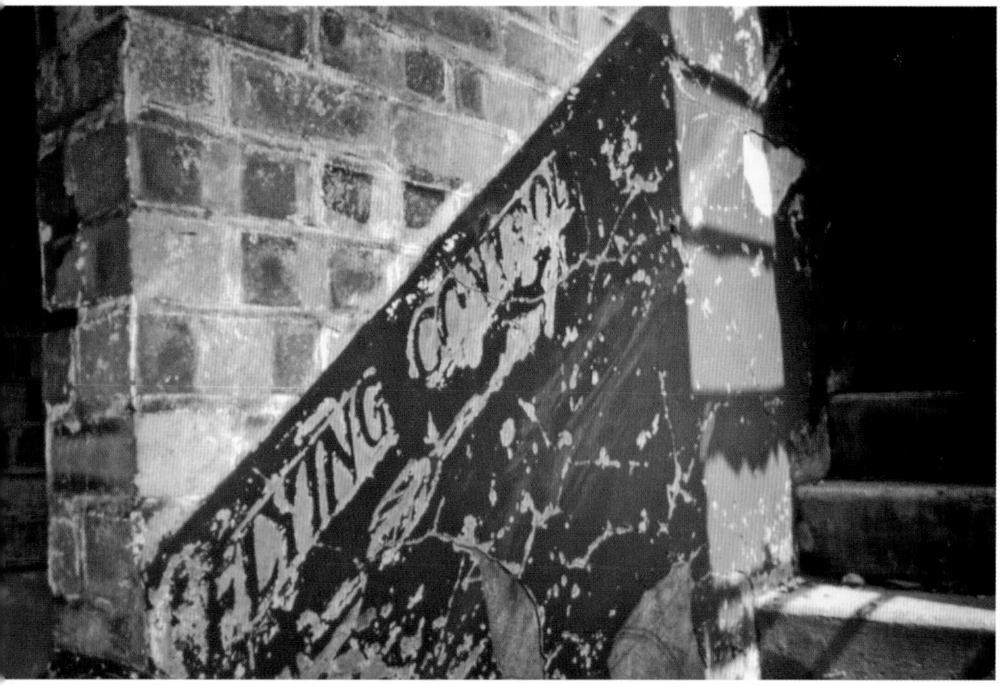
FLYING CONTROL

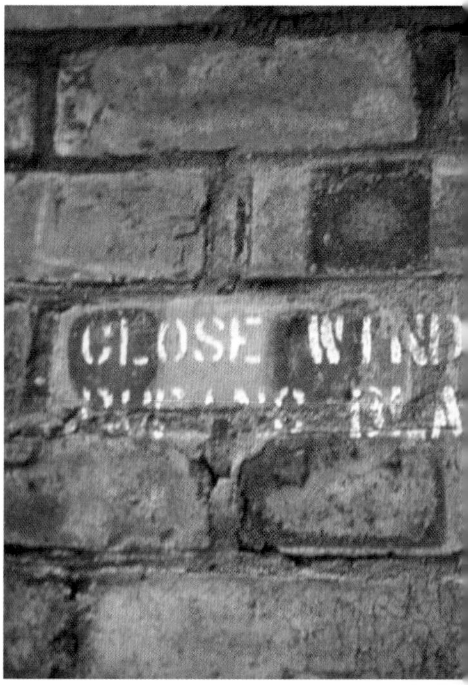
CLOSE WIND

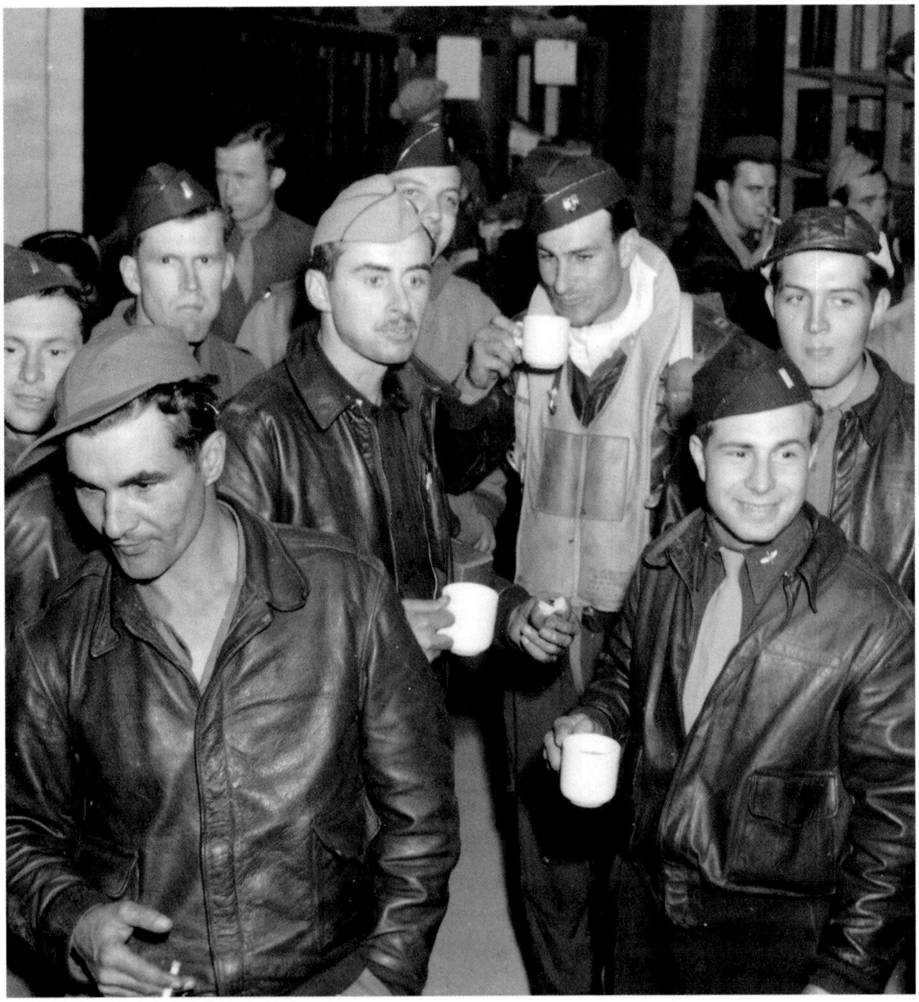

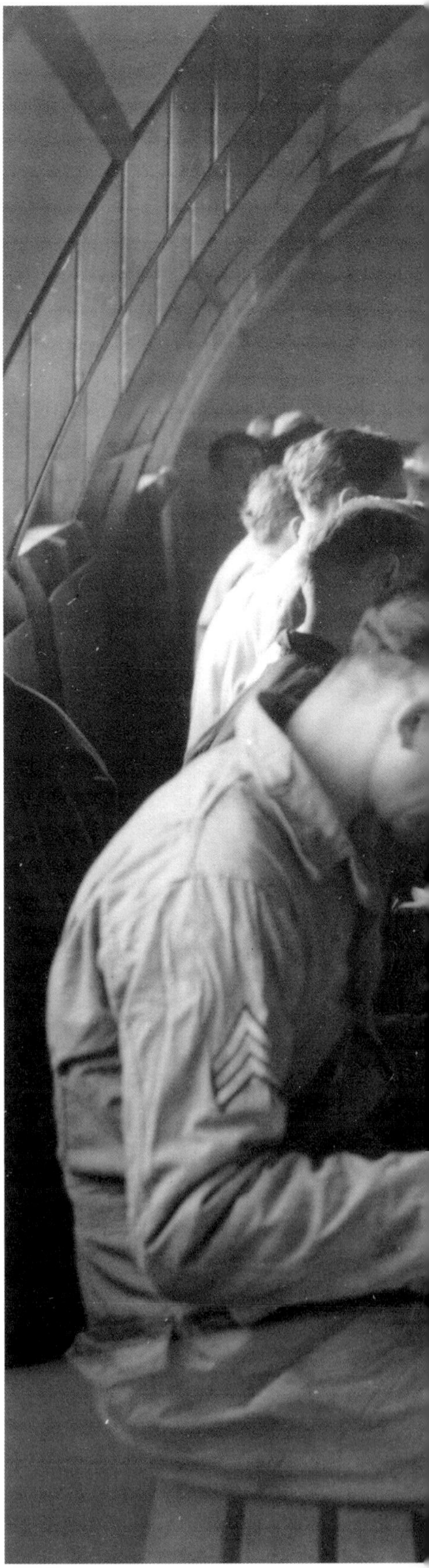

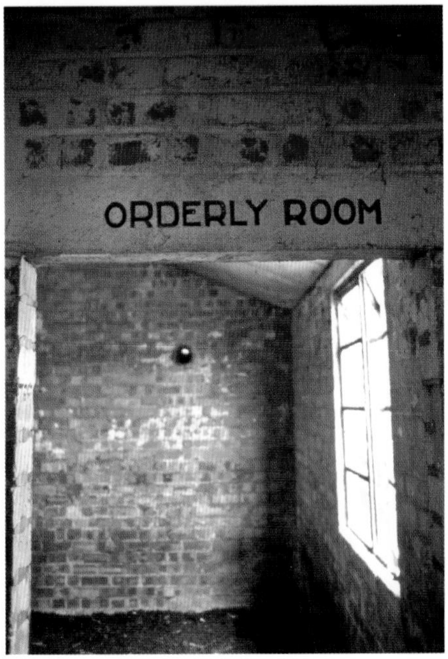
ORDERLY ROOM

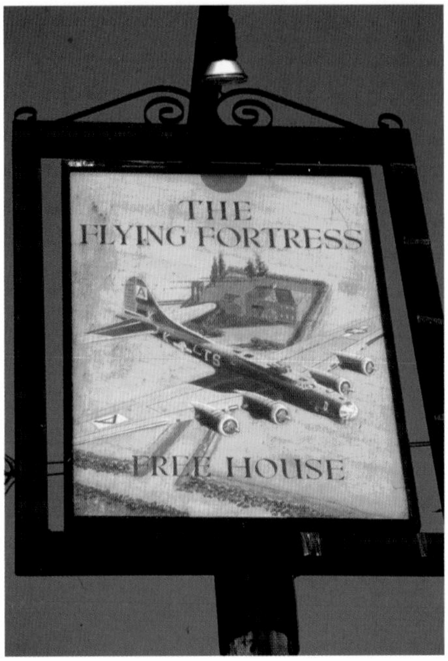
THE
FLYING FORTRESS
FREE HOUSE

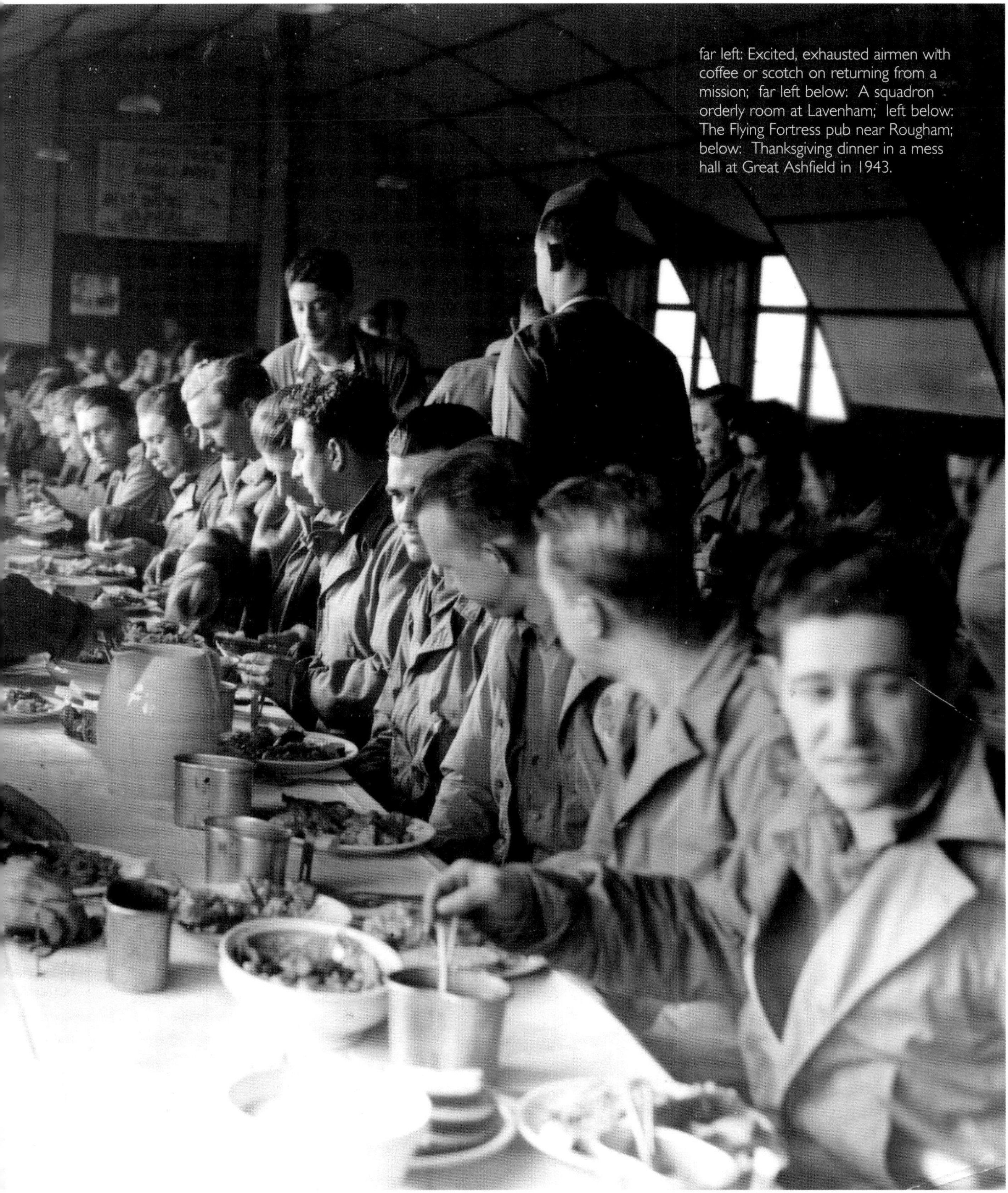

far left: Excited, exhausted airmen with coffee or scotch on returning from a mission; far left below: A squadron orderly room at Lavenham; left below: The Flying Fortress pub near Rougham; below: Thanksgiving dinner in a mess hall at Great Ashfield in 1943.

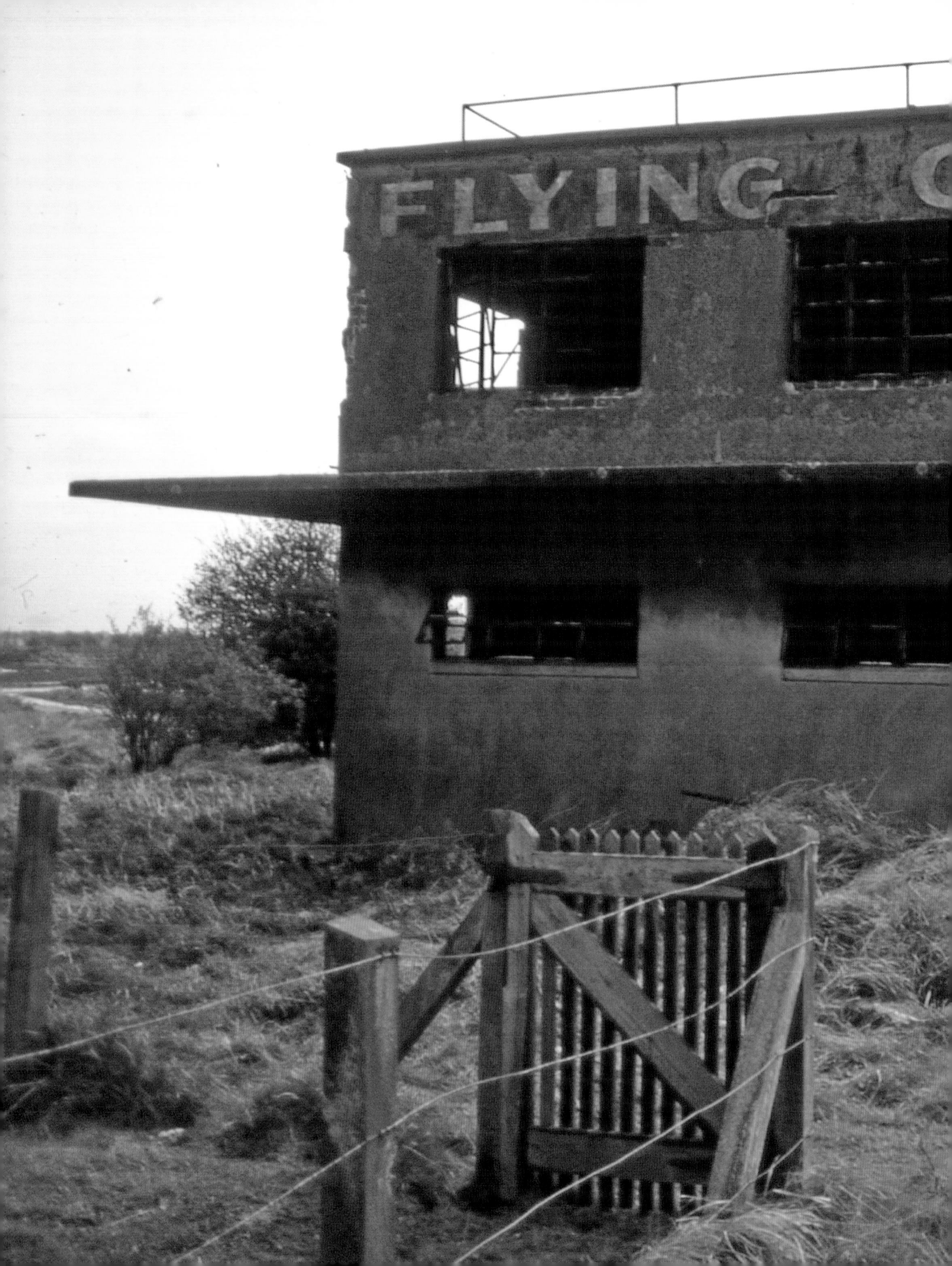
FLYING C

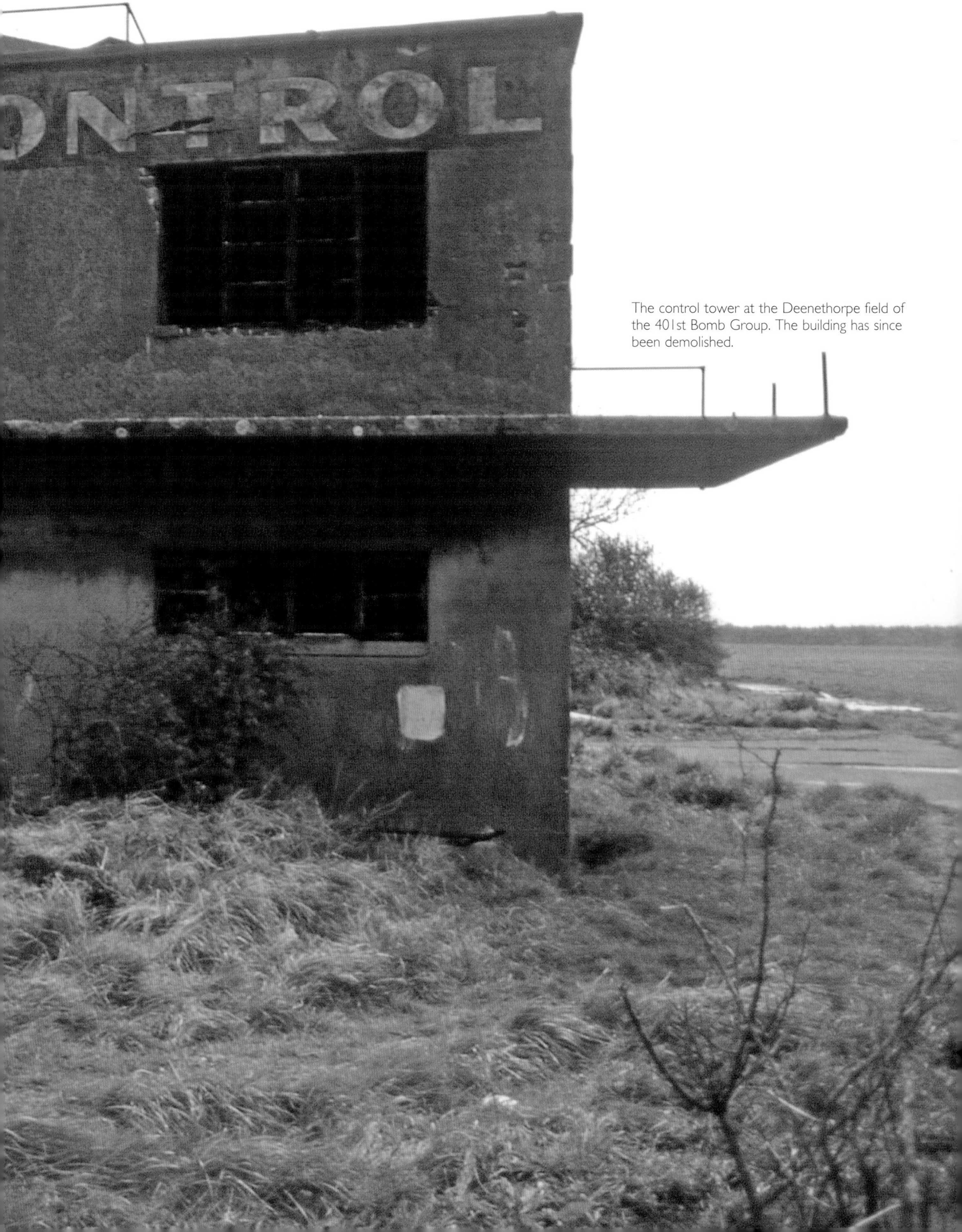
ONTROL

The control tower at the Deenethorpe field of the 401st Bomb Group. The building has since been demolished.

THE FLYING MACHINES

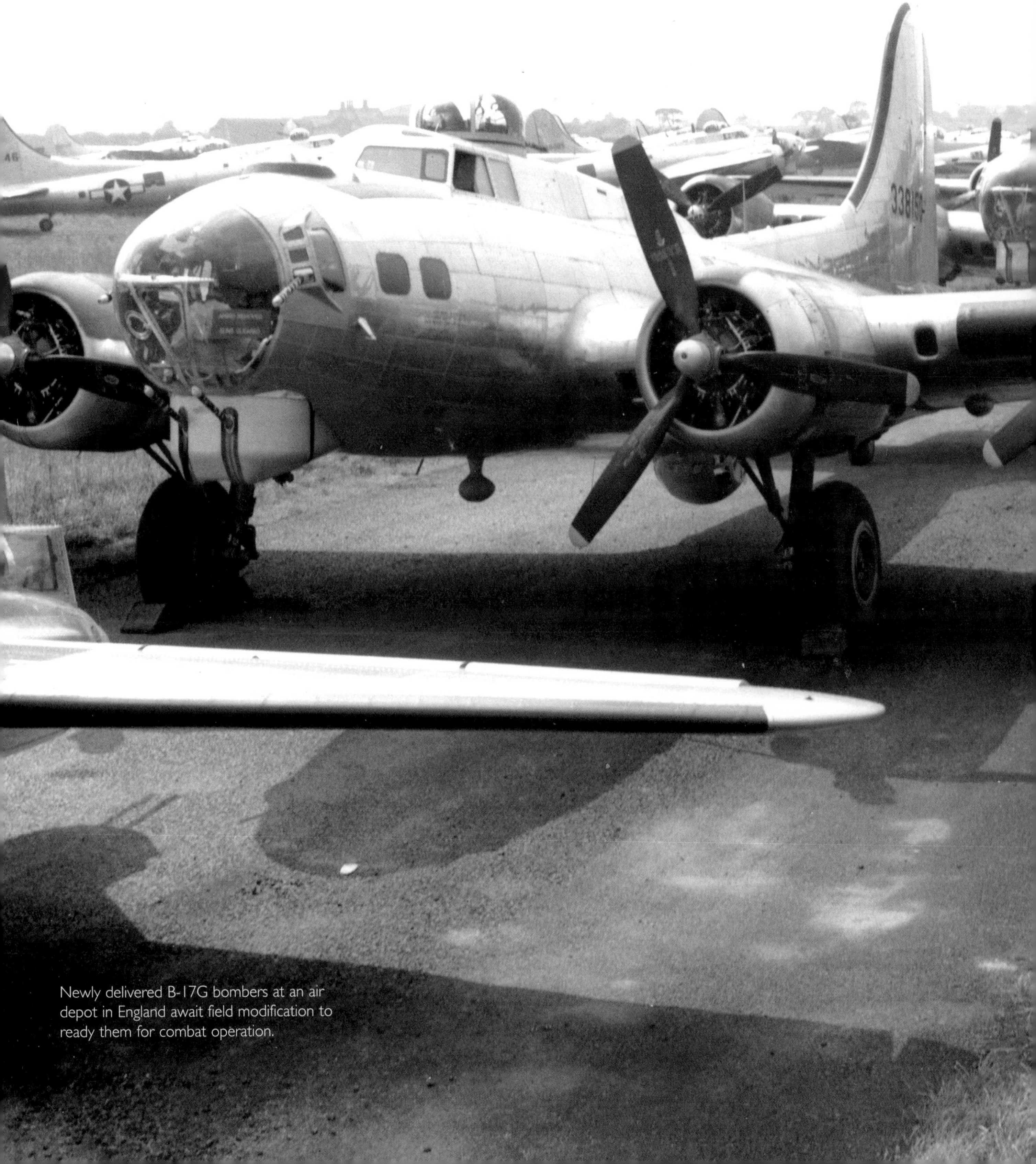

Newly delivered B-17G bombers at an air depot in England await field modification to ready them for combat operation.

AN ARGUMENT has simmered over the decades since the Second World War as to which was the better bomber, the American B-17 Flying Fortress or the Consolidated B-24 Liberator. The B-17 and B-24 were the long-range, high-altitude heavy bombers employed by the Americans in their daylight precision bombing campaign against Germany in WWII.

B-17 advocates have tended to boast about the massive firepower that was put out by the thirteen caliber fifty Browning machine-guns of the Fort, the superb gun platform it was, that it was easier to handle than the 24 and withstood battle damage better than the big and lumbering Consolidated plane. It also had a considerably higher service ceiling of 35,600 feet relative to the 28,000-foot ceiling of the B-24. Proponents of the B-24 have pointed to her ten-mile-per-hour greater top speed and thirty-three mile-per-hour greater cruising speed. And she had a slightly better rate of climb than that of the 17. Which was the better bomber? In general, B-17 crew members were partial to their airplane and most believed they had a better chance of returning safely from combat in it. For the most part, B-24 men were positively disposed toward their aircraft and liked it, although many of its pilots acknowledged that flying it could be quite an effort physically. Most airmen in that war were partial to the type of aircraft to which they were assigned.

How did these American heavies compare to the airplane that many believe to have been the finest heavy bomber of the war—the Avro Lancaster of the British Royal Air Force? Lanc crews thought their plane was the most efficient, effective bomber in that conflict. With its massive bomb-carrying capacity and the great amount of bomb tonnage it

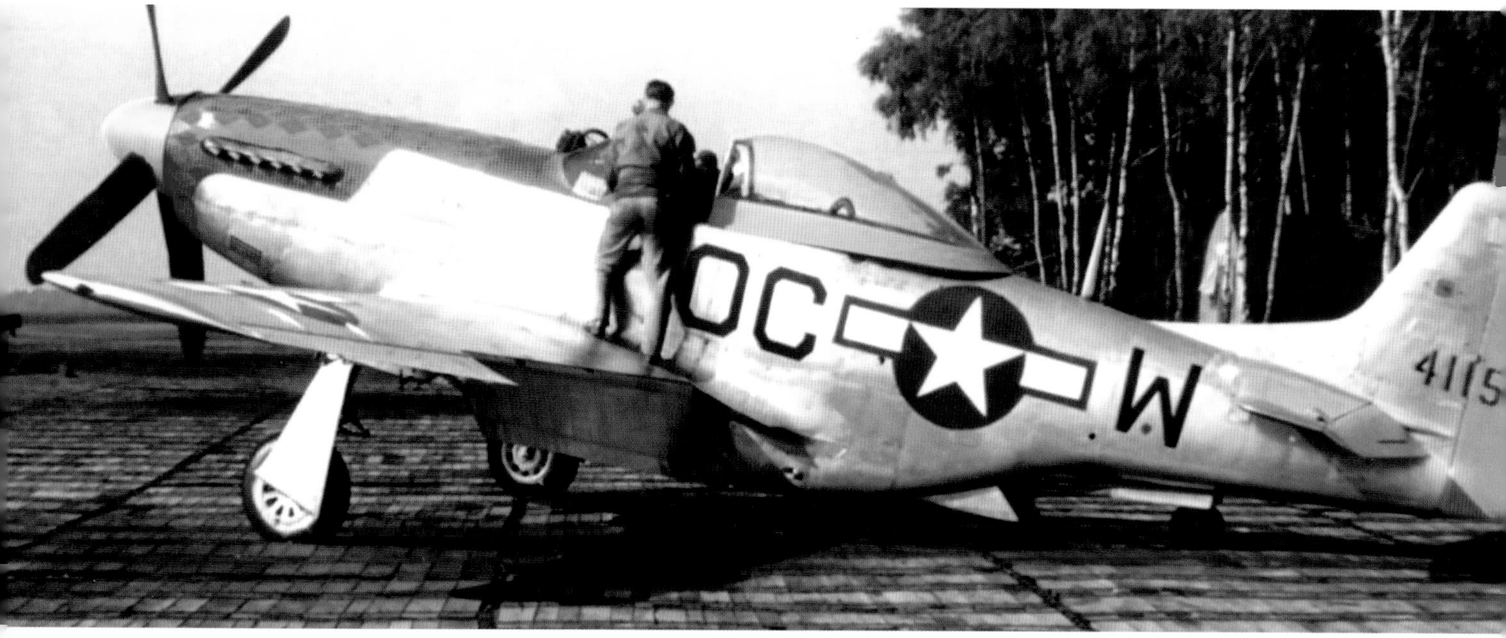
OC
W

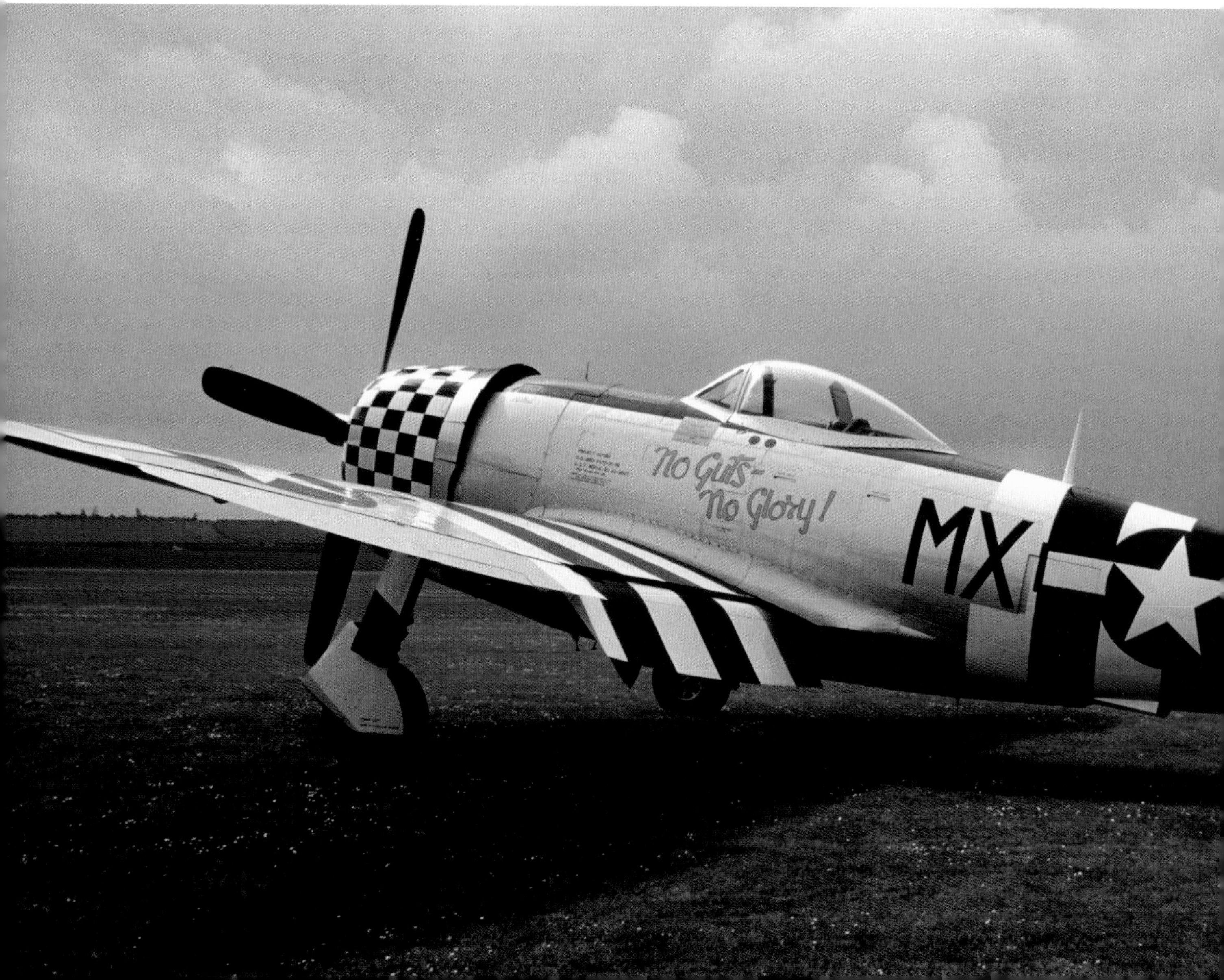
No Guts-
No Glory!
MX

left: A P-51D Mustang escort fighter of the 339th Fighter Group at Martlesham Heath; below left: A postwar-era P-47D warbird in the markings of the wartime 78th Fighter Group, which was based at Duxford, Cambridgeshire; below right: A Wright Cyclone turbo-supercharged radial engine of 1,200 horsepower. Four of these engines provided power for the Boeing B-17 bomber, a principal workhorse of the Eighth Air Force in the Second World War.

took to its many targets in Germany and German-occupied Europe, they saw its contribution to the ultimate defeat of Nazi Germany in that war as more significant than that of the two American heavy bombers.

In her performance the Lancaster was comparable to the Fortress and the Liberator, having a top speed of 287 mph and a cruising speed of 210 mph. Her rate of climb was not as good as that of her American counterparts, and her service ceiling was just 21,400 feet with a typical weight of 63,000 pounds. But her bombload on a typical long-range operation into Germany was 14,000 pounds, more than twice the load normally carried on a comparable mission of the Forts and Libs. An area where their specification differed substantially was armament. The B-17G, for example, with slightly greater armament than that of the B-24J, was equipped with thirteen caliber fifty machine-guns distributed in eight very important positions (two in a nose chin turret, two in nose cheek positions, two in an upper turret behind the pilots, two in staggered waist positions, two in a ball turret under the belly and behind the bomb bay, two in the tail, and one firing upward from the radio compartment ceiling). The thirteen guns of the Fort projected a very effective field of fire in nearly all directions. With

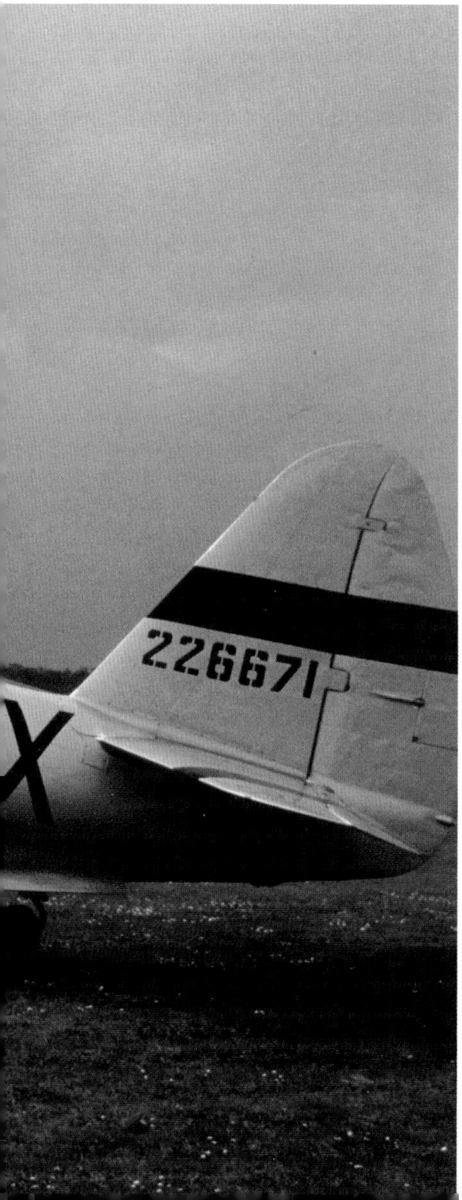
226671

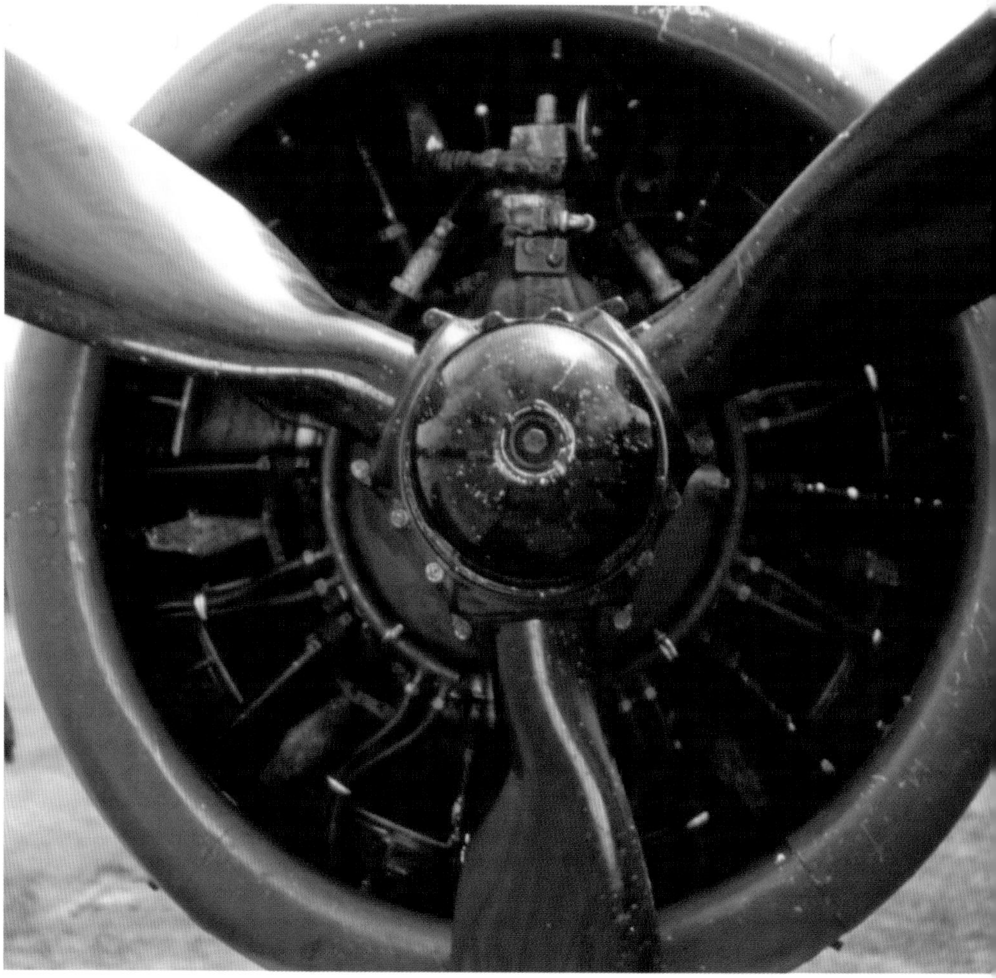

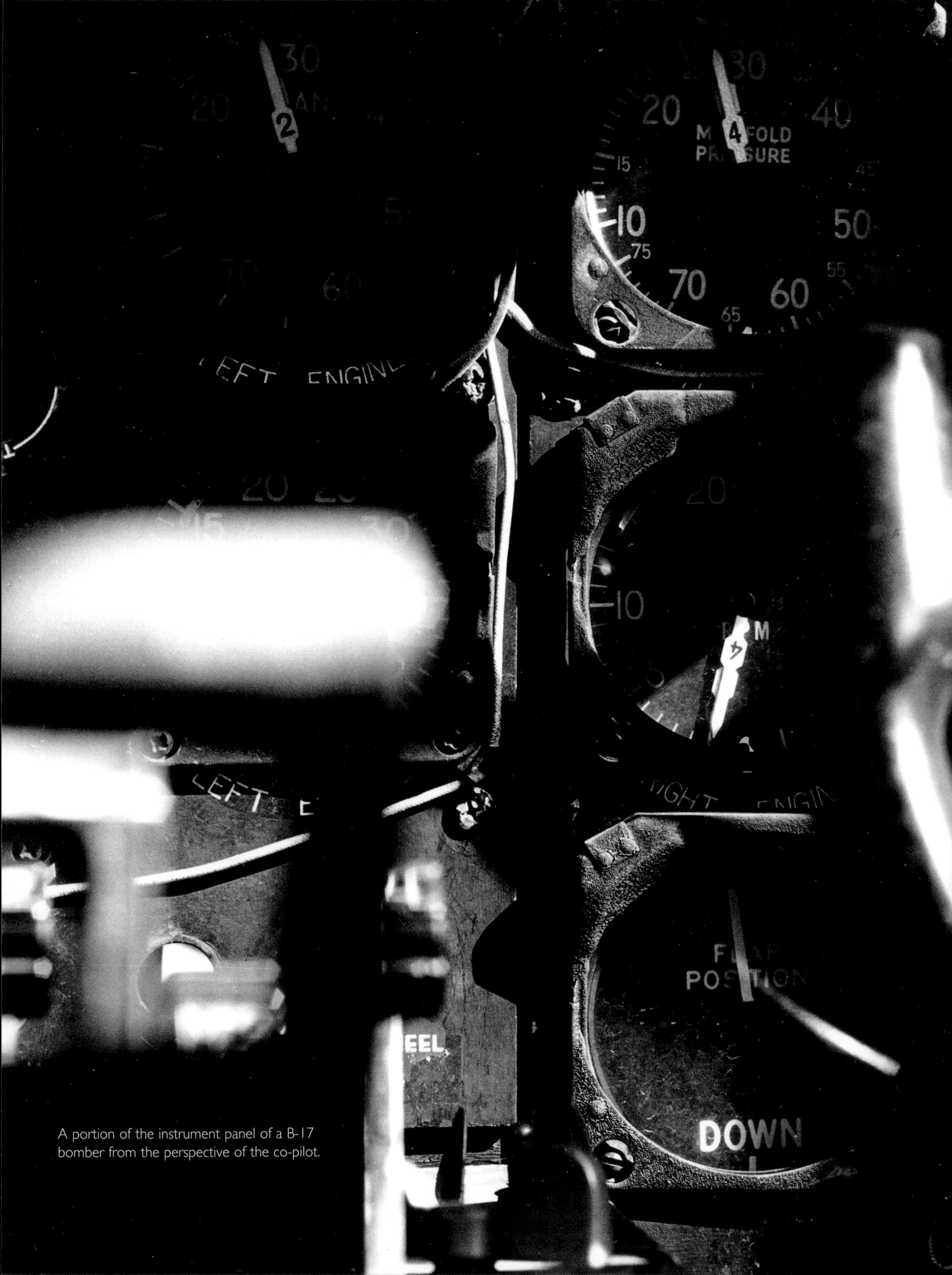
DOWN

A portion of the instrument panel of a B-17 bomber from the perspective of the co-pilot.

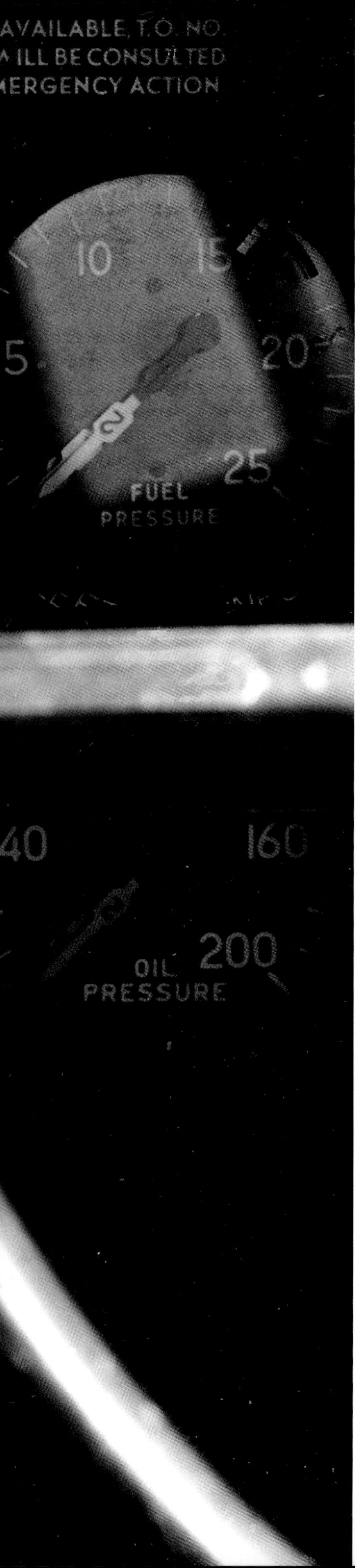
FUEL
PRESSURE
OIL
PRESSURE

her ten .50 machine-guns, the B-24 was nearly as well armed as the 17. The Lancaster I, on the other hand, was equipped with eight .303 caliber machine-guns—later changed to .50 caliber (two in a nose turret, two in a mid-upper turret, and four in a rear turret in the tail). She had no gun protection below and was thus quite vulnerable to the upward-firing guns of German night fighters.

Another significant difference between the Lanc and the American bombers was in crew composition. The Lanc was operated by a crew of seven (pilot, flight engineer, bomb aimer, navigator, wireless operator, mid-upper gunner, and rear gunner). The B-17 and the B-24 both had ten-man crews (pilot, co-pilot, bombardier, navigator, radio operator / gunner, engineer / top-turret gunner, ball-turret gunner, two waist gunners, and tail gunner). For the American bombers, more guns, ammunition, and body weight meant the penalty of less bombload weight, a major difference. And there is one other remarkable difference—the capability provided by the Lanc for its pilot to fly it almost like a fighter, in an unusual corkscrewing tactic used to evade attack by an enemy fighter. This was commonly resorted to as an emergency measure in Lancaster operations.

The Avro Lancaster resulted from a 1940 argument erupting when the British Ministry of Aircraft Production determined that the Avro and Metropolitan Vickers production lines should be re-tooled for the assembly of the Handley Page Halifax bomber. Those lines had been building the Manchester I, a twin-engined medium bomber deemed an operational failure by the RAF and RCAF for being underdeveloped, unreliable, and underpowered with its Rolls-Royce Vulture engines. The chief designer of Avro, Roy Chadwick, together with the directors of the Hawker Siddeley Group, were vigorously opposed to the move on the grounds that the Halifax and its engine choice of the Merlin X were a poor second to their own Manchester III (later to be renamed Lancaster), a new bomber they had been developing for nearly two years. They fought for MAP approval of the Manchester III and its R-R Merlin XX power and they won the argument in September 1940 with an MAP order for two prototype examples.

One of the two prototypes first flew in January 1941 and made a positive impression even though Avro was initially forced to power it with Merlin X engines due to the unavailability of the Merlin XX at that point. Chadwick had designed a superb performer in his Lancaster, just what Sir Arthur Harris needed desperately for his RAF Bomber Command. From mid-1942, the Lanc became the mainstay of the British bomber force, leading Harris to write a letter to the Avro Production Group at the end of the war: "As the user of the Lancaster during the last three and one-half years of bitter, unrelenting warfare, I would say to those who placed that shining sword in our hands, without your genius and your effort we would not have prevailed—the Lancaster was the greatest single factor in winning the war."

Lancaster heavy bombers dropped more than 60 percent of all the bombs dropped by RAF Bomber Command in that war; 7,374 Lancasters were built.

The Lancasters had been designed, built, and, for the most part, operated as night bombers, and under the direction Arthur Harris they conducted a campaign of area bombing on targets in the cities and industrial parts

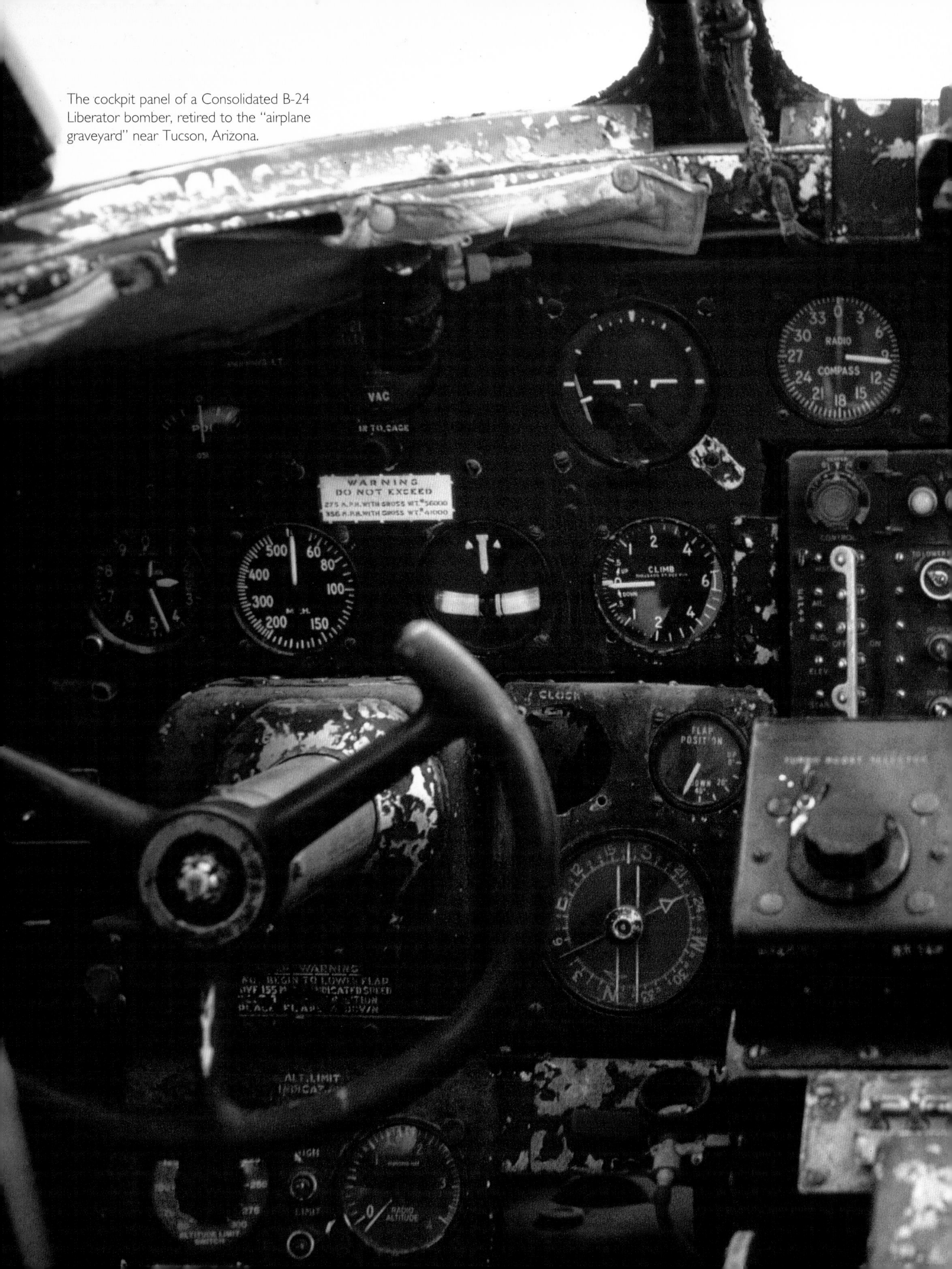
VAC
WARNING
DO NOT EXCEED
RADIO
COMPASS
CLIMB
FLAP
POSITION
CLOCK
WARNING
ALT. LIMIT
RADIO
ALTITUDE

The cockpit panel of a Consolidated B-24 Liberator bomber, retired to the "airplane graveyard" near Tucson, Arizona.

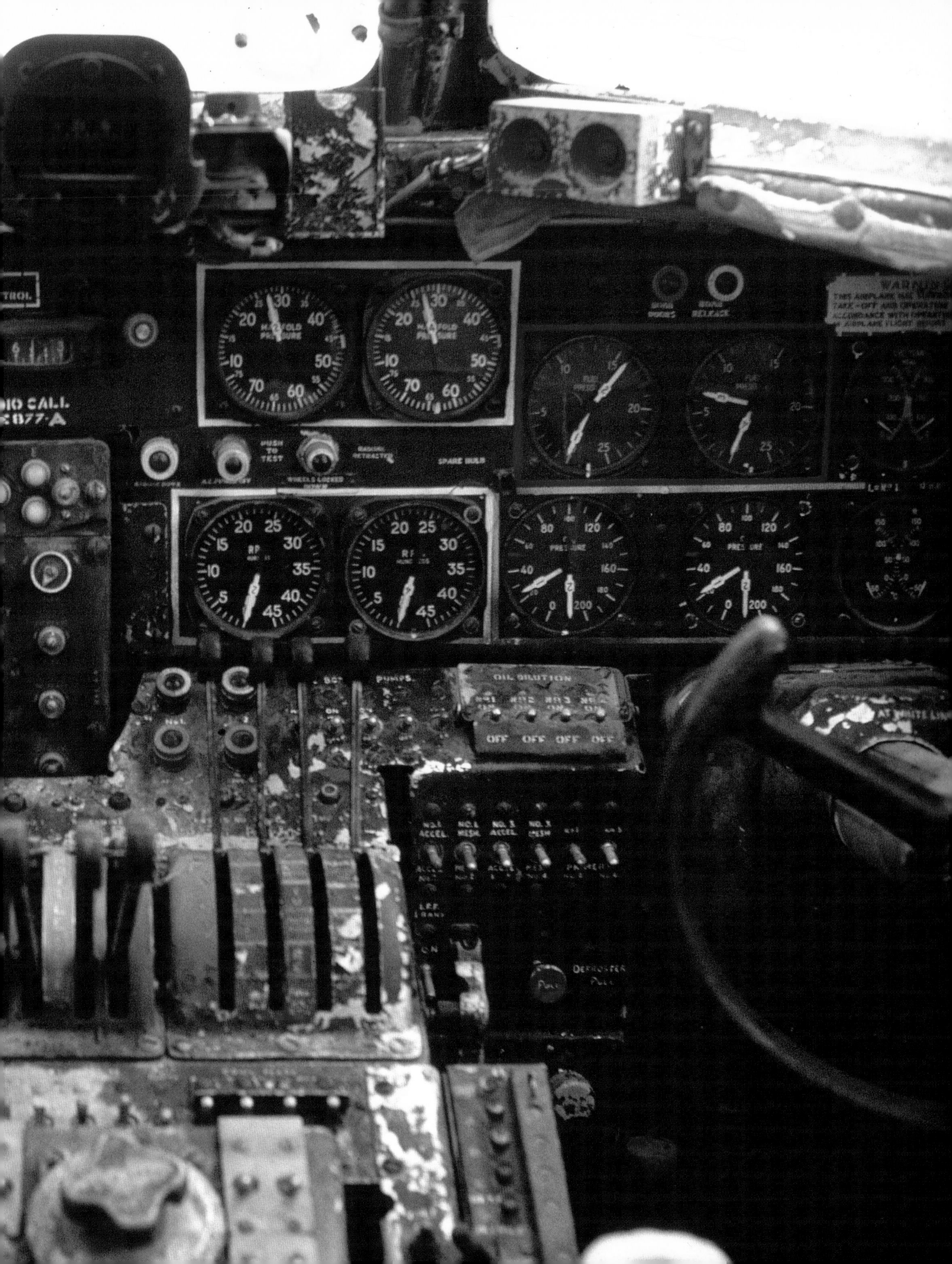
MANIFOLD PRESSURE
PUSH TO TEST
SPARE BULB
PUMPS
OIL DILUTION
OFF OFF OFF OFF
DEFROSTER PULL

Refuelling a B-17G on a field of the Eighth Air Force in WW2 England.

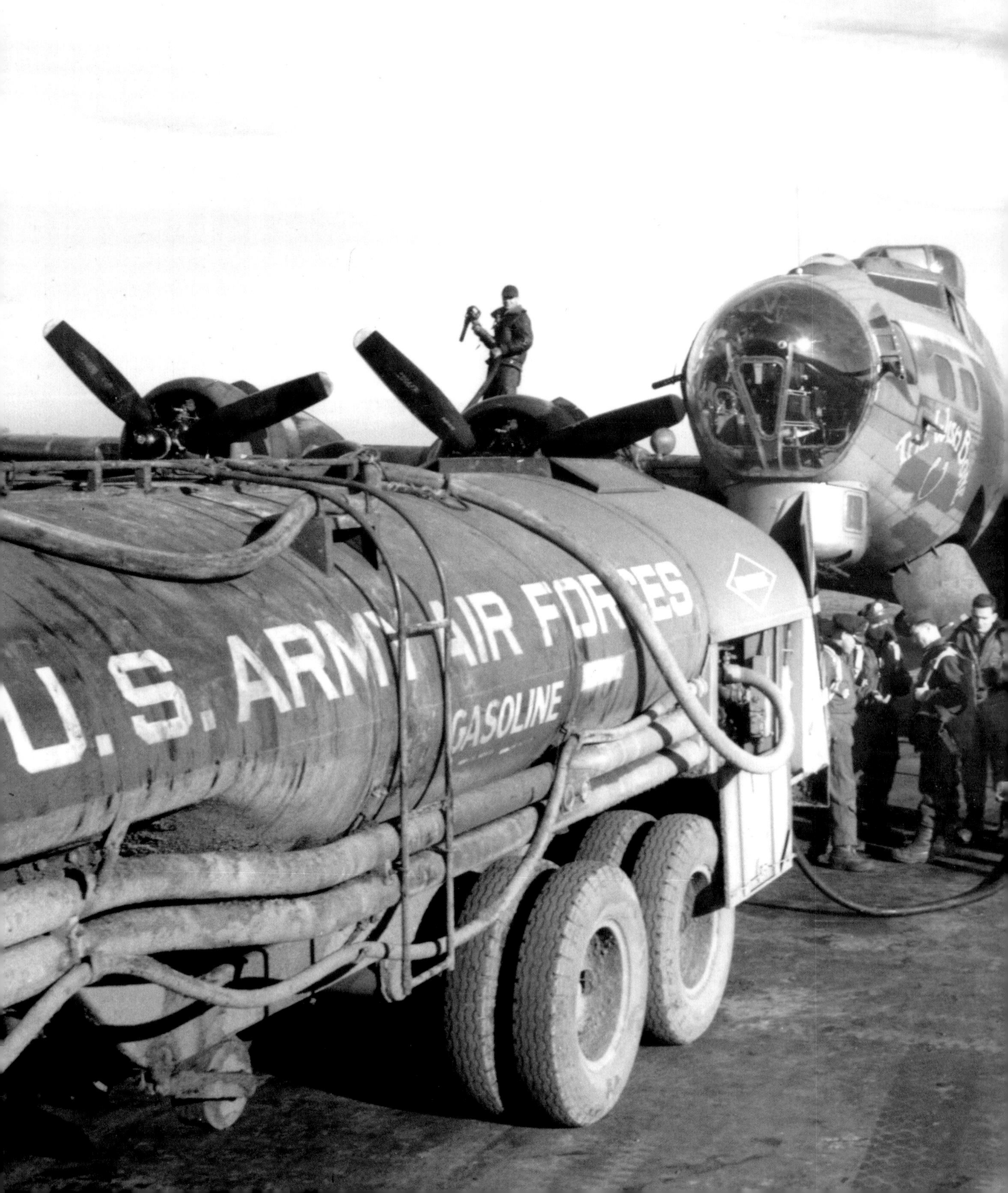
U.S. ARMY AIR FORCES
GASOLINE

of Germany. The B-17s and B-24s of the American Eighth Air Force played their part in the combined bombing offensive using an entirely different method. The Yanks believed in high altitude precision bombing, possible only in daylight through the use of their excellent Norden bombsight. In their first year of the European war, they believed too that their 17s and 24s were fully capable of defending themselves through the use of their powerful armament and flying tight box formations. They would be proven tragically wrong by the enormous losses they incurred during two raids in August and October 1943 on the ball-bearing industry plants at Schweinfurt, Germany, each raid costing the Eighth sixty bombers and six hundred crewmen. While the protection afforded the bombers by the fighter escort then available helped to an extent, the Spitfires, Lightnings, and Thunderbolts of the day all lacked sufficient range to accompany the bombers from England to the targets and back. True ultra-long-range fighter escort was on the way but would not arrive in the Eighth Fighter Command squadrons until early 1944. It came in the form of the North American P-51 Mustang, probably America's finest contribution to the European air war effort. With the Mustang going all the way to the deepest targets on the Continent, the Fortress and Liberator crews knew that at last they had at least a chance of surviving their tours of duty.

Both Boeing and Consolidated had built fine performers in the Flying Fortress and the Liberator, airplanes able to meet the outrageous requirements of the daylight bombing campaign. Easily the best of the B-17s was the G model, distinguished by its chin gun turret mounted under the Plexiglas nose; its guns fired by

the bombardier during frontal fighter attacks, unless he was hunched over the Norden bombsight—an optical, electro-mechanical gyro-stabilized analog computer—doing his job on the bomb run. When the bombardier fed the required variable factors into the Norden, it computed the precise release point for the aircraft's bombs and he was able to "fly" the airplane through the bombsight, maintaining the bomber's altitude and flight attitude during the bomb run. By war's end more than 4,000 B-17Gs had been built by the Boeing, Douglas, and Vega companies. The Gs were the epitome of bomber defensive firepower and crew protection, to the extent that such protection was possible in the circumstances.

In the execution of their precision bombing policy, they had to trade the sort of bomb tonnage delivery capability of the Lancaster for what they believed was the ability to hurt the enemy more through the precise surgical placement of their bombs on key resource, supply, and industrial targets. In terms of bomb tonnage dropped by the end of the European air war, B-17s had delivered 640,036 tons; Lancasters had delivered 608,612 tons. Clearly, the B-17s had to make more trips to achieve their total.

The first head of Eighth Bomber Command in England, General Ira Eaker: "The B-17, I think, was the best combat airplane ever built. It combined in perfect balance the right engines, the right wing and the right control surfaces. The B-17 was a bit more rugged than the B-24. It could ditch better because of the low wing and it could sustain more battle damage. You wouldn't believe they could stay in the air." An exceptional air leader during the combined Allied bombing offensive against Germany, General Curtis LeMay: "The Air Force

THE NORDEN BOMBSIGHT

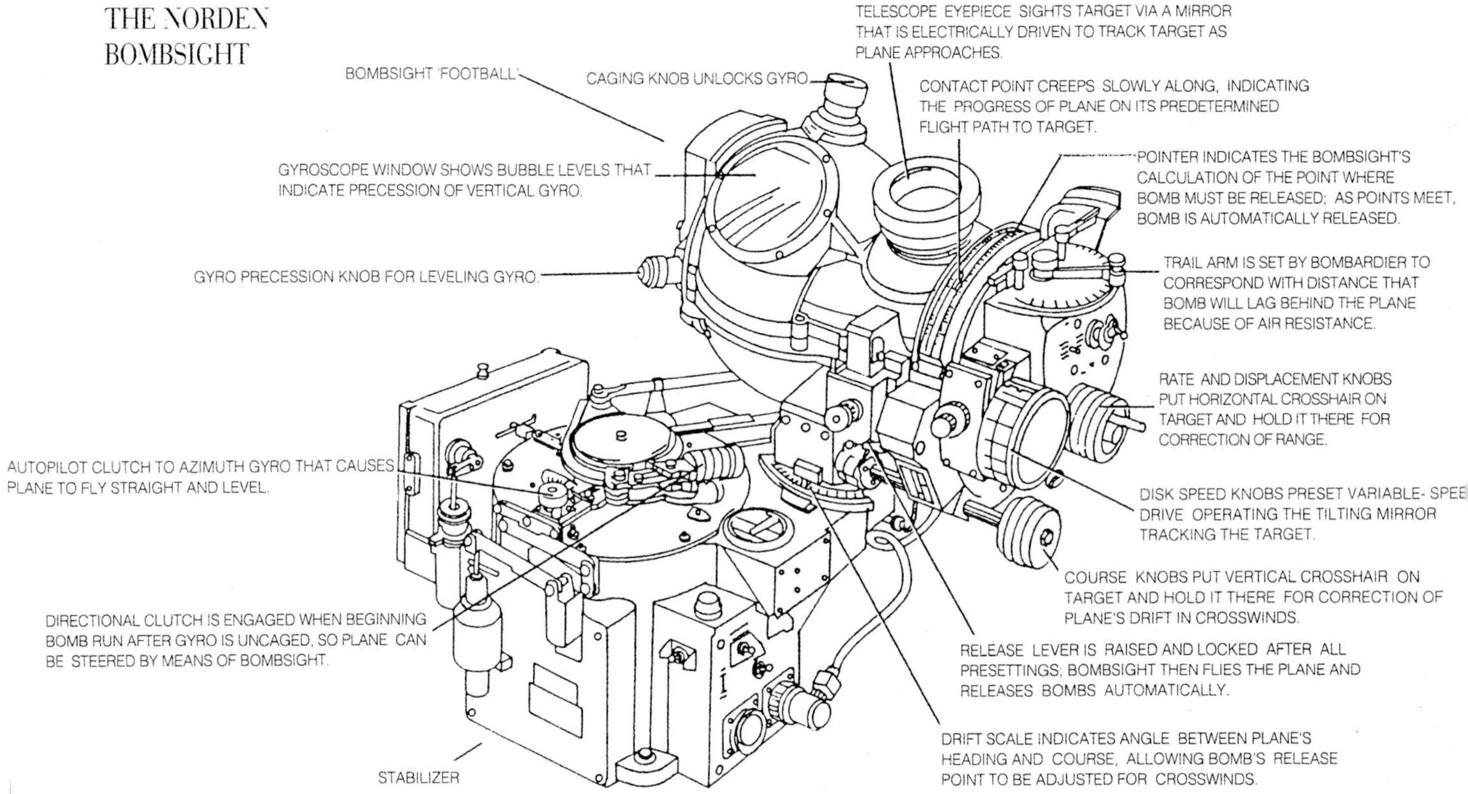
TELESCOPE EYEPIECE SIGHTS TARGET VIA A MIRROR THAT IS ELECTRICALLY DRIVEN TO TRACK TARGET AS PLANE APPROACHES.
BOMBSIGHT 'FOOTBALL'
CAGING KNOB UNLOCKS GYRO
CONTACT POINT CREEPS SLOWLY ALONG, INDICATING THE PROGRESS OF PLANE ON ITS PREDETERMINED FLIGHT PATH TO TARGET.
GYROSCOPE WINDOW SHOWS BUBBLE LEVELS THAT INDICATE PRECESSION OF VERTICAL GYRO.
POINTER INDICATES THE BOMBSIGHT'S CALCULATION OF THE POINT WHERE BOMB MUST BE RELEASED; AS POINTS MEET, BOMB IS AUTOMATICALLY RELEASED.
GYRO PRECESSION KNOB FOR LEVELING GYRO.
TRAIL ARM IS SET BY BOMBARDIER TO CORRESPOND WITH DISTANCE THAT BOMB WILL LAG BEHIND THE PLANE BECAUSE OF AIR RESISTANCE.
RATE AND DISPLACEMENT KNOBS PUT HORIZONTAL CROSSHAIR ON TARGET AND HOLD IT THERE FOR CORRECTION OF RANGE.
AUTOPILOT CLUTCH TO AZIMUTH GYRO THAT CAUSES PLANE TO FLY STRAIGHT AND LEVEL.
DISK SPEED KNOBS PRESET VARIABLE- SPEE DRIVE OPERATING THE TILTING MIRROR TRACKING THE TARGET.
COURSE KNOBS PUT VERTICAL CROSSHAIR ON TARGET AND HOLD IT THERE FOR CORRECTION OF PLANE'S DRIFT IN CROSSWINDS.
DIRECTIONAL CLUTCH IS ENGAGED WHEN BEGINNING BOMB RUN AFTER GYRO IS UNCAGED, SO PLANE CAN BE STEERED BY MEANS OF BOMBSIGHT.
RELEASE LEVER IS RAISED AND LOCKED AFTER ALL PRESETTINGS; BOMBSIGHT THEN FLIES THE PLANE AND RELEASES BOMBS AUTOMATICALLY.
DRIFT SCALE INDICATES ANGLE BETWEEN PLANE'S HEADING AND COURSE, ALLOWING BOMB'S RELEASE POINT TO BE ADJUSTED FOR CROSSWINDS.
STABILIZER

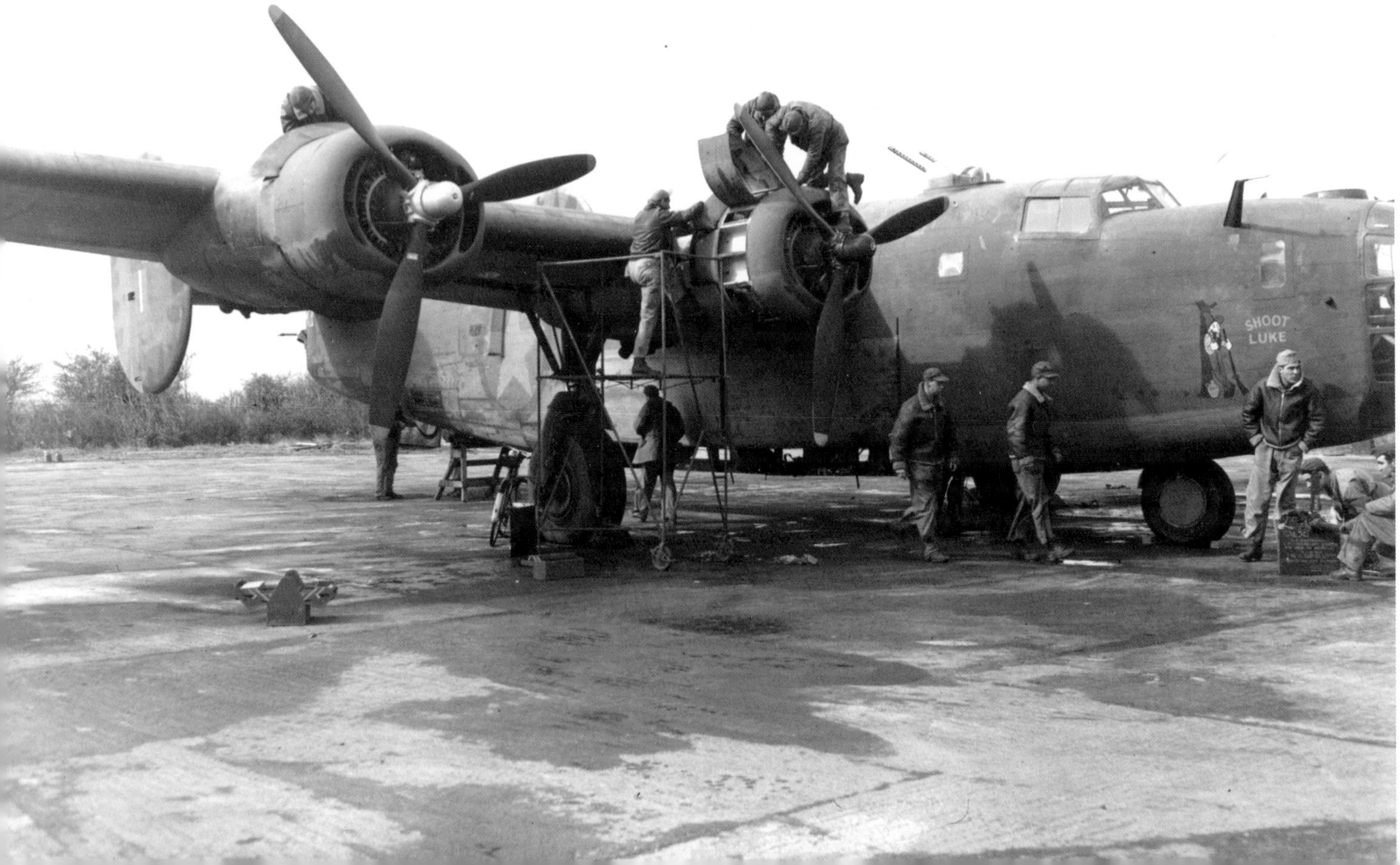
SHOOT LUKE

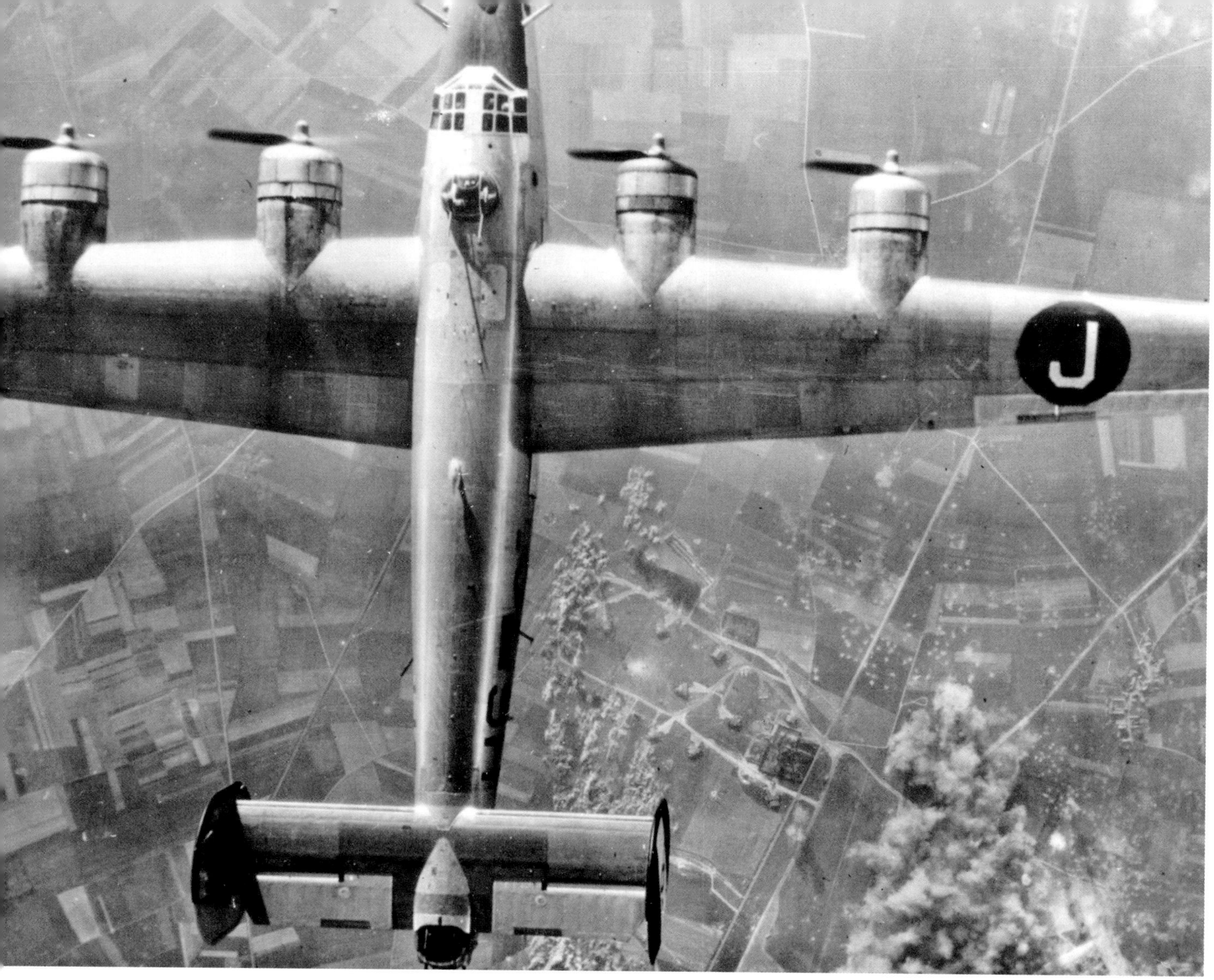

top left: A diagram of the secret Norden bombsight used by the Americans in WW2; top right and below: B-24 Liberators on operations against German targets.

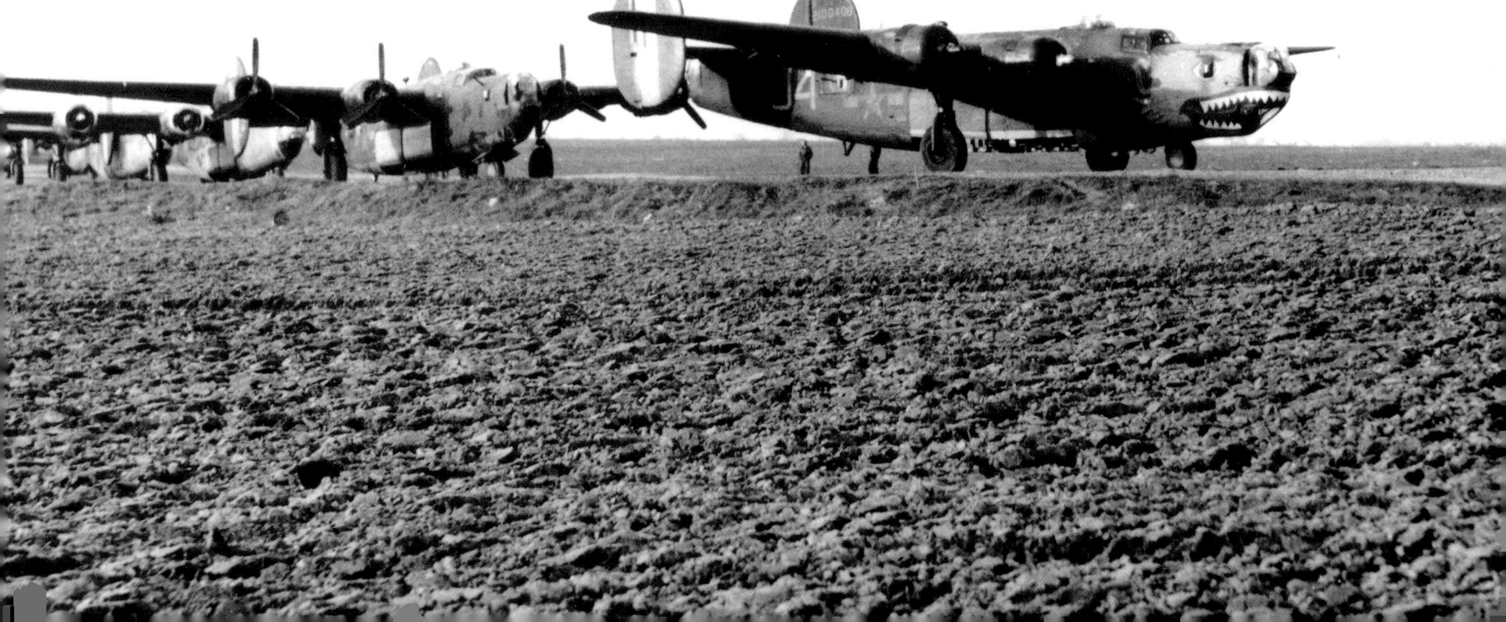

kind of grew up with the B-17. It was as tough an airplane as was ever built. It was a good, honest plane to fly—a pilot's airplane. It did everything we asked it to do and did it well."

The B-17 was the Boeing company's response to a competition launched by the United States Army Air Corps in August 1934 to design and build a new heavy bomber with a range of at least 1,000 miles, a speed of between 200 and 250 mph, and a bombload of 2,000 pounds. Boeing designated its entry Model 299 and it was to be a major gamble for the company. If its design did not win the competition and a contract order, Boeing would not be reimbursed for the project. It would not be the last time the company bet its entire future on the success of one airplane. Many years after the war it would take the same gamble on its 747 jumbo airliner.

The Model 299 incorporated many design characteristics of Boeing's earlier XB-15 bomber and its 247 passenger airliner. It was to be an all-aluminum airframe powered by four Pratt & Whitney 750 hp Hornet engines. The maiden flight of the Model 299 took place on 28 July 1935 and was followed on 20 August by a nonstop flight from Seattle to Wright Field, Ohio, completed in just nine hours. All went well in flight testing until it had accumulated about forty flying hours. The prototype crashed after an elevator gust-lock was not removed before the flight. Due to the crash, the Air Corps declined to place its order for sixty of the planes. But Boeing still received an order for thirteen airplanes designated YB-17A, followed by an additional order for thirty-nine B-17Bs. The guns of the B-17B were upgraded from .30 caliber to .50 caliber and the engines were changed to 850 hp R-1820 Wright Cyclones.

As the prospect of the Second World War grew in likelihood in the 1930s, so too did isolationism in America, where there was there was little political enthusiasm for a big, expensive new long-range strategic bomber. With the Munich Crisis of late September 1938, however, more and more Americans saw the apparent inevitability of U.S. involvement in the coming war, and in January 1939, President Franklin Roosevelt asked the U.S. Congress for a $300 million appropriation to buy 3,000 aircraft for the Army Air Corps. At the end of B-17 production, 12,731 of the aircraft had been built. By September 1944, twenty-seven of the forty-two Eighth Air Force bomb groups then operating, as well as six of the twenty-one bomb groups of the Fifteenth Air Force flying from bases in Italy, were equipped with B-17s.

"Being as tall as I am, there was only one place in a B-17 where I could stand up and that was directly under the astrodome. The navigator was supposed to use an astrocompass, getting lines of direction from the sun, but I never did have the astrocompass mount in there because this was the only place I could stand up and stretch out, so mine was always on the floor. And the one time that any flak came close to hitting me, it came through the bottom of the airplane and hit this astro-mount and ricocheted up in the airplane. Had the astro-mount not been there, I would have had to sleep on my stomach for two or three weeks. It would have come right up through the seat of my chair."
—W.W. Ford, navigator, 92BG, Podington

"We liked the B-17 a lot. When you compared it to a B-24, the B-24 was

A newly-built Lockheed P-38 fighter on the ramp at the company's Burbank, California facility. The P-38 Lightning along with the P-47 Thunderbolt, the P-51 Mustang, and the British Spitfire escorted the bombers of the Eighth Air Force on their missions to attack German targets.

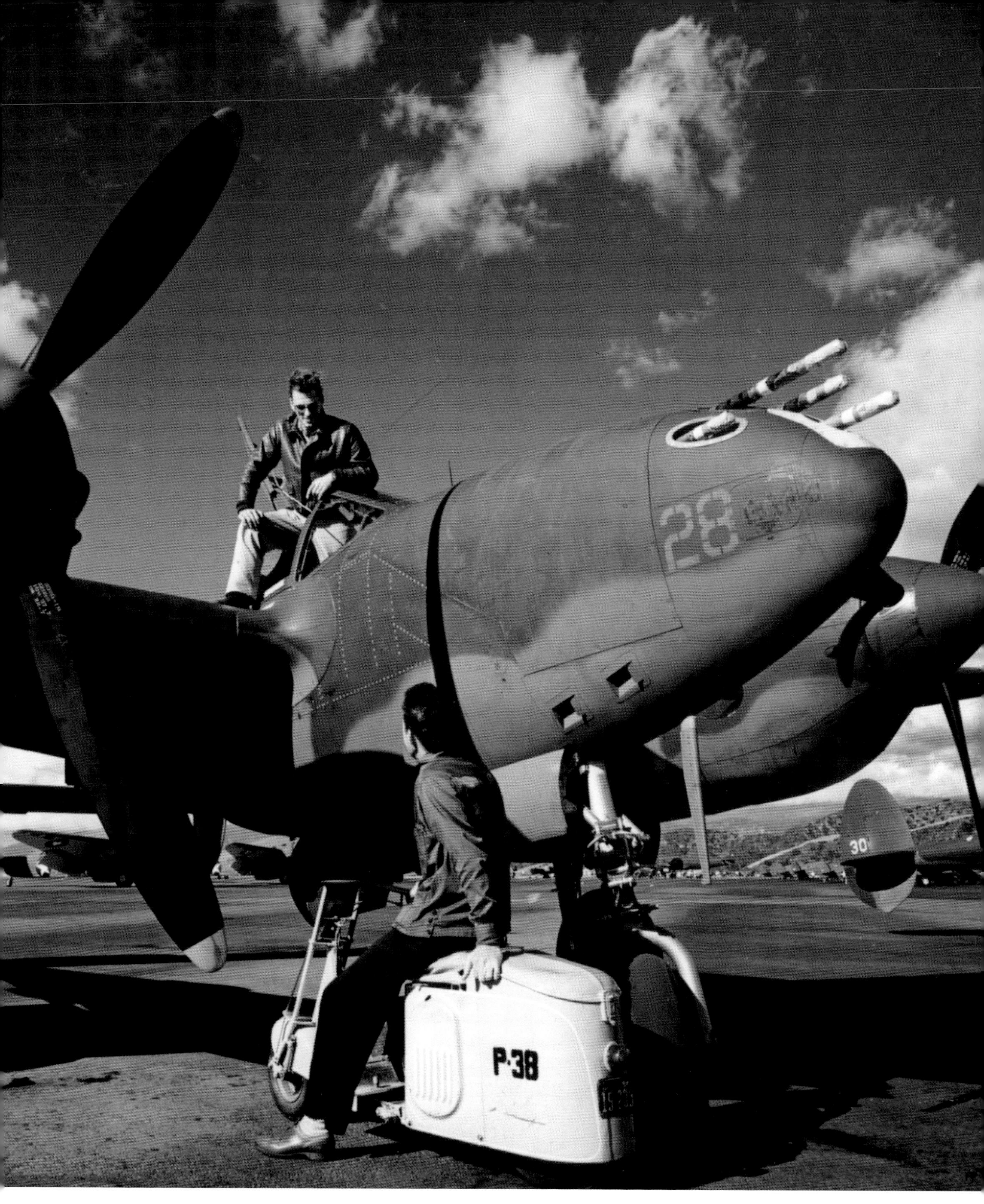
28
P-38
30

The North American A-36 Apache version of the famous Mustang, this example at the Inglewood, California company plant.

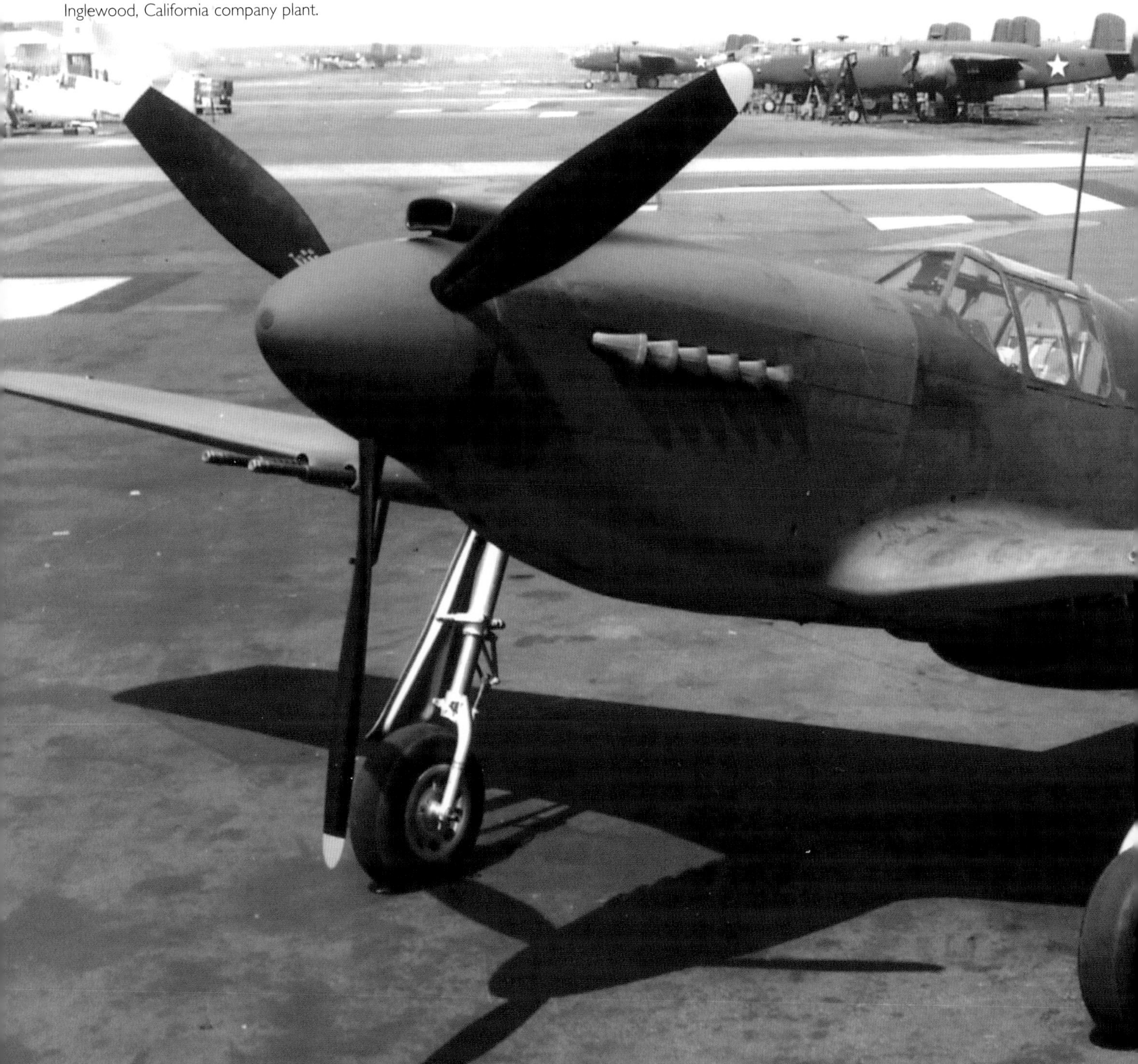

a faster airplane, about ten miles an hour faster, but it could get hit with anything and it would go down; the B-17 you could chop into little pieces and that son of a bitch would come back. You had a great affinity for it. The B-24 pilots said the same thing; that theirs was the greatest airplane in the world."
—Ray Wild, pilot, 92BG, Podington

Like the B-17, the B-24 Liberator was a product of the late 1930s. It was built in considerably greater numbers than the 17, with a total of 19,256 Liberators produced. The 24 first flew on 29 December 1939 and entered service in 1941. With a slightly longer

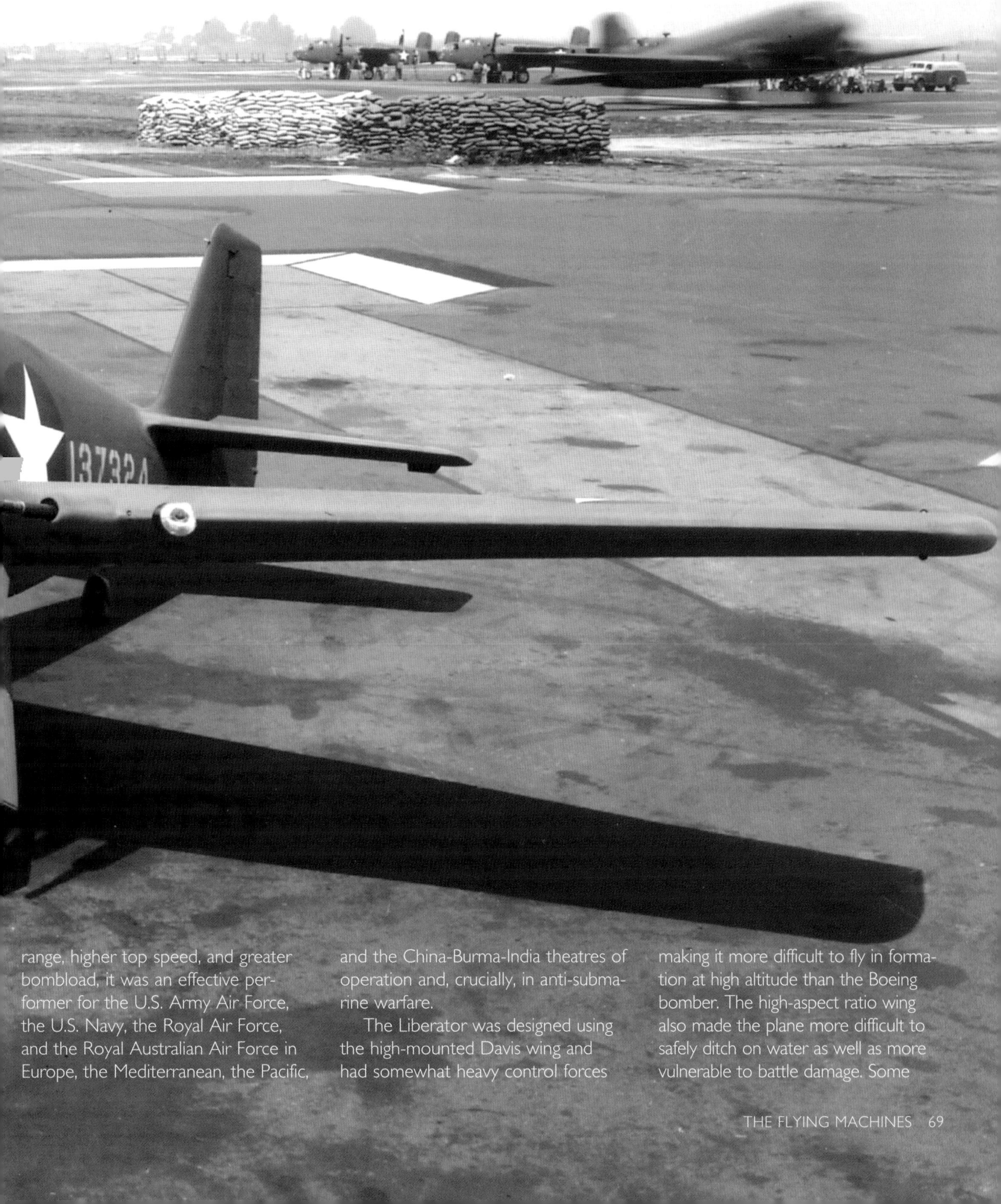
137324

range, higher top speed, and greater bombload, it was an effective performer for the U.S. Army Air Force, the U.S. Navy, the Royal Air Force, and the Royal Australian Air Force in Europe, the Mediterranean, the Pacific, and the China-Burma-India theatres of operation and, crucially, in anti-submarine warfare.

The Liberator was designed using the high-mounted Davis wing and had somewhat heavy control forces making it more difficult to fly in formation at high altitude than the Boeing bomber. The high-aspect ratio wing also made the plane more difficult to safely ditch on water as well as more vulnerable to battle damage. Some

A wonderfully restored North American P-51D Mustang escort fighter in the 21st century.

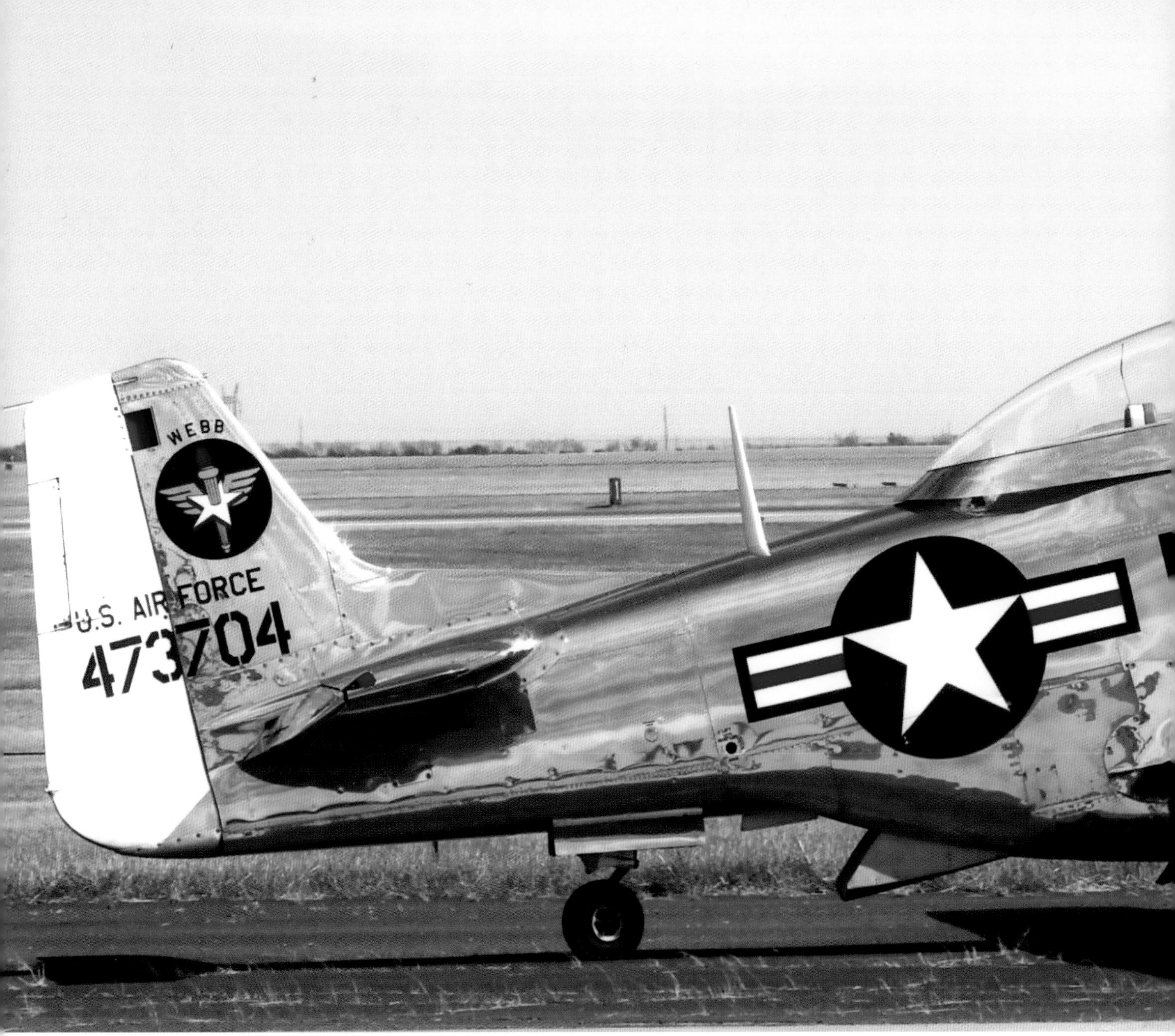
WEBB
U.S. AIR FORCE
473704

B-24 air crew members and some bomb group commanders felt, rightly or wrongly, that the airplane was not as rugged and as able to take punishment in air combat and flak as the B-17. The view from the top in Washington, however, seemed to favor the B-24 to some extent over the 17 and ordered nearly seven thousand more of the Consolidated bomber than its Boeing counterpart. Factory production increased dramatically in 1942–1943 at Consolidated's plant in San Diego and its new plant at Fort Worth, Texas, as well as a Douglas Aircraft plant at Tulsa, Oklahoma, a North American Aviation plant at Grand Prairie, Texas, and at the new Ford plant at Willow Run, Michigan. At peak production in 1944, the Willow Run plant was

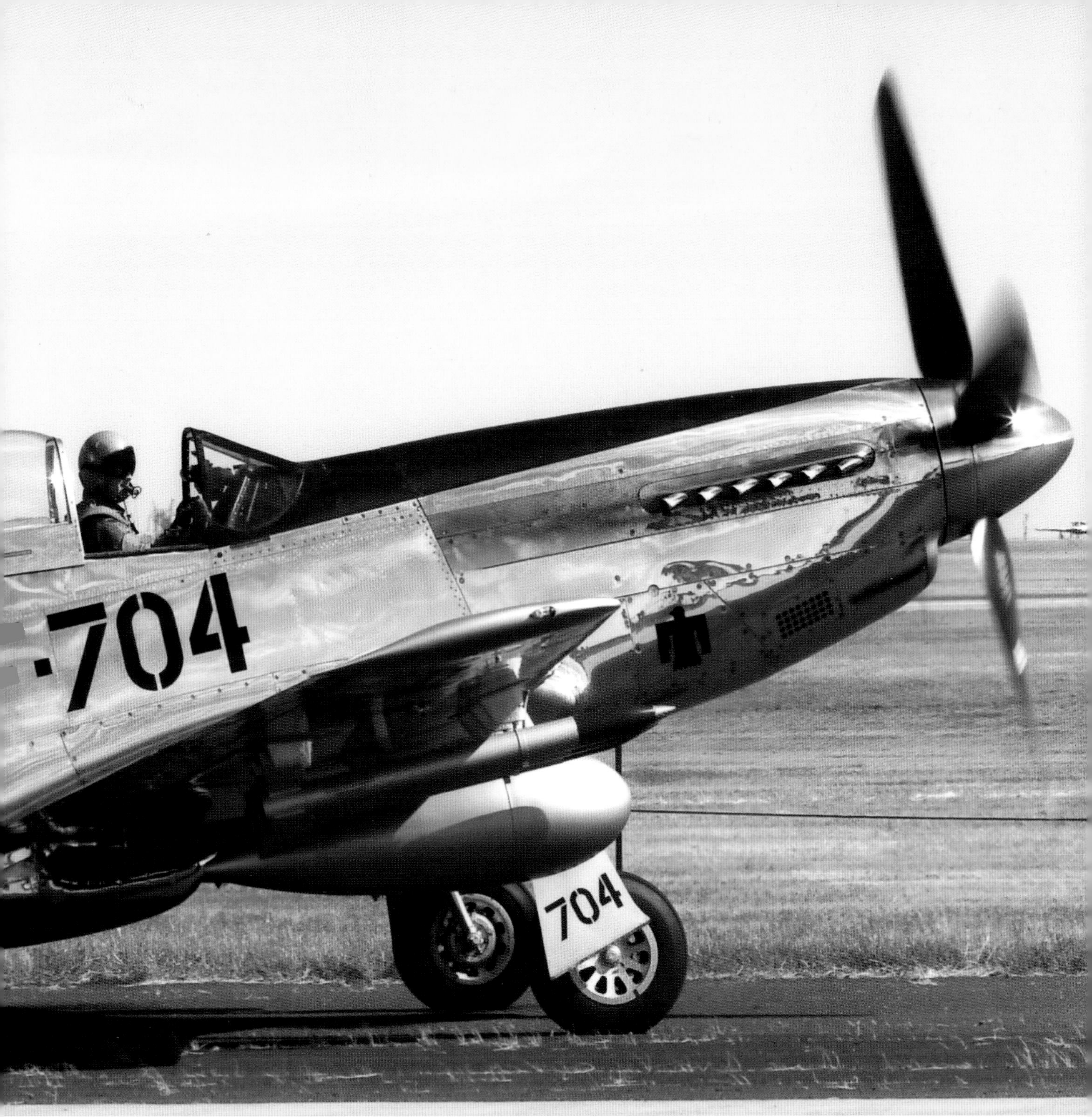
-704
704

producing one B-24 an hour and 650 a month.

Initially, the XB-24 failed to meet the contractually specified requirement, having a top speed of just 273 mph rather than the promised 311 mph. This led to a switch from mechanically supercharged Pratt & Whitney R-1830-33 engines to turbo-supercharged R-1830s along with a few other design changes.

"I had been in charge of people before, but I'd never really had a command before, prior to being a first pilot . . . it was not only being competent to fly the airplane, but being competent to command and to gain the respect of the crew. I elected fairly early to run a rather strict crew. Although we were about the same age and some were considerably older than I was, it was extremely important that when you told someone to do something, they'd understand to do it and do it right away because it's a life and death situation. On this particular day, our assignment was to practice emergency bail-out, which was extremely important because, with all the gear and equipment that everyone had—they're all strapped in and all in their little holes with all these wires and cords and oxygen on them—you have to be very quick to get out of an airplane like a B-24. You didn't have many seconds to get out of your seat and jump out before you were hopelessly trapped inside. It was such a cumbersome airplane, you couldn't hold it once it went out of control. So, the whole thing was to convince these people that if I pushed the 'jump' button, I meant jump, and not to wait. We went out to practice that day. We were in the mountains and we were flying at about five thousand feet. We had to fly formation, which keeps you very busy, and the crew were all in position, had strapped themselves in, and then I gave them the warning sign and, in so many seconds, to pass the test, they had to be ready to jump, so with the next signal they were gonna jump out of the airplane, parachutes on and ready to go. As the morning went on, instead of getting better at the procedure, they just got worse and worse, and I got angrier and angrier, and by the time we landed I was fighting mad. As soon as we landed I called them all together out on the ground and I just chewed them all out and I told them that they could either do it or just get the hell off the crew. They didn't say anything. I had just had enough of them that day. Anyway, I think it

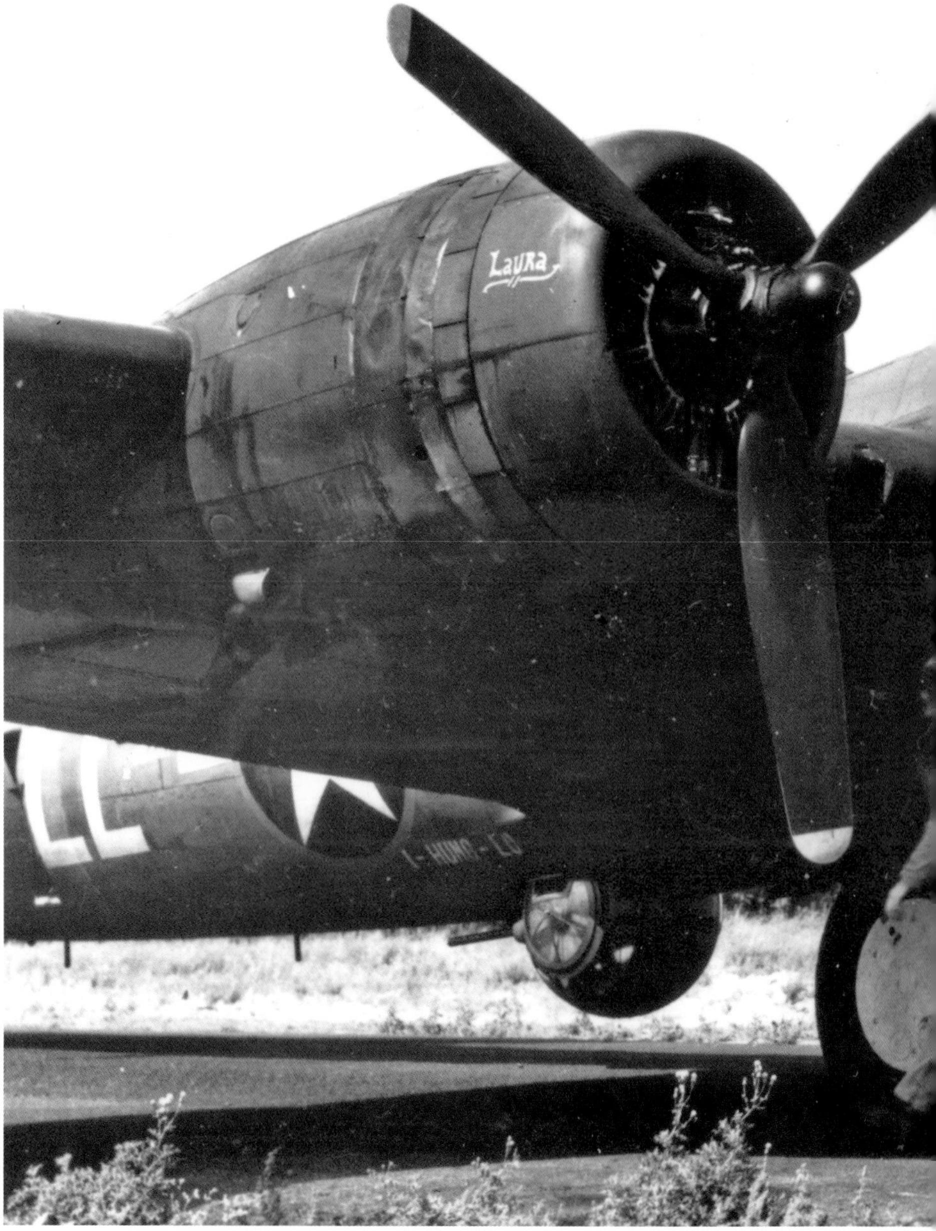
Laura

The pilot of the B-17 *Bomb Boogie* was twenty-four-year-old Lt Elwood Arp of Summer, Nebraska. The aircraft was assigned to the 91st Bomb Group at Bassingbourn, England, and was shot down by flak and enemy fighters over Stuttgart in May 1943.

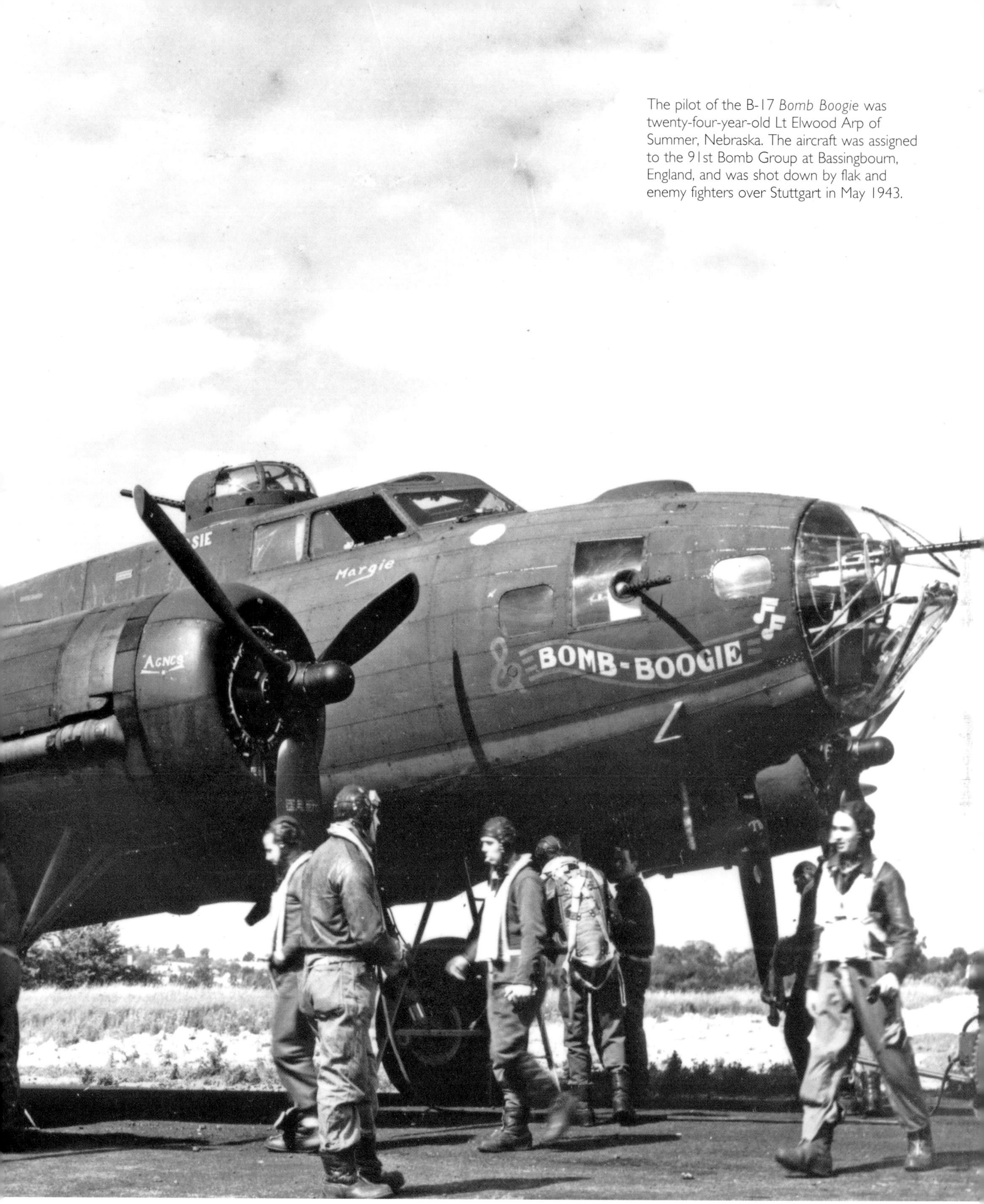
Margie
BOMB-BOOGIE

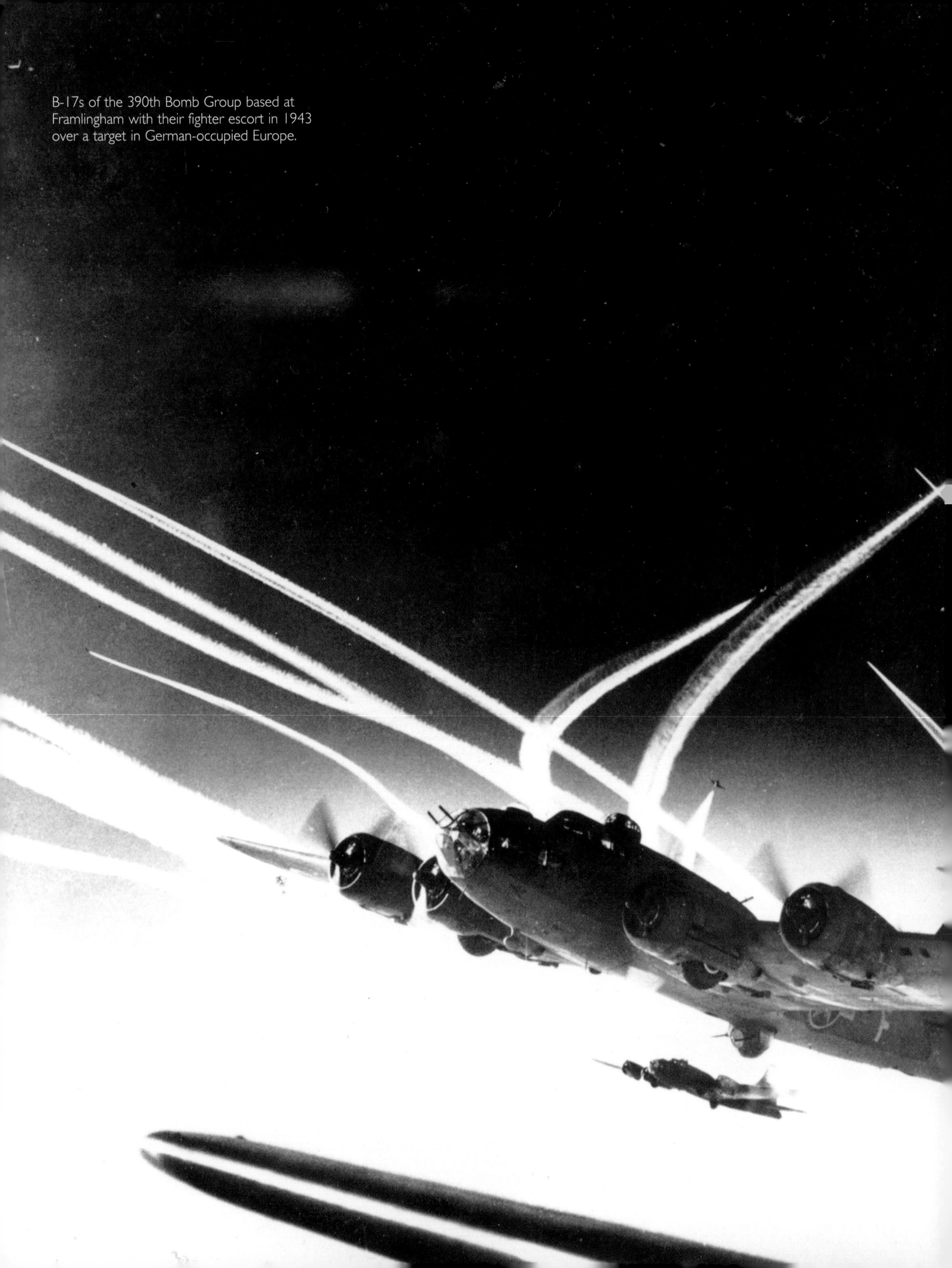

B-17s of the 390th Bomb Group based at Framlingham with their fighter escort in 1943 over a target in German-occupied Europe.

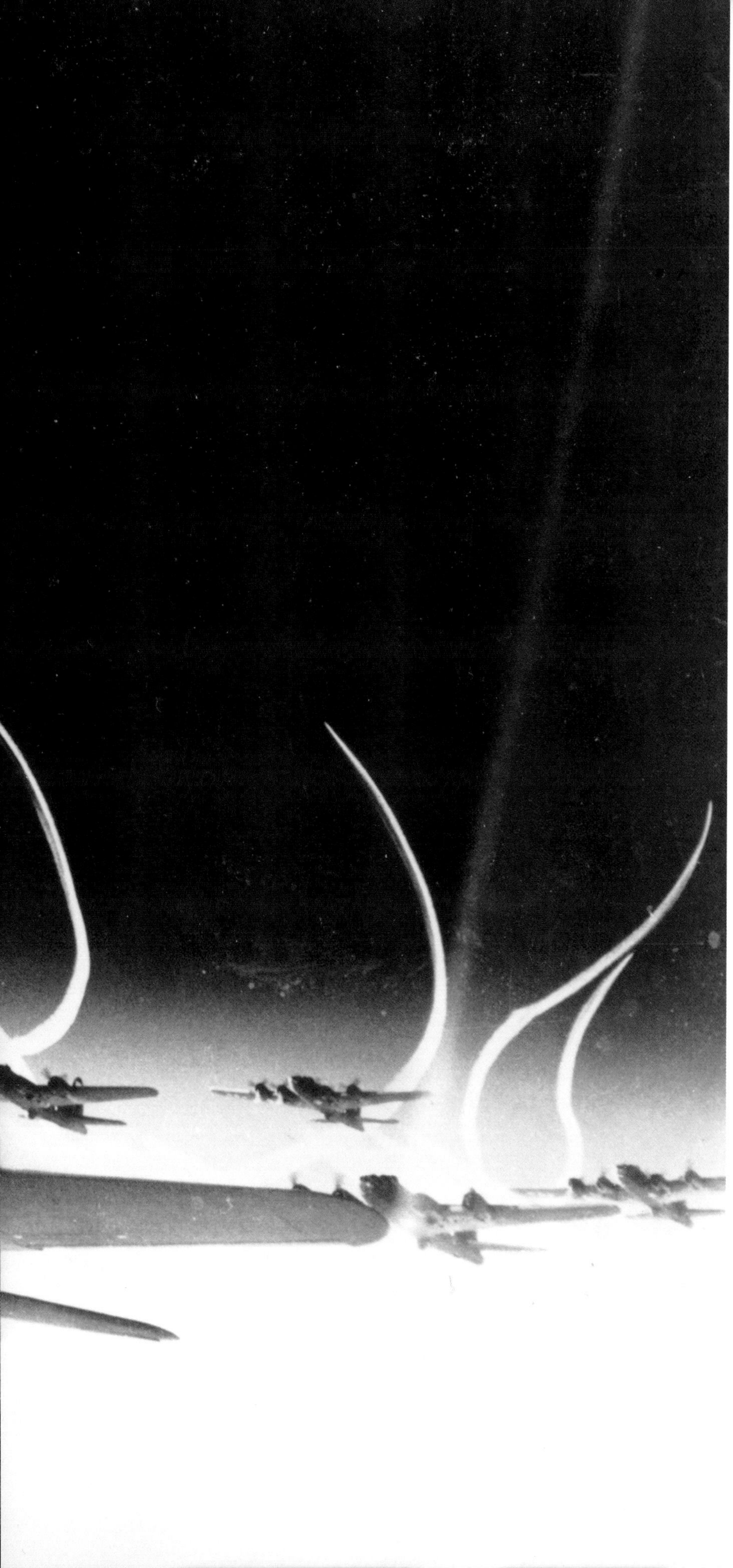

was a good sign on my part because at least I had accepted responsibility; I had to do something about this because I couldn't be responsible for people who couldn't do what they were told. The next time we went up they performed extremely well. What had happened, they had gone out the night before and got drunk and they couldn't perform. Anyway, that little experience helped create solidarity on the crew and helped make us a good crew."
—Cecil Johnson, pilot, 458BG, Horsham St Faith

Rex Smith, my co-author on an earlier air war book, described the takeoff experience in a B-24: ". . . the bombers when loaded had to be alternately bullied and coaxed, and had to be flown with a firm hand, alertness, and respect. The bombers had their disconcerting quirks, one of which was an understandable reluctance to leave the ground when overloaded. On the long runway—which at most English bases measured about six thousand feet—this could be trying. On either of the short runways—usually a little over four thousand feet—it was, as one pilot said, 'a real nail-biter.' This was especially true because of the high penalty for failure. A loaded bomber carried more than twenty thousand pounds of bombs and gasoline, which meant that a crew that failed to get one off the ground before reaching the end of the runway would be spoken of thereafter only in the past tense. It is therefore understandable that every such takeoff had the rapt attention of the three men charged with bringing it off—the pilot, co-pilot, and engineer.

"You have just taxied into position for takeoff from one of your field's short runways . . .

"With less distance for gaining

takeoff speed than you would like, you are eager to seize every advantage you can. Accordingly, you set the brakes and hold the airplane stationary on the very end of the runway and at the same time advance the throttles to full takeoff power. The engines thunder, the airplane begins to shiver, as someone once crudely put it, 'like a dog shitting peach pits,' and if the airplane is a B-24 (which has a nose wheel) its accelerating propellers pull it down into a belligerent crouch. Now there is much argument about whether this raucous procedure actually helps a takeoff run, but it certainly feels as if it does, so you run up the engines until the airplane strains to be released and to race bellowing down the runway. Then you release the brakes . . . and find the airplane to have been a liar. Instead of leaping forward it waddles. What had promised to be a charging bull is actually a fat lady beginning a languid Sunday stroll. You knew this would happen. It always happens. Even so, it exasperates you and you unconsciously hunch back and forth in your seat in an attempt to nudge the airplane forward.

"Slowly the heavy ship accelerates and becomes lighter on its feet. Standing behind and to the right of your seat, the engineer watches instruments reporting the engines' health and is ready to make instant corrections if he detects malingering. Sitting to your right, the co-pilot watches the airspeed indicator and calls out its advancing numbers, and you listen for those announcing arrival at certain critical speeds. The first of these is the speed beyond which you can no longer stop the airplane on the remaining runway and are committed to take off no matter what. It is a variable number determined by aircraft weight, runway length, and

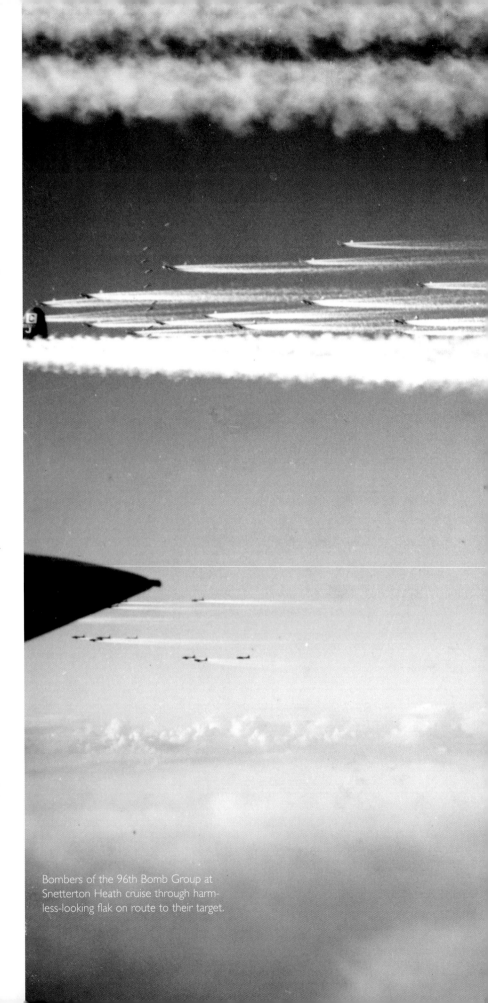

Bombers of the 96th Bomb Group at Snetterton Heath cruise through harmless-looking flak on route to their target.

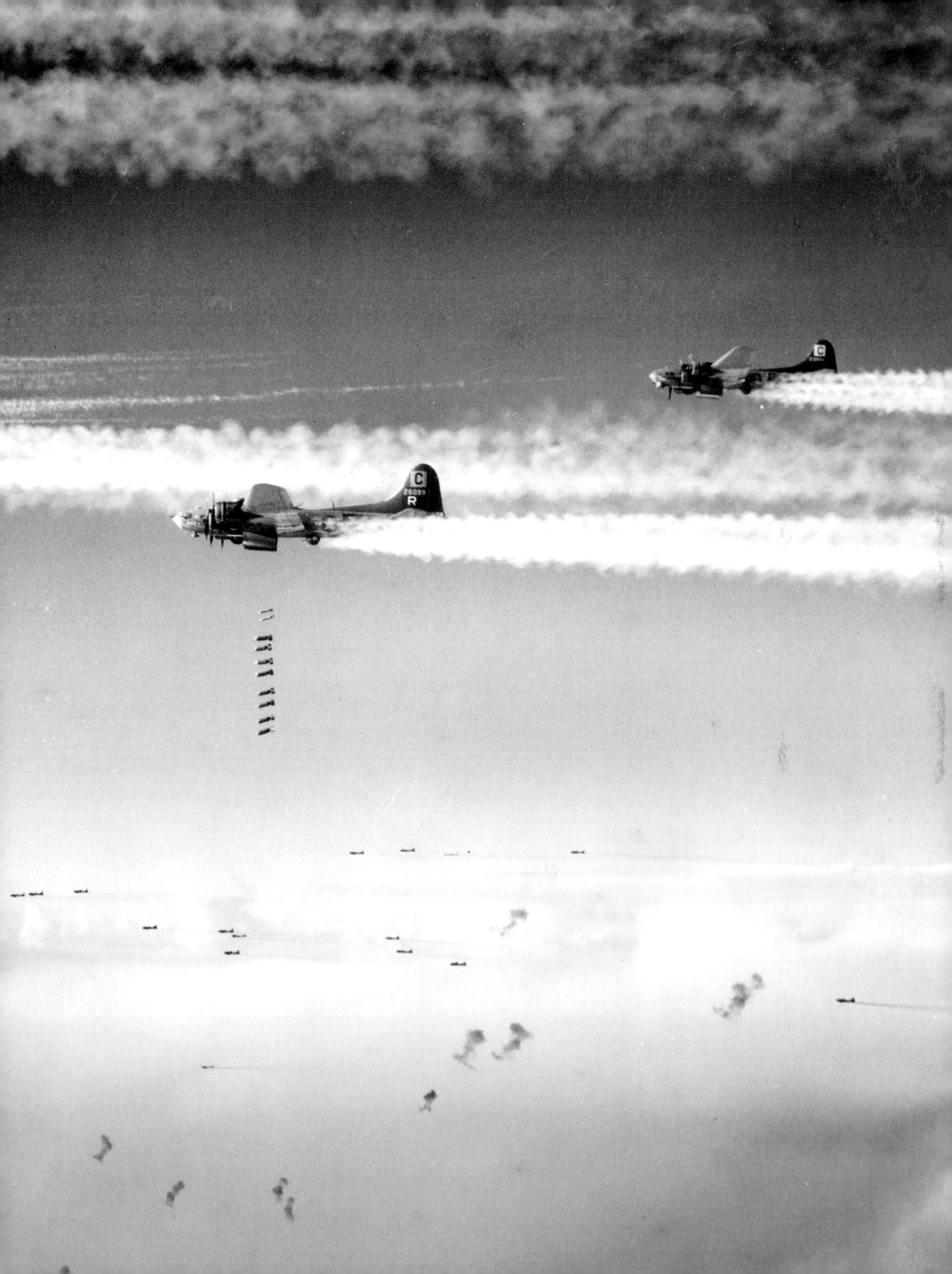
C
26099
R
C

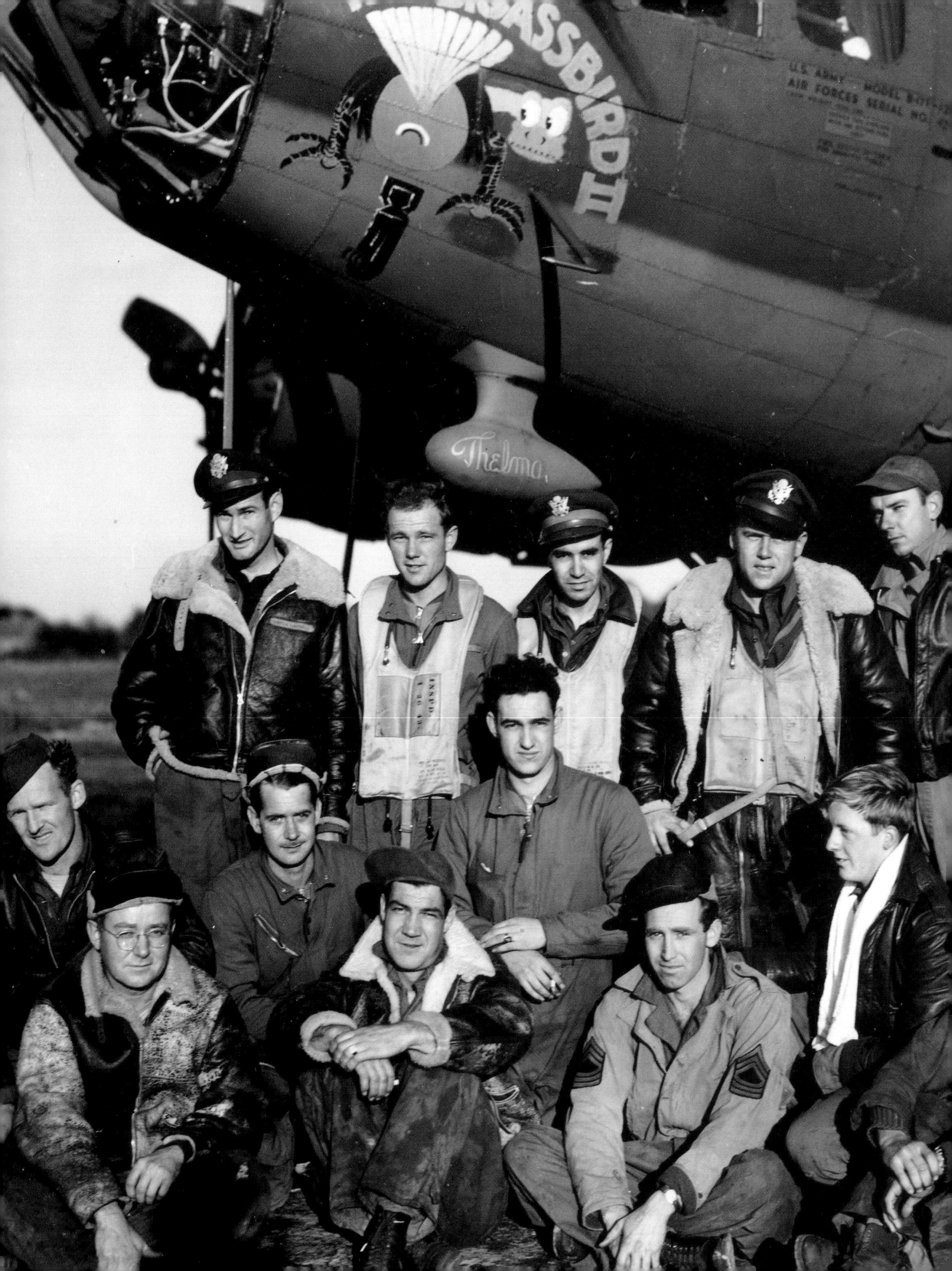
Thelma
U.S. ARMY
AIR FORCES SERIAL NO.

The crew and ground crew of *THE BIGASSBIRD II* at Thorpe Abbotts, home base of the 100th Bomb Group.

wind direction and speed, and today you figure it at about ninety miles per hour. Next is stalling speed, the speed above which the airplane will fly and below which it will retire from flying and become a thirty-five ton rock. It, too, is a variable that at today's weight and with landing gear and flaps extended you calculate to be between 105 and 110 mph. Finally, there is takeoff speed. For a safe (or even successful) takeoff, this needs to be well in excess of stalling speed. You figure today it ought to be at least 120 mph, and you will be very grateful for more if you can get it.

"With movements so automatic you are not aware of them, you hold the accelerating ship straight on the runway, and you listen to the numbers . . . 'seventy . . . eighty . . . ninety . . . ' Now you are committed. Even if you lose an engine you must still try to take off.

"The airplane is rushing now. Objects beside the runway whip past in blurred flashes. 'Hundred 'n five . . . hundred 'n ten . . . ' Now you have passed stalling speed and thereby have been led into temptation. The end of the runway is fast approaching. So, too, are the trees beyond the field. Instinct urges you to get the ship up now, before it is too late. You could get it up now. But would it stay up? The energy that lifts an airplane is robbed from its airspeed. Your margin of speed above stalling is still thin and if the act of lifting off consumes it all, the airplane will rise, then wallow and stagger and fall back to earth in a booming, pyrotechnic bankruptcy seen and heard by everyone in the neighborhood, excepting, of course, you and your crew. So, you master the temptation, and wait.

" 'Hundred 'n twenty . . .' You'd like more, but the end of the runway is too near. This will have to do. Easing the control wheel back, you lift the ship from the runway. It rises

so heavily that you feel you've lifted it with your own hands, but it rises, and to get rid of landing gear drag you immediately call to the co-pilot, 'Wheels up!'

"Now, even though you are off the ground you are not out of the woods. Not yet. Now you have additional problems, as described by one Eighth Air Force pilot: 'You really had to walk a tightrope. If you didn't build up additional airspeed before starting to climb you were liable to stall out. On the other hand, you had to climb enough immediately to get over whatever obstacles lay just beyond the field. Trying to do enough of each and not too much of either, you really could work up a quick sweat—especially if at the same time you ran into prop wash from the plane ahead of you. Once, I remember, we seemed certain to fly right through a farmhouse just beyond the field. Somehow we got over it, but I'll swear we dragged our tail on the roof as we went by!'

"Now you feel a sudden wave of affection for your airplane, even though moments ago you were thoroughly exasperated by it. Again, you've asked it to lift from a short runway a load that the book says it can't lift in that distance, and again the airplane has done it. Moreover, you've seen many of its kind become so battle-damaged they seemed held together only by their control cables, and yet still managed to get their crews safely home. 'These are tough old birds,' you think, 'the best bombers ever built,' and you'll defend their honor against anyone who tries to claim otherwise."

O build your ship of death. Oh build it! For you will need it. For the voyage of oblivion awaits you.
—from *The Ship of Death* by D.H. Lawrence

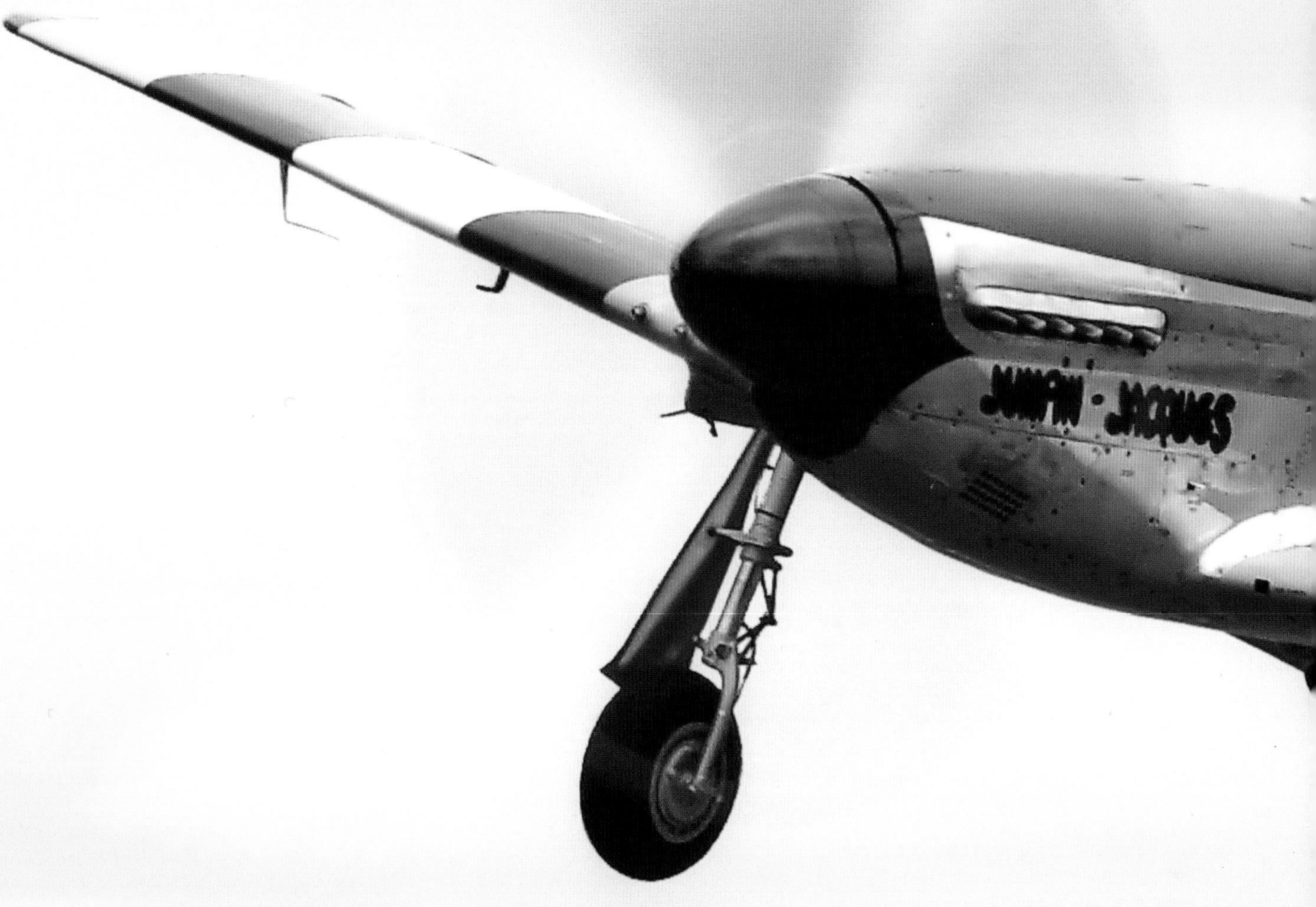
JUMPIN · JACQUES

A restored Mustang banking onto final approach to a landing at Duxford airfield in England.

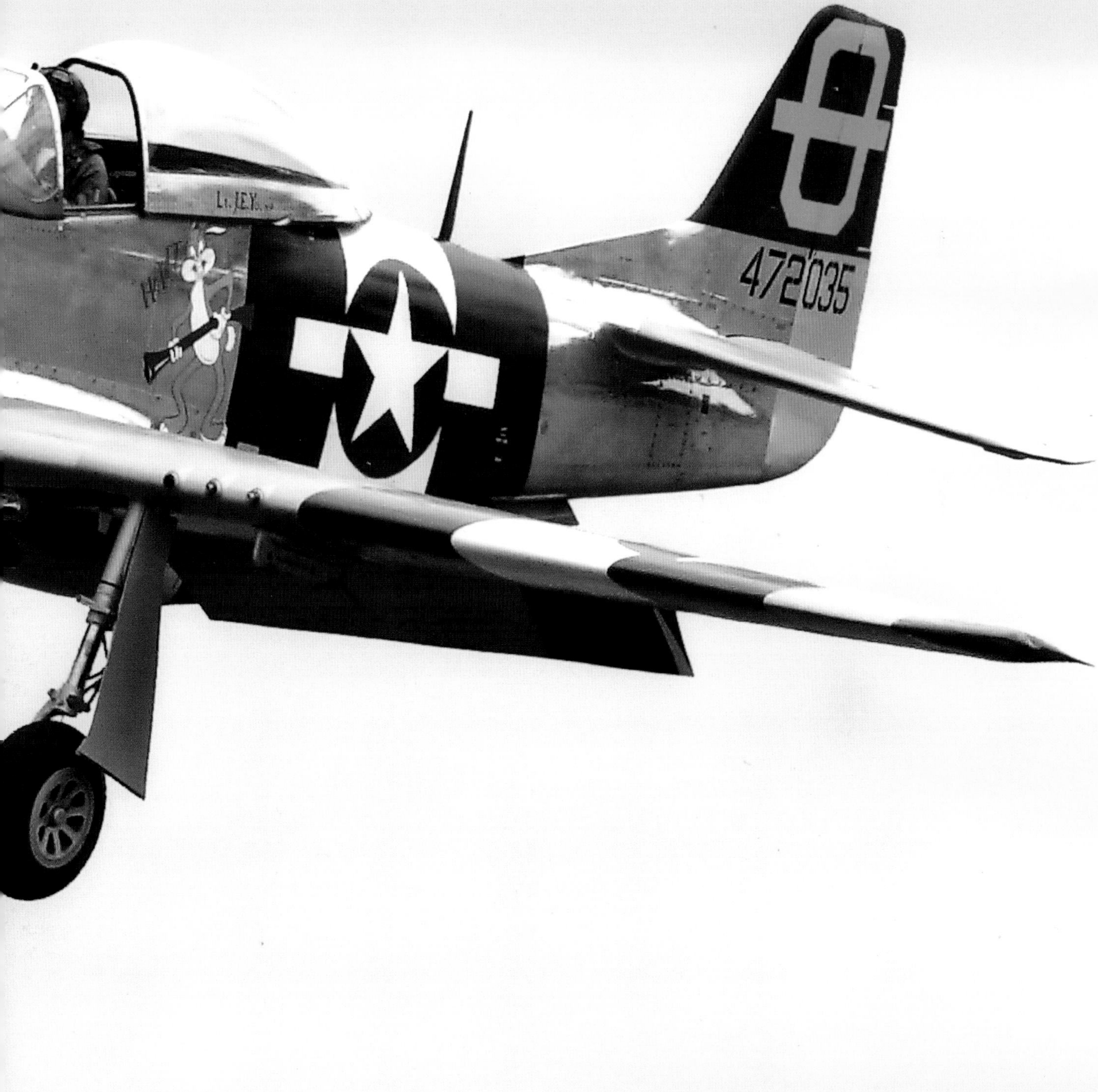
472035

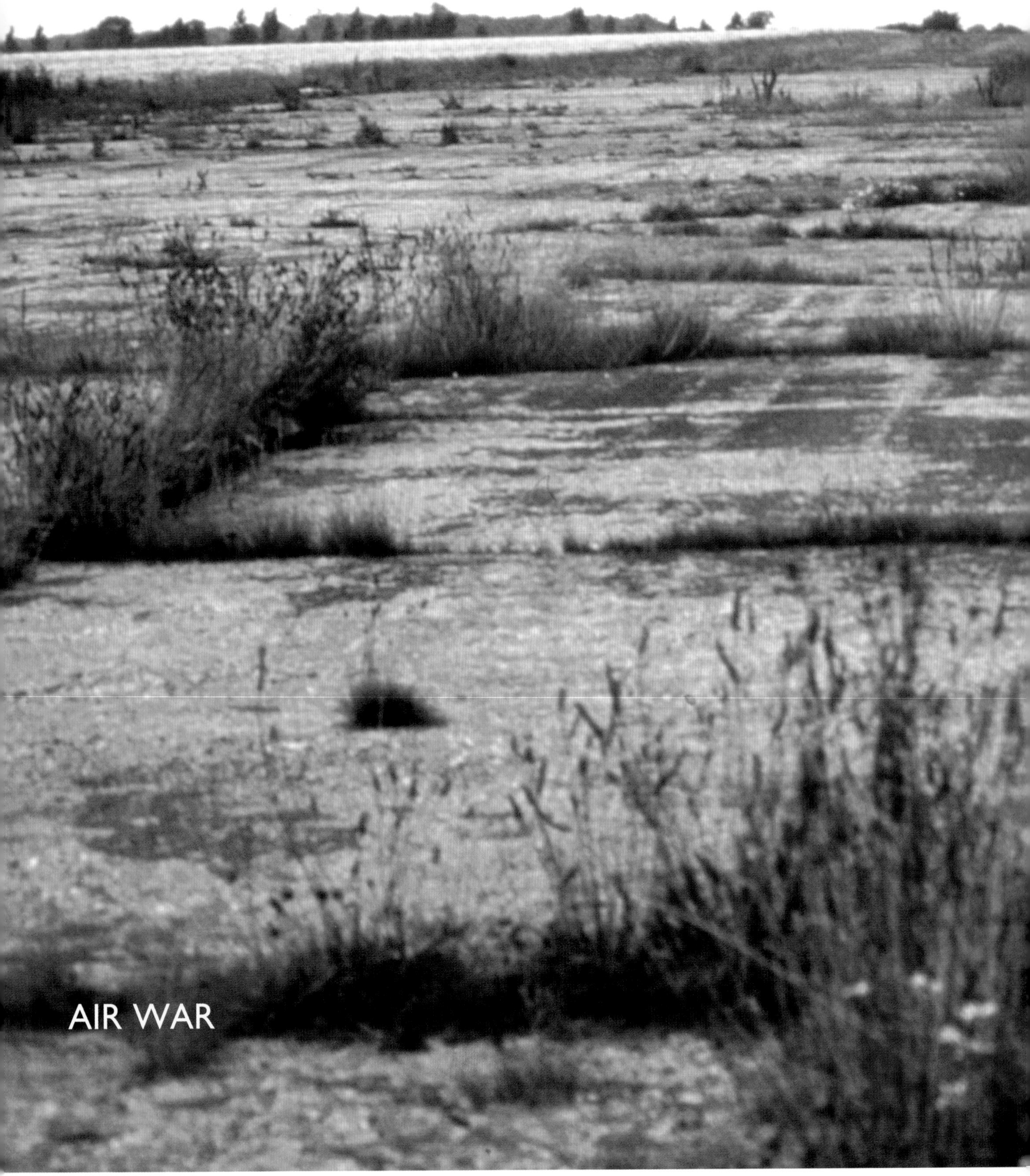
AIR WAR

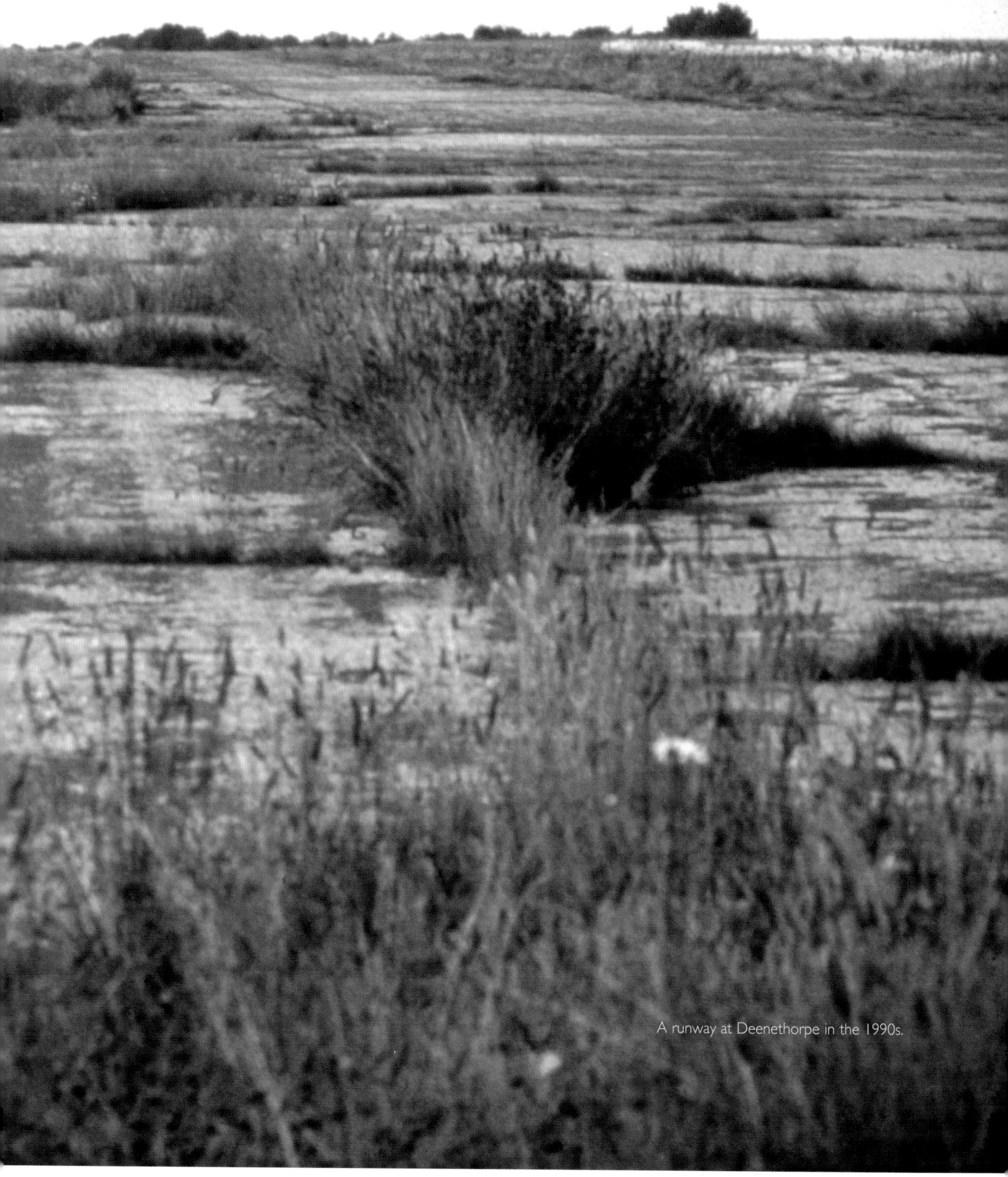

A runway at Deenethorpe in the 1990s.

"On the Kiel job I got my first close-up of a Fort blowing up. The flak tightened up on the group just ahead of ours, and right out at ten o'clock, not very far away, a great red wound opened up, and then the drifting pieces, and ten men and a couple of hundred thousand dollars' worth of airplane, powdered in a hundredth of a second. And while we were watching the streamers of flame from that one, another Fort nosed over straight down and started for the ground by the shortest road. It must have dived five thousand feet, and then by some miracle it pulled out, level and into a straight-up climb. It stalled out somewhere below us, and fell off on the right wing and spun in."
—Bert Stiles, 91BG, Bassingbourn

ON 17TH AUGUST 1943, just one year to the day since Ira Eaker and his twelve B-17s flew the opening Eighth Air Force mission of the European air war, a force of thirty times that number—the largest yet assembled—made the first American deep-penetration raid into the heart of Germany. In 1942, the objective had been barely forty miles from the Channel coast of France: the anniversary targets—the Messerschmitt factory in Regensburg and the ball-bearing plants in Schweinfurt—were both in Bavaria, and the route to the farthest passed over four hundred miles of hostile territory.

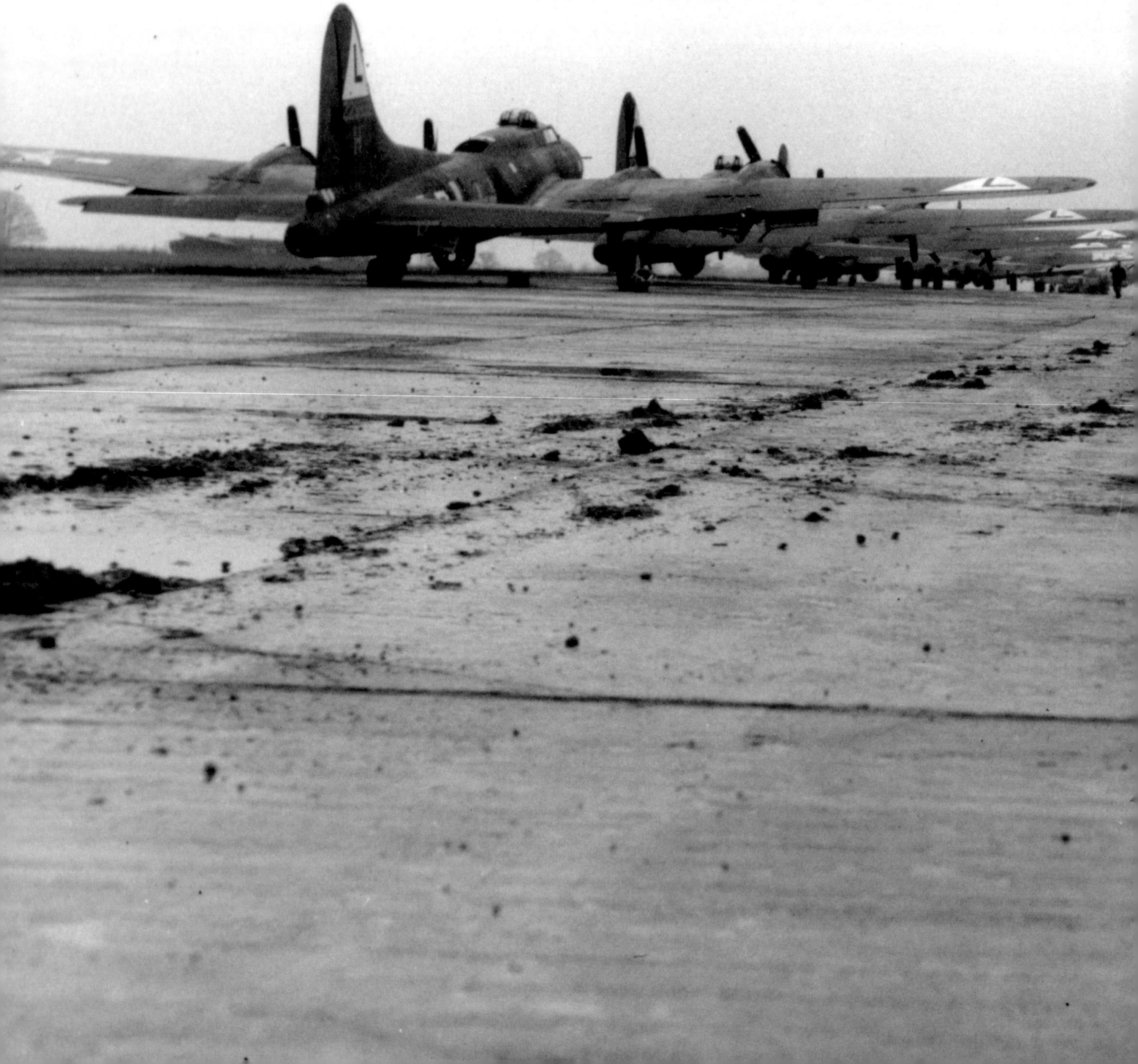

"The attacks were planned to begin simultaneously—at ten minutes before twelve noon—with the aim of splitting the fighter opposition, but, as every fighting man knows, few plans survive exposure to the enemy, and in this case, the enemy was aided by the weather. The skies over Regensburg were reported to be clear, while Schweinfurt was obscured by ten-tenths cloud. To the RAF bomber crews, that would have mattered little: using radar marking, they would have rained the bombs down just the same. Not so the Eighth: at that stage of the war, the edict of Pinetree, Eighth Bomber Command, was that bombardiers must see their targets.

"On the Regensburg mission 146 B-17s of the 4th Bomb Wing, flying in three combat box formations, were escorted by P-47 Thunderbolt fighters as far as the Belgian frontier. From there on, the bombers were subjected to a persistent onslaught by relays of German fighters with cannon fire and rockets. The Luftwaffe mounted a formidable defense: Messerschmitt 109s, 110s, and 210s, Focke-Wulf 190s, and Junkers 88s rose in their hundreds to repel the bombers. In the Fortresses, the intercoms crackled with urgent admonitions: 'Fire short bursts . . . don't waste rounds . . . lead them more.' At times, it seemed to observers that the sky was filled with the debris of aerial combat: pieces of airplane, both American and German, life rafts and fuel tanks, exit doors

B-17s of the Ridgewell-based 381st Bomb Group, in Essex.

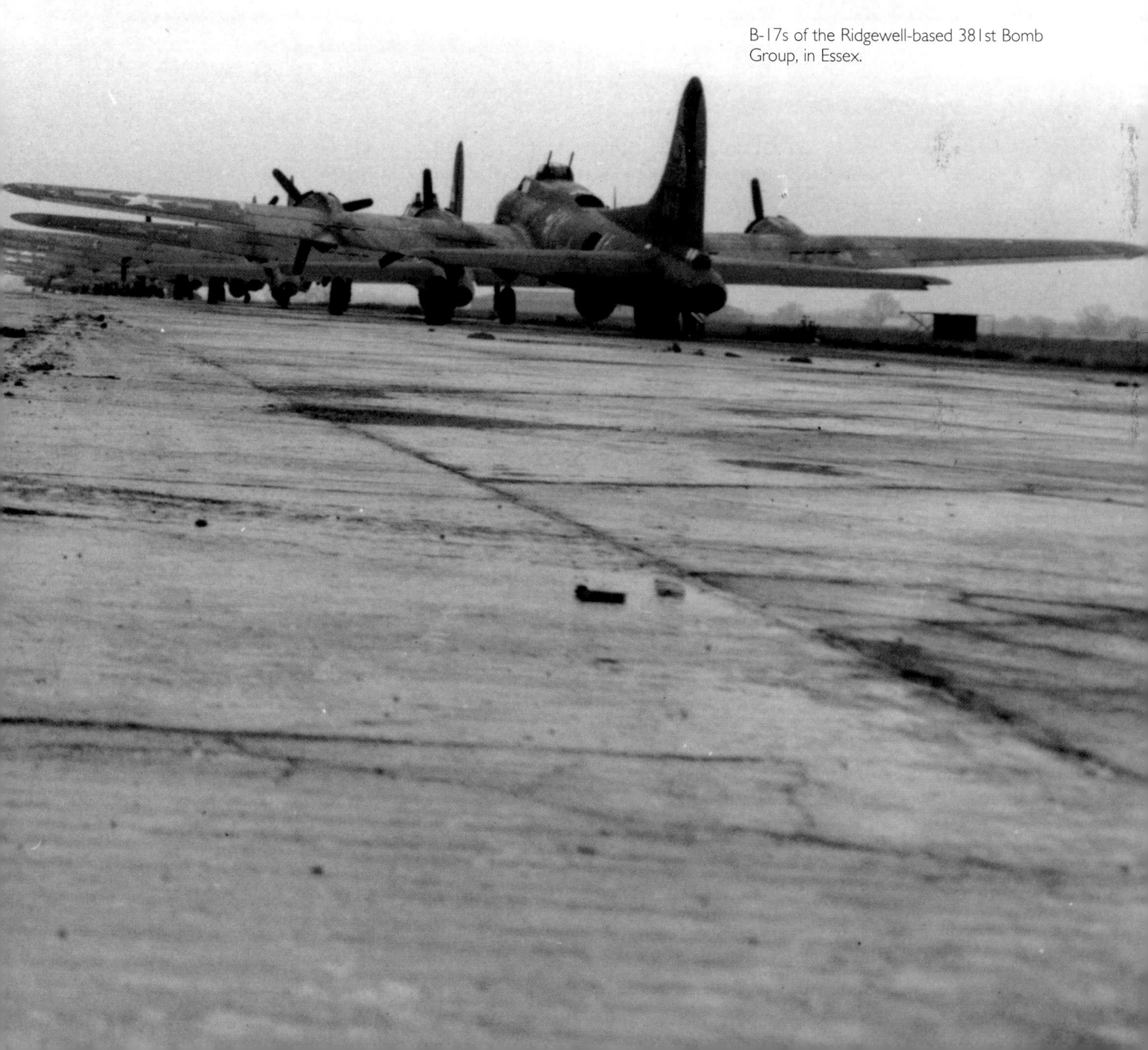

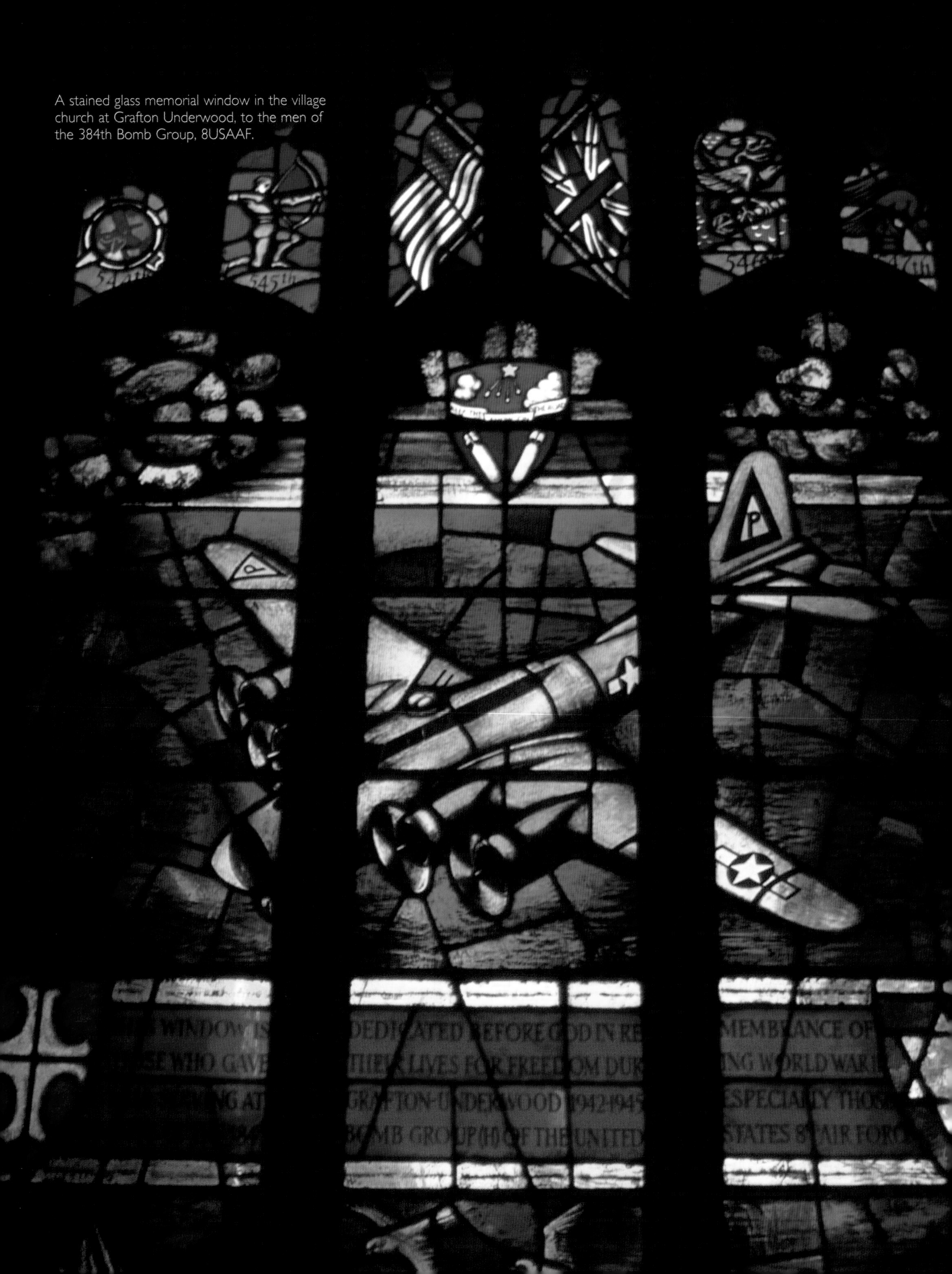
545th
WINDOW IS DEDICATED BEFORE GOD IN RE MEMBRANCE OF
WHO GAVE THEIR LIVES FOR FREEDOM DUR NG WORLD WAR
GRAFTON-UNDERWOOD 1942-1945 ESPECIALLY THOSE
BOMB GROUP (H) OF THE UNITED STATES 8TH AIR FORC

A stained glass memorial window in the village church at Grafton Underwood, to the men of the 384th Bomb Group, 8USAAF.

and hatches. Some men fell with parachutes, other men without. Black smoke columns towered from burning bombers in the fields below.

"After ninety minutes, the fighters broke away. Their controllers planned to re-engage the bombers on return. The B-17s swept on to Regensburg and, flying in the height band between 17,000 and 18,000 feet, released three hundred tons of bombs. The strike on the factory was well concentrated, and the results achieved by the 390th Bomb Group in particular, of fifty-eight percent inside 2,000 feet, were precision bombing of a high order.

"We were all on oxygen and the ship had shuddered like a dog shaking wet fur when eleven guns had been test-fired. I wondered how those big Wright Cyclone engines could continue their comforting roar in such numbing cold. Soon I began to hear foreign noises. The treacherous clouds built up below us and by the time we reached bombing altitude of 20,000 feet, we were just on top of that dirty, sinister scud. Now I knew that our engines were running rough—all four of them. Captain Algar and I exchanged helpless looks."
—Dale O. Smith, 384BG, Grafton Underwood

Two months earlier, sixty Lancasters of No. 5 Group, RAF, having bombed a radar assembly plant on the shore of Lake Constance, had flown on across the Alps and the Mediterranean to land in Algeria. Three nights later, refueled and reloaded for the homeward flight, they had bombed the Italian naval base at La Spezia en route. That force of Lancasters had flown the first shuttle mission of the war; the 4th Bomb Wing of the Eighth Air Force now embarked upon the second. Twenty-four aircraft had gone

down; the survivors landed safely on airstrips in North Africa.

Three hours after the attack on Regensburg had ended, the 1st Bomb Wing's force of more than two hundred B-17s made their delayed approach on Schweinfurt, 120 miles to the northwest. Ken Stone, at twenty years of age, was manning the ball turret of the 381st Bomb Group's *Big Time Operator*: "I was awakened at three o'clock in the morning by the operations officer at Ridgewell, Captain Robert Nelson. I ate a hearty breakfast and rode out to the briefing room. Then I cleaned and dried my guns in the armament shack and installed them in the ball turret. I donned my flying clothes and sat down and waited until the officers came out at 0545. Our plane was the lead ship and our regular pilot, Lieutenant Lord, was flying as tail gunner to check the formation. Captain Briggs was flying as pilot and Major Hall as co-pilot. They started the engines at 0600 and warmed them up. The control tower called and delayed takeoff one hour due to weather over the target. The engines were restarted at 0700, but before taxi time they delayed the mission again. I took a nap and the roar of the engines woke me up at 0900. Then a red flare was fired from control and the mission was once more delayed. A truck came out with some Spam sandwiches. I managed to eat two of them."

Marvin T. Lord's crew had first become acquainted with the *Big Time Operator* at Pueblo, Colorado, while they were undergoing the final phase of their training. They had flown her to England, and on sixteen missions since they joined the 381st. Ken Stone liked the airplane, and he liked his pilot; he particularly liked his pilot's name: "I'm flying with the Lord and

the Lord will protect me."

At 1130 *Big Time Operator* finally took off. Stone entered the ball turret and the twenty B-17s of the group formed up over England and joined the rest of the Wing. Again, the "little friend" fighters provided cover to the limit of their range, but from Aachen onward the bombers flew alone. The German fighters were ready and so was Ken Stone: "I watched them circle our group, sizing us up, and then they came in line abreast with guns blazing. In the first pass they came head-on at us; it was the first time they had done this. It was something new to us, and very effective. Then they flew underneath our plane and into the formation. They were Me 109s and Fw 190s. I had plenty of good shots, but I don't know if I got any—I was too busy shooting at the next one coming in—but I'm sure I didn't waste all my ammunition. Lord said one blew up after it passed us, and he figured I might have got it. Two wingmen were hit—Painter on our left and Jarvis on our right. The waist gunners waved to us and then they went down. Lieutenant Darrow's plane had an engine knocked out, but he managed to keep up with the formation. After what seemed like hours, the fighters disappeared.

"We were met by a medium amount of flak over the target. That was the scariest thing—when you had to go over the target and your bombardier controlled the plane. You had to fly steady, and you could see what you were headed into. It didn't deter our bombardier, Lieutenant Hester. He dropped his bombs and the other planes dropped theirs. The bomb bay doors were right in front of me, and I could always watch the bombs. I watched them fall all the way. It seemed like Hester hit the factory itself. The whole target was well

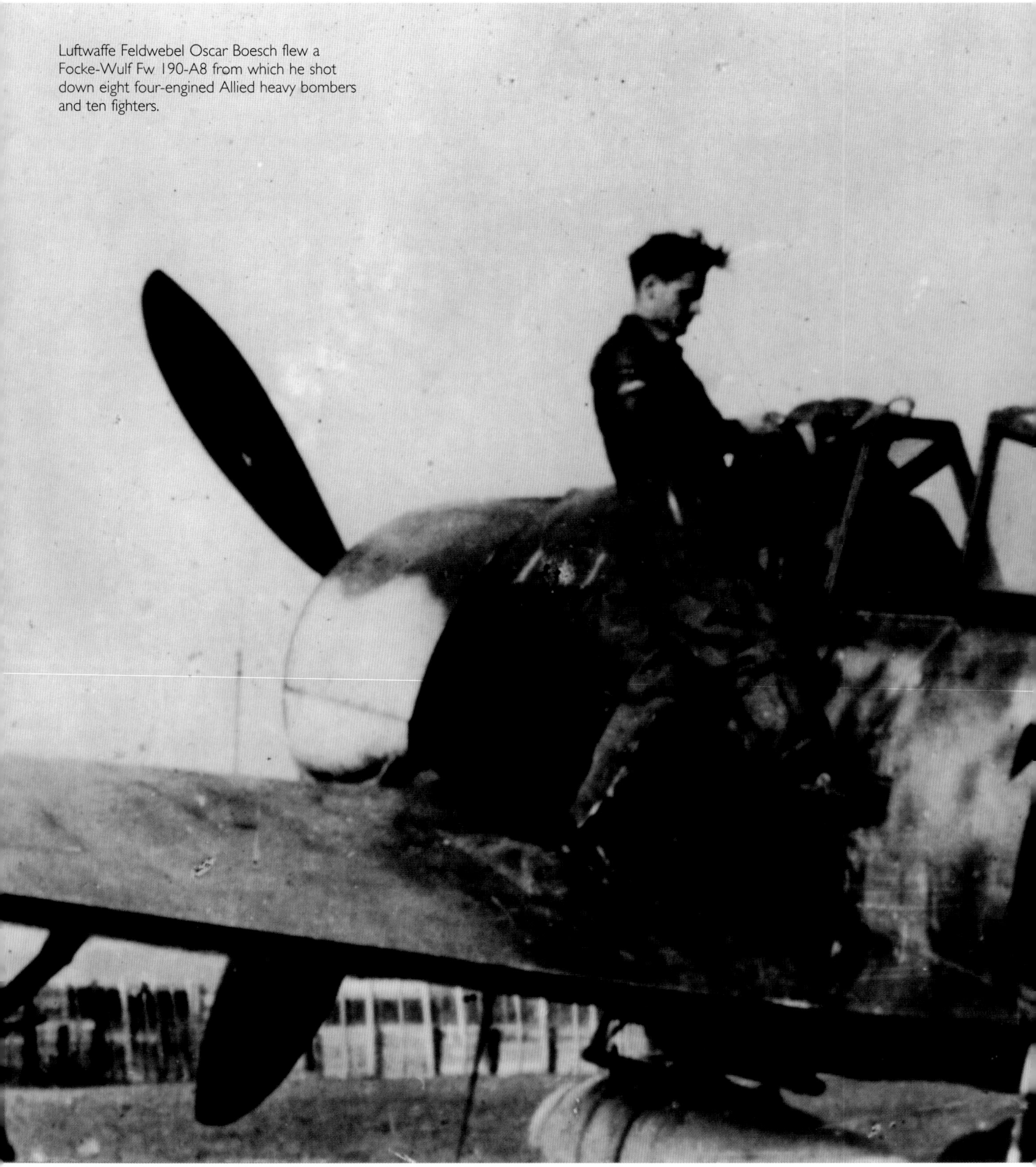

Luftwaffe Feldwebel Oscar Boesch flew a Focke-Wulf Fw 190-A8 from which he shot down eight four-engined Allied heavy bombers and ten fighters.

plastered and the smoke rose high. Lieutenant Darrow was still clinging on. I knew it wouldn't be long before the fighters returned. The tension was very great.

"Fifteen minutes later the fighters were sighted coming in from our right. I thought, 'This is it.' I never thought I'd make it back that day. I was really scared and I prayed to God to get me through this. They circled us once, lined up, and attacked head-on again. Chutes were going down all over the sky, brown ones and white ones; it looked like an airborne invasion. The fighters kept on coming in, passing under and coming around again. The odds were against us. It was not like in the movies, when you hear the fighters zooming and all the sound effects. You just hear your own airplane, its engines, and your own guns.

"At last the fighters left us. We flew on for about fifteen minutes more; then I saw fighters miles to our left and heading our way. I thought, 'Uh-oh, here we go again.' But they turned out to be our escort. They were angels from heaven. I turned the turret around. There were ten planes left in the group. Lieutenant Darrow was dragging along on two engines and dropping out to our left. It looked like he would have to ditch in the Channel. The white cliffs of Dover were the most beautiful sight in the world, and ten minutes later, when I got out of the turret, I was the happiest person in the world. We were safe and back in good old England."

Colonel Dale O. Smith, CO, 384BG, Grafton Underwood: "The clear weather we had enjoyed when leaving England had worsened. On crossing the Channel we found a solid undercast over the whole of the British Isles. On checking with our base we learned that it was socked in with thick fog and that there were no open alternates within range of our dwindling fuel supply. We'd been practicing instrument let-down procedures but they weren't honed to handle such low ceilings. If I attempted to get into Grafton I might prang several Forts on the hills and obstructions.

"I had anticipated such a nightmare situation and knew what I was going to do. By now I had relieved the other two groups from the combat wing box and the 384th was on its own. We had nineteen in the formation now, for which I was responsible. Not far from Grafton was the great bay on the North Sea called The Wash. I headed there and searched for a hole in the clouds below us. There wasn't much time. Our fuel was low. But luck was with us.

"A small hole appeared through which I spotted some whitecaps. I put the formation in a wide echelon to the right and told the pilots to follow me through the hole. Then I dove, pulling out just above the rough water. Soon the 384th was again in echelon below the clouds, skimming the water and heading for England.

"We made landfall and hedgehopped through the scud, just missing church steeples and power lines. It must have shocked the people of the villages we passed. Nineteen Flying Fortresses with seventy-six engines just overhead made a frightful thunder.

"The ceiling began to lift some and I sent the formation on to Grafton Underwood, while I landed at a nearby RAF field. I wanted to check that hole in my wing."

On the Schweinfurt raid, the German fighter planes had shot down twenty-one B-17s en route to the target, and destroyed fourteen more on the homeward flight. Although the target defenses were described by seasoned crews as negligible, yet another bomber fell to the Schweinfurt flak. The Eighth had lost more aircraft in a day than in its first six months of operations.

That night, RAF Air Chief Marshal Harris sent six hundred heavies to attack the Baltic rocket base at Peenemunde. It was the opening gambit in the Allied air campaign, later code-named Crossbow, which would be waged against the factories and launching sites of the enemy's "V-weapons."

The 4th Bomb Wing of the Eighth, returning from North Africa seven days later and attacking Bordeaux airfield on the way, was grievously depleted. In addition to the aircraft lost attacking Regensburg, another twelve had suffered damage beyond the resources of the African outposts to repair, and three from the shuttle operation were missing over France. For its fight against the odds, the whole Wing received a Distinguished Unit Citation, and Major Gale Cleven of the 100th Bomb Group, leading the rear formation, which had borne the brunt of the enemy attacks, was awarded the Distinguished Service Cross.

Throughout the dire Regensburg and Schweinfurt operations, the conduct of the crews could not be criticized: they had met the enemy fighter onslaught with enormous courage. The B-17 gunners had hit back with everything they had, and although the early claims were optimistic, as they often could be in the heat of battle (a Messerschmitt came in, many guns were fired at it, and, at the debriefing, several gunners claimed the kill), twenty-five of their attackers had been shot out of the sky. Both the main targets had been accurately bombed, but so efficient were the Germans at rehabilitation that the factories resumed production in a week and were almost back to normal in two months.

Assessed, therefore, as bombing operations, the attacks could be looked upon as qualified successes: in terms of economy in men and machinery, they could not be so regarded. Five hundred young Americans were missing in action

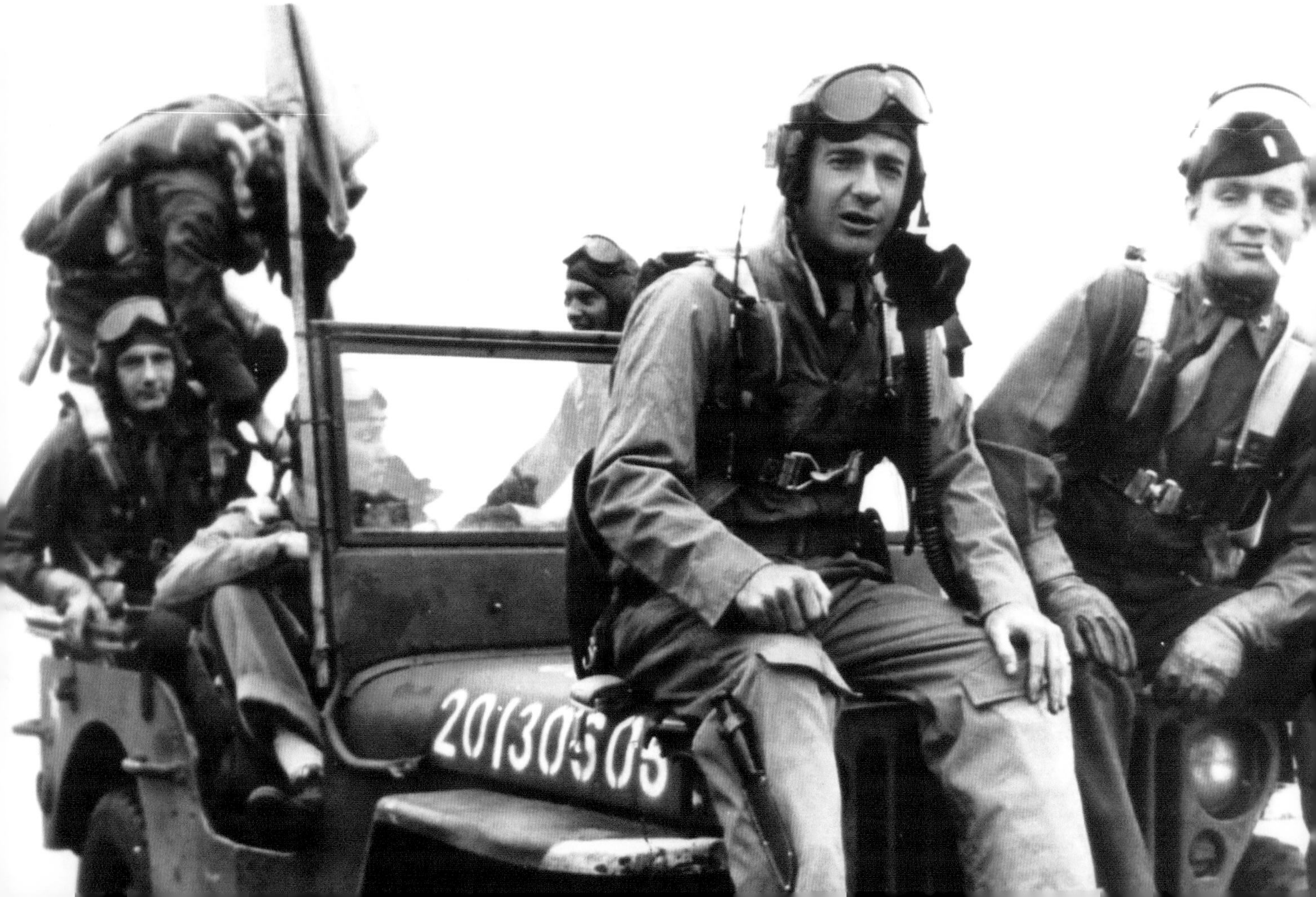

20130505

below: The flying goggles of an 8AF fighter pilot in WW2; bottom: A bomb fuze warning tag; below left: Fighter pilots hitch a ride to their planes on a squadron jeep.

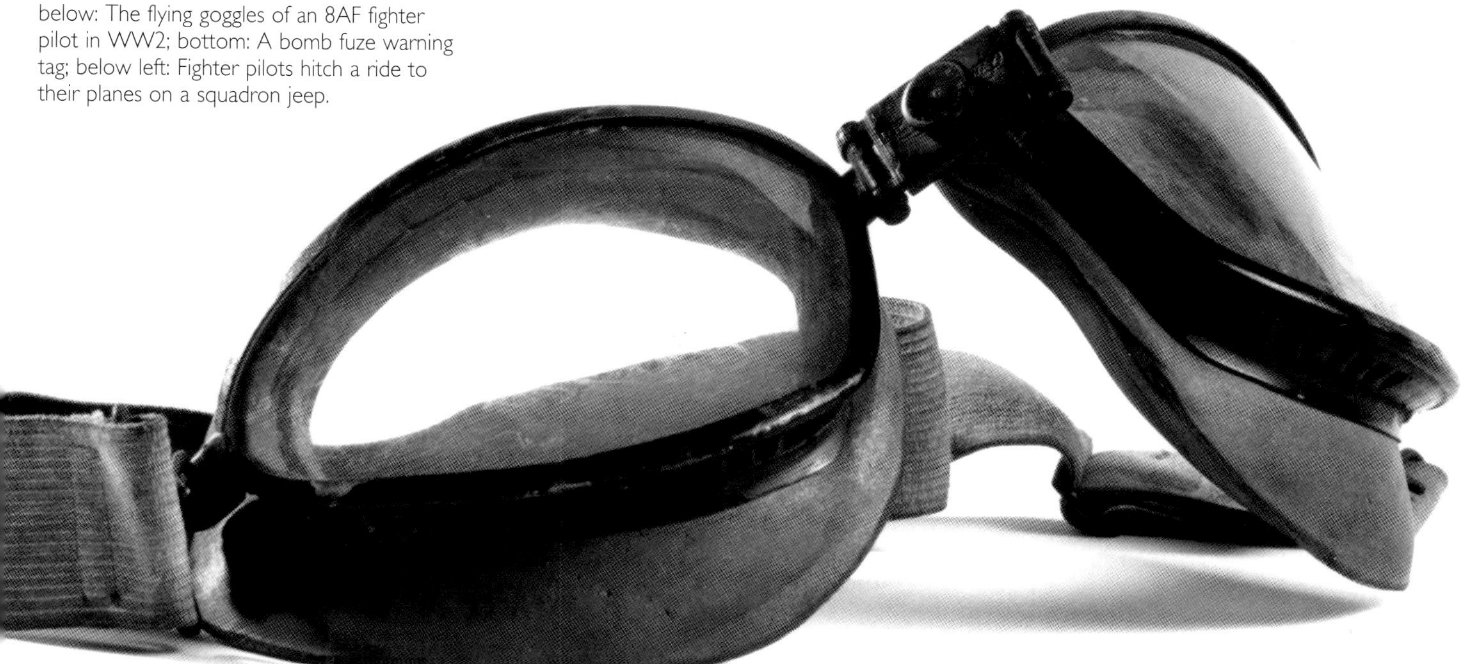

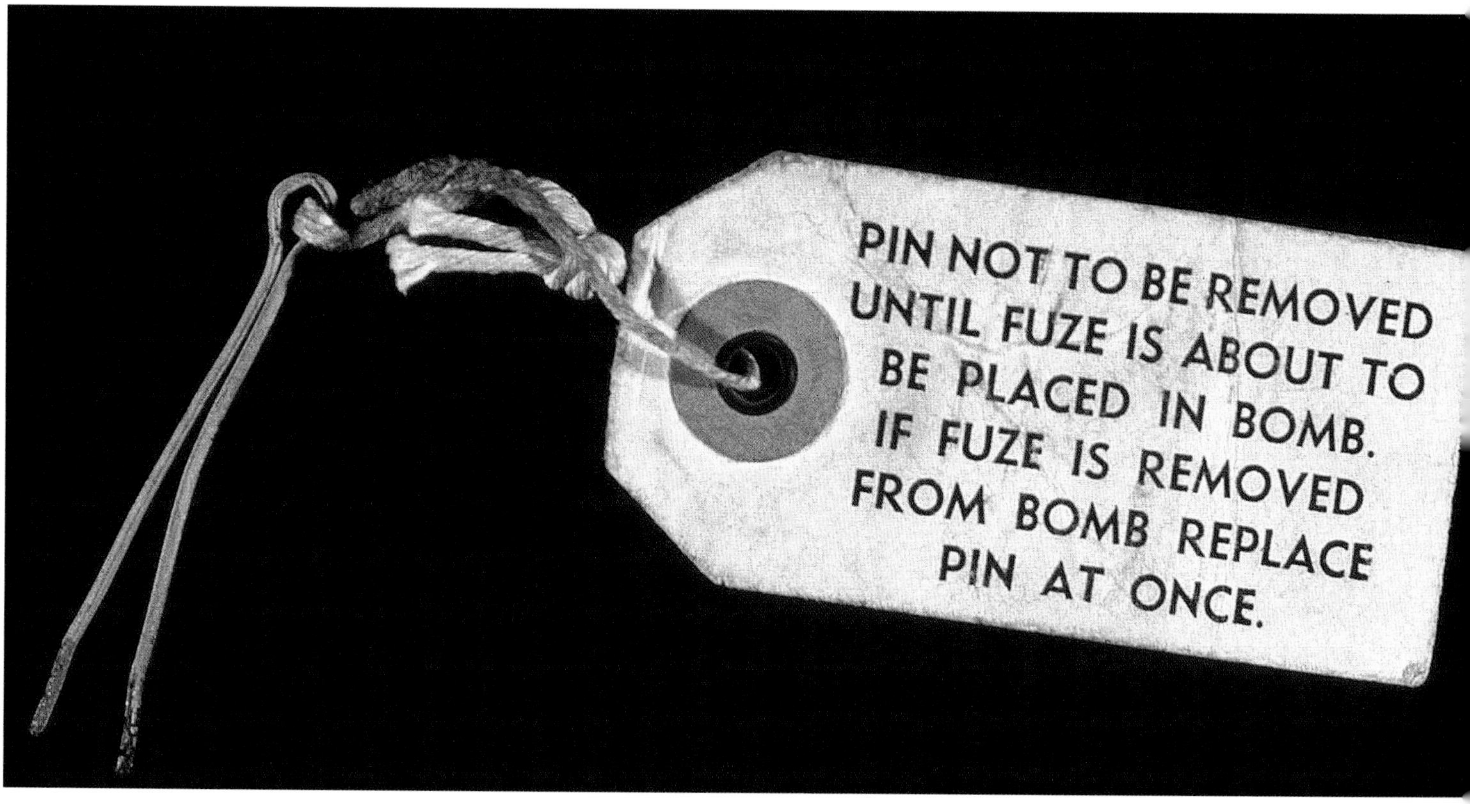
PIN NOT TO BE REMOVED
UNTIL FUZE IS ABOUT TO
BE PLACED IN BOMB.
IF FUZE IS REMOVED
FROM BOMB REPLACE
PIN AT ONCE.

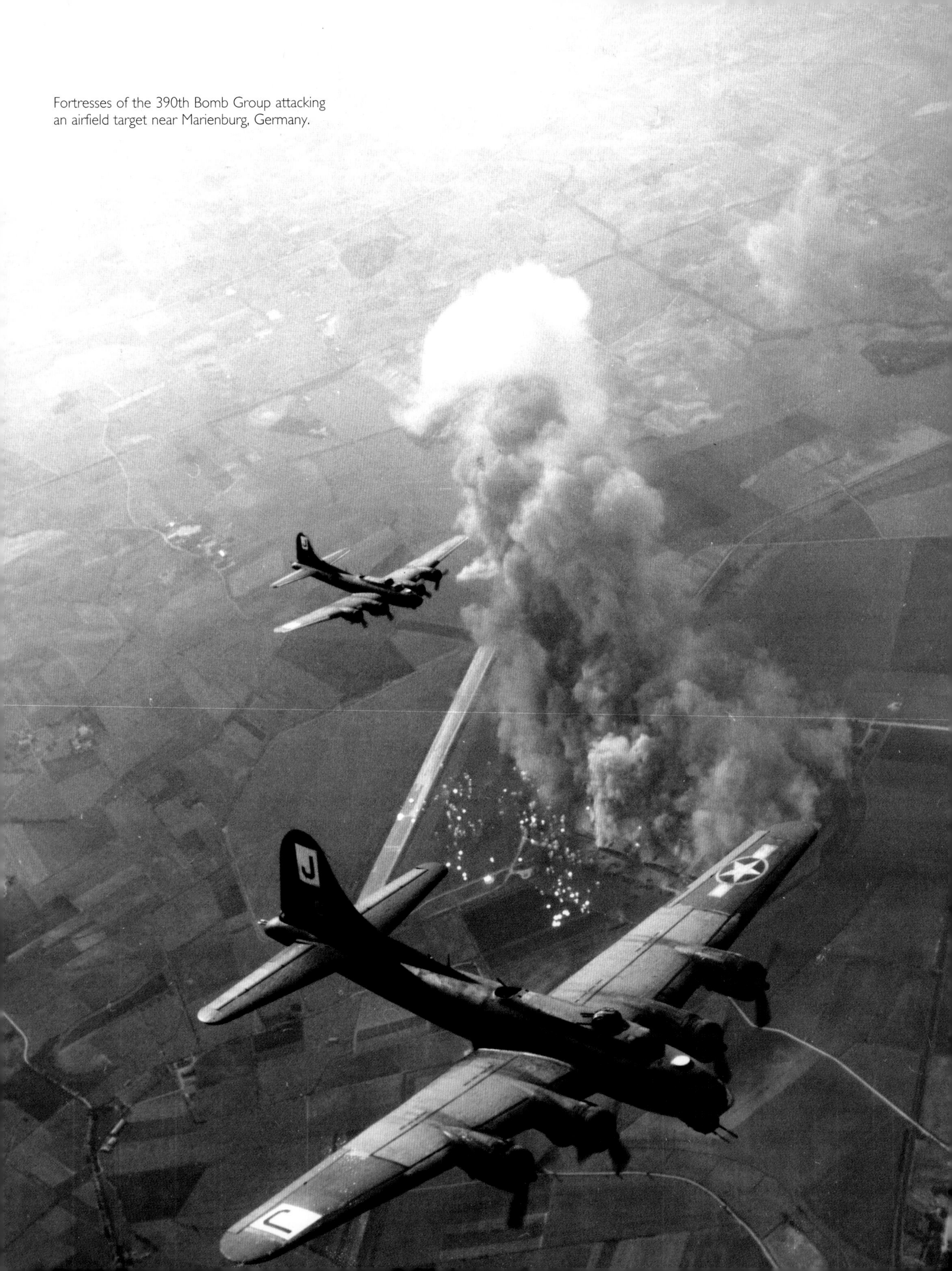
J

Fortresses of the 390th Bomb Group attacking an airfield target near Marienburg, Germany.

somewhere over Europe, and many homecoming aircraft had carried dead and wounded. Over 31 percent of the bombers had been lost, and others had suffered heavy battle damage. These were savage blows—as savage as any the RAF had taken in the early days—and the Eighth reverted to short-range targets for a while. The next big encounter with the enemy defenses came on 6th September, and was as costly as the last. The aiming point in Stuttgart was hidden under cloud, few crews found the primary target, and forty-five aircraft were lost in the attempt. Five more, with battle damage, were forced to land in Switzerland; another twenty-one, short of fuel, ditched or crash-landed in England.

Again, the Eighth stepped back and took a breath. For a few weeks, most of the targets selected were in France or on the German North Sea coast. In the next four thousand sorties ninety planes were lost, and a third of these went down on the only long-range mission: an attack on Münster's railways and canals. Eaker then decided that General Anderson's bombers must return to Schweinfurt and its three ball-bearing plants. On 14th October the crews were briefed for the follow-up attack. At Great Ashfield, Lieutenant Colonel Elliot Vandevanter spoke a few words of encouragement to the 385th Bomb Group. "This is a tough job but I know you can do it. Good luck, good bombing, good hunting . . ." From the seated ranks in the briefing room, a lone voice added ". . . and goodbye."

The 1st and 3rd Bomb Divisions dispatched three hundred B-17s to the primary target, while B-24s of the 2nd Bomb Division made a diversionary attack on Emden. Ray Wild was flying his third mission out of Podington with the 92nd Bomb

Group: "We were off to an early start. We reached altitude and got over the French coast. Somehow, we failed to pick up the low group of our Wing. As we were the lead Wing, the colonel decided we had better fall in with another group. We did a three-sixty over the Channel and, seeing fifteen planes ahead of us that didn't seem to be attached to anyone, we just tagged along with them. We picked up enemy fighters at just about the time our own escort had to leave. From that moment, it was unbelievable. For three hours over enemy territory, we had fighters shooting tracers and rockets at us. You could see those rockets coming. They were about eighteen inches long, and when they hit they would explode and set the plane on fire. Some twin-engine jobs at about a thousand feet above us were dropping bombs on the formation. There was no way they could aim at any one bomber—they were just dropping bombs into the group. And they were dropping chains or cables to foul our propellers.

"We were riding Ray Clough's left wing when he got hit. He dropped out, and twenty seconds later he burst into flames. Brown got hit and disintegrated; a great sheet of flame and then a hole in the formation. I took over the lead of the second element just prior to going over the target. Major Ott was riding on three engines and had to drop behind. I never saw him again. Even over the target, the fighters came on through the flak. It was one of the few times they did that. They were really first team, those guys. They had guts and they were damned good fliers. They'd come in close, and if you straggled by as much as fifty yards, you'd had it. You'd get hit by three or four guys.

"The main thing was, the lead bombardier did a beautiful job on the

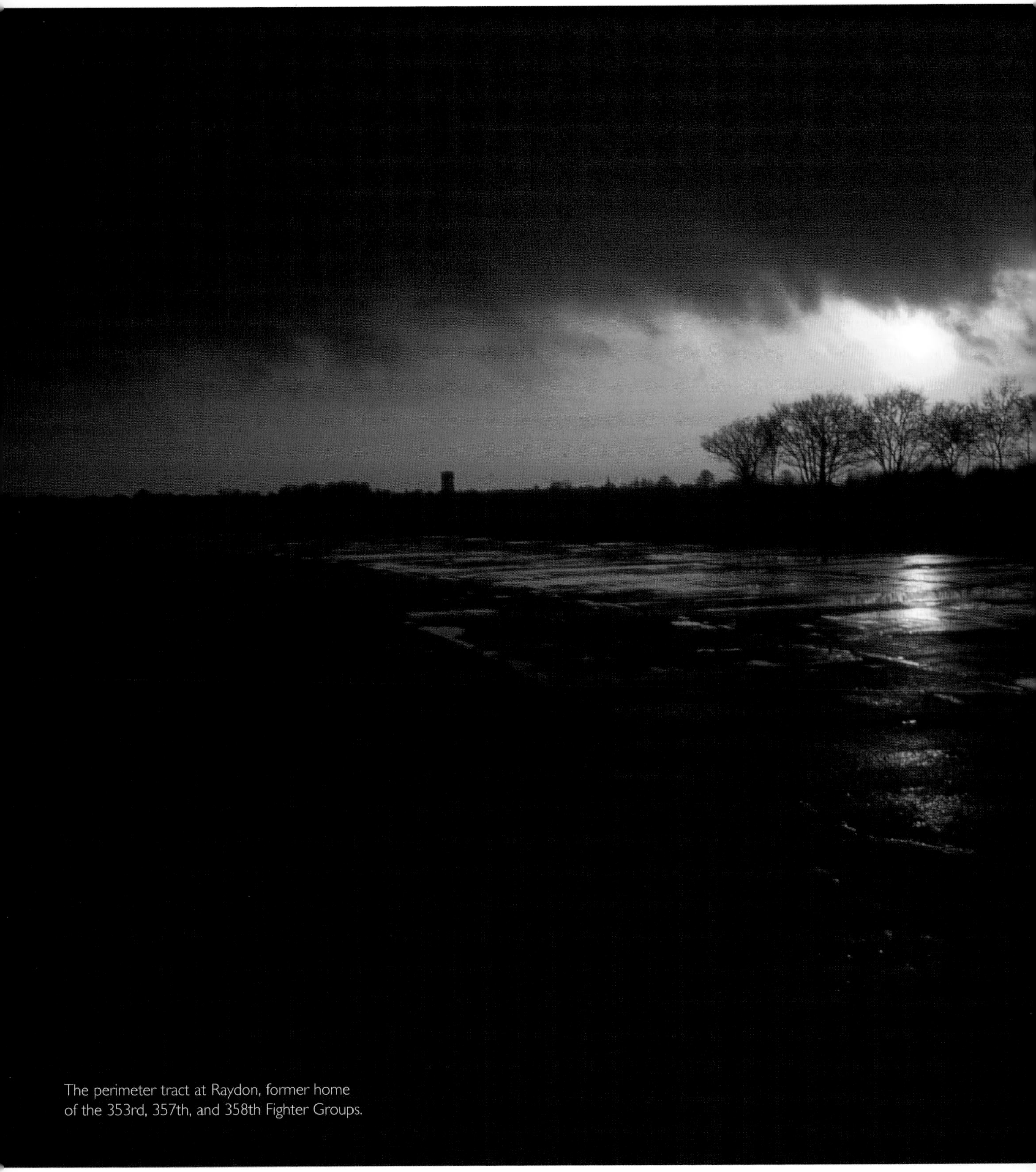

The perimeter tract at Raydon, former home of the 353rd, 357th, and 358th Fighter Groups.

target, but about three minutes later we got hit in number three engine. Due to loss of the prop governor control we couldn't feather it, and we began to sweat. We had to use maximum manifold pressure and 2,500 revs to stay in formation. We limped home as far as the Channel and started to let down into the nearest field. We got into Biggin Hill, southeast of London. Seven Forts set down there and they were all shot up. Several had wounded aboard and one had a dead navigator. We had fifteen holes in the ship and only about sixty gallons of gas left. After Schweinfurt, I thought the rest would seem easy."

The return to Schweinfurt had been yet another calamitous event: sixty B-17s had failed to return, more than twice that number had suffered battle damage, and over six hundred officers and men were missing, dead, or wounded.

It could have been a deathblow for precision daylight bombing; indeed, a partial switch to night bombing was considered for a while. At the end of the day, however, the USAAF commanders held fast to their philosophy, while the operations staff at Pinetree undertook a total tactical reappraisal. Stuttgart had indicated the need for pathfinder aircraft, equipped with a version—a better one if possible—of the RAF's H2S radar; all the long-range missions had shown a requirement for more firepower for the bombers and protection for the crews; the combat box formations must be flown tighter for mutual support; above all, the range of the "little friends" had to be extended.

Meanwhile, in Germany, the armaments ministry planned a wider dispersal of vital war industries and the urgent construction of underground factories. The Luftwaffe generals had also read the signs: despite their fear-

ful losses, the American formations were still hitting targets and knocking down fighters, and it seemed they intended to go on. There was only one thing for it: Berlin must be told that the production of fighters should immediately be doubled, and that the training hours for pilots had to be reduced. All these decisions, in England and in Germany, were translated into action in the ensuing months, and those that affected the USAAF fighters' range and the Luftwaffe training were to have a major impact on the outcome of the war.

Four months later, in what was to become known as the Eighth Air Force's "Big Week," Schweinfurt was to discover what bombing round the clock meant. On 24th February 1944, the 1st Air Division, heavily escorted by P-47s and the new Merlin-engined P-51 Mustangs, all with long-range fuel tanks, struck the ball-bearing plants; that same night Air Chief Marshal Harris, pausing briefly in the Battle of Berlin, dispatched his Lancasters and Halifaxes in two separate attacks with two thousand tons of bombs. The whirlwind had come, and the dead had been avenged.

"To her crew she has always been a graceful and beautiful creature. They have often talked about this 30-ton craft, of the manner in which she slides through the air in the clean sunshine high above earth. Under her glistening belly the ball turret turns slowly as she moves into German territory. In her transparent nose the bombardier prepares his equipment, checking for the run over the target of thirty to sixty seconds, the meaningful justification for this airplane and all the others to be plunging into Germany. He kneels before his bombsight like an acolyte before an altar,

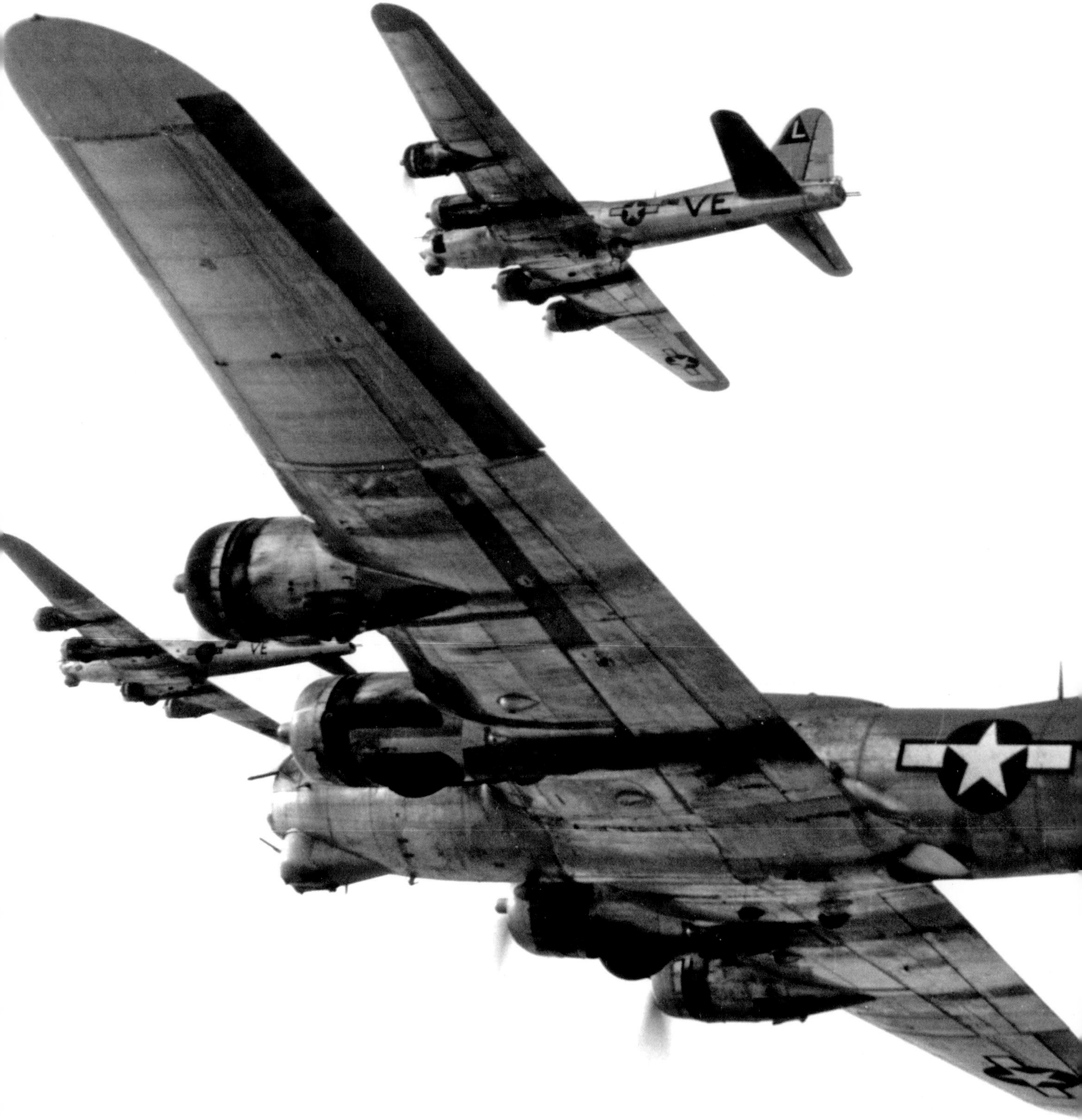
VE
L
VE

B-17s of the 381st Bomb Group form part of a combat box formation.

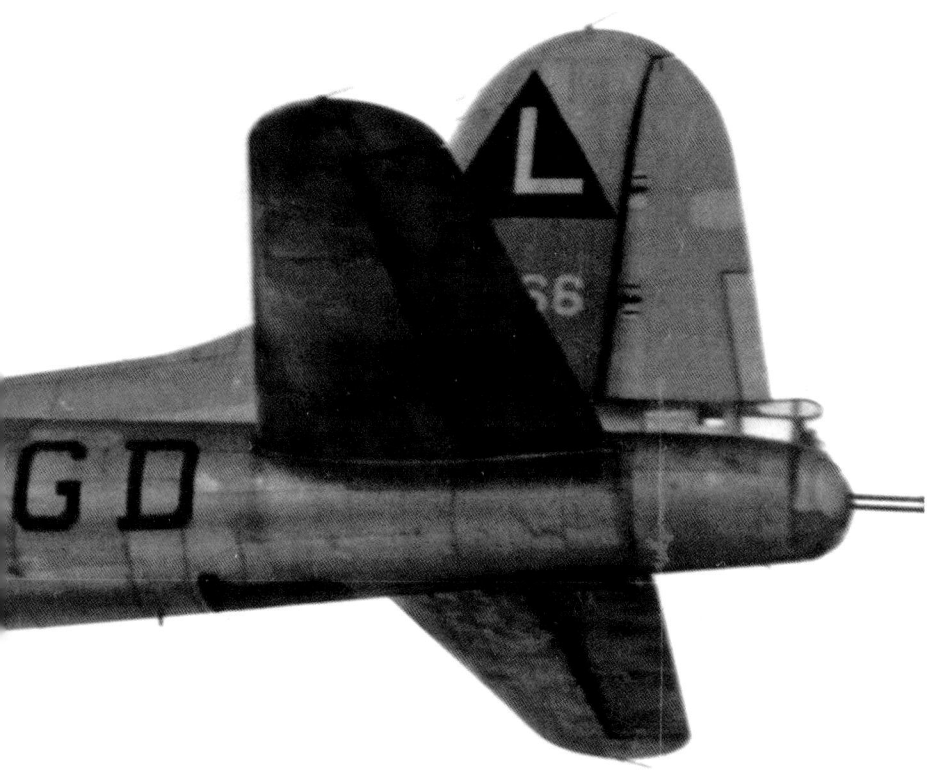
L
GD

just as intense, equally as concerned for proper obeisance to the delicate equipment. The livid yellow of his inflatable life jacket, the dark green of his oxygen mask, stand out sharply against all his bulky attire.

"The Flying Fortress does not seem to be occupied by men. They are beings from some other world, alien creatures with strange breathing systems dangling from beneath their faces. The rubber diaphragms of the oxygen masks expand and contract regularly like living lungs, delicate membranes exposed outside the body, fragile in puncture.

"Everything happens so quickly that it is blurred and chaotic. Movement and action are more instinctive than deliberate. Around this particular ship the bombers accept their punishment. Some die in violent agony; others absorb the deathblow with seeming stoicism, drifting out of formation, easing toward the earth far below, and never coming out of the long, gentle glide, dead airplanes before they smash into the earth.

"There is a terrible feeling when a bomber dies. Not just among the crewmen who, if not dead, are abandoning their machine in frantic haste before it becomes their tomb, but among those men in accompanying bombers who watch, helpless to assist, as a tongue of flame licks hungrily from a tear in a wing, feeds on fuel streaming backward, gathers strength, and throws itself through the rest of the airplane."
—from *Black Thursday* by Martin Caidin

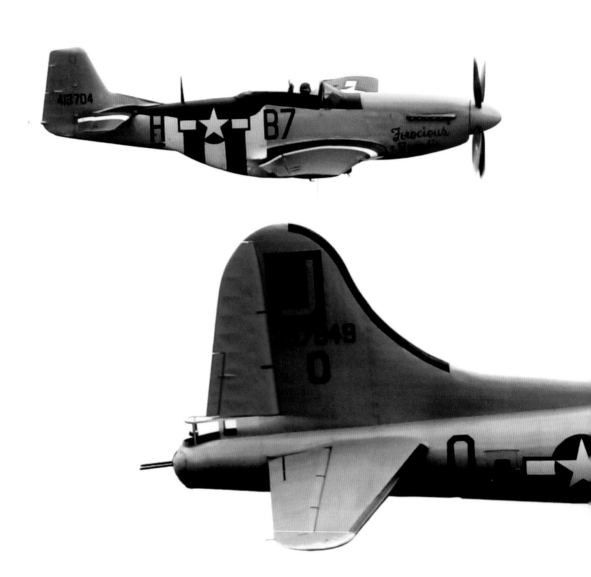

P-51 "little friends" escorting a B-17 'big
friend'—all superb warbird restorations.

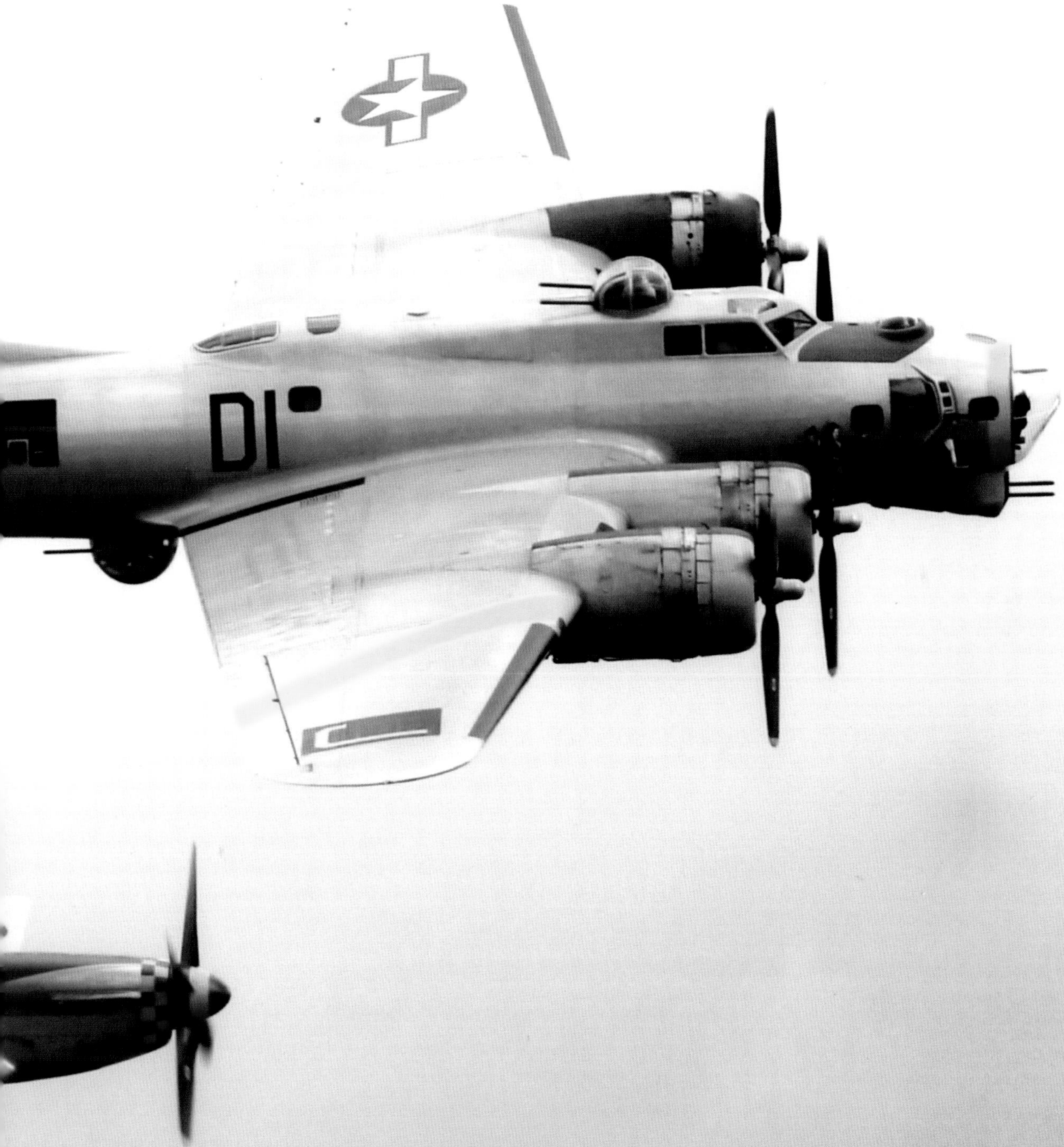
DI

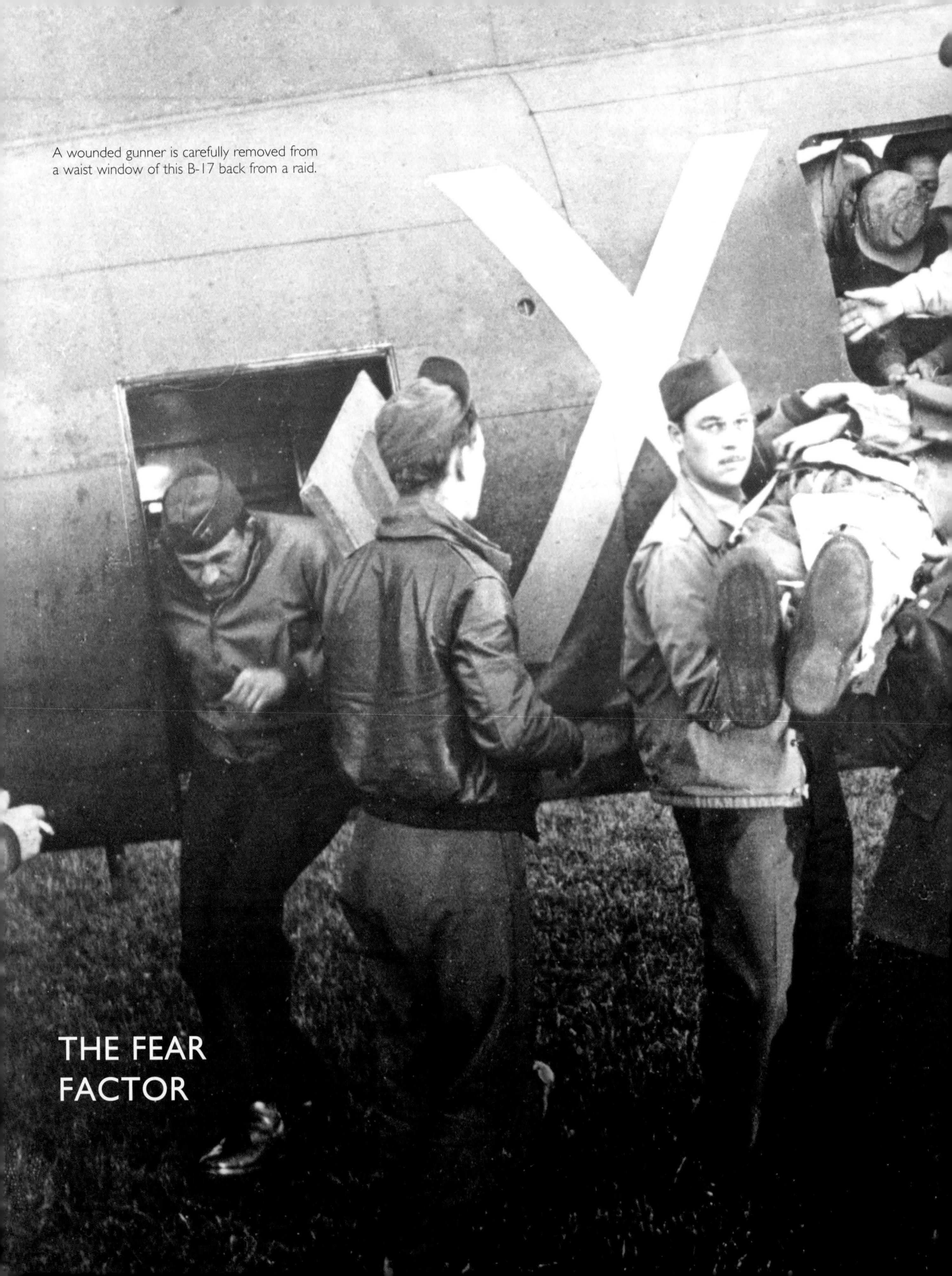

A wounded gunner is carefully removed from a waist window of this B-17 back from a raid.

THE FEAR FACTOR

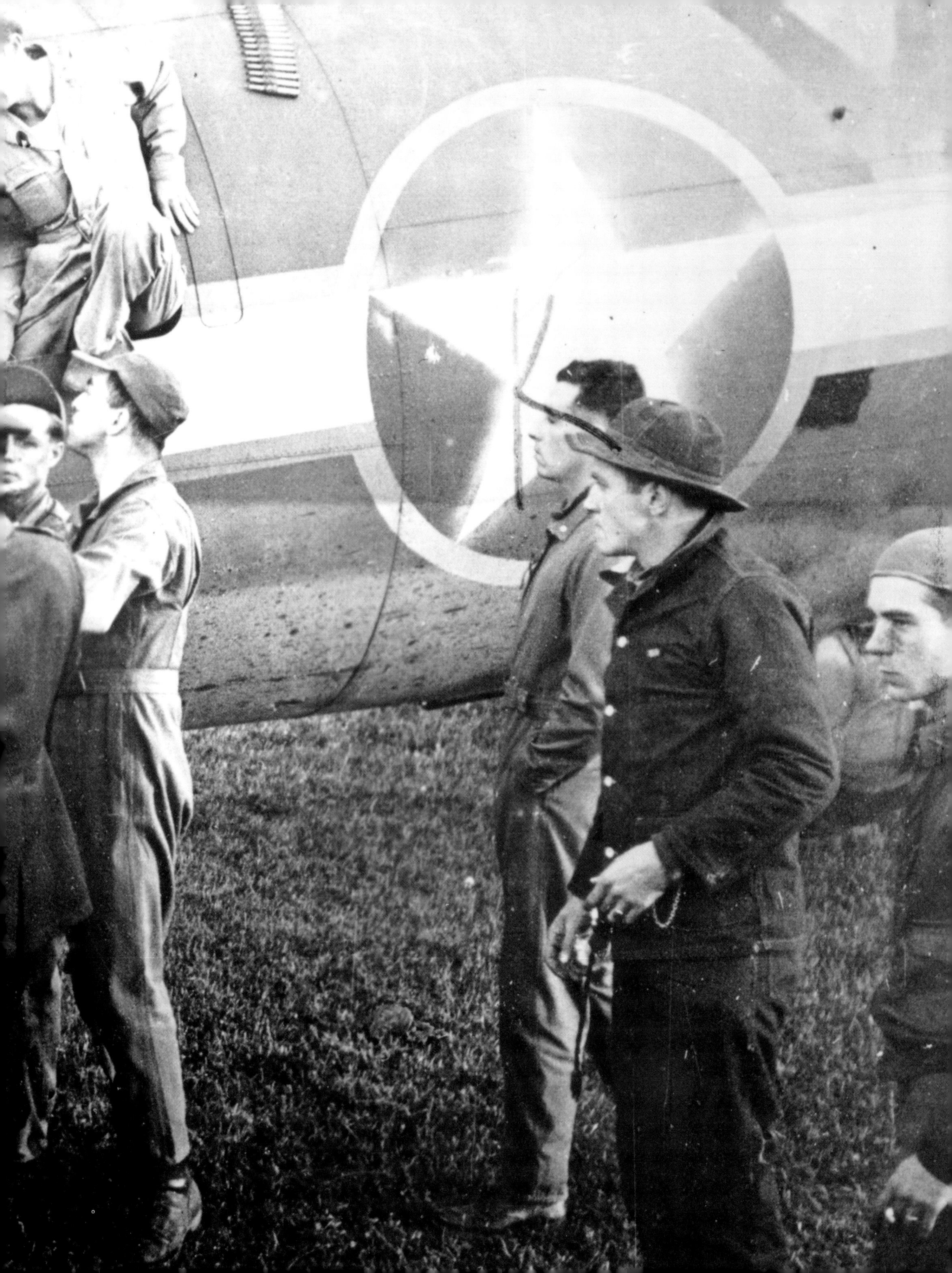

One in every ten American servicemen killed in World War Two combat was a member of the Eighth Air Force.

pucker string, n. an apocryphal part of the pilot's anatomy which when figuratively pulled causes one's buttocks to constrict in fear.

flak, n. German Flieger Abwehr Kanone (anti-aircraft cannon). Explosive or exploding missiles fired from anti-aircraft cannon.

"I DIDN'T REALIZE that you could get killed, believe it or not . . . you saw the flak, you saw one or two planes getting hit and veering off. A couple planes in our formation were just blown up—from then on I was frightened. From then on I really realized the danger. You know there's danger; you know there's the chance of getting hit. With fighters, you didn't have the fear. It was flak! Unpredictable and you knew you had to go through it. The first time we went to Berlin and we saw that box of black and you knew you just had to fly towards that box and keep on going, and once you got into that box you could see puffs trailing the formation. On a mission to Tours, France, we were bombing support for the troops and we got flak through the windscreen and also through the nose and the navigator had some flak go through his arm. I had just reached forward to cage the compass because we were doing some manuvers of some sort, and as I reached forward the flak came through and embedded in my jacket and my parachute pack behind me."
—Bill Ganz, 398BG, Nuthampstead

"The initial explosion caused my aircraft to go into a stall and we fell two thousand feet in a vertical fall, the

airplane out of control. The explosion happened just prior to 'bombs away,' and when we stalled out after that initial concussion, I reached over and hit the salvo switch to get rid of the bombload; I wanted to get as much weight off as quickly as I could, to recover from the stall without damaging the airplane. The ridiculous thing was that the bomb camera started right then, and when we came home and didn't have a single hole in the airplane, they were not going to give

us credit for having gone on the mission—they thought we'd been goofing off over France or something, because the reports were that all thirty-six airplanes had gone down, but when they developed the film out of our bomb camera, our bombs had hit approximately one hundred feet from the aiming point . . . purely an accident. There was no aiming involved. And as we were recovering and pulling back up to the outfit, the second series [of explosions] started and that's when they hit the number two aircraft and the whole group started disappearing right in front of us as we were climbing up to it. Self-preservation took over and I just tried to turn and get out of there as quick as I could . . . trying to figure out what it was going to take to save us . . . worrying about avoiding falling debris, concussion, the fire, and by the time we got out of the mess and the area and started looking around, we were into an area where the German fighters were starting to close in on us because we were a single. We started worrying about that . . . and [at that point] it was just genuine fear.

"There was one thing that [my co-pilot] laughed about. I was flying the plane the whole time with him following on the controls, as we recovered and climbed back up to the outfit. He said, 'Don't say that you never sweated in below-zero temperature.' It was forty degrees below zero and the perspiration had rolled down over my eyes, on the front of my oxygen mask and was caked on the top of my mask a quarter of an inch thick. At forty below zero, you can sweat! The heavy breathing and fighting the controls . . . trying to keep control of the aircraft so that I wouldn't lose it. The oxygen mask exhaust was under my chin and there was a huge layer of ice all down the front of my jacket down to my waist—condensed and frozen moisture coming out of my oxygen mask."
—Robert White, 390BG, Framlingham

"I can remember vividly on a raid, it wasn't Schweinfurt 'cause it wasn't that rough on our group, but it was terrible. We lost about half a dozen planes and one of them was right in front of me in the formation, and it just absolutely exploded. Nothing but a big ball of debris and you

could feel that debris hit your airplane. A very unpleasant sensation."
—David Parry, 390BG, Framlingham

"The target was the Villacoublay airdrome at Paris, France. The Germans were assembling the Focke-Wulf 190s there and it was a real important target. We were on the bomb run and just before we dropped our bombs we got hit by flak, which knocked out the two engines on the left side. Number one being on fire and burning, we stayed in formation, dropped our bombs, and as we were pulling away from the target, number four was shot out. We soon found ourselves a straggler with seven Fw 190s trying to finish us off. With the ship's load decreased as much as possible, we were indicating ninety-five miles per hour and losing five hundred feet per minute. We passed over the city of Le Havre on the coast of France at 4,000 feet and still going down. Finally, At 1,000 feet above the water, the seven 190s broke it off and left us. The RAF then picked us up with twelve Spits. We then ditched in the water and watched our B-17 sink within three minutes after ditching. We were picked up an hour and thirty minutes later by the RAF air-sea rescue and we were told we were the first B-17 crew to ditch and get the whole crew out and safe."
—Calvin Swaffer, 303BG, Molesworth

"We used to put on a thin silk glove, then a very thin leather glove, then on top of that a wool-lined leather glove. Any time you had to adjust a knob or work on a gun you'd take the heavy, wool-lined glove off and you'd still have the other gloves to protect you. But any time you touched anything with your bare hands—we were flying in temperatures of minus fifty or thereabouts and anything you touched with bare hands—you just stuck to it.

You'd get frostbite then and lose that skin and muscle tissue."
—Lawrence Drew, 384BG, Grafton Underwood

"You have a funny feeling when you see flak. You know that it can hurt, but you look out there and it's fascinating because it comes up like a little armless dwarf. There's a round puff and there's usually two strings that come out of the bottom like legs, and this thing will appear out of nothing. You don't see any shell; you don't hear anything. You just see a puff of smoke, and shortly after that it sounds like somebody is throwing gravel all over the airplane. You're fascinated by it. You know that it can hurt you; but you watch it. It's kind of like watching a snake; it kind of hypnotizes you."
—W.W. Ford, 92BG, Podington

"About three days after we got to Podington, we were in a briefing session down on the flight line in an operations office. They briefed us on the mission that had been flown that day, and a repeat of all the training we had had up to that point. It was fairly late in the afternoon and just as we were to be dismissed the airplanes that had flown the mission that day started coming back in and the briefing officer held us in the room until they brought most of the planes in. One of them had been hit pretty badly and it pulled directly up in front of operations because this was the closest place to the hospital. The co-pilot had been hit. A piece of flak had come in through the nose and seemed to have taken most of the back of his head off. I think he lived and was eventually fairly normal. And the tail gunner had been wounded. But they pulled this plane up right in front of where we, as a new crew, were being trained, and unloaded

these guys right there in front of us. It was a gory mess. On a combat mission there was not much time when a guy got wounded to take care of him. By the time you got to him he'd pretty well made a mess of himself. That was our 'introduction to combat.'"
—W.W. Ford, 92BG, Podington

"Part of our job was in the middle of the night, in the freezing cold and we couldn't wear gloves because of putting shackles on bombs and doing reasonably delicate work. It was extremely cold; we were always out on the hardstands where the bombers were being loaded with bombs, and at the very end, just before the flight crew arrived around six in the morning, ordnance people would arrive and put the fuses in because we never did that. The bombs were completely safe when we had them, except, there was one period when they had developed a new type of bomb which went off on impact without a fuse. The bomb truck drivers—their habit in unloading the bombs—was to back up the truck as fast as they could and put on the brakes so all the bombs would roll off. In the ordinary course of events, nothing ever happened, but one day they had this new shipment of bombs and it did blow up quite a bit of the air base and the poor guy who was driving the truck."
—Sam Burchell, 448BG, Seething

"We didn't see any flash or anything on the ground. We just got hit. They got us with their first burst. We didn't even see anything. They knocked out two engines. Unbeknownst to us, they got one of the landing gear and one of the tires, and many, many holes. And this was just one burst of flak. Obviously, we had to abort. You've always got a deputy—a follow-up lead—so we turned it over

to him. We made it back across the Channel and we ended up losing a third engine. We had dropped our bombs in the Channel. We made the base and landed with one engine. We landed with one gear up and one partially down, so we ended up doing a belly-landing, on one engine. We landed adjacent to the runway, in the dirt. Kicked up a lot of dust but nobody was hurt."
—Frank Nelson, 487BG, Lavenham

"We lost numerous aircraft in assembling our formations over the base where you had to do it under instrument conditions and with a ceiling of maybe even less than fifty feet. We had many instances of aircraft colliding with each other. In an instrument assembly, you took off on a particular heading which you maintained for a certain number of minutes, climbing at a specific rate of climb, and then assuming a different heading, and being in clouds. Generally, the aircraft would take off at about forty-five-second intervals. Taking off in clouds, and the element of human error or pilot error being such that it is, it was almost an impossibility to maintain exactly the rate of climb and exactly the heading for the specific number of seconds—as a result it wasn't uncommon to find yourself in prop wash from the aircraft immediately in front of you, and yet you couldn't see him. In some instances, we would form on top of cloud cover that was nineteen thousand feet thick. And, of course, the element of risk, of everything not going just exactly as briefed and as it was designated, the possibility of aircraft colliding was great and we did have some losses. You also have to consider that we had the whole group assembling at the same time and in a ten-mile area there were five to ten other groups that were assem-

bling at the same time. We did have instances where one of our aircraft collided with an aircraft of another group during those conditions."
—Donald Maffett, 452BG, Deopham Green

"We lost the hydraulics to the nose, the turret whipped around and the doors blew off. Ernie Devries was in there holding on for dear life to keep from getting sucked out. He was a cotton-topped kid from Roberts, Montana, about eighteen years old, and he used to call me Pa. Finally, he made his plight known to me, and I used the manual crank so he could get out. After that, he felt even closer to me."
—Charles Bosshardt, 458BG, Horsham St Faith

"On your first raid you go with a veteran crew and they leave your crew at home. I was flying as co-pilot, and the bullet that came through the bullet-resistant glass took the mask off the pilot and left a streak cross his throat that bruised the skin and hit me in the left arm, just like someone took a baseball bat and swung it with all his might. They had an expression at the time, 'If it hurts, don't worry, you're gonna live; if it doesn't hurt, say a Hail Mary because you're really hurt bad.' So, I wouldn't look at it. I kept it behind me and we went over in a dive. And he was laying all over the controls because it had taken his oxygen mask off and they were getting him portable oxygen. The flight engineer was fooling around with his parachute and I asked him what he was doing while I was fighting the damned airplane. I said, 'Get him some oxygen and the hell with that chute!' And he said, 'I'm just trying it on for size, Captain.'"
—Ray Wild, 92BG, Podington

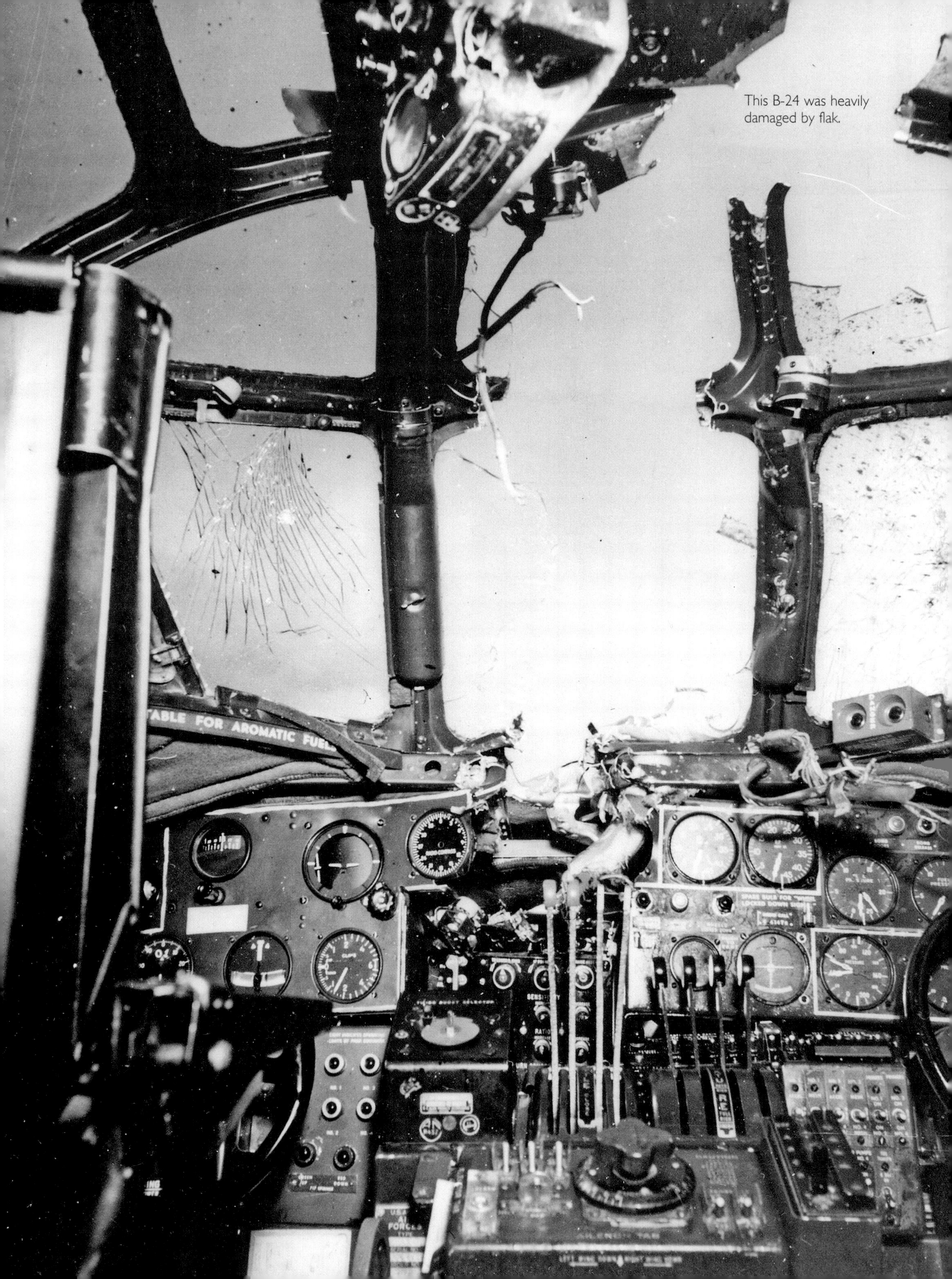
TABLE FOR AROMATIC FUEL

This B-24 was heavily damaged by flak.

"The Duke of Gloucester's home was being used as a 'flak house' or 'rest home'. That's where they used to send us when we started getting a little bit flak-happy and started pulling little things that were verging on dangerous. They'd send us down there for three or four days of rest and recuperation. It was real nice and we had a very wonderful time down there."
—Robert White, 390BG, Framlingham

"Coming off of Munich we were hit and we had only two engines left and then we got hit by fighters. But the fighters were not that good. I was

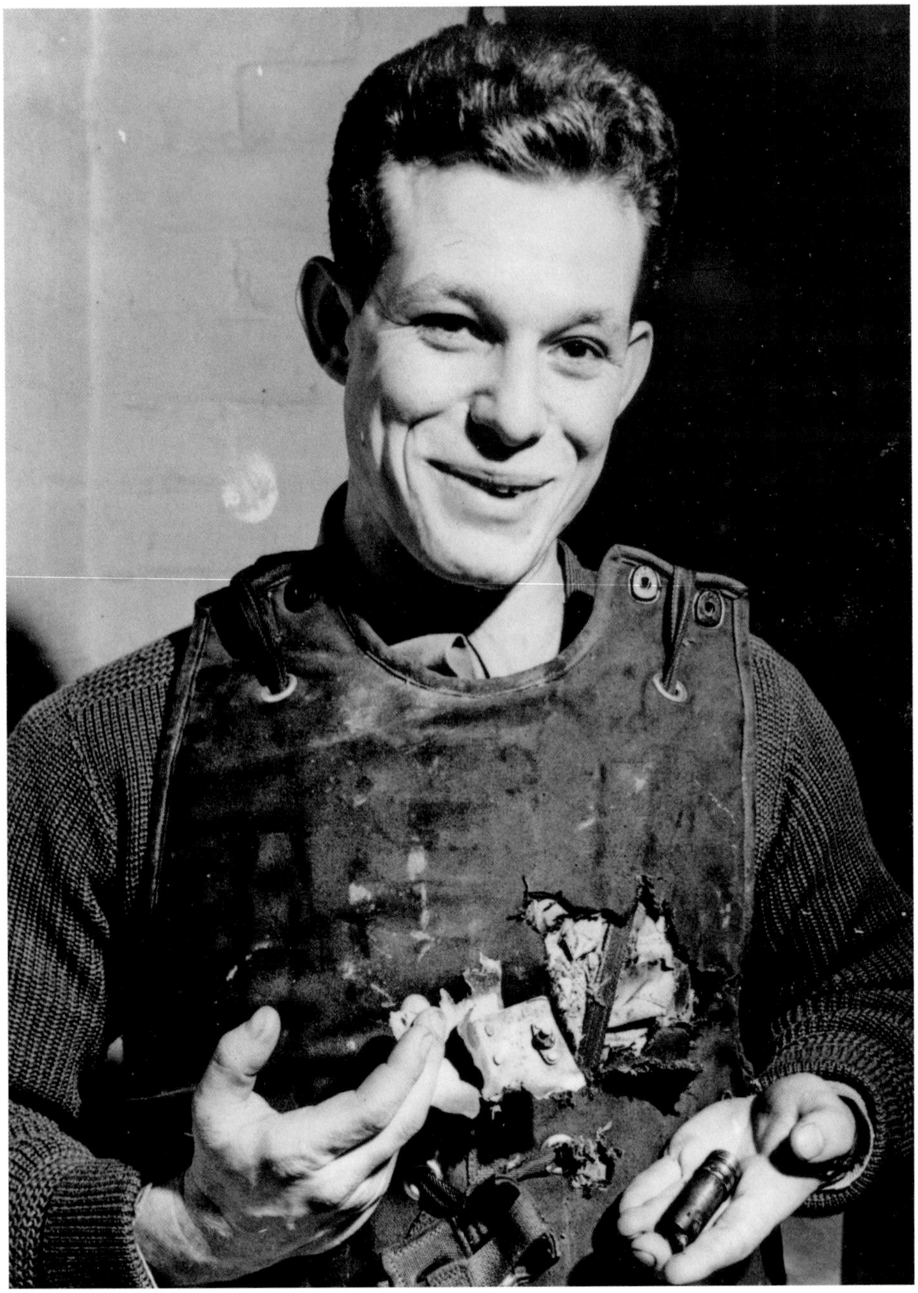

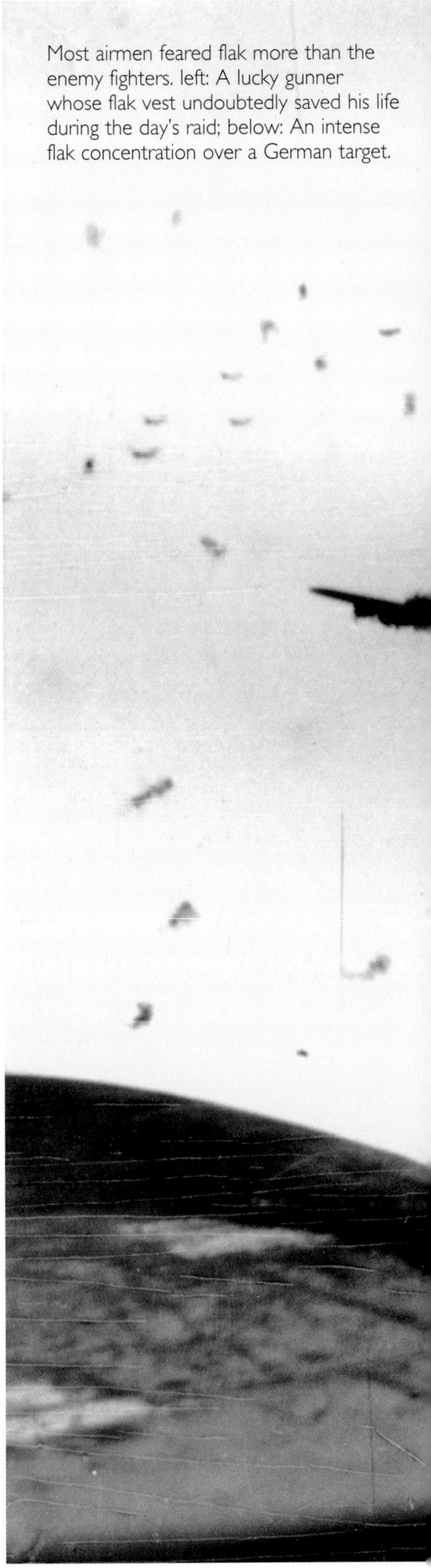

Most airmen feared flak more than the enemy fighters. left: A lucky gunner whose flak vest undoubtedly saved his life during the day's raid; below: An intense flak concentration over a German target.

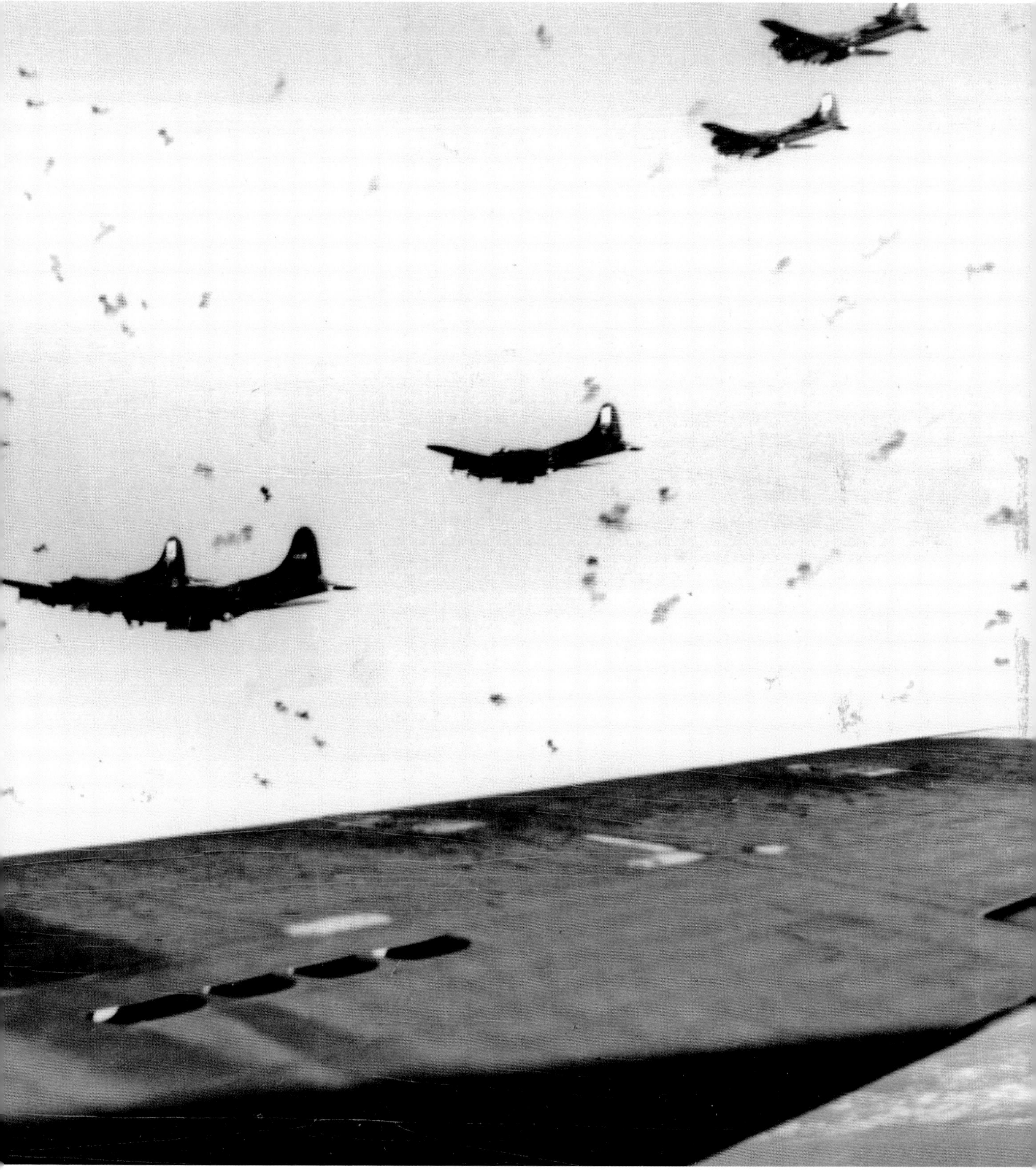

flying in the tail of the aircraft that day as an observer for the formation. The operations officer of the group was flying as command pilot and I said, 'Look, I'm five foot five. I'm a hundred and seventeen pounds. I'm not supposed to be a bomber pilot and I'll be Goddammed if I'm gonna fly in the tail of the aircraft.' So he said, 'Okay, Lieutenant Ganz, we'll court-martial you.' My colonel came around later and asked me what was wrong. I told him I was not happy with the situation and he said, 'Fly this mission. When you come down we'll write a letter to the Eighth Air Force asking for a transfer to fighters.' I flew the mission and, true to his word, I came down and the letter went all the way up to Eighth Air Force and came back down. They said, 'When this officer finishes his tour of duty in bomber pilots we'll transfer him to fighter pilots.' It was signed by General Eaker. I later had them transfer me to a Mosquito weather squadron."
—Bill Ganz, 398BG, Nuthampstead

". . . Kept telling myself, just the way I told the men, that it was going to be a lot better to fly straight instead of zigging. We'd get through the area where they could shoot at us more rapidly, and the enemy would necessarily fire fewer rounds. All in all, we'd have a better chance of getting off with whole hides—people and airplanes alike."
—Curtis E. LeMay, Commander, Third Air Division, 8USAAF

"If there was anything an outfit hated to do, it was to take a three-hundred-and-sixty-degree turn for a second run on the target, because one Fort going around alone takes time enough, but with a formation you almost had to multiply that time by the number of ships, and you had to multiply the

agony by plenty, too, because you'd thought the worst was almost over, and the fighters were still there, and the flak was still coming up, and it took forever. Oh, it was a nasty thing to have to do."
—from *The War Lover* by John Hersey

"As far as our going for a break at a flak house or rest home, we had a very democratic crew; we operated in a very democratic way, and we decided to finish our tour before we went so we could enjoy the rest and not have to think about going back and doing some more missions, so we did. The day I got there was so beautiful and it was such a marvelous place and I got sick, some flu or something, and spent practically our whole time there in the improvised infirmary, but I still remember it fondly. I've often wondered where they recruited the American girls there. They were such first-class beautiful girls. I guess they were Red Cross girls, but they weren't identified as Red Cross. I think they were daughters of commanding officers, a lot of them."
—David Parry, 390BG, Framlingham

"We were sitting up there cool and silver and almost home, when the black puffs started coming up. The Germans had wheeled in a mobile battery and they had us zeroed. I could see the dull flashes right outside the window. The ship lurched and gagged and I could hear the stuff hitting the wings. Little slivers of glass splintered around the cockpit. The right wing bucked and I looked out there and saw smoke curling out of the oil cooler. 'Number four's on fire', came over interphone, loud and scared. 'Just smoke,' Spaugh said cooly. 'Smoking bad, sir.' I looked down and we hadn't moved. We were standing still over France, and they were pouring it at us."
—from *Serenade to the Big Bird* by Bert Stiles

B-17 crewmen treating this wounded gunner aboard their aircraft. Their first aid kit contained morphine syrettes, like very small toothpaste tubes with a needle in the end for easy application and rapid pain relief.

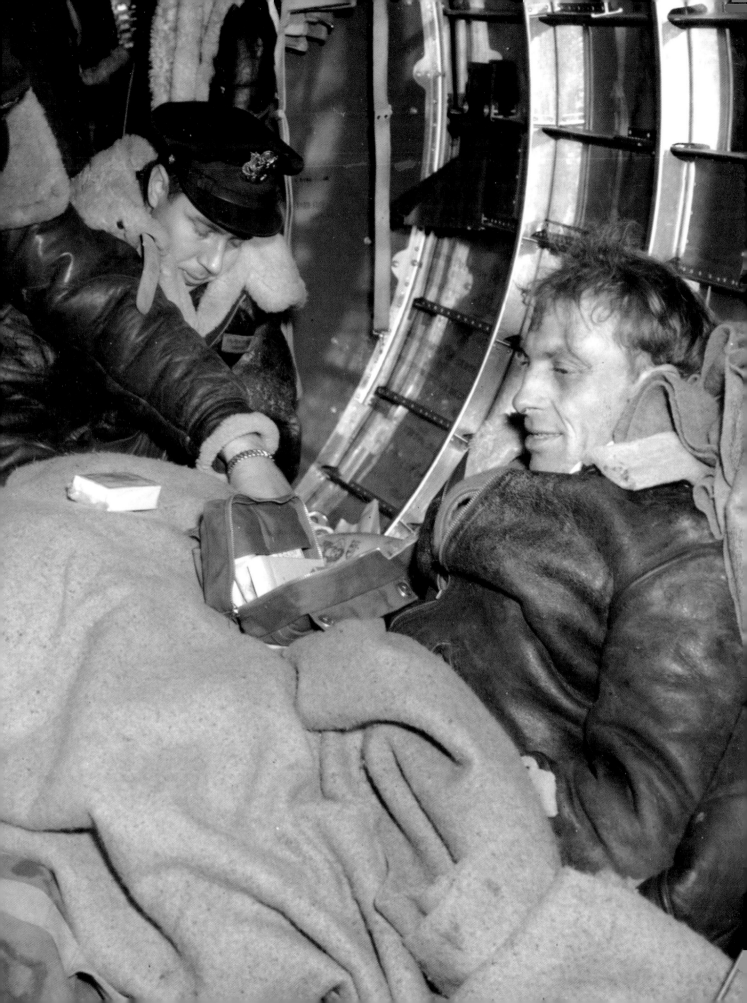

"Flak has a terrible fascination. There is a five-ball burst, and the black smoke rolls out like a plume dancing in a heavy wind. Then it is caught in the slip stream and disappears. If it is close enough to hear, it is a rather subdued 'pooh.' The pieces sound like hail on the plane. But when it first starts it is generally low and ahead. Step by step it advances up. Then you find yourself saying, 'The next one is it. Can't miss this next time. This is it. Next one.' Well, so far the next one hasn't done all it was expected to do. Perhaps there hasn't been a 'next one,' although we've had damage on the bomb doors. A fellow gets a detached air while watching those angry black puffs. Can't do a thing about them so you relax and observe, hypnotized by them. If I'm flying, I can't resist a corner of the eye glance to see how close they are."
—Keith Newhouse, 467BG, Rackheath

"I could hear him yelling, 'I've been hit. I've been hit.' He was standing there on the middle of the floor. He had his hands between his legs . . . he was jumping up and down and yelling 'I've been hit.' "
—Larry Bird, 493BG, Debach

"There were, of course, a couple guys—I felt so sorry for them at the time—who just realized 'This is it! I'm not gonna be able to do any more.' And they'd just go and say 'I'm sorry. Count me out.' It was very difficult. They weren't ostracized, but obviously they felt ostracized, and I can sure understand why the commanding officers could not be sympathetic . . . the matter of morale. It was very difficult. They were in a terrible position. Everybody was. But I don't think fear really ever entered into it."
—David Parry, 390BG, Framlingham

"It was a relatively short mission into France and as we went over the coast I was enthused about seeing Europe. It was the first time I'd ever flown over Europe and, boy, I was looking out the nose and navigating, and I saw these flashes down on the ground. And I said, 'There's a flak gun down there.' It looked like a three-battery job to me, and about that time there was a big black puff over here and a big black puff over there. That didn't bother me too much. Then there were a few more black puffs and we got a little flak and I could hear it hit the aircraft. There wasn't any major damage on that first mission. I wasn't concerned. After that mission, we came back and talked about it. Some of the crew members would honestly build up in their minds a fear of that flak. They would get 'flak happy.' Everybody hated the flak worse than the fighters. You couldn't do anything about it. You just went on in and you had to go through it. A pilot, you could shoot back at. Flak, there was just something about it. The philosophy I developed: you've got twenty-five missions to fly over here. You've got to do your job. That's your number one consideration. If you are going to be shot down, so be it. But don't worry about it. Worrying about it is the worst thing you can do. So, every mission I went on, I wasn't particularly worried about getting shot down. I saw a lot of B-17s shot down, and real close to me too. I saw them blow up, but that's war. You just have to keep your job as your number one consideration. Some people couldn't develop that philosophy. They were always worrying and as a result some of them had to be sent home or be grounded because they were nervous wrecks."
—Frank Nelson, 487BG, Lavenham

"We had two B-17s collide in mid-air and the nose was taken off of one, the roof of the nose, and the floor was still there. No one was hurt, it just sheered it right off. And the navigator and bombardier who rode in the nose were suddenly just out in the open without anything around them at all. The navigator simply reached under his table and picked up his parachute pack. You wore the harness all the time; the chest pack parachute itself was stowed away and he picked it up and snapped it on the harness of the bombardier and then just took his foot and pushed him

right over the edge of the plane. We were over Brussels at the time, so the bombardier went down over Brussels and the navigator later jumped too, he had to jump, there was no way he could hang on. They had two or three good days in Brussels and then they came back home."
—Lawrence Drew, 384BG, Grafton Underwood

"They all agreed that what happened seemed to happen very slowly. The Fortress slowly nosed up and up until she tried to climb vertically and, of course, she couldn't do that. Then she slipped in slow motion, backing like a falling leaf, and she balanced for a while and then her nose edged over and she started, nose down, for the ground. The blue sky and the white clouds made a picture of it. The crew could see the gunner trying to get out and then he did, and his parachute fluffed open. And the ball turret gunner—they could see him flopping about. The bombardier and navigator blossomed out of the nose and the waist gunners followed them. *Mary Ruth*'s crew yelling 'Get out, you pilots.' The ship was far down when the ball turret gunner cleared. They thought the skipper and the copilot were lost. They stayed with the ship too long and then the ship was so far down that they could hardly see it. It must have been almost to the ground when two little puffs of white, first one and then the second, shot out of her. And the crew yelled with relief. And then the ship hit the ground and exploded. Only the tail gunner and

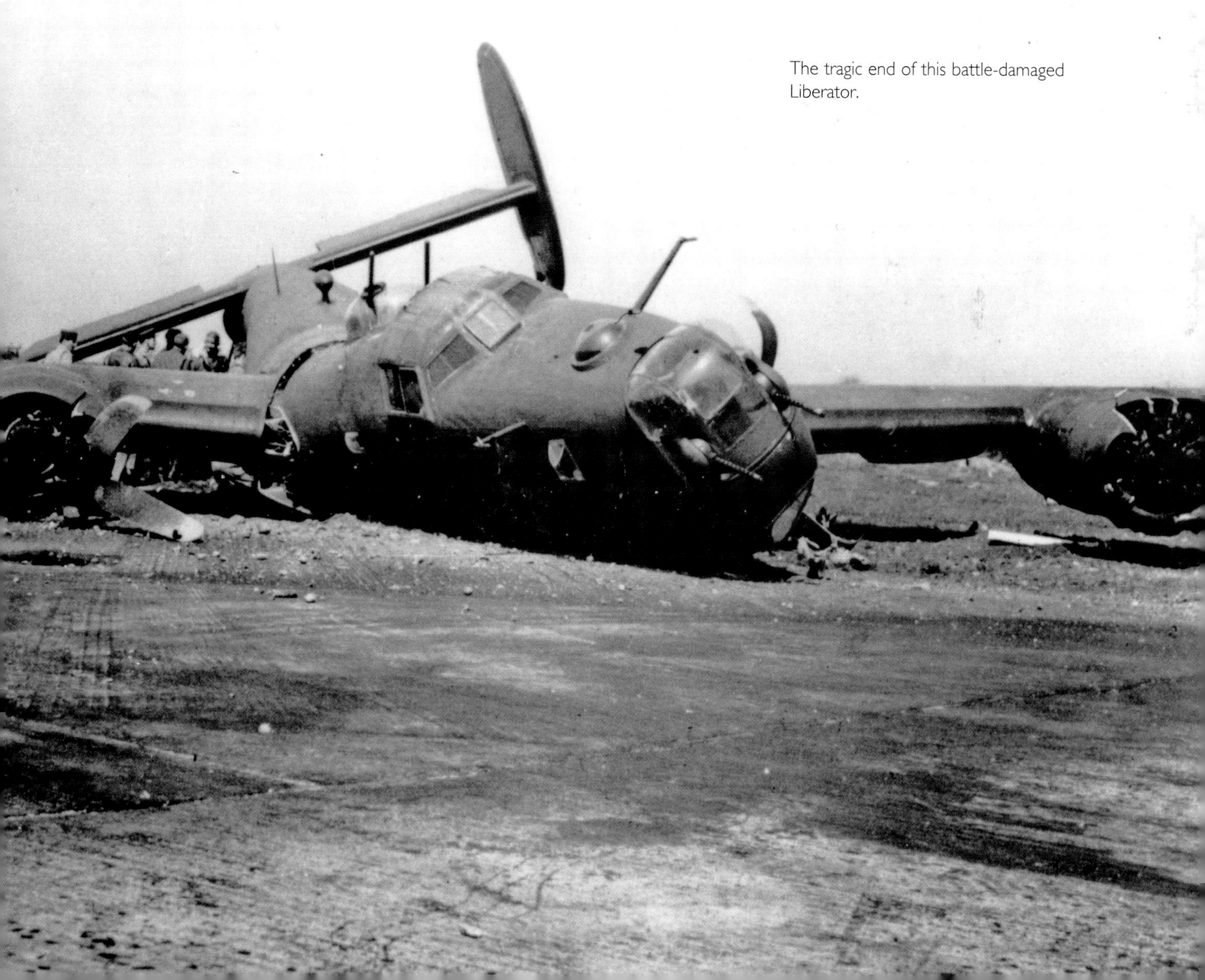

The tragic end of this battle-damaged Liberator.

the ball turret man had seen the end. They explained it over the intercom."
—from *Once There Was a War* by John Steinbeck

"When we came to a wide bay we saw the German smoke pots cloaking our target, Wilhelmshaven. Out of the smoke rose a storm of flak, rocking *Tondelayo*, sending fragments through its metal skin, biting into her delicate electric nerves."
—from *The Fall of Fortresses* by Elmer Bendiner

"We left the States in January and got snowed in in Iceland for twelve days. Went in to Valley, Wales. Got into Podington early in March. We trained for about three weeks and I got a real good twenty-first birthday present— our first mission over enemy territory. The Ruhr Valley—the target was Recklinghausen and the flak was real heavy that time and I figured that twenty-one years was all the good Lord was gonna leave me and this was it. We got back and debriefed and my whole crew said that the flak was heavy, and the debriefing officer, when we got through telling him how heavy the flak was, gave us the debriefing notes from some of the experienced crews and it seems that we were experiencing light flak. Of course it looked like it was solid to us."
—W.W Ford, 92 BG, Podington

"Maybe once every month or two we would get a weekend to go to London, which wasn't that far away, but under wartime conditions it could be a six- to eight-hour train ride. I remember once, I was with a couple of guys and we were eating in a restaurant when the sirens went off and the room emptied. Everyone went to the shelters, I guess, and we were just sitting there 'cause this was our first time in London. We didn't know what was going on. There

were a lot of bombs going off. They referred to it as the 'Little Blitz.'"
—Sam Burchell, 448BG, Seething

"The 'Twenty-Seven-Eighty-Blues' was a condition where a B-17 would hold 2,780 gallons of fuel, topped off, and that meant you were going WAY in there. We were going into Berlin and they had put us the maximum gas load and the maximum bombload that the airplane would carry. We were number six in line for takeoff. The first two airplanes lined up on the runway and got off all right. The third airplane started off all right, and Podington had a hump in the middle of the runway, so you are going uphill when you start off. And the third airplane gained enough speed to partially lift off the ground to partially lift off the ground at the top of the hill, but he stalled and came down alongside the runway. Apparently the tire was damaged and had not been changed, and the tire blew; the gear collapsed and the airplane went down the runway on its belly, and sparks and a ruptured fuel tank added to that. We were two more airplanes back in the line to take off, and didn't see any of this. We got a red flare which means 'hold'. About five minutes after the red flare, there was an explosion. It looked like the whole end of the field had blown up, and of course, we're sitting there not knowing what was going on, sitting in the nose of a B-17. We got a call from the tower and the pilots were instructed to go on around to the short runway and there was a cross-wind takeoff, and we had to leave the field with a full bombload, a full gas load, a cross-wind take-off, from a short runway. We were supposed to ride the takeoff in the radio room, but due to my size and the narrowness of the bomb racks in the B-17 bomb bay, it was always

very hard for me to get through, and when I went through I had to take off my parachute and my parachute harness. So, I decided that morning, 'The heck with it . . . if I'm gonna get it, I'll get it up front.' I wasn't gonna worry about going back there, when I could get out of the nose just about as easy as I could get out of the rear. So we sweated that out and our pilot bounced the wheels and at the last minute on that runway he pulled it back just enough to get the wheels up and popped just enough flap to it to give it that extra goose and we just got over the tops of the trees at the end of the runway. Later on I found out that that plane that bellied in, they got the crew out and got everybody away from the airplane and the full bombload had gone when we saw the explosion and when we got back that night the wreckage of what was left of that airplane was still there. It consisted of a hole in the ground, two wingtips, and the tail and that was all."
—W.W. Ford, 92BG, Podington

"On one particular lead crew we had a bombardier by the name of Wolf, and we had flak vests that we put on when we were in a flak area; they just covered the front and back of you. He'd line up that crawlway with flak vests and he'd sack out there until we got within five or ten minutes of the IP and then he'd come up and do his thing. He just hated flak, except when he was on a bomb run and then, of course, with that bombsight, the run was the only thing he was concerned with and it would take his mind off it. This one day, he was all hunkered up there in the crawlway with his flak vests and we got hit by some flak, and a couple of pieces came through the nose and one of them banged around up in the nose; it was just about spent, and

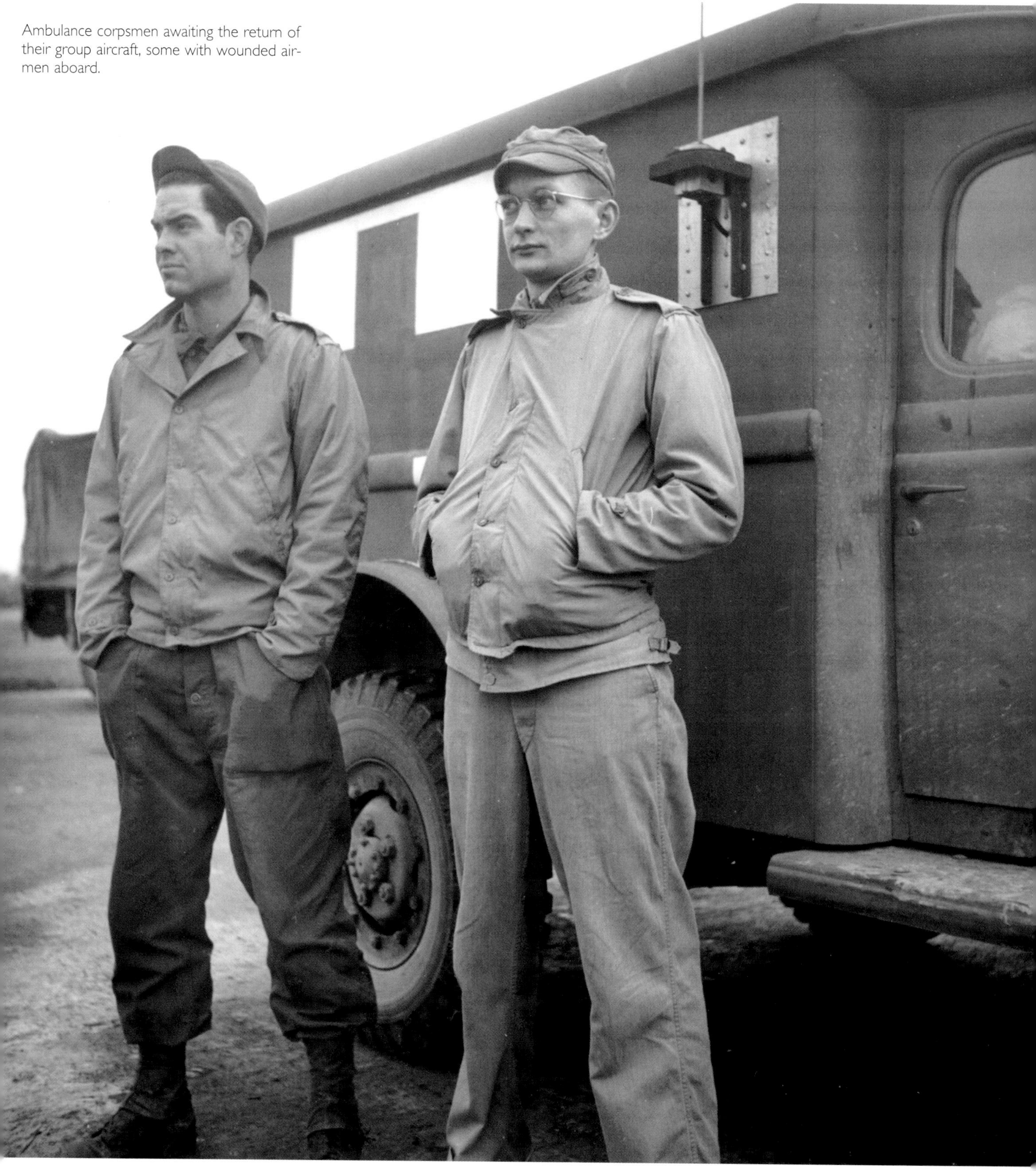

Ambulance corpsmen awaiting the return of their group aircraft, some with wounded airmen aboard.

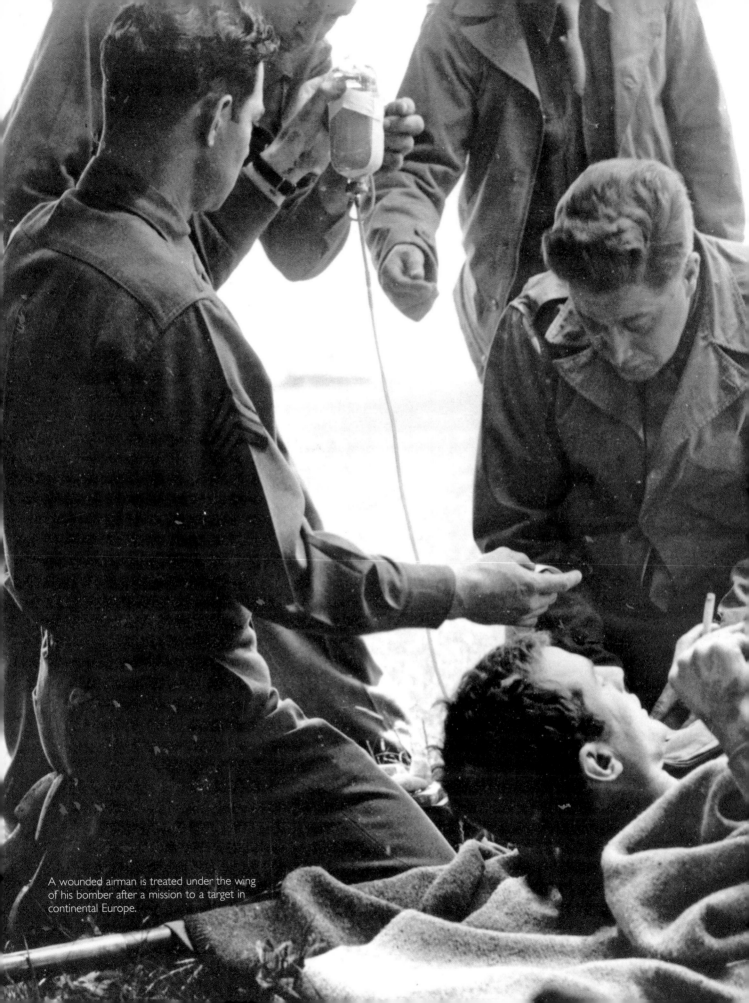

A wounded airman is treated under the wing of his bomber after a mission to a target in continental Europe.

it hit him right in the cheek of his ass. He got on the intercom and yelled, 'I'm hit in the ass.' And the pilot said, 'Frank, see what the problem is.' I got my knife, and this was when we had on the heated 'blue bunny suits,' and I cut his suit, pulled it back and looked, and all it was, it was just pinked a little bit. I suppose it gave him a pretty good bounce. But, that's all that happened to him and he thought he'd lost one whole cheek of his ass."
—Frank Nelson, 487BG, Lavenham

"On returning from missions, we had aircraft that were badly crippled when they landed and there was a possibility of fire, the landing gear collapsing, brakes being shot out, many other conditions that resulted in accidents on our base. We did lose people who actually jumped from an airplane as it was proceeding down the runway after landing and was on fire. They just wanted to get out as fast as they could and they actually just jumped out of it through fear."
—Donald Maffett, 452BG, Deopham Green

"The eighty-eights which were, I think, used for flak, were tremendously accurate, just fabulous. They used two types. One was predetermined; the other was barrage. In barrage, there'd be a flock of guns and they'd shoot at one spot in the sky and keep shooting at it. In predetermined they were aiming at planes. The most frightening was barrage where they were shooting at a spot in the sky. You had to go through that spot when they weren't shooting. Emden, Kiel, Wilhelmshaven, Munich, Berlin. . . I think they did both at all five of those targets. But Schweinfurt was murder. I'm sure they shot barrage there because they had so damned many guns. The German fighters stayed pretty much out of the flak, but on Schweinfurt they did come through the flak. That indeterminate flak. There was nothing you could do about it. This was something that was gonna happen. It was impersonal as hell."
—Ray Wild, 92BG, Podington

"'Doesn't this world ever make you want to throw up, Doc?'
'Constantly. Once upon a time,' he said, 'there was crow with the appetite of a condor, or perhaps a goat. It didn't care how things tasted, but only how they looked. It liked bright objects, silver and shining blue things, and one day it ate a lady's ring, a nickel a child had lost by the roadside, a priest's collar button, a sequin, a violinist's mute, a juke-box slug, and a lot of other junk like that. In the afternoon the crow began to feel nauseated, and he said to himself, 'Must be something I ate.' His crop got more and more uncomfortable, and finally he oopsed everything. The morsels he had thrown up looked so pretty that he wanted to eat them all over again, but believing that one of them had made him sick he decided not to eat any of them at all, and he flew away with a sense of forfeited pleasure. Do you know what the moral of this fable is?'
'Don't eat breakfast before going on a mission?' I said.
'Wrong,' Doc said. 'The moral is: People don't know what's bad for them until after the fun's gone out of it.'
'Doc,' I said, 'You're the God-damnedest man I ever met.'
—from *The War Lover* by John Hersey

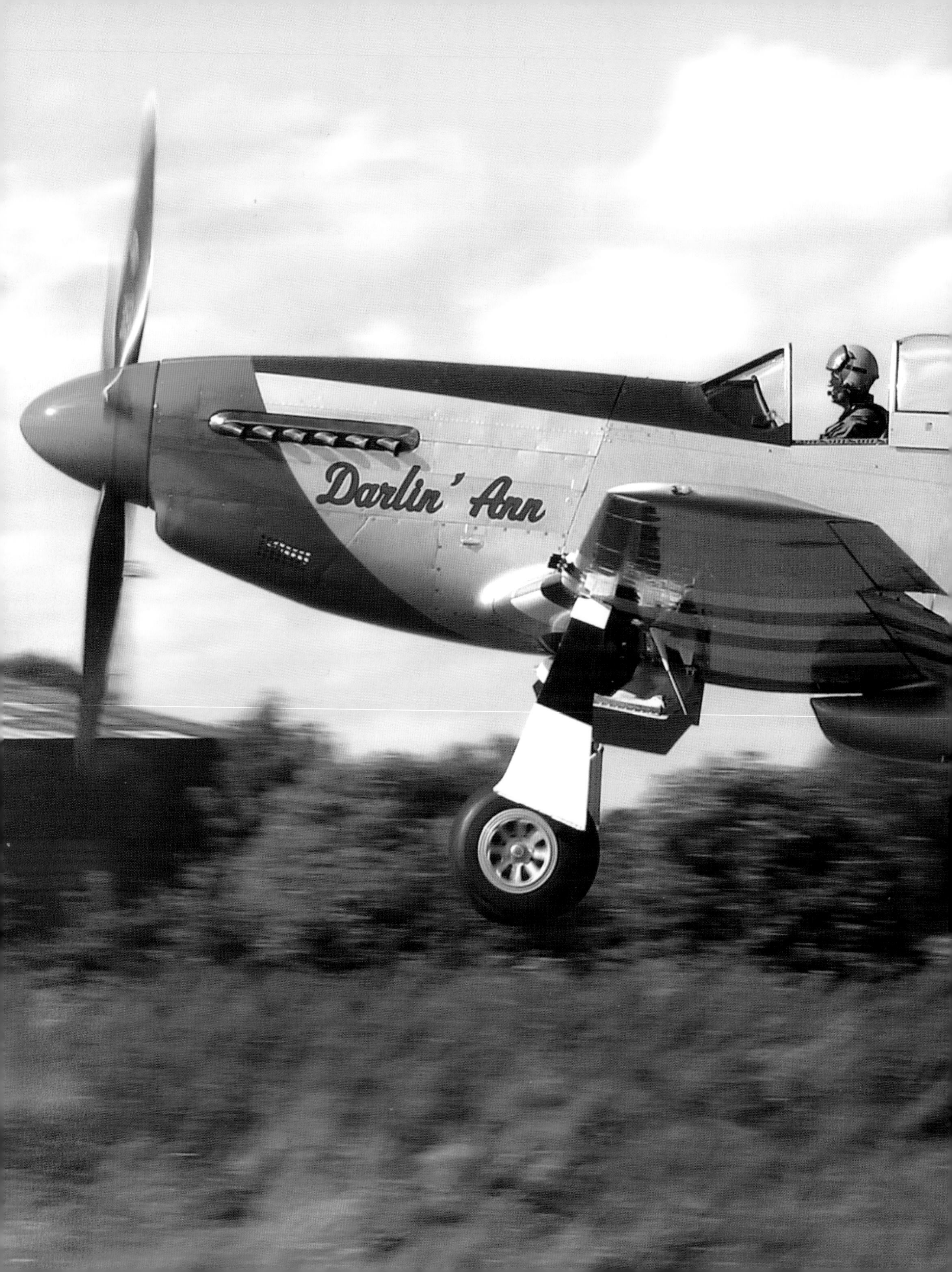
Darlin' Ann

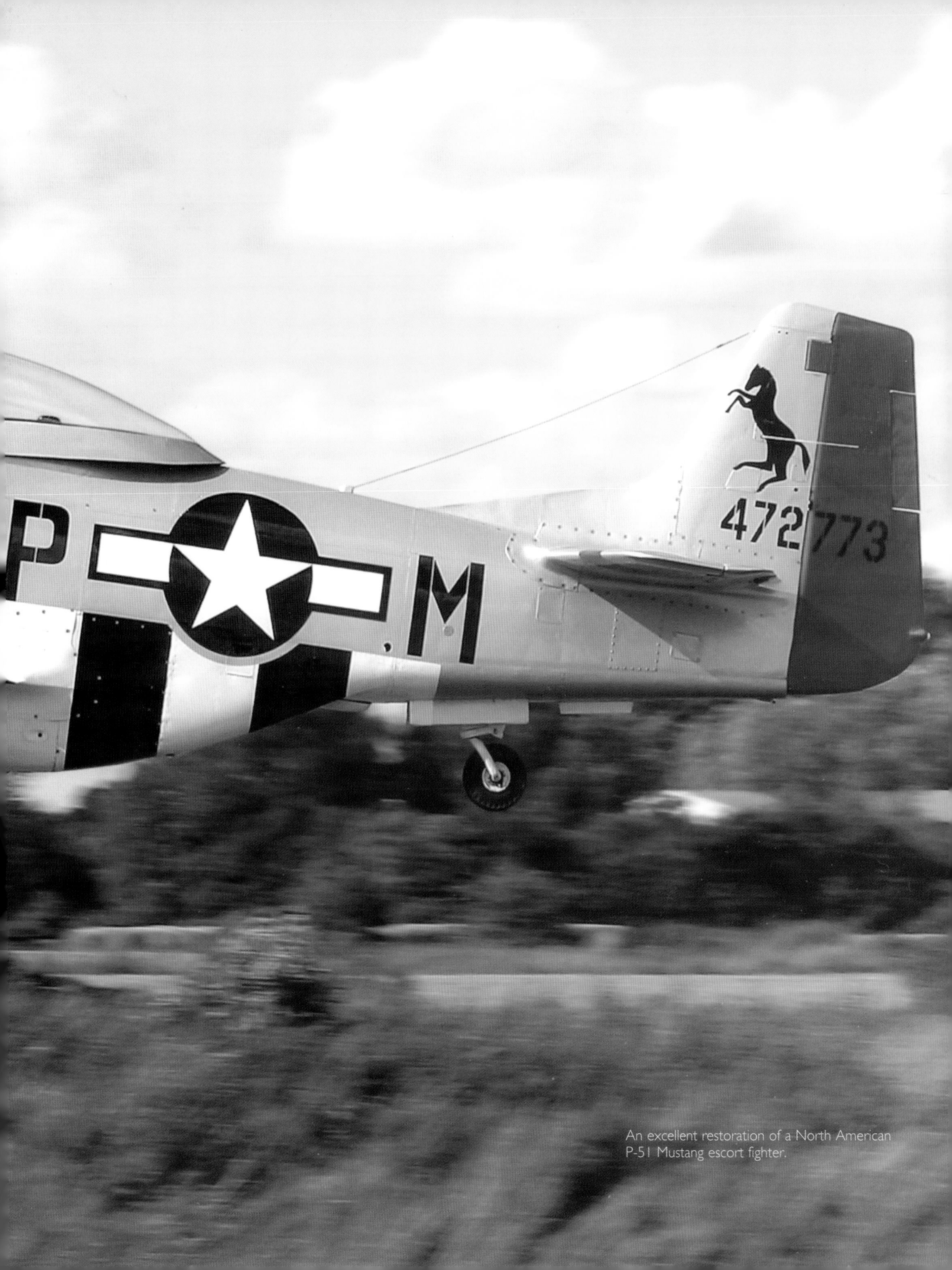
P
M
472773
An excellent restoration of a North American P-51 Mustang escort fighter.

FLIERS

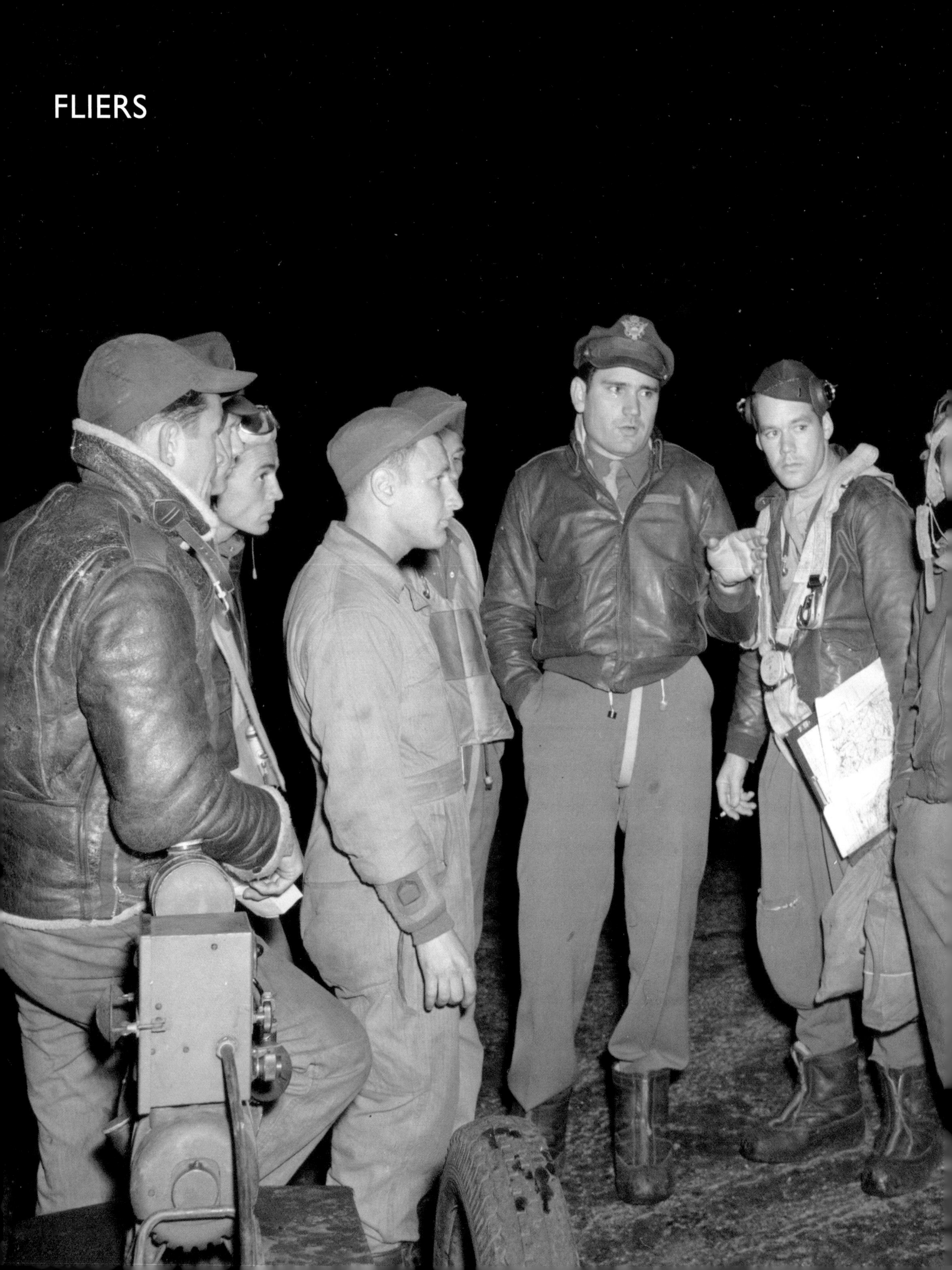

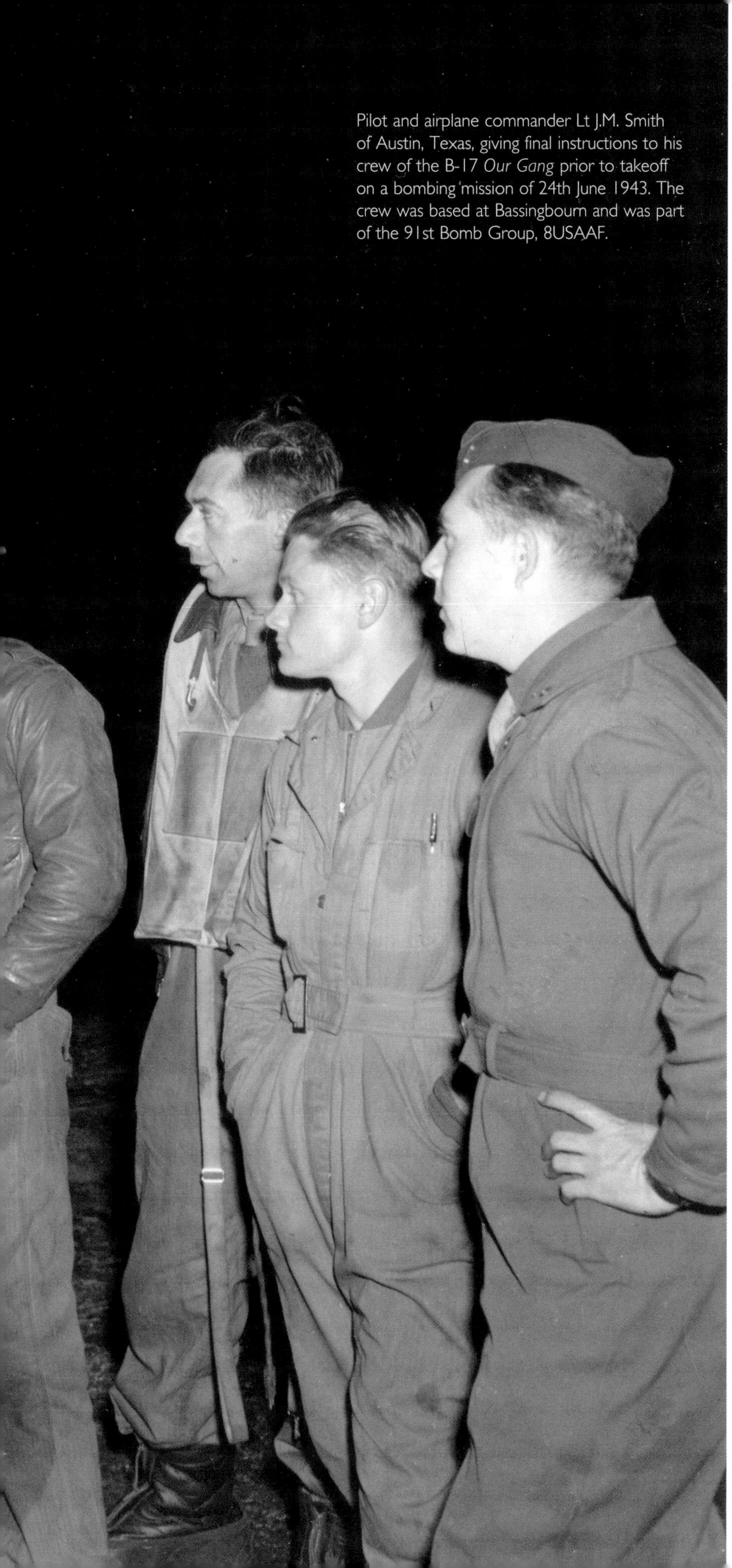

Pilot and airplane commander Lt J.M. Smith of Austin, Texas, giving final instructions to his crew of the B-17 *Our Gang* prior to takeoff on a bombing mission of 24th June 1943. The crew was based at Bassingbourn and was part of the 91st Bomb Group, 8USAAF.

IN THE SECOND WORLD WAR, the most effective fighting units were usually small: infantry platoons, submarine crews, commandos, and bomber crews. It is almost certainly true that, of those examples, the bomber crews did more damage to the enemy, with a greater effect on the outcome of the war, than any other. Most of those airmen were volunteers; all of those in the Royal Air Force were. All of the aircrew were highly trained, intelligent, fit, and adventurous; most were enthusiastic and high achievers. Every man knew he was essential to his team, whether that team was the ten-man crew of a Flying Fortress or Liberator or the seven-man crew of a Lancaster or Halifax, and each man knew that a mistake, sometimes even a minor one, could mean the death of all of them. Their unique interdependence was the glue that held them together.

When such a man was trained in the U.S. Army Air Forces to become a pilot, a navigator, or a bombardier, his training as an officer proceeded in sync with his training as a flier: his failure in either aspect would prevent him graduating. Those crew members—and the co-pilot in an Eighth Air Force bomber—were to be commissioned officers; the gunners of the crew were all enlisted men, sergeants. It was different in the Royal Air Force, where many crews were entirely composed of non-commissioned officers, while some crews were made up of mixed ranks, but the pilot, regardless of his rank, was always the captain and commander of the aircraft. Laurence Pilgrim, RAF: "It was really a matter of luck, whether you got a good crew or not to start with. Once they were formed, it was up to the captain to mold them into the sort of crew he wanted. If the crew didn't turn out well, it was the captain's fault. It was essential to go out together quite often, to have a drink together and be as friendly as possible. Of course, the pilot had to have the crew's respect—not as NCOs to officer, but as crew to captain—so that if he said something in the air, they did it, immediately, without question."

303rd Bomb Group pilot Dave Shelhamer: "I said that if anybody on my crew fouled up, and it was some little thing, admonition and that would be it. But anything serious, and that person would be off the crew. Now, whether they believed I would do that, I don't know. But when Keaton really pulled a lulu and I summarily removed him from the crew, it was a kind of shock to them. After that I had a crew that worked like a well-oiled machine. They were just beautiful."

A typical RAF all-NCO crew was that of Alan Forman, who flew thirteen operations with No. 103 Squadron in the final stages of the war. Forman was the son of a Lincolnshire farmhand, and he had never expected to be a bomber captain: "I put in for air gunner, but there was an old First World War flier, an air commodore, on the selection board, and he told me I ought to try for pilot. I told him I left school at fourteen and my maths was pretty poor, but he said not to worry about that. I was very lucky. I passed the course in Canada, while a lot of people failed. They ended up as navigators or bomb-aimers. I went through operational training and got my own crew: a Scotsman, two Yorkshiremen, three Australians, and me. Apart from the gunners, they'd all been to better schools than I had, yet there I was, twenty-one years old, commanding a crew in which the navigator was an old Etonian and the rear gunner had already done a tour of ops and had a DFM. The war was a great leveler."

From the beginning of 1943, the RAF replaced the co-pilot in its four-engined bombers with a new flight engineer, who managed the fuel system, assisted the pilot with the engine handling, and generally acted as Mister Fix-it in the air. In the USAAF, however, the co-pilot was always an integral member of the crew, with the added task, in lead planes, of checking the formation from the tail turret while the lead pilot occupied his right-hand cabin seat.

Bill Ganz, who flew thirty-two missions with the 398th Bomb Group, was fully qualified to fly the B-17, but, in his time at Nuthampstead, he seldom got the chance to make a takeoff or a landing: "My pilot always wanted the takeoff. I read out the checklist and made sure he went through the standard operating procedures. It was the same with the landing. Once we got off, either he or I would fly to altitude while the other watched the instruments and after we formed up, we would split the formation time. That was the most tiring thing of all—flying formation."

The standard British bomber crew included two air gunners—who (unlike their USAAF counterparts) received special training in deflection shooting air-to-air. Wireless operators were also trained in gunnery, and could replace an injured man in either turret if required. The front gun turret was seldom used on normal operations—it was manned by the bomb-aimer on those rare occasions—and many pilots thought that it served only to supplement the aircraft's "built-in head wind."

Eighth Air Force gunners, of whom there might be six or seven in a crew, often had a dual role, doubling as engineer, armorer, radio operator, or "toggleer"—a designation which entered the vocabulary when the

German non-commissioned officer fighter pilots of the Second Staffel, JG52, on the Channel coast of France in 1940.

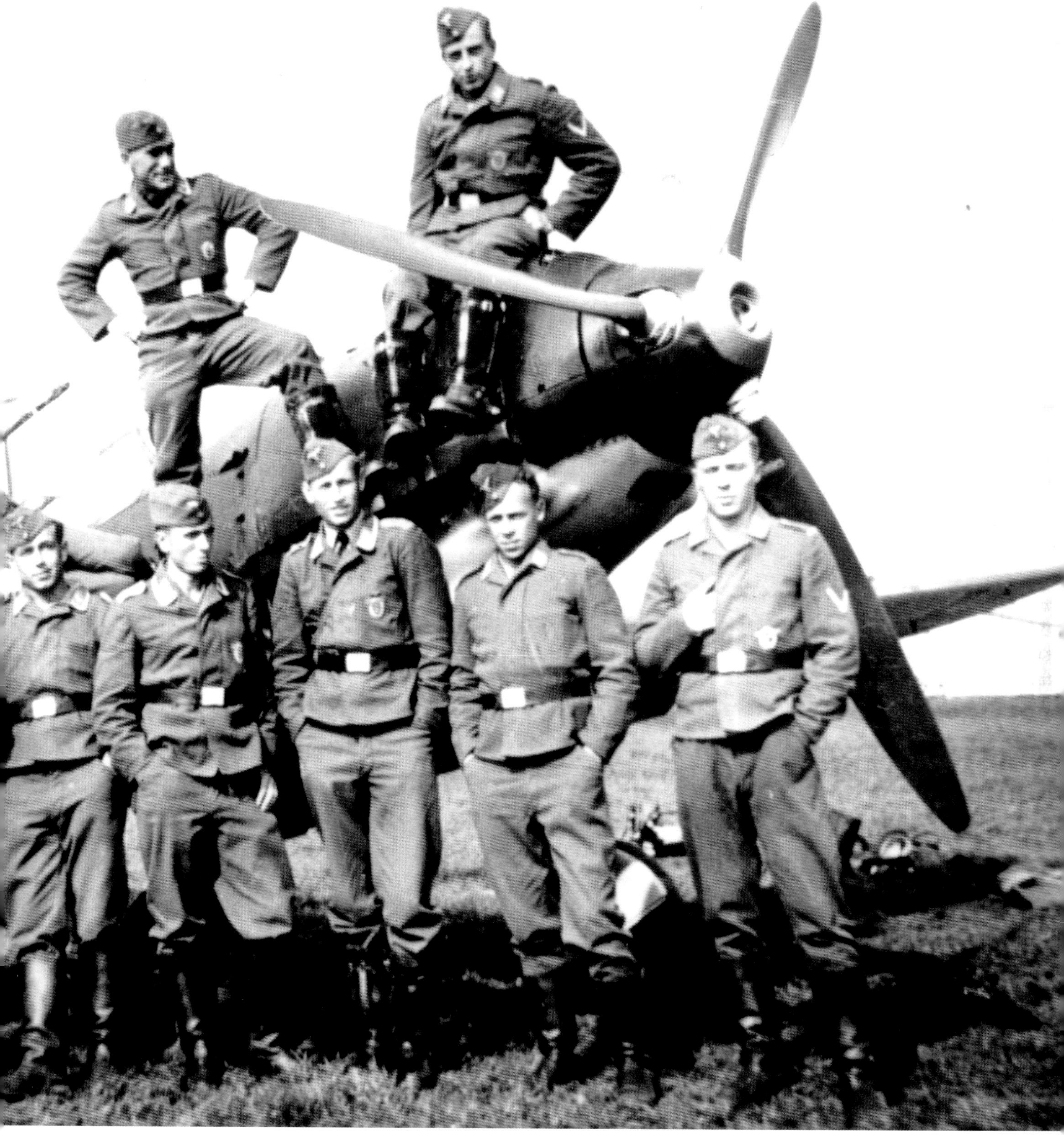

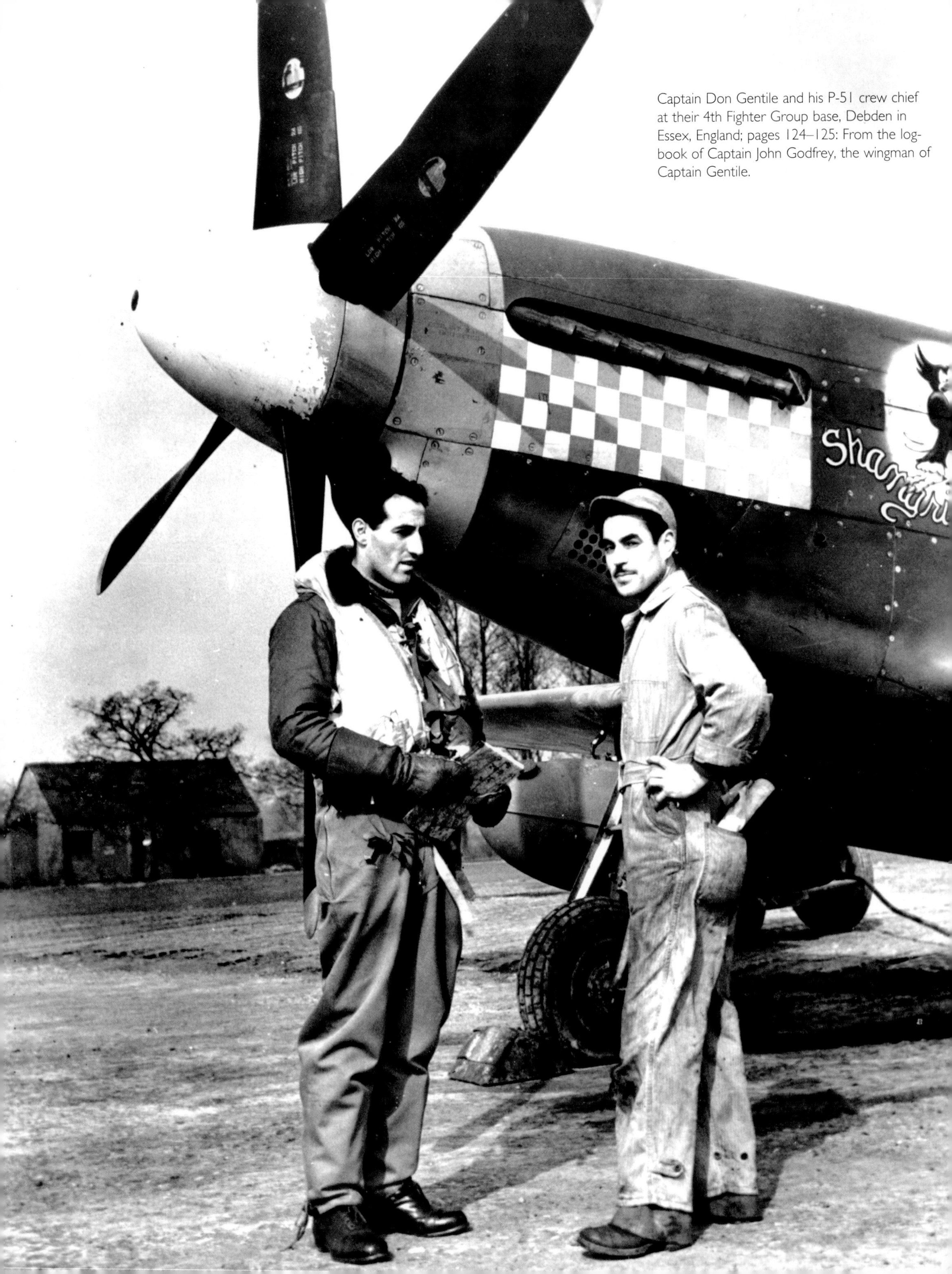

Captain Don Gentile and his P-51 crew chief at their 4th Fighter Group base, Debden in Essex, England; pages 124–125: From the log-book of Captain John Godfrey, the wingman of Captain Gentile.

Eighth developed the technique of formation bombing to a point where trained bombardiers were only needed in the lead and deputy lead crews. In an emergency, any man except the pilot might be required to fire a gun.

The rapidity with which a newly graduated USAAF pilot reached a bomber squadron contrasted sharply with the progress of his British counterpart. The American could occupy the left seat of a B-17 or B-24 within weeks of being awarded his pair of silver wings; the RAF man, on the other hand, after graduation underwent further courses on twin-engined aircraft before he ever got to fly a Lancaster or Halifax. There was certainly a need for overseas-trained pilots to become adjusted to the weather, the blackout, and the enemy's proximity, but 180 flying hours spread across six months seemed more than enough, certainly for those who had been trained in America. Perhaps the British Air Staff had not fully realized how much more air experience the USAAF Arnold Scheme provided than the Empire schools.

"Honest John" Searby was the second-tour commander of an elite RAF pathfinder squadron and a master bomber. He took the view that Bomber Command stood or fell by the quality of its navigators. "A competent, confident navigator," he wrote, "was a powerful factor for morale. Courage, determination, and the will to press on in the face of flak and fighters was one thing, but only the skill of the navigator could ensure that the effort was taken to the vital spot. So much depended on him, yet we all took him for granted. He was expected to produce the answers at the drop of a hat."

At the age of twenty-one, navigator W.W. Ford of the 92nd Bomb Group was the fourth oldest member of his crew: "The engineer was twenty-six, the co-pilot twenty-five, and the armorer-gunner twenty-three. The aircraft commander was the youngest. He was all of nineteen—and the rest were between nineteen and twenty. We had all denominations. The pilot was a staunch bluestocking Presbyterian, we had a Jewish boy from Brooklyn, one gunner was a Mormon, the engineer was a Southern Baptist, I think the tail gunner was a Methodist, the radio operator and one of the waist gunners were Catholics, the other waist gunner was a Protestant, and I was in the Episcopal church. As for the co-pilot, I'm sure he was at least an agnostic."

In May 1944, Keith Newhouse, by then a deputy lead pilot: "We flew a practice mission and took along the navigator who had just been assigned to us. He was not operational yet, and was as green as England's rolling hills. Had him lost any number of times. It was only his second trip in a B-24, and his first time at altitude. He had lots to learn."

Navigator Sidney Rapoport arrived in England in the late summer of 1944, and was at once required to undertake a radar course. "The first thing at Alconbury was indoctrination—you had to forget whatever you learned about navigation in the States. We started from scratch and it was a crash program." Discovering a talent for operating the Mickey system, Rapoport passed the course with flying colors and was assigned to the 94th Bomb Group at Bury St Edmunds (Rougham) where he joined a pathfinder crew of the 333rd Squadron. At first he flew practice missions every day: "We went up to 25,000 feet and made a lot of bomb runs—the library in Cambridge, Oxford University, and many other points. British radar was checking us and giving us the score. Then we would fly a mission and get a seventy-two-hour pass. That was a marvelous privilege."

Fred Allen's Halifax crew was formed during training in the customary RAF do-it-yourself way: "There were probably three hundred in the room, and you don't know who's who. You just started walking about and if you liked the look of someone: 'Have you got a gunner?' The pilot was six foot three and I thought, he can handle anything. We hit it off and that was that. Then me and another gunner talked and I said, 'I'll go in the tail if you like.' He said, 'That suits me, I'll go in the mid-upper.' We picked the engineer up at a heavy conversion unit. At thirty-eight, he was an old man, nearly twice our age. But he knew engines, plus he played piano and he had an accordion. He was always useful and a good man to have in the crew."

In common with every crew that cared about survival, Allen's crewmates in *Friday The Thirteenth* were sparing in their use of the intercom: "We wouldn't say a word that wasn't absolutely necessary. We had a spare bod on board once, and he kept thinking his intercom was busted, because he couldn't hear anything. He said afterward he'd never flown with a crew that were so quiet. We thought if we kept the intercom clear, it would be there when we needed it. You didn't want to have to say, 'Oy, get off the intercom, this is important.' Too late then. Fractions of seconds counted. Maybe that's why we did thirty-eight ops and came back."

Paul Sink of the 493rd Bomb Group, 8USAAF, confirmed Fred Allen's view: "Usually in the airplane it was very quiet. The only time we had much conversation was while we were under attack, calling out positions, type of aircraft, losses, or whatever. For the rest of the time

Aircraft		Pilot, or 1st Pilot	2nd Pilot, Pupil or Passenger	Duty (Including Results and Remarks)
Type	No.			
—	—	—	—	— Totals Brought Forward
-51	UF-Z	Self	卍 卍 卍 卍	F.O. #483 Escort Green #3
51	UF-T	Self	卍 卍	F.O. #487 Escort Blue #1 Hit by 7.9 in Head
51	UF-F	Self		F.O. # Escort Red #3

Grand Total [Cols. (1) to (10)]

.... Hrs. .... Mins.

Totals Carried Forward

SINGLE-ENGINE AIRCRAFT				MULTI-ENGINE AIRCRAFT						PASS-ENGER	INSTR/CLOUD FLYING [Incl. cols. (1) to (10)]	
DAY		NIGHT		DAY			NIGHT					
DUAL	PILOT	DUAL	PILOT	DUAL	1ST PILOT	2ND PILOT	DUAL	1ST PILOT	2ND PILOT		DUAL	PILO
(1)	(2)	(3)	(4)	(5)	(6)	(7)	(8)	(9)	(10)	(11)	(12)	(13)

5:10 Escort Libs to Brunswick - Green section
Free Lancing - Glass & I split up & got 8 trains
down & A/D Strafing. Shot down a Me109 w
two guns - He blew up at 2,000 FT. (Beautiful Sig
claim 8 Locomotives damaged
3 Ju52's Destroyed
3 Ju52's Damaged
1 Me109 Destroyed

6:00 Escort Forts to Berlin - Thay Freelance deci
Went down to 10,000 ft. Shot down a Me410 - Pilots c
did not open - Strafed A/D near Berlin. Was hit by 7.9
Engine also - Primed it all the way back - Prettyn
bailed out - Jettisoned canaby - Thanks to Fred &
I'm back!! Landed at Beccles shot up.
Claim - 1 Me410 Destroy
1 Me109 Destroyed
1 Ju88 Damaged

5:40 Escort Beaufighters on strike to Norc
Watched them beat up Convoy. Not one
Jerry seen - Lum hit by 20MM. Made it bac
Lost 3 boys

| (1) | (2) | (3) | (4) | (5) | (6) | (7) | (8) | (9) | (10) | (11) | (12) | |

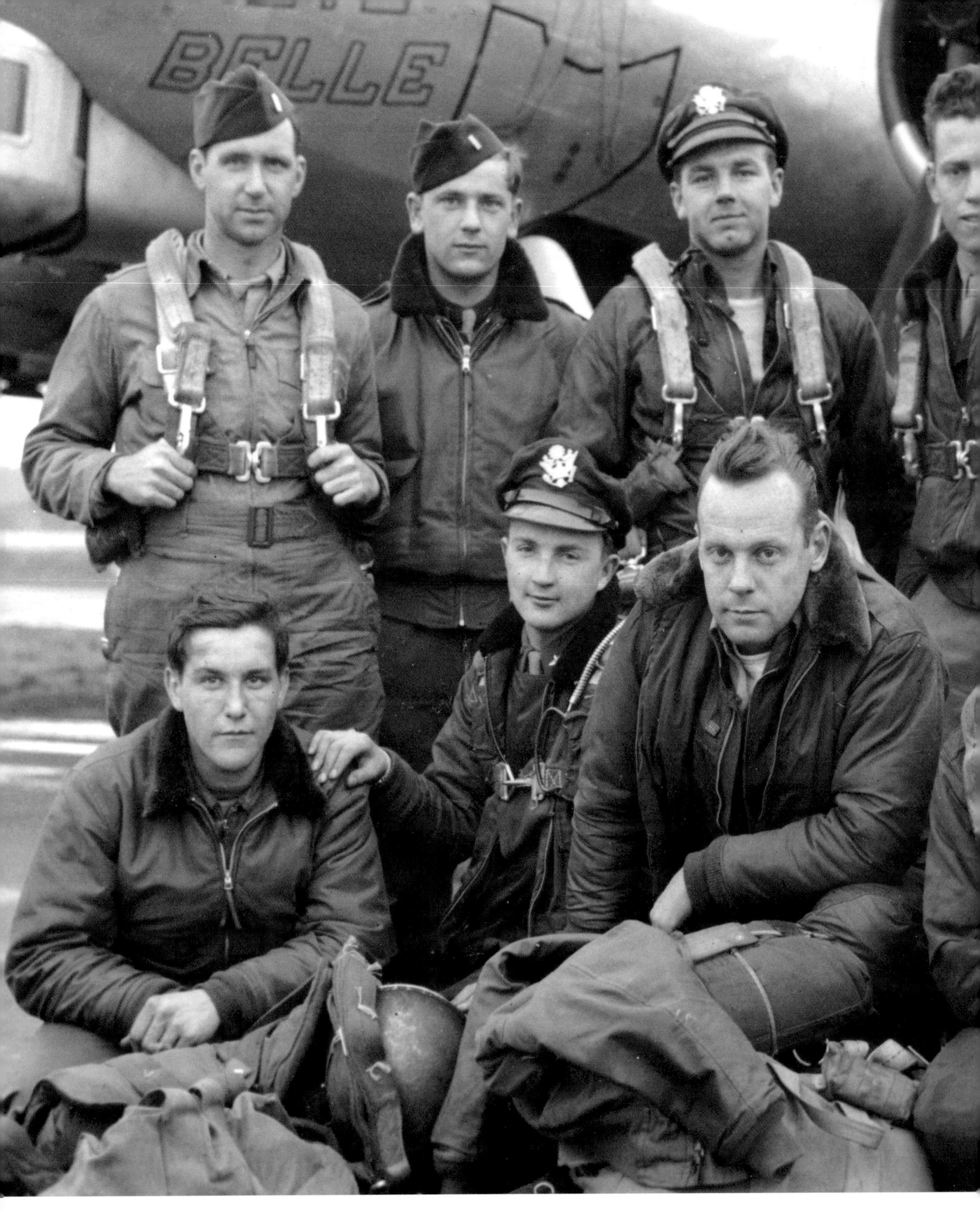
BELLE

The crew of the B-17G *Buckeye Belle* at the 384th Bomb Group base, Grafton Underwood.

the intercom was kept very clear."

With two engines giving trouble, Allen's crew once landed at a USAAF base, and he chatted with the Fortress gunners. "We wouldn't go up at night," they told him, "Don't know how you can do it." Allen examined the B-17's ball turret with interest. "The gunner was a bit tight in there," he commented. "He needed somebody to help him out. We saw them come back from a trip the next day and one of those ball turrets was shot away underneath. There was half a body in it. And they couldn't understand us going at night."

Although in Air Force circles, the ball turret was referred to as "the morgue," but statistics show that the occupant's chances of survival were slightly better than the other gunners'. For his part, Ken Stone of the 381st was content with the position: "I could turn through 360 degrees; I could go down, turn around, and go back up, so I had vision all the way around the plane. I could see everything."

Comparing it, however, with the isolation of the ball and tail turrets, and with the numbing chill of the waist positions, Larry Bird favored the toggleer's location: "There was a hot air vent in the nose, and I didn't need to wear an electric suit or any of that stuff. Sitting in the nose there, you had the most beautiful views in the world—the Swiss Alps, Lake Constance—I was in a very good spot. I didn't have to worry about the bombsight. My job was to handle that little button and keep my eye on the lead plane. As soon as I saw his bomb doors open, I'd open mine. Everybody opens in unision. So when the bombs go, they go together, and they make a pattern of explosions on the ground, same shape as the formation."

It wasn't every man who had the mental stamina to go on, mission after mission, knowing that the odds against survival were increasing all the time. Sometimes resolution failed, to no one's surprise. What was surprising was that so relatively few combat fliers ever quit and said, "The hell with this. I'm not doing it anymore." One RAF pilot who flew a tour of operations at a time when Bomber Command's losses were at their worst, said: "I knew of only three among the thousand men who must have come and gone in those eight months. None of us blamed them or derided them—in fact, I remember someone saying 'I wish I had the guts to go LMF,' and not entirely as a joke—but those three chaps were treated pretty harshly. They were sent away to some corrective establishment, they lost their rank and privleges, and their documents were labeled 'lack of moral fibre.' I expect the stigma stayed with them for life."

In the treatment of its weaker members, the RAF's posture was different from the USAAF's, which was less censorious and a great deal more humane. In the Eighth Air Force, "combat fatigue" was a condition to be recognized and treated with compassion. Larry Bird of the 493rd Bomb Group knew one crewman at Debach who decided, halfway through his second tour, that the time had come to stop: "His buddy was killed, and he just wouldn't fly anymore. You never heard anybody say a word against him. Everybody was as friendly as they ever were." Tail gunner Paul Sink corroborated this: "I never heard of anyone who was mistreated or ostracized when he got to the point where he wouldn't fly anymore. They came into the mess hall like everyone else did. I had some good friends who got to that point, and I had a lot of sympathy with them because I knew what it was like."

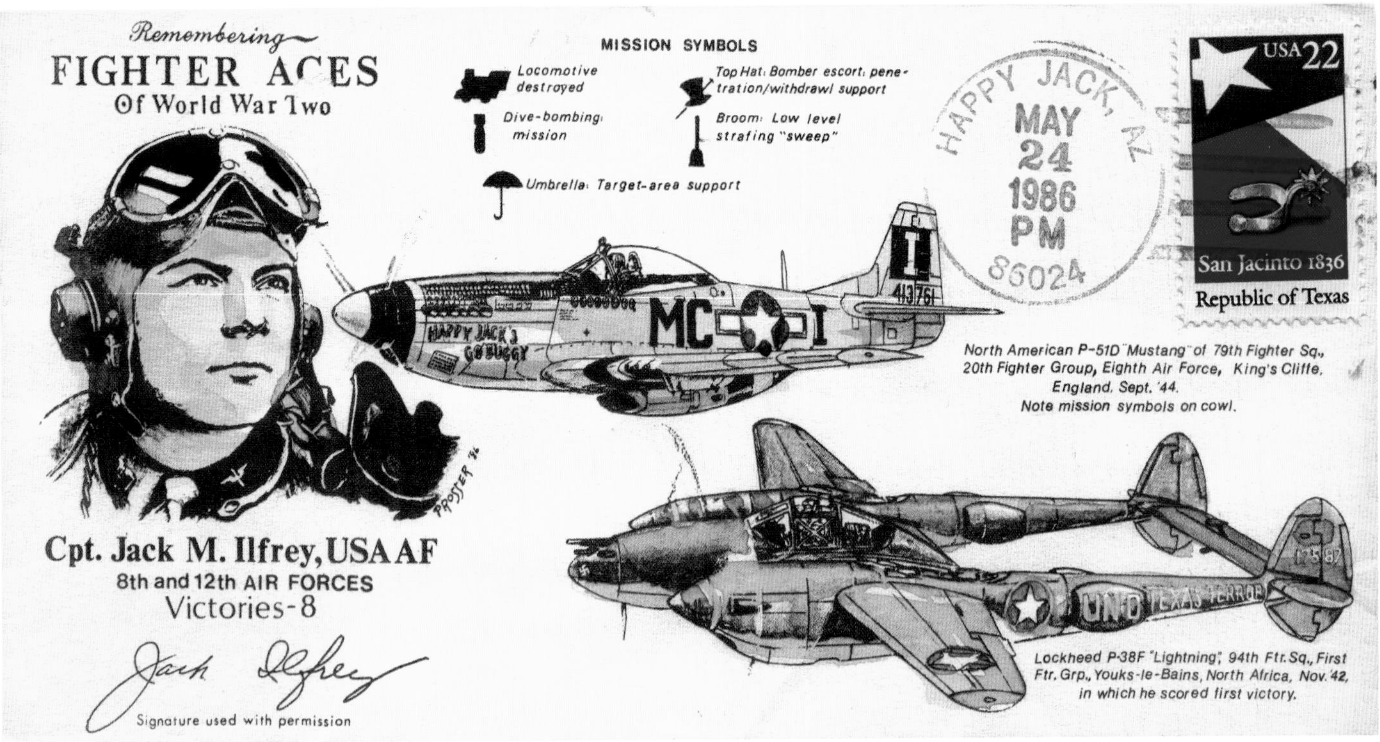
Remembering
FIGHTER ACES
Of World War Two
MISSION SYMBOLS
Locomotive destroyed
Dive-bombing mission
Umbrella: Target-area support
Top Hat: Bomber escort: penetration/withdrawl support
Broom: Low level strafing "sweep"
HAPPY JACK, AZ
MAY
24
1986
PM
86024
USA 22
San Jacinto 1836
Republic of Texas
HAPPY JACK'S GO BUGGY
MC
I
413761
North American P-51D "Mustang" of 79th Fighter Sq., 20th Fighter Group, Eighth Air Force, King's Cliffe, England, Sept. '44.
Note mission symbols on cowl.
UN O
TEXAS TERROR
Lockheed P-38F "Lightning", 94th Ftr.Sq., First Ftr. Grp., Youks-le-Bains, North Africa, Nov. '42, in which he scored first victory.
Cpt. Jack M. Ilfrey, USAAF
8th and 12th AIR FORCES
Victories-8
Jack Ilfrey
Signature used with permission

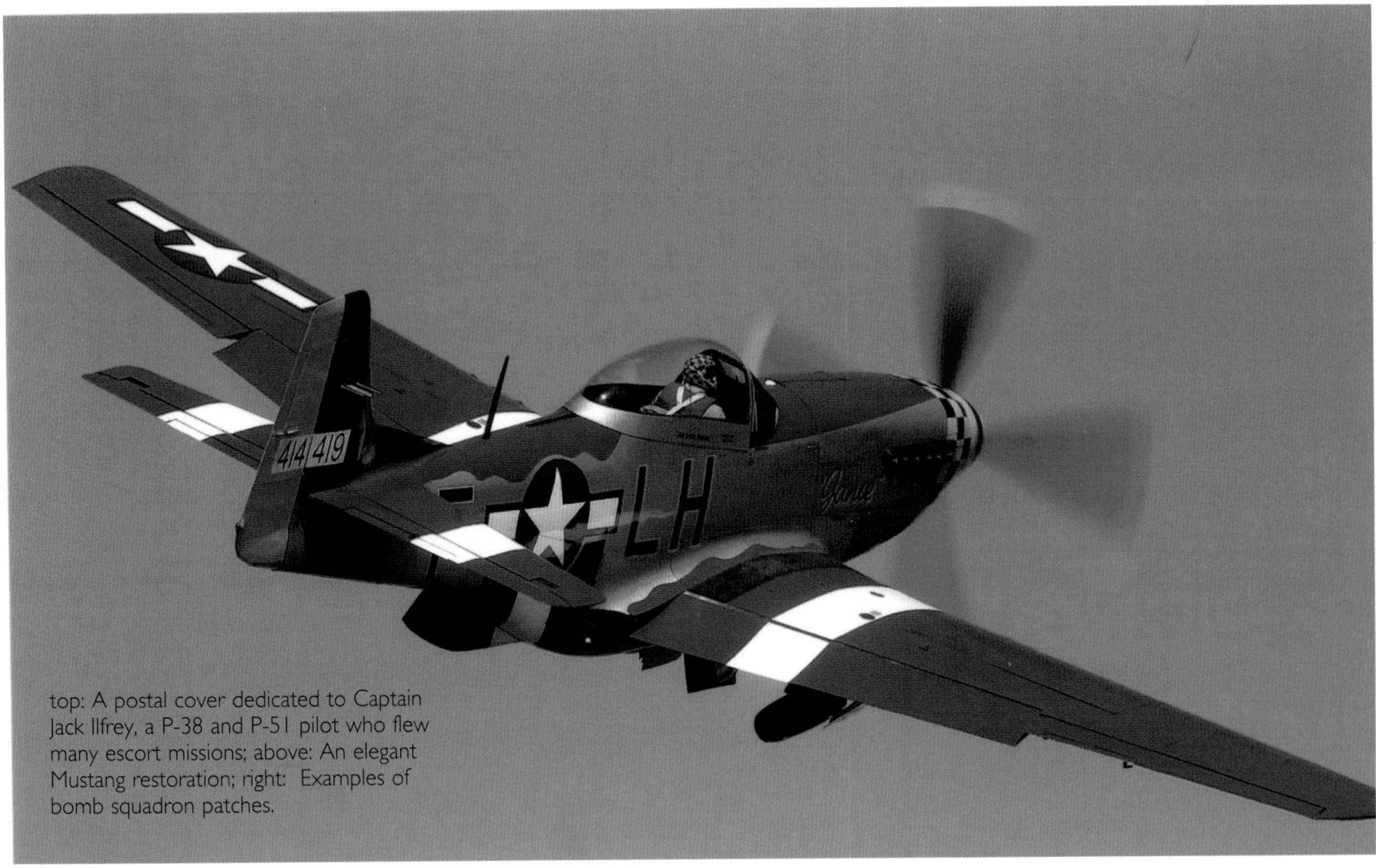
414419
LH

top: A postal cover dedicated to Captain Jack Ilfrey, a P-38 and P-51 pilot who flew many escort missions; above: An elegant Mustang restoration; right: Examples of bomb squadron patches.

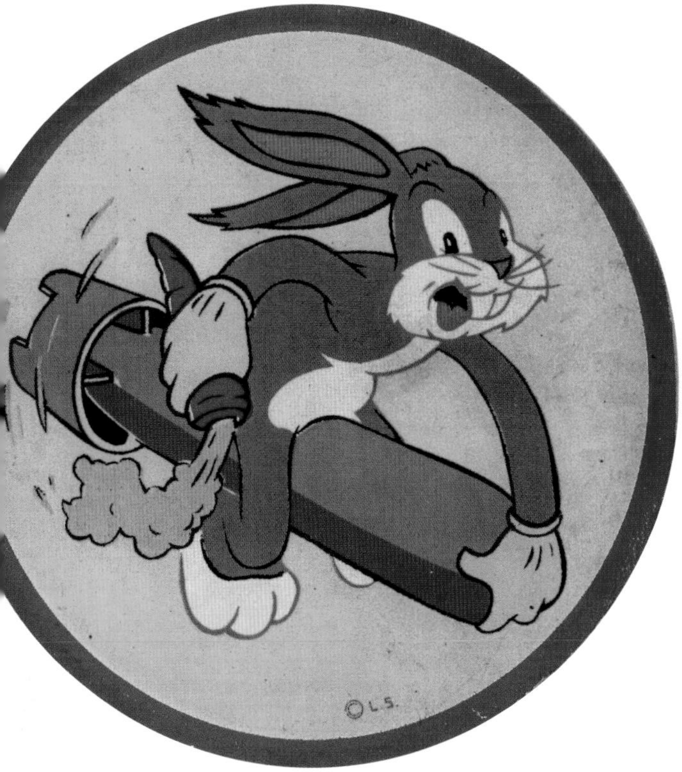
©L.S.

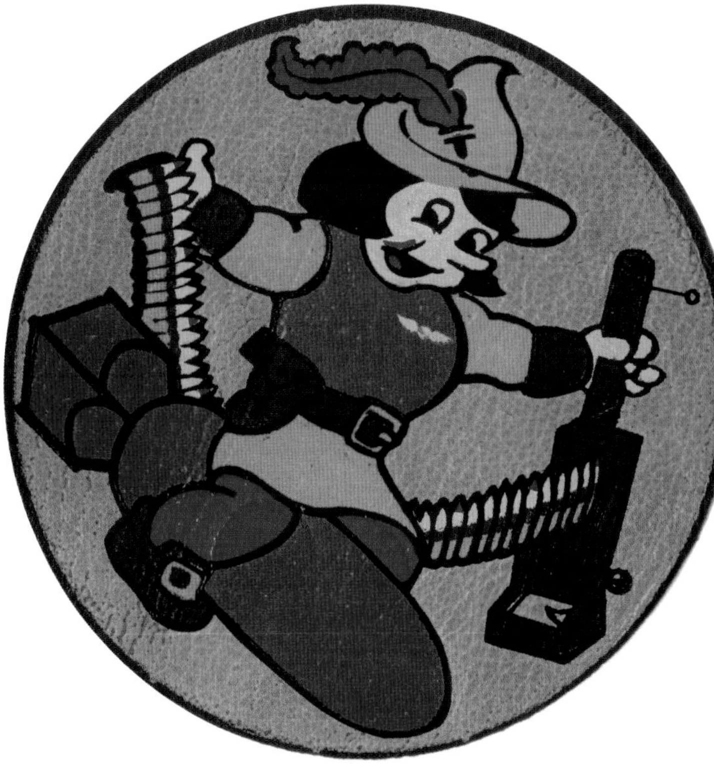

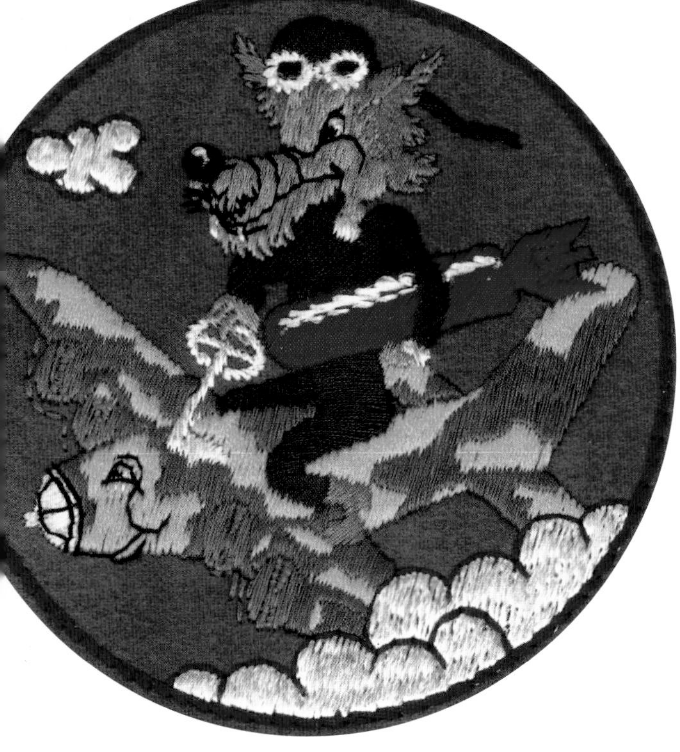

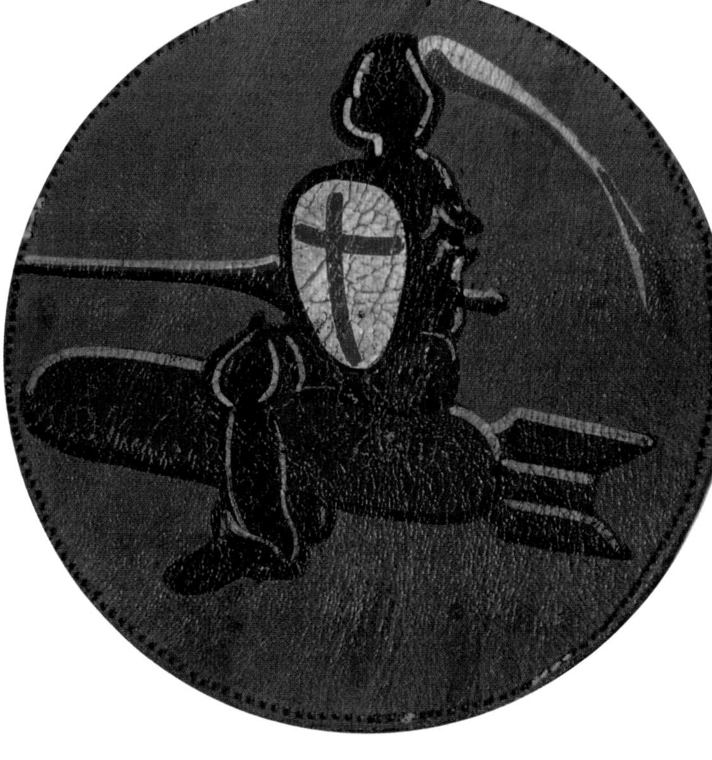

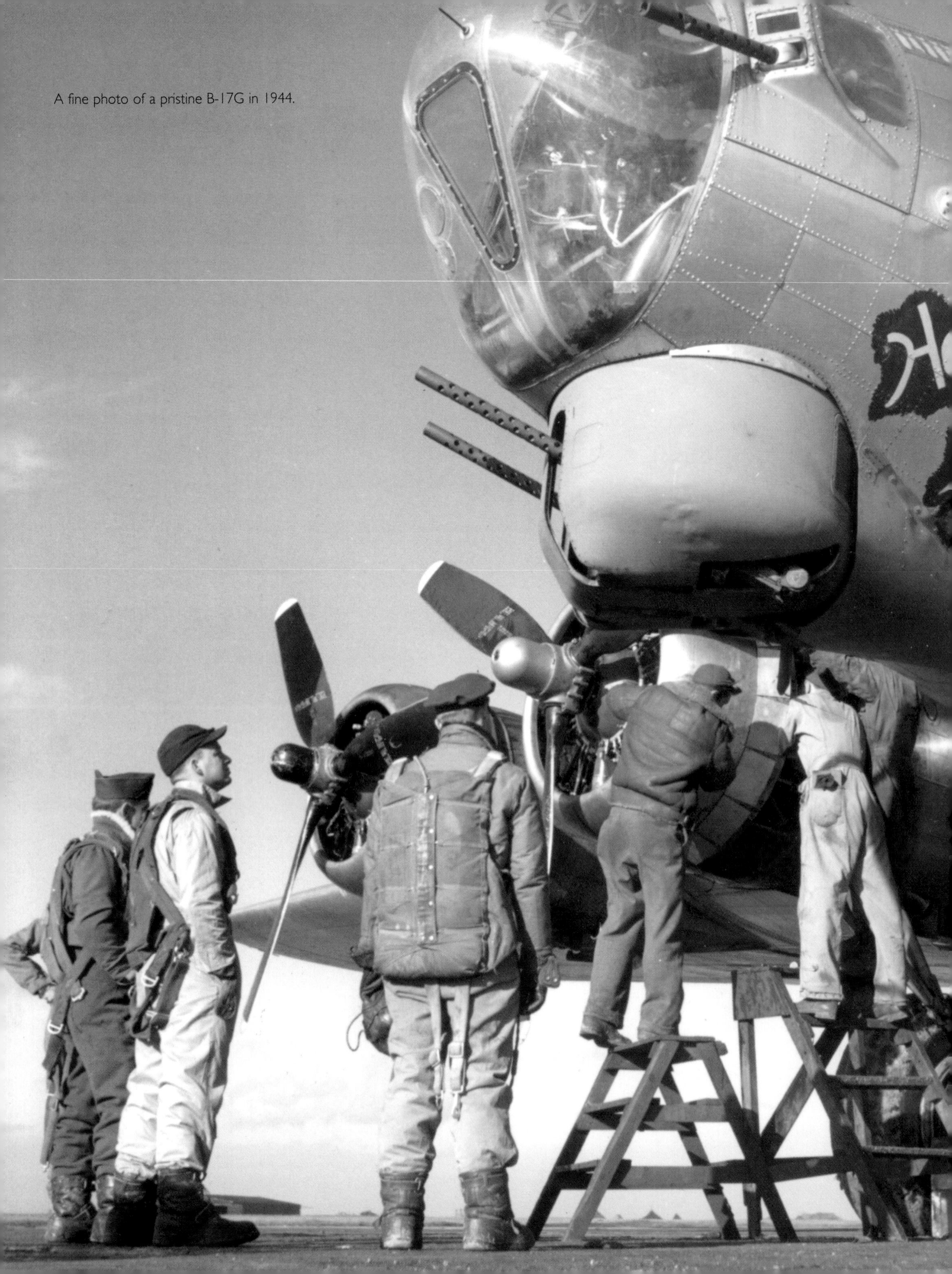

A fine photo of a pristine B-17G in 1944.

It was RAF practice, when a new crew joined a squadron, to give the pilot his first experience of action by flying as "second dickey" with a seasoned crew, while his own men stayed behind, hoping they would see him back again. Some Eighth Air Force bomb groups followed that procedure: in others the process of initiation was reversed. Navigator Charles Bosshardt observed: "What they did with a new crew was to send them on their first mission with an experienced co-pilot, while their own co-pilot went with another crew. Our first co-pilot was a guy named Leo Hipp from New Jersey. The plane he went in suffered some hits and had one or two engines out. In trying to land it at the base, it got out of control and Leo and all the crew but two were killed. That made us all superstitious about flying with anyone other than our own pilot."

Paul Sink: "The crew was very congenial. We were very close. If a person didn't meet the expectations of the rest of the crew, he was replaced. We took classes together and spent a lot of time together. When we weren't flying, we'd go to the tower and watch the group take off. Sometimes we'd split in half and each group would do what they wanted to do, but most of the time we were all together. You got to know those people very well. After you flew missions with people, especially in combat, you got to know what their reaction would be in any given circumstance."

"I will always remember my thirtieth and last mission. I definitely was more nervous than on all the other twenty-nine missions."
—Chuck Bednarik, 467BG, Rackheath

Robert F. Cooper was a B-17 co-pilot with the 385th Bomb Group at Great Ashfield, Suffolk in 1944–45: "There were only six officers in our Nissen hut—Ray Shattenkirk, pilot, myself, and Howard Giberson, navigator, and from our crew; and Alex Rusecky, pilot, George Burger, co-pilot, and Art Axelrod, navigator, from another crew. We arrived within a few days of each other and were constant companions and hutmates from late December until the end of February. We had friendly competitions, played softball, went on bike rides, told each other our life stories, went to the Officers' Club together, and often just huddled, all six of us, around the coal stove, trying to keep warm. I was especially friends with Burger, my fellow co-pilot, who was exactly my age and a happy-go-lucky type.

"On 1st March 1945, both crews were scheduled to fly, Rusecky as part of the Lead Section, Shattenkirk in the Spare Lead Section. We would not fly unless Rusecky (or another member of the Lead Section) had to abort. Even so, we had to go all the way through the starting procedure, including 'Start engines.'

"But Rusecky had developed a problem: he couldn't awaken his navigator, Art Axelrod. That was because Art was dead drunk! He had been out on a bender the night before, even though he knew his crew was to fly a mission the next morning. He probably came in around midnight, worrying the hell out of Rusecky. When the sergeant came in to awaken us at about 0300, he tried to wake Art but failed. His pilot said he'd take the responsibility to get him up. But Alex was unable to, and in fact, we all tried to. Art was totally out of it, and very quickly Alex realized he wouldn't be any good on the crew anyway. So pilot Alex had to call at the last possible moment for a replacement

B-17 crew members included, clockwise from right: waist gunner, top-turret gunner, ball-turret gunner, pilot, radio-gunner, waist gunner. Not shown: Co-pilot, navigator, bombardier, and tail gunner. With the introduction of lead crews later in the war, many bombardiers were replaced by toggleers. B-24 crews were mostly similar in composition.

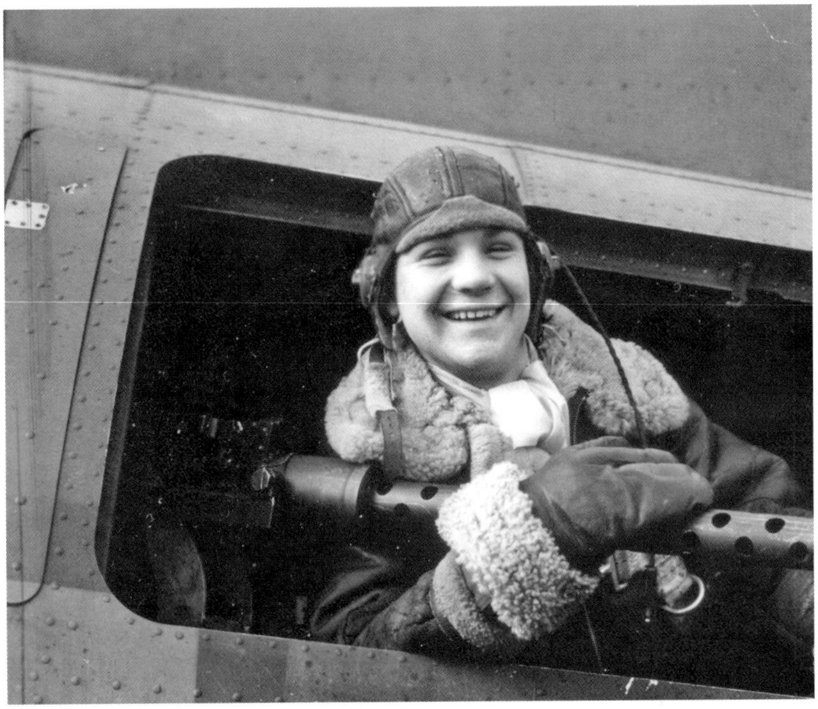

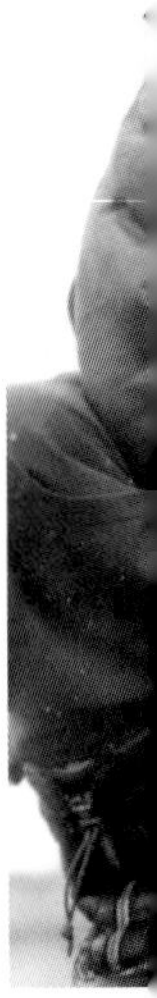

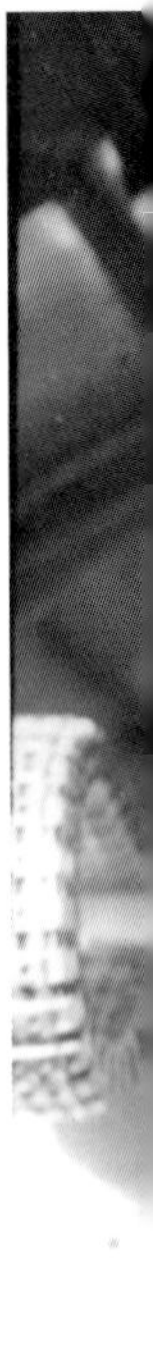

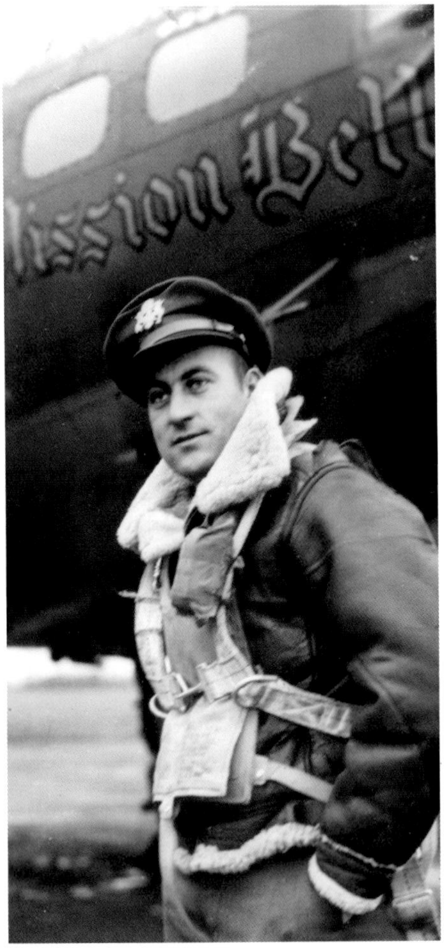

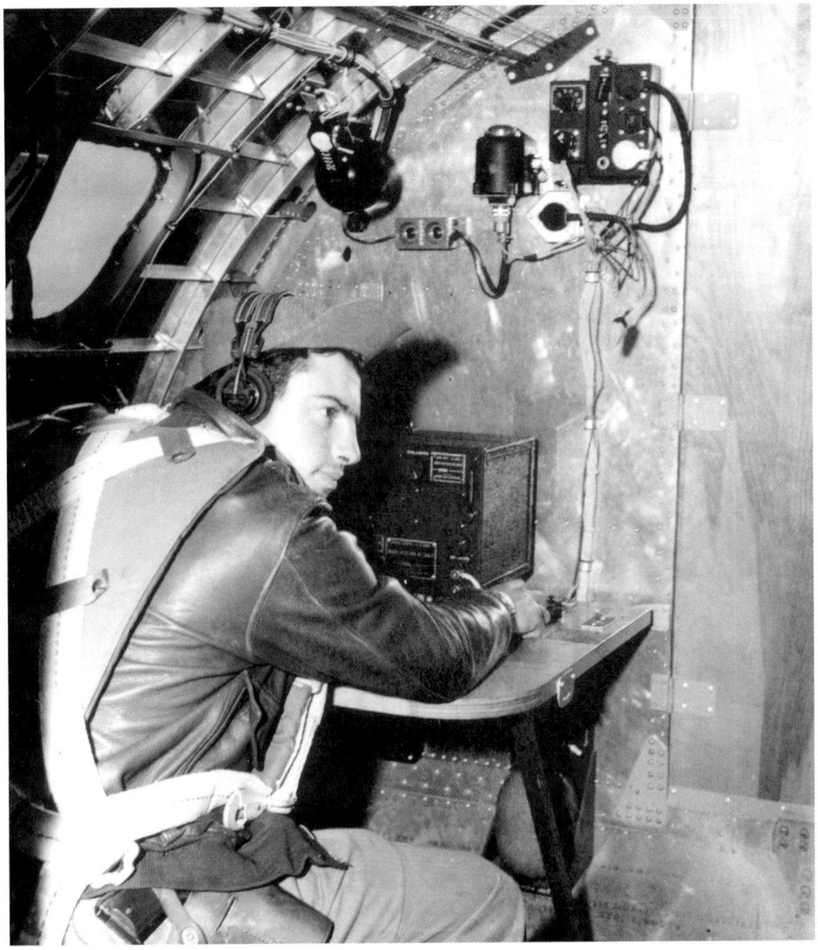

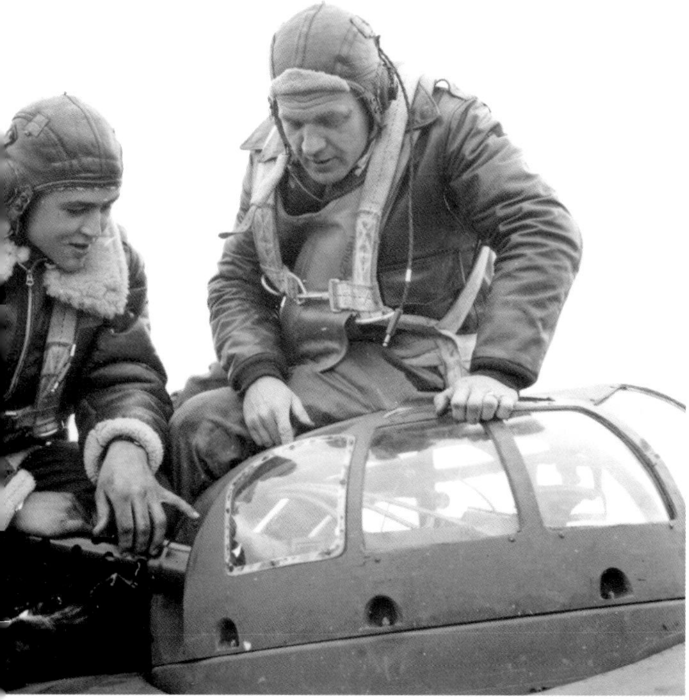

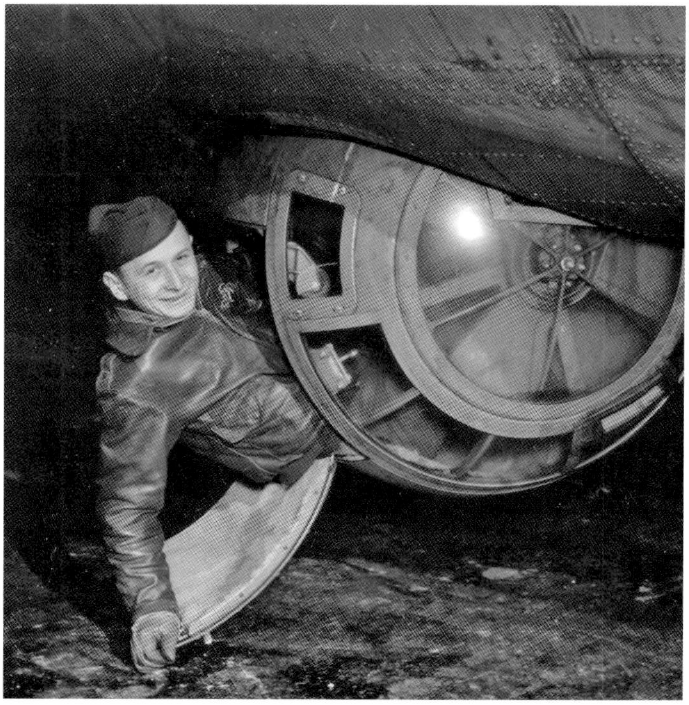

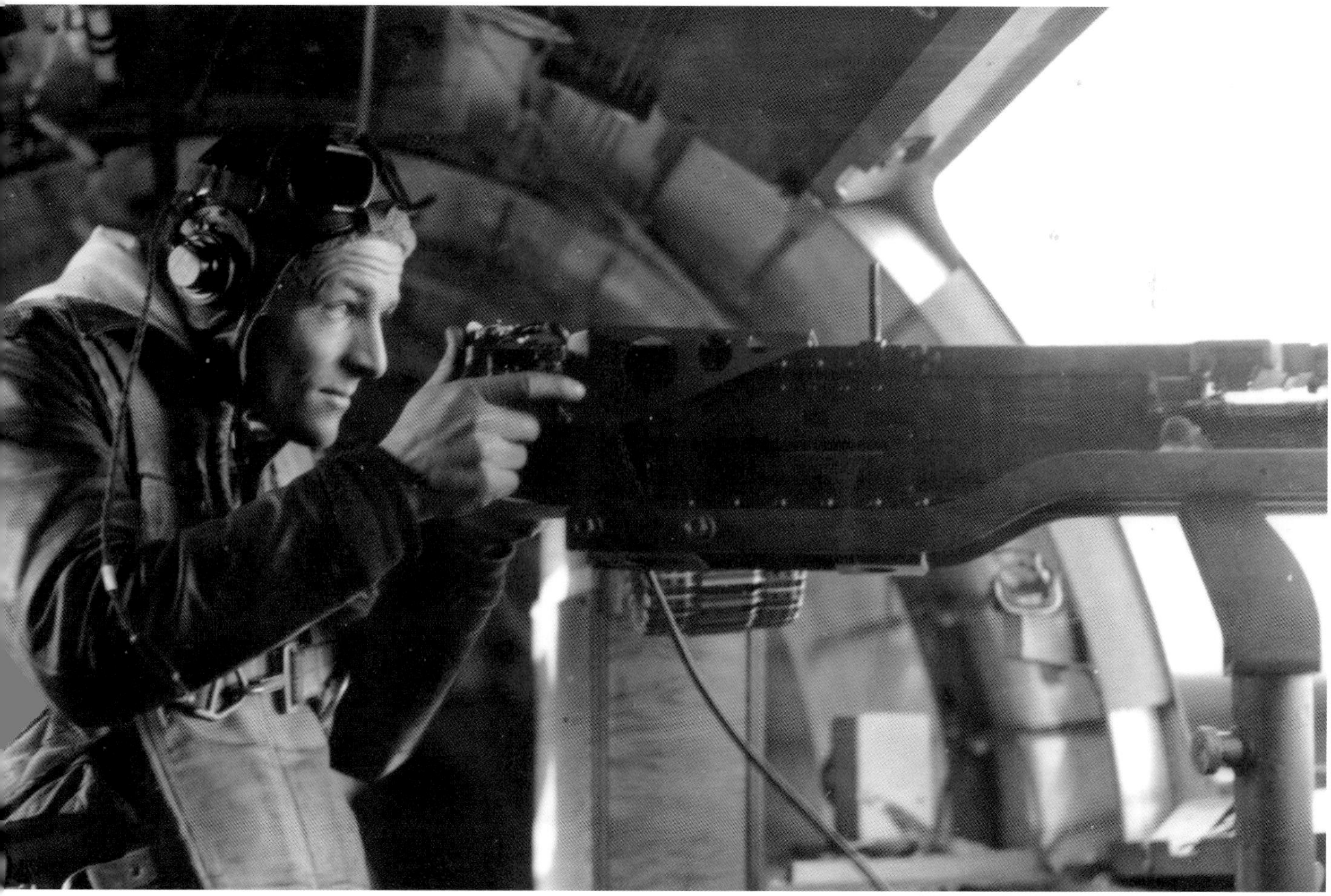

navigator, some poor guy from the Squadron who hadn't thought he would be flying that day. The rest of the five of us left for the mission briefing, etc., leaving Art snoring away in his bunk. At the flight line, we started engines, but no one aborted, so we were able to come back to our barracks around 0600 and pile back into our bunks for another few hours sleep. Art was still snoring, still drunk, out of it.

"The bad news came to us at lunch. Rusecky's plane and Armbruster's plane had collided while assembling, and both planes had gone straight down. Of the eighteen men on both planes, only one parachuted safely—the tail gunner from Armbruster's crew. The other seventeen were dead. We all felt very badly indeed, but if we felt that way, imagine how Art felt. My pilot and I talked with him just a bit that afternoon. He said he was utterly devastated by the loss of his entire crew, but also utterly thankful that he hadn't been with them. Art didn't want to talk much about it, and he was gone almost immediately. The brass probably figured he wouldn't be welcome around the squadron much. I don't doubt that this event (which just amounts to getting drunk one night at the wrong time—or perhaps the right?) changed Art's life forever. I never saw him again."

Wake, friend, from forth thy lethargy; the drum beats brave and loud in Europe, and bids come all that dare rouse, or are not loath to quit their vicious ease and be o'erwhelmed with it. It is a call to keep the spirits alive that gasp for action, and would yet revive man's buried honour in his sleep life, quickening dead nature to her noblest strife. All other acts of worldlings are but toil in dreams,

begun in hope and end in spoil.
—from *An Epistle to a Friend, to perswade him to Warres* by Ben Jonson

Former B-17 pilot Bill Harvey was assigned to the 384th Bomb Group at Grafton Underwood, Northamptonshire, in World War Two: "I have never forgotten the green, 'Farty shades of green,' the Irish would say. After months of training in the western deserts of the U.S., I couldn't believe how beautiful Ireland and England looked then.

"We arrived at Grafton on a beautiful Saturday morning in early June 1943, two or three weeks after the rest of the crews. By this time they were old hands with a mission or two under their belts. The next day, Sunday, was another beautiful day so my navigator, Dick Sherer, and I decided to go to Kettering, the closest town of any size, then take a train to Leicester, a nearby city, and be tourists for a day. At the Kettering station, I read the schedule and there was a train returning at six that night, getting us back to the base before dark. After a looksee at downtown Leicester, we stopped in a hotel and they were having a tea dance. This turned out to be our first chance to see English girls. They were pretty and friendly and we had a great time. Five-thirty came all too soon and we had to leave for the station. I checked at the ticket window to see if the six o'clock train was on time and was advised that this being Sunday there was no six o'clock train and the next one was at midnight. I never could read a train schedule. Back to the dance. We took two of the pretty girls to dinner and the movies, arriving back at the station in time for the midnight train. Our only thought was, we'll never get a taxi so late at night, so we'll have to walk out to the base—which we did.

"As we got near, we could hear the

The 100th Bomb Group crew of the B-17 *Piccadilly Lilly II*: top row left to right: 2nd Lt J.S. Neal, 1st Lt R.J. Flack, 2nd Lt H.J. Quilici, 2nd Lt A.H. Campion; bottom row left to right: S/Sgt G.A. Perez, S/Sgt J. King, S/Sgt E.P. Hall, S/Sgt J.S. Berrick, T/Sgt C.R. Contreras, and T/Sgt W.L. Tee.

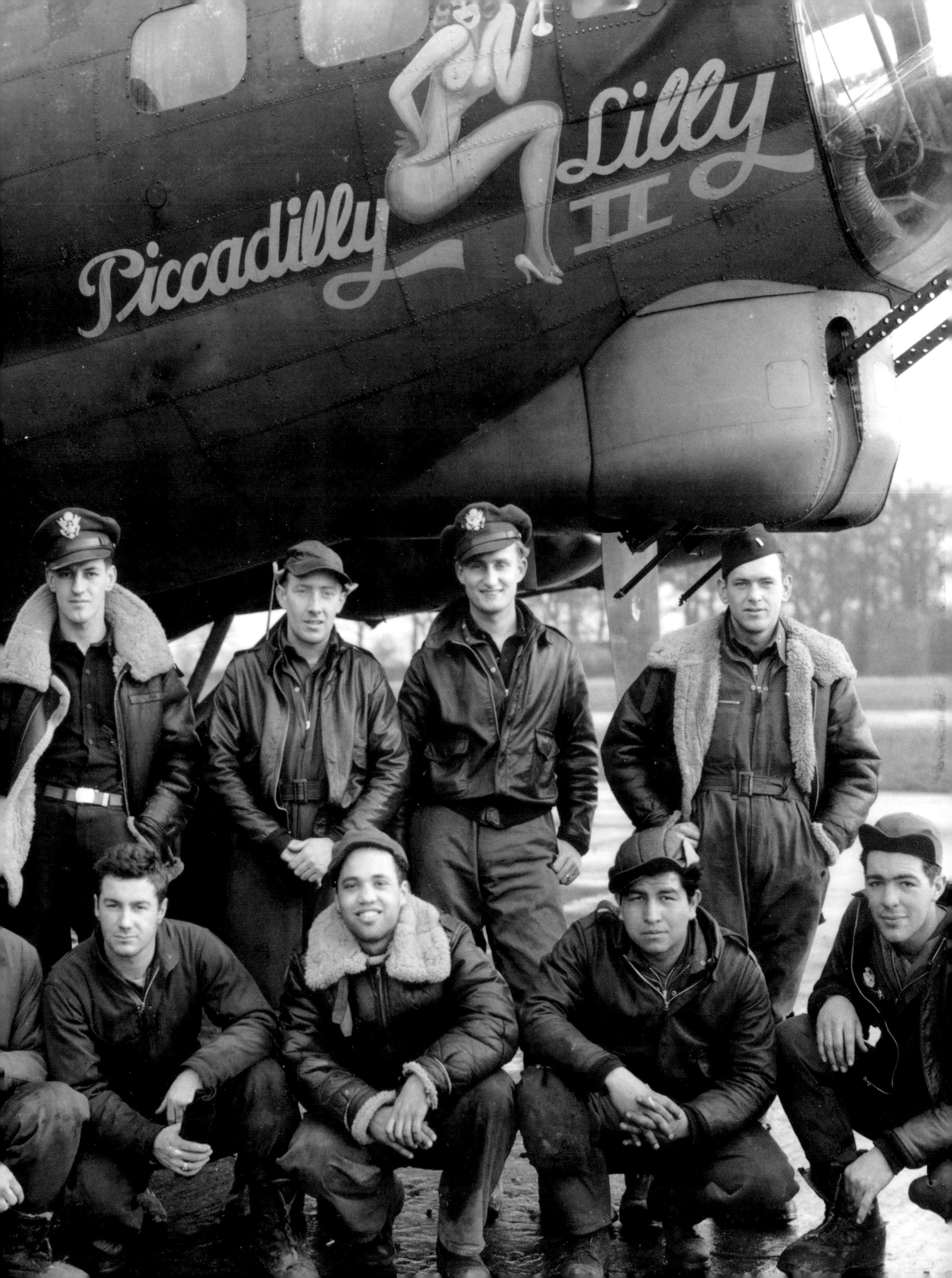
Piccadilly Lilly II

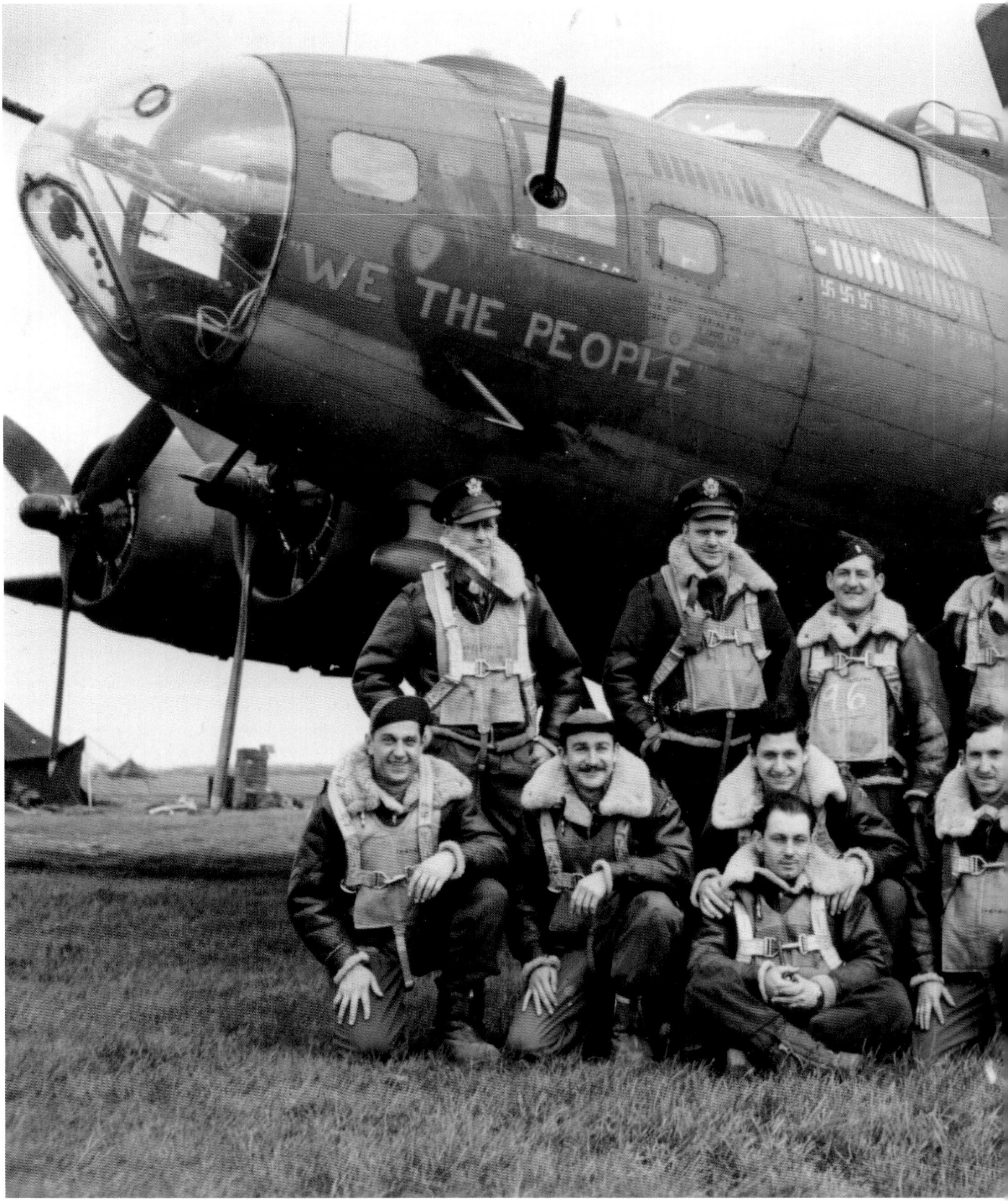
"WE THE PEOPLE"
96

The B-17F *We The People* and her crew at Chelveston, home base of the 305th Bomb Group.

roar of many engines. Deciding there must be a mission on, we walked down to the flight line to watch the planes take off. We had only been there a couple of minutes when our Squadron Operations Officer saw us and said, 'Where the hell have you fellas been? We've been looking all over for you. Your plane and crew are on this mission and we've had to find a replacement co-pilot and navigator to go in your place.' We couldn't believe it. We had only arrived yesterday. We hadn't even had an orientation flight. How could they send our crew? We weren't ready, not even one practice mission. This is crazy. Crazy or not, there was our plane taking off and we were sick. He told us to go to our quarters until the Squadron Commander could see us. It wasn't long before we were standing at attention in his office. We felt terrible. We knew we hadn't done anything wrong, but he told us that the Group CO was really upset. After hearing our explanation, he said, 'I'll do my best to save your asses.' We were sent back to our quarters and told to stay there until the Colonel could see us.

"Hours later the mission was due to return and we said, 'To hell with it. Let's go down to the flight line and watch the planes land.' One after another the Forts came in and landed. Two didn't make it back—one of them was ours. God, then we really felt terrible, thinking that, if we had been along, maybe we could have done something to bring the plane back. Just then the Colonel spotted us and called us over. He said, 'I was all for court-martialling you two, but I can't because you really haven't broken any rules and I know how bad you feel. Anyhow, your squadron CO was the one who really saved your asses because I wanted to make an example out

of you.' What a way to start a tour of duty! As badly as we felt, we also knew that we were damned lucky to be alive. I would let someone else read the train schedules from then on.

"The next three months were the most frustrating of my life. Whenever a co-pilot was needed for a crew, I was picked. Seven times I started a mission and seven times we aborted and returned to base. There were, of course, many reasons for these abortions . . . engine problems, control problems, weather, but the really bad one was mental problems. Some pilots just lost their nerve when they got close to enemy territory and they would use any pretense to turn back. This was rare, but it happened. That was my luck on my fifth, sixth, and seventh aborted missions. My pilot must have had a premonition that he was going to be shot down. He would drop out of the formation and turn back for the least little reason. After his second abort, I went to the Squadron Commander and asked to be taken off the crew. I didn't want to fly with that pilot again. The CO said, 'Harvey, fly with him one more time. If he aborts again I'll relieve him.' I reluctantly agreed and a couple of days later we were off on another mission. We hadn't even reached altitude when the pilot said, 'Look at the RPM indicator; it's jiggling all over the place.' It looked okay to me, but he said, 'We are going back to base.' I pleaded with him to let me take the controls, but all he would do was shake his head. That was the last time I spoke to him. After landing and taxiing to our hardstand, I got out of the plane and reported to the CO. The pilot was removed from command and a few days later was flying co-pilot for another crew. His premonition was right. He never came back. I vowed that if I ever made first pilot, I would never abort.

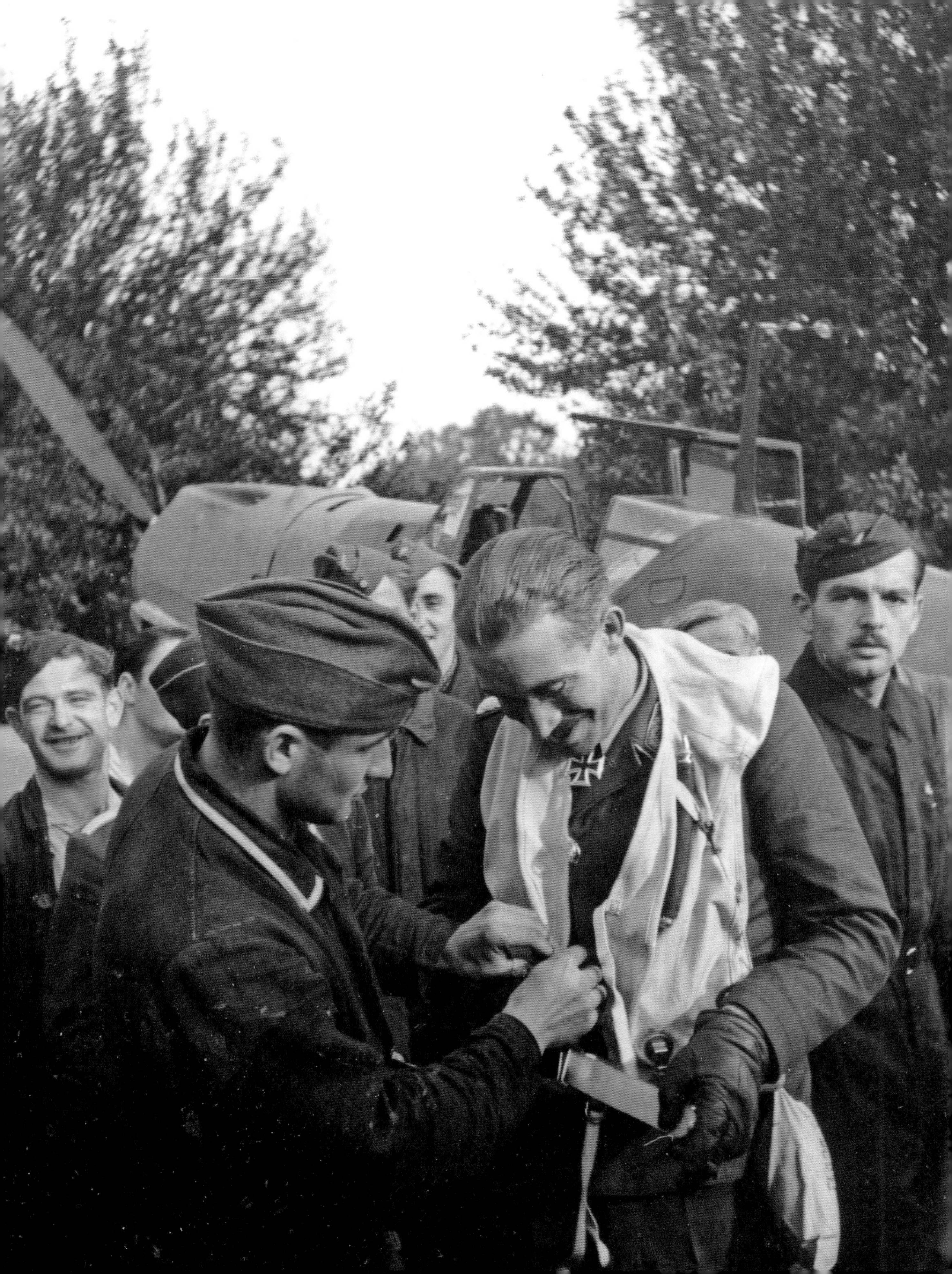

"One day the CO called me in and said, 'Harvey, you've had enough experience now so I'm going to make you a first pilot, but I'm not giving you a crew. We need some experienced instructor pilots to fly with the new crews, anywhere up to five missions. If you think the pilot and crew are ready before that, that's okay too. Teach them well. As you know, most of our losses are on the first five missions. We should cut those losses with an experienced pilot aboard.' I was so happy to be a first pilot that I didn't even think about having to fly with inexperienced crews all the time. I thought about it many times later.

"24th April. My twenty-fifth mission. This was the sixth crew I had trained and my second time out with them. They were about ready to go on their own under their pilot, Bob Brown. The target for the day was an airfield and manufacturing plant in Oberpfaffenhofen, a suburb of Munich. We were leading the low squadron that day with Colonel Dale O. Smith leading the group and the wing, which consisted of three groups. The high squadron in our group was led by Bud MacKichan, who was married to a girl from Saginaw, Michigan, where my parents lived. Bud's wife and my mother had become friends.

"The takeoff was normal, but shortly after beginning our climb to altitude we lost the supercharger on one of the engines and as a result my low squadron began to lag behind the group. Colonel Smith radioed to close it up, but I just couldn't do that while climbing. I thought that once I reached altitude we'd be all right and I could close up then. During this time I began to think about aborting the mission, something I had never done as a first pilot. I had had enough of those as a co-pilot. Also, I had five planes flying formation on me and they were all

inexperienced pilots with very few missions. I probably should have aborted, but I didn't. We finally got to bombing altitude, and, little by little, we were closing in. I could see Paris below and to the south of us. It was a perfect spring day, not an enemy fighter in sight, and our own escort of Mustangs and Thunderbolts all around us.

"Suddenly the sky below was filled with little black puffs, those innocent-looking little clouds were anti-aircraft shells exploding just beneath our group. Just then our B-17 lurched and I knew we had been hit. I looked around and the back of the cockpit was on fire. This had happened to me on a previous mission and I had been able to put it out, so I told Brown to take over and I would go back and try to put out the fire. No luck this time, so I rang the alarm and told the crew to bail out, grabbed Brown by the arm and said, 'Let's go.' The bombardier and the navigator already had the forward escape hatch open and were waiting for my signal. A thumbs-down sign did it and the four of us were out and away.

"When we were lectured on how to parachute, three things were stressed. Number one: 'free fall' as long as possible so the enemy fighters can't follow you down and shoot you. Number two: free fall so that the ground forces can't follow you down and be there to meet you as you land, and number three: save the ripcord as a souvenir. The first and second, I did; the third I didn't. When the chute opened, and I thought it never would, it gave me a helluva jerk. I realized I hadn't tightened my leg straps enough and they were really cutting into me. I would lift one leg at a time to relieve the pressure, which helped, but in the meantime I was swinging back and forth and starting to get airsick. I couldn't see any other parachutes in

the sky no matter where I looked, but I thought that Bud MacKichan must have seen what happened and would be able, through his wife, to tell my family that the plane didn't explode, that he had seen parachutes and that I probably would be okay. That report never got home, however. Bud was killed a few minutes later."

left: German fighter ace Adolf Galland was credited with shooting down 104 Allied planes and later was made General of the Luftwaffe Fighter arm; below: A B-17 pilot, 2nd Lieutenant R.E. Bennett.

The relief and elation of a B-17 crew on the completion of their twenty-five-mission tour of duty. In June 1943 these men experienced the welcome realization that, unlike so many of their friends and associates, they had survived their combat committment.

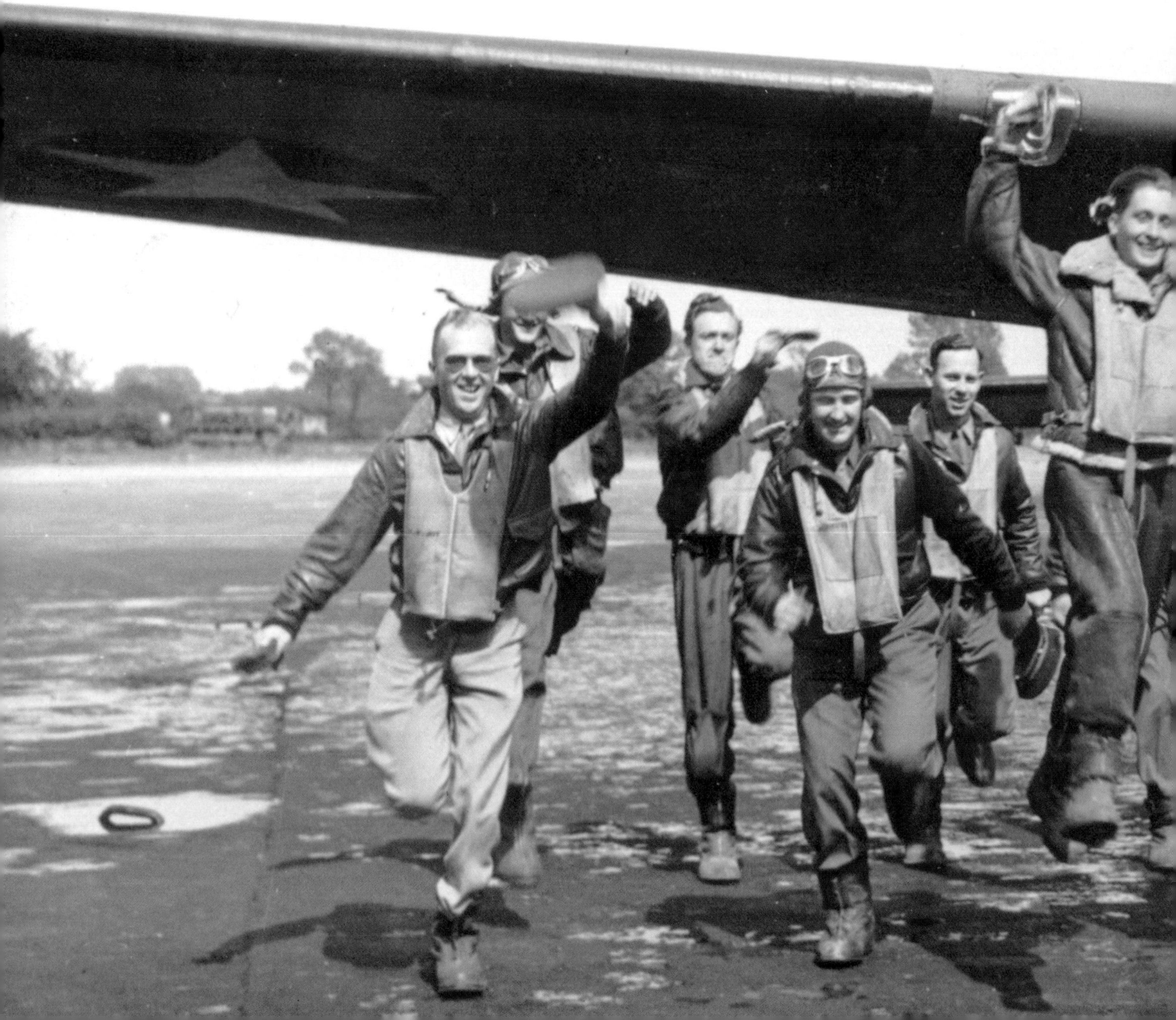

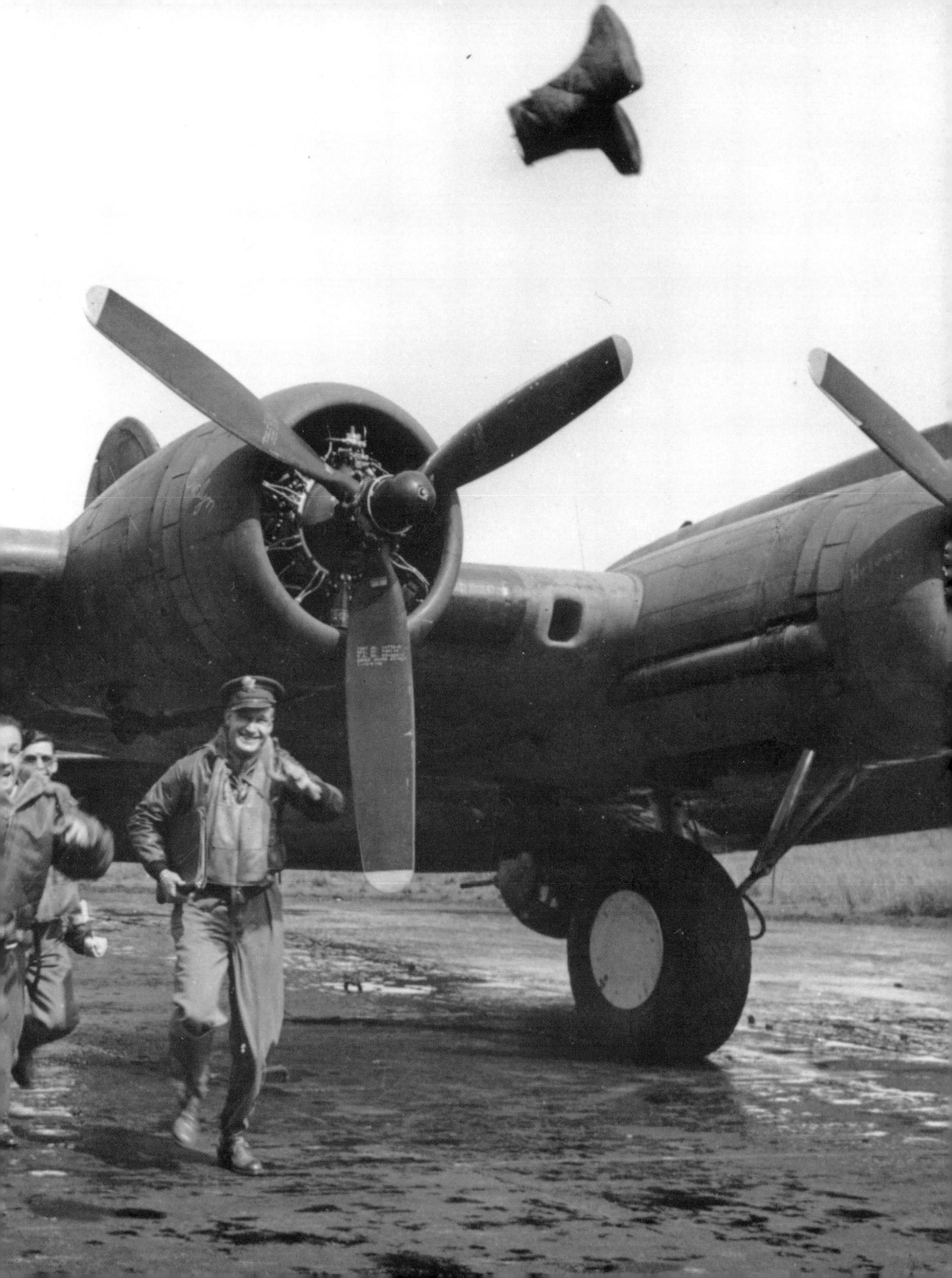

HAVE GUM WILL TRAVEL

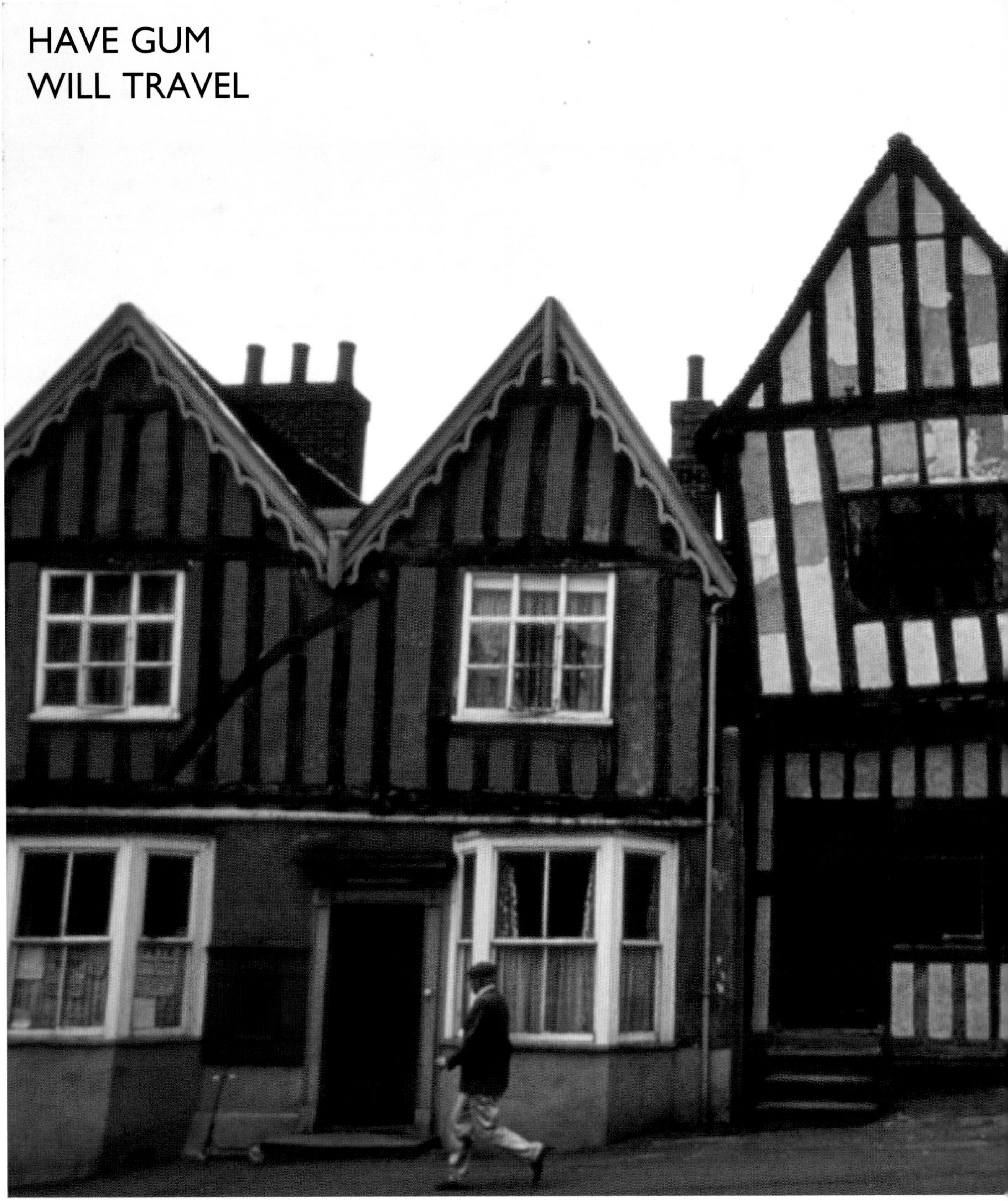

The charming village of Lavenham, Suffolk, adjoins the airfield that shared its name and played host to the 487th Bomb Group in the Second World War.

"I still remember the Yanks almost more than I do the war."
— A Suffolk woman

"They brought colour into our lives, and when they went away it was all grey again."
—An Englishwoman recalling the American forces in England in the Second World War

SINCE 1066, Britons have faced the prospect of invasion on seventy-three separate occasions. The likes of Edgar Aethling, Sweyn Estridsson, Eustace the Monk, France on several occasions, Lambert Symnel, Perkin Warbeck, Spain, the Netherlands, John Paul Jones, and others . . . all had an eye for Blighty. In 1940, Hitler's Nazi Germany got as far as occupying the Channel Islands and might have attempted to invade England had it not been for the outnumbered fighter pilots of the Royal Air Force who prevented the Germans from gaining air supremacy over the British Isles. Such threats appeared to fade for a time after the Luftwaffe Blitz on Britain in late 1940–1941—until early 1942 and the arrival of distant relations from the American colonies. They were a trickle at first, but over the remainder of the Second World War more than 350,000 Americans served in the Eighth Air Force in England. Their contribution to winning that war was immense; their accomplishments legendary. . . the impact of their presence on the British people unforgettable.

Back in 1940, with the Nazi army paused across the Channel, the British stood ready to greet them with pitchforks and ploughshares, but the RAF made that encounter unnecessary. Another threat arrived two years later, though, to their innate

insularity and reserve.

The American "invaders" were benign but unfamiliar; open-handed and gregarious; with very few inhibitions. They greeted the British with "Hi" and smiles. In comparison with British servicemen, they were well dressed, well off, and well fixed for Chesterfields, Camels, or Lucky Strikes. Many seemed to chew gum, drink cold beer, dance the Jitterbug, and have ready access to perfume and nylon stockings. Many drawled like certain well known film stars. With all their peculiarities, the British mostly thought of them as friends and certainly as strong and welcome allies. Some less charitable locals tended to discount them as "overpaid, oversexed, and over here." In response, some Yanks referred to their hosts as "underpaid, undersexed, and under Eisenhower."

One young evacuee from London, who was billeted in Woodbridge, Suffolk, when the Eighth Air Force was arriving, wrote: "If there was no flying, the Yanks would hit the town. Usually they came in jeeps and six-by-six trucks, but more often on bicycles, caps on the backs of their heads, slacks rolled up below the knee and sporting fancy cowboy boots. They came in crews—young officers side by side with weathered non-coms and non-shaving boy gunners, all eager to find a pub that was not 'officers only,' as many were. There were fights over local girls, fights with British servicemen, and fights between drunken buddies for the hell of it. We couldn't understand them, but the old soldiers among us did. The clues were out there in the craters made by crashed aircraft in the Suffolk mud."

One thing did endear the Americans to the locals who noticed it. It was their attitude to the British kids. Ira Eakin, a crew chief, remembered: "When we was on that fighter base we adopted a little blond-headed girl. Her parents got killed and our captain found out about it somehow. The cutest little girl you ever saw. She was just an angel. The captain would call down at this orphanage that had her and they'd let her come up to the base for the weekend. We had Red Cross women on the base and they looked after her at night. The guys were kicking in a pound or so and the captain came in and said, 'Hell, you can do better than that. I gave sixty pounds and I want at least ten from you cats.' And we did. We got it all fixed up and sent her back to the States. I often wondered whatever happened to her."

B-17 gunner Paul Sink: "We would land in the afternoon and there was a road around the base to kind of separate us from the surrounding countryside. These little boys, ten, eleven, twelve years old, would be standing there, peering through the hedgerows, watching us get out of the airplanes. We'd have the heavy flying kit, flak jackets, oxygen masks hanging from our helmets. I guess we did look pretty strange."

The Yanks provoked a variety of reactions from the distaff side: some females made no bones about it—they didn't care for them; some had British boyfriends or husbands in the armed forces and remained true to them—in their fashion anyway. Others had the time of their young lives when the U.S. Army Air Force came into town or threw a party on the base. Casual acquaintanceships at such events often evolved into romances and sometimes into marriage proposals. After the war ended, more than 70,000 GI brides followed their American husbands to the States and a whole new and different life there. Not all such meetings resulted in that way, however. Ira Eakin: "I met a pretty English nurse shortly after I went over there and I dated her most of the time. We almost got married, but it ended up we didn't. She said my folks would think she'd married me just to come to the United States. I asked her if she felt that way about it and she said, 'I would like to go to the United States but I wouldn't marry anybody just to go there.' I found the English girls real good, just real understanding. Sure, they liked to go out and have a good time, dance and all this, and a few other things, but not that big a difference."

"Love is an ocean of emotions, entirely surrounded by expenses."
—Lord Dewar

Bombardier Larry Bird: "I went with this girl, Jill. She was a dancer, about eighteen or nineteen and very independent. We used to go out in London and get caught in the air raids. We spent nights in the subway, and got home in the morning. Her parents didn't mind. They were so doggone nice. I'll never forget them. They were people of some standing. They had a car, and not everyone in England had a car in those days. It was up on blocks in the yard on account of no gasoline. Most people depended on the bicycle. If you had a bicycle, you had transportation."

B-17 radioman Roger Armstrong: "After we had been at Bassingbourn two or three weeks, we learned where the pubs were that welcomed American fliers. Actually, I never went into a pub where we weren't treated well, once the regulars realized we weren't troublemakers. Many of them told us they counted our ships leaving on missions, and on return again. They were very concerned about our well-being. I also enjoyed the dances

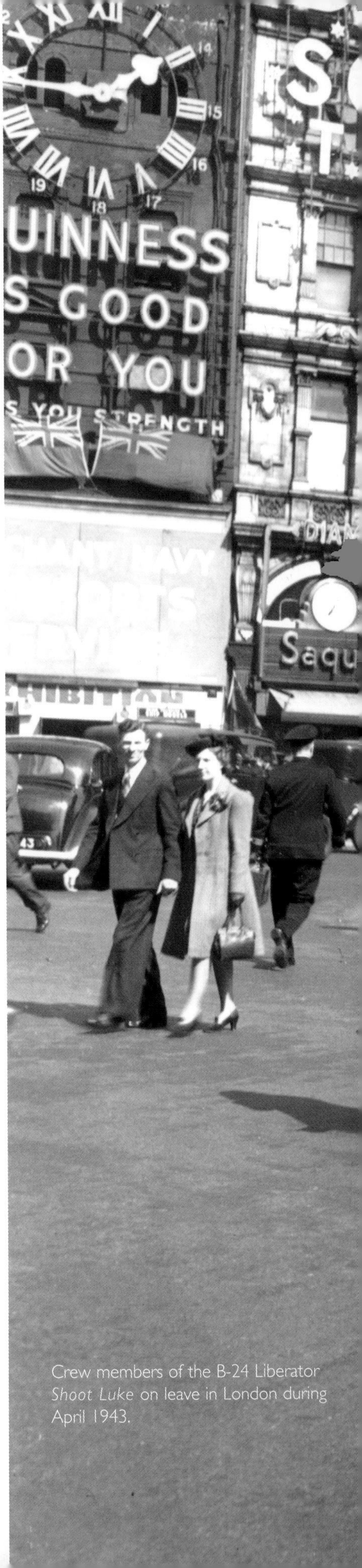
UINNESS
S GOOD
OR YOU
Saqu

Crew members of the B-24 Liberator *Shoot Luke* on leave in London during April 1943.

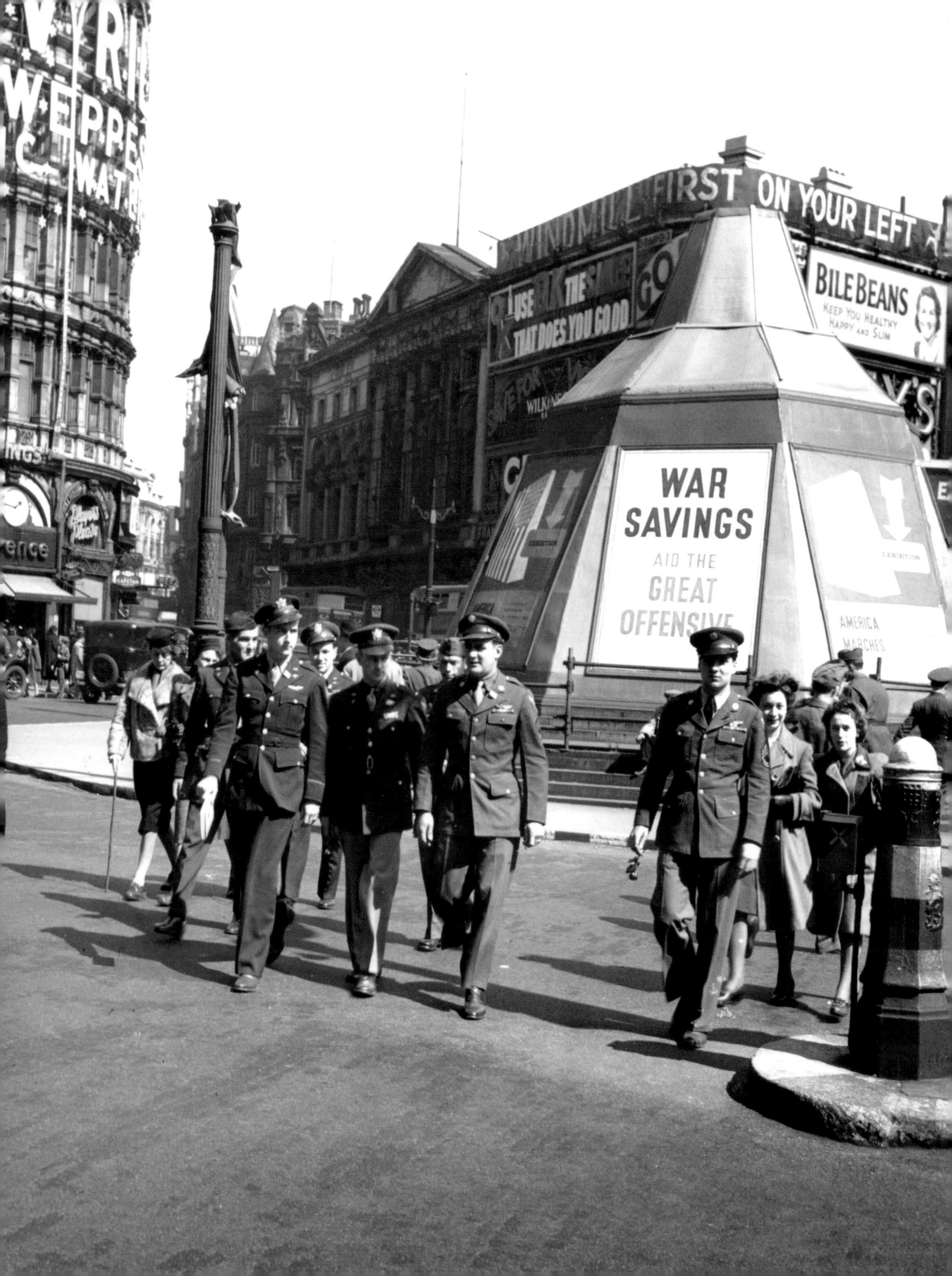

FIRST ON YOUR LEFT
BILE BEANS
KEEP YOU HEALTHY HAPPY AND SLIM
USE THE
THAT DOES YOU GOOD
WAR SAVINGS
AID THE GREAT OFFENSIVE
AMERICA MARCHES

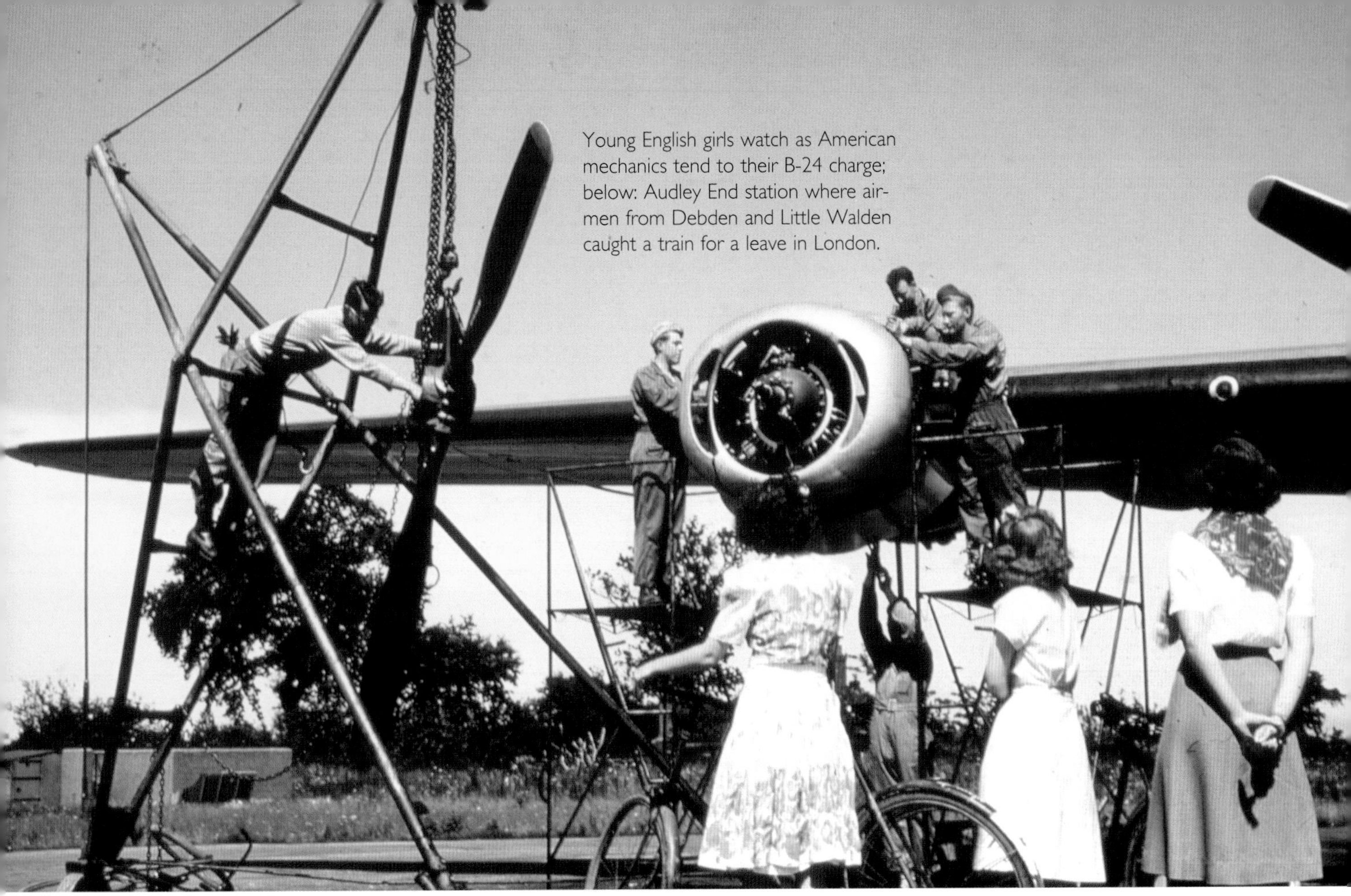

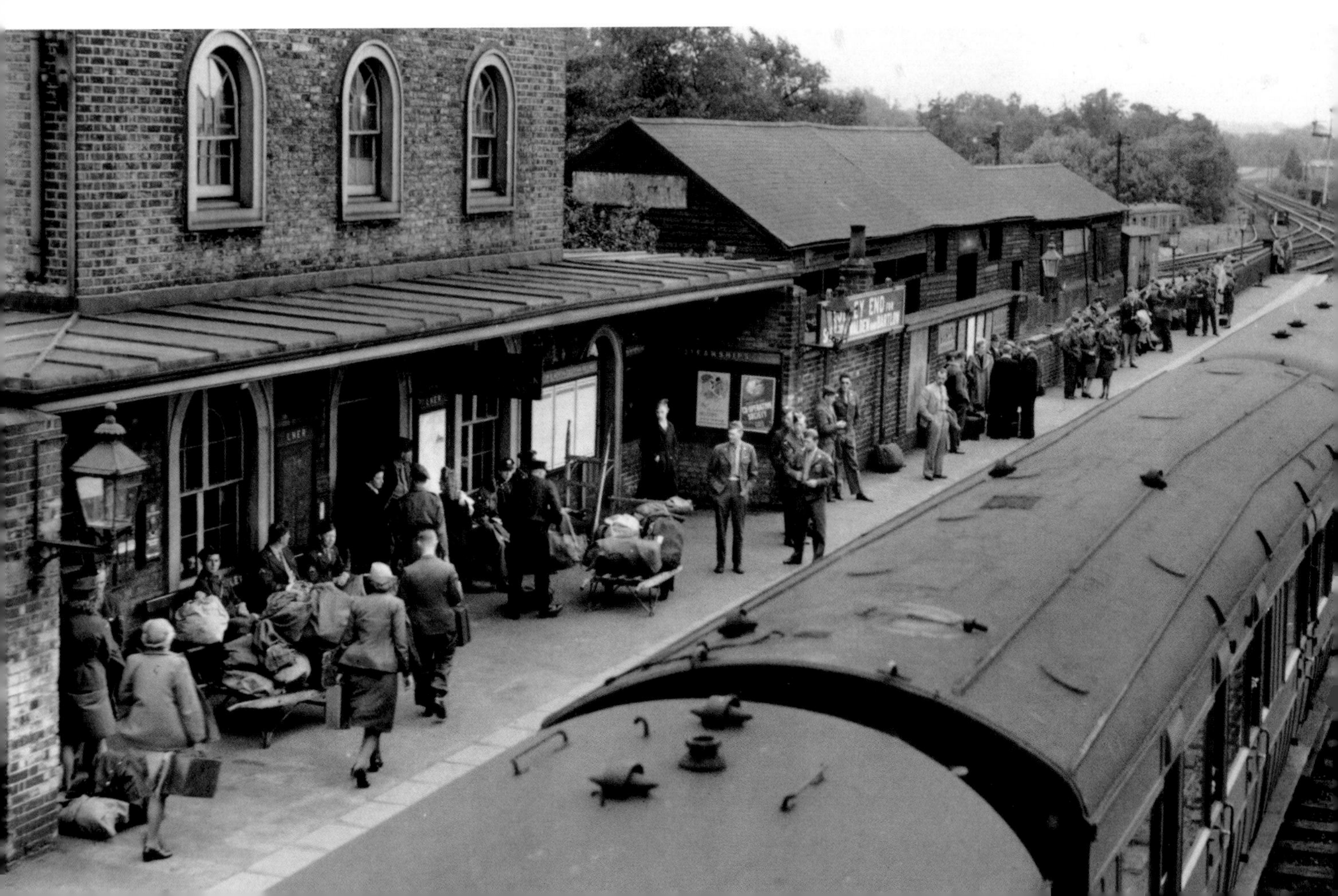

Young English girls watch as American mechanics tend to their B-24 charge; below: Audley End station where airmen from Debden and Little Walden caught a train for a leave in London.

at a large hall in Cambridge. The girls were good dancers and the band played music that was popular in the States. They served beer at the dances, and there was a brand called Nut Brown Ale that was pretty heady stuff, so one had to be careful about how much one drank. We had to be back to catch the shuttle truck by eleven p.m. as many of the flight crews were on the alert list for the morning mission."

Ira Eakin on the local waters: "They had a beer, Worthington Ale. I drank that and I drank a lot of scotch and soda. I got drunk one time on Irish potato whiskey and I'll never do that again. Me and this buddy of mine, ol' Owen M. Close, we went out to the pub and they'd run out of their ration, so we had a few big mugs of that mild-and-bitter—the stuff they should pour back in the horse—and we got to drinking that and chasing it with Irish whiskey. I thought I was gonna die for a whole week later. Close slept in the bunk across from me, and he had a little bald spot on top of his head. First thing every morning he'd put on his little GI cap to cover that bald spot and keep his head from getting cold. Hell, for two weeks later, he'd raise up in bed, put that cap on and say, 'Oh, shit.' You could tell he was suffering. That was the last time we ever tried that Irish whiskey."

The V-1 flying bombs, or doodlebugs as the British called them, brought a new dimension to the air raids Britain was experiencing. Navigator Frank Nelson: "The Germans used to send those damned buzz bombs over. They sounded like a BT-13 trainer, and as long as you heard them, no sweat. But when that sound cut out, you knew it was coming down. This one came at night and it sounded like it cut out right over our field. We had

slit trenches outside of the Nissen huts there, and you saw nothing but bare feet and white butts heading for those trenches."

From the diary of B-24 pilot Keith Newhouse: "Thursday, 13th April 1944. We had time off today and wandered into Norwich early, got off the bus in the middle of town and just ambled about. The streets are narrow, the sidewalks narrower and the shops flush with the walk. Traffic, of course, flows opposite to ours, and bikes are more of a hazard than cars. Little side streets meander off in every direction, but still and all orientation is easy because everything branches from the center of town. The points of interest are all extremely old buildings and churches. Shopping is done by sweating out long lines outside the shops, which have little to sell. Not 'How much does it cost?' but 'How many coupons?'

"In the towns, one can't help noticing the number of baby carriages that crowd the walks. Women with perambulators and two or three little mites swarm through the streets. These Englishmen may be away to the war most of the time, but they surely aren't wasting any leave time or shooting many blanks.

"The tea shop was a flight of stairs down from street level, very cramped and informal. The brew was excellent, and we had a sort of gingerbread with raisins, and toast with honey. The honey was tangy, milky in color and granulated. I prefer it to our own. The assortment of crumpets, cookies and the like was rather poor and I imagine rationing has done that, but we shall undoubtedly return.

"Lou went in search of some books for his little son. He picked up A.A. Milne's *When We Were Very Young* and *Now We Are Six*. The two of us laughed all the way home, swap-

ping the stories back and forth.

"Sunday, 16th April. Trees are popping buds, flowers are in bloom and fruit trees are all a-blossom. It is lovely and growing more so. The thing that forces itself on the observer here is the system of fences. They appear in all forms, sizes and lengths. Every little plot has its perimeter defined by some manner of pickets, lathes, wire, stone wall or shrubbery—anything to form a dividing line. A Westerner would feel he had been set down in somebody's idea of what a child's world should be like. The whole scene gives a rather cozy feeling.

"Saturday, 13th May. The London leave was perfect. The number of cabs and the crowds on the street impressed us at first. I've never seen as many cabs, even in Chicago. We never had any trouble getting one, and they were cheap until blackout time. Then the sky was the limit. A trip that cost about thirty cents in daylight ran about $1 after dark. We didn't have much trouble getting a hotel room and had excellent food in one of the officers' clubs. We bought some clothes down at the big PX and then went in search of liquor. We finally bought Booth's dry gin and some good scotch at $13 a fifth for the gin and $17 for the whiskey. So, for about $50 we managed to get stinking enough not to be interested in the stuff next day, and to go to *Something for the Boys* the following evening. It was a fair show, but the chorus saved the day. What seductive legs, and of course we were only three rows from the front.

"We traveled to Lou's field by train. Their cars are called coaches, and are about half the length of ours. Six people sit in a nice first class compartment. The seats are feather soft, with arm rests, and the upholstery is a delicate, flowery broadcloth sort of weave. The toilets are twice the size of American train closets and kept spick and span. Most of our travel back to home was in the top of a double-decker bus. We had box seats for the lovely panorama that is the English countryside. This island is beautiful."

Ira Eakin: "I've heard a lot of bad remarks about the English people, but don't believe it. They're great in my book. They really treated us well. They would come around those bases every weekend and invite so many GIs to their homes, and a lot of times they'd take you out there and fix you a good meal, and they were doing without themselves, we found out later." Paul Sink agreed: "The English made a lot of sacrifices for the Americans there in World War Two."

"Mrs Kirby's weekly food ration comprised four ounces of bacon; two ounces of butter plus four ounces of margarine or lard; two ounces of tea; eight ounces of sugar; one shilling and tuppence worth of meat, which amounted to about thirteen ounces or less depending on price; and a cheese ration which varied considerably during the war, but averaged around two or three ounces a week. In addition, she was entitled to one egg; one packet of dried eggs; eight ounces of jam; and twelve ounces of chocolate or sweets. Milk was 'controlled' at around two or two and a half pints per person per week. Potatoes, bread, and fresh vegetables were not rationed, but the latter were scarce and distributed on a controlled basis. Tinned and packet foods were on 'points.' Mrs Kirby was entitled to twenty points per four-week period. One packet of breakfast cereal, one tin of pilchards, half a pound of chocolate biscuits, one pound of rice, and one tin of grade three salmon added

up to twenty 'points' and so, would exhaust Mrs. Kirby's entitlement for a whole month. At twenty-four points for a one-pound tin, stewed steak was a luxury available only to housewives with several ration books at their disposal. For a nation of tea drinkers, the meagre ration of two ounces a week was probably the greatest hardship. Otherwise, the draconian rationing system equalized hunger, as it were; no one starved, and the health of the British people actually improved, which said much about the pre-war British diet, inequalities and deprivations of the unemployed and the poorly paid."
—from *Yesterday's Gone* by N.J. Crisp

The men of the Eighth Air Force were generous in sharing their rather more liberal rations with their English friends, including candy, chocolate, and cigarettes. Some of them came to the local farms and helped the farmer in his fields. And the Yanks used their more ample resources to give parties for the local villagers and especially for the children. At Christmas nearly every bomber and fighter group gave a party for the kids, with nearly all the airmen saving up their candy rations so each child would have something to take home.

In his book *Suffolk Summer*, American airman John Appleby wrote: "By British standards, we were pampered. Our food was much better than theirs. Our pockets bulged with candy and chewing gum, and we gave the impression of having more money than we knew what to do with."

Among the English, there were some who made known their opinion that Americans were relatively uncivilized, and were johnnies-come-lately in a war they ought to have been in from

the beginning. Had there been no more to their association than this, the Eighth and its English neighbors simply could not have gotten along at all. But there was much more. Beneath the superficial behavior the English perceived, the Yanks were impressed with them and felt a sense of "home-coming" in Britain where much of their own customs, language, laws, and literature had originated. And the English were, unquestionably, grateful for the American assistance and involvement in the war. Yes, some of the English continued to have strong reservations about the Americans, but in general, they came to regard them as "their own lads." As one young farm girl put it, "When the boys were returning from a raid, we never felt at ease until all of them had landed. We called those boys, 'our boys.' When the war was over, as quickly as they had come, they departed. They went shouting, singing and waving. We could hear them as they went along the road to the station . . . farther and farther away, then everywhere became silent. The Yanks had come—and now they were gone! One moment it was all noise, then dead silence, with everything deserted. We walked back home across the runway. There was no one in sight. It was just as if everyone had fallen asleep. We shall never forget the boys who had come so far from their homes in America, many of them never to return."

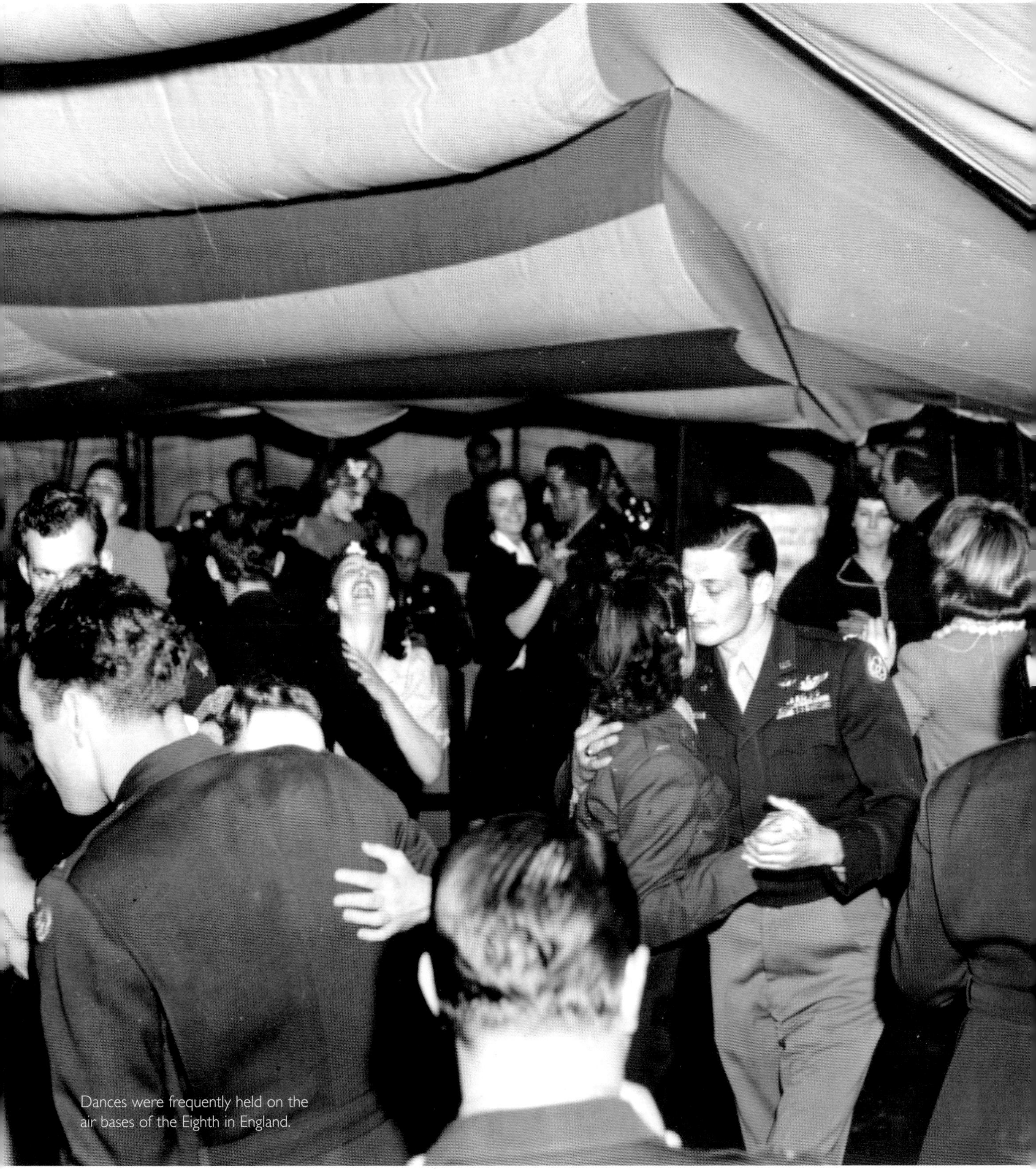

Dances were frequently held on the air bases of the Eighth in England.

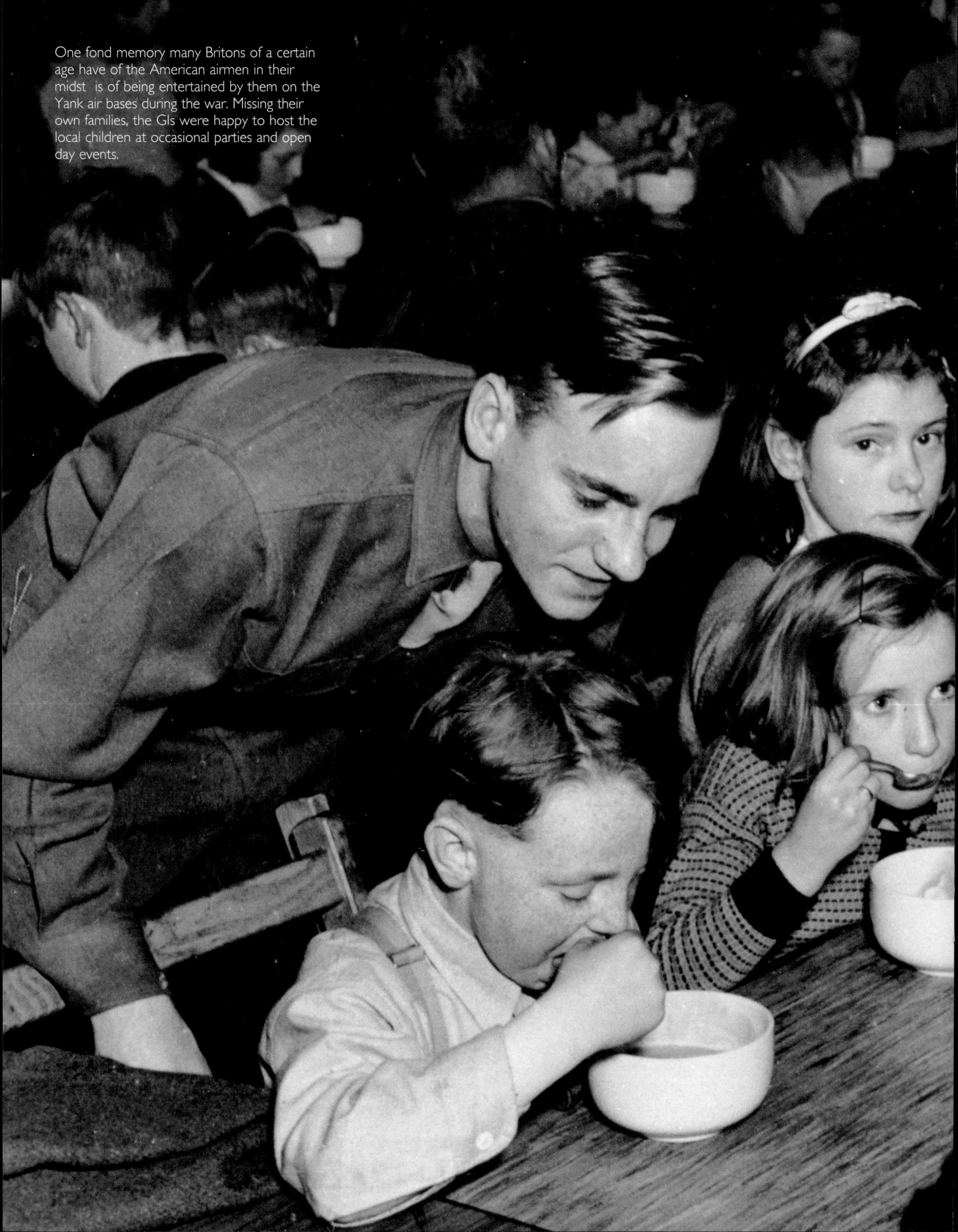

One fond memory many Britons of a certain age have of the American airmen in their midst is of being entertained by them on the Yank air bases during the war. Missing their own families, the GIs were happy to host the local children at occasional parties and open day events.

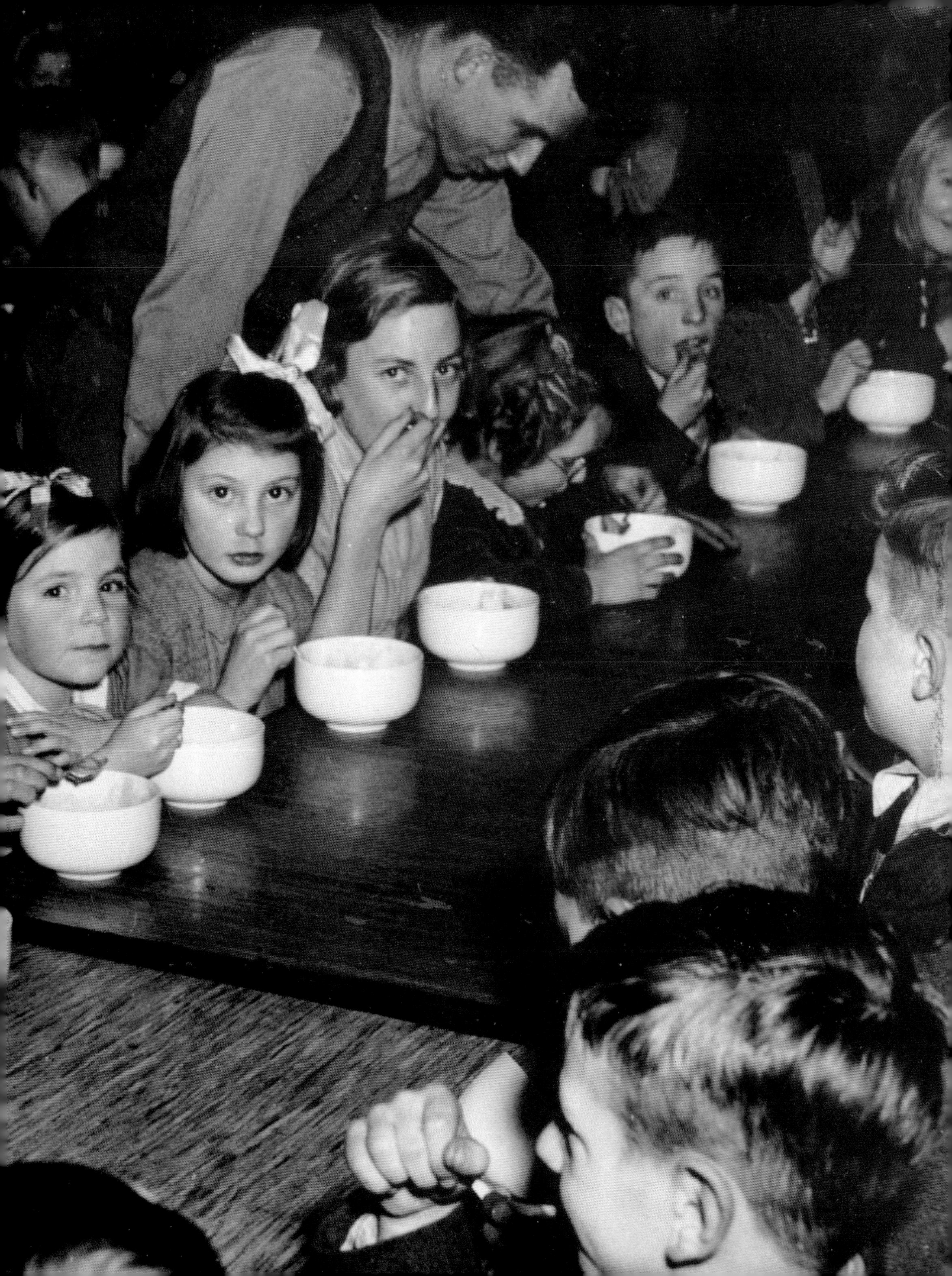

“Every gun in a B-17 was designed to give the group maximum defensive fire power. That’s what I mean by group integrity. When you pull a B-17 out of the formation the group loses the defensive power of ten guns. A crippled airplane has to be expendable; the one thing that is never expendable is your obligation to this group. This group, this group, that has to be your loyalty, your only reason for being.”

HOLLYWOOD GOES TO WAR

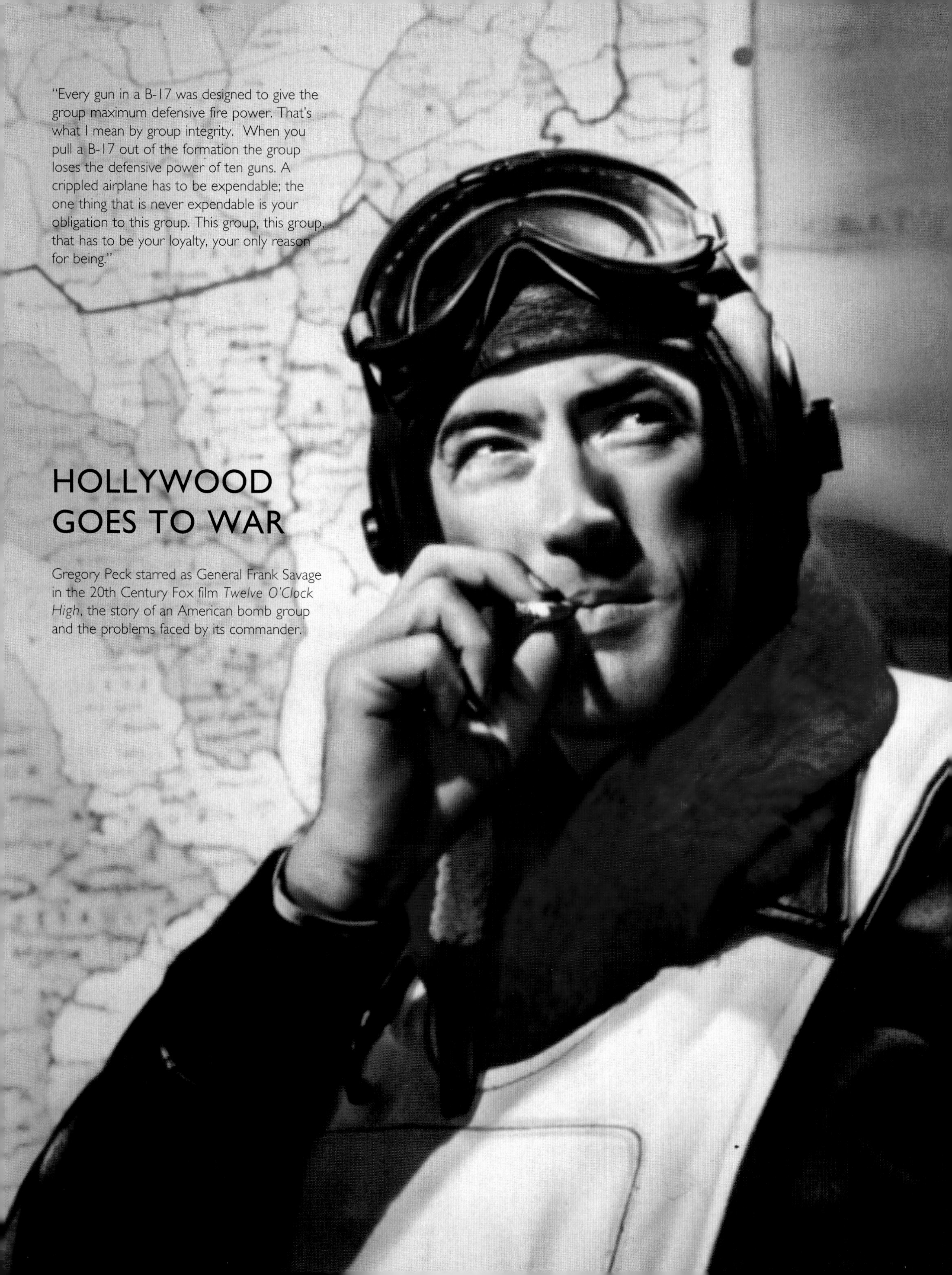

Gregory Peck starred as General Frank Savage in the 20th Century Fox film *Twelve O’Clock High*, the story of an American bomb group and the problems faced by its commander.

THE CELLULOID PULP THRILLERS of the 1930s, movies like *Flying Aces*, *Shadow of the Eagle*, *Fighting Devil Dogs*, *Tailspin Tommy*, *Hell Divers*, *Above the Clouds*, *West Point of the Air*, *Men with Wings*, and *Captains Courageous*, and others were the motion picture industry's effort to exploit the growing air-mindedness of American youth in the years just before the Second World War. Most war films—including most of the air war films—made up to and through WW2 were of the heavy-duty propaganda variety. It wasn't until 1949 and the production of perhaps the finest war film ever that the industry finally achieved a breakthrough.

In that year, a motion picture was made which has become one of the most highly acclaimed, widely respected and durable films of all time. *Twelve O'Clock High* is arguably among the very best motion pictures of any genre. It was based on the book of the same title by Beirne Lay Jr. and Sy Bartlett, both of whom had served with the American Eighth Air Force in England during the Second World War. While a work of fiction, most of the events depicted in the film actually happened. As Lay and Bartlett stated in the foreword of their book: "Although the characters and events in this novel are fictitious, the story closely follows the actual ordeal of the real-life men with whom the authors served in England. Many are living. Many are dead."

The film: In the fall of 1942, the Eighth Air Force, a neophyte American organization operating from a half dozen bases in southern England, was fighting in the skies over Europe. Undermanned and inadequately equipped, its very survival was being threatened by the poor performance of one of its bombardment groups. If the trouble in the 918th

were to spread to the other groups of the Eighth, the entire American air campaign against Nazi Germany could collapse. American film historian James Farmer wrote of *Twelve O'Clock High*: "The premise of the 1949 film from Twentieth Century Fox was historically accurate. The commander was real. The moving portrayal of the emotional climate and the all too-human resolve of one individual was authentic, economic, and delivered with rare insight. Well received in its day and having passed the uncompromising test of time, all the requisites are present for the recognition of *Twelve O'Clock High* as a true American film classic. The film's human message of man's psychological limits remains as valid today as when it was first screened—more than five decades ago."

The plot: In the summer of 1948, Harvey Stovall, a lawyer from Columbus, Ohio, found himself aboard a train bound for the village of Archbury in the English Midlands. On the seat beside him was a box tied with stout cord. In it was a Toby jug, a beer mug depicting a robber with a black mask over his eyes and a green Robin Hood hat. Stovall had noticed the Toby in the window of an antique shop in London's Burlington Arcade and had purchased it for fourteen shillings. At Archbury he walked to the Black Swan pub where he borrowed a bicycle from the bartender. Resting his package in the basket on the handlebars, he pedalled out of the village on a country road bordered with hedgerows and thatched-roof houses, the low, puffy white clouds parting to let the sun thaw the crisp, cold air. A breeze came up and dried his forehead as he pumped the bicycle over the occasional low hill. Finally, he turned off on a country lane and rest-

ed the bike against a low fence. He bent to climb through the fence and walked slowly through the tall grass out onto an enormous, flat unobstructed field.

Presently he stopped and stood at the head of a wide, dilapadated avenue of concrete, stretching in front of him with gentle undulations for more than a mile. A small herd of cows was nibbling at the grass which had grown up through the cracks between the concrete squares. He remembered it looking quite differently. He noted the black streaks left by the tires, where they had struck the surface, smoking, and nearby, through the weeds which nearly covered it, he could see the remaining stains left by puddles of grease and black oil on one of the hardstands evenly spaced around the five-mile perimeter track, like teeth on a ring gear. And in the background he could make out a forlorn olive green control tower, nearby a tattered tan windsock and behind that a pair of empty hangars, a shoe box of a water tower mounted high on stilts, and a cluster of squat, ugly Nissen huts.

There was no one, not a soul, save the cows, and no sound at all to interrupt the great quiet. In that strange moment Stovall was no longer in a blue suit, but now in an olive drab uniform with the leaves of a major on his shoulders, the adjutant of a heavy bomb group.

The sounds of aircraft engines starting filled his ears and a wind began bending back the tall weeds behind the hardstand near where he was standing. A few quick tears blurred his eyes. Through the blur he saw and felt the ghostly presence of a B-17 bomber on each empty hardstand, with its whirling propellers throwing back a powerful slipstream, its tires bulging and sagging under the weight of the tons of bombs and gas required for a raid deep into Germany.

At the living site he entered what had been the quarters of the group commander, a privileged accommodation with its own bathroom, sitting room and fireplace, now cold and rusted. In the office of the adjutant, he thought he recognized the middle-aged ghost of himself there on that deserted air base.

The moment passed and Harvey Stovall walked back to where he had left the bicycle. Confused, distracted, he then came to the realization that here on this base, America might have lost the war . . . how close it had come, with the events here at Archbury to destroying what was to become the most powerful air combat force in history, which, in the view of its opponent, was the decisive factor in the German defeat.

Back on the bike, Stovall pedalled down the runway, turned off at the far end onto a concrete lane toward an oversized Nissen hut he knew to have been the officers' club. Here he thought he saw ghosts of airmen who had sought a haven from the harsh reality of their day jobs, a place in

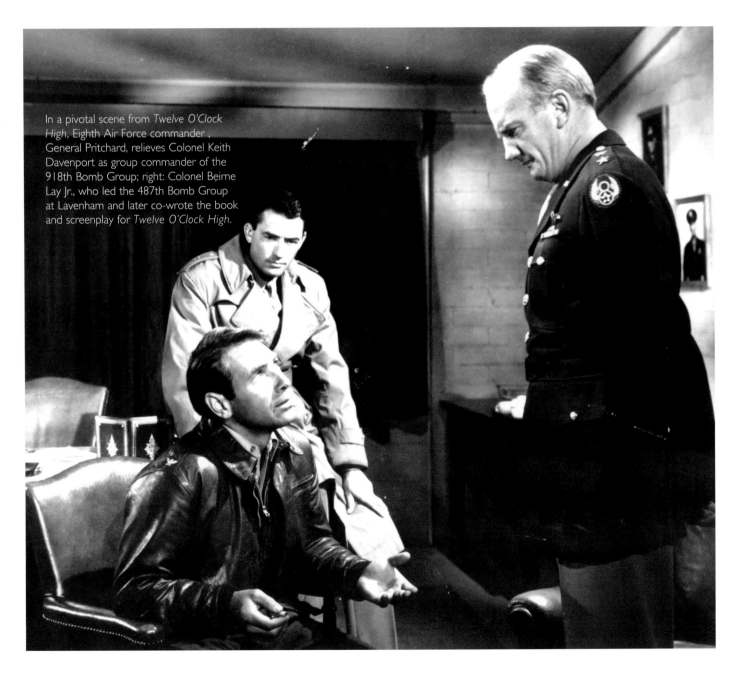

In a pivotal scene from *Twelve O'Clock High*, Eighth Air Force commander , General Pritchard, relieves Colonel Keith Davenport as group commander of the 918th Bomb Group; right: Colonel Beirne Lay Jr., who led the 487th Bomb Group at Lavenham and later co-wrote the book and screenplay for *Twelve O'Clock High*.

which to relax with a drink, play cards, listen to the radio, and write letters. Then he noticed the mantelpiece.

Returning to the bicycle, he took the box from the basket, untied the cord, and removed the brightly decorated Toby jug. He reentered the club and walked straight to the mantel where, using his handkerchief, he cleaned the dust from a place on the center and placed the Toby reverentially with the masked robber facing into the room. Stovall turned and walked rapidly to the door. He paused for one last look at the jug that leered back at him. Closing the door he got back on the bike and slowly rode away.

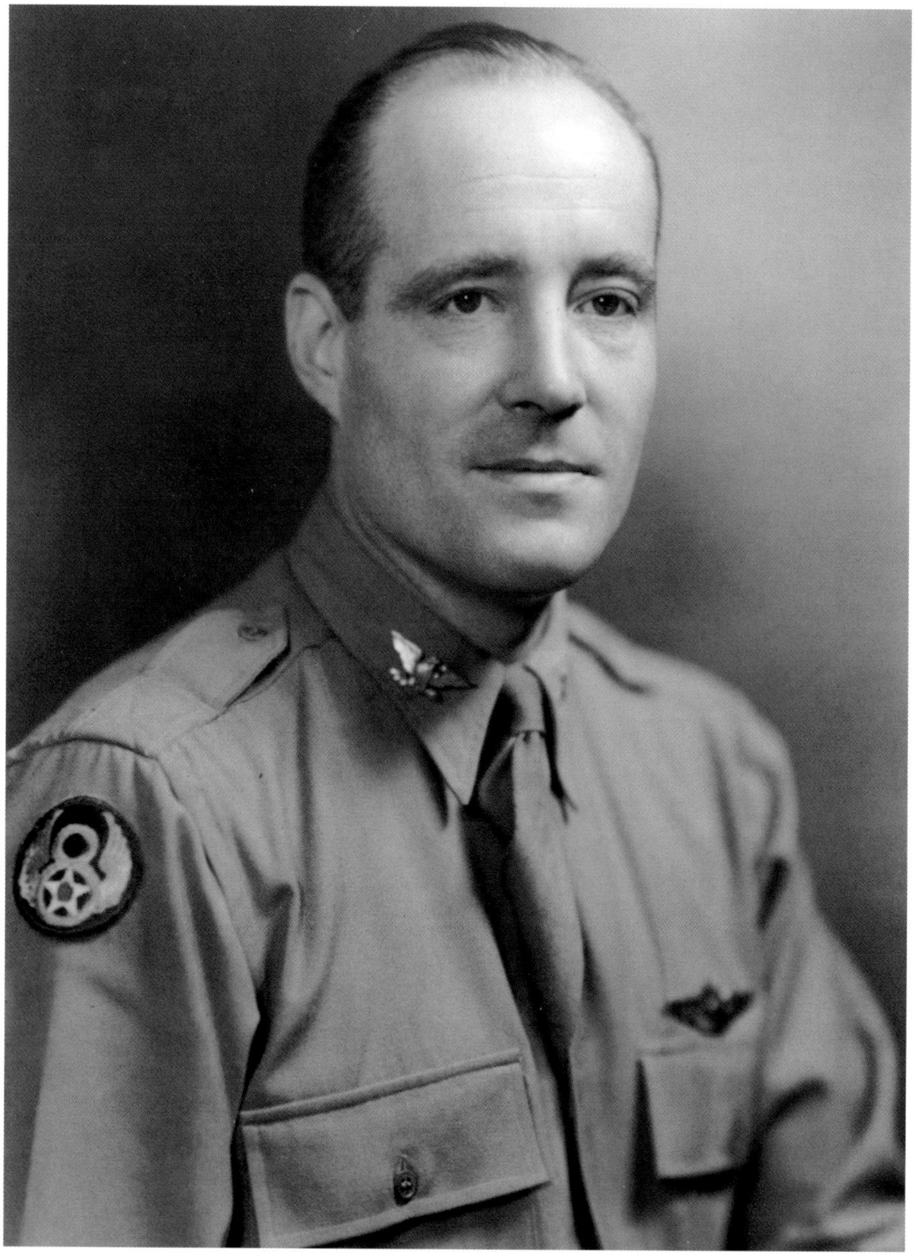

Screenwriter and author Beirne Lay Jr. and writer / producer Sy Bartlett had both been serving officers in the U.S. Eighth Army Air Force during the Second World War. Colonel Lay was one of the original members of General Ira Eaker's cadre, sent to England early in 1942 to help establish the new Eighth Air Force there. Lay was a B-24 bomber pilot and had been a commander of the 487th Bomb Group, based at Lavenham in Suffolk. He had led the group on a number of missions in attacks on German targets in occupied Europe. He was shot down over France and had spent three months evading capture with the assistance of the French Underground. He later served as Chief of the Eighth Air Force Film Unit, supervising production of William Wyler's *The Memphis Belle*. In addition to his collaboration with Bartlett on the book and screenplay for *Twelve O'Clock High*, he wrote the book and screenplay for the William Holden film *I Wanted Wings*, as well as the screenplays for *The Young and the Brave, The Gallant Hours, Toward the Unknown, Strategic Air Command,* and *Above and Beyond*. Lieutenant Colonel Sy Bartlett was Aide-de-Camp to General Carl Spaatz, and was among the first American Army Air Force officers in the European Theatre of Operations. He served on the Operations Staff of Eighth Bomber Command and participated in many combat missions with both the American and British air forces. Towards the end of the war in the Pacific he was a member of a B-29 crew commanded by General Frank A. Armstrong, flying several bombing missions over Japan. After the war, Lay and Bartlett combined to write the novel *Twelve O'Clock High*, largely based on the experiences of General Armstrong in the air war against Nazi Germany.

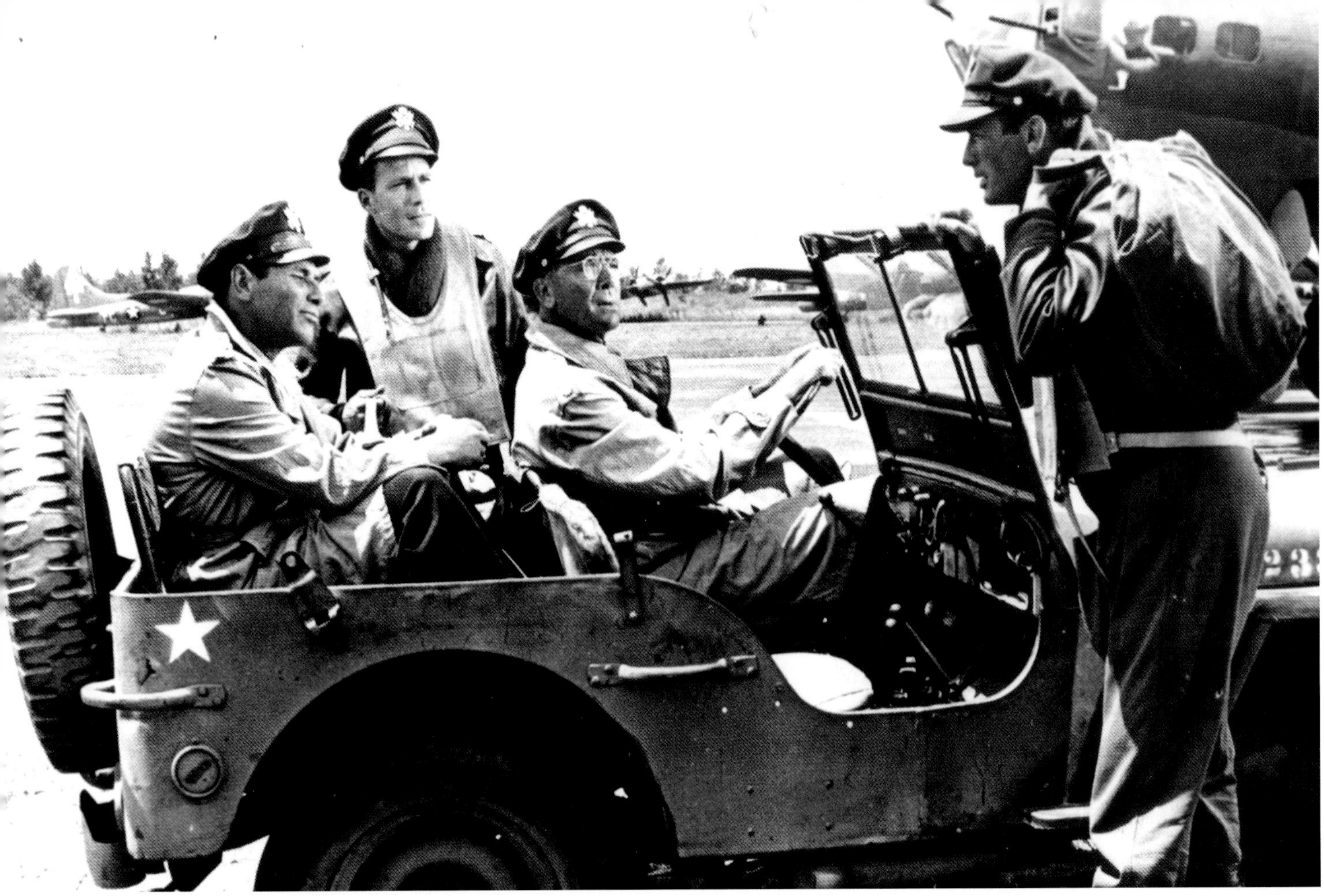

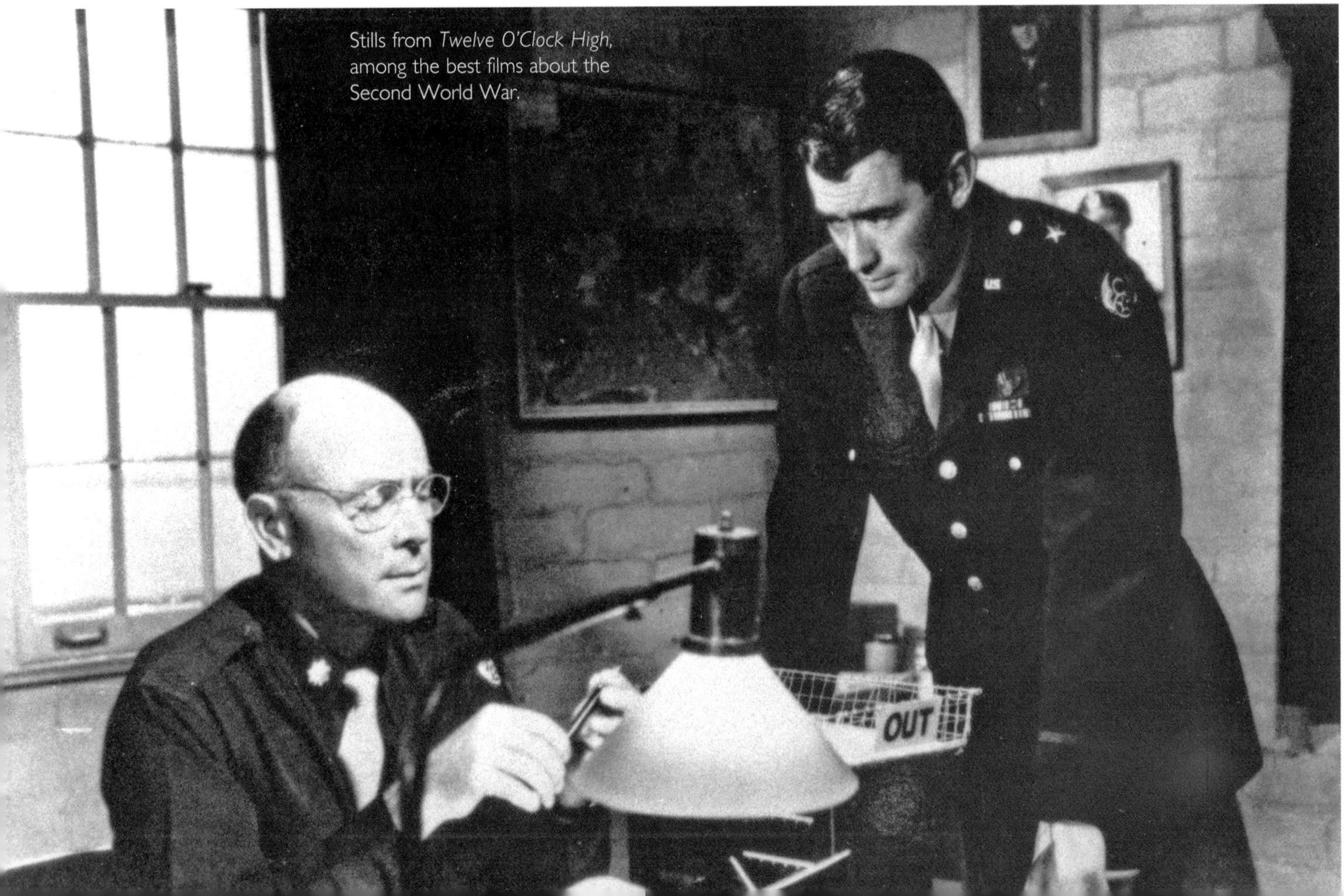
OUT

Stills from *Twelve O'Clock High*, among the best films about the Second World War.

Drawing on the fresh memories of their own experiences in the Eighth Air Force of World War Two, they wanted to pay tribute to the men, their friends, and to one combat commander in particuler, Brigadier General Frederick W. Castle, Medal of Honor recipient, who was killed on 24th December 1944 while leading the largest attacking force of aircraft ever assembled. It was his thirtieth mission.

The character of General Frank Savage in *Twelve O'Clock High* was inspired by actual events in the life of General Frank Armstrong who did, in fact, take over command of the 306th Bomb Group at Thurleigh, near Bedford, in January 1943, at a point when the morale and performance of that group had reached rock bottom. The leaders of the fledgling Eighth Bomber Command realized that, should the problems of the 306th spread to the other U.S. bomb groups in England, the American daylight bombing campaign would be finished before it had even begun. The character of Colonel Keith Davenport was based on Colonel Charles B. Overacker Jr., who was replaced by Armstrong.

According to Beirne Lay: "There wouldn't have been any book and no screenplay except for Sy Bartlett. He put me on the rack, forced me to write it. Right after the war I said that we didn't have a chance with a book about the war. But he was bound and determined that he was going to get this thing done." In 1946, Bartlett was working as a screenwriter at Twentieth Century Fox Studios during the day while working nights with Lay on the book. When serving in England during the war he had developed a great friendship with then-Colonel Frank Armstrong who, as group commander of the 97th Bomb Group, had led the first Eighth

Air Force mission of the war, to the Rouen-Sotteville marshalling yards in France. Early in 1943, Armstrong was sent to take over and shape up the 306th Bomb Group at Thurleigh. Less than a month later he led the newly-rejuvenated 306th, and the other four heavy bomb groups of the Eighth, in the first American raid on a target in Germany—Wilhelmshaven. Sy Bartlett was so impressed by Armstrong's achievements that he felt the story had to be written in novel form. As the book neared completion, the Fox producer and life-long aviation enthusiast Louis D. "Bud" Lighton read it and was excited about the possibility of bringing it to the screen. At Lighton's request, Fox head Darryl Zanuck purchased the film rights and signed Lay and Bartlett to do the screenplay. Lay: "You would have thought it would be a breeze to write the screenplay when you had written the book—not so. Bud Lighton, every inch of the way, made us justify and rejustify everything that went into it. He made us refine our central idea. Here, Bartlett and I had written a whole novel, and we never adequately answered that question. He insisted that we establish this in a paragraph, or preferably in a line, or even four words. Well, Sy and I took nearly two weeks. We did get it down to four words—*the disintegration of Savage*. Lighton then insisted that he didn't want one inch of film that did not contribute to telling that central idea. The key word was disintegration. The story was to tell of the forces that could tear a strong man apart. Savage was to be a very humane, warm-hearted civil kind of guy, saddled with the dirty, bloody job of sending nice young kids out to get killed. It was to be the tension between these two forces that would tear him apart."

One of the most important reasons for the critical acclaim the motion picture received is the outstanding cast whose rivetting performances appreciably raised the standard of the war film genre. Darryl Zanuck hand-picked the principals: a youthful Gregory Peck for the lead role of General Frank Savage; veteran film and stage actor Dean Jagger, who agreed (with some misgivings) to take on the role of Major Harvey Stovall, the group's Ground Executive Officer; Gary Merrill, who got the part of Colonel Keith Davenport, the likeable Commanding Officer that Savage would replace; and Hugh Marlowe, who took the part of Savage's whipping boy, the Air Executive Officer demoted to command pilot of the B-17 *Leper Colony*—all of them contributed immensely to the power of the film.

Henry King directed *Twelve O'Clock High*. The U.S. Air Force had offered both complete co-operation and the use of Eglin Air Force Base in Florida to the filmmakers. But when King, an experienced private pilot, and his cinematographer, Academy Award-winning Leon Shamroy, went looking for a location where they could shoot the opening scenes of the film, they were faced with the undeniable fact that Florida and the American south do not look much like England. Still, King spent several long days flying out of Eglin in his Beech Bonanza with Shamroy, location manager John Adams and technical advisor John H. DeRussy, scouting possible sites. They were looking for an abandoned former wartime airfield with at least one macadam runway that was overgrown with grass. King: "When I was searching for a suitable location for an abandoned air base that had grown up in weeds, I was flying across Alabama and saw the Ozark air base. It seemed

When asked by Fox studios producer Bud Lighton to establish the central idea of the screenplay for *Twelve O'Clock High*, co-authors Beirne Lay and Sy Bartlett thought about it for two weeks and finally boiled it down to four words—*the disintegration of Savage.* As the film nears its conclusion, Frank Savage finds himself a victim of the same psychological trauma that toppled his predecessor.

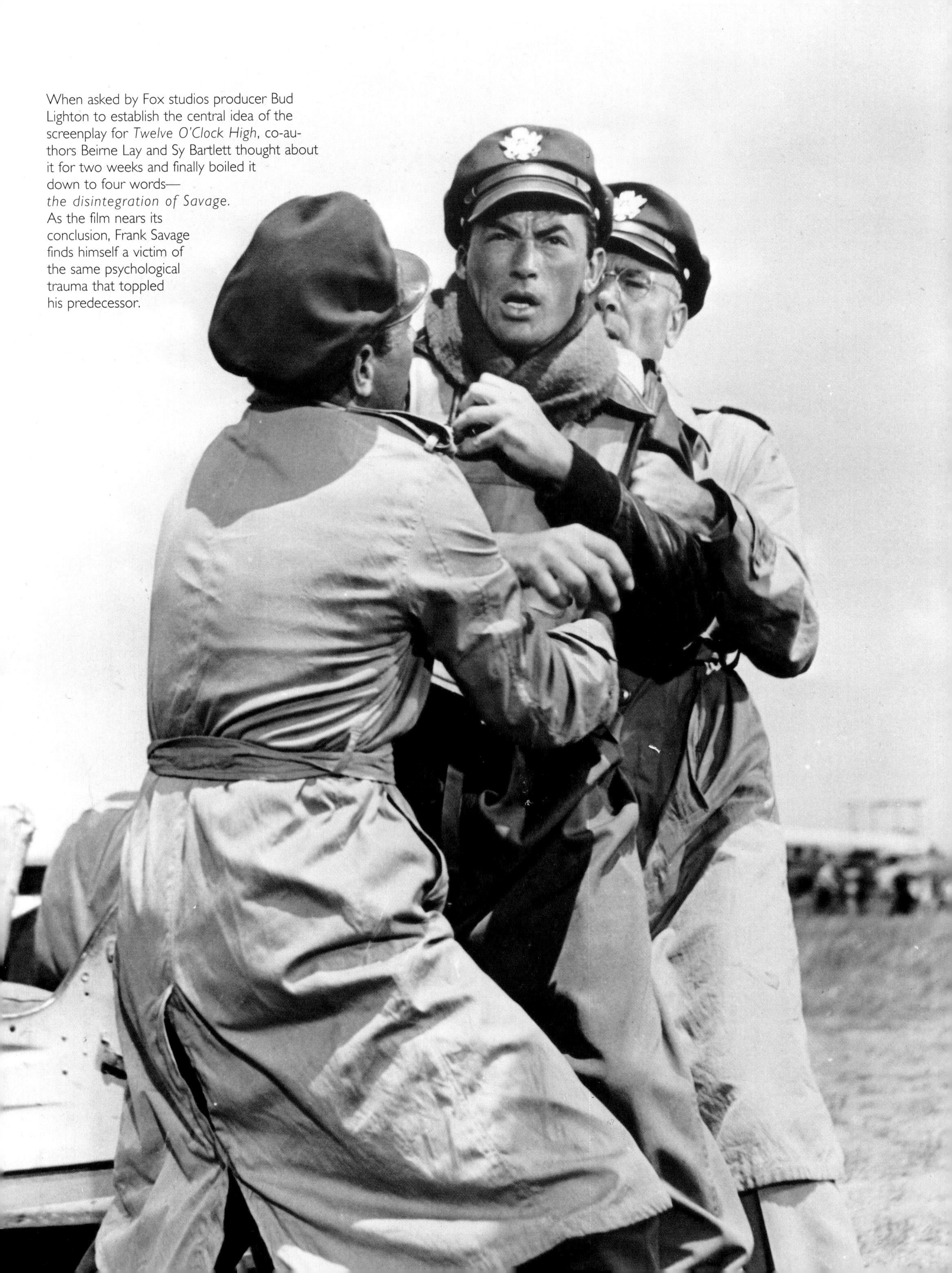

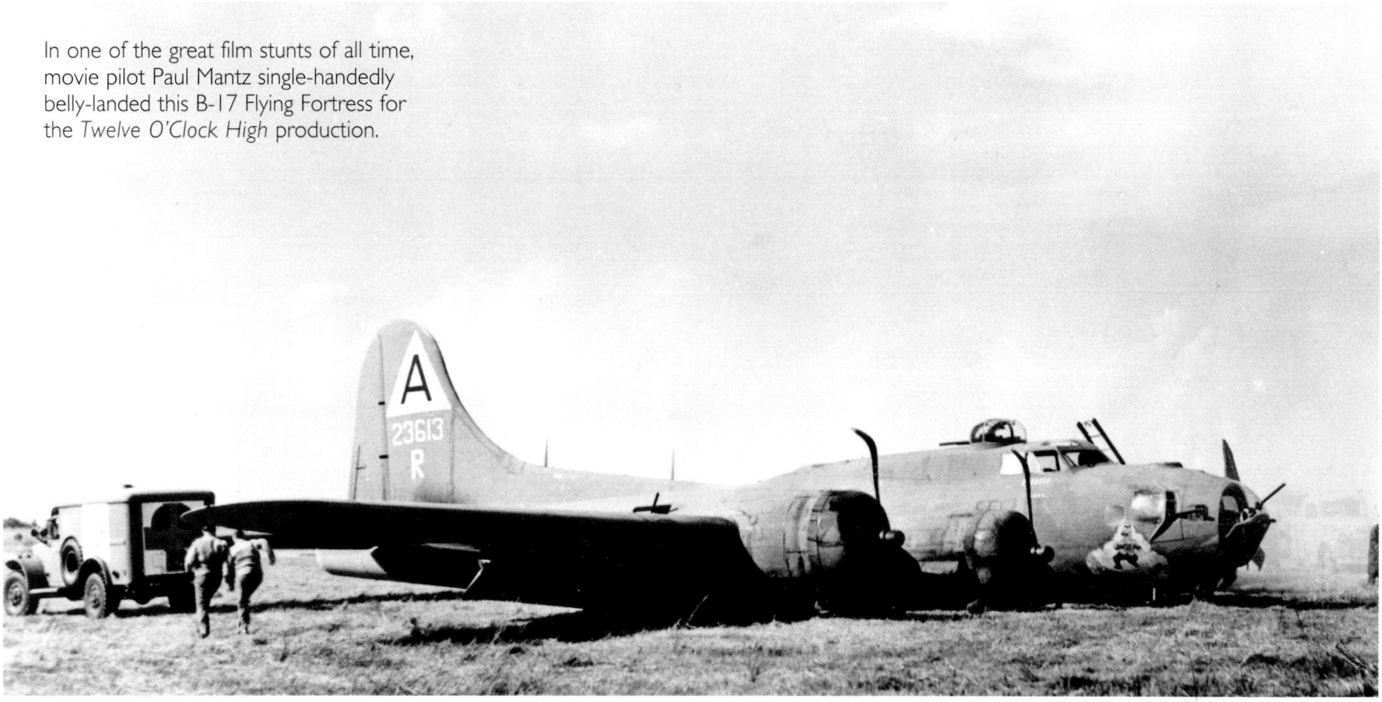
A
23613
R

In one of the great film stunts of all time, movie pilot Paul Mantz single-handedly belly-landed this B-17 Flying Fortress for the *Twelve O'Clock High* production.

deserted and was closed. I landed there and, after looking around, decided it was exactly what I needed. The grass and weeds around the runway were several feet tall. I took off and went back to Eglin to get permission to use this deserted base, only to learn that it was not an Air Force base at all, but an Army base. Had I remained on the ground at Ozark another ten minutes, I would have been placed under arrest for landing on a closed field without permision. The public relations department at Fox, however, straightened this matter out and secured permission for us to use Ozark."

The Air Force loaned Fox twelve B-17s complete with crews for the filming. Many of the planes had come from the 3205th Drone Group at Eglin, aircraft destined to be destroyed in ground-to-air missile experimentation of the time. Some of them had taken part in the early postwar atomic bomb tests at Bikini Atoll in the Pacific and still carried low levels of radiation.

Hollywood stunt pilot and aviation entrepreneur Paul Mantz played a controversial part in the making of the film. Technical advisor DeRussy: "Upon hearing that the Air Force intended to provide B-17s for the film, Mantz wired USAF Headquarters threatening legal action because he had the capability of supplying aircraft and crews to Twentieth Century Fox. Indeed, the Air Force did consider withdrawing their support until the studio received a quote of cost from Mantz. Based on this estimate, they informed the Air Force that it would be monitarily impossible to complete the film without the Air Force aircraft and crews. The Air Force decided to provide their support. They did, however, rule out the use of any USAF or USAF Reserve pilot in the filming of the famous belly-landing scene near the beginning of the picture. Mantz ultimately got that job."

Colonel John DeRussy had been Operations Officer of the Eighth Air Force's 305th Bomb Group in England during the war. Probably no one knew the details of the daily routine on the bases of the Eighth better than him. He was the perfect choice to be the technical advisor on the film.

Motion picture historian James Farmer: "The film was an immediate success with American critics and audiences. Bosley Crowther observed: 'The saga of our Air Forces and their accomplishments in the recent war already has inspired a number of pictures . . . but there hasn't been one from Hollywood which could compare in rugged realism and punch to *Twelve O'Clock High*.' Based for the most part on hard historical facts and given special life and credibility by two talented writers who had 'been there,' the film was nominated for four Academy Awards in January 1950.

The nominations included Best Picture of 1949, Gregory Peck for Best Actor, Dean Jagger for Best Male Supporting Actor, and Thomas Moulton for Best Sound Recording. Many at the time felt that a fifth nomination should have gone to director Henry King and a sixth to Lay and Bartlett for their writing."

Beirne Lay did not see the film again for many years. When he did he commented: "I thought it stood up well. Bud Lighton used to say 'there is one adjective every filmmaker hopes and prays might be associated with his film and that is 'unforgettable.' 'There are not many motion pictures that come in this category, but if there is even one scene in this picture that's unforgettable, then we haven't wasted our time. If we strike one

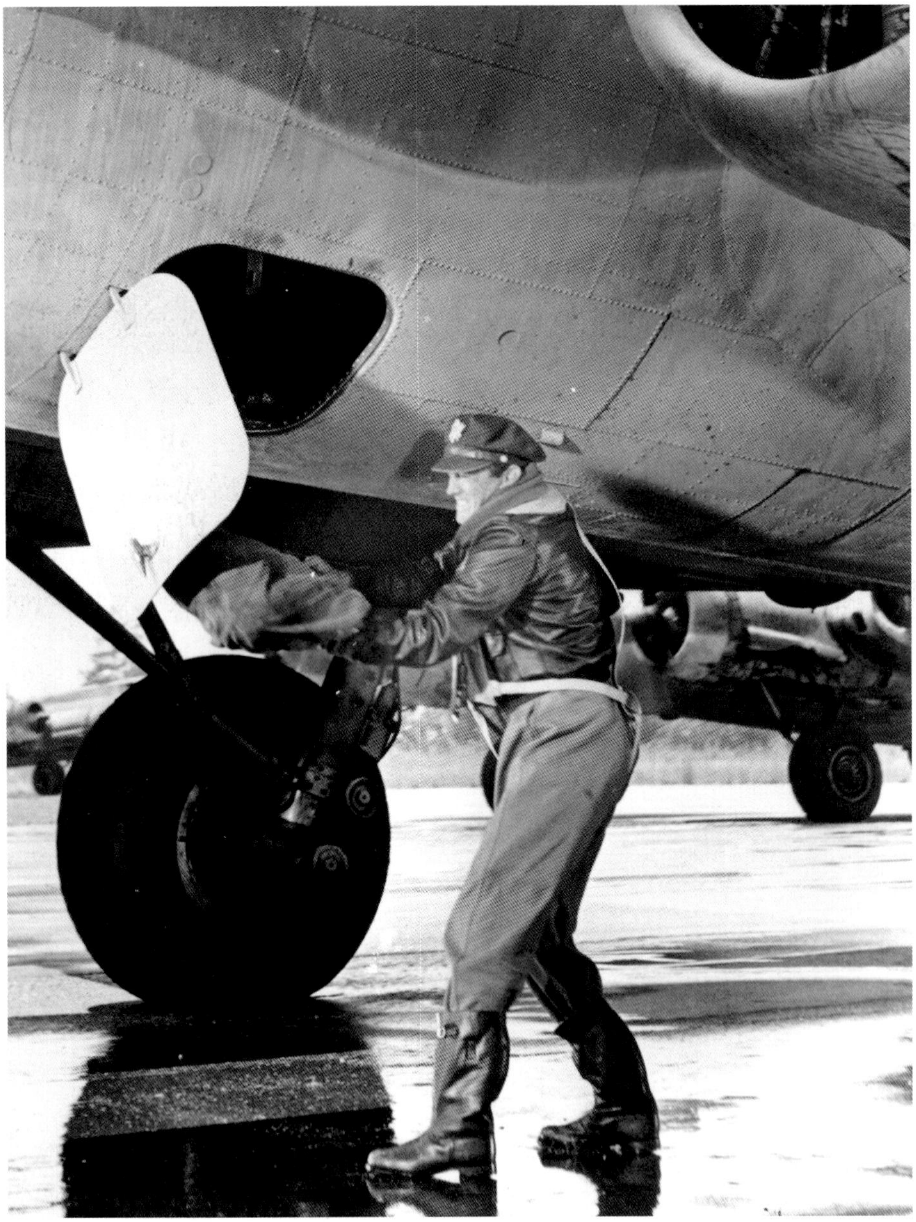

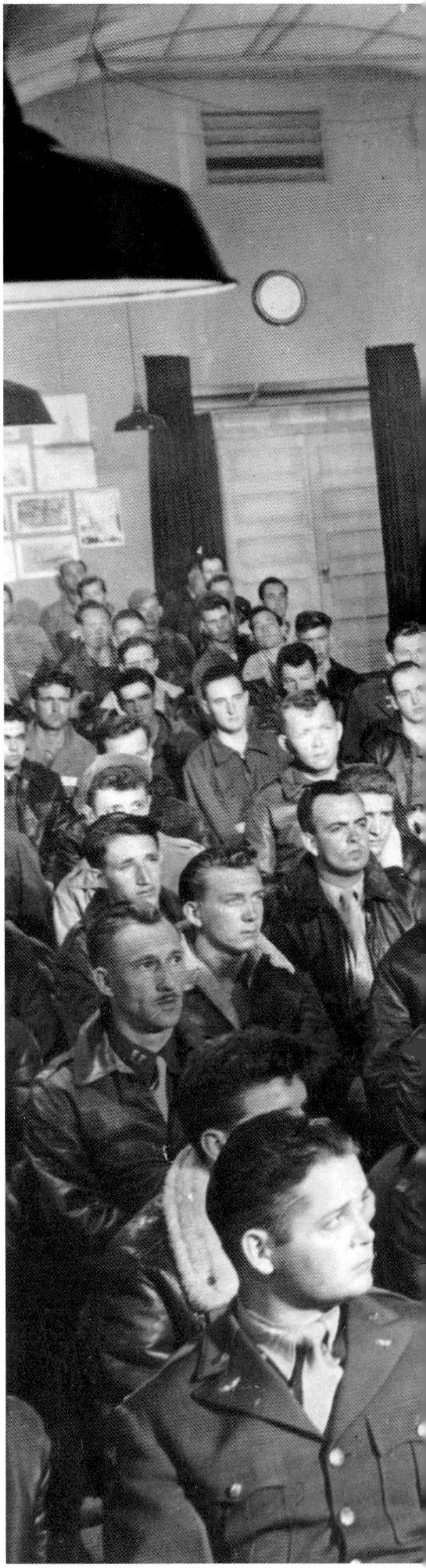

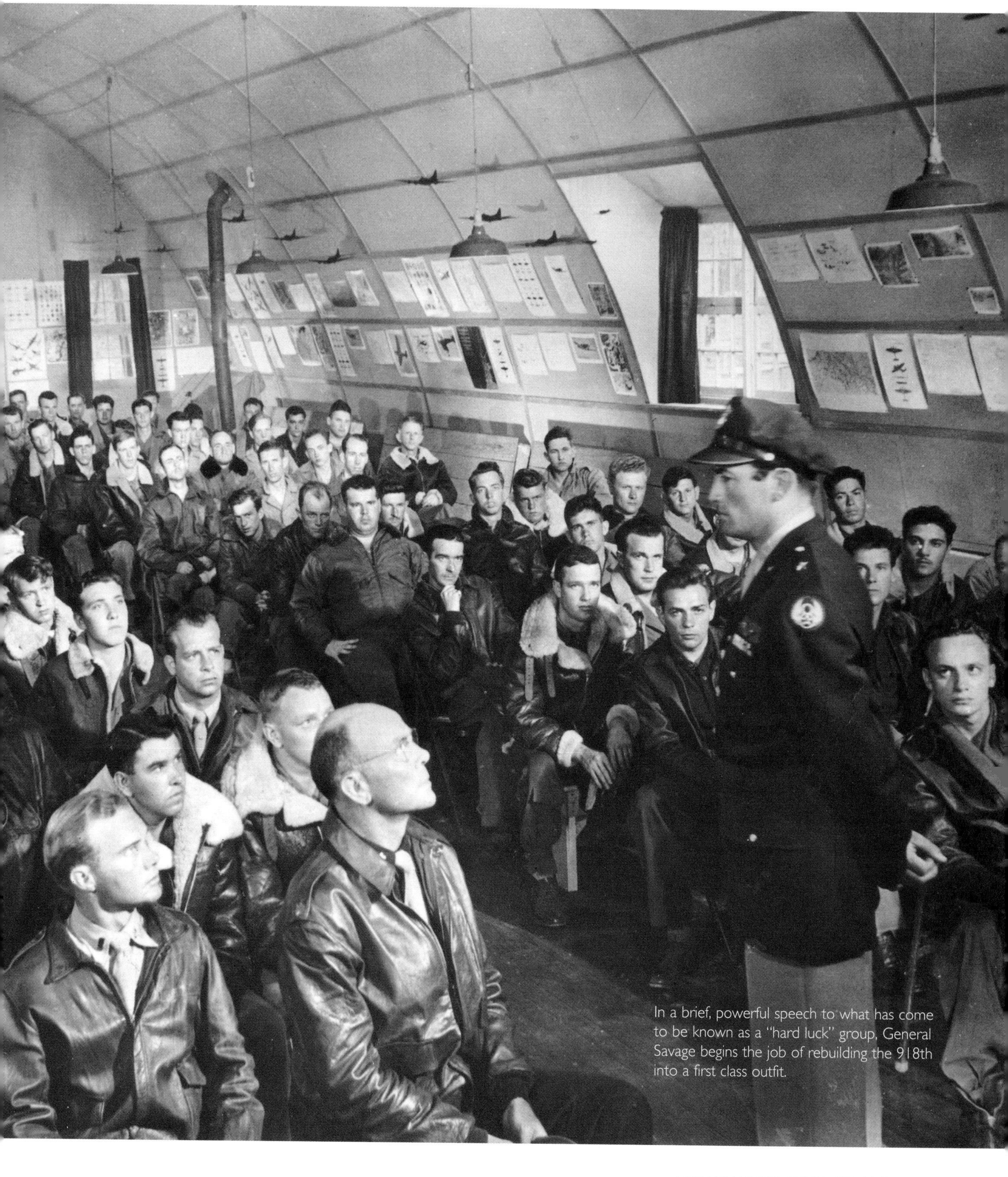

In a brief, powerful speech to what has come to be known as a "hard luck" group, General Savage begins the job of rebuilding the 918th into a first class outfit.

false note anywhere in the screenplay, all our work is down the drain because audiences aren't stupid and you've lost them!' I thought, when I saw it again, that it retained your confidence from beginning to end." Gregory Peck observed: "It is gratifying to be part of a film that is still being shown more than twenty-five years after we made it. I think the picture still has meaning for audiences because of its integrity. We managed to dramatize a true story without resorting to false theatrics and sentimentality." Other evidence of the film's amazing durability and appeal is its continuing use by such diverse organizations as the United States Air Force and the U.S. Navy, business corporations and self-improvement companies in their leadership training efforts—that, and the enduring popularity of the film among the general public more than half a century after its release.

From the screenplay shooting script of *Twelve O'Clock High*:

Briefing room. The room is packed with combat men, buzzing with conversation. Doc Kaiser and Chaplain Twombley sit with the Adjutant, Major Stovall, near the rear door. It is within seconds of eight o'clock. General Savage enters the rear door.

Stovall: "Ten-SHUN!"

The men rise indifferently and raggedly to their feet, as Savage, looking alert and fresh, strides down the center aisle in the long walk to the platform. He ignores the steps, leaping intead, to the platform. He faces the crews.

Savage: "There will be a briefing for a practice mission at eleven hundred this morning." (there is a quiet hum) "Yes, practice." (he looks straight at them) "I've been sent down here to take over what has come to be known as a hard-luck group. I don't believe in hard luck. So, we're going to find out what the trouble is. Maybe part of it is your flying, so we're going back to fundamentals. (his eyes sweep the room)

"But I can tell you now one reason I think you're having hard luck. I saw it in your faces last night. I can see it there now . . . You've been looking at a lot of air lateley and you think you ought to have a rest. In short, you're sorry for yourselves. (he lets that hang there for a minute)

"I haven't much patience with this what-are-we-fighting-for stuff. We're in a war—a shooting war. We've got to fight, and some of us have got to die. I'm not trying to tell you not to be afraid. Fear is normal. But stop worrying about it and about yourselves. Stop making plans, forget about going home. Consider yourselves already dead. Once you accept that idea it won't be so tough. If any man here can't buy that, if he rates himself as something special, with a special kind of hide to be saved, then he'd better make up his mind about it right now. Because I don't want him in this group. I'll be in my office in five minutes. He can see me there."

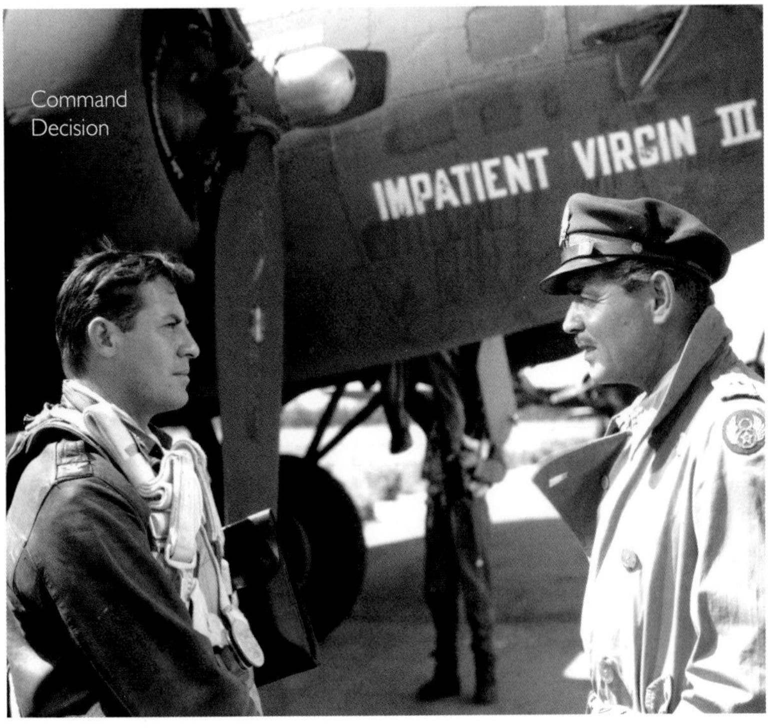
IMPATIENT VIRGIN III

Command Decision

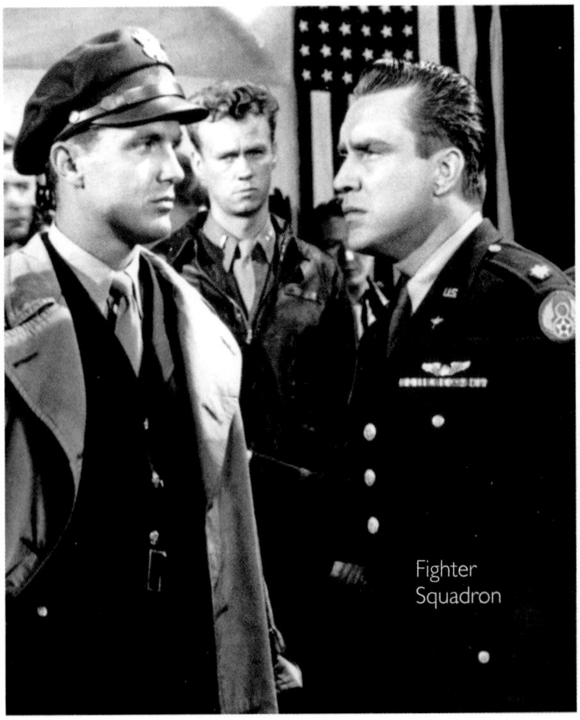

Fighter Squadron

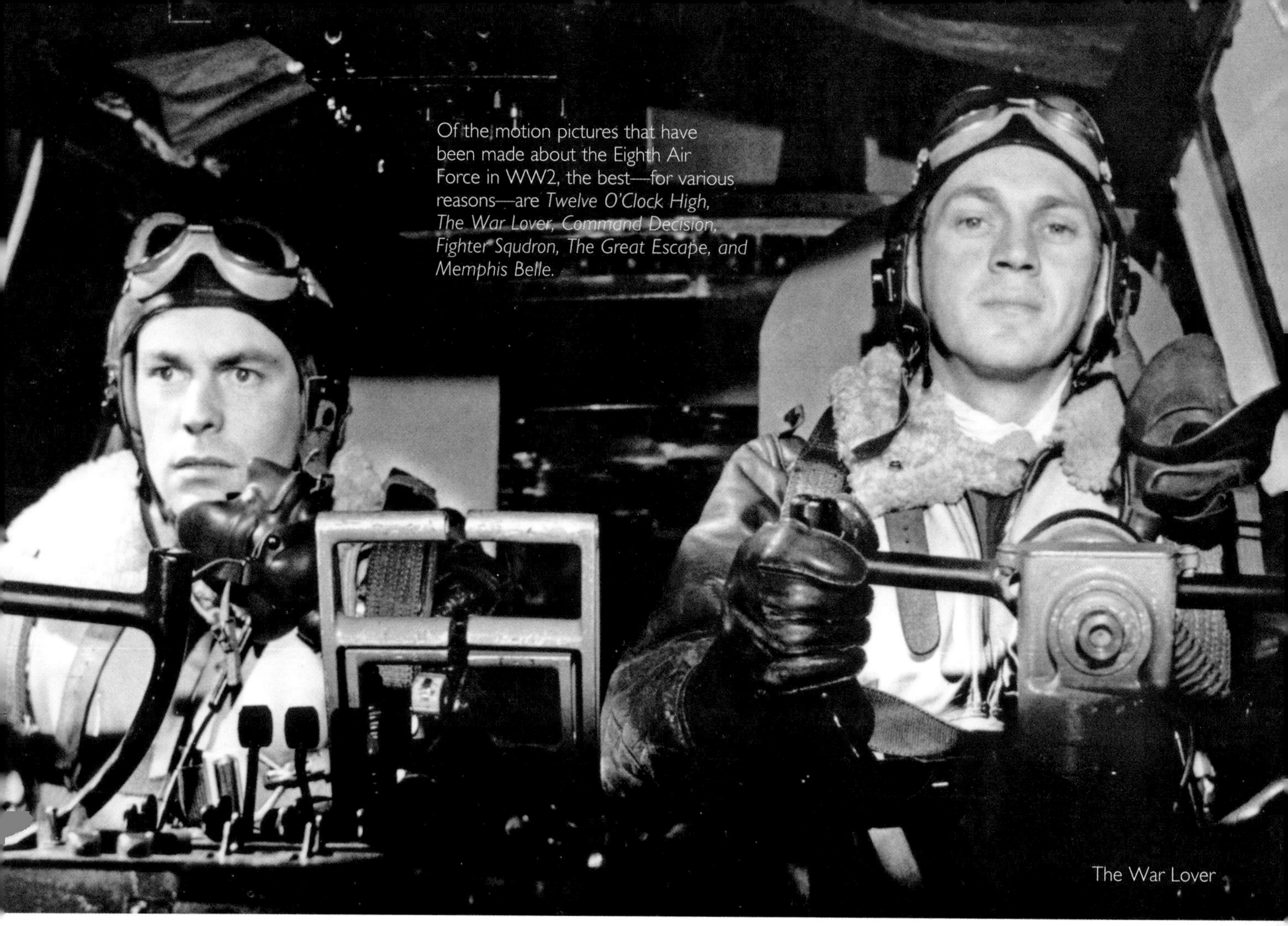

Of the motion pictures that have been made about the Eighth Air Force in WW2, the best—for various reasons—are *Twelve O'Clock High, The War Lover, Command Decision, Fighter Squdron, The Great Escape,* and *Memphis Belle.*

The War Lover

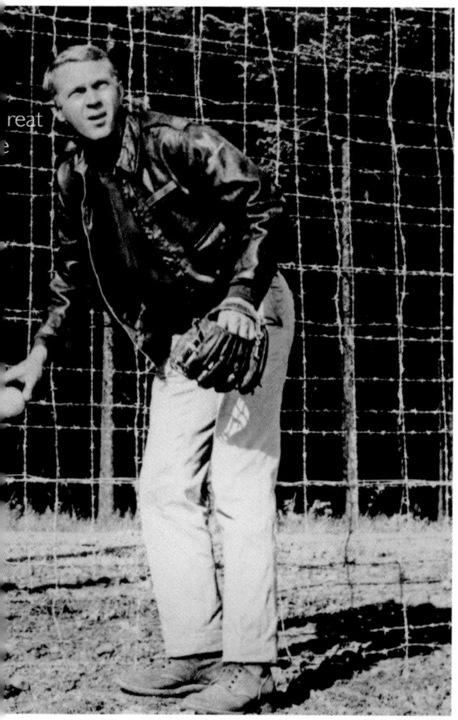

reat
e

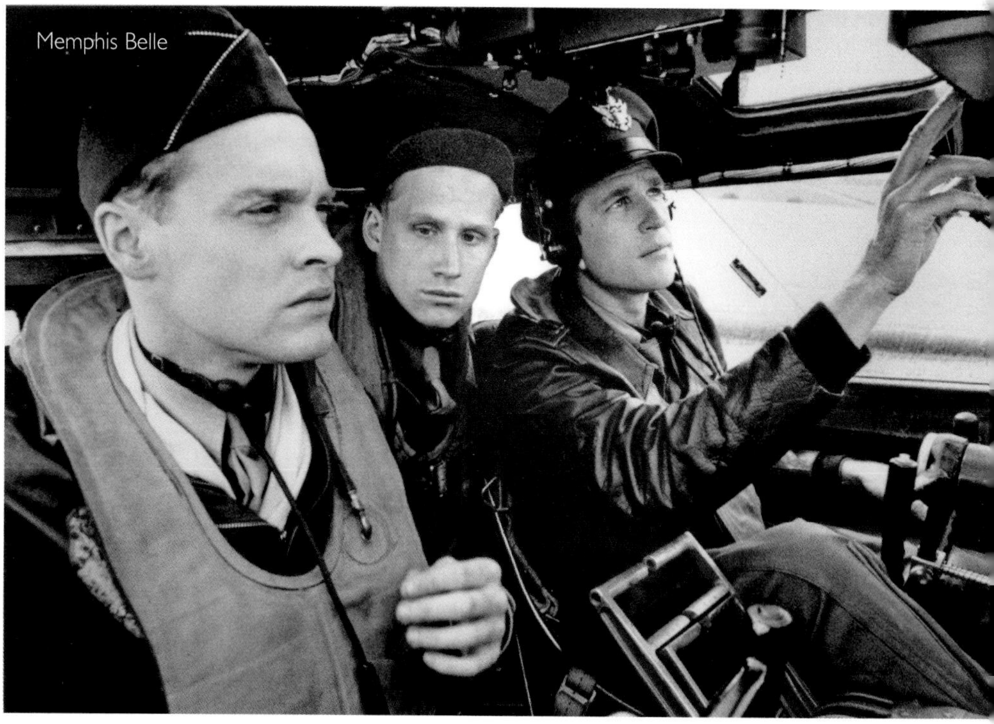

Memphis Belle

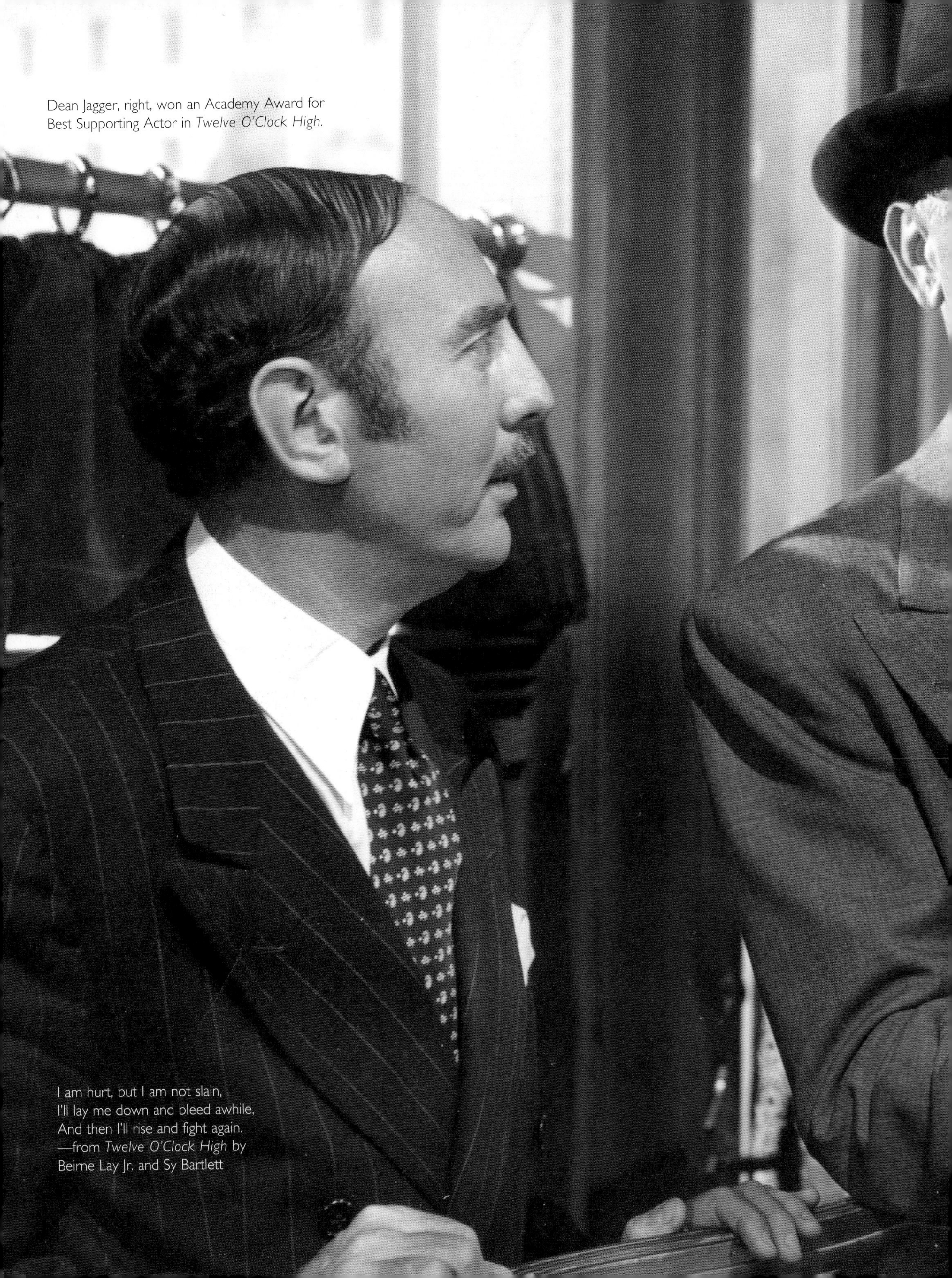

Dean Jagger, right, won an Academy Award for Best Supporting Actor in *Twelve O'Clock High*.

I am hurt, but I am not slain,
I'll lay me down and bleed awhile,
And then I'll rise and fight again.
—from *Twelve O'Clock High* by
Beime Lay Jr. and Sy Bartlett

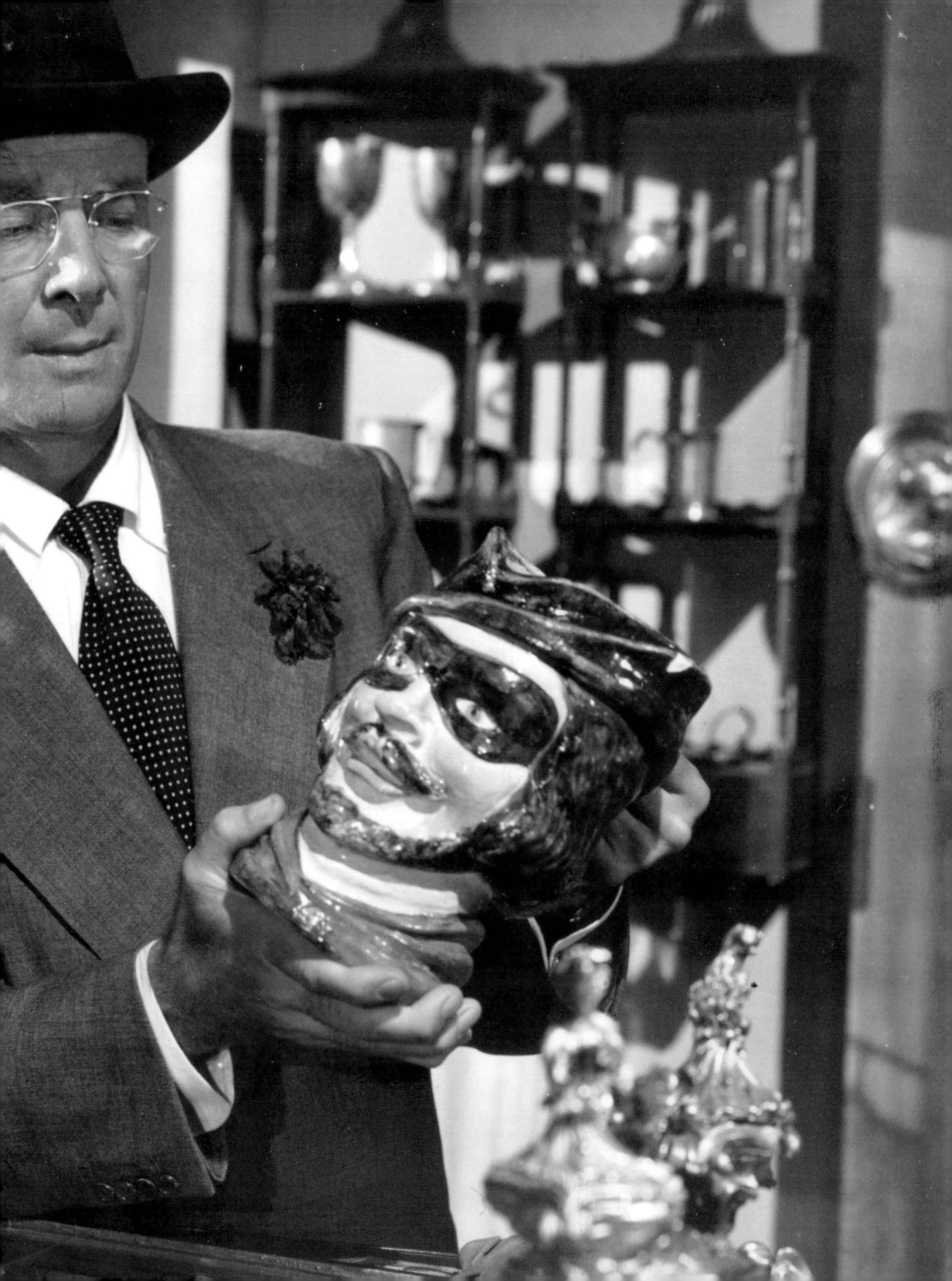

ELMER'S WAR

ELMER BENDINER flew as navigator of the B-17 *Tondelayo* with the 379th Bomb Group based at Kimbolton in the English midlands. He and his crew took their heavy bomber to Schweinfurt in Germany on 17th August 1943 as part of an American bomber force sent to do what damage they could to the several firms that made ball bearings for the German war effort, with a goal of depriving the Germans of their war-making ability and bringing the Second World War in Europe to an early end. Bendiner later wrote a fine book, *The Fall of Fortresses*, about his experiences with that bomb group during the height of the air war: "For two weeks after Schweinfurt the Eighth Air Force dared not venture beyond the sheltering umbrella of P-47s and Spits. It was a time for 'simpler tasks,' as military historians have come to label our attacks on Watten, Villacoublay and Amiens, missions deadly only to those who died.

"By September 6, however, Generals Eaker and Anderson felt that the transfusion of fresh men and planes had restored us to a condition of health in which we could again carry the flag deep into Germany. It is said that we could not afford another Schweinfurt just then. But if so, why did we go to Stuttgart, where the risks were almost as great and the promise of victory not nearly as meaningful? The distance was actually greater than to Schweinfurt, and almost all of it over heavily defended parts

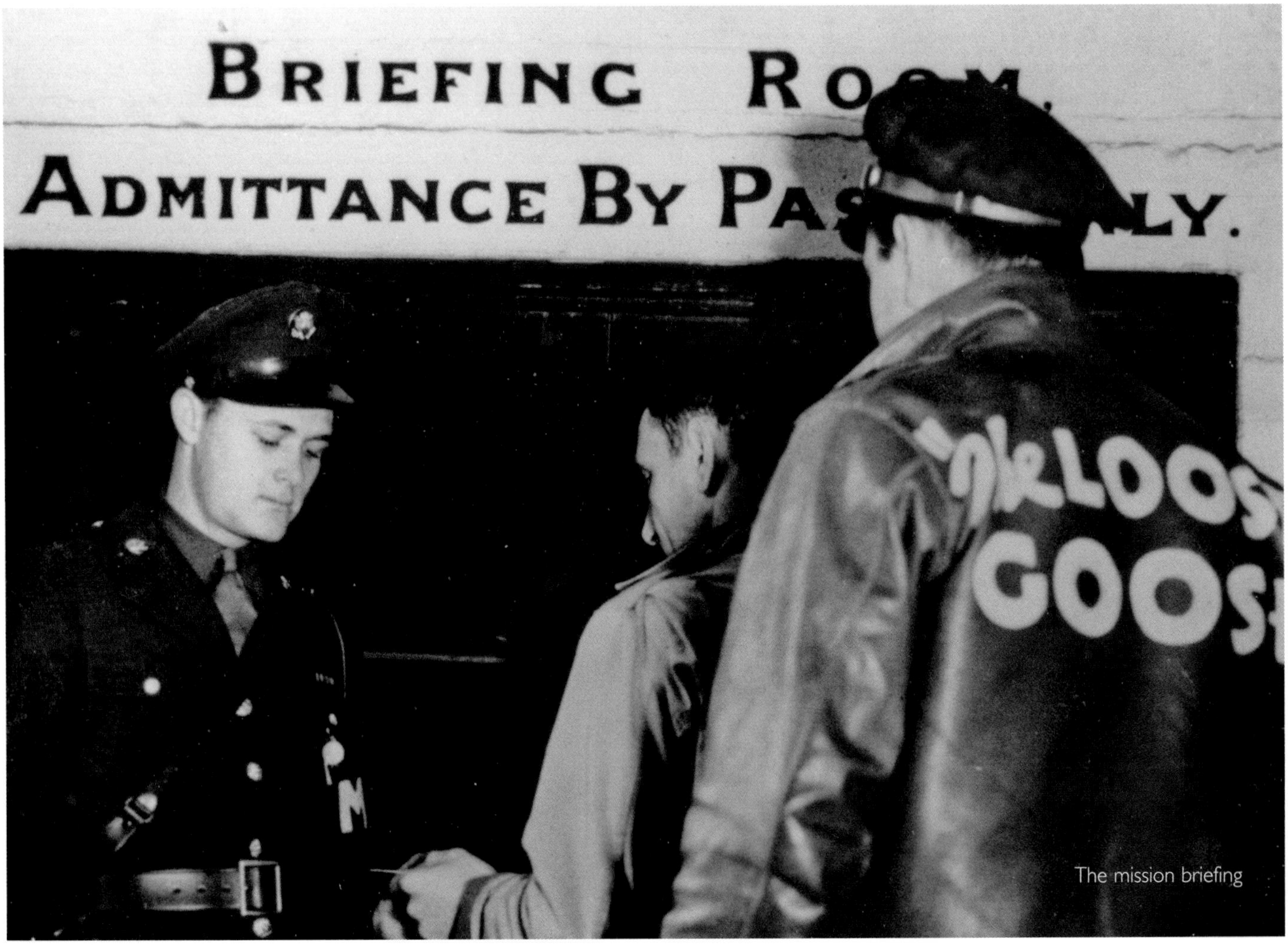
BRIEFING RO
ADMITTANCE BY PA
LY.
The mission briefing

of Germany. As a target Stuttgart offered some aircraft factories and some ball-bearing plants, but these were not nearly as important as those in Schweinfurt.

"Evidence indicates that the trip was decidedly more important than its destination. We were to show our friends and enemies that two weeks after suffering a devastating loss of six hundred men and sixty planes we had the replacements, the spirit and the sense of theater to leap through other hoops of fire.

"Part of the charm of the air war lay in its circus atmosphere. On some occasions we swung from a flying trapeze not to get to the other side of the tent but to win applause or tears, depending on the finale.

"The circus aspect of the war was a symptom of our innocence. We believed in the political importance of brave gestures. We were appallingly juvenile.

" . . . a letter to my wife written within a few days after Stuttgart. Some of the chipper tone may have been laid on to win Esther's admiration, and some aspects were omitted for what I considered reasons of military security. The story is still valid, but it has the theatricality and the omissions that flaw most first-hand accounts. I must therefore interpose material from my notes, from my more sober recollections and from those of my crew to lend weight to this too glib account, written by the young man I used to be.
—Somewhere in England, 1943.

"Dear Esther:
I know that I began to tell you all about the Brevet Club some days ago but I was interrupted by a bit of duty. Between then and now I have fallen into the sea and been daringly rescued, and what with one thing and

another I don't feel much like rattling on about polite society at the Brevet.

"The whole story is pretty melodramatic and I feel silly telling it in the first person. But, in as unpurple language as I can manage this is what happened.

"The mission was the longest, the deepest penetration into Germany ever undertaken by Forts, and in talking it over among ourselves and with Carlson and the chaplain just before takeoff, I remember that I was advocating with considerable heat that this time we couldn't possibly choose

to bail out or make for Switzerland or do anything but return to England because in scarcely any time at all the baby would arrive. (I've been bragging in public again.)

"Just after the target we were heavily attacked . . .

"That goes much too quickly. It tells of Waterloo without mentioning Napoleon. It is altogether too bloodless a report.

"Stuttgart lies some five hundred miles inside Germany. A heavily loaded B-17 flying at a moderate

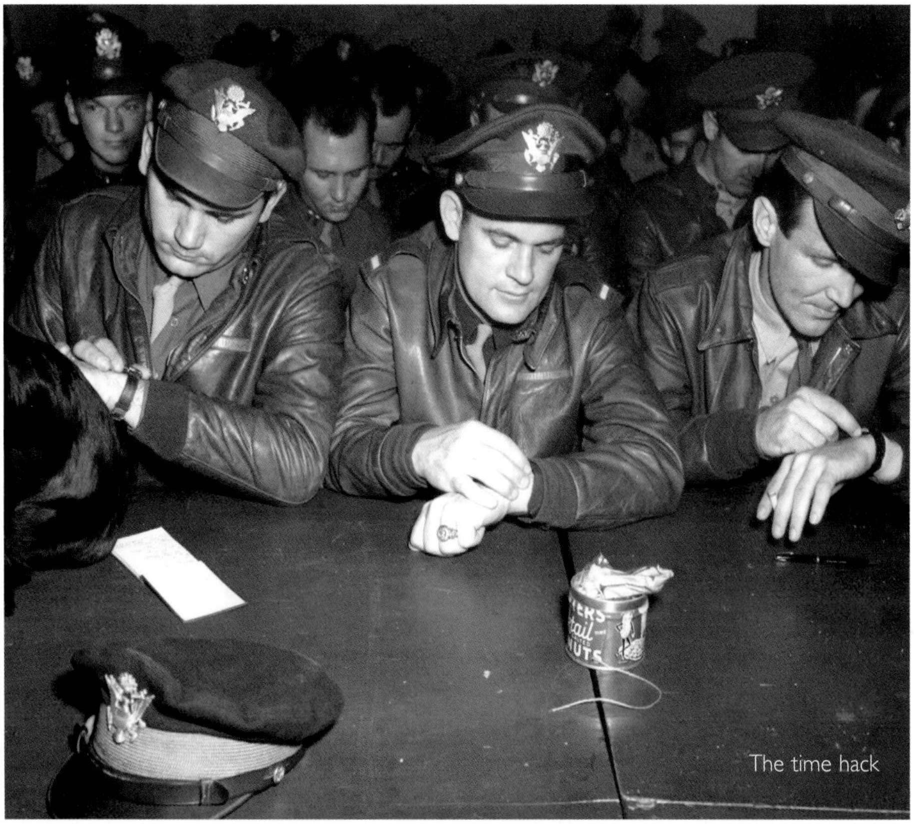
The time hack

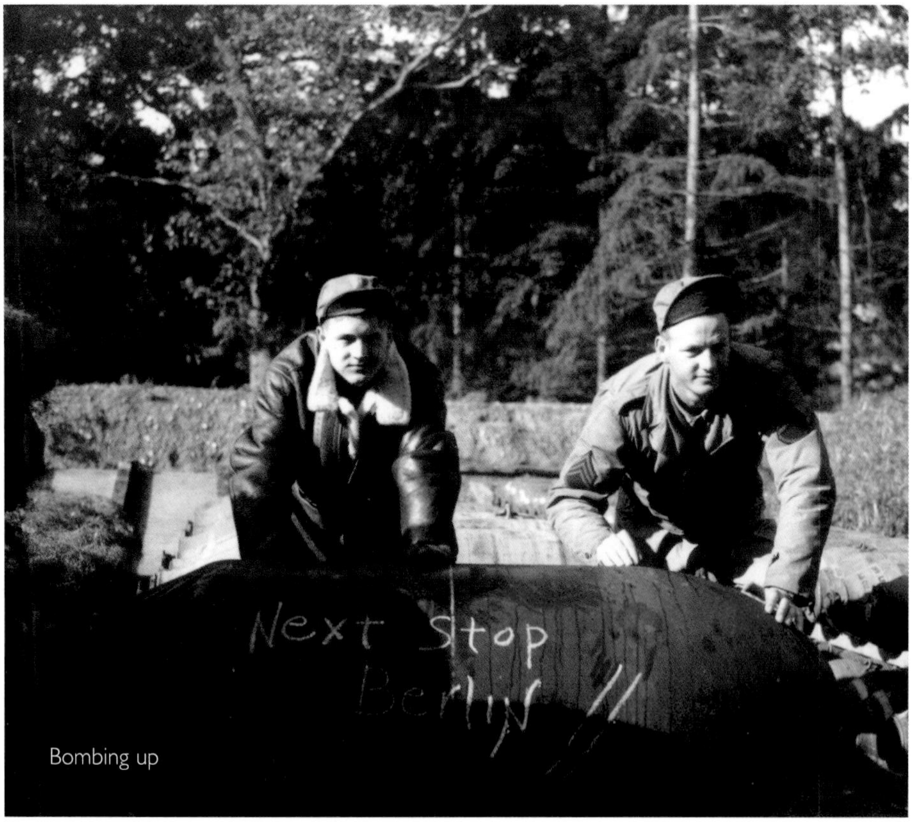
Next Stop
Berlin
Bombing up

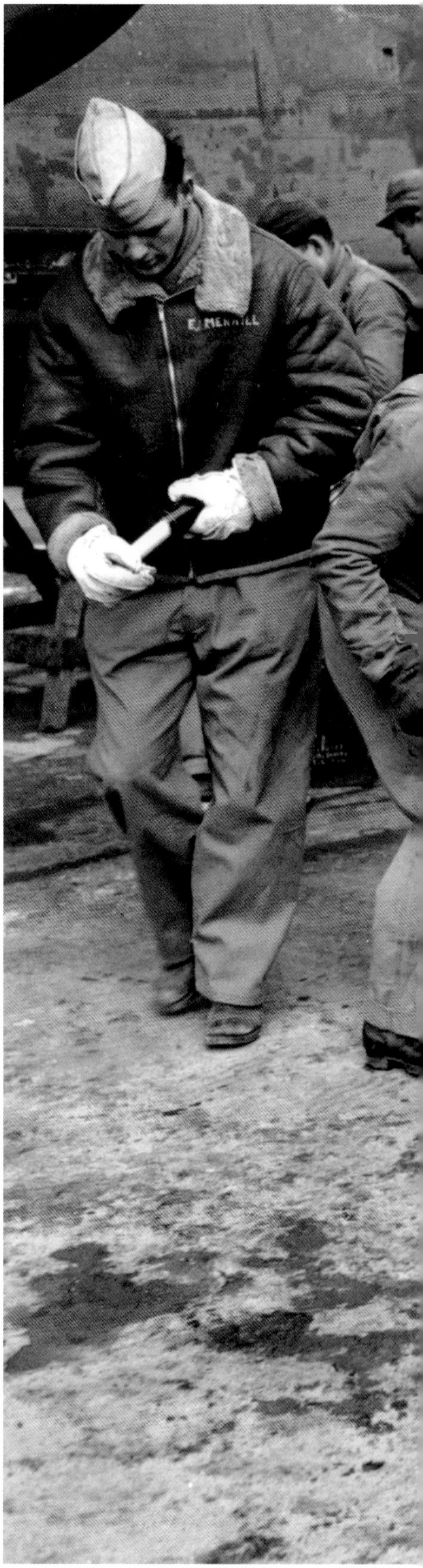

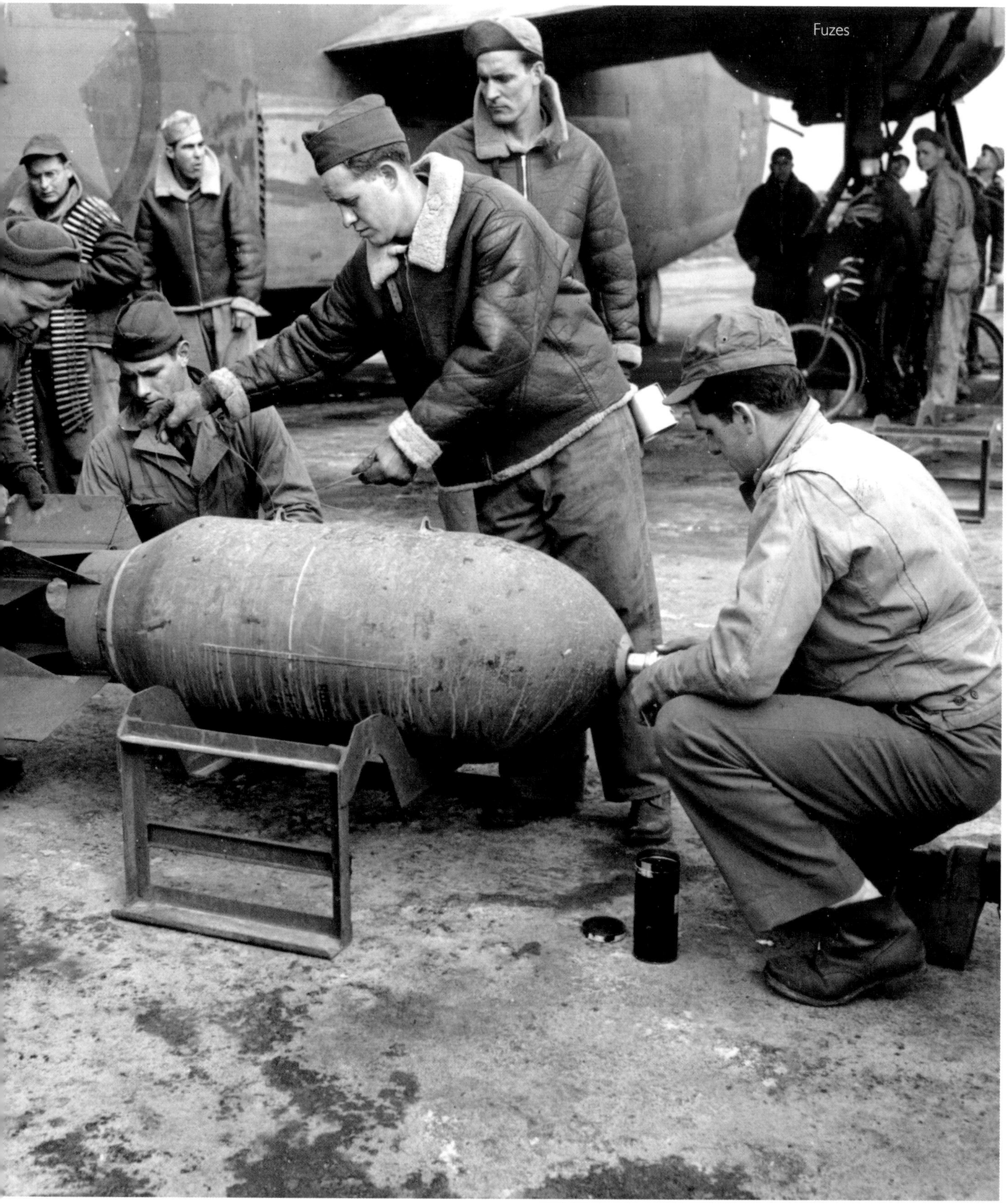
Fuzes

altitude—say, seventeen thousand feet—in formation, zigging and zagging in evasive action, might be expected to make the round trip but would land with fuel tanks perilously close to empty. There would scarcely be a gallon to spare for a foolish mistake or a bit of horseplay.

"The mission was being led by Brigadier General Robert Travis. I had nothing against the General before Stuttgart because I knew very little about him except for his legendary talent at poker. After Stuttgart many of us had a great deal against him. He added to our anxieties—or at least to Bohn's [*Tondalayo*'s pilot]—from the very inception of the mission by announcing his intention of following a newfangled theory developed by someone at Bomber Command. A great deal of fuel was being wasted by climbing to altitude with full tanks, it was reasoned. Why not climb at a later point when the tanks would be lighter?

"My second-lieutenant pilot could have told the General why not, but he wasn't asked. To fly in the thin upper air a plane needs the added strength of its superchargers. If those superchargers are out of order it is best to realize that incapacity when you are over friendly territory and can drop down to a lower altitude and head for home. It is not wise to wait until one is at altitude over enemy territory to find that you cannot stay in formation.

"Travis, untroubled by such technical considerations, led us across Europe at ten thousand feet until we were close to Tübingen, from which we would turn onto the target. Then he began to climb steeply and we followed him. Our superchargers worked. The record does not show whether others failed, because how can one distinguish in the fall of a Fortress the various ingredients of a disaster—enemy flak or 20mm shells or rockets or simple mechanical failure?

"We were flying low and on the outside of the formation. Travis and his lead group were in view ahead of us. As we rounded Tübingen I noted clouds moving across the Black Forest. Outside my starboard window the Neckar River was still plainly visible snaking its way to the target.

"Stuttgart lay before us in checkered sun and shadow. It was close to noon. The flak came up, but not too heavy. Then as we neared the target white clouds capriciously intervened. Bob had no concerns; he would drop on the leader's bombs. But those clouds must have disconcerted Travis's bombardier, all set as he was to fix the primary target on the cross hairs of his bombsight. Could he switch at an instant from visual bombing to instruments?

"We read the answer in the spectacle of our lead group passing over the target with bomb-bay doors open and no bombs falling amid the furious black flak.

"Travis was going around for another try, and the formation would wheel behind him. All very well for Travis and the happy few at the hub of that wheel. They could describe a nice, tight circle. But to us on the outward rim it meant a fearsome strain to keep up with the formation, and a serious drain of gas. We had to fly perhaps an extra forty or fifty miles at full throttle, using gas at very nearly the rate required for a take-off, just to keep our position in the formation.

"We could have come in closer to the hub, shortening the radius of the swing and saving considerable fuel, but we dared not slip under the open bomb-bay doors of Travis and his group. His bomb-bays, like ours, were loaded with incendiaries. (This too seems odd, for ball bearings and the machines that make them do not burn.) The incendiaries were ingeniously packaged in clusters with a timing device so set that, at a predetermined distance below the bomber that hatched them, the firebombs would spread out and cover a wider area.

"No one could be sure just when those incendiaries would tumble out, their clusters flying apart. We swung out in a wide arc. Why the General did not close his bomb-bay doors is yet another unanswered question of the city.

"On the second time around, the incendiaries fluttered down, and smoke billowed up in black clouds from the city.

"As we turned away from the target the Luftwaffe made its belated but emphatic appearance. Fighters came at us head on and blazing. Bohn was one of those pilots who believed ardently in evasive action. (There are some contrary schools of thought, which declare that it is better to fly straight and level as if on parade, following the model of the Light Brigade.) As the German planes came at us from high out of the sun, Bohn pushed *Tondelayo* to climb and pitch. This seemed to throw the attackers off momentarily. But they—or others like them—came at us again, three or four abreast. Bohn recollects that he saw a puff of smoke from the engine of one of the German fighters and in response nosed *Tondelayo* into her dance. In retrospect he much regrets that he did not accurately interpret the puff as an indication that the German pilot had cut his throttle and was waiting for us to come down from our jump while he slowed his run at us. He caught us cold and raked *Tondelayo* from nose to tail.

"When he left us one of our engines was on fire; our co-pilot of the day, Chuck, had had his leg torn

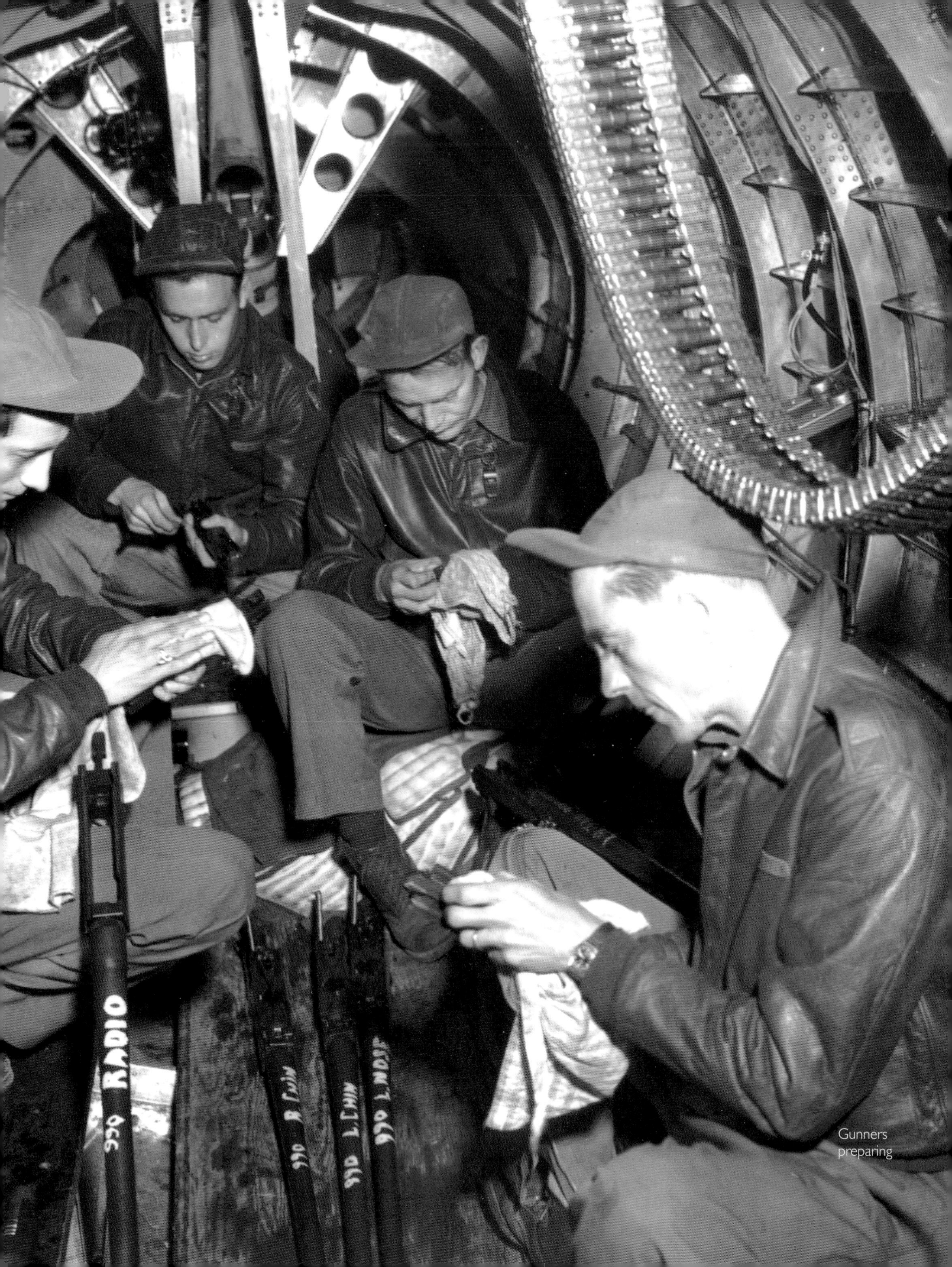
990 RADIO
990 R.CHIN
990 L.CHIN
990 L.NOSE

Gunners preparing

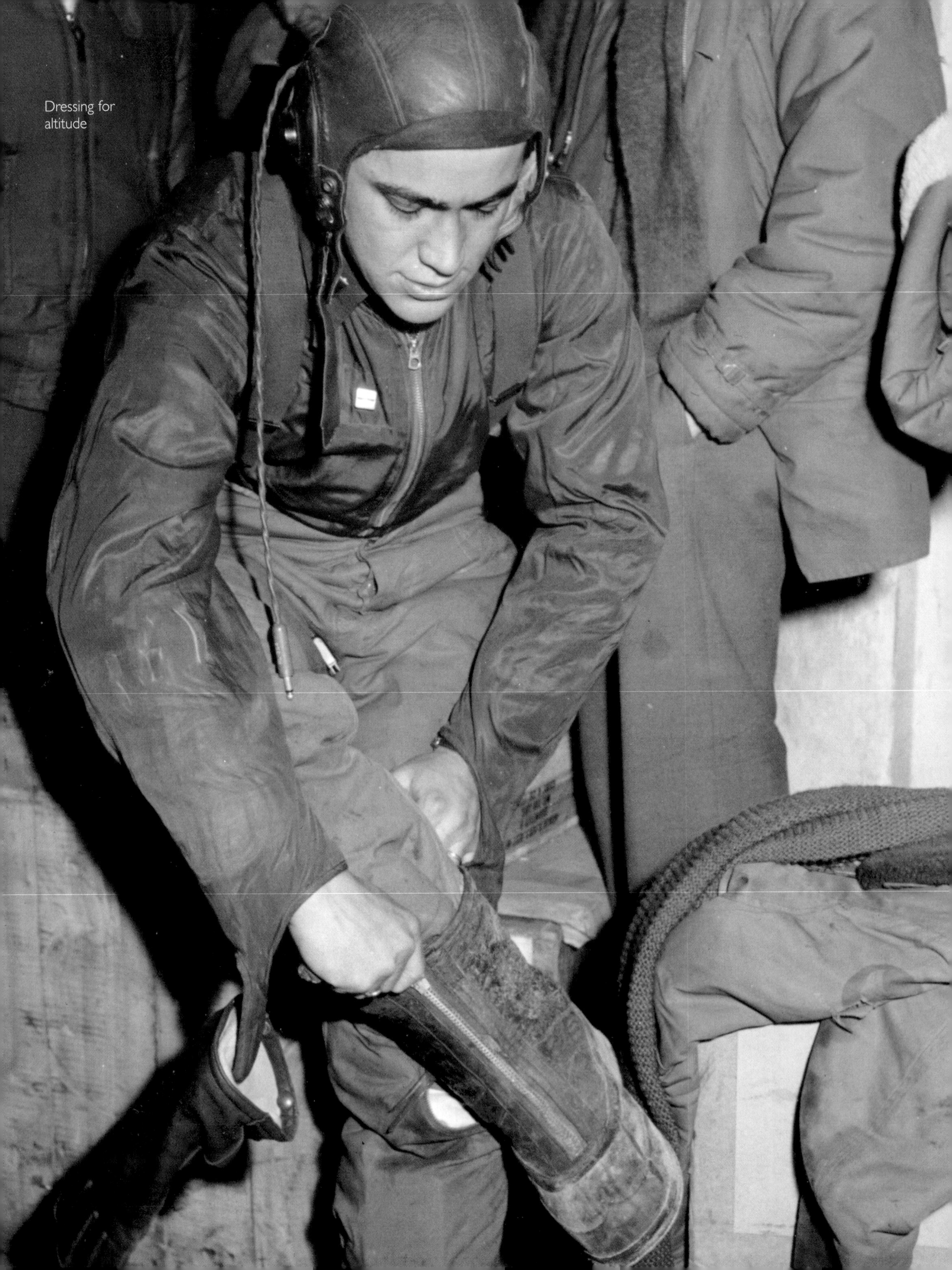

Dressing for altitude

by a 20mm shell; the oxygen lines in the rear of the ship had been cut, and the oil pressure gauge was down to zero because our oil line had been severed.

"Now, it is the oil pressure that enables the pilot to change the pitch of the propellers. And if the pitch cannot be changed the propeller stands like a rigid paddle in the teeth of hurricane winds. If it spins without lubrication the friction can build up enough heat to melt metal. Then the propeller blades might turn into a deadly missile and slash the frame that held us.

"It was clear that we could not stay in formation. To put out the fire in our engine we would have to work up an airspeed of at least 235 mph. We could have done so only in a dive. (We had been at that deadly extremity before.) In any case we would have to drop to lower altitudes with half our crew deprived of oxygen. (We had been there before as well.)

"At the first lull in the fight we waved away our wing man and dived until the fire was out.

"Now we can pick up the letter to my wife.

"'. . . We had to drop out of formation and fight our way across Europe by ourselves. As it developed, we didn't so much fight our way out as sneak out, running for every cloud cover we could see. The spot decision right then was up to Fawkes. He could have asked for a course to Switzerland. The lovely snowy, blue and white peaks of the Alps were plainly visible, towering almost up to our altitude, although quite a way off.

"I must interrupt again. Technically it was up to Bohn, but not actually as it turned out. Bohn was our commander—and a very good one, which is to say that he almost never gave an

order. We talked this situation out, weighing the pros and cons as if we were civilians around a table. While we talked we flitted from cloud to cloud over Europe. I had given Bohn a heading, but he could scarcely keep to it while chasing clouds. I had to follow every twist and turn he made, altering our headings accordingly and still aiming for England by the shortest route.

"It was plain from the most casual glance at our fuel level, at our ground speed, at our low altitude and at the distance we had to go that we could not make it back to Kimbolton. We had three choices to discuss. We could head for the Alps, where we would be interned for the duration. (General cheers over the intercom.) Choice number two: we could bail out over France. We all carried civilian passport pictures. (I liked mine because I had borrowed a very un-Army, tweedy jacket for the purpose.) We could hope to land among the French Resistance and follow their lead to the Channel coast, where we might thumb a ride on a fishing boat. Our intelligence captain had described this alternative as an easy walk across occupied Europe for which we were well armed with a snapshot and a .45-caliber pistol. (Dead silence for that option.)

"Last possibility: we could fly as far as our fuel would permit. I told everybody I was sure we could reach the Channel. We would have to ditch, take our chances against riding down with the plane straight to the bottom of the Channel, and take our further chances on being picked up by friends, not foes, at sea. I argued for that proposal. Everyone knew it was a personal matter with me. I could see no other way to get home to my wife and shortly forthcoming child before the war's end. I might grow old while my child grew up.

"'Poor Benny—he's got to see his kid.' Real sympathy poured over the intercom disguised as mock tears. Bohn supported me from the start. Mike and Duke pitched in, and the others followed cheerfully.

"I accepted such sacrifices without a qualm. I was young then. Would I now try to persuade others to make so risky a choice on my account? Not likely.

"We knew then that our co-pilot's wounds were superficial, but would not Switzerland have seemed the safest bet for him? We could have made a case for internment. Why didn't we?

"Back to the letter:

"'. . . Bohn asked for a heading home and I was glad of it even though with fighting and one thing and another I was a bit vague as to our precise position at the time. We dived down into the loveliest heaviest cloud imaginable and stayed in it as long as possible, while I feverishly worked away to establish our position and improve on the course I had originally set. The cloud gave out, and for a time we sailed at low altitude over the grain fields, forests, towns and rivers of France. Some of these checkpoints seemed to bear out my theoretically estimated position and some of them contradicted it. It was beautiful country; it seemed to be of a different color from that of England or Holland or Belgium.

"We were playing hide-and-seek in the clouds over France. And in the open spaces our gunners were anxiously watching for German fighters who were looking for us but who miraculously failed to see us before other clouds came up to hide us. However, ground radio was tracking us and we had to shift course to clear what I thought would be heavy flak areas. We could see flak on both

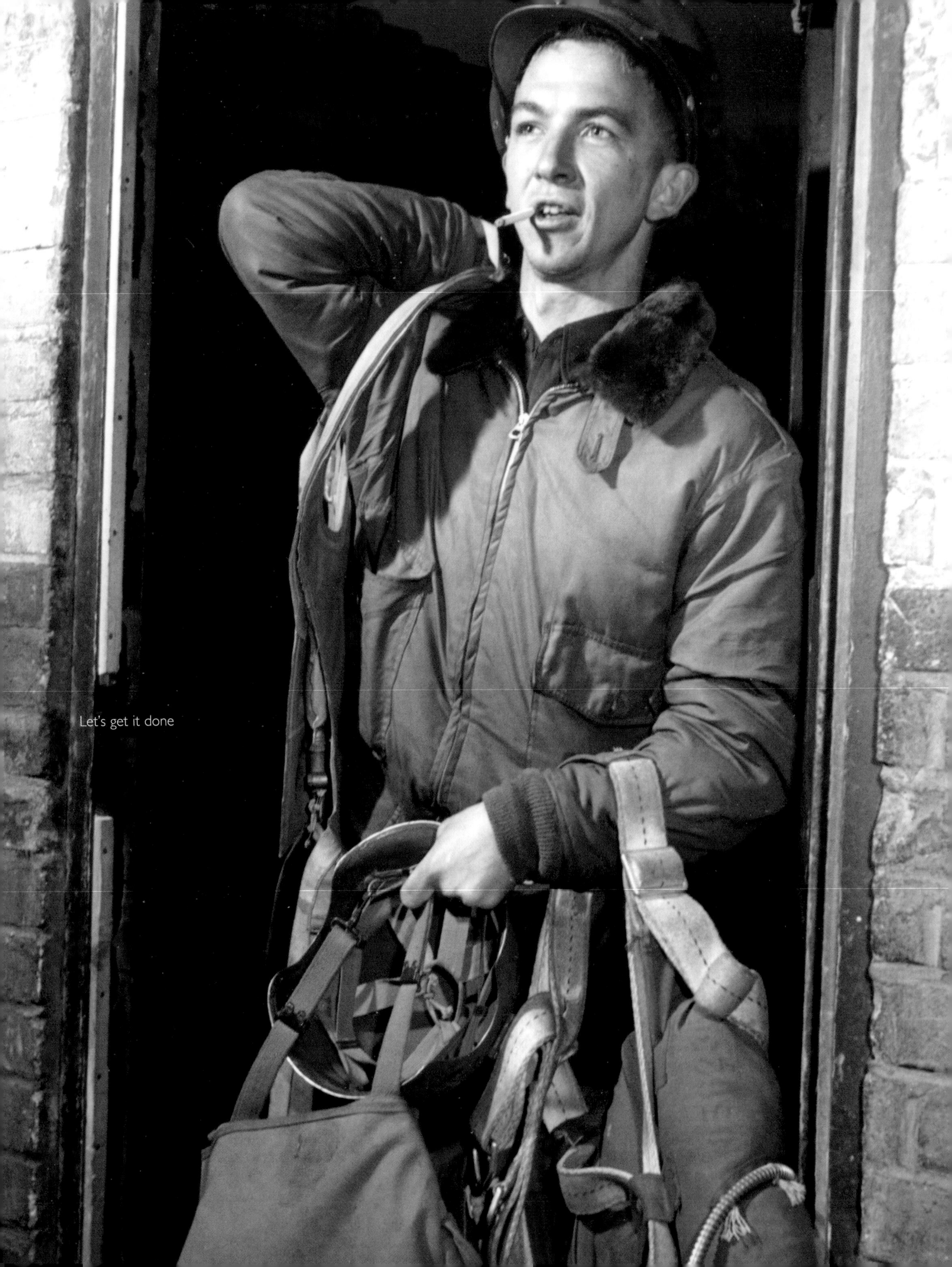

Let's get it done

sides of us, largely to signal fighters, we thought . . .

"At this point I must defer to Bohn, who remembers clearly an incident which I recall only dimly. We had been flying through cloud for some time when he asked me where we were. He says that he could see no way in which I could be sure of anything. And he was right, of course. I had followed our zigs and zags as best I could, but how could I be certain in that fog to which we clung? Then I had my answer from the Germans. The gray-white nothingness was punctured by black flak explosions all around us. 'Ah,' I said. 'Rouen.' We both laughed.

"Just before we crossed the coast Fawkes called up and suggested that anyone who didn't want to take his chance in the water could still jump. None of us did. I could see water ahead, but we ran up along the coast to avoid a large seaport and heavy coastal flak. Duke, our radioman, was sending out an SOS and asking radio stations to take a fix on us. They did and he reported it to me, but it seemed to me to be way off. And Duke asked for another, which was just as bad. I realized then that no one in England knew where we were. I gave Duke our estimated position, but he couldn't get it through . . .

"Actually the British shore stations were asking us to move some thirty miles north where they could get a proper fix on us. They did not know it, but they were asking men to fly without wings. When we crossed the coast we had only one engine working, and in a B-17 that is a few minutes away from none. I gathered a few of my belongings—a chart of the Channel coast, which I folded and slipped into the pocket of my cover-

alls, a pencil or two, my gloves (gauntlet types that were more elegant than warm) and Esther's picture. Then I clambered out of the nose, up the hatch behind Bohn, and through the bomb bay to the radio room.

". . . We were over the sea now and our four engines ran out one after another. When I left the nose, two of them were already motionless—a most disconcerting thing to see in an airplane. Back in the radio room we all took our previously assigned positions, bracing ourselves for the shock. I crouched behind the radioman's armor plating and talked to Mike, who was crouched next to me. Up to the last minute Mike retained his faith in *Tondelayo* and couldn't believe we would really have to ditch. He asked me whether we were headed toward England. I said we were but I knew we couldn't make it. We chatted like that, looking up through the open hatch to the great, gray, swirling clouds, wondering how near the water we were and when the shock would come . . .

"As we dropped closer to the sea Bohn turned to our co-pilot and asked him whether he had ever landed a plane in water. Chuck shook his head. Would he like to? With the last bit of power in *Tondelayo* Bohn maneuvered to land along the crest of a wave. To hit a wave broadside is very like flying into a stone wall. We skimmed the crest, then sank into the trough of a mountainous wave. We sank, then rose, buoyed by empty gas tanks.

"From the cockpit Chuck saw his fondly crushed pilot's cap in the hatchway leading to the nose and seemed about to try to fish it out. Bohn recalled looking at him doubtfully as if to say, 'You're on your own.' No

window in the cockpit of a B-17 is made to allow a grown man to wriggle out of it unless he is in the extremity of desperation. Both Bohn and Chuck made it to the wing.

"Someone should have pulled a lever to release the dinghies from the fuselage. No one had. Bohn quickly scanned the directions on the metal plaque above the wing. He pulled the appropriate lever as per instructions, but nothing happened. He and Chuck pulled, twisted and clawed the dinghies out, then started the inflation, which should have been automatic. Could it have been ten seconds or thirty? None of us remembers how long it took to climb out.

". . . We lit lightly at first and only a bit of spray seemed to come in. Mike stood up, and we all yelled to him to get down. But it was too late. After skipping along the water the ship finally plunged, throwing Mike forward so that he gashed his forehead. Then the green-gray water rushed in. I felt nothing so much as surprise. In drills there had been nothing to suggest such a torrent of ocean running through our airship. I tried to stand, but the force of the water knocked me down, and when I did get up, some of the precious things I had gathered were floating.

". . . Everyone was on his feet, everyone excited and clambering toward the hatch, everyone shouting that there was plenty of time and to keep calm. Mike stood next to me and I saw that his head was bleeding badly. A piece of floating B-17 had clipped me and scratched my forehead. For an awful moment I thought that Mike and I, who were wedged in a corner, would never get out. Mike finally managed it. By that time the water was up to my chest and rising rapidly. Our bombardier,

Bob, was still in there. I hoisted myself up on one side while he made for the other. I remember that I failed to make it the first time and I could hear Mike hollering outside. 'Where's Benny?' Then I clambered out. The wings were already under water.

"I clung to the fuselage for a second or so and watched Fawkes and the others, who had extracted one of the rubber dinghies and were maneuvering it away from the wings of the sinking plane. Then I plunged into the water. The dinghy was scarcely more than a stroke away from the ship. But I had overlooked one detail that might have proved disastrous. I had neglected to inflate my Mae West . . .

"The Channel was as rough that day as it ever gets, and the swell was dark, towering and fearful to look at. It was worse to feel. We became violently seasick. That is, all except Bob and one gunner who increased our miseries by remaining obtrusively and volubly high-spirited. Before giving way to utterly abandoned wretching and writhing we paddled with our hands toward the other dinghy so that we

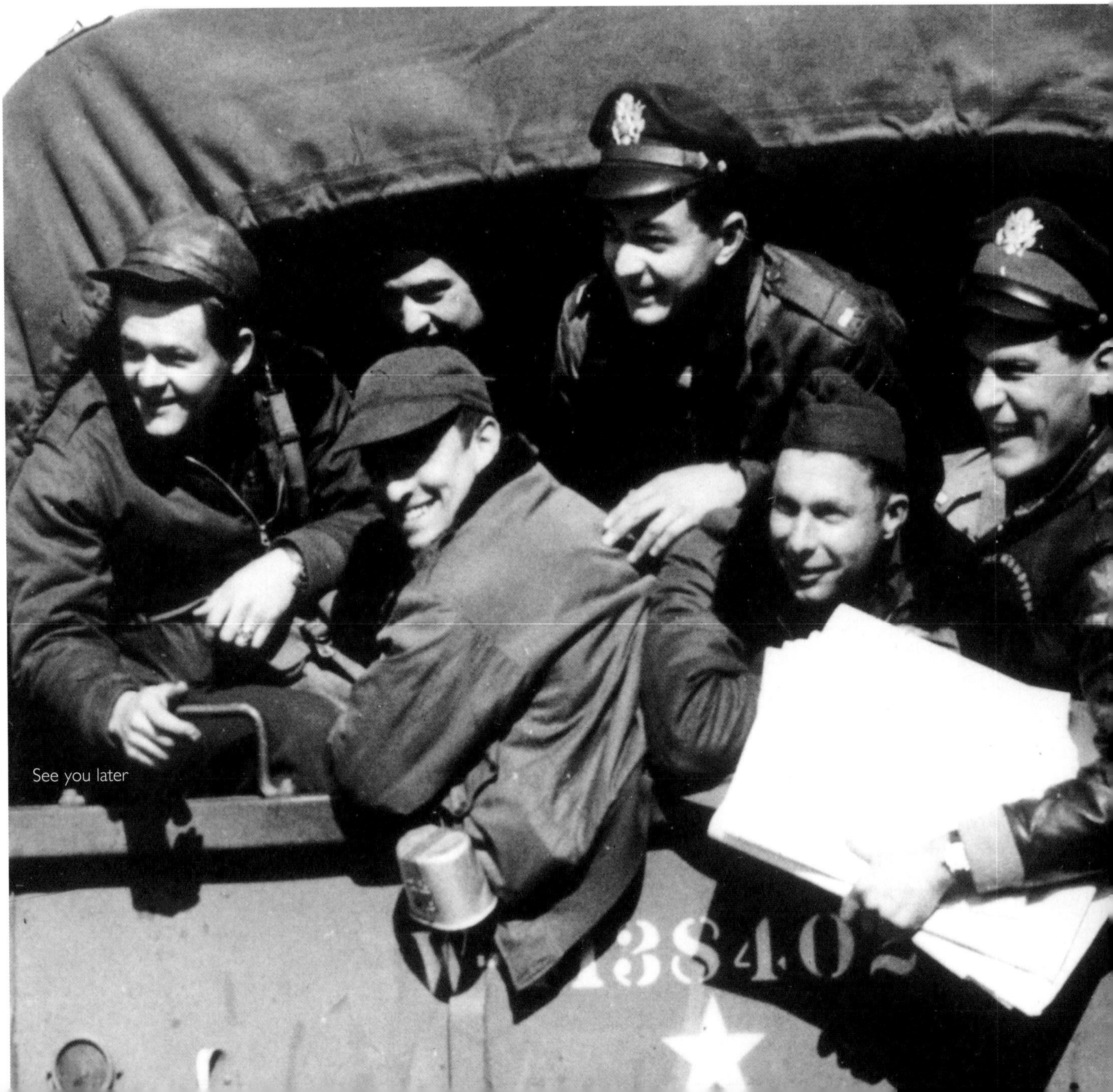
W-138403

See you later

could lash the rafts together . . .

"Dinghies are equipped with oars, but we could not find them. Eventually they turned up at the very bottom of a heap of tightly stowed, largely unworkable gadgetry.

"In between spasms, when I could lie with my head back and not feel too sick, I could watch the endless

seascape and the barren sky. Bob was cranking our portable radio frantically but in vain, because we had lost the kite to raise our aerial; we knew then that we could send no signal at all.

"Toward the end of the afternoon we were all resigning ourselves to spending a night on the water. I, at least, was convinced that no one in England had any idea of where we were. Earlier we had seen a flight of bombers, but they were very high and no one aboard could possibly have seen our signals. It was a little more than five hours after we ditched that we sighted a squadron of fighters. Larry had the flare pistol out and ready to shoot. Duke shouted that they might be Germans. Some of us told him to shoot and others yelled at him not to . . .

". . . Larry fired. The fighters were already past us, but one blessed pilot was looking back for an unknown but providential reason. We watched the fighters fly on and then noted that one peeled off, and the others followed.

"They came in low over the water toward our flare—a magnificent affair of parachutes, red balls of fire and smoke like a Fourth of July celebration. Those Spitfires were the most meaningful, beautiful things I have ever seen. They swooped down and circled above us. Sick as we were, we stood up, waved and yelled at them, and came very near to upsetting the dinghies altogether. One of the Spits circled high above us to radio our position while the others continued to make passes over us by way of sustaining our morale. It was wonderful. We would cheer and laugh and get sick again, then laugh some more. I have never been so happy and so miserable at the same time.

"We had been in the water about nine hours when Mike suddenly shouted

that he saw a light. Fawkes saw it too, when we rode the crest of a swell. We sent up another flare and then waited. Then we heard the dull throb of a motor, and a beam of light reached out near us but not quite on us. Dinghies are pitifully small things to spot on an ocean. We fired another flare, this time into the wind so that it fell back directly over our heads. The beam swung around and picked us up. Then while the light came nearer a terrible thought struck me and most of the others, I suppose: What if the vessel were an enemy ship? To have traveled all that distance across Europe alone, to have dived *Tondelayo* into the sea, to have spent nine agonizing hours on a raft, all to avoid capture and then to be picked up by the wrong ship—that would be too bad. We shouted and soon heard someone answering. 'Ahoy,' said a voice behind the light. Apparently our collective Minnesota, Pennsylvania, Massachusetts, Texas and New York accents made themselves known, and the voice answered jubilantly, 'OK, Yanks. We're coming.'

"We clambered aboard the boat, fumbling awkwardly up the swaying rope ladder. There were a dozen happy angels dressed in blue RAF uniforms and turtleneck sweaters saying 'Bloody good show,' and cinematic things of that sort. They had hot soup and dry clothes ready for us. I couldn't swallow the soup and, since I paused on deck for one last mighty heave of what was still in my innards, I came down too late for the clothes. But I stripped to the skin and they wrapped me in warm fleecy blankets . . ."

EIGHTH AIR FORCE A2 JACKETS

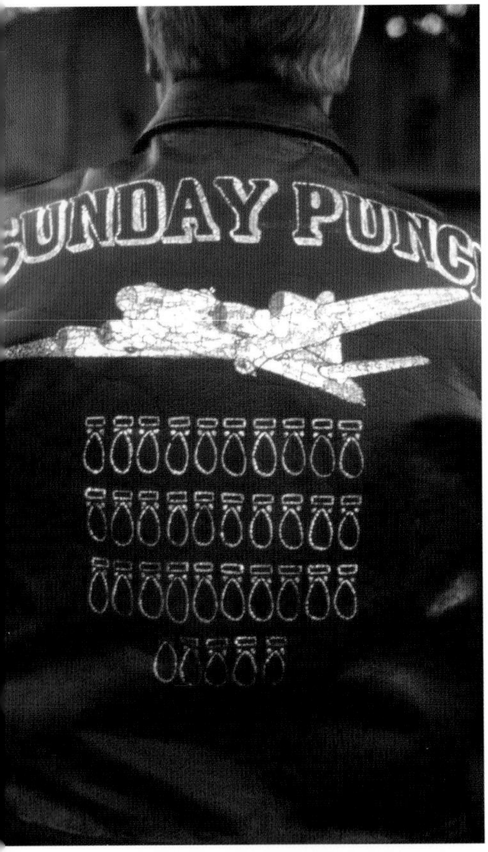
UNDAY PUNC

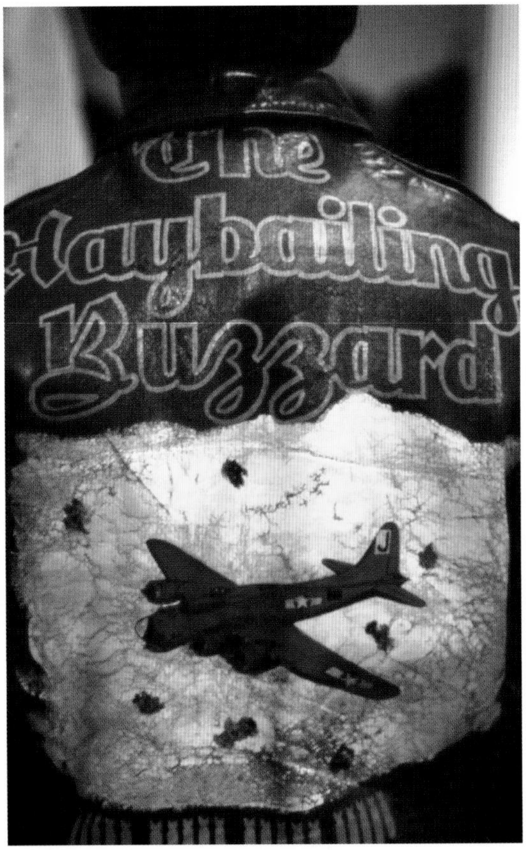
The
aybailing
Buzzard

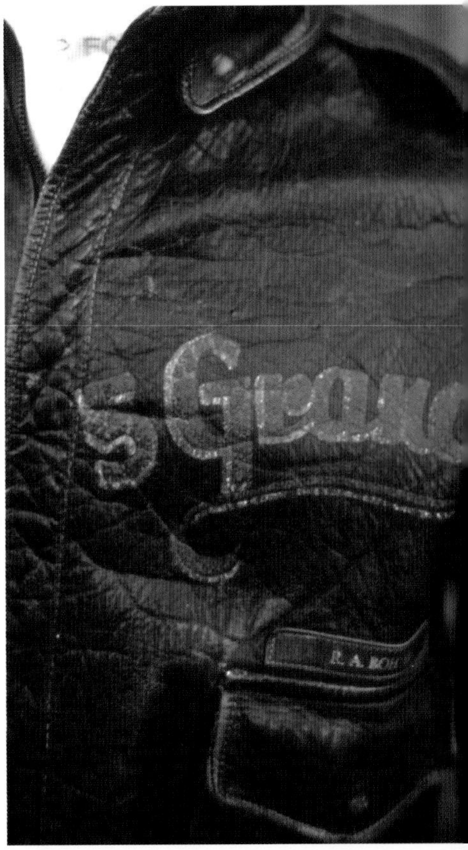

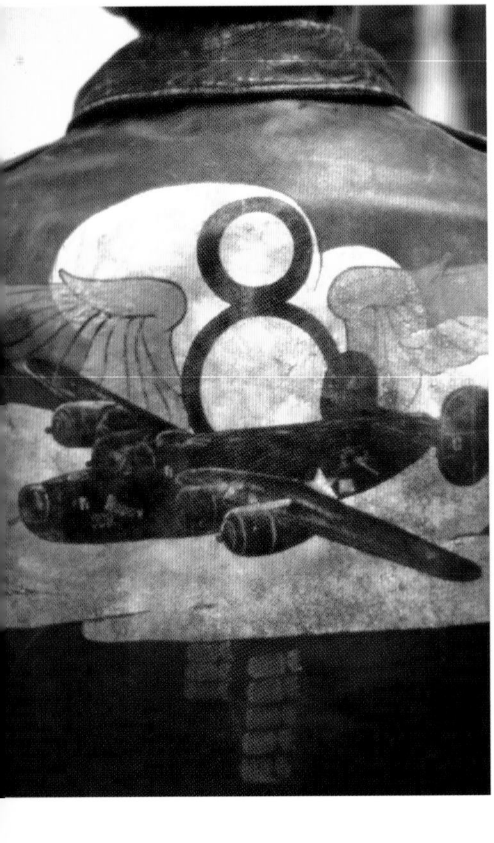
8

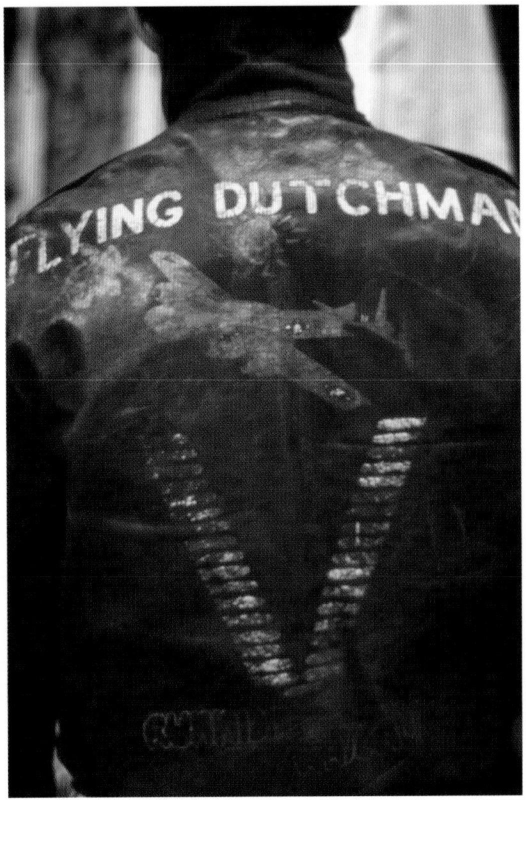
LYING DUTCHMA

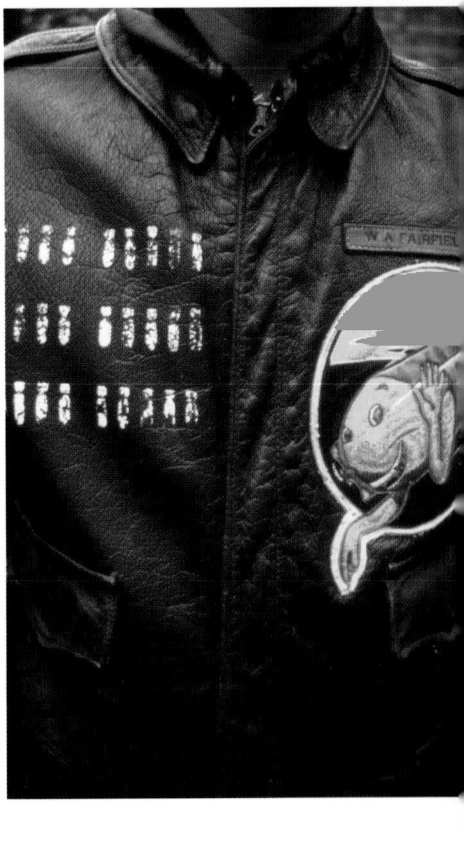

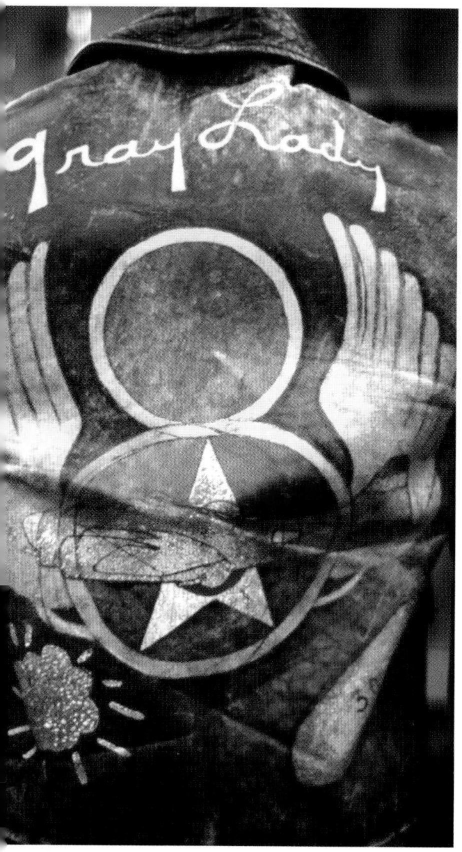
gray Lady

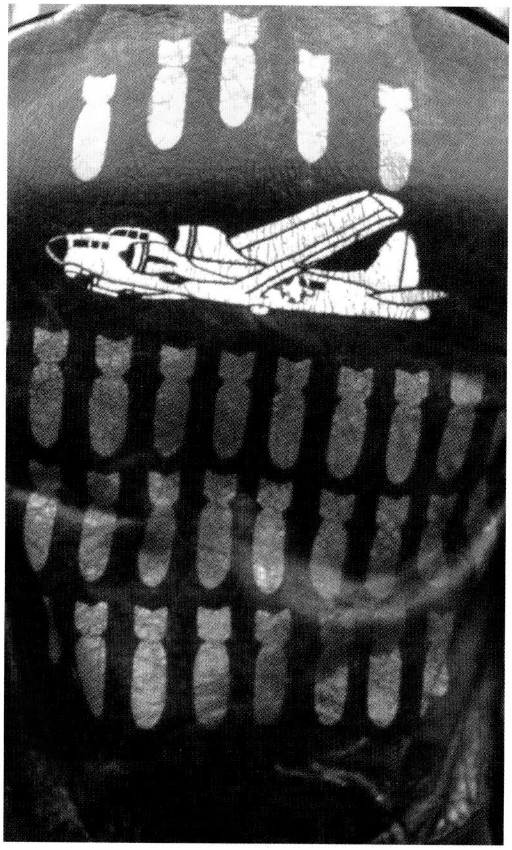

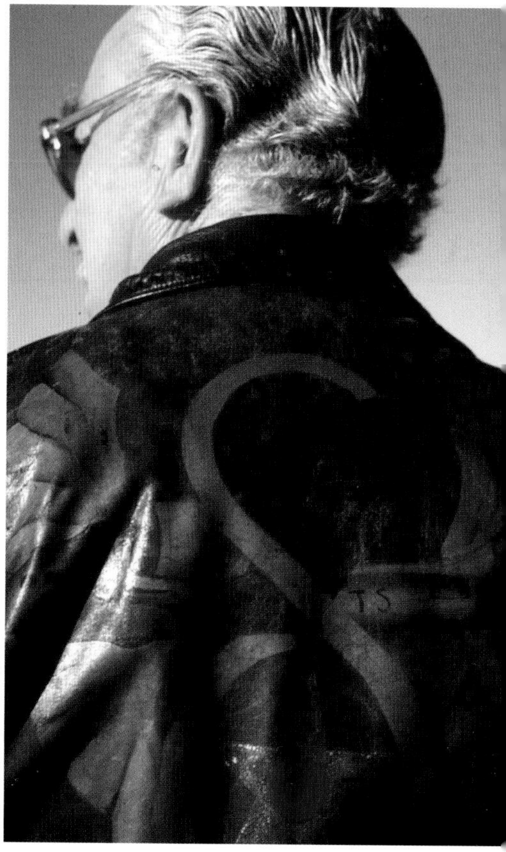

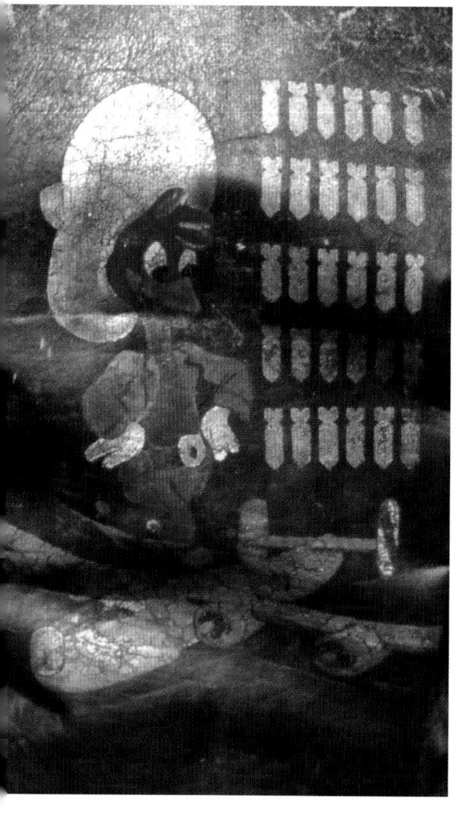

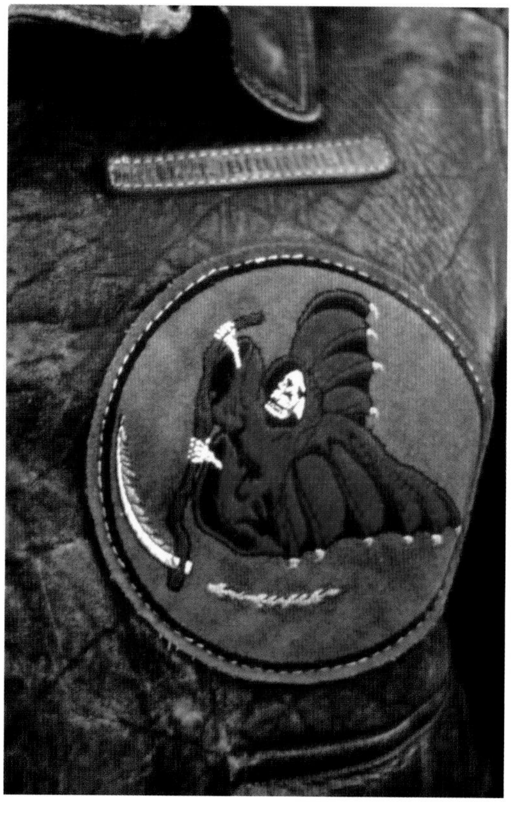

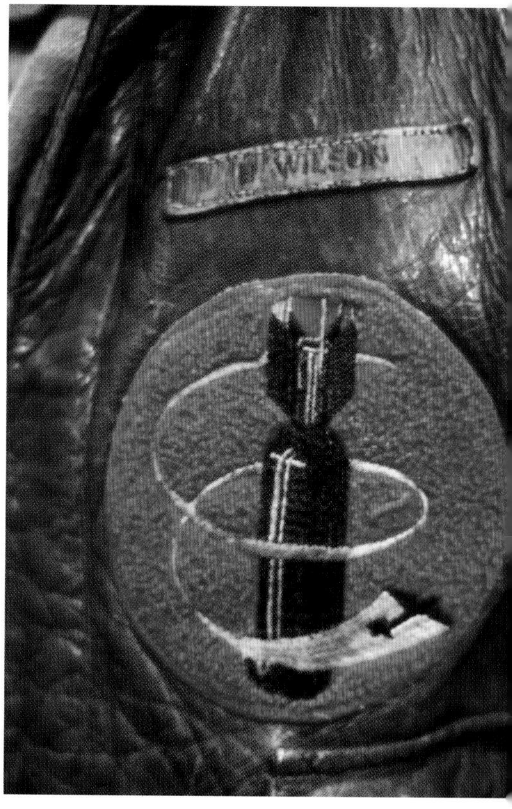
WILSON

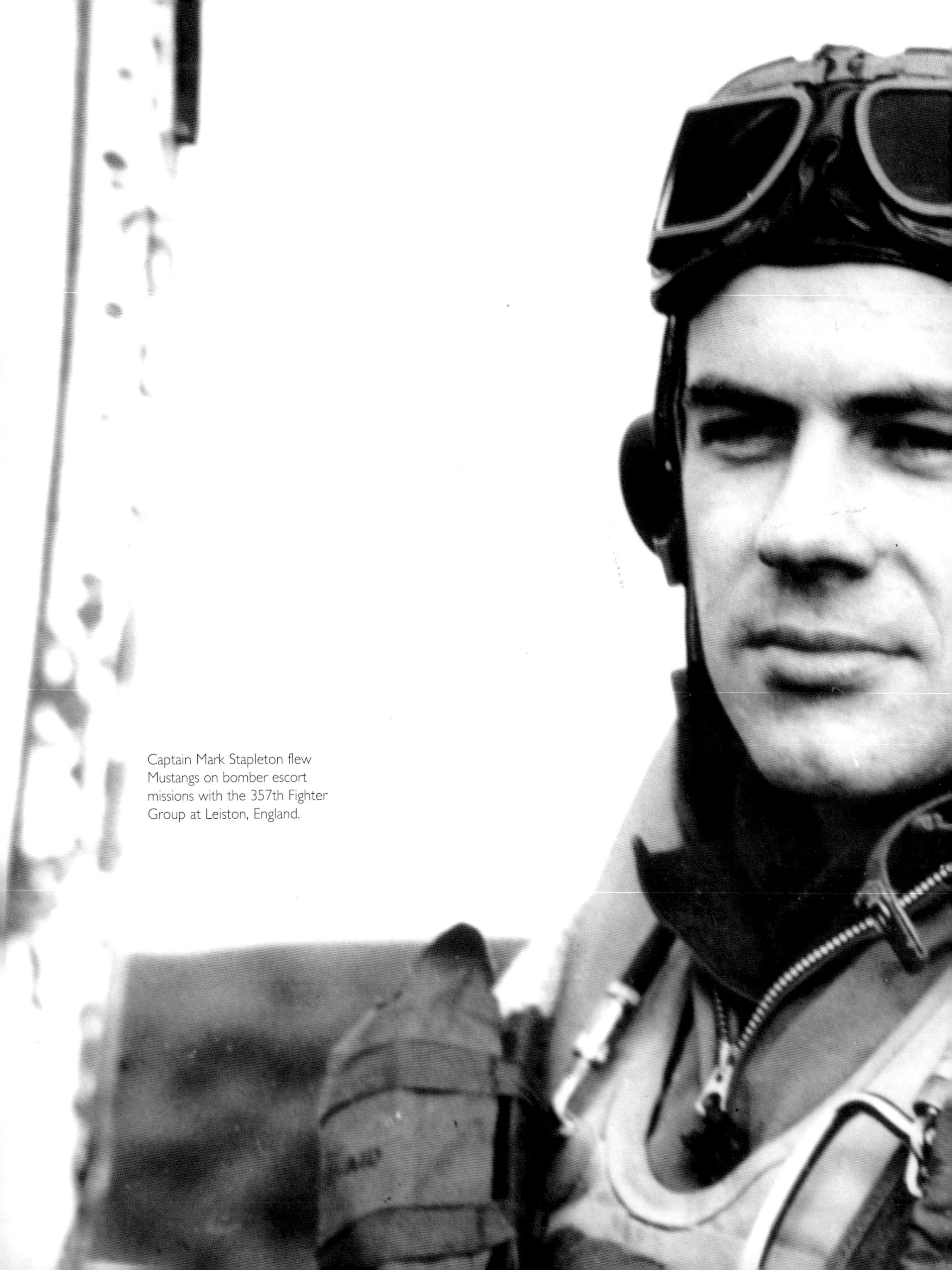

Captain Mark Stapleton flew Mustangs on bomber escort missions with the 357th Fighter Group at Leiston, England.

LIFE ON LEISTON

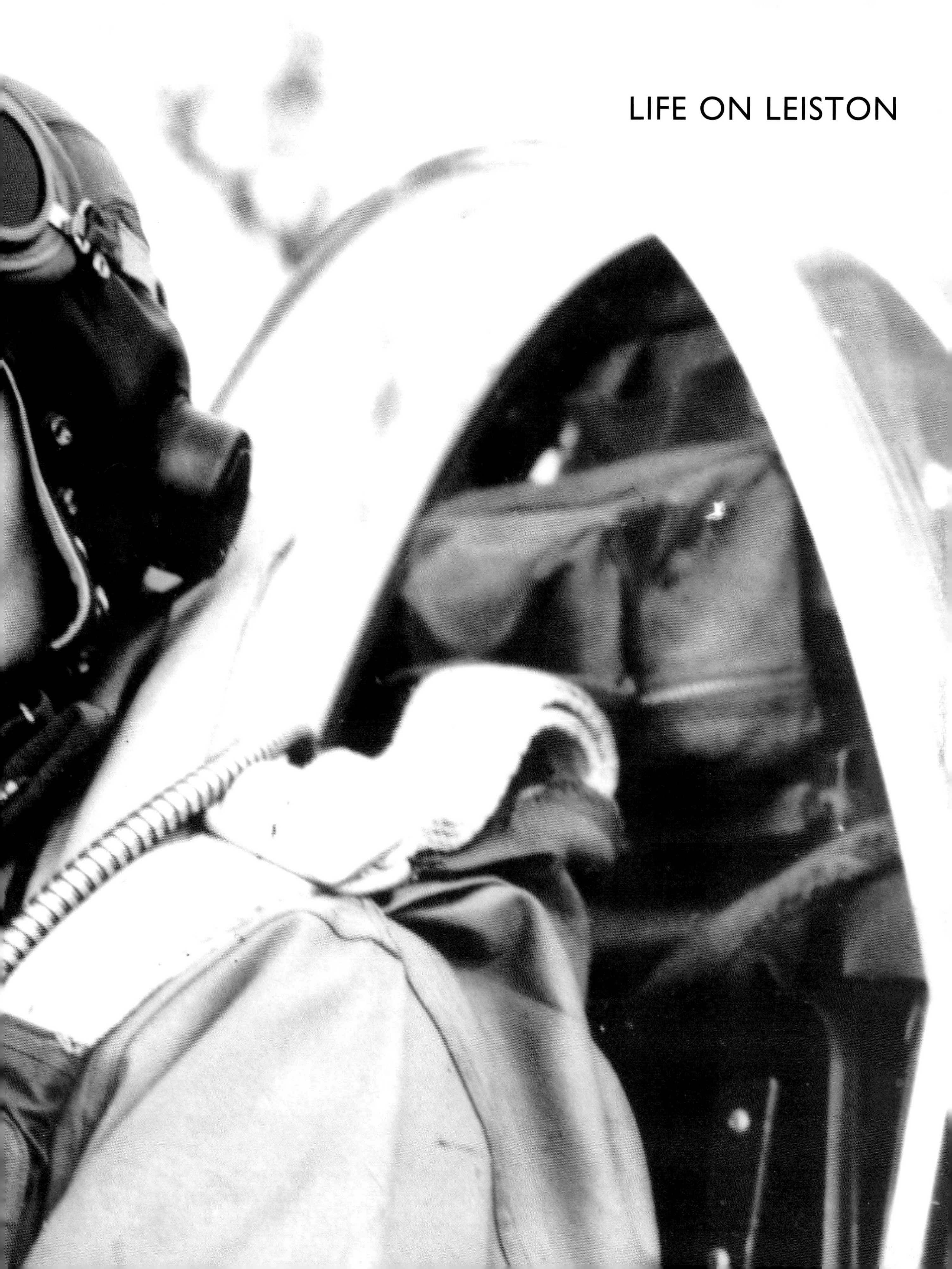

Leonard "Kit" Carson flew a Mustang named *Nooky Booky IV* with the 357th Fighter Group in WW2. He was credited with 17.5 enemy aircraft destroyed in flight.

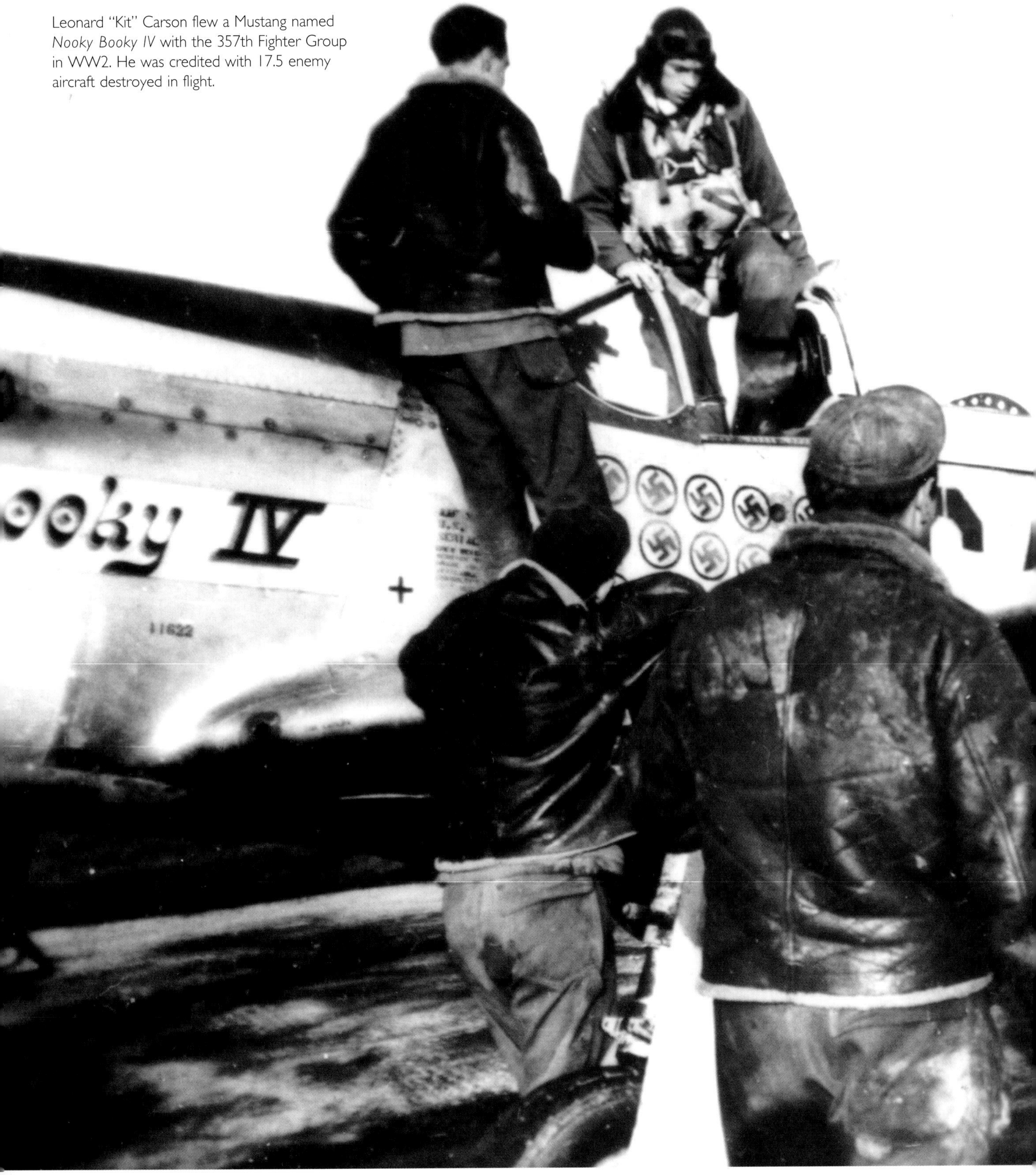
ooky IV
11622

P-51 MUSTANG crew chief Merle Olmsted served with the 357th Fighter Group at Leiston, England in the Second World War: "November 1944—the third year of war for a still angry America, the fifth year of war for the British Commonwealth nations, most of the nations of Europe, and for a German Reich tottering on the edge of ruin. To the British Isles, many changes had come. The dark days of 1940 were but a memory, albeit a recent one. The blitz was over, but there was the problem of the V-1 buzz bombs, which had been falling on London since June. However, it was possible to counter and defeat the V-1 and although the cause of much death and destruction, the little pilotless bombs were to be of little strategic consequence.

"Food and fuel and most of the luxuries of life were scarce, and the casualty lists were still depressingly long, but there was no longer any likelihood of defeat. Among the changes which had come to the islands was the presence of the United States Eighth Air Force, which had become a dominant factor in the eastern counties, for better or worse. Near the peak of its strength, the Eighth sprawled across East Anglia in a vast complex of airfields with well over seventy major installations, and many smaller ones, stretching north from London almost one hundred miles to The Wash.

"The names of English towns and villages, which had meant little to anyone except their inhabitants, now assumed an unexpected importance to thousands of Americans. For the rest of their lives they would remember such places as Mount Farm (7th Photo Group), Great Ashfield (385th Bomb Group), Nuthampstead (55th Fighter Group and 398th Bomb Group), Bassingbourn (91st Bomb Group), Martlesham Heath (356th Fighter Group), Snetterton Heath (96th Bomb Group), Steeple Morden (355th Fighter Group), and dozens of others which were home for a brief and exciting period of their lives.

"For the men of the 357th Fighter Group at station F-373, there were two names: Leiston, the closest town to the airfield; and the village of Yoxford, a bit further away, but chosen by the Nazi propaganda agency when they dubbed the 357th Group the 'Yoxford Boys,' a name its veterans still bear with pride.

"In retrospect the Yoxford Boys were a typical unit of its type, now nine months through the calendar from the time it had become operational in February with P-51s, the first Eighth Air Force group to equip with the legendary Mustang. It was, by now, a veteran outfit, having taken its losses and applied considerable punishment to its assigned enemy, the Luftwaffe. The Operational Summary

at the end of October stated proudly that 'enemy aircraft destroyed has reached 400, the highest monthly average of any group in the air force for a similar period.'

"Throughout Eighth Air Force operations out of England and over the Continent, the weather had always imposed severe hardships, and was responsible for a great many casualties. Bad weather posed especially difficult problems for fighter pilots, many of whom had only minimal instrument training. It was a wise fighter pilot who realized early in his career that skill in flying the gauges might improve his chances of survival more than his skills in gunnery. The final three months of 1944 were particularly bad, far worse than the same period of the previous two years. During November, the heavies of the Eighth were held to their fog-shrouded bases more often than not, managing to operate on only eighteen days, with most bombing being done through cloud by radar. Bombing priorities went to the oil campaign and to the new emphasis on the continental transport system. Of the eighty-seven major oil installations, over half had been put out of production by the end of the month. The greatest fear of Albert Speer, Germany's production genius, was being realized.

"Life on base at Station F373 had long ago settled into a routine, the 1,000 men of the fighter group, plus many others of the 469th Service Squadron, the signal, quartermaster, ordnance, medical, military police, and other essential companies had built an American community in the English countryside. In common with other bases the living areas were a mile or two from the technical sites and airfield proper. There was a movie

left: Gun camera images of an enemy aircraft destroyed; below: A restored P-51D Mustang fighter in the markings of the 357th Fighter Group of World War Two.

theater, an officers' and an NCO club. The Red Cross had a large recreation facility called the Aero Club and staffed by several genuine American girls. There was a small post exchange, all of these housed in the usual Nissen hut type half round structures.

"A central mess hall fed all enlisted personnel, the quality of the food being quite good, and all in all life was reasonably satisfactory for the army of support people. Nevertheless, few

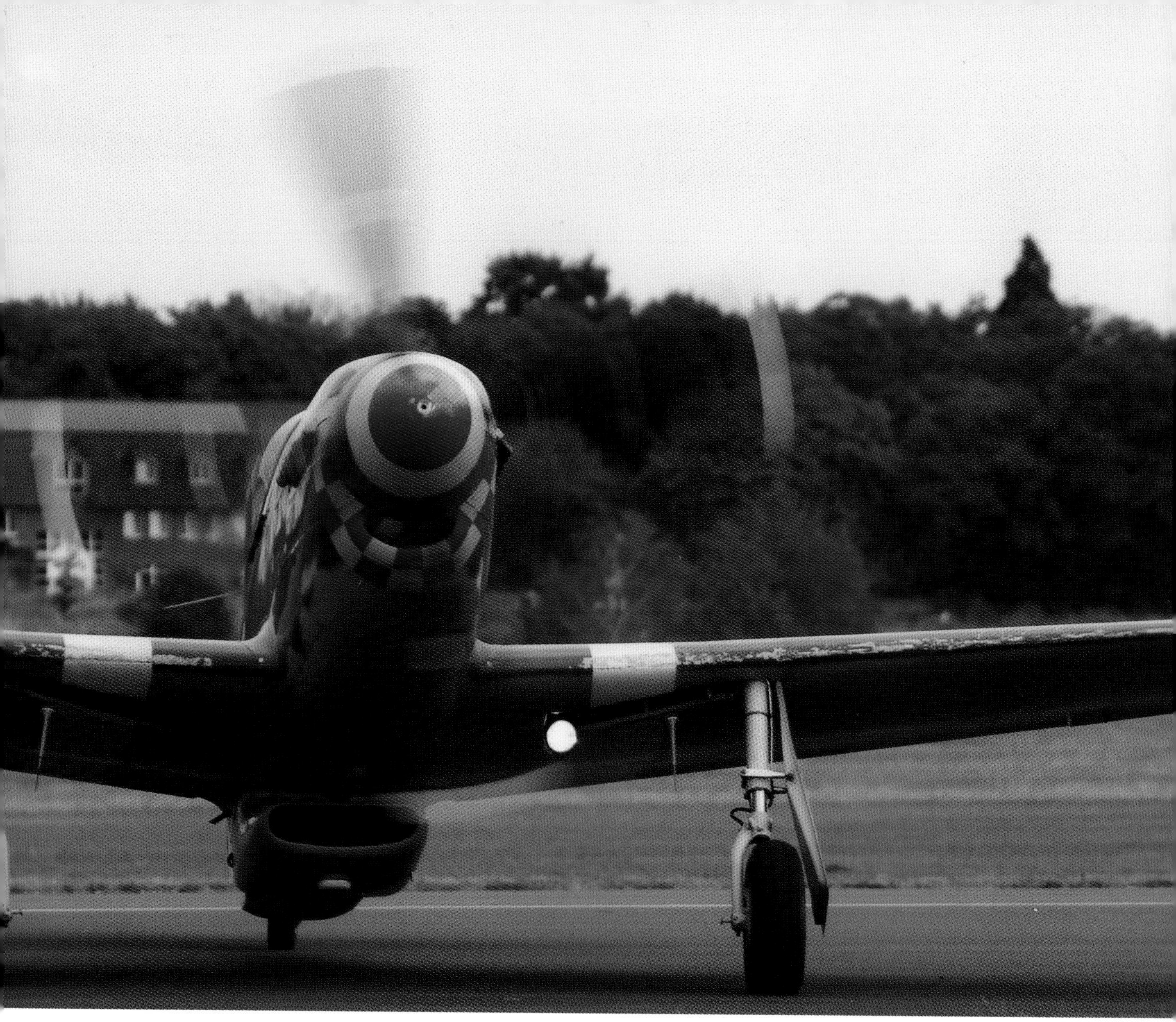

recognized the unique experiences they were living. The common desire was to see the war's end, so we could all go home.

"The majority of Americans used their occasional day off to venture forth into the surrounding villages in search of pubs, girls, or historic culture, either charming or annoying the natives, depending on the disposition of both. The rare three-day pass provided the time to visit London, some sixty miles south.

"In retrospect, life on an Eighth Air Force base during those years was an interesting study in contrasts. On base, one was surrounded by the paraphernalia of the air assault on Germany, while just beyond the perimeter track lay the quiet English countryside and indeed, the two were intertwined, most bases having active farms within their boundaries. Every effort was made to avoid disturbing the farming, whose products were badly needed by the English economy.

"Providing an audio canopy over the whole was the almost constant roar of aircraft engines, at night the muted thunder of hundreds of RAF bombers bound for the Reich; during the day the sounds of Wright Cyclones and Pratt & Whitney Wasps of B-17s and B-24s, mingled with the closer distinctive snarl of Packard Merlins.

"With the worsening weather

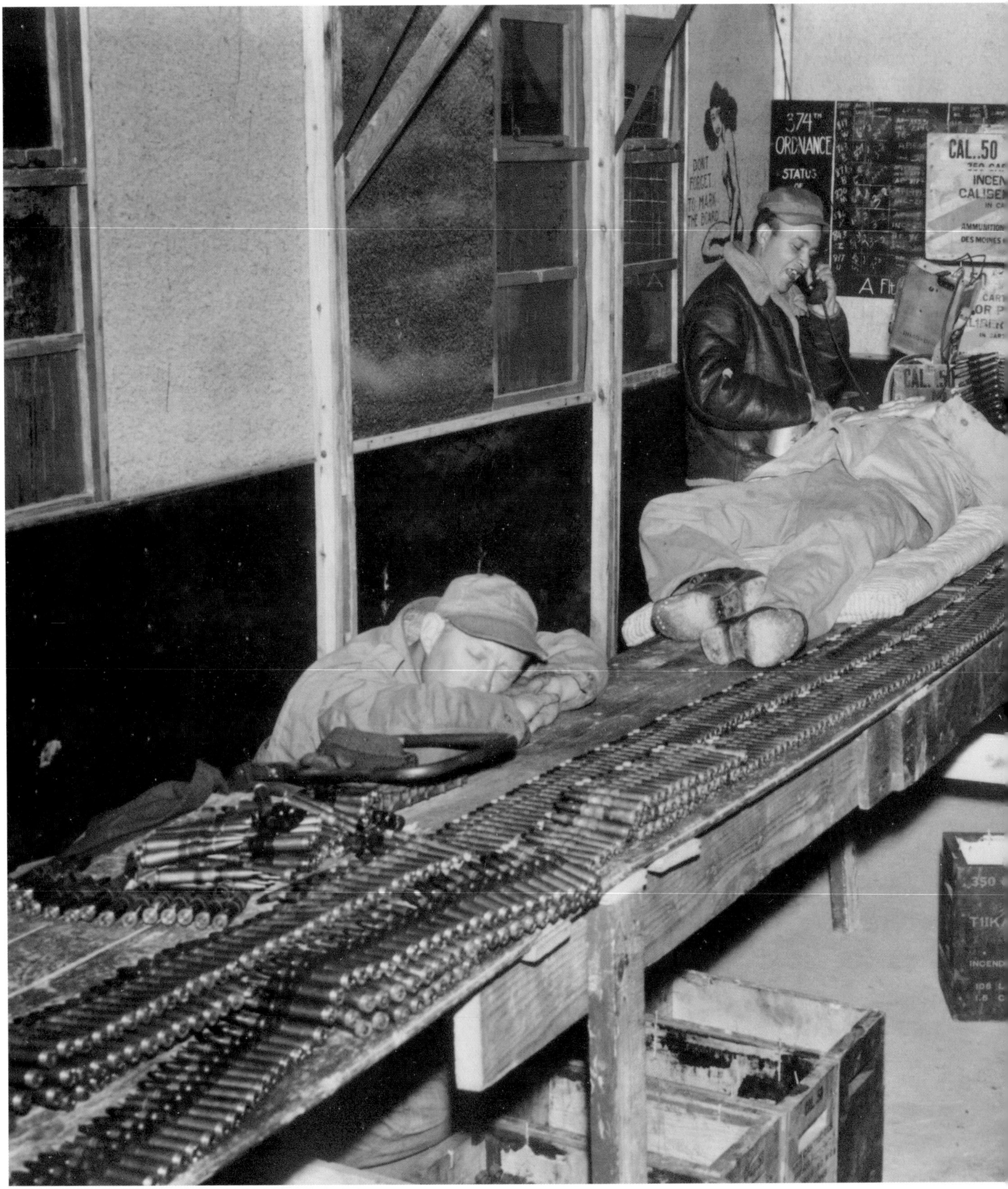
374TH
ORDNANCE
STATUS
DONT FORGET TO MARK THE BOARD
CAL..50

In the armorer's shack of an Eighth Air Force fighter station somewhere in England in 1944.

there were fewer operational days, and on those days when the teletype did not clatter out a Field Order in the early morning hours, air and ground crew members could sleep a bit later—'crew chief weather,' we called it. Even with 'blotto' weather and no ops, there was usually maintenance to be accomplished on the P-51s, even if only to adjust and tighten canopy and wing covers, which never did fit properly.

"On mission days the ground crews, jarred out of their sleep by the intrusion of the squadron CQ (Charge of Quarters), were usually breakfasted and on the line about two hours before scheduled briefing time for the pilots.

"The crew chief, or assistant crew chief, whichever arrived first, started the pre-flight inspection which was always concluded by an engine run and topping off the fuel tanks. The armorer had by then arrived and checked and charged his guns. With the pre-flight completed, the windshield and canopy adjusted, it was just a matter of waiting until the jeeps and weapons carriers, loaded to the fenders with pilots and their gear, arrived to begin the day's operation.

"Some pilots did a walk-around of their aircraft, others did not, trusting it had all been done. Most took the opportunity to relieve themselves (it was always a long ride, and the relief tube stowed under the seat was almost useless). With the pilot settled in his seat, belt and harness secured, oxygen and radio hook-ups complete, it was waiting time again—this time for engine start. All engines in the group started at the same time. More waiting, until time to pull chocks and edge into the proper place in the line of P-51s snaking their way around the perimeter track to the active runway.

"At takeoff time, the mission lead-er and his wingman were waved off together, the remainder of the force following in pairs as the pair ahead broke ground.

"With the departure of the mission, quiet descended on Station F373 except for the distant sound of other groups forming up and climbing out Channel-bound.

"The P-51 was unique among WWII fighters by virtue of its great range, five-hour missions not being unusual. This meant that most of the mid-morning or midday period was one of suspended animation. The time provided was often used to unpack and prepare the 108-gallon pressed paper drop tanks for future use (several days' supply was kept on hand at each dispersal point). The tanks arrived without attachment points, which were secured by light gauge metal bands around the tank. Fuel and air line (the tanks were pressurized) elbows had originally been aluminum, but these sometimes failed to slip out of their hoses on tank release, causing the tank to hang up or swing back and strike the wing. Glass elbows were substituted and were found to break clean, or sometimes slip out of the hose.

"The crews who waited on hardstands and dispersal areas at dozens of airfields across East Anglia, for their charges to return, were a vital part of the vast air offensive. In hundreds of photos of those long-gone days, it is remarkable how much alike they all look. Clad in usually ill-fitting coveralls, baseball-type fatigue caps, and mechanics–issue leather jackets, they present a singularly unglamorous appearance. The aircrews are the stars and the cutting edge of any military flying organization, but the ground crews are fully their equal in importance—no one will fly for long without them.

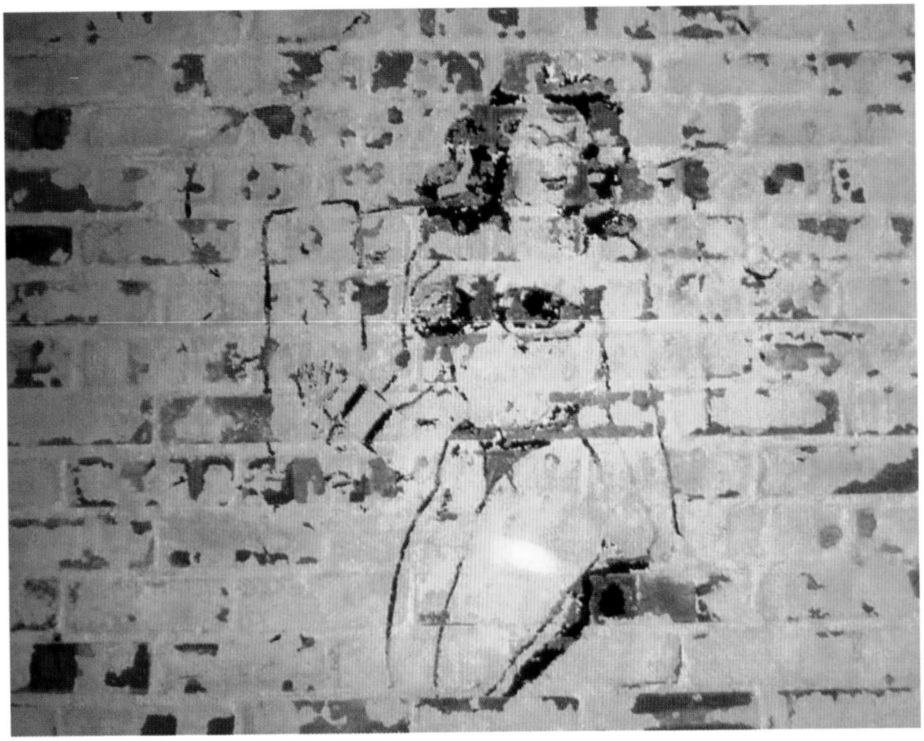

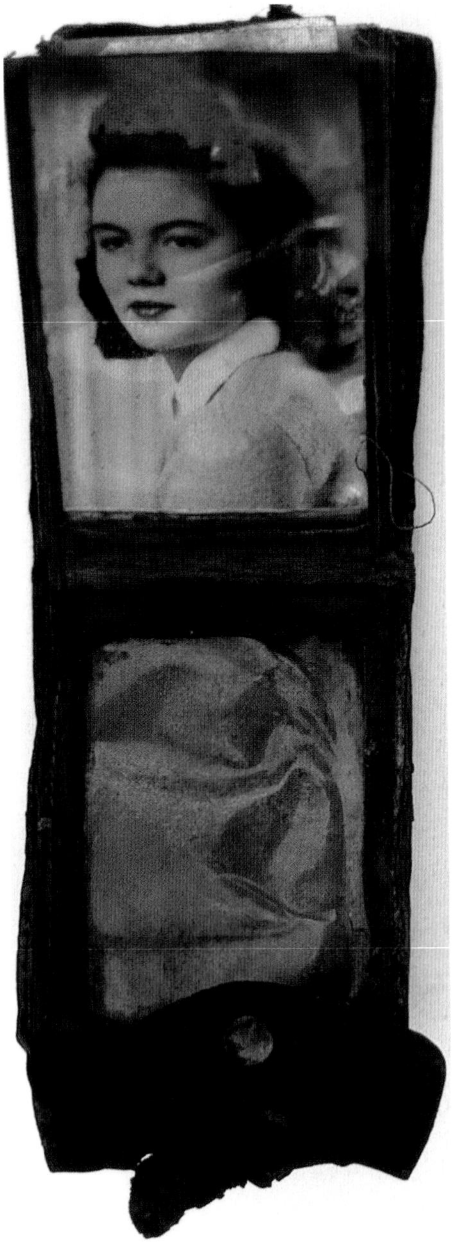

"Mission return time was known by the crews and all were back on the line long before this. If the group had flown an uneventful operation, the Mustangs usually arrived over base in formation, but often returned as small groups, or ones and twos if there had been action. Landing and taxiing aircraft were always scrutinized carefully for damage, or for missing tape from the gun muzzles, or heavy oil streaking along the fuselage from the crankcase vents, an indication of violent maneuvers.

"All aircraft, of course, returned to their own hardstands, but if Leiston air base had absorbed crippled airplanes from other units, which parked in the first available spots, it could generate considerable confusion, with returning P-51s finding their 'home' occupied by a damaged Thunderbolt or other stranger.

"With the ground crews briefed on aircraft condition and highlights of the mission, the pilots departed via roving jeeps and weapons carriers, for debriefing. If the airplane was reported serviceable, new tanks were installed and fuel system serviced to full 485 gallons. All fluid levels were checked and the fuselage washed down with 150 grade gasoline. The armorer attended to cleaning and servicing his guns and loading ammo cans. Guns were not charged until the following day's pre-flight.

"The Merlin engine and 150 grade fuel were tough on spark plugs, and plug changes were common on post-flight inspections. Overall, however, the Mustang was not a maintenance hog and crews were usually finished with their duties by early evening.

"It had been a day of heavy fighting, with Eighth Air Force fighters claiming 114 enemy aircraft destroyed. For the 357th and its Third Division 'big friends' it had been a ride to

top right: Wall art remaining at the Knettishall base of the 388th Bomb Group; above: The wallet of a downed airman; top right: A sticker promoting the sale of American defense stamps to raise money for the U.S. war effort.

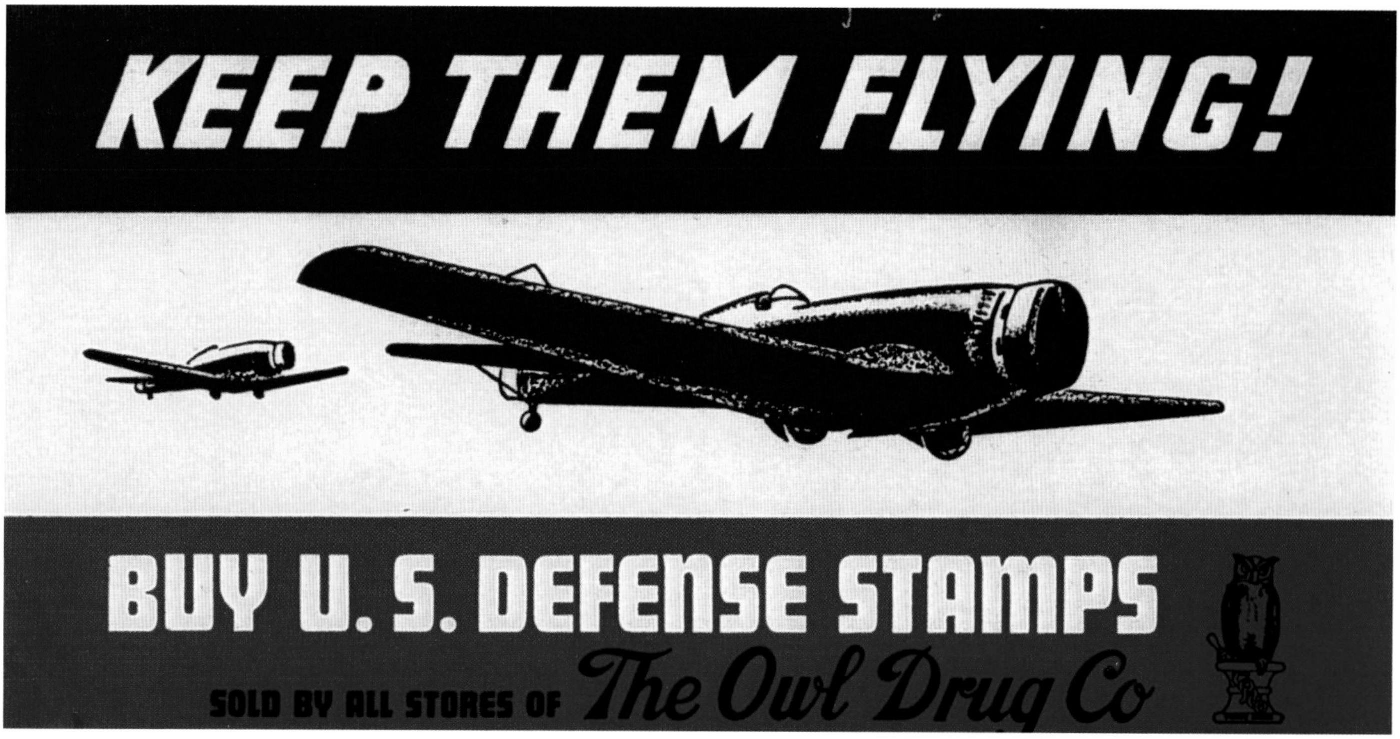
KEEP THEM FLYING!
BUY U. S. DEFENSE STAMPS
SOLD BY ALL STORES OF The Owl Drug Co

Hamm with no interference from the Luftwaffe. The B-17s bombed the marshalling yards through cloud, and by 1430 the forty-nine Mustangs were on the ground at Leiston. It would not be so quiet on the morrow.

"There was one major social event during November, a two-day celebration of the group's first anniversary in England. The affair took place on the 25th and 26th. A first-run and very popular movie of the time, *Double Indemnity*, was shown twice, and there were parties at all three clubs. Army Special Services presented a strictly GI show with a cast of twenty-two which was well done, and enjoyed by most of the troops. The celebration finale was provided Sunday night by a stag show in the officers' club, and a huge dance for the enlisted men was well attended by local civilian girls and by the women of the nearby British Army AAA batteries.

"On Monday morning, it was back to war, and in a big way—a strafing operation against an oil depot at Annaberg. It was unusual in that the Yoxford Boys were teamed with the 353rd group, only recently transitioned from P-47s to P-51s. Heavy Luftwaffe reaction on this date would change the mission objective, and it was to be a big day for both groups. Takeoff was late in the morning, at 1107, with Group Ops Officer Major Broadhead leading fifty-four Mustangs, soon reduced to fifty-one by aborts.

"The oil depot was forgotten. There was bigger game afield. At 1245 about fifteen miles southwest of Magdeburg, three gaggles of enemy aircraft were encountered; the two low gaggles, of seventy-five and one hundred-plus respectively, and the third fifty-plus as top cover. These enemy aircraft appeared to be coming from the Brandenburg area and were forming up. The combat took place from 30,000 feet down to the deck. The enemy aircraft took no aggressive action. The lack of aggressiveness by the pilots of the 109s and 190s is a common thread running through many of the encounter reports for the day. It may have been indicative of the low level of Luftwaffe training at this stage of the war, or possibly they were under orders to avoid combat with Allied fighters.

"The experiences of Major Andy Evans and Lieutenant Cliff Anderson tend to support the former theory. Each claimed an Fw 190, and in both cases the 190 pilots lost control while being chased at low altitude and crashed without being hit. In his encounter report, Anderson said he counted over thirty aircraft burning on the ground. The 353rd group claimed twenty-one and a half and the 357th thirty Me 109s and Fw 190s. Several

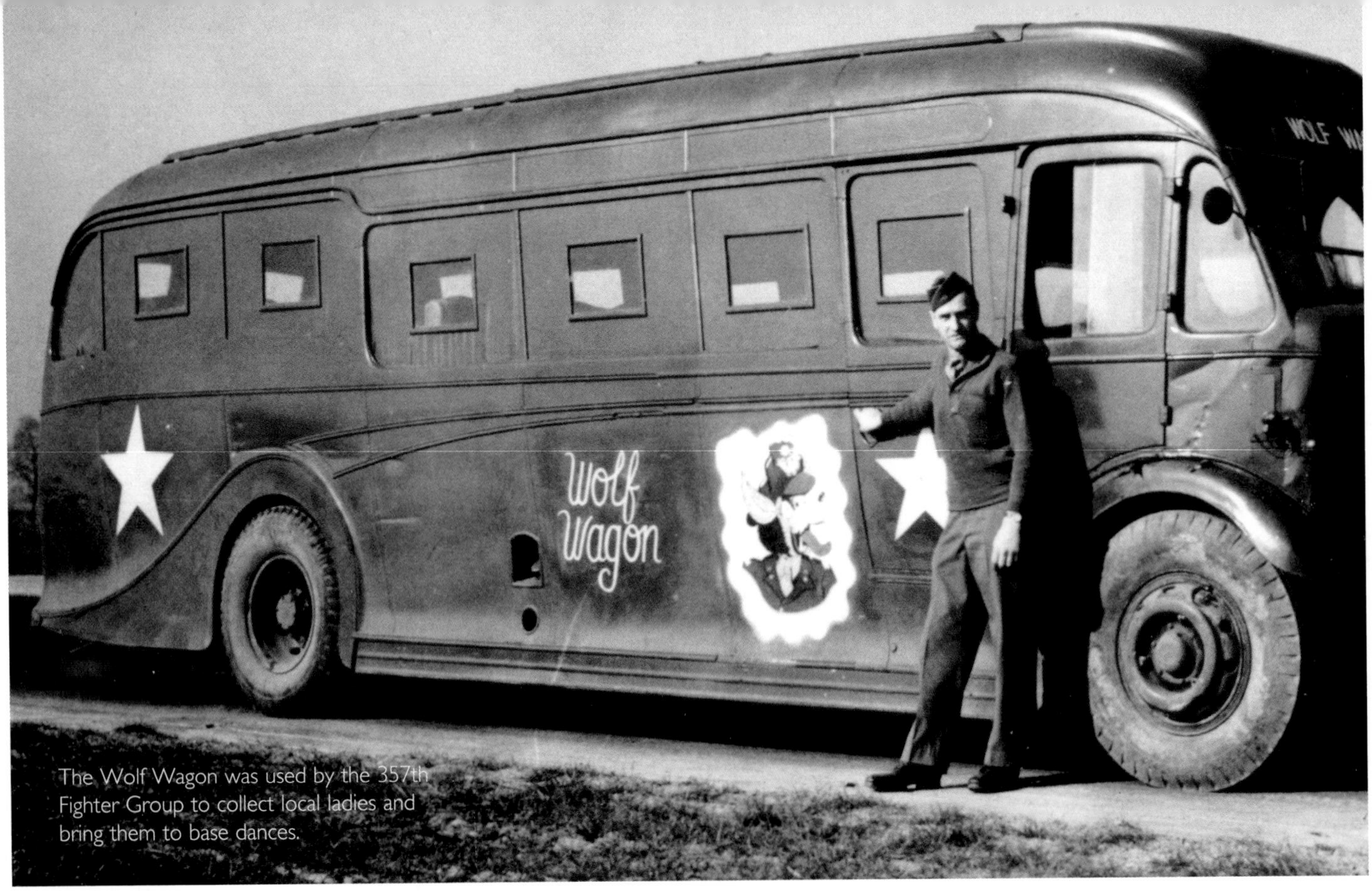
Wolf Wagon
WOLF WA
The Wolf Wagon was used by the 357th Fighter Group to collect local ladies and bring them to base dances.

pilots claimed multiple victories, the highest being Captain Leonard Carson with five. All of Carson's victims were 190s, with three of the pilots effecting apparently successful bailouts. John England claimed four, as did Chuck Yeager, with others claiming doubles and triples.

"The 353rd group reported two P-51s lost, and the 357th one. This last casualty of the month was Lt Frank Gailer. Gailer had been with the group since August and now, on the 27th of November, was a competent veteran flying his forty-fifth mission, as element leader in Red Flight. Early in the melee, having lost his wingman, Gailer shot down two 190s in rapid succession and then picked up a stray 55th Fighter Group P-51 as a wingman. Six months later, Gailer was able to file his encounter report for 27th November: 'We climbed up to 28,000 feet trying to find some stragglers from the other enemy gaggle. An element of two ships made a head-on pass at me. I thought they were P-51s, but not being sure, I did not break, but kept ready to fire in case they were bandits. As we closed in the lead plane coming at us fired, shattering my canopy, knocking out my oil line and wounding me in the right shoulder. They were P-51s that knocked me down, of the 352nd group. I got back as far as Kassel, where my prop and engine froze. I bailed out at about 7,000 feet. The 55th group pilot stayed with me all the time. I called my squadron before bailing out and told them of the two victories.'

"Gailer's bailout was a textbook operation. Only the day before he had attended a lecture on bailout procedures, and having paid attention, found that it worked exactly as advertised. Frank Gailer spent the remaining six months of the war in Stalag Luft I at Barth, and although being shot down and wounded by friendly fighters was a personal disaster, ultimately he was the most fortunate of our November casualties—the only one to survive.

"Although the end of the war in Europe was only five months away, no one could know that. In those remaining months the Yoxford Boys would take more losses and add to their accomplishments. The last mission was flown on 25th April, and it all ended officially on 8th May 1945 with a teletype message clattering into Group over Jimmy Doolittle's printed signature: 'Effective immediately, 1st, 2nd and 3rd Divisions are stood down from any further bomber and fighter offensive operations in the European Theatre.'"

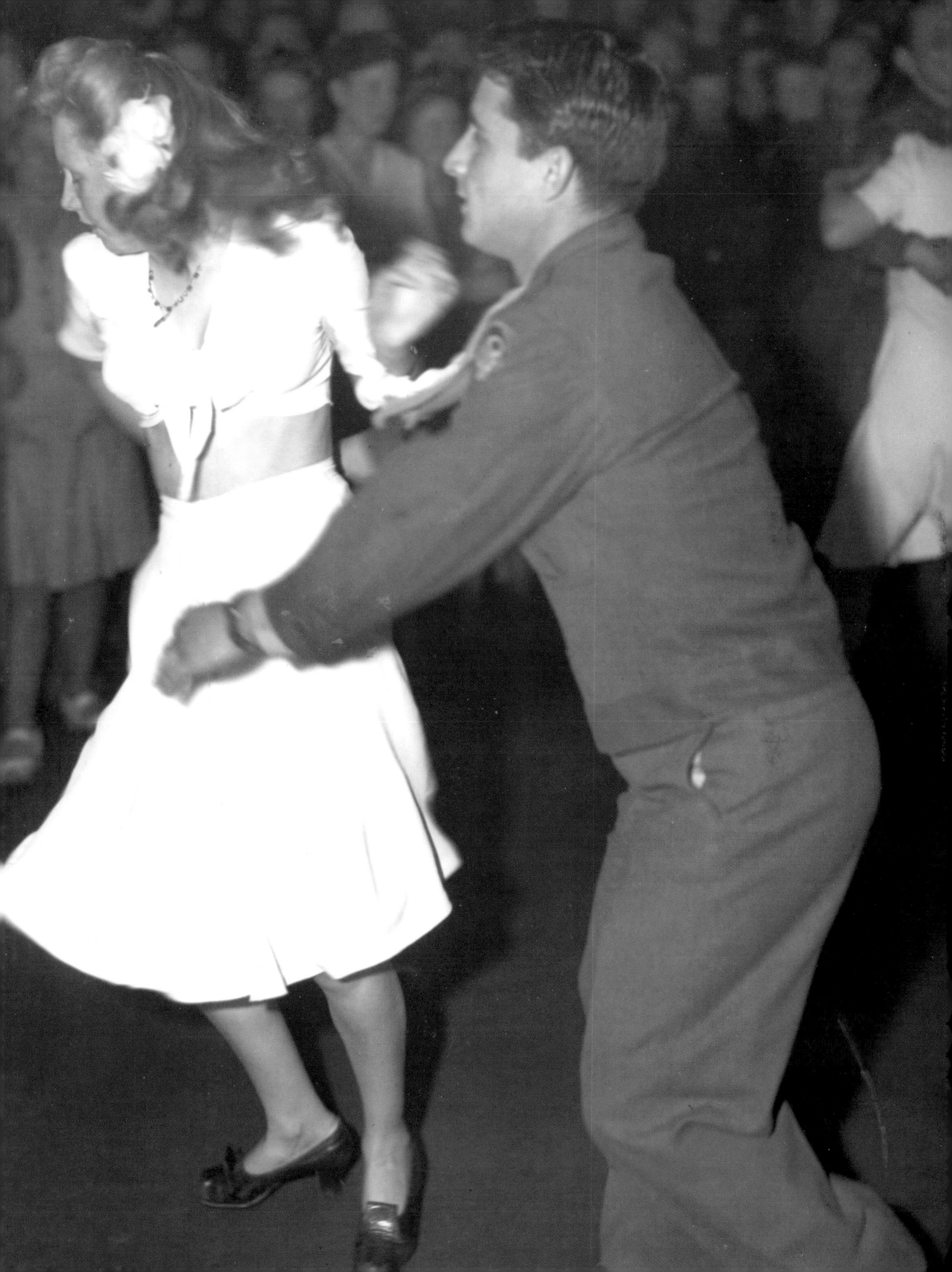

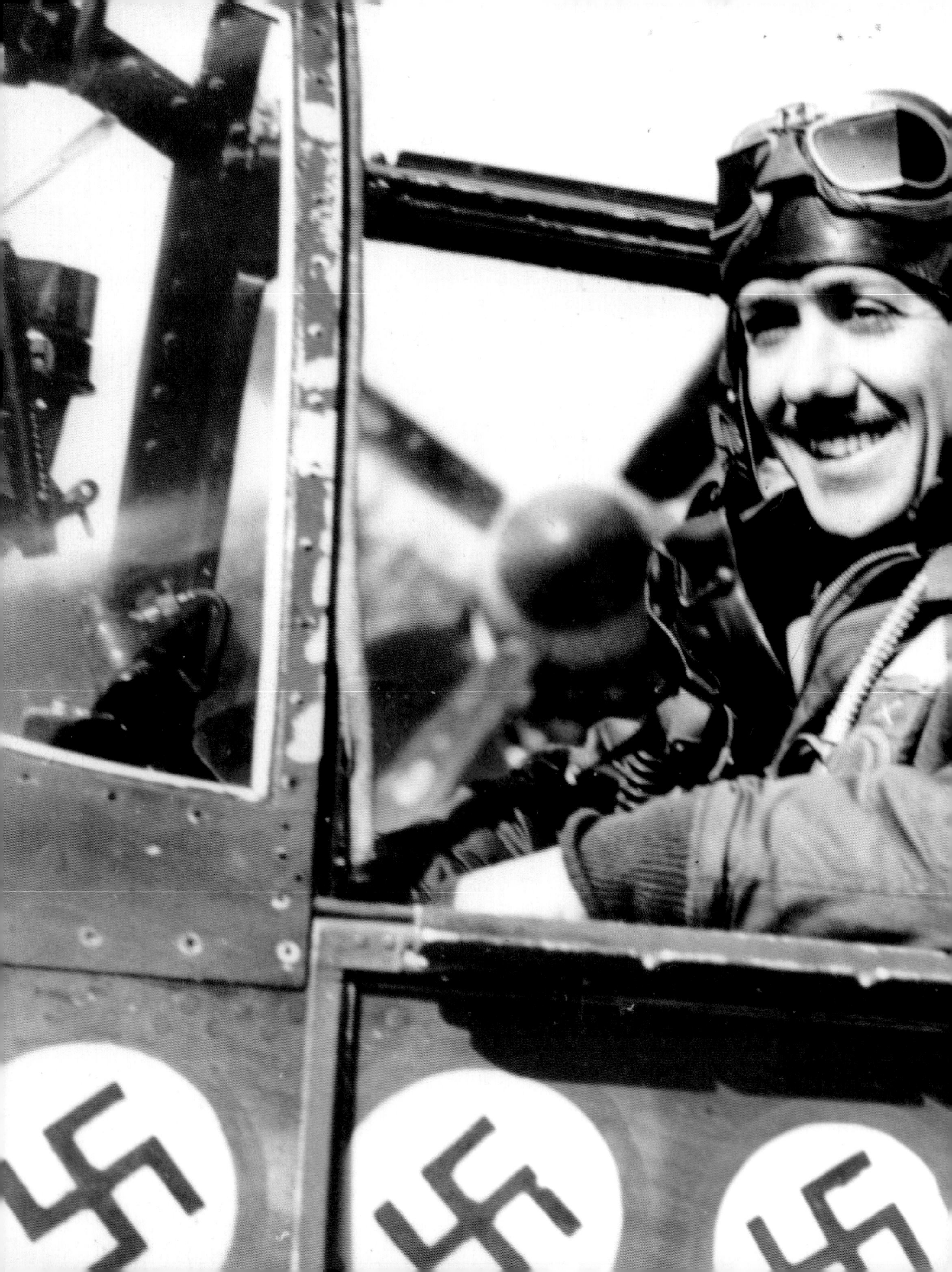

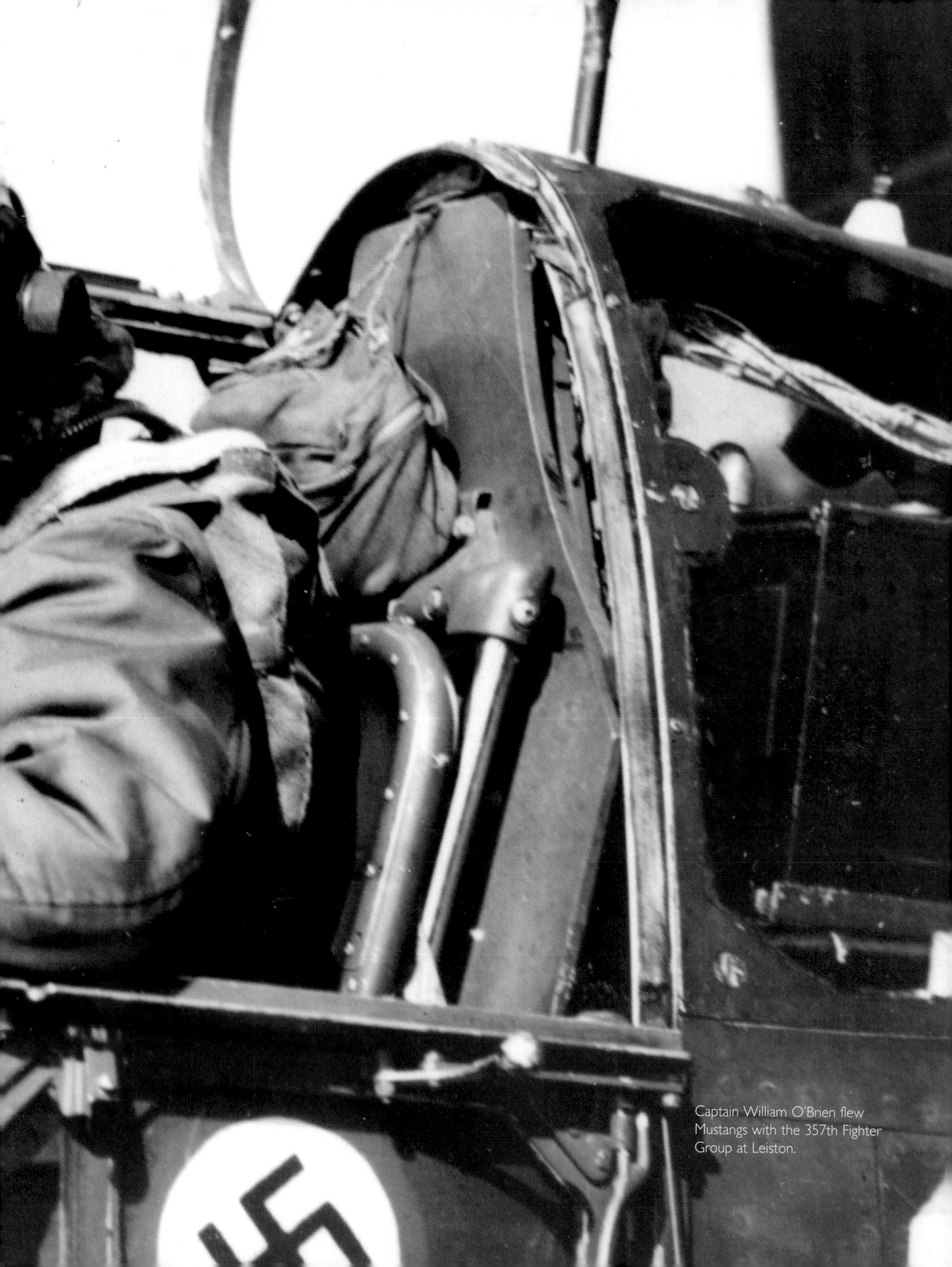

Captain William O'Brien flew Mustangs with the 357th Fighter Group at Leiston.

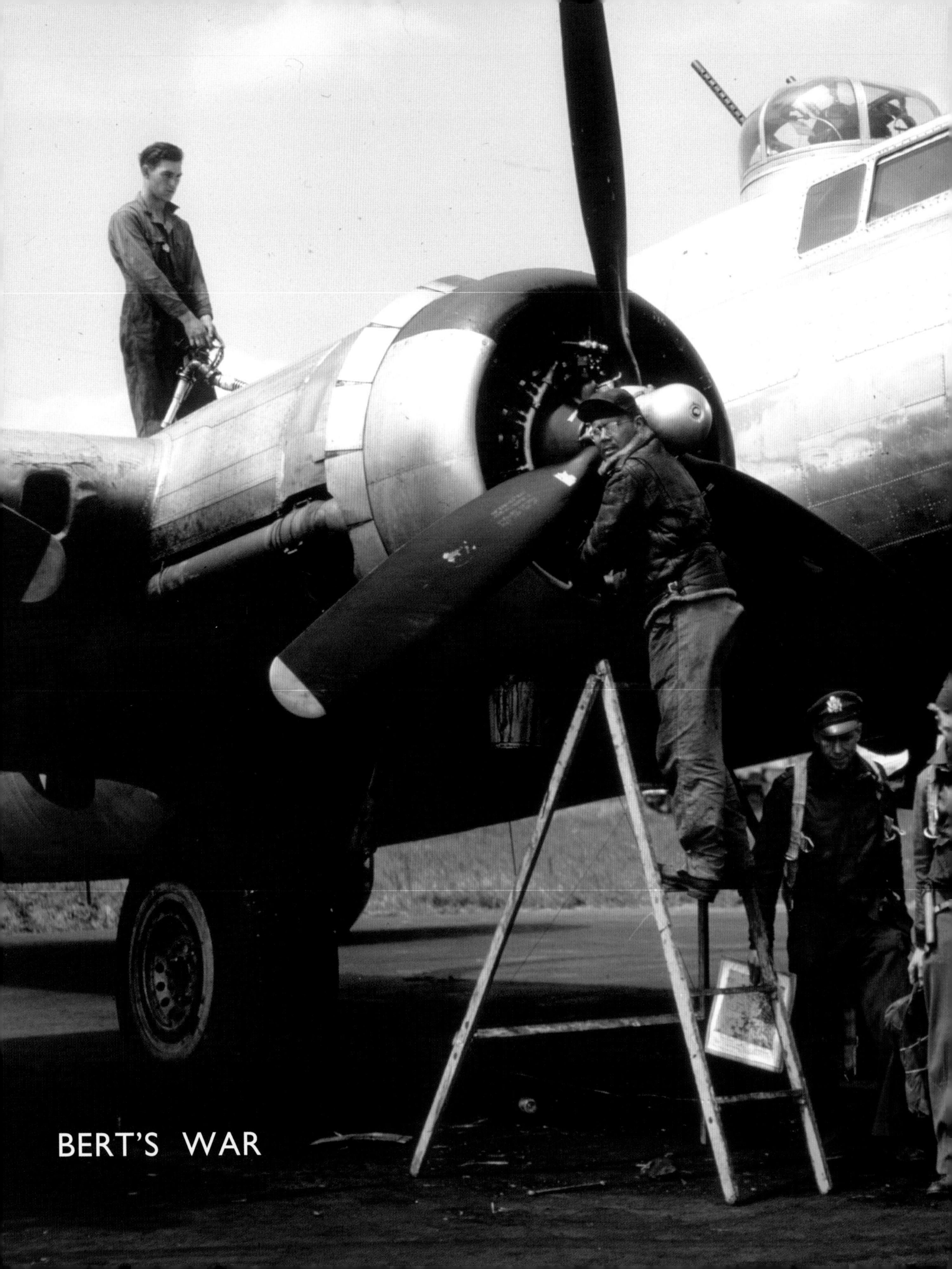

BERT'S WAR

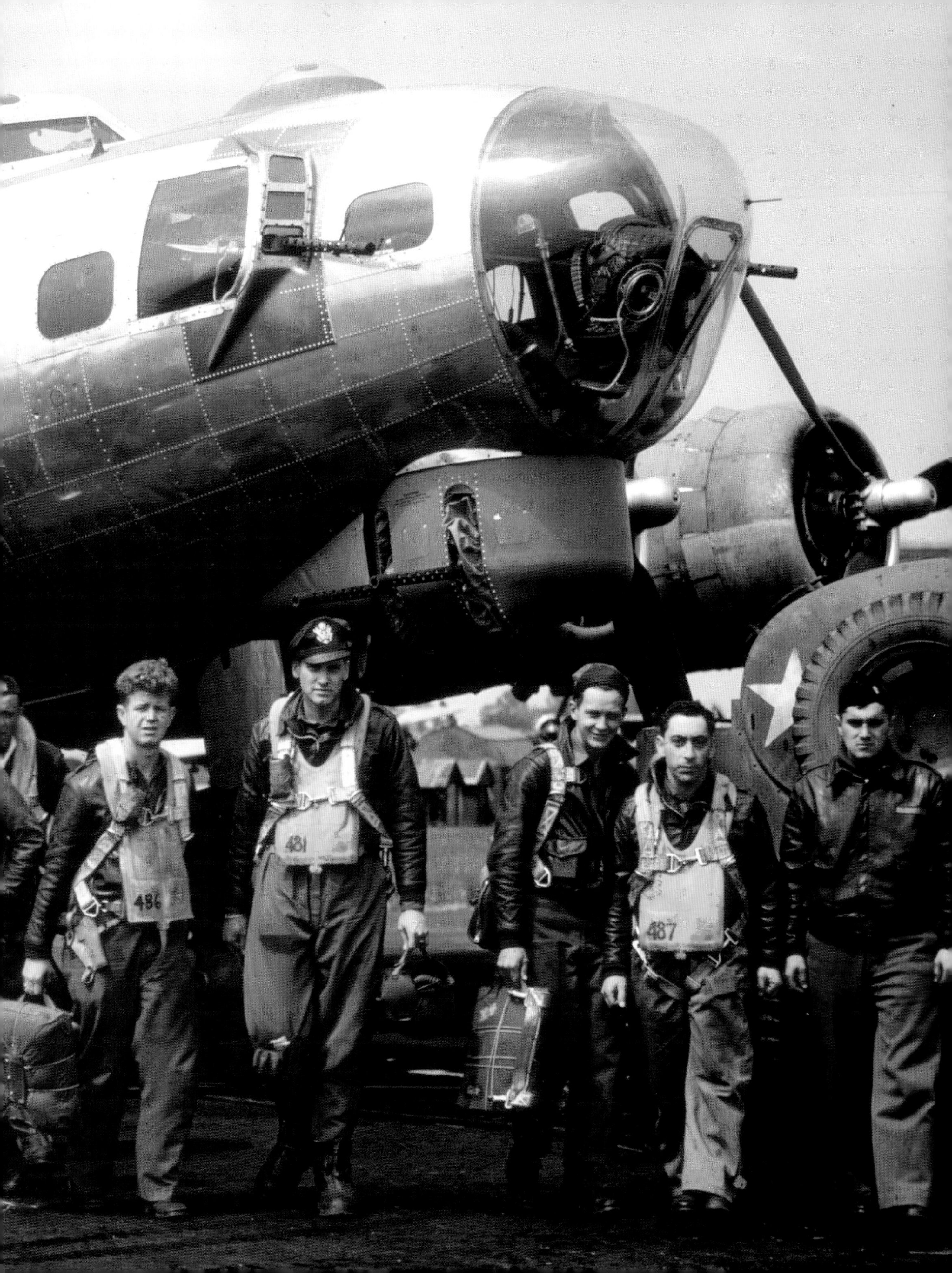
486
481
487

OF ALL WHO HAVE WRITTEN about war in the air, perhaps the greatest of these are Cecil Lewis, Richard Hillary, and Bert Stiles. Much of their greatness is in their ability to articulate and recreate an historic experience, the impact of which changed the world, and crucially with each of them, it was an experience they had lived; they were writing about their own personal air war. Bert Stiles may be the least well-known of the three, but his contribution to the literature of war in the air is as affecting and significant, and as powerful as that of the others. Stiles flew as co-pilot on the Sam Newton B-17 crew with the 91st Bomb Group in the Second World War. On completion of his thirty-five mission tour of duty he requested to be transferred to fighters rather than being rotated back to the United States for reassignment there. He was shot down and killed in a P-51 Mustang on 26th November 1944 while on a bomber escort mission to Hannover. He was twenty-three. Here are two examples of his work, reprinted with profound thanks to Robert F. Cooper and Roland Dickison.

"There were three new crews in the squadron, Black's, Newton's, and Hanna's. We belong to Newton, Sam Newton. All the first pilots were feeling pretty serious, but the rest of us didn't quite believe it yet. Our first mission, finally.

" The major gave us a little talk about how we might as well start sometime, and were there any questions, and told us to just fly that baby in there close and you'll come home. Most of the time.

"I'd only flown formation in a 17 twice, once in phase-training, and once this afternoon, and I'm no flash.

"Sam was all right. Big Sam. I've known him a long time. We were fraternity brothers at school—Colorado College.

"I wasn't scared. Not yet. I was just wondering a little, what the hell I was doing here. I'd been building up to this night for a long time. I used to dream about it in school, sitting there drinking Cokes with Kay, reading the airplane magazines. I used to think about it all the time in Aviation Cadets. And now we were really here, ready to go to war. We were going to kill the Germans.

"And I knew right then that I didn't know a thing about killing, or about being killed. I didn't feel like those Polish Spitfire pilots we met one night in Watford, Iceland. Those Polish kids had it bad. They wanted to kill everybody, and I know a Pole would choke Nazis all day long with his bare hands.

"But I've never been shot at, or bombed, and my folks live on York Street in Denver, a hell of a long way from war. The only way I knew about this war was through books and movies and magazine articles, and listening to a few guys who came back.

"It just wasn't in my blood yet. The whole idea was to blow just as much hell out of Germany as possible, tomorrow, and kill just as many good German workers as possible, and if any women or little kids get in the way, and get their legs torn off, or their faces caved in, tough. T.S. for them.

"From way up high, it wouldn't mean a thing to me. The more I thought of it, the uglier it looked, and I've thought about it a lot of times before today. What I wanted to do tomorrow was ski down the Canyon Run on Baldy up at Sun Valley, or wade out into the surf at Rosarita, and get all knocked out in the waves, and come in and lie in the sun all afternoon, and maybe love someone in the moonlight.

"Instead I was going to the war. World War, number II.

" 'Come on,' some joker said, at two the next morning. 'Breakfast at two-thirty, briefing at three-thirty.'

"Nick poked his head out from under the covers. 'Drag the Luftwaffe up and give 'em a blow for me.' He was on pass, and he could lie there all day.

"Bell, co-pilot on Black's crew, and I walked over to the mess hall through the dark. The stars were out and it was pretty cold. When we get up early for a mission we eat at Mess number one, with the colonels and the majors, and since they were not around so early, they don't care. I forgot my eggs, so Bell loaned me one of his. They check out six eggs to each man every Thursday.

"Bell and I were the first ones there. So we had a whole hour to eat before we had to go to the briefing.

"The 91st Bomb Group holds its briefings in a big overgrown Nissen hut, and it was almost like the briefings we had back at Alexandria in phase-training. The formation was drawn up on the blackboard and I copied down our squadron. We were flying right wingman in the high squadron. Smitty was leading, his 30th.

"The navigators went somewhere else for their own briefing. Sam went to change his pants, and I queued up in the co-pilot's line for escape kits. The gunners were somewhere else getting the same treatment.

"They had the route marked out with yarn on the big wall map, and it looked like a long way in to me. It was only a six-hour job, and we were supposed to have a record number of escort P-47s and P-51s alongside us, but it was Germany, and the Germans didn't want us over there at all.

"Everybody was talking and laughing and swearing, and we felt as if we were ready, sort of like this is what we came for, and let's get the show on the

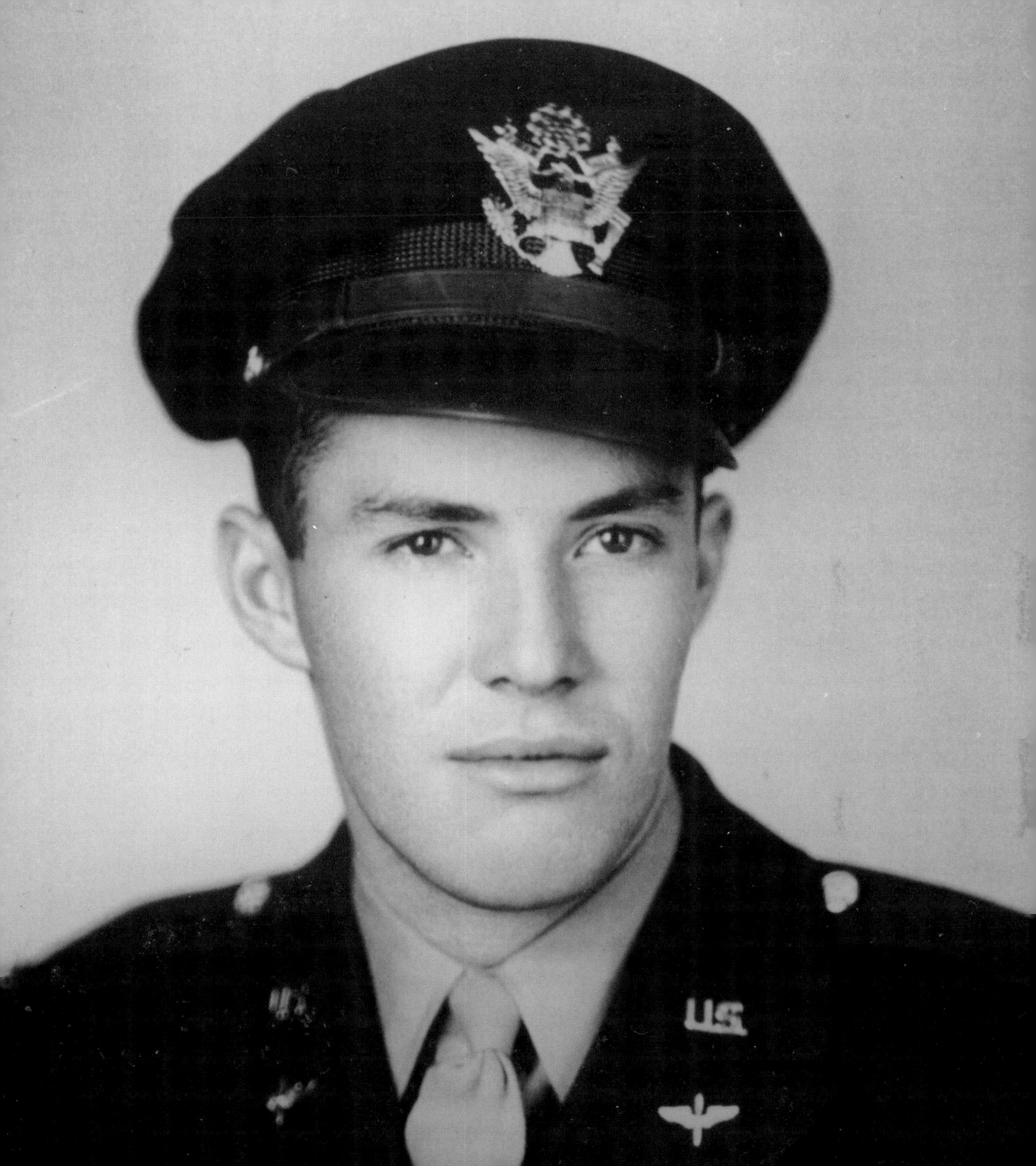

Lt Bert Stiles flew as co-pilot on the crew of Sam Newton from Bassingbourn. At the end of his tour he transferred to a Mustang group and was killed in an air combat incident; page 198: Eighth Air Force airmen in flight gear

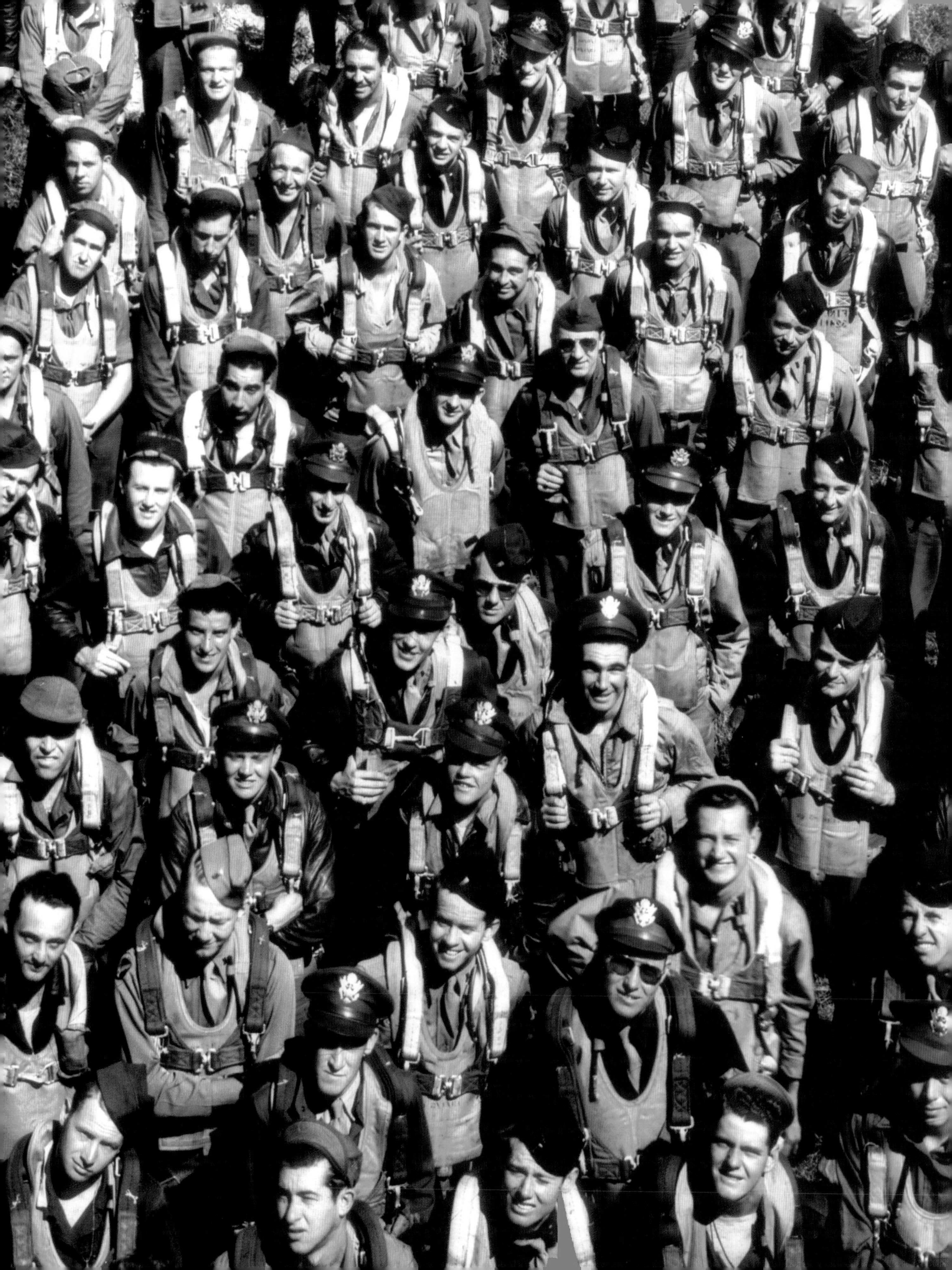

road. Getting ready to go in a Fortress is a rugged job, especially in the dark.

"Lewis was trying to get his guns in, while I was trying to get my flak suit set under the seat where I could reach for it fast. My 'chute kept falling off the hooks in the back of the co-pilot's seat, and I couldn't find my helmet.

"Don Bird and Grant Benson (bombardier and navigator) were all tangled up in the nose getting their guns in. Sam was the smart one. He stayed outside and talked to the crew chief.

"We were flying *Keystone Mama*. I turned my flashlight on the brown lady with no clothes on her chest, painted on the side, and decided they were short of artists at this base. But she was a good airplane.

"We were hauling ten five-hundreds, blunt-nosed and ugly, and deadly too. Spaugh patted them and laughed. He looked like a fighter, a big red-headed Carolinian.

"Ross (radioman) was the last one to get his gun set, and then we all huddled up back by the tail. It was sort of like the locker room before a high school ball game, only not as tense.

"Crone said he hoped those Fws and Me 109s came in on his side. He's a bloodthirsty little guy, a good man to have along. I wanted to see a Focke-Wulf sometime, but I didn't care about seeing one today. A museum would be a good place, after the war.

"Beach didn't say anything at all. He's a sleepy little guy, and older than the rest of us. He comes from Denver, like me, and in some way that makes us closer. He doesn't look like a killer, but he can wheel that ball around.

"We started engines at six o'clock. They rang off, start one, mesh one, start two, mesh two . . . right down the line. Four good engines.

"Our call sign was Hot-Pants-J-for-JoJo that day, and we were flying off Hot-Pants-S-for-SEXY, Smitty's ship.

His co-pilot gave us the wave when they came by, and I unlocked the tail wheel and Sam drove her out on the taxi strip.

"There was plenty of daylight when we got to the takeoff position at the head of the runway. Sam ran the engines up and the mags checked and the superchargers checked; and we gave the props their warm-up exercise.

"Then we were on the line, gyros uncaged and set, generators on, and superchargers set. I watched the instruments and called off the air speed and Sam herded her down the runway. We were bouncing all over before the needle hit 120, but Sam held her and then we were airborne.

"Grant Benson gave me the heading over interphone and we started climbing on course. I forgot to put the gear switch in neutral and Lewis reached up and did it for me.

"Assembling a group of eighteen planes is a madman's business. They fly around and around, and nobody seems to be getting anywhere at all, and then miraculously they're all in, flying off their respective wings, trying to look pretty.

"Our group got lined up with the wing, but the wing must have been off the beam someway, or some other wings were way out of line, because just as I was about to sit back and look around, we went driving in on a collision course into another wing. For a few seconds there were airplanes everywhere, and we were flopping around in prop wash. Then they were gone.

"We didn't even get over breathing hard when it happened again. Bird yelled over interphone, 'Here they come again,' and then I heard him tell Benson he didn't want to die this way. Nobody got hit but nobody was very far from it.

"Somewhere down in the forma-

tion the lead navigator was sweating out his check points, and the various squadron leaders were sweating out keeping their boys out of prop wash and in the right position, and all we had to do was hang on that wing. And that was plenty. I was hot, and my oxygen mask was driving me nuts, and I over-controlled on the throttles, too far forward, too far back, trying to keep the star on Smitty's wing centered.

"Sam could sit there, and move those throttles a quarter of an inch and still keep us in there. But flying across cockpit, heaving that big lady around, I really made work out of it. And jockeying for position uses up gas, and Forts need lots of it.

"We flew across the channel and crossed the coast of Holland. Intelligence had routed us nicely, and the lead navigator was on the ball, so we didn't see a sign of flak until we were out in the Zuider Zee, when another wing off to our right caught some, pretty black puffs in a blue sky. Harmless-looking stuff.

"We were flying into the sun, and our top window was dirty, and I couldn't see out of it. The front sheet of bullet-proof glass was dirty, too, and it was rough trying to see anything in that sun.

"'Fighters, three o'clock high,' came over the interphone. They were P-47s, ours, and they skated on by into the sun.

"We were over the fatherland. The country was all chopped up into little fields and little towns, and the fields were just as green as those in England, just as green as Iowa, too. They used the same sun, and the same moon, and the sky was just as blue and just as beautiful over here as over Pikes Peak. But the God damn people down there were Nazis.

"Sam signalled me to take the throttles for a while. The wing on our left

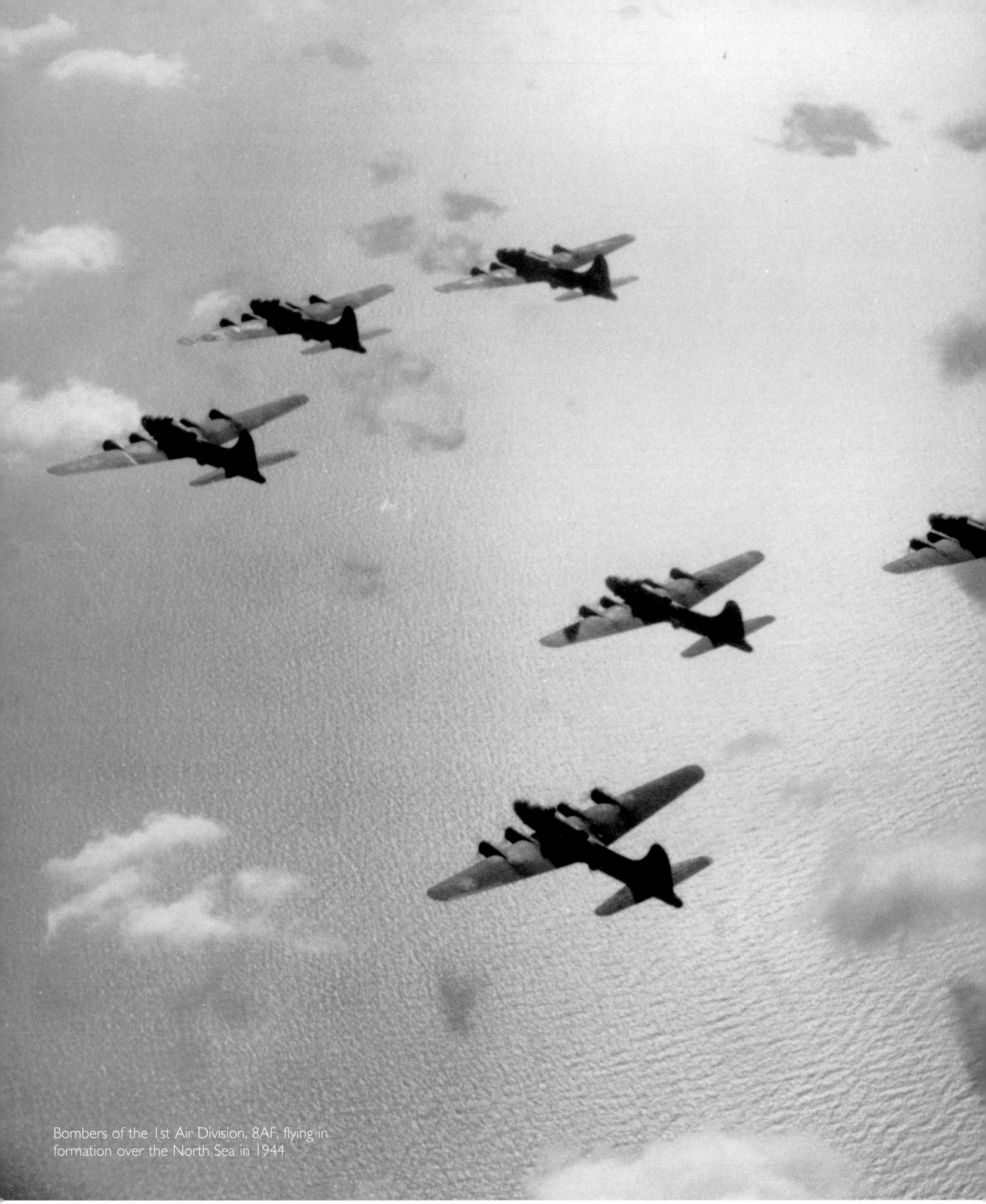

Bombers of the 1st Air Division, 8AF, flying in formation over the North Sea in 1944.

was doing some cagey flying, swinging in front of us, and then back again, and it threw a wrench in the works for me. Once, I almost overran Smitty, and stayed throttled back too long, and when I hit the power again, we had faded away.

"I looked up into that dazzling sun and knew, right then, we were meat for the Luftwaffe. I jacked up the RPM and poured the petrol to her, and we moved back in, slowly.

"When you take a quick look at a formation, it always looks good. Static death, standing still in the air. Even the ships out of position look right. Then if you watch a minute, you'll see the constant swing and play, back and forth. Hundreds of pilots are easing up on their throttles, or easing back, or horsing up or heaving back.

"B-17s in formation are something to see, because the 17 with its wheels up is a beautiful airplane, slim, and lovely, a machine dealing out death high in the sky. But it's work to keep one in position, especially when you haven't tried but a couple of times. It's nothing but work, with the sweat oozing down your armpits, down in back of your knees.

"Sharpe called off flak at seven o'clock. 'Look at that stuff,' he yelled. 'All over hell.'

"The sky is a big place, and keeping seven hundred airplanes at the right altitude, over the right check points at exactly the right time, is a hell of a job, and nobody was exactly right that day. Wings were swinging off for their targets in front of us, and behind us, and a couple of them looked like they wanted to go through our formation, and we were trying to get lined up on the Initial Point (I.P.), our point of bomb reference.

"I thought here's where we get left with a bombload. I didn't think there was a target anywhere around. Then

I saw Smitty's bomb bay doors open and their bombs fell. A second later Bird yelled that ours were gone too.

"'Radioman', Sam yelled, 'See if all our bombs dropped out.'

"'I can see 'em,' somebody yelled from the back end. 'Look at all that smoke.'

"Everyone was yelling. It was a lousy demonstration of interphone discipline. We had the RPM jacked up, and we were turning off the target. There was no flak.

"All the bombers were throwing out radar chaff, to throw the aim off from the anti-aircraft jockeys below. We were letting down a thousand feet so we could get the hell out of their country a little faster.

"A couple of wings off to the left were catching some flak, and somebody had knocked hell out of a town to our right.

"We flew out of Germany into France, and I couldn't tell the difference. It all looked the same from 30,000 feet.

"There were a lot of planes in sight when we came in, but going out, there had been thousands. Every direction, up, down, or sideways, there were airplanes, big ones and little ones.

"Over Belgium, I remembered my flak suit. I was a little late, but I finally struggled into it. It was heavy on my neck, and when Sam turned the plane over to me, I thought I was going down. My neck hurt and my shoulder was tired. About two minutes later, I took the flak suit off. It was better to die fast than slow.

"Two P-51s came jazzing by looking for game. I got the same old hopeless feeling that hits me every time they come close. I was supposed to drive one of those little ones once. I went through the single engine advanced flying school, and I'd sell my soul to end up in a P-51 or a P-47. So here I am on the right hand side of a B-17.

"After awhile, the coast came into sight. Sometimes one of the gunners would call flak to the left or right, but our lead navigator was really hot that day, and they didn't even come close.

"There were three straggling B-17s down with a B-24 Liberator, but the fighters were herding them home.

"I had to tell myself over and over that this was war. This was really it, and somewhere down there in that crazy, lovely patchwork of farms and towns there were a lot of hard-eyed bastards who would have sold out to get at us.

"We crossed the coast and started letting down, The formations began to come apart then, and I suppose it didn't matter much. In the old days, eight months ago, you didn't loosen up or the Abbeville kids were on you, right off the coast, when the tired bomber boys tried to stretch their legs.

"At sixteen thousand I took off my helmet and ate my candy bar. It felt wonderful to get that soggy oxygen mask off my face. There was a puddle of drool in the chin cup.

"We tightened up again when we hit the English coast, because they had told us at briefing we had to look good when we came in, because Doolittle and Spaatz were down there, and maybe Mr. Stetinius, maybe even Churchill.

"I've never been so tired. The lead navigator took us home and we circled the field while the squadrons peeled off, and then it was our turn. I put the wheels down and tried to remember what I hadn't done.

"Sam made the best landing he's made in England.

"We'd been to war and we were back from it now, safe in England, safe on this big wide runway. I forgot about the generator switches and Lewis had to tell Sam to knock them off.

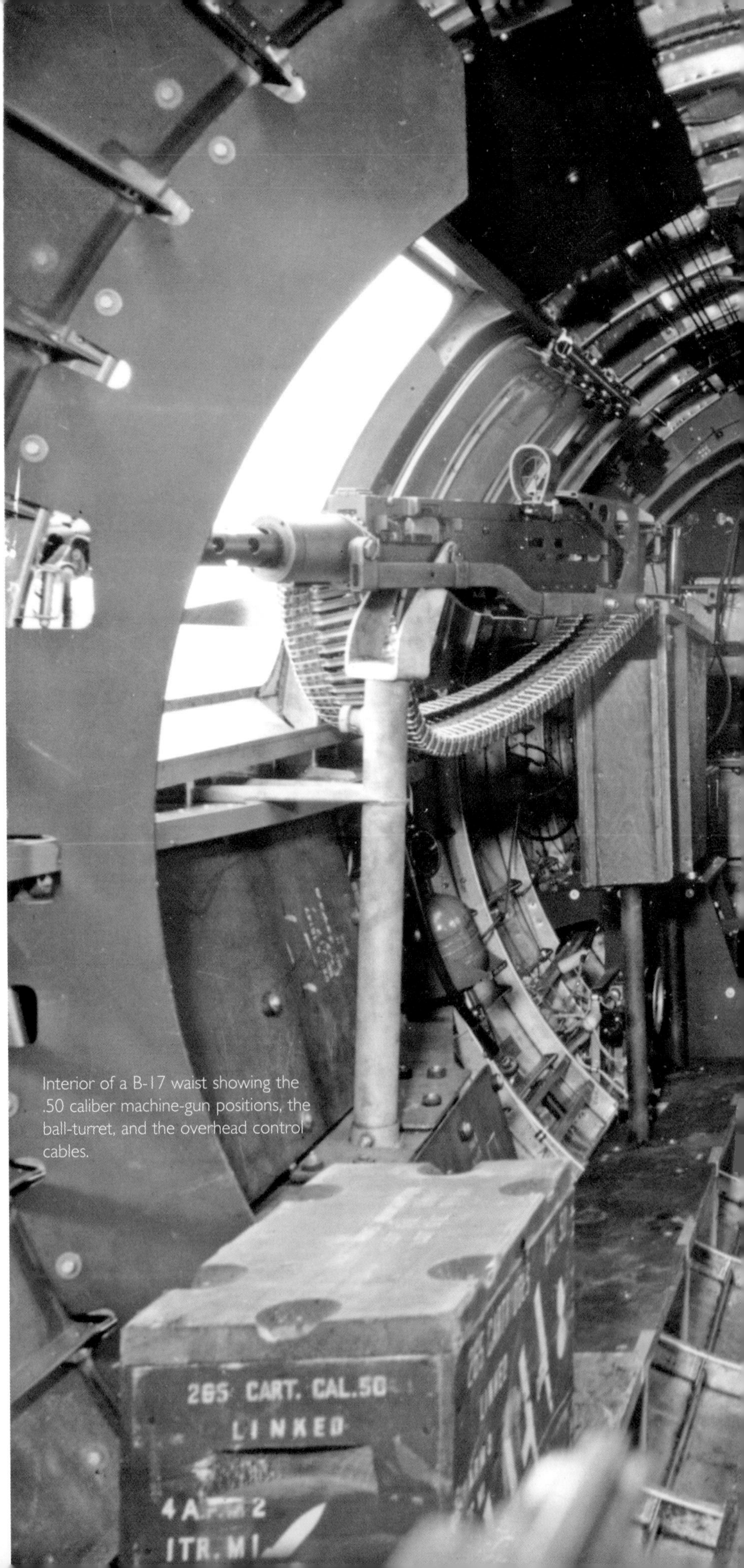
265 CART. CAL.50
LINKED
Interior of a B-17 waist showing the .50 caliber machine-gun positions, the ball-turret, and the overhead control cables.

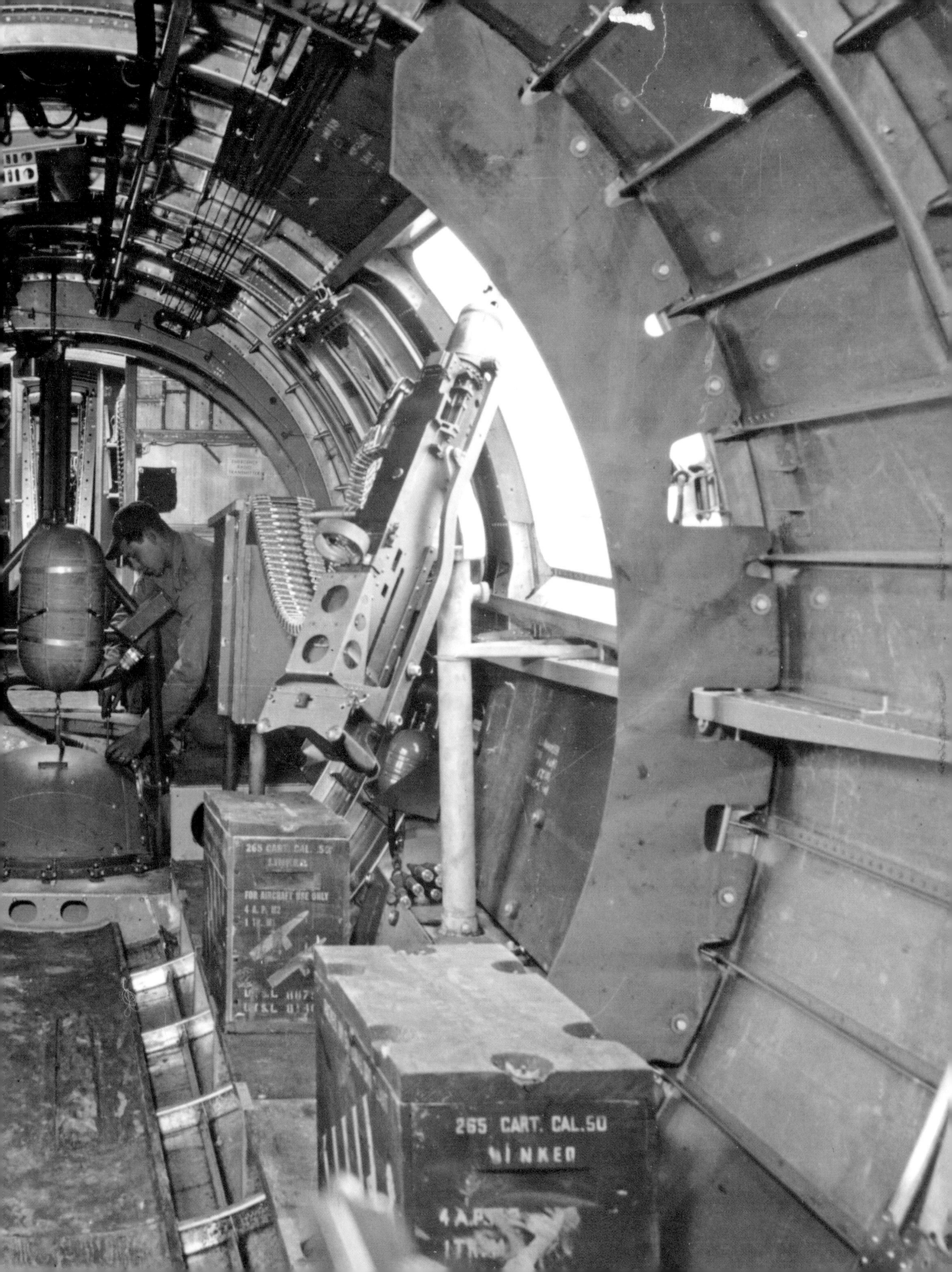
265 CART. CAL.50

"We got the plane back in its stall in the dispersal area, and gave it back to the ground crew.

"I wondered if we'd killed anybody. I wondered if we'd smashed anything. I was so shot I didn't want to move. My flying had been lousy. My hair was caked with sweat, and my eyes ached from looking into the sun.

"While I sat there a plane taxied by with half its tail blown off. It was one of ours. I didn't believe it. Those guys had been in the war, too, but they were back now.

"Lewis got his guns out, and we threw the flak suits on the ground, and let the parachutes down easy, and got ourselves and all our junk on the truck.

"Sharpe said, 'Well, we're not virgins anymore.'

"We'd been there and we'd come home. I lay back in a pile of flak suits and let go. We were all here, and there weren't any holes in us, and right then I didn't want to be anywhere else in the whole world, and these were the people I wanted to be with, these guys, Sammy Newton's crew.

"Air crews are just like people. They have to grow up sometime. Before Wednesday, the 21st of June, nobody thought a hell of a lot of Sammy Newton's crew, except the guys on the crew, and even they didn't make any great claims.

"They were just nine guys assigned to an airplane. They got along all right, because there's a war on and you have to get along with the guys you fly with.

"Since the Luftwaffe has taken itself deep into the homeland, and taken to being coy, crews have been known to go through twenty or thirty missions without even speaking to a Me 109 or an Fw 190. Of late, fighter escort has been so beautiful, only one or two wings of bombers get any business all day. With a certain amount of luck, and

by availing yourself of all the short rides to France, you stand a good chance of keeping your health in this league, especially if your group flies a good tight formation over Germany.

"The odds on getting shot up by fighters are lesser now than they were in the old days when the Abbeville Kids were waiting at mid-channel, and the battling bastards from Brunswick were sitting on top of the overcast, and the air battles went all the way around.

"With little fighting, it doesn't matter a hell of a lot who stands by the guns, and swings the turrets around, and looks out the windows. Pilots tend to forget they may need gunners in some dark hour. Gunners tend to not give a damn, and tend not to be eager about keeping their weapons clean.

"Most of May 1944 was a cinch. Sammy Newton's crew flew a lot of missions, but except for the 24th on a trip to Berlin when the Focke-Wulfs came through from one o'clock and blew off the rear escape hatch, and gave the tail gunner a bloody pair of shorts, most of the hazard was mental, wending through the flak-gardens at the target, and sweating out the chow lines, now swollen out of all shape by new crews.

"'What this place needs is a strafing mission to Berlin,' some old joker (two months) would say. 'This crop needs some thinning.'

"But from just before D-Day and for about a week after, the big birds had a soft life. They had to get up at ungodly hours, but they were usually back for a late breakfast and a couple of hours of sack time before noon.

"And then the high command decided some more strategic bombing was in order and sent the 17s back to Hamburg, and those flak opera-tors turned out to be a checked-out bunch of boys. They put it in your lap

at Hamburg, and they kept putting it up there for several of the best years off the end of a lifetime. Two trips to Hamburg, and then the Forts went back to Berlin.

"Wednesday, the 21st, was the day, and Sammy Newton's crew went along on their third trip to the capitol, with a thousand other Fortress crews, and a thousand or more fighter boys.

"By this time, Newton's crew had visited most of the better known hot spots in Europe—Kassel, Hamm, Munich, Metz, Brunswick, Ludwigshaven, Kiel, Paris, Dassau, Leipzig, Cherbourg. They dropped bombs, and sometimes brought bombs home. There were a couple of abor-tions on the record. They flew in for-mation and out of formation.

"The officers had been doing their jobs, and the enlisted men had been going along for the ride.

"But on the 21st of May, Sammy Newton's crew had to grow up or fold up. There was still a Luftwaffe. The Luftwaffe got up early on the 21st and they were coked-up and eager for battle.

"These are the men who flew on that mission—Pilot: Sam Newton of Sioux City, Iowa; Co-pilot: Jack Oates of Waco, Texas; Navigator: Edward Parsons of Watanda, Pennsylvania; Toggleer: Gilbert Spaugh of Winston Salem, North Carolina; Engineer: William (Jack) Lewis of Grand Island, Nebraska; Radio Operator: Ed Ross of Buffalo, New York; Ball Turret: Gordon Beach of Denver, Colorado; Waist Gunner: Basil Crone of Wichita, Kansas; and Tail Gunner: Ed Sharpe of Hot Springs, Arkansas.

"And there was a passenger: Lieutenant A.A.B. Maclemore of Mississippi. Mac was the base Public Relations Officer, along for the ride. He knew how to operate a .50 caliber machine gun and was adept at spotting incoming German fighters. He couldn't help, though, in anticipating flak before it arrived.

"The ride across the North Sea on that day was pretty normal. It is a long haul, but you don't have to go on oxygen until about half way across, when the wings start to climb to bombing altitude. The sea is restfully free of flak-batteries. Everything was going smoothly so far that day.

"When the formations turned in at the coast, the VHF set began to carry tidings of bandits. Somebody up ahead was catching some hell from some fighters.

"Sammy Newton's Fort, the *Times A-Wastin'*, was flying in the low squadron, and about that time the low squadron leader began to get a feeling of insecurity and tucked up under the lead squadron pretty tight. The lads on both sides began to swing in, and the three-way squeeze was on, from the sides, and on top and down under. And there was prop wash! After almost chewing off the element leader's trailing edges, and in turn almost having his own chewed off, Lt. Newton consulted Lt. Oates and they decided to get the hell up to a vacancy in the high squadron.

"They had to do some finessing to get the job done, but they finally eased out into the clear and pulled up. On the way around they noticed a large formation of planes heading the wrong way. At our briefing there had been a lot of talk about the RAF tagging along behind on this one and really cooling Berlin town for all time.

"'Look at those damn Mosquitoes,' Sam said. 'I guess they did come today.'

"'Those lucky bastards are on the way home,' another crewman chimed in.

"'Formation at nine o'clock level,' the tail gunner called in.

"Somebody else called them when they got around to seven. They were

silver, and they looked peaceable and went about their business in an orderly manner.

"About that time Crone checked in with: 'Mosquitoes, hell. Them are Me 410s!'

"They were 410s all right, new ones with no paint. They came through on a tail pass, just as *Times A-Wastin'* was slipping into formation.

"Sharpe squeezed down on the first one, and that first one did the same to Sharpe, and they kept shooting at each other, hard and fast and furious.

"Then Sharpe forgot to shoot anymore and yelled over interphone, 'I got one, I got one, Jesus God I got one of those sonsofbitches.' The Me sagged off and began to come apart and the pilot bailed out.

"And then Sharpe remembered there were more of them.

"The 20 millimeters were sparkling all over the sky. Up ahead, Forts were beginning to falter. One nosed out of formation in the group on the left and began to give birth to chutes. Nine of them. One old painted job out at three o'clock had a fire in his left Tokyo tanks. Another tipped off on a wing and split-s-ed out of formation in a spectacular dive.

"The fighters weren't going much faster than the Forts and both sides were throwing everything. Sharpe's left feed-way snafued on him, but he kept on shooting the right gun.

"'Every time our ball-turret opened up I thought we had it,' Crone said later. 'I could feel those twenties chewing my tail.'

"The ammunition covers fell off the ball-turret, making it impossible to swing the guns straight down because the ammunition would fall out.

"Beach was going crazy. 'God damn these . . . coming in at nine o'clock low . . . get him, Crone . . .' He never got in a complete sentence before he had to

above: 8AF wall art photographed at Lavenham (top), and at Horham.

sound off a new attack.

"Ross knocked his 410 off when the joker tried to pull into our formation while he lobbed shells into the group ahead.

"'I could have conked the pilot with my gun barrel,' Ross said later. 'But I decided to shoot him.' The German fighter blew up.

"Lewis tracked a 410 across the tail with the top turret, saw the pieces begin to chip off, and smoke belch out of the engines, and the pilot came out streaming silk.

"'Coming in at nine chimes,' Maclemore said. It was an Fw 190 going under to mop up a crippled Fort. Crone teed off on him low and straight away. The 190 flipped over into a spin, spilling smoke, and spun on into the ground.

"'I watched him all the way,' Crone said. 'I just stood there and watched him with one eye, and waited for that other bastard with the other.'

"That other bastard came in from two o'clock high on the front end. Maclemore swung the right nose gun into position and tagged him fair and saw him crumple. Lewis called in to report a bailed-out pilot and a falling wing.

"Most of the business was back by the tail. Spaugh kept his guns swinging and did a lot of shooting, but they were all long, wishful thoughts, and he didn't claim anything more than a couple of scare-a-ways.

"'They can tell when I wink at 'em when I get this turret wound up,' Spaugh said.

"All the guns were blazing, and there were Forts and fighters throwing up all over the sky, with 20 millimeters dancing around.

"Newton and Oates were about going nuts in the cockpit. 'Where are they?' Sam yelled. 'How you doing?' 'Are we hit?' 'Tail gunner?' 'Waist gunner?' 'Where are they?' 'What the hell is going on back there?'

"The 410s made two more passes, and several minor feints and the side-lines were thick with stray 109s and 190s looking for easy meat, waiting for wounded Forts to stumble.

"Little Friends came on the scene about that time, P-38s over the top, and P-51s in from ten o'clock high. Sammy Newton's crew breathed a collective sigh of relief and passed on into the comparative safety of the Berlin flak-area.

"Sharpe was soaked with sweat. Crone wiped his forehead and came away with a cupful.

"After Hamburg, they thought the flak over Berlin would be minor league. But the flak was major league all the way and it was everywhere. Nothing but black puffs from there to hell, not trailing behind, but poking up to powder our nose.

"The VHF set announced more bandits after bombs were away, but the Luftwaffe was all through for the day with Sammy Newton's crew. The Luftwaffe was ready for the sack.

"'Oxygen check,' the tail gunner said. 'Everybody still living? Check in.' He was number one.

"'Two okay.'

"'Three okay.'

"'Four, roger.' And so on. All present and accounted for.

"'We got one little hole in the right stabilizer,' Crone said. 'It ain't much.'

"'It ain't nothin',' Beach said.

"'Godamighty, how'd we do it?' Sharpe said. His hands were shaky and the sweat was draining down his back and pooling up in his electric shoes. He turned the electricity off, and he still oozed.

"Lt. Newton crawled back through the bomb bay on a health inspection tour.

"Crone was stroking his gun kindly. Beach was moaning about his gun covers. Sharpe was still sweating.

"'Hey, Crone,' Sharpe called up. 'I guess you checked out that goddam shooting iron today.'

"Nobody was hurt. Only a few holes. Sam shook his head. 'Got a roochie?' he asked.

"Ross pulled out a soggy pack of Luckies and everybody had one. Some of them had two, a tricky job in an oxygen mask. Lewis had his semi-annual drag in the top turret.

"The rest of the ride to the coast was uneventful. The letdown was smooth. The formation loosened up out in the channel and there was a stark taste of relief in the air.

"At twelve thousand feet, Oates told everyone to take off his oxygen mask. It was time for a Hershey bar.

"'I never saw anything so Goddam pretty', Spaugh said when England came through the mist.

"There was scotch at the interrogation, and everyone got slightly jagged. Everyone was talking with both hands and drinking coffee and dunking doughnuts, and spilling coffee and trying to think of a way to get more scotch.

"The interrogating captain got teed-off because he couldn't hear the answers to the questions he was asking and because every time he got someone steadied down to coherent accounting, somebody from the outside would come in and paw the boys and ask if it was really true, did they shoot down five of those bastards.

"'Probably six', Sharpe said. 'Lewis is only claiming one, but he got two.'

"'Maybe,' Lewis said.

"'That guy was most definitely got,' Sharpe said. 'I saw him.'

"Finally the S-2 officers cleared the briefing room and those who didn't belong had to stand at the door to watch Sammy Newton beam on his club. He was also pretty glad to be alive.

"Every ten seconds somebody else would say, 'Brother, I thought we'd had it.'

"Or: 'I was half-way out that hatch.'

"Or: 'Did you see those poor bastards on fire?'

"Or: 'You should've seen me.'

"Or: That's nothing, you should've seen me.'

"Madhouse.

"There was a Red Cross girl passing out doughnuts who had most of the requisites of A-1 stuff, really nice, sort of warmly cool, friendly to all, not too friendly to any of the charmers to the exclusion of the rest.

"Sharpe came out of the breifing hut with most of his clothes off, talking to Crone who was talking right back at him. Two guys from another crew came up and grabbed them. One of them said, 'That sure was a sweet job of shooting.'

"Sharpe laughed, 'You ought to see my left gun-barrel.'

"'Like a goddam corkscrew,' Crone said. 'No kidding, bent all to hell.'

"'First time I knew you could cuss and pray in the same sentence,' Sharpe said."

Rather than return to the United States to be a flying instructor following his tour of duty in bombers, Bert Stiles signed up for a second tour, transferring to fighters. He was then based at Fowlmere in a Mustang outfit and on 26th November 1944, he was flying *Tar Heel* (below) when his squadron encountered more than forty Focke-Wulf Fw 190 fighters near Hannover. Stiles engaged one of the enemy planes in combat and shot it down. It is believed that he followed the Fw down and became disoriented, crashed, and was killed.

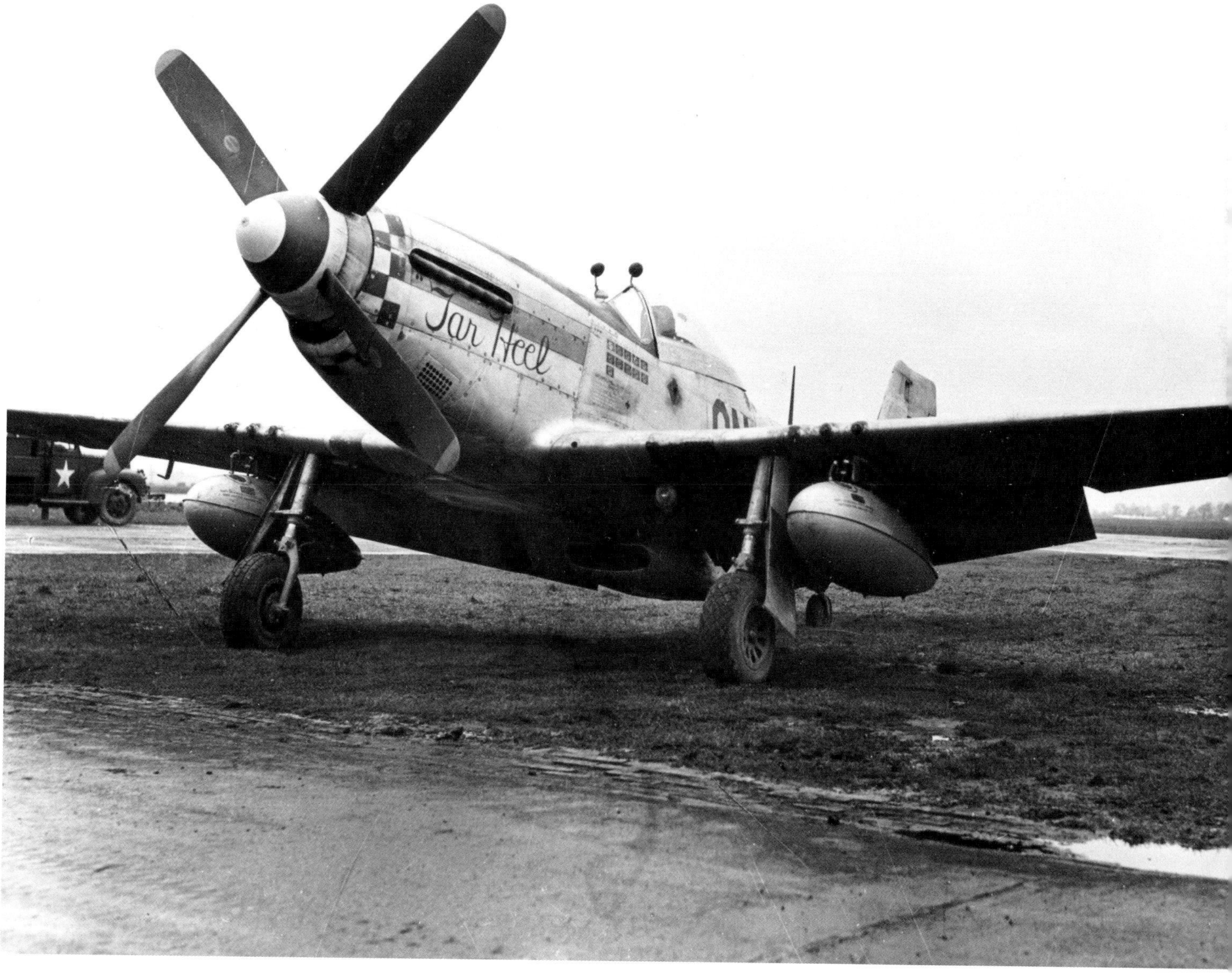
Tar Heel

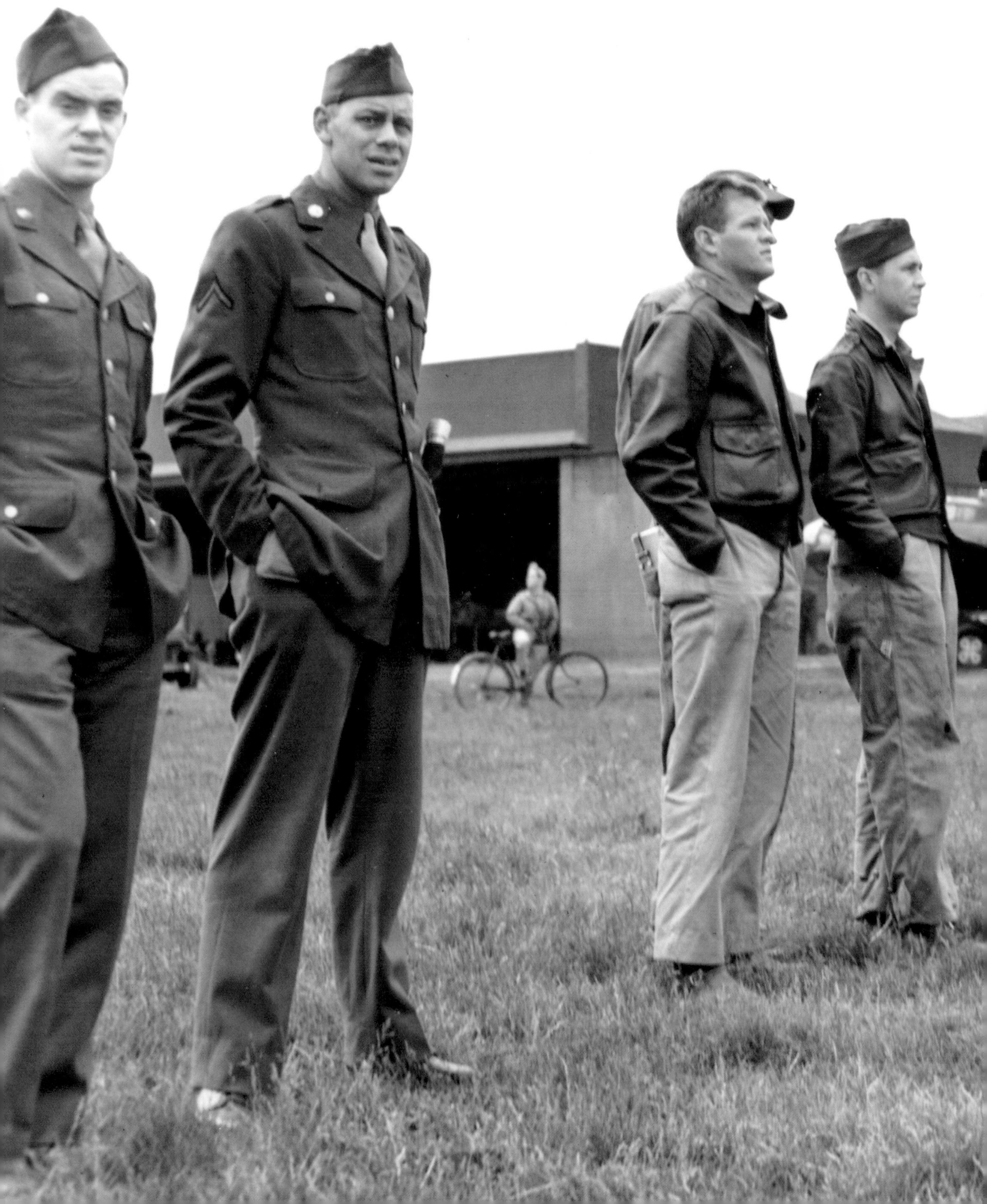

Common practice on the airfields of the Eighth was that of ground personnel and those not on the flight schedule that day to gather on the field and "sweat out" the return of the group's planes and aircrews.

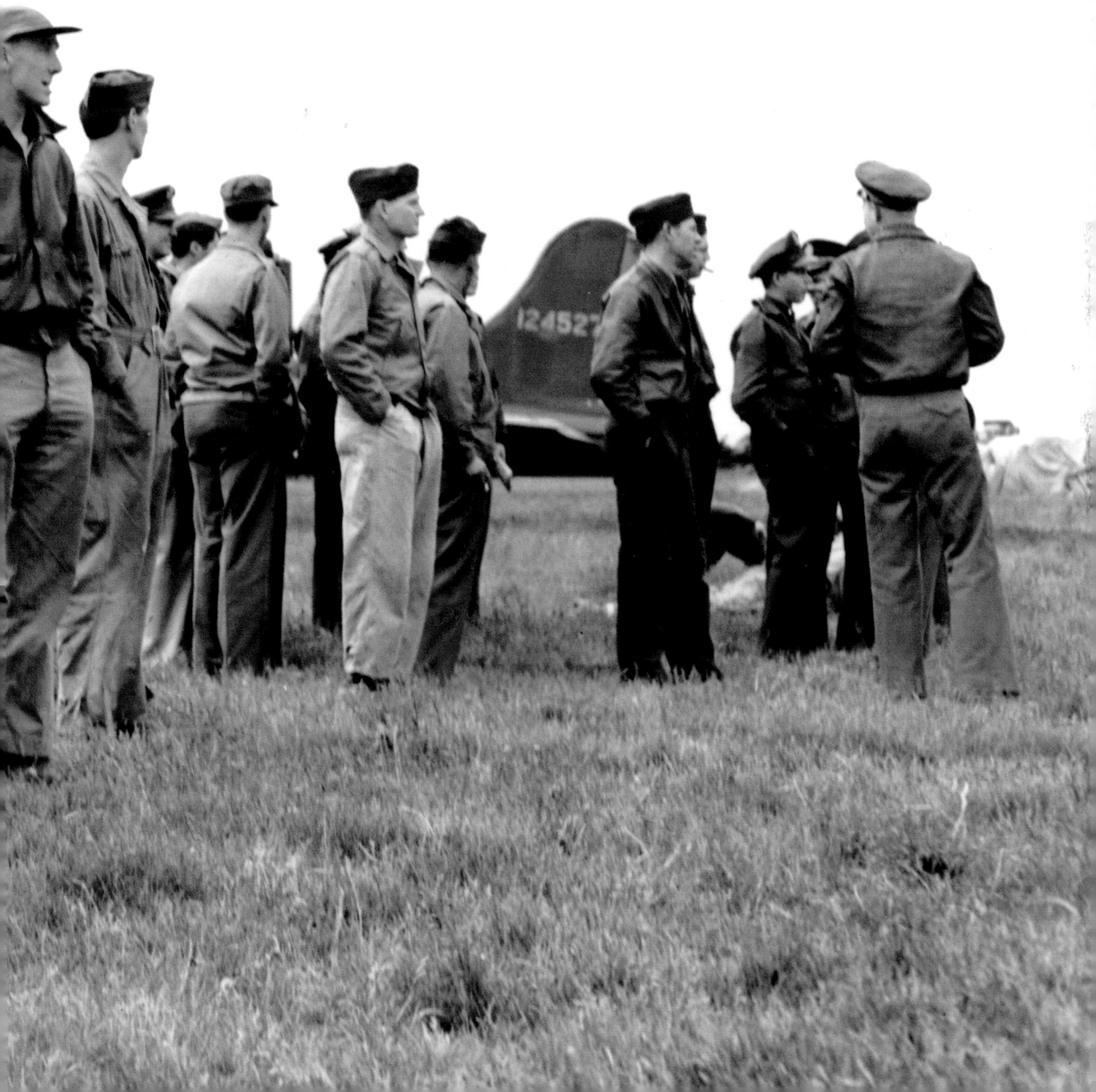
124527

GRAFTON UNDERMUD

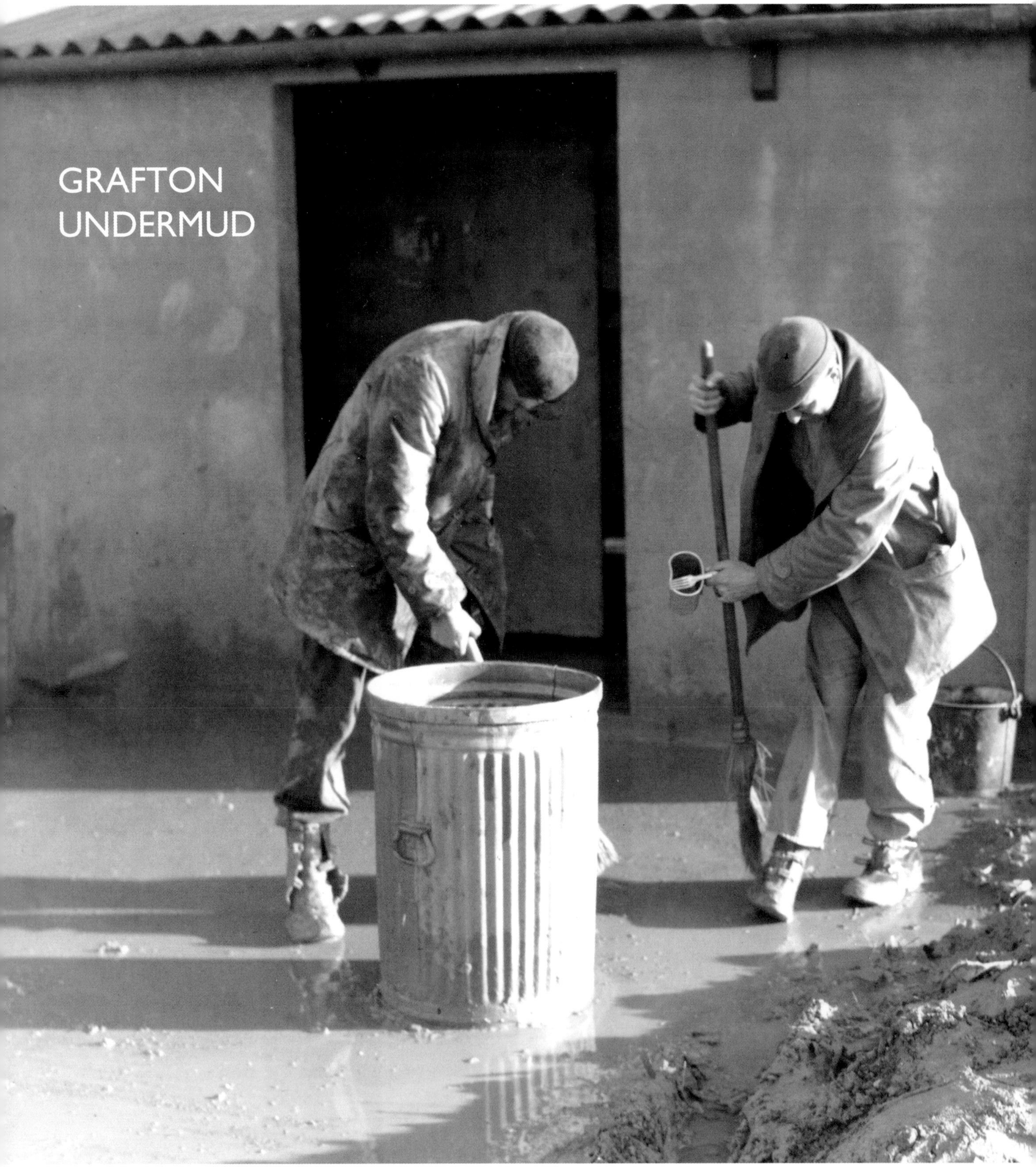

There was no shortage of oozy, gooey, miserable mud at Grafton Underwood . . . until Colonel Dale O. Smith took command there.

WHEN COLONEL DALE O. SMITH took command of Station 106, Grafton Underwood, in November 1943, it was mud everywhere: "It wasn't located in a bog, but the clay soil held the frequent rains and the place was a sea of sticky brown muck." Life and daily routine on the base were, at best, difficult, and mostly irritating and depressing. In later years, Colonel (now Major General) Smith recalled how virtually all personnel left their caked overshoes inside the doors of the mess halls, but still the mud found its way into all buildings and dried on the floors. Rarely was one able to retrieve his own overshoes. The pervasive mud did nothing for the base morale.

While cleanliness and discomfort mattered, safety was the greater concern. It was the tires of the big, five-ton trucks whose business it was to roam the concrete lanes, taxiways, and perimeter track of the airfield, and various personnel sites, that made the problem so serious. They tracked the thick, gooey stuff from the taxiways onto the hardstands where the B-17s were parked and it consistently accumulated on the wheels of the bombers. When that nasty fresh mud froze on the landing gear of the planes as they climbed through the frigid air to their cruising altitude, it could and sometimes did cause the gear to stick in the up position, creating a potentially deadly situation when the aircraft returned to Grafton. Colonel Smith had to find a solution.

Initially, he got many of his hundreds of station personnel out with shovels to dig the mud off the miles of concrete lanes, pavements, and taxiways. The men grumbled at the added chore, but slowly the surfaces began to clear. Smith orderd that all trucks and other vehicles were to stay on the pavement at all times

and to pass only at the concrete turnouts. Violators were summarily dealt with and the violations soon ceased. The colonel had the CO of the first offending driver bust the man from sergeant down to private, making an example of him. He would later restore the man to his former rank, but ordered the man's commanding officer not to inform him of that pending restoration. The draconian punishment further reduced Colonel Smith's already crumbling popularity with his men (in the wake of the enormous mud-shovelling project). But the men of the 384th Bomb Group got the message and the trucks conducting the ground business of the group stayed on the pavement. Morale improved as the personnel were soon able to walk the pathways of the base without wearing overshoes. Bicycles began to be used, more and more salutes were exchanged . . . until, without warning, the mud returned to immerse the pavements once again.

The colonel went out in his beat-up Ford staff car to inspect the station and soon came upon a massive dump truck "loaded with muck and oozing mud onto its caked double wheels and thence onto the road. It wasn't a military vehicle. Where had it come from and where was it going? I followed it to a field where it dumped its load and to another field near our hangar, where a large power shovel loaded it with more mud from a mound. There were several such dump trucks, and each traversed the base from end to end. It hadn't taken long to undo weeks of labor and again leave Grafton Undermud."

When the colonel checked with his ground exec he was told that nothing could be done as the mud movers were apparently in the employ of the owner of the land on which the air base sat, the Duke of Buccleuch. The ground exec also informed Colonel Smith that the U.S. Army Air Force was paying the Duke a monthly rental of some thirty thousand dollars for the use of the property: "'Okay, let's call the Duke and politely ask him to cease and desist.' Moving mud from one field to another didn't seem to be a high-priority effort during a hot war." The ground exec had already tried that approach, to no avail.

When Colonel Smith tried to reach the Duke by phone, he was told that His Excellency was "shooting in Scotland." He asked the Duke's manager to stop the mud-hauling trucks but the man said he could do nothing without the Duke's approval. "I didn't like his manner. He showed no concern for our problem. In fact, he was rather curt and uncooperative. I gathered that the war was a dreadful bore to him, particularly with those Yanks everywhere. I instructed the exec to put guards on the gates to those mud fields and not to let a single one of the Duke's trucks pass. Within hours all hell broke loose. High-ranking Brits from the Air Ministry in London called me; the Duke was a member of the royal family. Generals from Eighth Air Force headquarters admonished me. I couldn't do that, they told me. The rental agreement allowed the Duke to use our roads. I was hindering good relations with our British allies, etc."

Colonel Smith then told his immediate administrative boss, Brigadier General Robert B. Williams, Commander, 1st Bomb Division, that, as long as he (Smith) was in command at Grafton, there would be no more mud tracked on the roads there and if he (Williams) wanted Smith's order changed, he (Williams) would have to relieve him of command. "Bob Williams took this insubordination with his usual good grace, and as

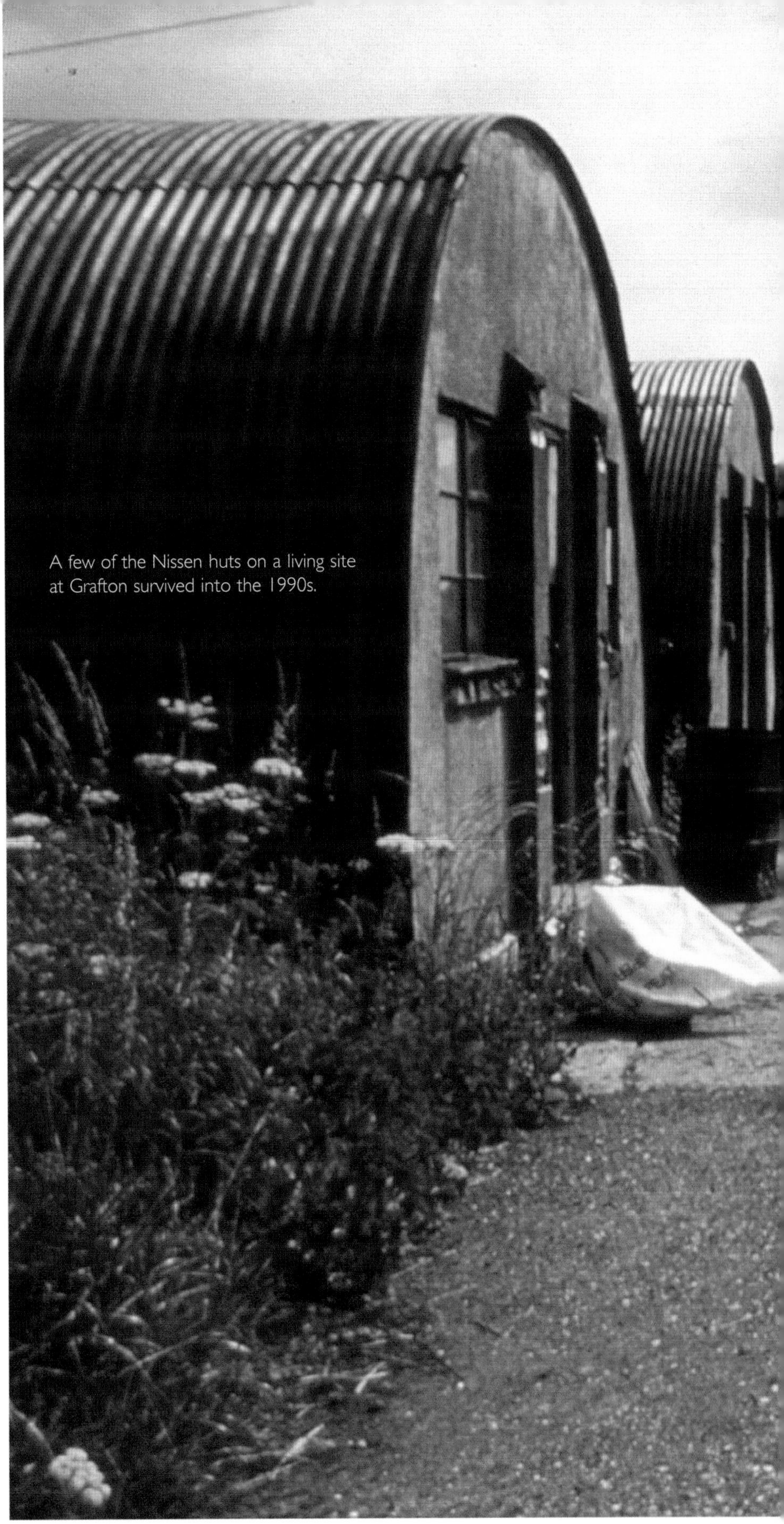

A few of the Nissen huts on a living site at Grafton survived into the 1990s.

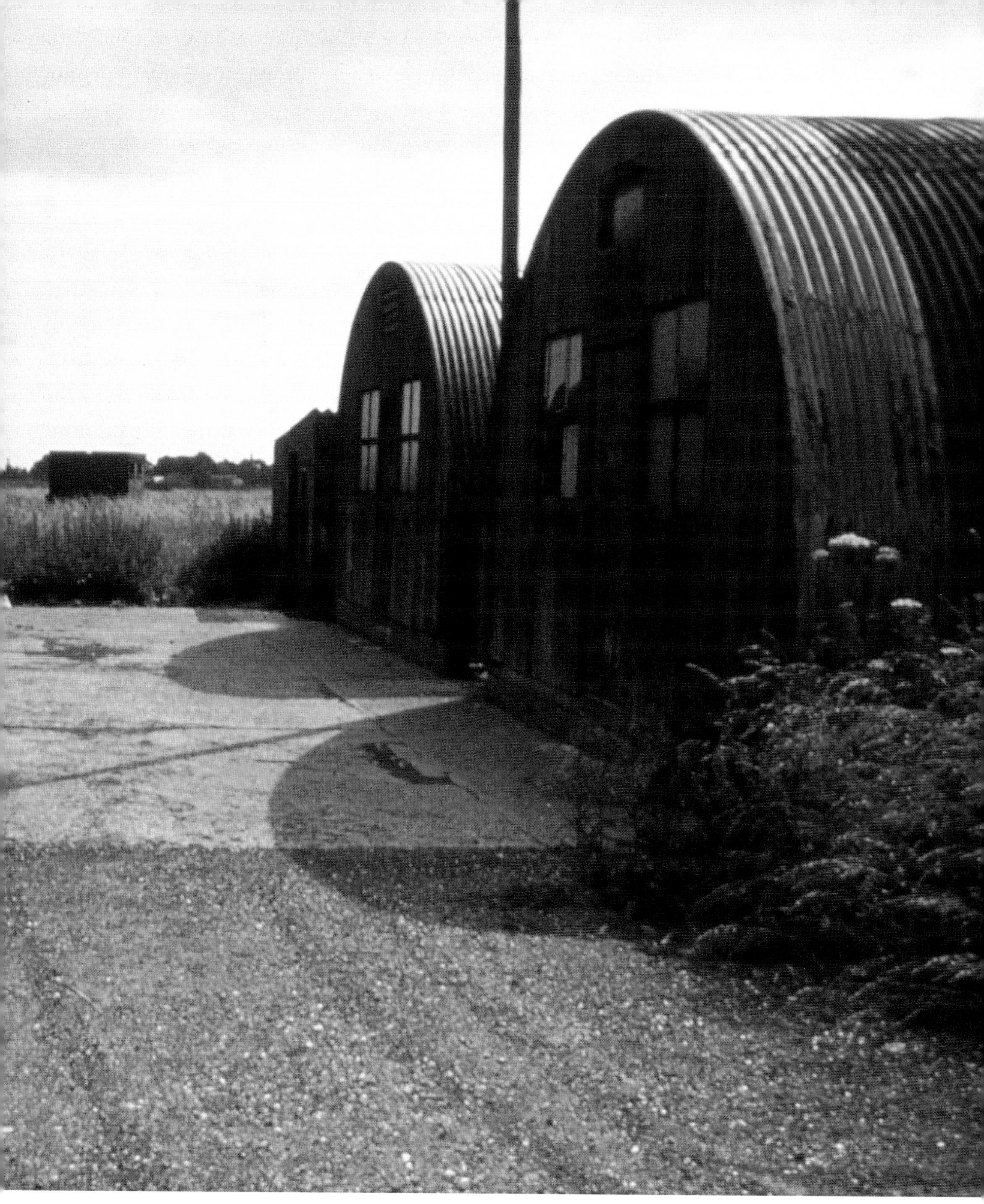

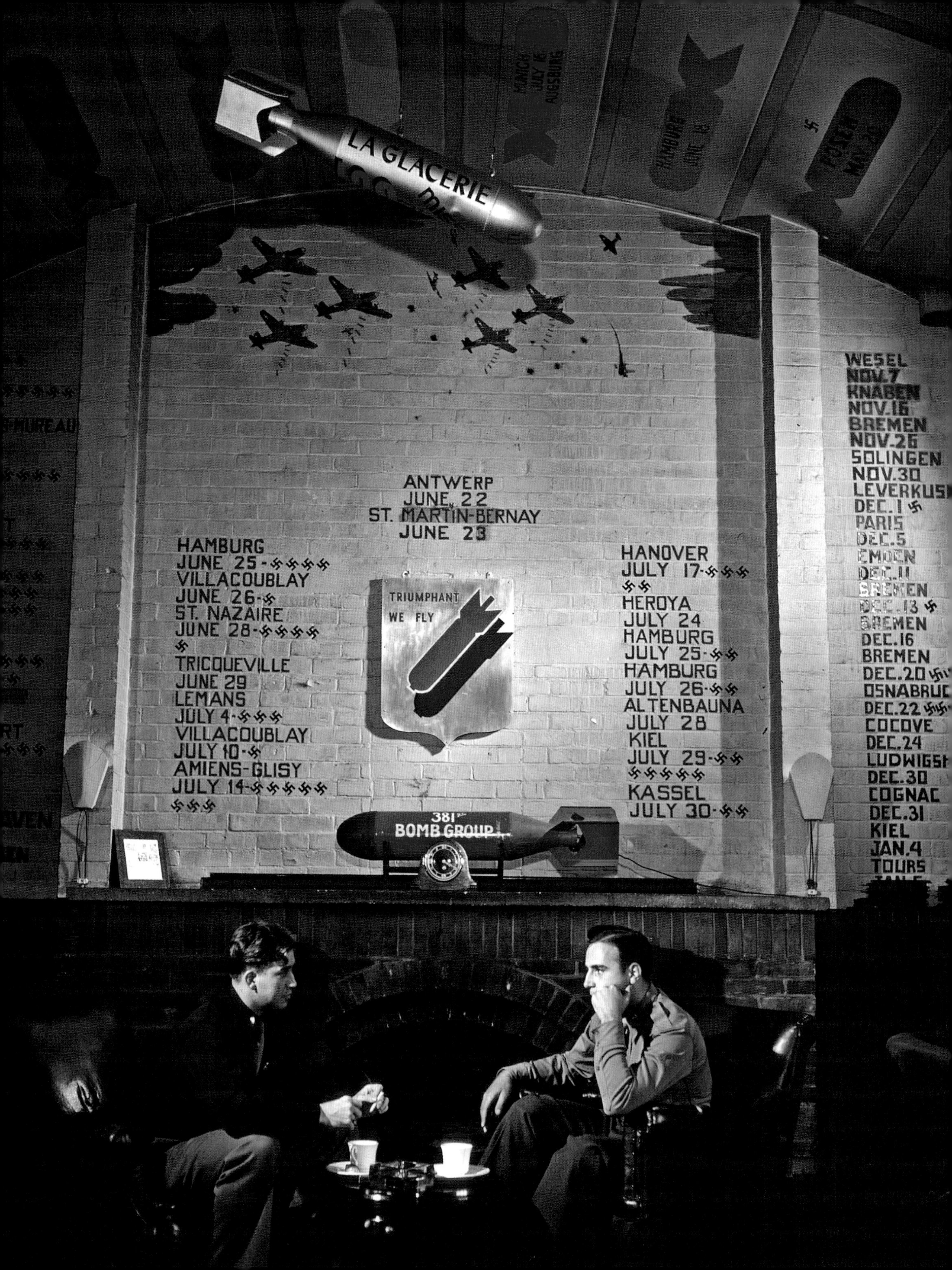
LA GLACERIE
MUNICH JULY 16 AUGSBURG
HAMBURG JUNE 18
POSEN MAY 29
ANTWERP
JUNE, 22
ST. MARTIN-BERNAY
JUNE 23
HAMBURG
JUNE 25-
VILLACOUBLAY
JUNE 26-
ST. NAZAIRE
JUNE 28-
TRICQUEVILLE
JUNE 29
LEMANS
JULY 4-
VILLACOUBLAY
JULY 10-
AMIENS-GLISY
JULY 14-
TRIUMPHANT
WE FLY
HANOVER
JULY 17-
HEROYA
JULY 24
HAMBURG
JULY 25-
HAMBURG
JULY 26-
ALTENBAUNA
JULY 28
KIEL
JULY 29-
KASSEL
JULY 30-
381ST
BOMB GROUP
WESEL
NOV.7
KNABEN
NOV.16
BREMEN
NOV.26
SOLINGEN
NOV.30
DEC.1
PARIS
DEC.5
EMDEN
DEC.11
BREMEN
DEC.13
BREMEN
DEC.16
BREMEN
DEC.20
DEC.22
COCOVE
DEC.24
DEC.30
COGNAC
DEC.31
KIEL
JAN.4
TOURS

above: Colonel Dale O. Smith arrived in November 1943 to take charge of the Grafton Underwood air base. He rose to the considerable challenge and, in the end, his will prevailed. right: A leather flying glove found by the author near one of the remaining hardstands at the Grafton airfield; left: An example of an officers' club on an Eighth Air Force heavy bomber station, this one at Ridgewell, Essex.

the days went by without my receiving transfer orders I realized he had gone to bat for me in his talks with the Olympian powers in London."

The Duke's trucks and power shovel remained dormant in that field and the roads of the air base were again cleared. That was still the condition eleven months later when Colonel Smith left the station for his next assignment, to be Chief of the Bombardment Branch in the Pentagon.

The fall of 1942 was not the best

of seasons for turning farmland into bomber bases, and the remark of an airfield engineer came right from the heart: "Where there's construction, there's mud; and where there's war, there's mud; where there's construction and war, there's just plain hell."

Each airfield needed 100,000 tons of aggregate, many miles of drainage pipes, and concrete foundations for some four hundred buildings. John Skilleter, an evacuee from London, watched the construction of the

Eighth Air Force bases in the quiet Suffolk countryside. At every opportunity he accompanied the driver of a Bedford truck on his haulage trips: "We collected shingle and carted it at breakneck speed to the airfield sites. The drivers did the maximum number of trips per day because they were paid accordingly. Every truck owner in the area was earning good money at that time. As the Americans got into their stride, so the airfields multiplied: Eye, Great Ashfield, Leiston,

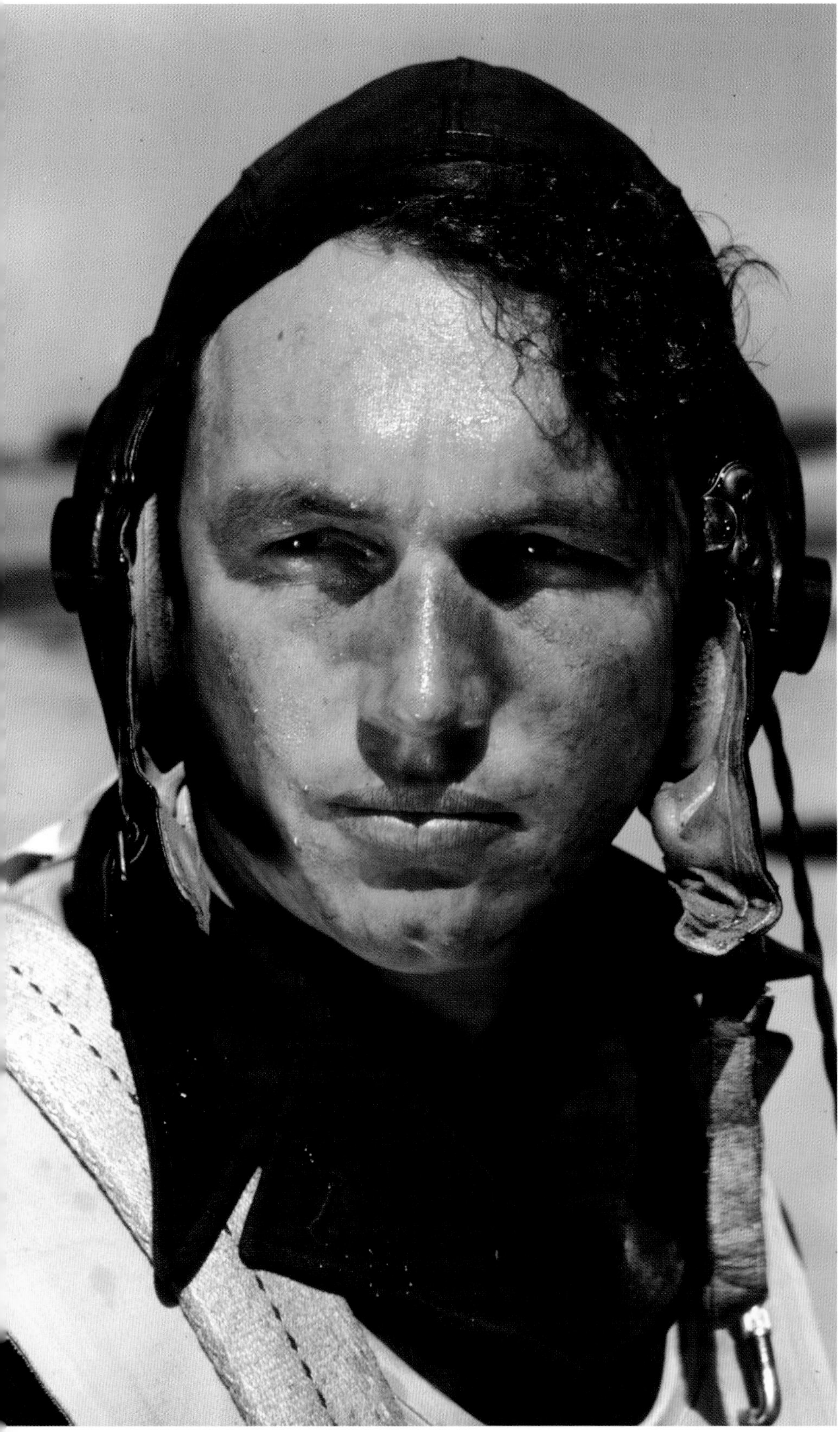

Framlingham, Mendlesham, Boxted, Debach, and many others. The U.S. Army engineers were quick-fire, happy-go-lucky guys who never failed to hand out chewing gum to us sweet-starved kids.

"When the B-17s arrived, I would sit on top of the truck and watch the splendor of the squadrons moving in line astern around the perimeter track, with baseball-capped gunners in the waist positions and concerned-looking pilots fingering their throat mikes as they talked to the tower. Ground crews squatted on the tarmac by the runway and waved them off with V-signs. Sometimes, about an hour after takeoff, the aborts would trickle in—aircraft with feathered props. Jeeps tore alongside the machines as they turned in to the hardstandings. At other times, the only activity would be around a grounded B-17, as mechanics tried to cuss its entrails into life."

The stars were out that night. I liked that very much because it meant a hard freeze and out of the mud for at least two or three days. Also it sent a message to the combat crews: get ready for a mission in the morning. With that in mind I set out my mission clothes and equipment. Most combat men developed superstitions about clothes or some special talisman they always carried on a raid. I remember one gunner who wore the same coveralls each trip and refused to have them washed. Somehow the unwashed coveralls had become his security blanket.
—from *Combat Crew* by John Comer

When it rains, all unpaved roads, paths and barracks areas become gooey quagmires, and it rains a lot. Also, the latrines and showers are in Nissen huts separate from the barracks; the mess halls and other

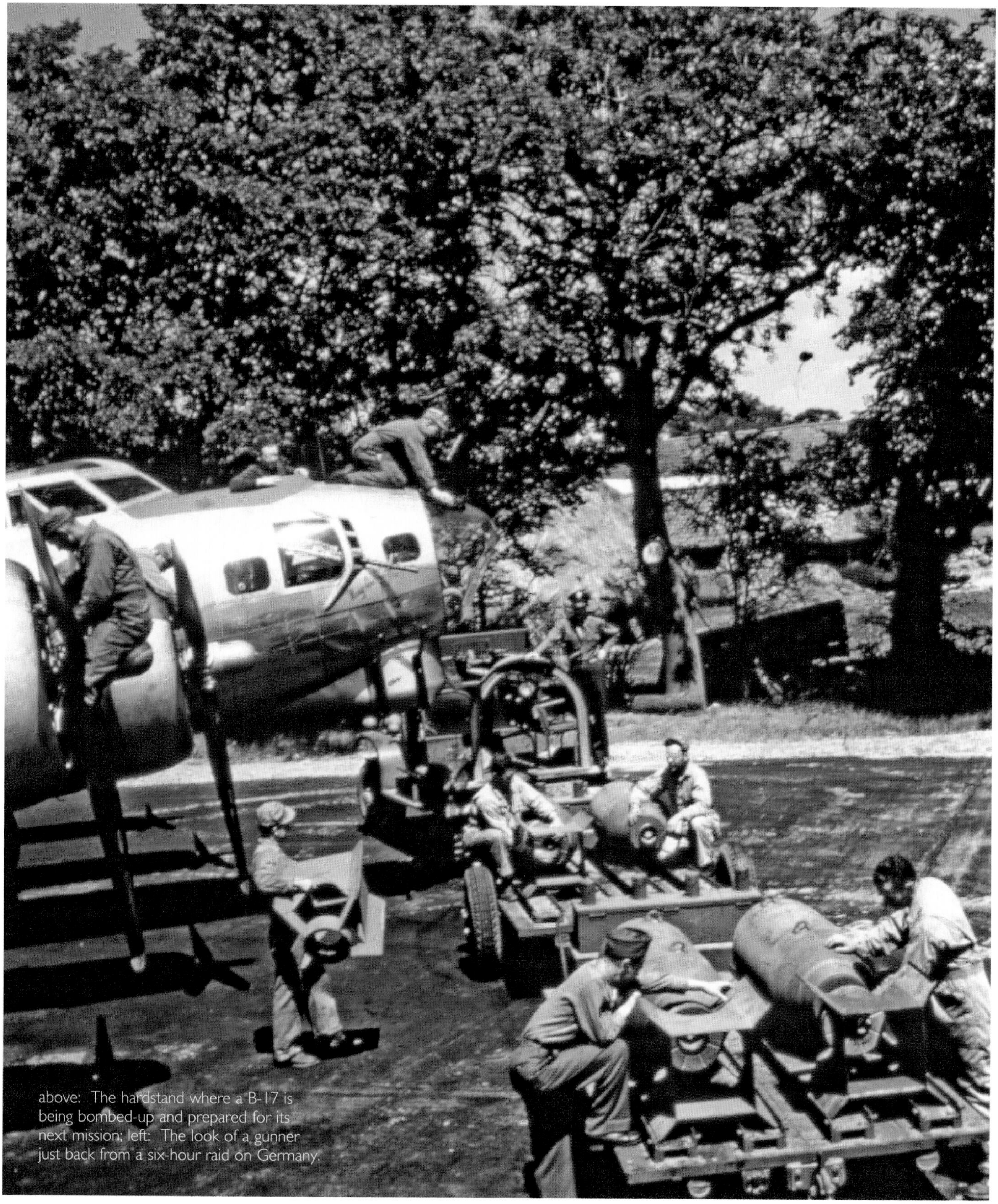

above: The hardstand where a B-17 is being bombed-up and prepared for its next mission; left: The look of a gunner just back from a six-hour raid on Germany.

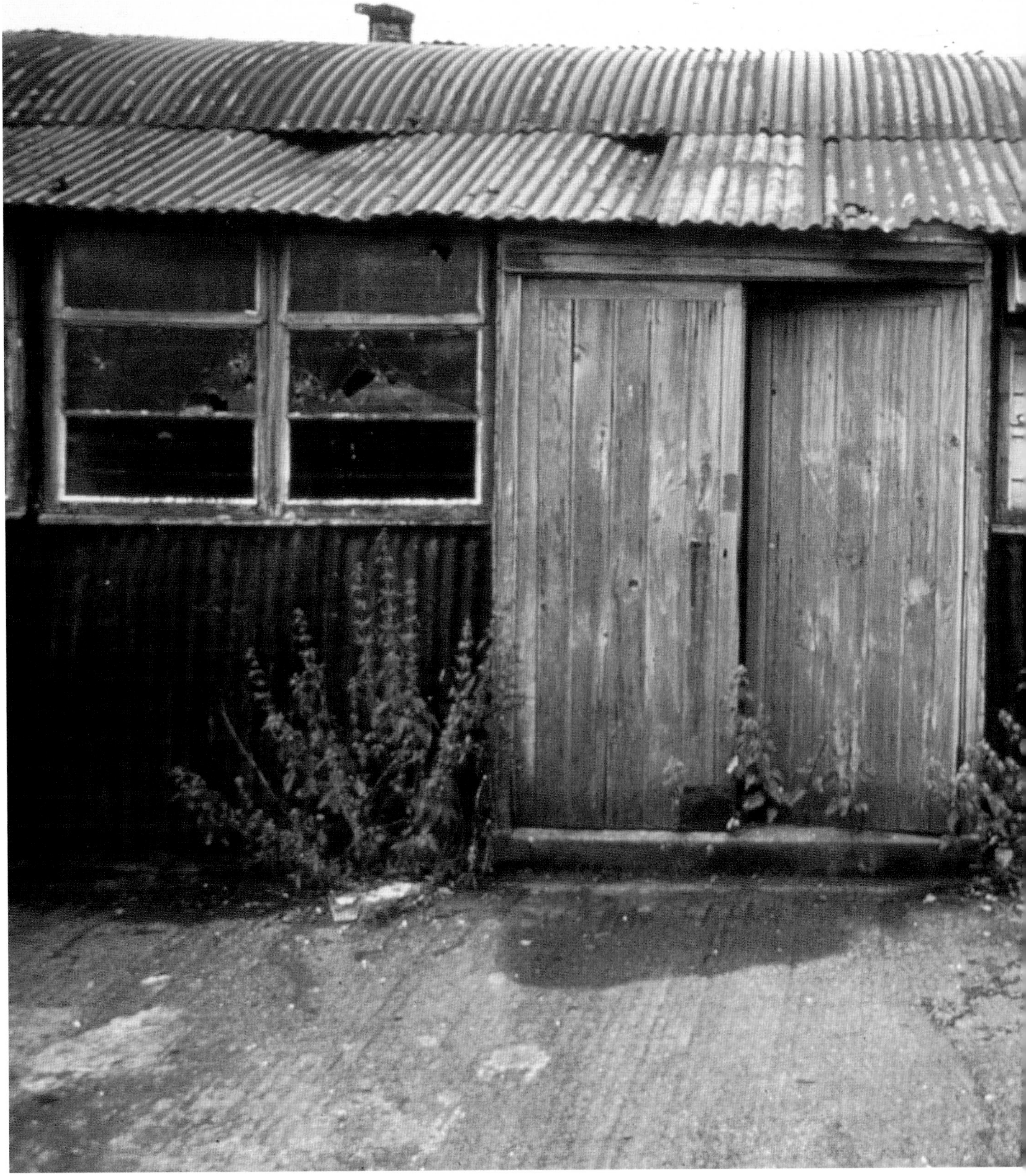

One of the big Nissen huts at the 401st Bomb Group base, Deenethorpe.

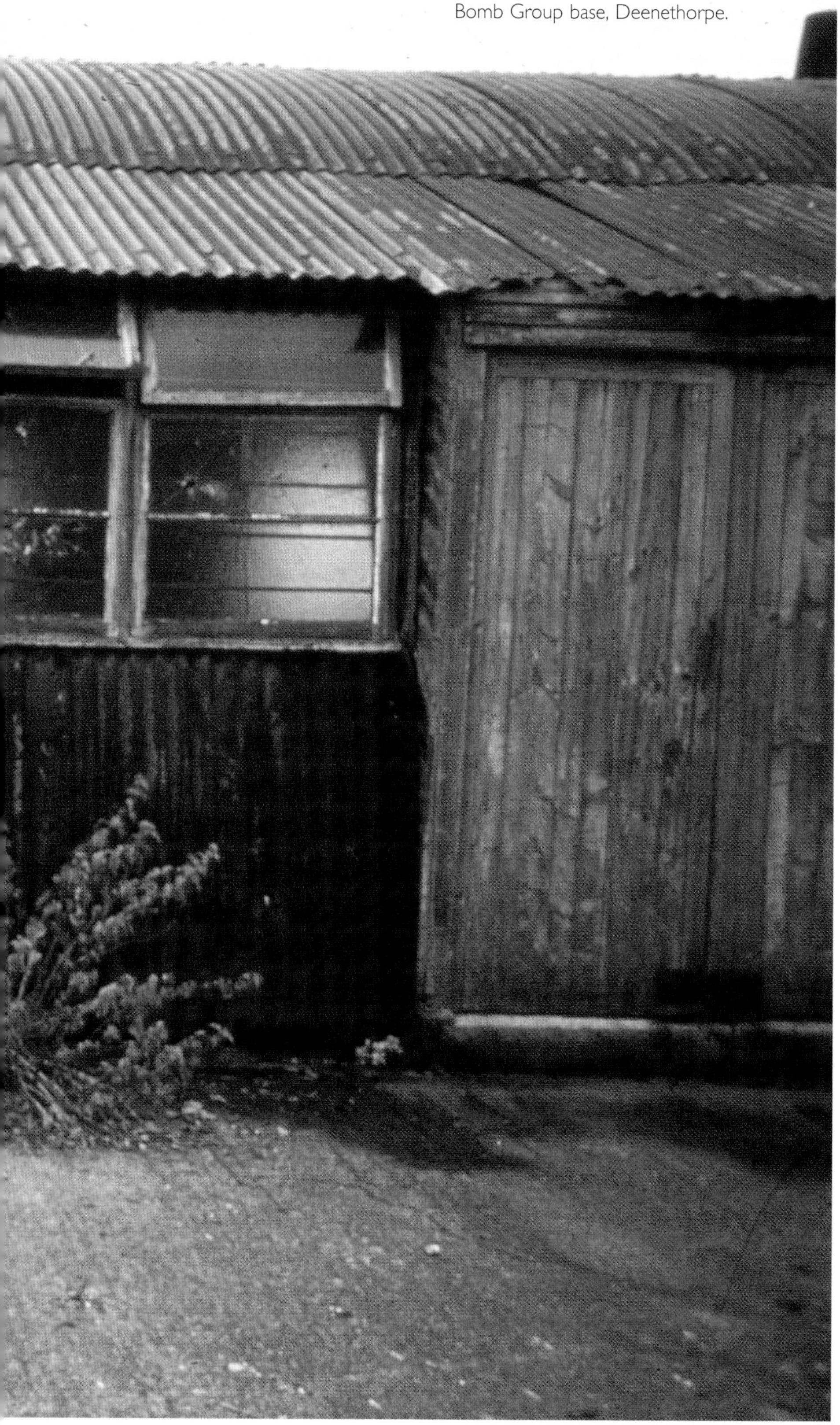

such base facilities are, in most cases, at a considerable distance from the housing sites, and especially in cold or muddy weather this inconvenience is the inspiration for a good deal of inventive and colorful language. On all but a handful of the Eighth's English bases, officers and enlisted men alike lived in scattered clusters of Nissen huts. Nissens came in three sizes, of which the housing Nissens were the smallest—sixteen feet wide, eight feet high at the center, twenty-four or thirty feet long—and when veterans of the Eighth recall those huts it is seldom with kindness. They were dark, their concrete floors usually were littered with tracked-in mud, and their mingled odors of cigarettes and cigars both past and present, damp woolen clothing, and socks too long unlaundered gave them, said one pilot, "the heady aroma of a goat-barn."
—from *One Last Look* by Philip Kaplan and Rex Alan Smith

The rain slanted under the wing on a raw northeast wind. Of Cambridgeshire we had only an impression screened through the deluge—somber flatness, and mud; mud oozing up over the edge of the asphault circle where we were parked; mud in the tread of the jeep, which rolled away on twin tracks of ocher, leaving us marooned; a vast plain, or lake, of mud stretching off toward a cluster of barely visible buildings.
—from *The War Lover* by John Hersey

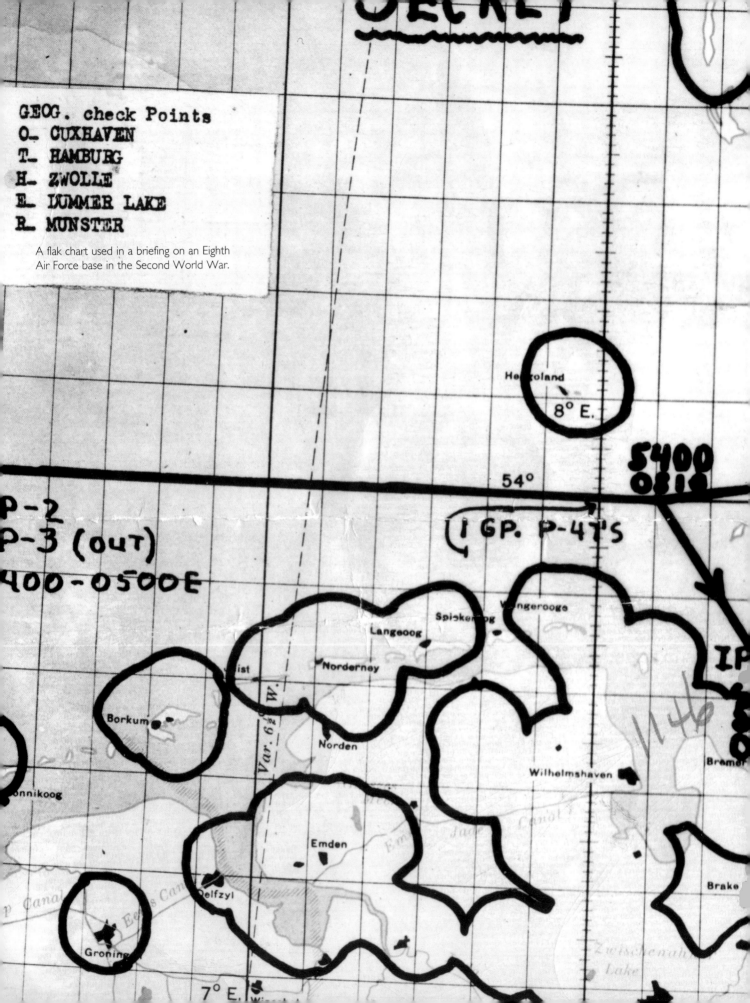

SECRET

GEOG. check Points
O. CUXHAVEN
T. HAMBURG
H. ZWOLLE
E. DUMMER LAKE
R. MUNSTER

A flak chart used in a briefing on an Eighth
Air Force base in the Second World War.

Helgoland

8° E.

54°

5400
0818

P-2
P-3 (OUT)
400-0500E

1 GP. P-47'S

Wangerooga
Spickeroog
Langeoog

IP

Norderney

Borkum

Norden

Wilhelmshaven

Bremer

onnikoog

Emden

Canal

Delfzyl

Brake

p Canal

Eems Canal

Groning

Zwischenah
Lake

7° E.

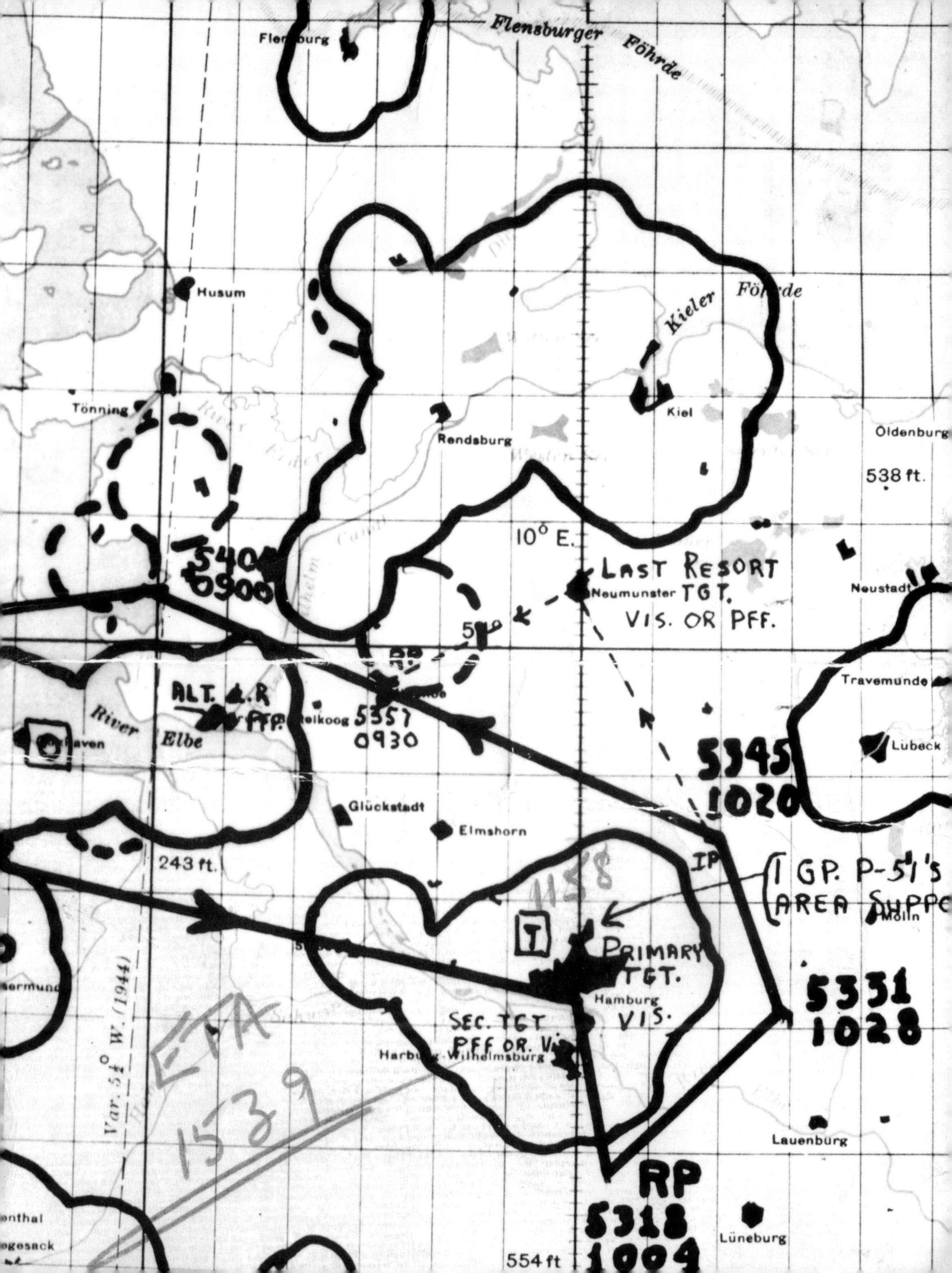

Flensburger Föhrde
Husum
Tönning
Rendsburg
Kieler Föhrde
Kiel
Oldenburg
538 ft.
10° E.
LAST RESORT TGT. VIS. OR PFF.
Neumunster
Neustadt
0900
5357
0930
River Elbe
Travemunde
Lübeck
5345
1020
Glückstadt
Elmshorn
243 ft.
IP
1 GP. P-51's AREA SUPP
Mölln
PRIMARY TGT.
Hamburg
VIS.
SEC. TGT PFF OR. VIS.
Harburg-Wilhelmsburg
5331
1028
Var. 5¼° W. (1944)
ETA
1539
Lauenburg
RP
5318
1004
Lüneburg
554 ft

ON THE NOSE

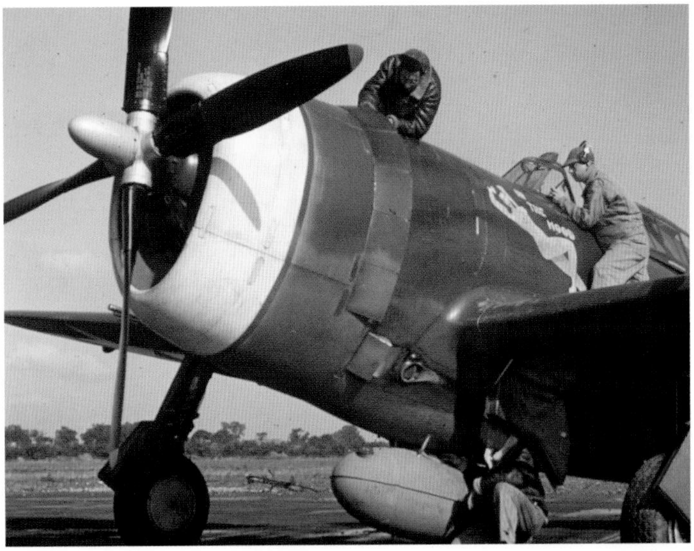

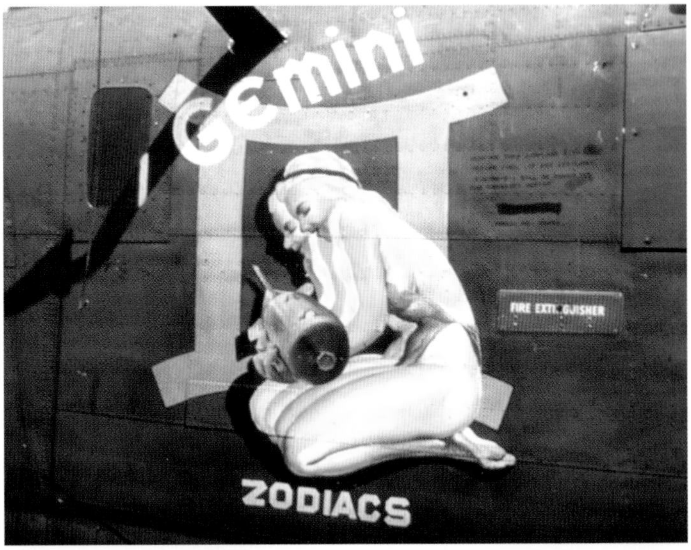
Gemini
ZODIACS

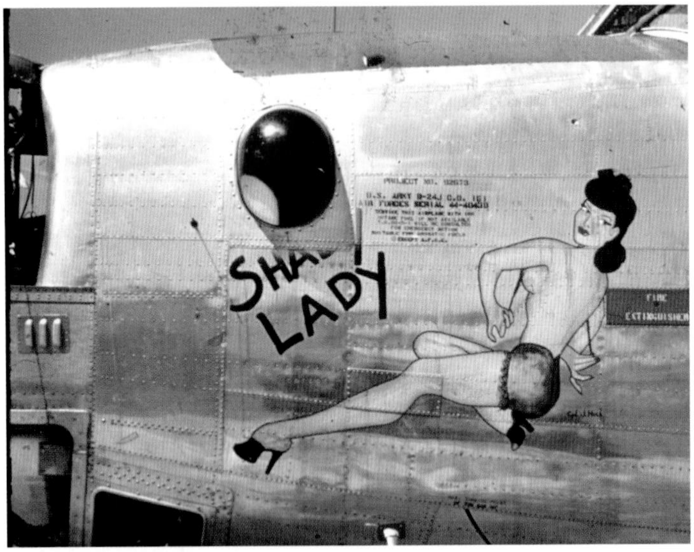
LADY

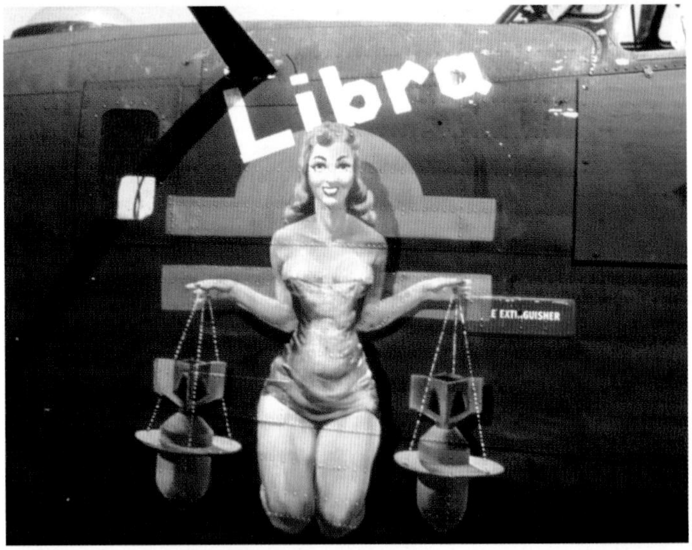
Libra

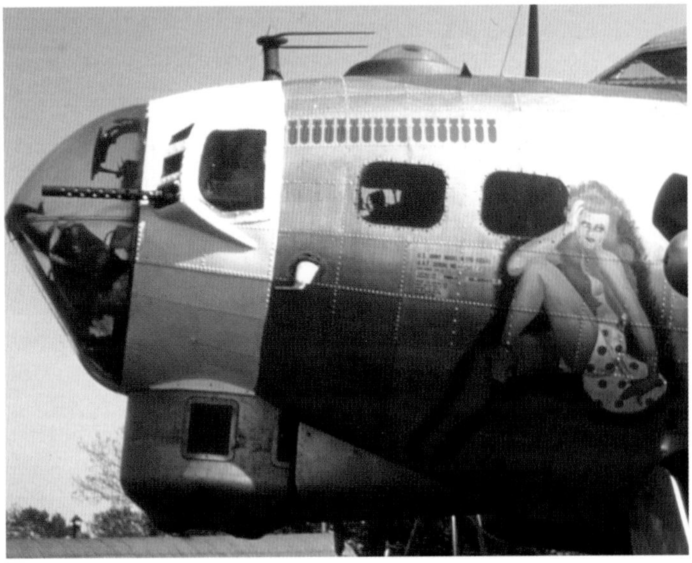

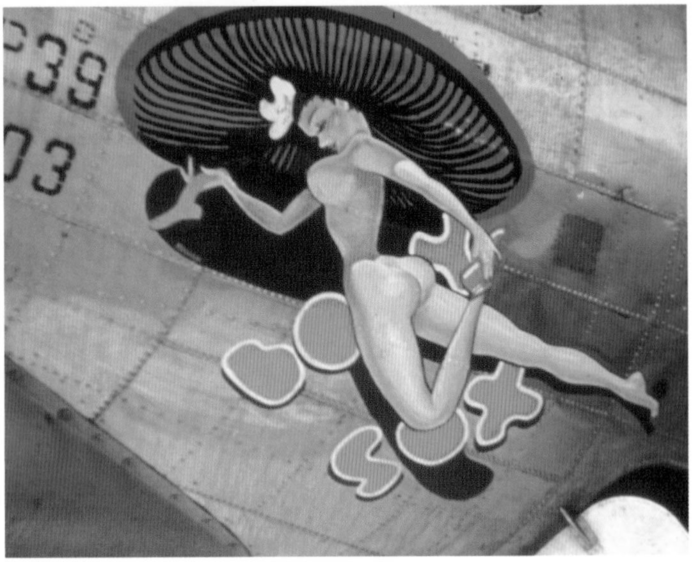

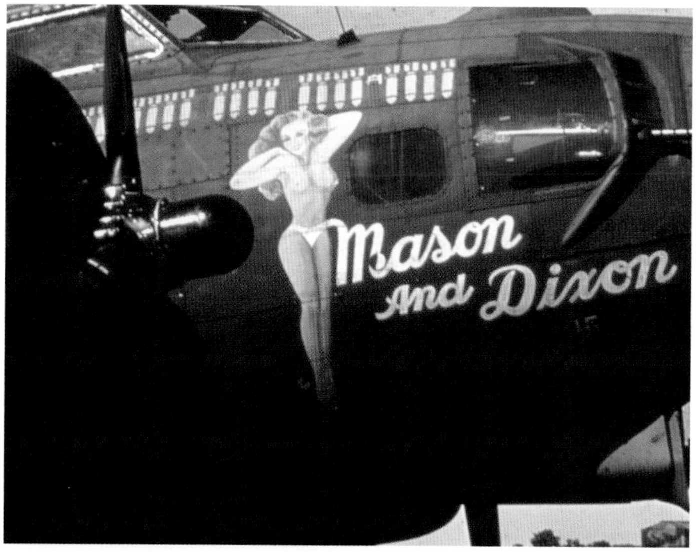
Mason
And Dixon

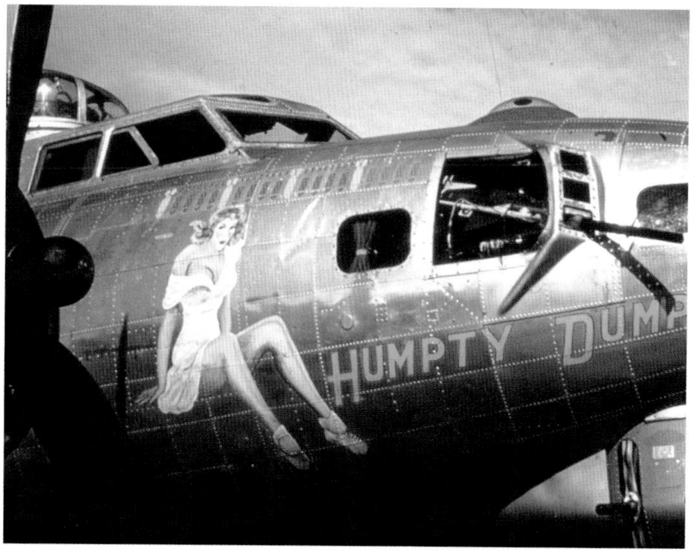
HUMPTY

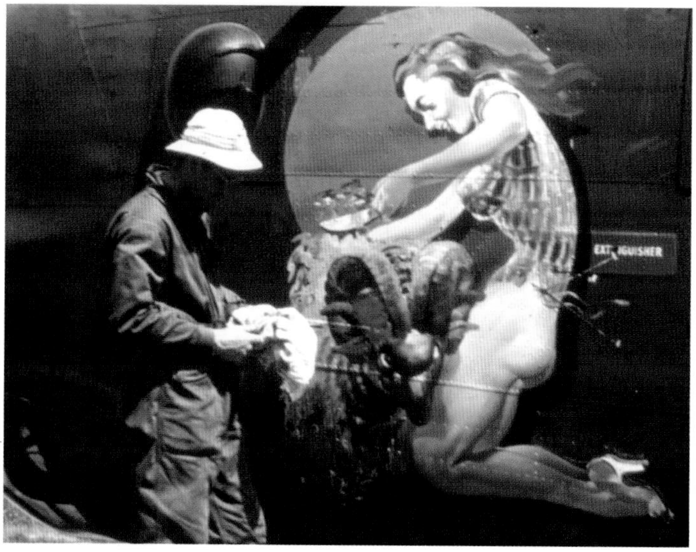

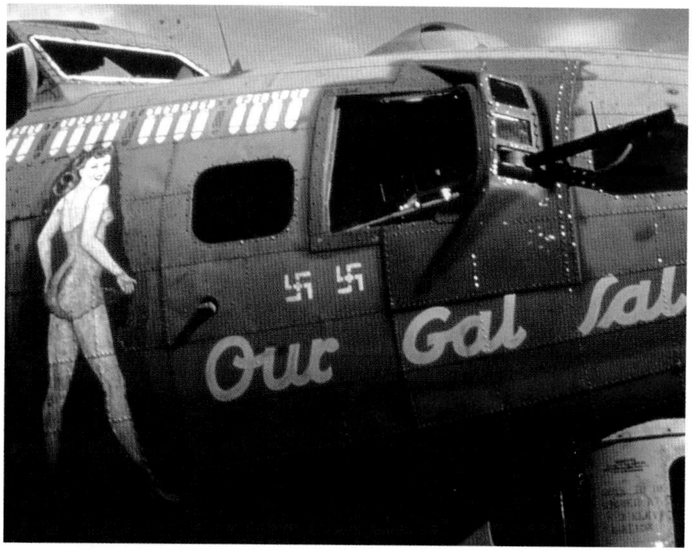
Our Gal

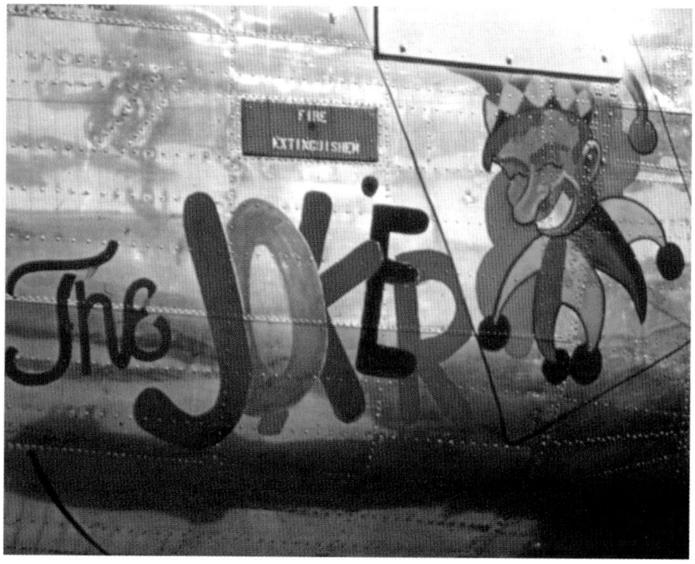
The JOKER

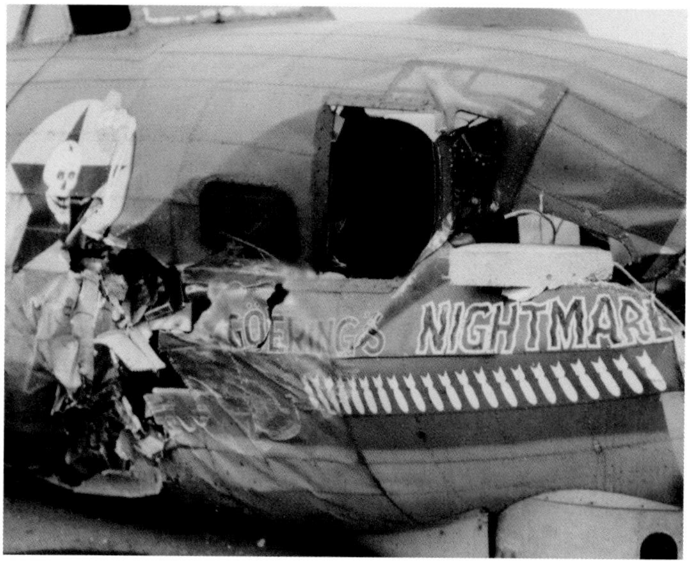

CASTLE

HE SAT IN THE co-pilot's seat of a B-17, in command of the largest force of bombers and escort fighters ever sent on a combat operation, 2,046 B-17s and B-24s, and 853 P-51 and P-47 escort fighters. Brigadier General Frederick Walker Castle had only held that rank for a few weeks before Christmas Eve 1944, the day of this historic attack by aircraft of the Eighth Air Force on German airfields and elements of Field Marshal von Rundstedt's forces. This was the greatest air armada ever assembled. It was General Castle's thirtieth combat mission.

Those who knew Fred Castle thought of him as exactly the opposite of the typical hard-nosed war leader commonly found in the upper echelons of an organization like the Eighth Air Force. Quiet, with exceptional humility, he was probably perceived by many as the antithesis of the larger-than-life hero so often portrayed on the big screen by stars like John Wayne, Gregory Peck, John Mills, and others.

Castle was a beneficiary of a fine old West Point custom. His father, Lieutenant Ben Castle, had attended the United States Military Academy and was, along with his friend Lieutenant Henry H. "Hap" Arnold, a member of the class of 1907. Both men were then posted to duty in the Philippines, where in 1908, Castle's wife gave birth to their son, Benjamin Frederick. By West Point tradition, the first boy born to a class member after graduation automatically becomes the Class Godson. Thus, young Fred was the recipient of 236 godfathers. With time both Arnold and Castle redirected their military careers into avi-

ation. Hap Arnold ultimately rose to become the "father" of the U.S. Army Air Forces, while Castle went on to become American Aviation Attaché in Paris after the First World War.

Fred Castle followed a similar military route to that of his father, winning a place at West Point, which he entered in July 1926. On graduation and commissioning, he first served with the Engineers and was later accepted for pilot training in the Army Air Corps. His first posting after winning his wings was a pursuit squadron at Selfridge Field, Michigan. But in the postwar years, flying time was strictly limited and he was required to supervise a group of unemployed men in a forestry project of the U.S. Civilian Conservation Corps as a part of a larger unemployment program. Disatisfied, and with little chance of another flying assignment, he elected to resign from the Army.

In the civilian world, Castle went to work for the Allied Chemical and Dye Corporation as a statistician and assistant sales manager. He progressed well and, in September 1938, was invited to join the staff of the Sperry Gyroscope Company as assistant to the president. The Sperry Company was making specialized equipment for the armed forces, including the ultra-secret Norden bombsight, as well as gun turrets for aircraft. Through this association he came into contact with his godfather, Hap Arnold, who was highly impressed with young Castle.

Castle, while having resigned from the military, had remained a member of the Army Reserve and had since been promoted to the rank of 1st lieutenant. With the entry of the United States into the Second World War in December 1941, he was eager to return to active duty and, probably thanks in part to his connection with

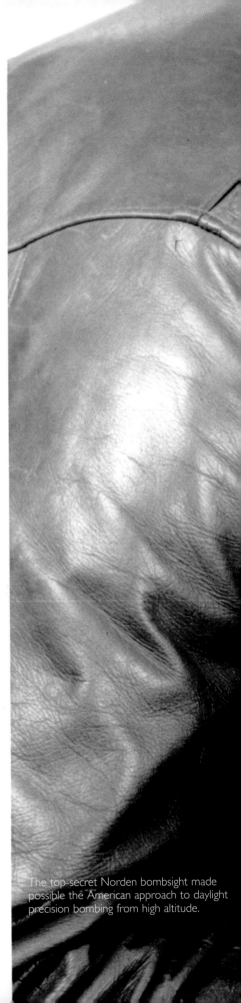

The top-secret Norden bombsight made possible the American approach to daylight precision bombing from high altitude.

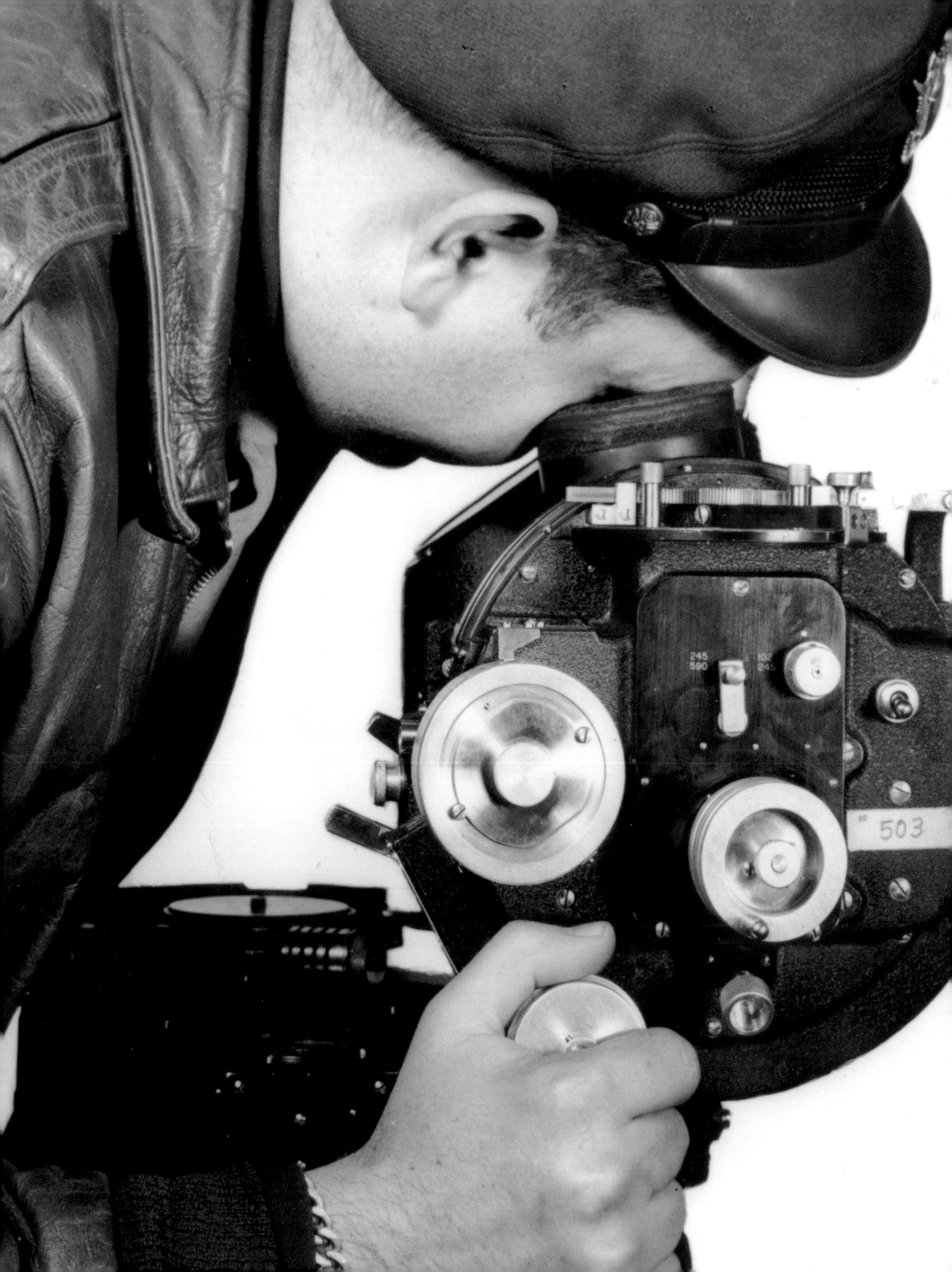
245
590
102
245
503

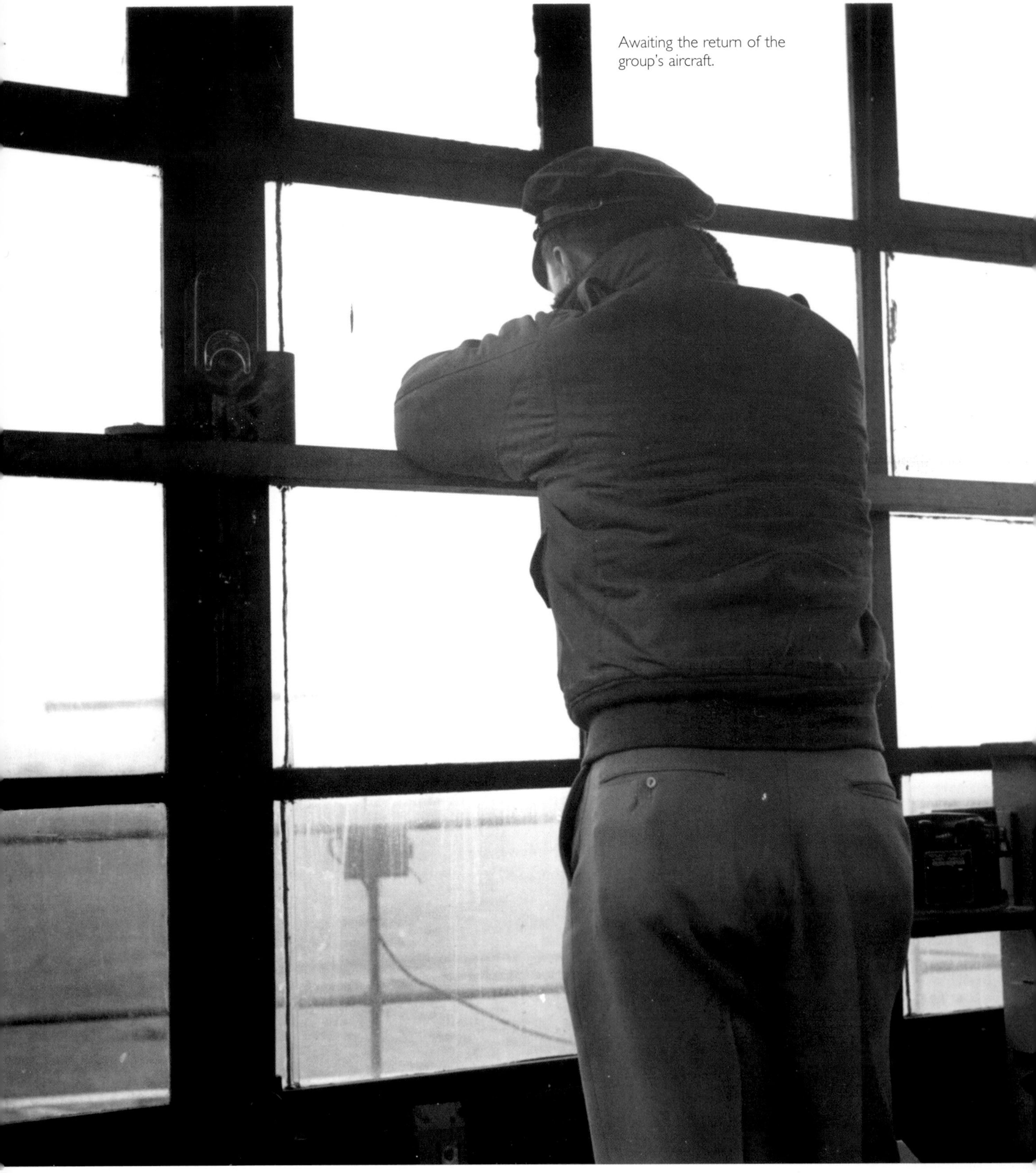

Awaiting the return of the group's aircraft.

Arnold, would be offered a promising opportunity.

At this point, a colleague of General Arnold, Brigadier General Ira Eaker, was preparing to take a small cadre of officers to England where they would begin to establish and form the new American bomber organization to be designated the Eighth United States Army Air Force. The job of the Eighth was to be the daylight strategic bombing of Germany from the United Kingdom. One of the men Eaker had chosen to go with him to England was Lieutenant Harris Hull who, as a civilian, had also worked for Sperry Gyroscope. Eaker was impressed when he learned from Hull that Fred Castle, though still quite young, was so well regarded by the top brass at Sperry that he was being considered as a future president of the company. Eaker knew Castle's father and, after briefly investigating the young man, was convinced he would be an ideal choice to handle the logistics of the Eighth in the UK. Eaker got Arnold to recall Fred Castle to active duty and gave him the challenge of organizing the bases and depot facilities the Eighth would require in England, a challenge he responded to enthusiastically. Now with the rank of captain, Castle would, within a year, rise to full colonel and be given the role of Chief of Staff for Supply.

To say that Fred Castle was hard-working and dedicated to his challenge would be to grossly understate. Historian Roger A. Freeman wrote of him: "Castle conscientiously persevered by working exceedingly long hours, causing fellow officers, such as Beirne Lay, to be concerned for his health. But Castle was not easily prevailed upon to take life easier. He possessed such dedication that he could not rest while matters remained outstanding. This dedication to duty was reflected in his personal conduct. His speech was guarded, his dress correct, and behavior always that becoming of an officer, following the code of conduct taught at West Point. However, Castle's propriety tended to be viewed as stiffness by some fellow officers."

But as good as he was at the work he was doing, Fred Castle aspired to a combat command, and the toughest, most demanding job in the Eighth was that of a group commander, the man responsible for the administration of between two and three thousand men on his station, and was also expected to fly as a combat leader. Soft-spoken gentleman that he was, though, Castle would occasionally raise the matter of such a possible command with General Eaker, in the hope that he might soon be relieved of his current job and given a combat group command. In the early summer of 1943, such an opportunity was developing.

The newest B-17 wing, comprised of three combat bomb groups, was made operational in May and was soon a matter of concern due to its poor performance. The groups were all producing inadequate bombing results and suffering high losses. Confidence, air discipline, and morale were all well below par; attrition was high and climbing; and Eighth Bomber Command was determined to fix the situation. One of the three groups, the 94th located at Rougham near Bury St Edmunds, was taken over by Fred Castle in a situation similar to, but not as severe, as that in which Frank Armstrong had been called upon to salvage at the 306th Bomb Group earlier that year. It was there, at Thurleigh, where the events that later inspired the book and motion picture *Twelve O'Clock High* occurred.

The change of command at Rougham was greeted with cool resentment by the officers of the 94th when Castle arrived on 20th June to take charge. In a scene reminiscent of one years later in *Twelve O'Clock High*, he addressed the officers in the briefing room and found them in an unmilitary mess of assorted attire, an exact contrast to his neat, precise, utterly correct appearance. Colonel Castle efficiently laid out what he expected of them in future operations, in their conduct as officers and gentlemen and in their uniform attire. As in the film, some in the audience were heard to mutter their dismay, displeasure, and clear disapproval of their new commanding officer. When word got around the base of Castle's educational and military background (West Point and Army supply), the men of the 94th were, to put it mildly, rebellious.

Castle's introduction to combat missions with the group began the next morning when it was ordered on a mission to Hüls, an attack on the German synthetic rubber plant there. The colonel went along on the raid and elected to fly in the B-17 piloted by Captain Franklin Colby, who at forty-one, happened to be the oldest combat pilot in the Eighth Air Force at the time. Colby's bomber was the lead airplane of the high squadron. Normally, a pilot of his age would have been assigned to either a transport or training role back in the States, but for whatever reason that was not so in this instance. Castle had quickly decided that Colby was likely the most competent of the pilots in the group. The colonel perched on a camp stool, crammed behind the pilots. Colby later recalled this flight and how Castle, "cool as a cucumber," calmly continued making notes while enemy fighters repeatedly attacked the American formation.

That the flying officers of the 94th had pre-judged and mis-judged their new leader as some sort of hopeless novice began to become apparent during the interrogation following the Hüls mission. A visiting officer and former associate of Castle at Eighth Bomber Command HQ happened to be visiting Rougham that day and sat in on the interrogation session. In conversation there with some of the group officers, he mentioned that Castle had flown a number of combat missions. But the relationship between the colonel and many of his officers continued to deteriorate. They resented what they perceived to be his excessive propriety and thought him aloof and distant. Most wanted nothing to do with him.

It was not immediately a marriage made in heaven, but Colonel Castle was certainly pleased to have the new command. In a letter he wrote to his family three days after taking over at Rougham: "I've been trying for several days to write the wonderful news of my new job, you have probably already guessed it. I am commanding a Bomb Group! I don't believe there could be a tougher job in the world, but I love it. The first raid on which I led my outfit will always be the high water mark of all my experiences. This job is the one I have worked for ever since I've been here, and I'm happy. But it keeps me working morning, noon and night, so for a while my letters will be brief." Typically, he plunged into the job and looked into every aspect of life and work on the base, as well as in operations, his primary concern. He was determined to resolve the obvious and the more subtle problems that were or

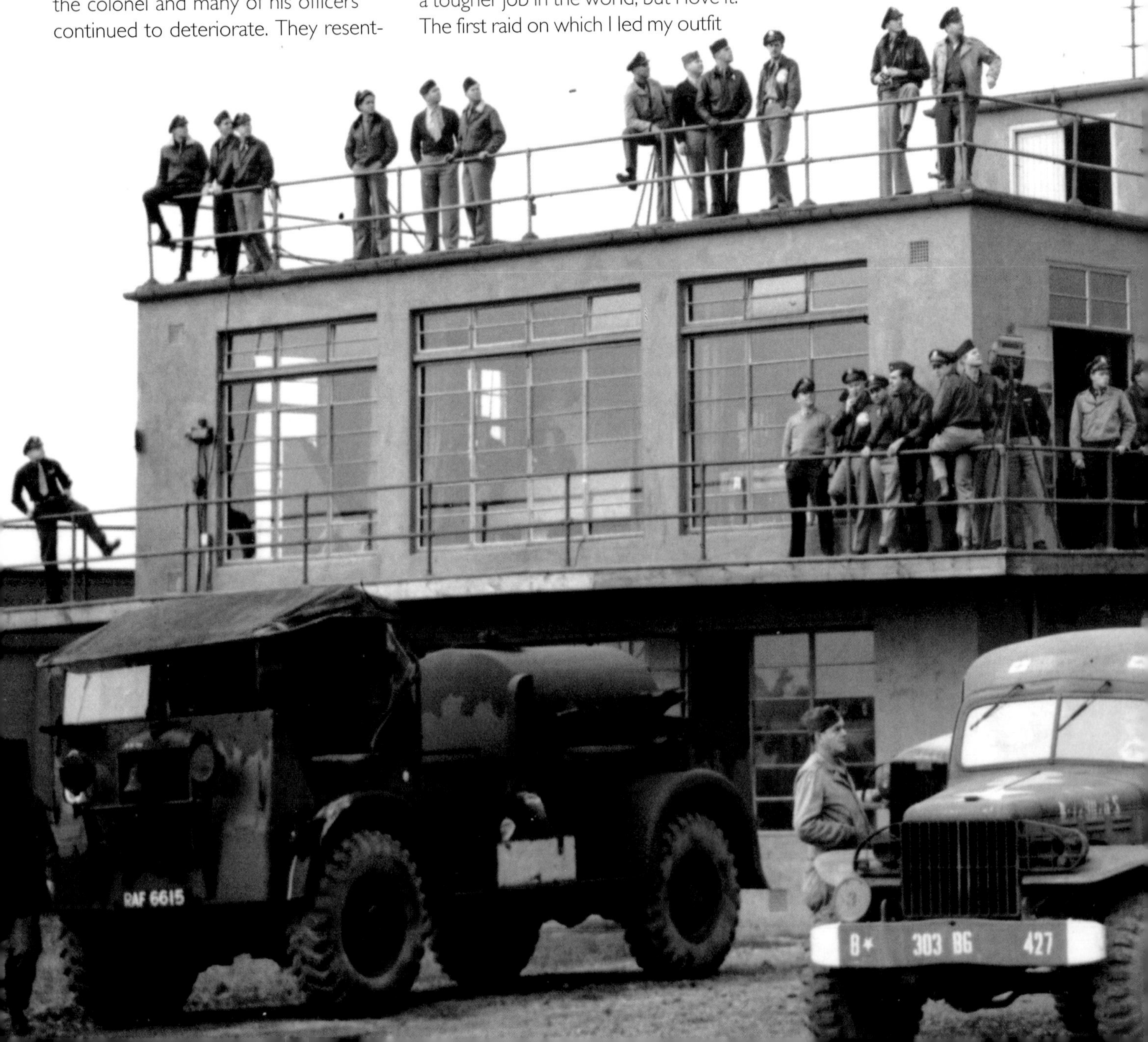
RAF 6615
B ✦ 303 BG 427

The flying control tower at Molesworth, home base of the 303rd Bomb Group in WW2.

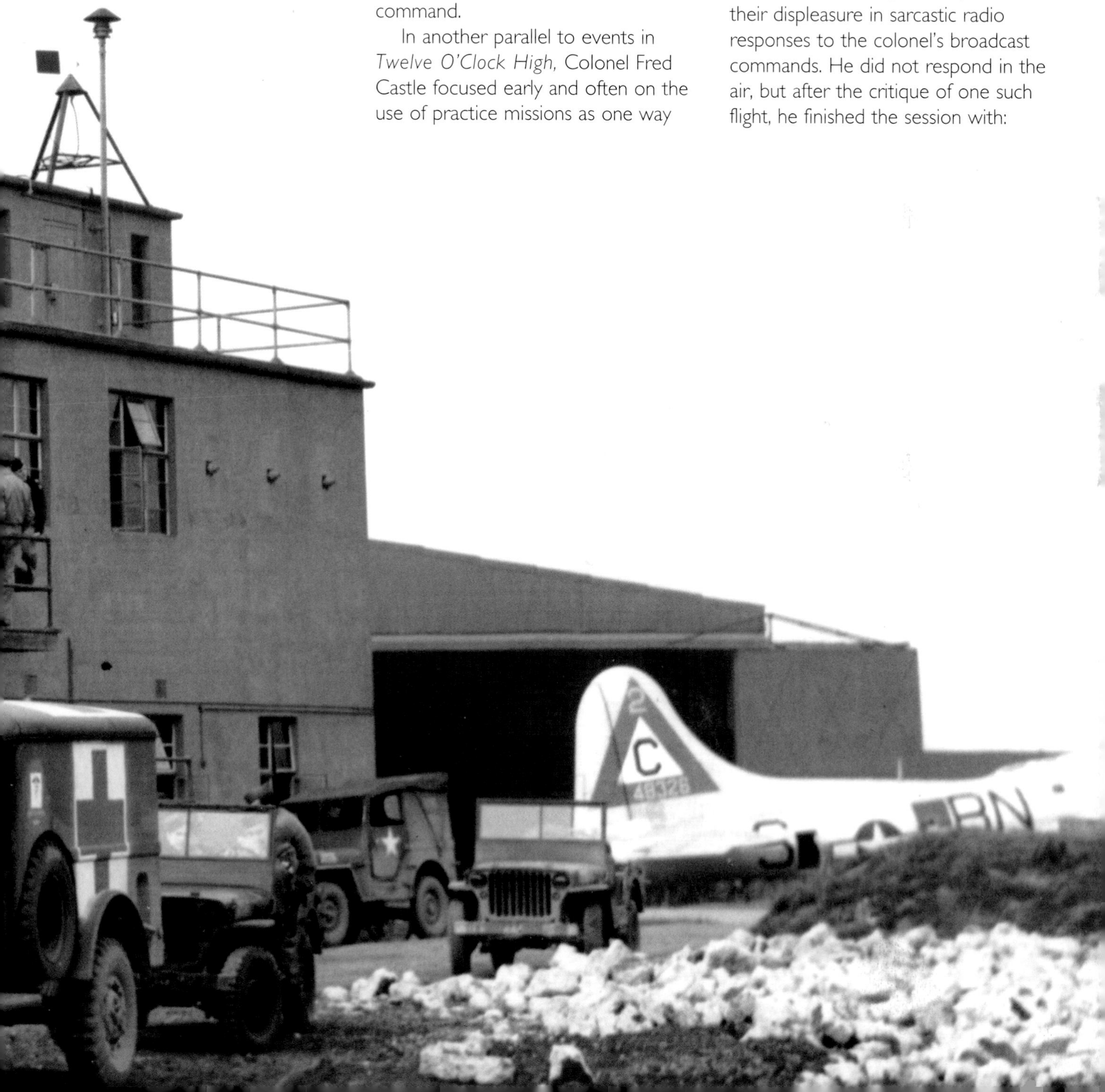
C
48326
BN

might be affecting the performance and efficiency of his crews. To that end he deployed his proven reliance on statistics. He required his staff to provide him with constantly updated records on all aspects of group operations, supply, and maintenance, to be entered in what he called his Command Book. He relied on this system, which had served him well in his prior business career, to get to grips with the situation in his new command.

In another parallel to events in *Twelve O'Clock High,* Colonel Fred Castle focused early and often on the use of practice missions as one way to improve the performance of his crews. Having already flown several actual combat missions most of the crew members were not pleased to have the added burden of what they thought were unnecessary practice flights and were frequently vocal in their displeasure. But practice they did, and Castle flew with them on most practices, giving instructions over the radio. Some of the pilots expressed their displeasure in sarcastic radio responses to the colonel's broadcast commands. He did not respond in the air, but after the critique of one such flight, he finished the session with:

"By the way, gentlemen, I consider the remarks made over the air to me today as beneath the dignity of the officers under my command." That did the trick and there was no further heckling over the air waves.

While many of his officers might say and think what they did of their commander in those early days with the 94th, their grudging respect for him as an air leader grew as he made a point of taking on the all of the most difficult and demanding missions. One example was the raid of 28th July 1943. The group was briefed for an attack deep into Germany to hit the Focke-Wulf fighter factory at Oschersleben. Clear weather over their part of eastern England soon gave way to layered stratus cloud over the North Sea, seriously disrupting the American formation. The chaos was compounded when the force was met by ranks of German fighters. When the airplanes of the 94th finally reached the coast of Germany theirs was the only group still essentially

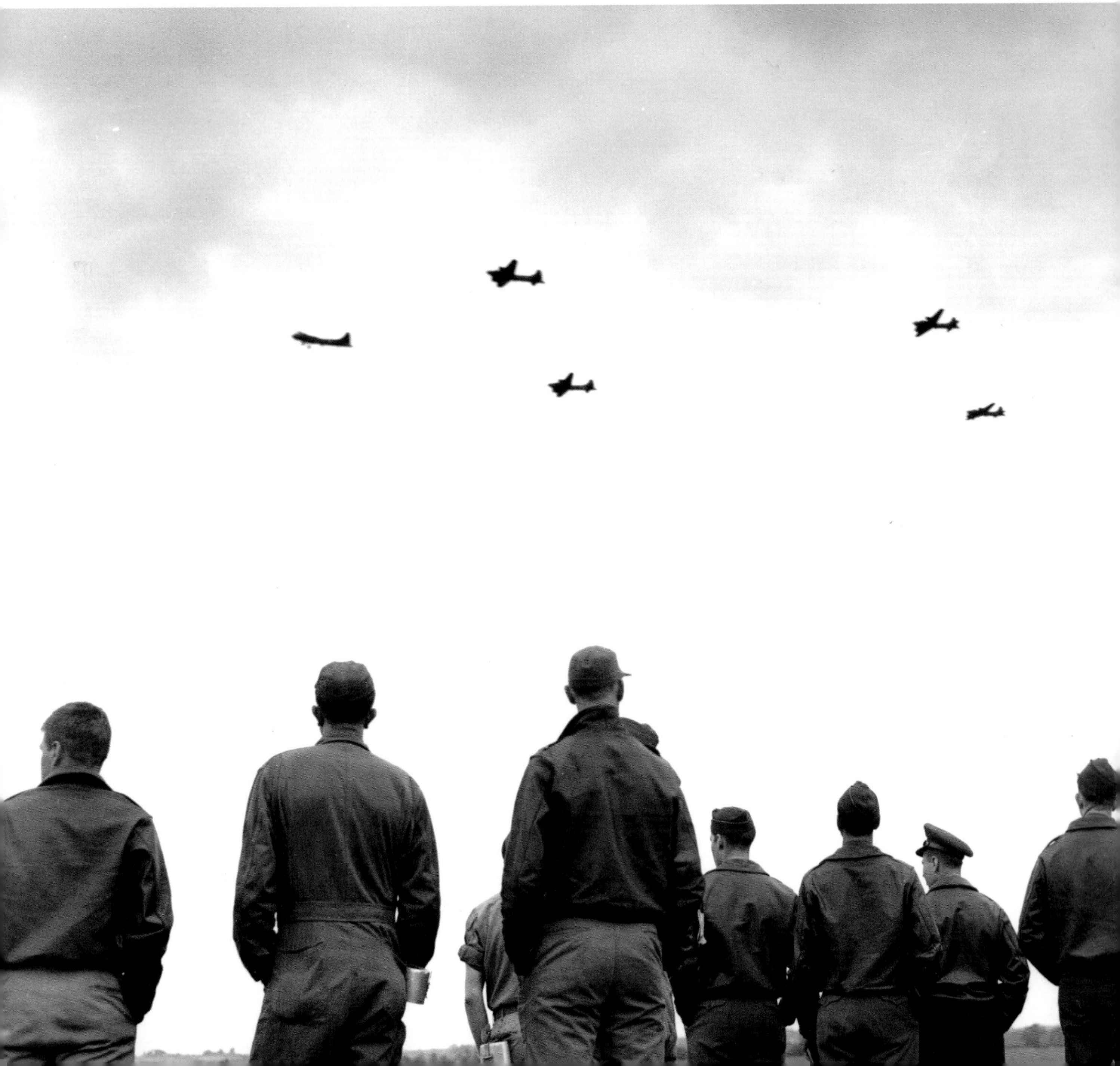

intact, together with elements from a few of the other bomb groups. As air leader, Colonel Castle this day had again chosen to fly with Captain Colby and, despite the depleted numbers in what was left of the formation, decided to continue to the target, which they struck and heavily damaged without facing further interference from the enemy fighters or incurring any losses. On their return to Rougham, Colonel Castle was reprimanded for having gone on to the target with a reduced force. Later, he was awarded the Silver Star for having led the mission. With typical modesty, he wrote to his family: "Did you hear I had been awarded the Silver Star? It was for the trip where we went close to Berlin to hit a plane factory. I am naturally very proud, but feel that it should be considered more an award to my outfit than to me. They're a swell bunch of lads."

As time wore on the officers and men of the 94th became accustomed to and more comfortable with the

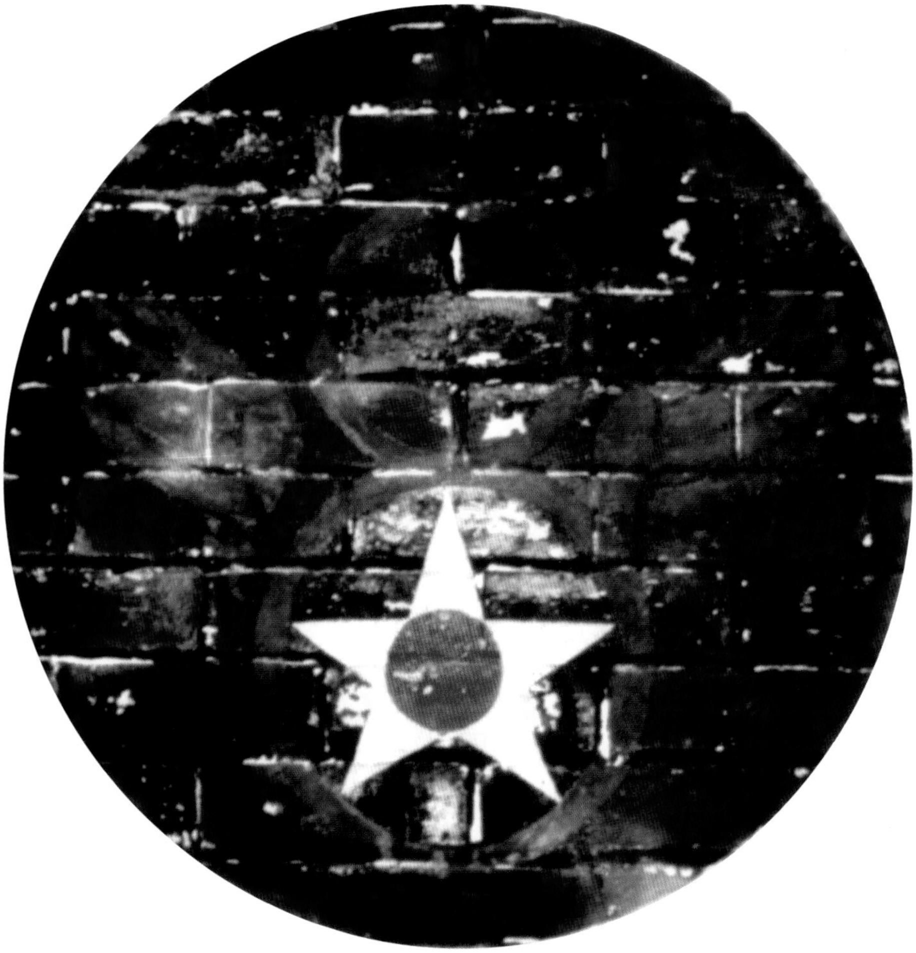

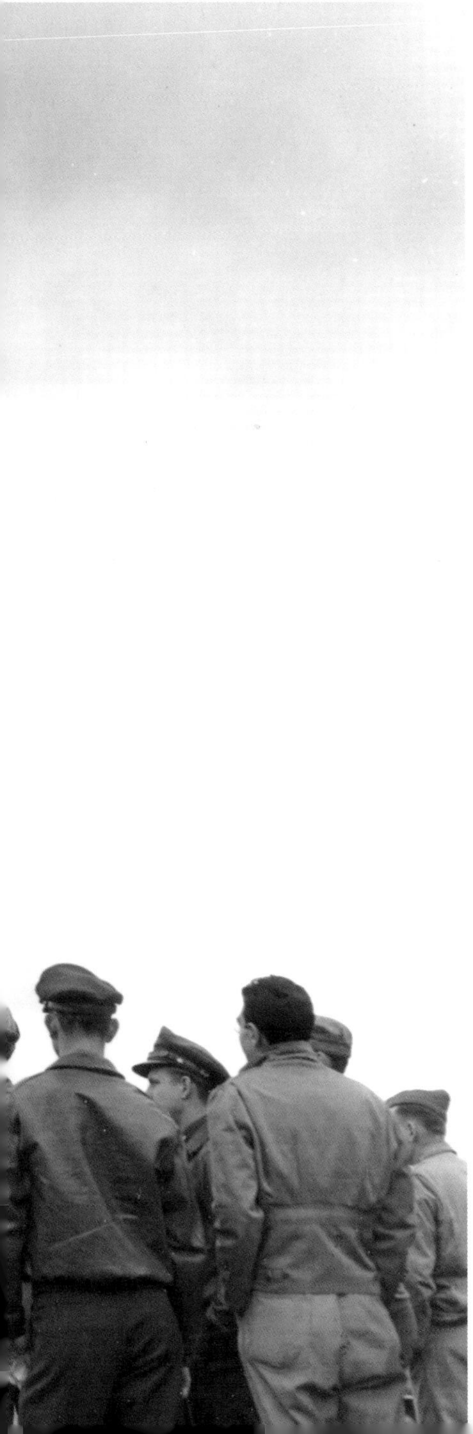

Sweating them in at the Chelveston base of the 305th Bomb Group.

The flaming demise of a B-24 Liberator bomber over Germany.

nature, personality, and characteristics of their commander and many grew closer to him, developing a level of respect for the man they could not have imagined possible during his early days with the group. They admired his practice of choosing to lead all of the toughest, most threatening missions. Even his most staunch critics among the flying officers, those who scorned anyone with West Point in his background, grudgingly admitted that Fred Castle was, in fact, a very tough, highly competent, proficient air leader; a dedicated, intelligent, efficient, fair-minded commander who was both dedicated to getting the best possible results in their bombing, and to the welfare of his crews. Still viewed as aloof by some of them, he was the finest sort of example of a West Point officer and gentleman, moving through his life and career to his own particularly high standard. He chose friends carefully and tended to

limit them to the better educated, more intellectual types. Though a very effective and tireless worker, he knew how to relax when time and opportunity allowed. He played tennis and squash, enjoyed theater and dances and the occasional late night poker session. His favorite pastime when he was able to make time for it was walking in the lovely countryside. Among his most favorite haunts in the area a few miles south of Bury St Edmunds were around the delightful village of Lavenham and the cozy bar in the Swan hotel. The walls in that bar have been decorated with the signatures of American and British airmen who served on the nearby bases and today a large framed photograph of Castle hangs in that hallowed room.

After a mission, Colonel Castle was often to be seen, still in flying clothes, eating with the enlisted men in their mess. But again, as in *Twelve O'Clock*

High, he was sensitive to what he saw as the danger of camaraderie with the officers and men of the group and finding himself identifying too closely with them.

If he could be faulted, it might be for his habit of over-working, flying too much, and going on too many of the more dangerous raids. But his desire to improve the performance of the group drove him to spend extra time on problems such as making the assembly and formation of the bombers of various groups safer and improving the instrument climb-out procedures in bad weather.

By April 1944, Fred Castle had been promoted to command of the 4th Combat Bombardment Wing, the headquarters of which would be there at Rougham. Soon the division consolidated five further bomb groups into Castle's Wing, making it the largest B-17 Wing in the Eighth Air Force. With that move came a well-de-served promotion for him to brigadier general. Those in command at division hoped that his new and added responsibilities would reduce the need he felt to fly so many missions.

With December came a spell of brutal wintry weather in much of western Europe. In Belgium, the Germans were mounting their largest offensive action since the time of the D-Day landings at Normandy, hitting at American Army positions in the Ardennes forest, with a goal of keeping the Allies from taking the port of Antwerp. The timing of the German operation was tied to a period of particularly bad weather which they believed would keep most British and American aircraft grounded while the Germans were on the move. That weather worked in the favor of the Germans until 23rd December when it began to lift, and by Christmas Eve the Allies were at last able to mount a maximum effort air attack on the communications targets supporting the enemy offensive. For the Eighth Air Force it was to be an all-out, no-holds-barred effort utilizing more than 2,000 B-17s and B-24s and more than 800 fighters in the biggest raid of the war.

Stress, extreme fatigue, the demands of his new job, and over-work had caused Castle's doctor to insist that the general take things easier, to which Castle responded by going out to visit other groups under his command. When he returned to Rougham he learned of the massive raid being prepared and, inspite of his fatigue, he insisted on personally leading the raid, and the Eighth Air Force, on it.

A thick frost coated the thin twigs and branches of the woods along the edge of the Lavenham airfield, home to the 487th Bomb Group, lying on a plateau just above the tiny hamlet of

Alpheton, Suffolk. General Castle was driven along the narrow winding road to the perimeter track and onto the icy hardstand where the B-17 and crew that were to lead the raid awaited him in that pre-dawn of Christmas Eve. In the bleak chill, the Fortress sparkled with a thin frost partially coating it. It was specially equipped with an H2X "Mickey" radar set and other specialized instrumentation. Sergeant James Ackerman, crew chief of the bomber, had assured its pilot that "she would fly hands-off without trimming and the auto-pilot was perfect."

Unlike most of the heavy bombers of the Eighth, this one sported no artwork or nickname on her nose. The crew simply referred to her as *Treble Four* for the last three digits of the serial number on her tail. On this trip she would carry a nine-man crew, including two navigators—one being the Group navigator, the other a radar navigator. General Castle rode in the co-pilot's seat on the right-hand side of the cockpit. The co-pilot would ride in the tail turret as an observer / gunner. Takeoff would come at 0900 hours.

The weather was good but, for whatever reasons, some aircraft of the Wing did not arrive on schedule at the rendesvous points, causing the lead formations of the huge force to be about fifteen minutes behind schedule in the climb across the English Channel and over Belgium. It left the 487th group, with Castle's plane in the lead, struggling to make up the lost time in order to rendezvous with the fighter escort before the whole assemblage crossed the battle lines. With no warning, the number four engine of *Treble Four* begin to run rough. For the time being, though, the pilot, Lieutenant Harriman, was able to hold position at 22,000 feet and retain the lead. Then as it approached the front, a row of

Me 109 fighters dropped down in a sudden attack out of the sun. All of the aircraft were still over Allied territory and, at that point in the war, it was unusual for enemy fighters to intercept Allied raiders there, but there were as yet no Allied escort fighters on hand to help.

When the German fighters attacked, it is believed that Treble Four may have been hit in the faltering number four engine because it began to vibrate severely and lost power. Now the airplane was unable to keep up with the formation. General Castle radioed the deputy leader, Captain Mayfield Shilling, and told him to take over the lead. He then told Lt. Harriman to let Treble Four drop back and fly at the rear of the formation. But Harriman was now having trouble maintaining control of the airplane, which was drifting to the left of the other nearby bombers. The German fighters soon returned to make further attacks on the damaged B-17. As Castle directed Harriman to try evasive action, a cannon shell shattered the Plexiglas of the nose, wounding the navigator. Harriman tried to pull the airplane back toward the relative protection of the formation but it was subjected to a third attack by the enemy fighters and was hit many times all over the airframe; the radar operator and the co-pilot in the tail were both wounded in the attack. The fighters hit the numbers three and four engines, setting them on fire, and General Castle came on the interphone to calmly order the crew to bail out. Castle took over the controls and ordered Harriman to get his parachute and bail out. He lowered the landing gear to reduce the flying speed and make it easier for the crew to leave the stricken aircraft. Most of the crew had left the plane and oxygen bottles were burning

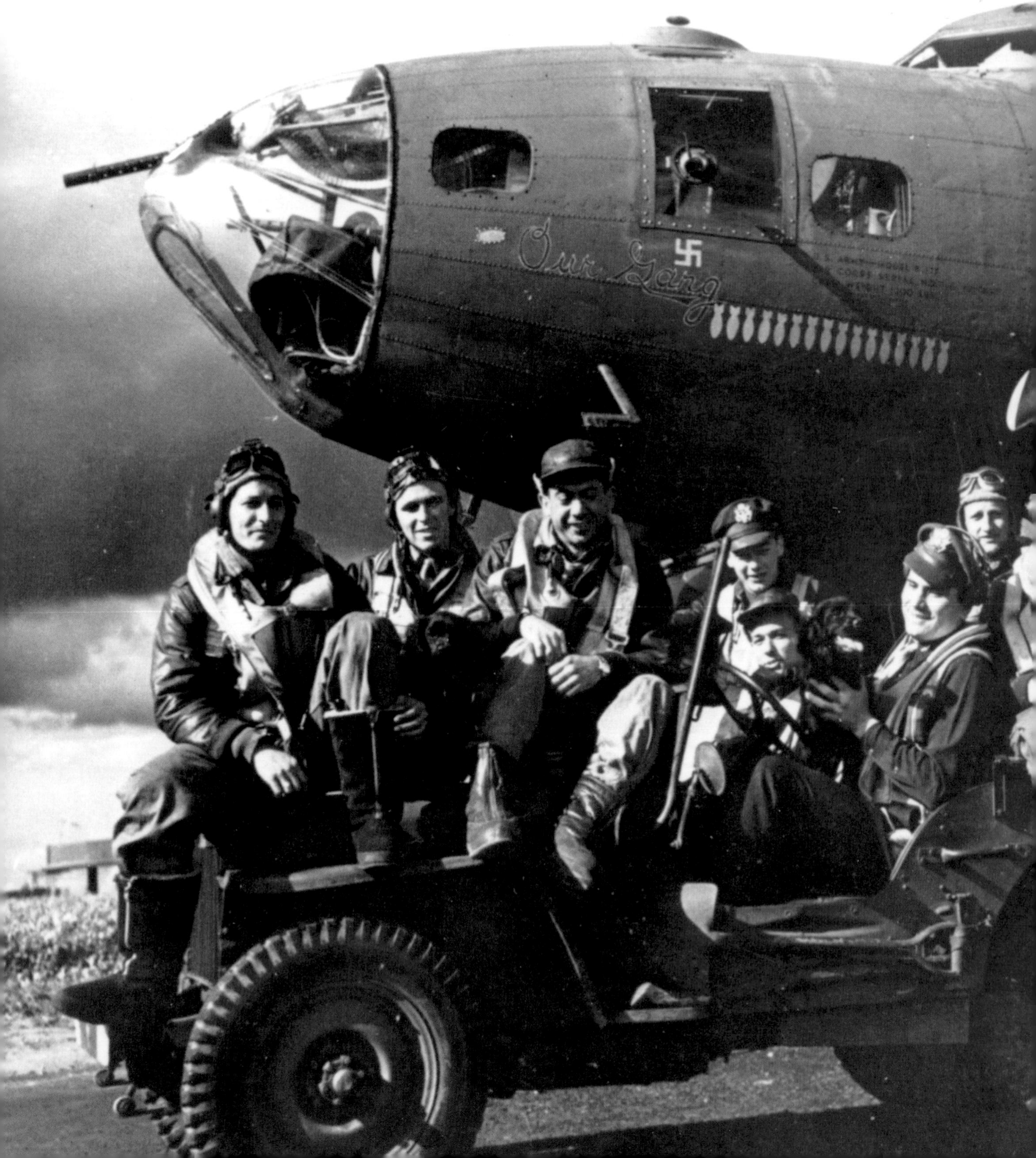
Our Gang

back in the fuselage. Before Harriman could escape, the right wing fuel tank exploded and Treble Four fell into a spin from which she would not recover. The B-17 crashed near a chateau at Hods in Belgium, killing both Harriman and Castle.

Of General Fred Castle, historian Roger Freeman wrote: ". . . it was typical of the man, of his humility and integrity, to risk his own life for those of others. Frederick Walker Castle seemed to many to be a strange man because he did not conform to the general pattern of social behavior amongst fighting men. He was unlike the hard-talking types that tended to dominate the combat commands in the Eighth Air Force. Yet he gave his life to leadership and had a combat record few other men of his rank could equal. As a man to whom duty was paramount he would have wanted nothing better than to be remembered as the only General in his country's history to die in a direct act to try and save the lives of his subordinates."

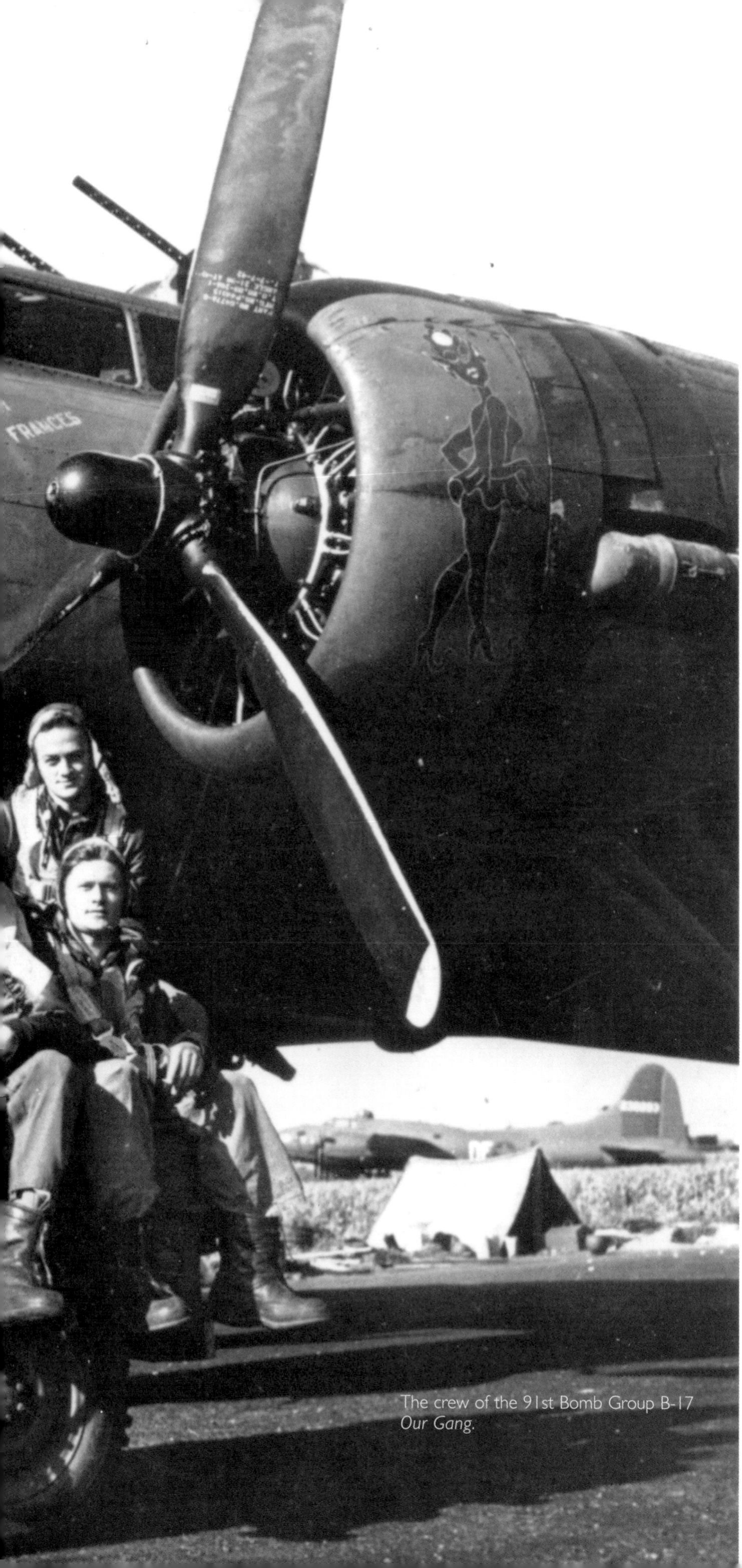
FRANCES
The crew of the 91st Bomb Group B-17 *Our Gang*.

EVADERS AND POWS

PARACHUTING has become, since the war years, a popular pastime. In free fall, with static lines, from various altitudes, individually or in teams, people have taken to jumping out of airplanes for the fun of it. There was, however, no fun in jumping out when you had to—when there was no alternative. In air war of the 1930s and 1940s, thousands of young men had that experience of placing their trust in a seemingly fragile silken canopy and its shroud lines to carry them down to safety from a doomed or crippled aircraft. Most of the time what awaited them on the ground—in addition to the possible injury they might incur on landing after doing something they had never done before—was an alien environment, one with the enemy in charge and perhaps an even greater threat posed by an angry and vengeful civilian population. Their duty, they had been taught, was to evade and escape, to bury their parachutes, remove all distinguishing badges, lie low in daylight, travel by night, and if possible, make contact with the underground, try to get to neutral country, get from there back to their squadron in England and back in the fight.

Among the highest-achieving heavy bomb groups in the Eighth Air Force, the Kimbolton-based 379th flew more sorties, dropped more bombs on target, and had fewer turn-backs in its month of combat operations than any other bomb group in the Eighth. It also lost fifteen B-17s in that month. On 16th August 1943, the day before the first historic raid on Schweinfurt and the ball-bearing plants there, twenty-one bombers of the 379th participated in an attack on the fighter airfield at Le Bourget, the field where Charles

Lindbergh had landed in 1927 after his history-making solo trans-Atlantic flight.

For twenty-nine-year-old Californian Albert Tyler, it was his fourteenth mission as a top turret gunner / flight engineer. His crew's regular pilot had been killed on a recent raid, and this would be their first combat mission with their co-pilot in command.

While flying in a height band between 26,000 and 28,000 feet, the formation of B-17s had a head-on encounter with several enemy fighters. Of their new pilot, Tyler recalled: "He was a helluva nice guy and we all liked him, but I guess he panicked. He did a real no-no. He pulled back on the yoke and drove right up. We were on our own up there, with no protection from the other B-17s. We were sitting ducks."

With methodical precision, pairs of the German fighter planes attacked the lone bomber, raking it with cannon fire from nose to tail. A hydraulic reservoir blew up in the fuselage, lodging some of its shattered metal in Tyler's leg. The oxygen bottles exploded next, filling the cockpit cabin with fire. Tyler grabbed his parachute pack and clipped it on his harness, burning canvas cover and all. Realizing that both pilots had already left the airplane (another no-no), he took it upon himself to order the rest of the crew to bail out, helping the bombardier and navigator to escape the burning Fortress: "I went out of the open bomb bay doors. Jumping from that height, I should have delayed pulling the ripcord, but I didn't want to take a chance on the chute catching fire, so I pulled it immediately. I soon passed out from the lack of oxygen, but it could only have been seconds before I came to again."

As Tyler floated down, two Focke-Wulf Fw 190 fighters made passes at him. Then, as he continued to descend, an Me 109 banked carefully around

him. Tyler saluted the German, who returned the gesture. As he drifted down he saw forest and the River Oise, and in the fields below he spotted German trucks and soldiers. He was a good swimmer and tried to steer his chute toward the river, but in common with most airmen, he had been given no training in manuvering a parachute: "I pulled the shroud lines the wrong way and I ended up in the tallest tree, right on the banks of that river. There were no Germans around that I could see. In fact, I didn't see anybody for a while. Then a dog started barking, and a group of people gathered under the tree. With my leg the way it was, I couldn't get down."

Once convinced that Tyler was an American, the Frenchmen on the ground below him dispersed, taking one of his fallen flying boots with them as a souvenir. One sturdy youth, whom Tyler came to know as André, climbed the tree, half held and half dropped the airman to the ground. There he concealed the American behind a pile of rocks. A few hours later, Tyler heard someone whistling Yankee Doodle. Two small children came through the forest carrying a basket of bread, cheese, fruit, and wine. Having improvised a crutch, André found clothes suited to the role of a peasant which Tyler, for the time being, would adopt.

Resting in a hayloft that night, they heard shouts of "Achtung, Achtung," as German soldiers searched the area. The next morning he and André moved to a cave near the river and there were joined by another member of Tyler's crew, who was escorted by the village mayor. Tyler was concerned: "Johnny was not our regular bombardier, and he was a very uncooperative guy. I thought he would be a real danger to me."

André left for a few days and the two airmen spent three nervous days

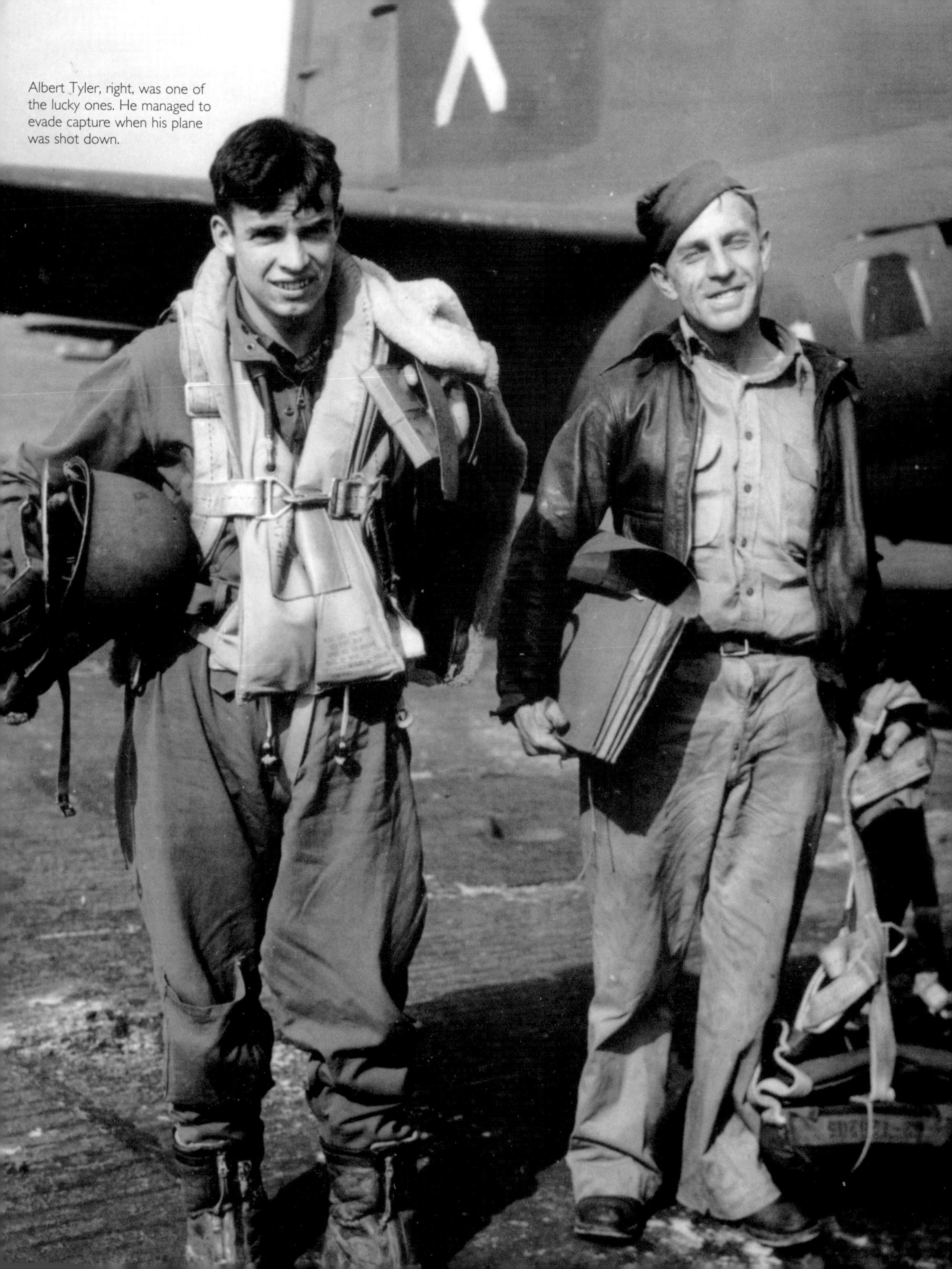

Albert Tyler, right, was one of the lucky ones. He managed to evade capture when his plane was shot down.

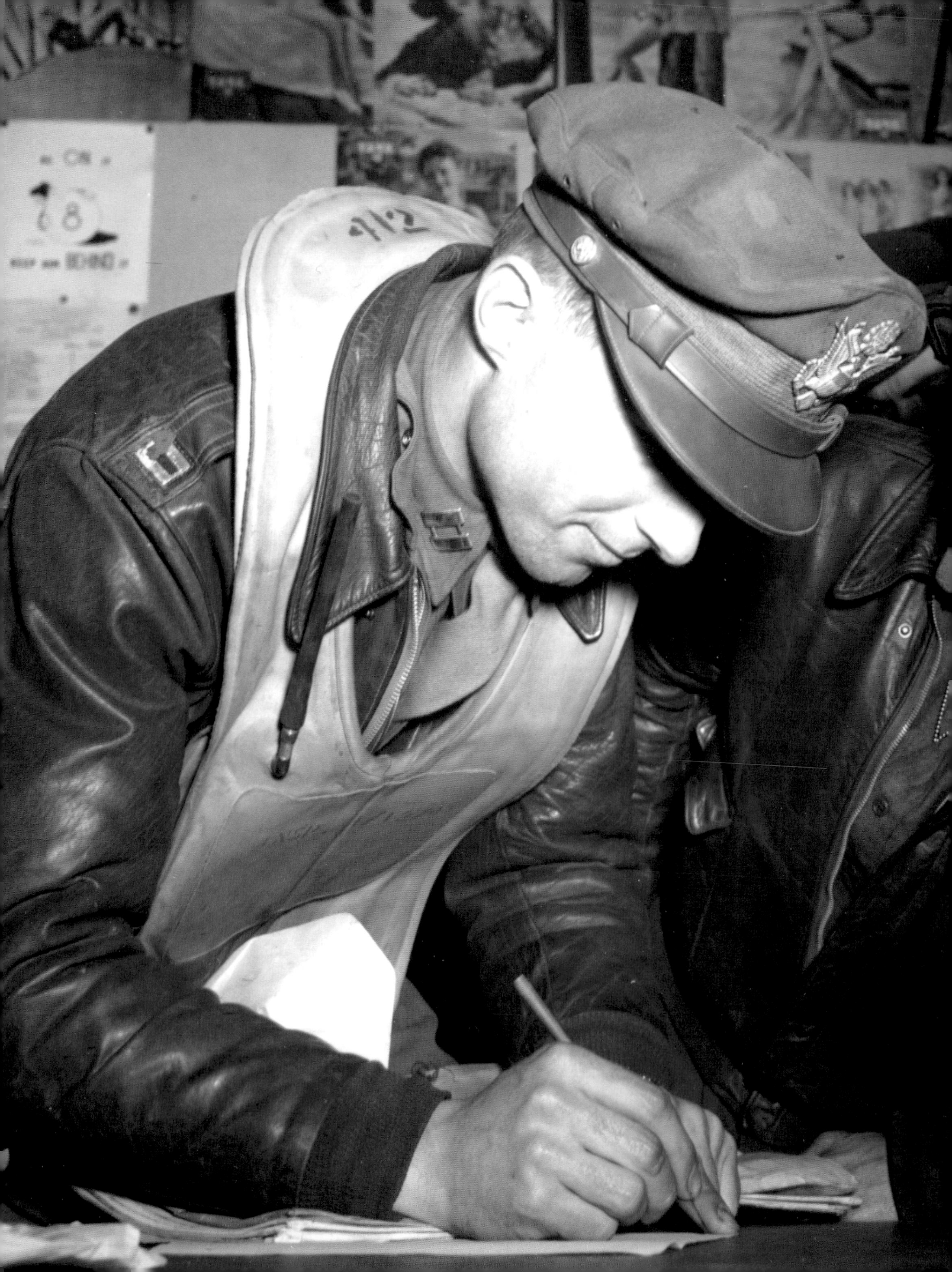

On returning from a raid on Leipzig, Germany, on 20th February 1944, Captain Alan Tucker signs for his wallet.

in the riverside cave. Then André returned with rail tickets for Paris. Though the train was packed with German soldiers, they paid no attention to Albert and Johnny. Albert was not required to employ the deaf-and-dumb act he had rehearsed with André.

In the urinal at the Gare du Nord, Johnny and Albert exchanged a few words in English: "A German officer then emerged from a cubicle and put a pistol up against my kidneys. Without saying a word, André came over and jammed a hunting knife into the German's back and we left in a hurry."

André took his charges to the apartment of a female member of the French Resistance: "There was a big, open courtyard, and our bedrooms were right off a balcony that went round the house. Madame gave us everything we wanted to eat and drink. At the same time she was hiding and feeding a bunch of escaped French prisoners of war. A very brave lady."

Meanwhile, the Resistance was planning the next move, which was almost a disaster. In a Paris suburb, they had to jump from a window in the middle of the night to evade a German search party. Their next port of call was an elegant townhouse a mile or so from the Eiffel Tower, and the two weeks they spent there were the highlight of their French adventure.

"Every day, Juliette surprised us with something—a duck, a lobster, and I mean a big one. It was very enjoyable. Her husband got a big kick out of taking us for a stroll around the sidewalk cafés in the afternoon. The trouble was that when the German's saw Johnny's blond hair, they thought he was one of them, and tried to strike up a conversation. He could have been picked up real quick. I suggested shoe polish, but he didn't want his hair blacked. That guy fought us tooth and nail. I had to

hold him down."

They then accompanied Marcel, another member of the Resistance, on a journey south of Paris where they watched him lay explosives on a railway line that carried German traffic. They watched as Marcel choked a sentry with a length of piano wire.

Two days before the time came to move on, they saw barrage balloons rising over Paris and watched from Juliette's patio while B-17s bombed the Renault engine plant across the Seine. On the train to central France, they were escorted by a priest. Arriving in Ville, they were welcomed by the mayor, who promptly threw a party. The whole town attended, much champagne was drunk, and Tyler, not America's most accomplished pianist, played the "Marseillaise" fortissimo until the more cautious townsmen persuaded him to stop.

Their next stay was at a castle on a hilltop where, over a bottle of Jack Daniel's, they discovered that their host, having made an illicit booze fortune in the States, was making amends to society by collecting starving children from the poorer parts of Paris and fattening them on the products of his land: "He and his beautiful wife would take them back to town and pick up another load. That guy was some character."

Their priestly guide then left them with instructions to take a certain train to Toulouse. In the compartment, Tyler's deaf-and-dumb act was successful until a stout lady, in rising to depart, happened to tread on his foot. Tyler yelped, "Oh, shit," at which two Frenchmen got up from their seats, muttering "Allez, allez," and hustled the Americans away.

They were then taken to a farm-house below the northern foothills of the towering Pyrenees. That afternoon, with twenty more evaders and a guide, they set out to make a crossing into

Spain. On the third day of the journey, they were halted by a blizzard during which their guide decamped taking not only his fee but also the party's store of food. While some of the men chose to continue on their own, Albert and Johnny returned to the farmhouse for reprovisioning. Their next attempt to reach a neutral haven was eventually successful, but not without its hardships.

"We were eating leaves and grass to supplement our rations. I ended up with diarrhea like you wouldn't believe. And they told me, we can't stop, we have to go on. The Germans were patrolling those mountain trails with light aircraft."

At last they reached Andorra, a neutral, if venal, sanctuary. It took Tyler's check for two hundred dollars, written on scrap paper, to purchase travel documents and a passage to Madrid. From the Spanish capital, the British vice-consul drove them to Gibraltar, and an RAF transport did the rest: "They put us up in a hotel in London and squeezed every bit of information out of us. The second night there I got deathly ill. The doctor said I had eaten too many little Spanish pastries."

Another airman of the 379th Bomb Group at Kimbolton was radio / gunner William R. McCarran. On a bitterly cold December day in 1943, the Eighth Air Force was mounting a strike on the shore installations and U-boat pen shelters at Bremen, a maximum effort involving more than two thousand heavy bombers and nine hundred American and British escort fighters: "The spare B-17 assigned to us appeared more like a sick pigeon than an attacking eagle. Patched and battered-looking, it was parked in the furthest revetment. We busied ourselves in the area of our responsibility.

I reported the intercommunication outlets were equipped with low-altitude microphones for what was to be a high-altitude mission. This condition would make it necessary to remove oxygen masks before 'pressing to talk,' rather than using the high-level choker-type mikes to pick up throat vibrations. Talking without oxygen for a moment was not dangerous—the resulting delay could very well be. The pilot was anxious to go along with the group (or embarrassed to abort). He chose to ignore the problem. Strike one?

"We were behind the others because of the switch in aircraft, and armorers hurried to load the bomb bay with incendiaries. Though small, these little candles from hell raised havoc when dropped on an area already blasted by high explosives. They defied ordinary fire-fighting equipment. We checked our guns; mine was the fifty-caliber machine-gun mounted

in the open hatch above the radio section. Parachutes were next along with oxygen lines, heated suits, transmitters and receivers, flare gun, and code books. Worriers worked harder than others, but maybe lived longer, I reasoned.

"The takeoff was a respite—but not from our practice of sweating out the performance of the pilot. We sweated out everything he did . . . formation flying or landings. We knew the pilots were only a year away from their desks or hot rods and everything about flying was new to them (sudden death would also be new to us).

"The engineer / gunner called the pilot's attention to a faulty supercharger, a condition bad enough to slow the ship should a burst of speed be needed for evasive action. Again, as captain, the pilot chose to ignore something that could prove disastrous. Whether or not this determined later events, those of us at the middle and rear of

Catching a lift on a bomb carrier.

the plane would never know. Strike two?

"It wasn't long until flares dropped by the lead plane indicated the beginning of the run over the target. We began the approach. The bomb bay doors opened okay. They were never to close.

"'Bombs away' came over the intercom and down went the incendiaries from a bay already afire. I remember thinking it strange to see aluminum burning. 'Bomb bay doors closed' came the order. This from the front of our staggering and flaming B-17 (these messages were delayed because of our microphone problem). There were more hits and more explosions. The confusion began. Strike three?

"It took time to inform the pilot that the doors were jammed. The instruction came back, 'Close them by hand.' It was my assignment and I went for the crank clipped to the partition between the radio room and

the bomb bay. Before moving, I had to connect my oxygen to a walk-around bottle. The communication foul-up continued. The top turret gunner / engineer came back through the walkway. He had neglected to use the emergency oxygen system and passed out in the fire-filled bay. He had to be revived and led back to the relative safety of his gun position.

"Because of the brake-like action of the open bay we were falling behind the protection of the formation and were being clobbered by fighters. I couldn't budge the doors with the crank and returned to the radio room. I didn't fully comprehend the danger when I saw an unexploded 20mm shell beneath the transmitter. I just stared at it. It blew and the force threw me facedown into the opposite corner. I was stunned. Couldn't get up until the thought came—'My mother would be sad if I stay here.' I got to my feet, and, following another series of hits, decided

to leave. There was then no contact with the front of the aircraft. I had no orders. I knew any place had to be an improvement and figured, if fire could melt aluminum, it could certainly burn my ass.

"I lurched back through the smoking and shuddering wreck. The waist gunners were sprawled near the guns. The ball gunner was up and out of his turret. Their faces were a weird greenish color. Indicating my intention to the others, I kicked open the escape hatch. I saw them lined up behind and pushed out into space. I went nowhere. I hung suspended by a broken cable while fire from the inboard engine crackled around me. One of the waist gunners, although badly wounded, managed to help me up and back in, where we loosened the wire. He was tremendous, and I was lucky he was there.

"I pushed out again, this time free . . . to what seemed the quiet of an arctic waste. We had been told that to escape continuing action, we should delay pulling the release cord. I dropped as far as I dared before doing so. There was no sensation of going down, and when the chute opened, it was as if my umbrella and I went up from wherever we were at the time. I heard afterwards that those in the front of the plane had left before us. The waist gunners reported that the ship exploded seconds after they left. Those in front survived and were taken prisoner with the exception of the co-pilot. He was killed in his seat at the time of the original problem with the bomb bay.

"There were other parachutes in the sky. Some were darker than the white one over me and looked like lighter-than-air toadstools. Guessed them to be those of the enemy. The enemy became real when a Messerschmitt 109 roared past. The pilot waved. He banked, made another pass, and was gone.

"It was heartening to see land when old worrier me half-expected to see the icy waters of the North Sea. There was a covering of snow, a village way over, and a church steeple. I figured the church was gonna get me one way or another until I saw the tree rushing towards me. I remembered instructions on how to guide the contraption and pulled on the lines to steer it one way or the other. Didn't alter my course an inch. I noticed I still had the ripcord and threw it away. Then, kerrunch . . . rippp . . . crash . . . there was the would-be hero . . . upside down in a tree, in Europe.

"There was no one in sight. I struggled to free myself. The chutes were difficult under normal circumstances, but I was upside down and my weight put too much pressure on the straps of the harness. I was helpless. I realized I had been working with only one hand and removed the glove from my left

hand. The wrist and hand were bleeding badly. I didn't remember getting hit. It must have been fragments from the 20mm shell. Still did not hurt. I had also sustained a puncture wound on my thigh. This stopped bleeding on its own with no real damage to the bone or leg muscles.

"Gave up on the harness and took a possum's eye view of the area. People were approaching. They had shotguns and pitchforks. Some of them wore wooden shoes. They stopped a short distance away and asked, 'Pistola?' I did have a .45 when in the plane, but now its holster was empty. I replied 'no pistol' and two teenagers were sent to release me. They noticed the blood and the crowd came closer. It took the excited young men a while to release me. A young soldier joined the group as I got to the ground. Until then, there was only the very young or the very old. A lady asked where the planes had struck; her family was in Bremen and she was concerned for them. I gave no answer. They still had the guns and pitchforks, but at no time did they threaten to use them. They pointed the direction they wanted me to go and I went. Captured by women and children yet.

"I was led to a farmhouse where the family, after cutting the sleeve of my suit, splinted and wrapped my arm. The bones of the wrist and hand were shattered, but the bleeding had stopped. They tore a pillowcase for a bandage. Each window in the kitchen was filled with a German face. The lady of the house showed a picture of a young man in a German army uniform. She cried. They gave me water and offered cookies. The young boys had gathered the parachute from the tree and brought it to the farmhouse. I hoped they would be able to keep it for the care they had shown me.

"A pompous older man entered,

Bringing a deadly special delivery to a waiting Fortress.

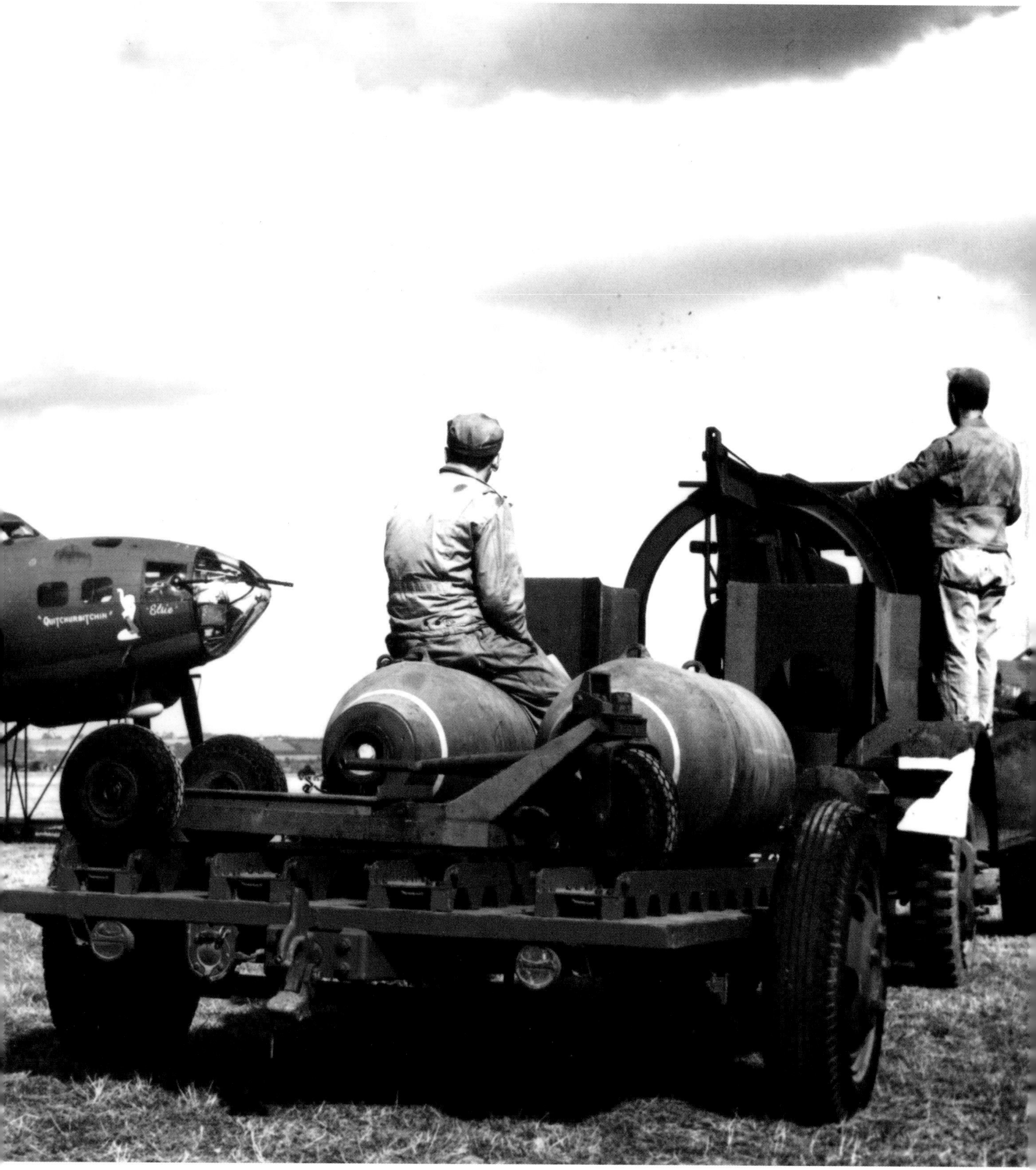
"QUITCHURBITCHIN"
"Elsie"

To all Prisoners of War!

The escape from prison camps is no longer a sport!

Germany has always kept to the Hague Convention and only punished recaptured prisoners of war with minor disciplinary punishment.

Germany will still maintain these principles of international law.

But England has besides fighting at the front in an honest manner instituted an illegal warfare in non combat zones in the form of gangster commandos, terror bandits and sabotage troops even up to the frontiers of Germany.

They say in a captured secret and confidential English military pamphlet,

THE HANDBOOK OF MODERN IRREGULAR WARFARE:

". . . the days when we could practise the rules of sportsmanship are over. For the time being, every soldier must be a potential gangster and must be prepared to adopt their methods whenever necessary."

"The sphere of operations should always include the enemy's own country, any occupied territory, and in certain circumstances, such neutral countries as he is using as a source of supply."

England has with these instructions opened up a non military form of gangster war!

Germany is determined to safeguard her homeland, and especially her war industry and provisional centres for the fighting fronts. Therefore it has become necessary to create strictly forbidden zones, called death zones, in which all unauthorised trespassers will be immediately shot on sight.

Escaping prisoners of war, entering such death zones, will certainly lose their lives. They are therefore in constant danger of being mistaken for enemy agents or sabotage groups.

Urgent warning is given against making future escapes!

In plain English: Stay in the camp where you will be safe! Breaking out of it is now a damned dangerous act.

The chances of preserving your life are almost nil!

All police and military guards have been given the most strict orders to shoot on sight all suspected persons.

Escaping from prison camps has ceased to be a sport!

and I couldn't believe it when he actually clicked his heels and shot out his arm in the Nazi salute. 'Just like the movies,' I thought. Even more when he said, 'Heil Hitler.' It was my introduction to the uniformed insanity of National Socialism. He asked questions of the people. He took charge and ordered me out of the house and onto the road. He pointed a small gun at my back and the two-man parade went down the street. The small man in a natty uniform and me in my bunny-like heated suit with its cord dragging in the snow. I had a burned helmet and floppy oversized flying boots. From the reaction, it seemed my captor was no more popular than his prisoner.

"We walked a mile to the next hamlet where I was searched in a one-room schoolhouse by members of the Volkstürm (home guard). When they discovered the escape kit we all carried in a leg pocket . . . one would have thought they had Eisenhower. They 'ach'd' and 'so'd' over each article: a map, sulpha drugs, some concentrated food, and a small amount of German money. From there it was to a jail-house fire station nearby, and I heard a lock click behind me for the first time."

Gunner John Hurd of the 401st Bomb Group at Deenethorpe, Northants: "While flying near Hanover, Germany, on 11th April 1944, and still heading toward the target, my squadron was hit hard by flak. We lost four B-17s in this action. There were many flak bursts around our ship, *Battlin Betty*. From my ball turret position I was able to watch under the wings for fires. Immediately the number three and four engines started smoking and shortly after, my ball turret was hit and I was injured on the right buttock. Our bombs were salvoed to guard against an explosion as one of our B-17s blew up. *Battlin Betty* finally came

clear of the flak and we were slowing down and losing altitude. I was then asked to leave the ball turret so the radio operator could have a look at my injury. He was not able to do anything as I had too many clothes on. About this time the pilot gave the order to bail out. I hooked on my chest-type parachute and placed my GI shoes inside my chute harness. We were over flat country somewhere east of Hanover. I looked out of the bomb bay and decided to jump out the waist door. We were somewhere between 15,000 and 18,000 feet. The two waist gunners and I were waiting to jump when I heard a loud crash noise. The ship started to rock to the left and knocked us against the left side. I thought to myself, 'It's now or never,' so I gave a big push and all three of us went out the door. It was very noisy as I left the ship and shortly after, I pulled the ripcord. The chute opened and the world was quiet. About this time I heard some machine-gun fire and I looked around but did not see anything. I looked down and there was a river or canal directly beneath me. I wondered if I would land in the water. I looked up and the bombardier was very close to the top of my chute canopy, so we talked to each other on the way down. My favorite B-17, *Battlin Betty*, with twenty-five missions completed, buried itself in the river as I watched from my parachute. I drifted away from the water and as I neared the ground it came up with a rush. I hit the ground and finally came to rest on my back. I struggled for several moments getting to my feet as I wanted to keep my injured right buttock out of the dirt. The bombardier landed nearby and I walked over to him. He started to look at my butt and tear a bandage from his chute, and I started to put my shoes on when a German officer came up to us and motioned

for us, and two other crewmen, to walk over to the military vehicle, an open touring car, and get in."

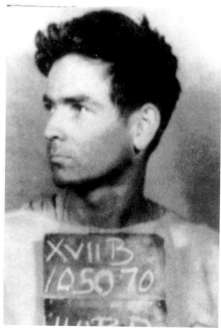

John Hurd became a prisoner of the Germans in 1944. He had been a gunner with the 401st Bomb Group based at Deenethorpe.

ROGER'S WAR

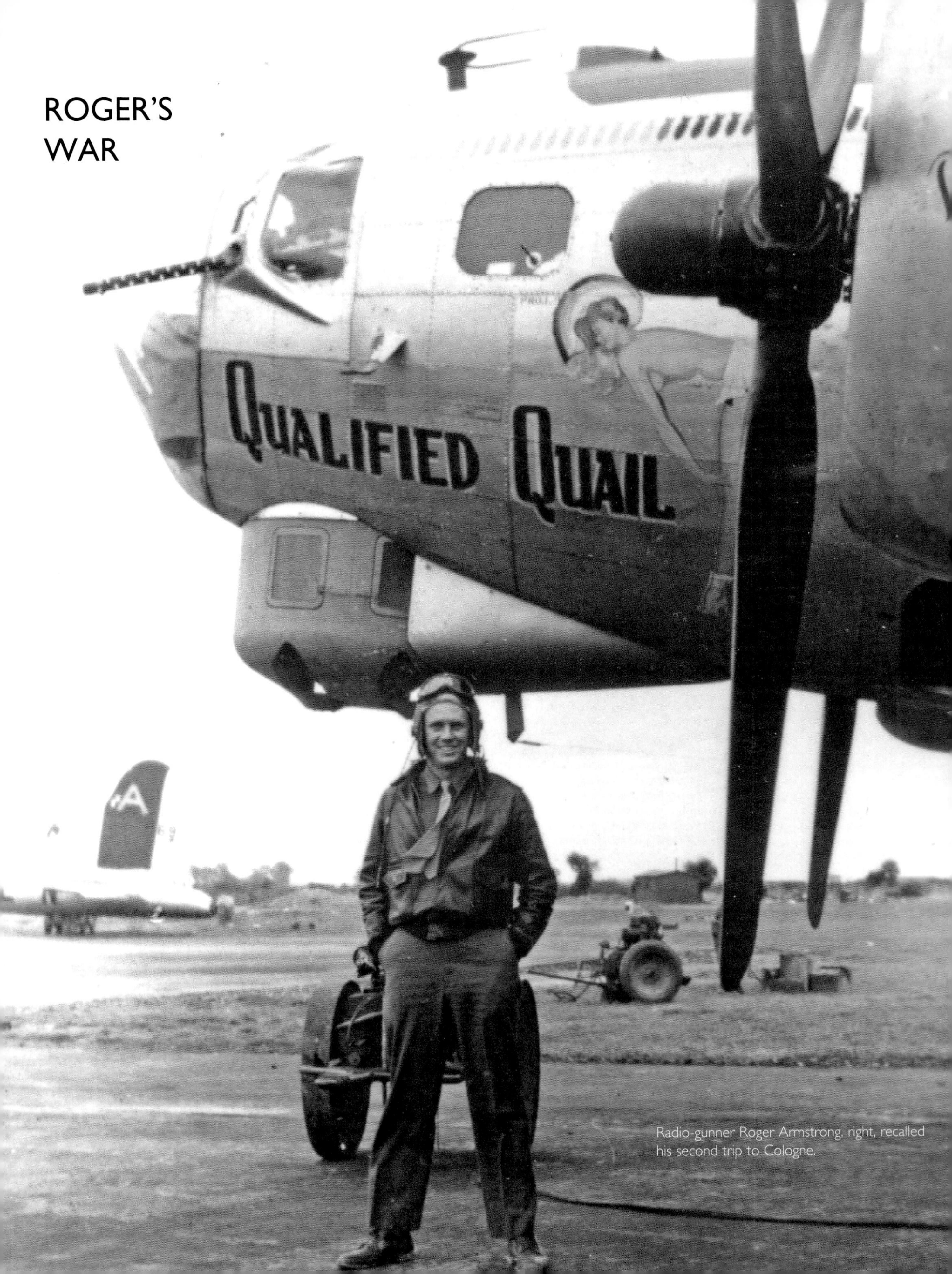
QUALIFIED QUAIL

Radio-gunner Roger Armstrong, right, recalled his second trip to Cologne.

WHEN THE TRUCK STOPPED and I saw the aircraft we would fly, I was stunned! Of all the planes, we got *Tinker Toy*. No one wanted to fly that plane. It was the jinx ship of the 381st. The tales of her raids read like a book of horror stories. No crew had ever flown her on a routine mission. Invariably it was a life and death struggle to get back. Most people would say there's no such thing as a jinx, but they weren't there to witness the dead men pulled from *Tinker Toy*, or to observe the heavy damage she suffered raid after raid.
—from *Combat Crew* by John Comer

B-17 radio operator / gunner Roger A. Armstrong was a member of the John Askins crew, the crew of *Qualified Quail* with the 91st Bomb Group based at Bassingbourn, England, in October 1944: "I felt a tug on my shoulder, and before I could open my eyes and come out of the wonderful dream I was having, someone tugged again. He put his mouth close to my ear and shone a flashlight in my face. I realized I was not in Sioux Falls, necking with a beautiful brunette in Sherman Park. I was in the 401st Squadron barracks at Bassingbourn, looking at the duty corporal. 'Breakfast at 0300,' he said, 'briefing at 0400, stations at 0515.' And he was gone.

"I shouldn't have been surprised. The day before, on 14th October 1944, we had dropped 'nickels' on Cologne; among them were copies of *The Stars and Stripes* printed in German, with a message to the Luftwaffe from General Doolittle, calling them a bunch of cowards and challenging them to a battle over Cologne the next day. Hilmer Beicker, our flight engineer, was born of German parents in Houston, Texas, and he had read the whole thing out to us over the intercom. We had all pitied the crews who would be going on the next day's

mission after an insult like that.

"While brushing my teeth, I admired the clean, yellow tiling in our latrine, and I thought how lucky we were to be stationed at a permanent base built by the Royal Air Force in 1938. The latrines were never crowded and we had central heating, so no battles with pot-bellied stoves like we had in basic training.

"As I dressed quickly in a suntan shirt and old OD pants, I couldn't help feeling fear, deep inside. I was ashamed to admit that I was afraid, but I found in later years that you weren't normal unless you had that feeling. It was really dark when I went outside. I tested the temperature, and put on my fur-collared B-10 jacket. My bike was in a rack outside the door, but the light batteries

were dead so I had to steer with one hand, with a flashlight in the other, as I rode to the combat mess hall.

"All the combat crews ate at the combat mess so the Air Force could control the types of food we ate. Nothing was fed to us on mission days that would cause gas in the stomach or the intestinal tract, because the gas would expand as your plane climbed to altitude. No one liked the powdered eggs, especially when there were green spots on them. There was a large grill outside the serving line where we could fry eggs to our taste. We purchased our own eggs from the farmer whose backyard was right behind the hardstand of our B-17. When the pilot or the crew chief ran the engines up, the prop wash struck

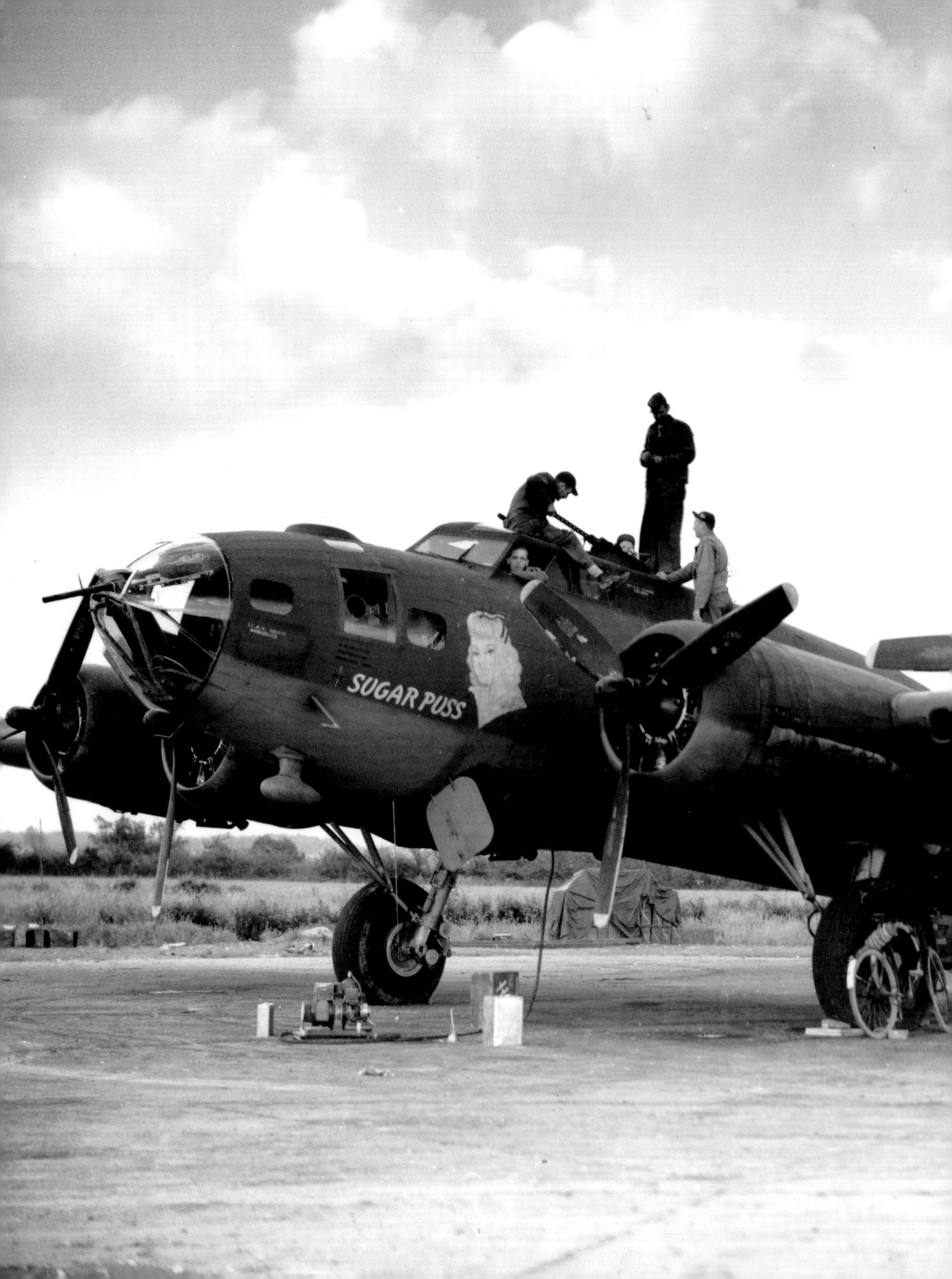
SUGAR PUSS

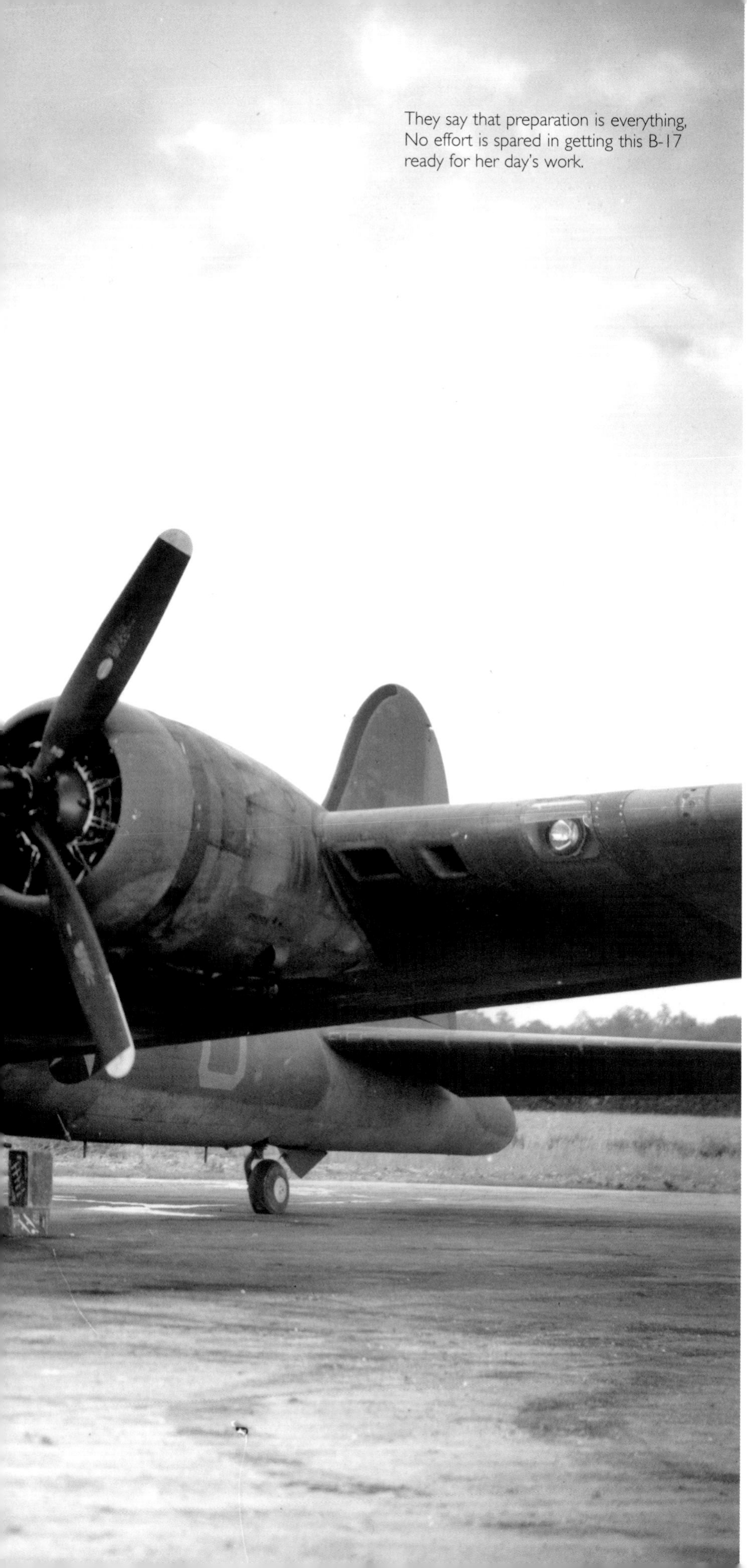

They say that preparation is everything, No effort is spared in getting this B-17 ready for her day's work.

the chicken coops and the feathers really flew. We could never figure out how those hens could lay with all that going on. When the farmer was out of hen eggs, we would buy his duck eggs out of desperation, to avoid those horrible green and yellow powdered eggs.

"After breakfast we drifted over to the briefing building, the only Quonset hut on the base. It was a king-size hut because it had to seat thirty-six or thirty-seven crews. There was a mission map of the British Isles and the Continent on a large board set on the stage, with a curtain hung over it. I sat down with Hilmer and the rest of my crew: the pilot, John Askins, came from Oakland, California; the co-pilot, Randall Archer, from Chester, West Virginia; the navigator, Anthony Delaporta, from Philadelphia, Pennsylvania; the bombardier, Paul Collier, from Hamilton, Texas; and the gunners—Hilmer Beicker, from Houston, Texas; I came from Sioux Falls, South Dakota; Ralph Azevedo, from Mill Valley, California; Roy Loyless, from Houston, Texas; Robert Webb, from Dyer, Tennessee; and James Primm, from Redondo Beach, California.

"I noted that the time was just 0400. Right on cue, one of the Headquarters officers barked, 'Tenshun.' Colonel Terry walked in at a brisk pace, stepped onto the stage and said, 'At ease, gentlemen.' He gave us a pep talk and turned the briefing over to the S-2.

"The S-2 walked over to the map, carrying his pool stick, and pulled the curtain up ever so slowly, as if he savored every moment of the anxiety he was causing in his audience. The red yarn indicated we were going to Cologne, and the reaction was a moan, which gradually crescendoed. The target was the marshalling yards, and we were to disrupt the supplies of armor, artillery, and troops to Aachen, where our soldiers were fighting. There were pieces of red plastic on the map which represented the areas of heavy flak. It bothered us that the S-2 officer would sometimes shift those pieces around, as though he wasn't sure of where the concentrations were. We all knew they were around the large cities; the problem was that no one knew how much mobile flak had been moved into the target area on flatbed train cars.

"The weather officer said that the cloud over England was about 19,000 feet thick but not too bad over the Continent. The operations officer gave a time hack so we could set our watches to Greenwich Mean Time, and then we were dismissed. On the way out, we had to pass the three chaplains. Now, I didn't particularly want to be reminded that I might soon meet my Maker, so as we passed I looked the other way. When we got into the fresh air I realized how warm a room could get when the men in there all became concerned about what fate might hold for them that day.

"There were other briefings for the pilot, co-pilot, navigator, bombardier, and me. I reported to the communications building to pick up the codes of the day, the verification codes that were sent when messages were transmitted or received. The communications officer gave me an aluminum briefcase containing the codes, along with log sheets and pencils for recording my messages while on the mission. The codes were printed on rice paper so you could eat them if you were shot down. The officer mentioned that the Germans broke most of our codes within twelve hours. I was also given the colors of the day for the Very lights, which we fired when passing over a convoy or a naval vessel so they wouldn't mistake us for a German plane.

"In the equipment room, we collected our Mae Wests, parachutes and harness, oxygen masks, headsets and throat mikes, goggles, gabardine coveralls, heated suits, leather helmets and steel helmets with ear-flaps that covered your headset. There were heated felt inserts to go inside the sheepskin and leather flying boots, and silk gloves to wear inside the heated leather gloves. We stowed the gear in our equipment bags, and then we picked up the escape kits, which contained a silk map, a razor, high-energy candy, a plastic bottle, water purification tablets, and translation sheets in Flemish, Dutch, French, and German.

"They had taken photos of us when we arrived at the base, which you were to give to the Resistance if you were shot down, so they could make you an identity document. I never took my photos along (a chief German interrogator told me recently that they could tell your bomb group by the civilian coat you were wearing the day they took your photo). We didn't take the .45 caliber Colt automatics along, either, because S-2 had found the possession of a gun had given the Germans an excuse to shoot you.

"It was a five-minute ride in a six-by-six truck from the hangar to the dispersal area where our B-17, the *Qualified Quail*, was parked. We all had our own thoughts and everyone was quiet on the way. It was a gray, depressing morning, and the overcast was down to 100 or 150 feet. The driver stopped in front of our plane. It carried the markings of the triangle 'A' on the tail and our squadron letter 'K.' The wing tips, tail plane, and stabilizer were painted red, which indicated we were in the 1st Combat Wing. The markings helped the group to assemble and then to find our Wing. We all looked in the bomb bay to see what kind of bombs we were carrying: if you

carried delayed-action bombs, you had to take off anyway, even if the weather changed, and drop them in the North Sea. We had a full load of 250-pound bombs and two clusters of M-17 incendiaries on the top shackles.

"I put my heated suit on over my coveralls, and this was a mistake, because as soon as I climbed into the plane to check out the radio room I always got the call of nature. As usual I found a semi-secluded spot to take care of that. At the same time I could hear Beicker throwing up. He said, 'I don't know why, but once I enter the waist door and smell the interior of the plane, I get sick at my stomach.' I told him what it did to me and not to worry about it. It was that smell—of oil, gas, canvas flak suits, and ammunition boxes.

"In the radio room, I checked the spare chest-type chute pack, the walk-around oxygen bottle, and the four-by-four piece of armor plating the crew chief had found for me. My radios and rack of frequency ranges were all in place, and so was the frequency meter, in case I needed to check the accuracy of what a dial on the receiver read.

"John and Randy, with Beicker and the crew chief, checked the exterior and interior of the plane, while the gunners checked their guns and ammunition. When the engines were started, I heard them cough and splutter before they started to run. We put on our headsets and checked the intercom, and then John ran the engines up while the ground crew stood by with fire extinguishers. The plane vibrated and became very noisy. I heard the sound of the brakes being released as John moved onto the taxiway and fell in behind the ship we were to follow in the line for takeoff. I turned on my radios and the IFF. I would monitor the Division frequency druing the mission: the IFF would send a continuous code while we were over friendly territory so the coastal defenses wouldn't shoot at us.

"The lead squadron took off at 0600 and by 0622 all twelve were airborne. John turned onto the runway and ran the engines while he held the brakes on. The plane kind of jerked into a rolling start as he released them. Runway 25 was 6,000 feet long, but it seemed he was never going to lift that heavy load off as we gathered speed. Then the plane broke loose from the pull of gravity and we were airborne. I noticed I had held myself stiff while we were moving down the runway, but now I relaxed. Watching out of the radio room window by my desk, I saw we were higher than the village church steeple, then suddenly we were in the overcast and flying blind.

"John had to fly at a given speed and rate of climb for so many minutes, then turn right while still climbing, and turn again so we were making one big square around the Bassingbourn Buncher beacon. It was quite nerve-racking in the overcast. It was so thick, I could barely see the left wing tip. A voice on the intercom said, 'Submarine at nine o'clock level.' It was Azevedo, the right waist gunner. No one answered. The plane bounced around and we knew it was from the prop wash of another B-17 out there somewhere.

"Randy's voice came over the intercom: 'Co-pilot to crew, we are passing through 10,000 feet, so oxygen masks on, please.' A few minutes later he said, 'Oxygen check,' and we answered to our names from tail to nose: Loyless okay, Azevedo okay, Webb okay, and finally Collier okay.

"We broke out of the overcast for a few minutes, and saw twenty or thirty B-17s around us. The third squadron from the 91st was just below us. Then, we were climbing back into

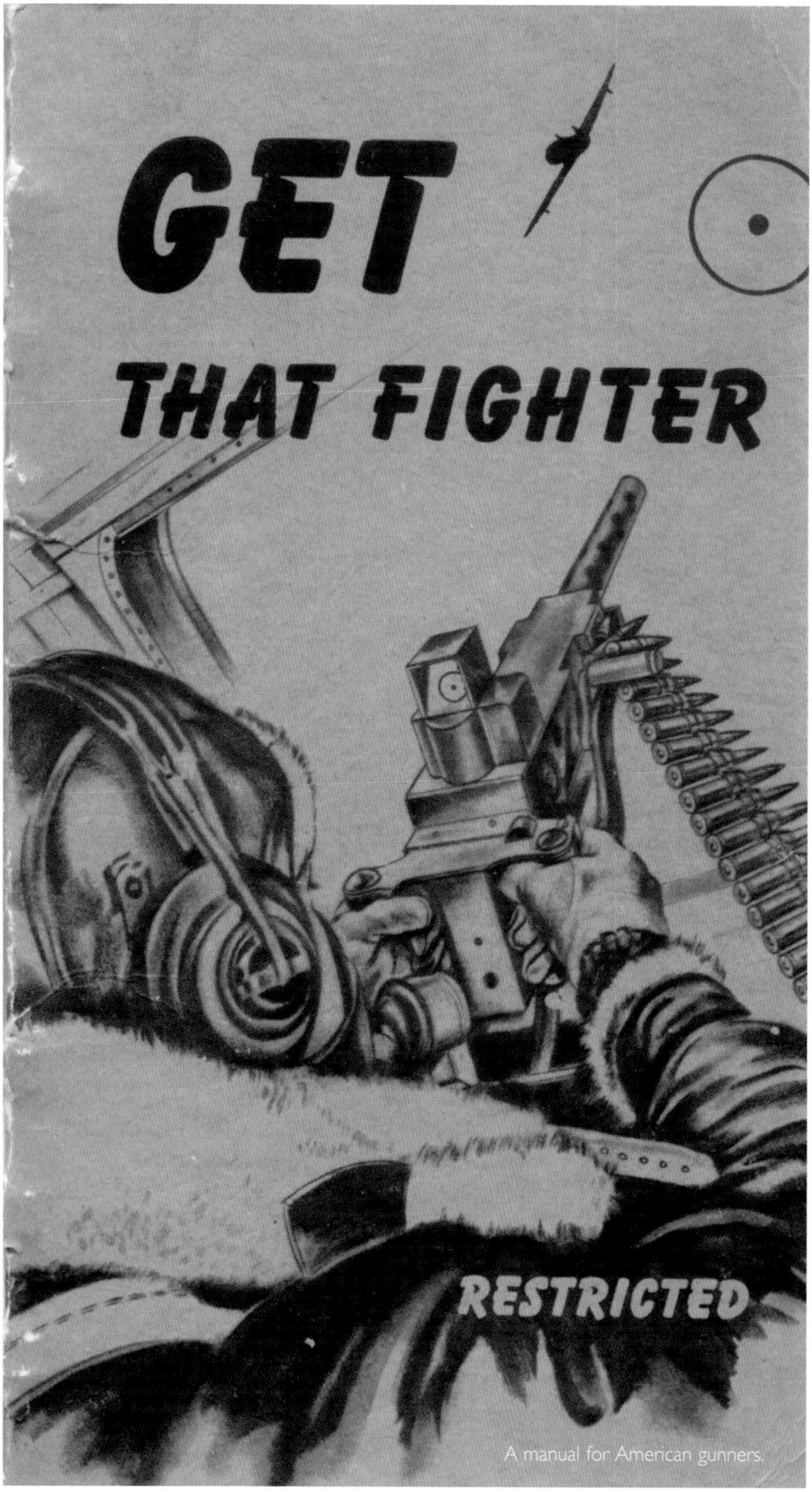
GET
THAT FIGHTER
RESTRICTED
A manual for American gunners.

the cloud, still making squares over the base Buncher. Finally it began to look a little lighter and we popped out of the mess. We were to fly high squadron of the group, and the group was to lead the 1st Combat Wing, with one wing ahead of us. Collier saw the lead squadron forming up and we located our element leader of the high squadron. It was still hazy, but with just sufficient visibility to get the group formed, and we set course for Clacton at 20,000 feet. The 381st and 398th Bomb Groups had taken off after us, and our group leader did a series of 'S' turns to let them catch up and form the combat wing.

"We left Clacton two minutes early at an altitude of 21,000 feet. The winds over the Channel were greater than briefed, and John told Tony, the navigator, that the whole wing was doing another 'S' turn because we were catching up on the wing ahead of us. We were at 27,000 feet when we arrived at point two on the route to Cologne, still two minutes early but with everyone spaced at normal intervals. Over the bomber channel, I heard the weather ship, *Buckeye Blue*, report that the route weather was good but that contrails were forming at the bombers' altitude. Then *Buckeye Red* said that Cologne was overcast and

that the PFF ships would be needed to locate and zero in on the target with radar.

"Out over the Channel, just before we reached the Continent, the gunners had test-fired their guns. They had charged their guns before we reached high altitude, because the barrel shrank at low temperature, and if you didn't have a shell in it, the gun probably wouldn't fire.

"As we flew toward Cologne, Tony called John and said: 'We're running parallel to the front lines, that's why we can see flak up ahead.' I thought, why aren't we flying on the Allied side, instead of over the German lines?

Falling in flames, a B-17 begins her final descent; right: Ground crewmen watching for the return of their charges.

Meantime, I was copying a message for the wing commander in the lead ship from the 1st Air Division. There were about a dozen German ground operators jamming the frequency, but Division was sending the Morse on a modulated tone that sounded like a big truck horn honking. You soon got used to that tone, and the jamming didn't really bother you.

"We had put our flak suits on as we entered German territory, and I snapped the check pack on the right ring of my harness. It left an area vulnerable, but I felt the chute would absorb low-velocity flak or even a bullet fired at long range. Suddenly the plane rose and fell four or five times. There was flak below us, not doing any damage but it was worrying me. I concentrated on copying some of the German code, because the busier you were the less you thought about getting hit, but they were just holding their keys down or tapping out a series of v's. I lost interest and got back to trying to get rid of the ache in my chest, thinking about the curtains of flak we would be going through at Cologne.

"The wing commander started a series of 'S' turns to throw the German gunners off, and John told us what was happening. We all felt John was the best pilot in the group, and he was also a good communicator. He always advised us what was going on. We in turn watched out from our positions and told him if we noticed any mechanical or structural problem with the plane.

"I listened in on the group voice channel and heard the pilot of the lead PFF ship in the low squadron say, 'We have lost our bombing radar.' The lead command ship said, 'Drop on our smoke bombs at the target.'

"We were getting both tracking flak and box barrage flak as we flew past Cologne to the south and picked up our IP, where we started our run in to the target. The plane was really bounc-

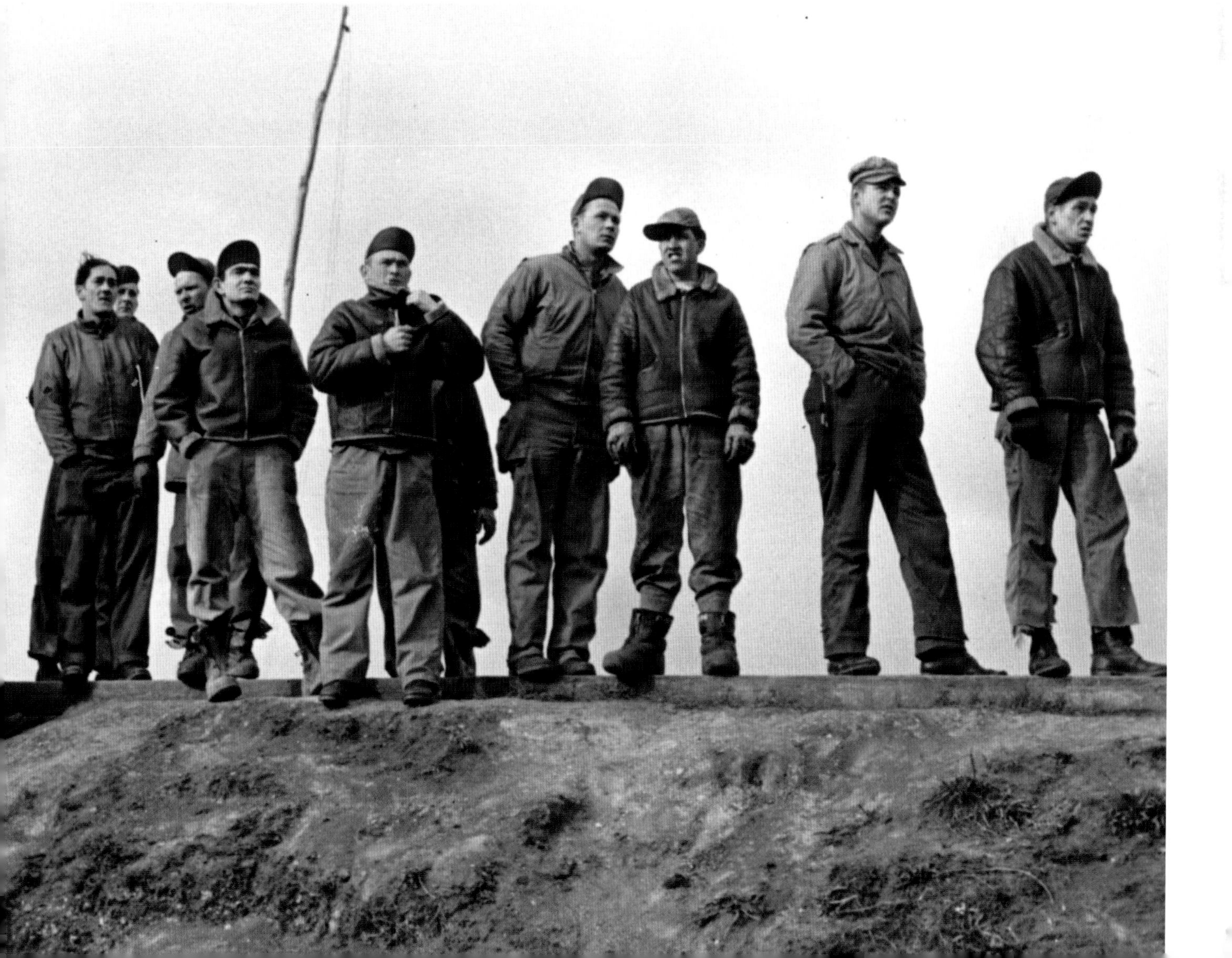

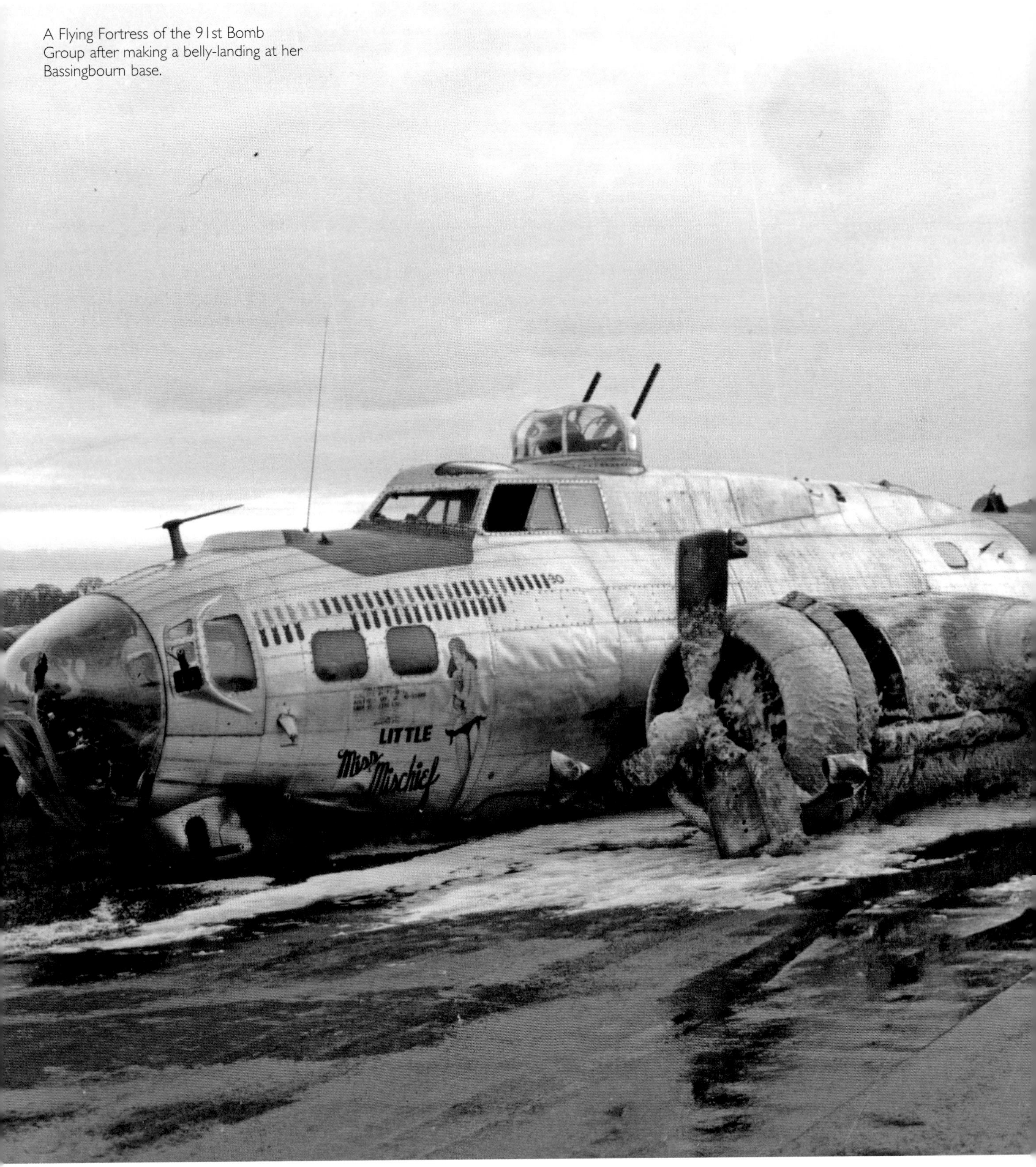
LITTLE
Miss Mischief

A Flying Fortress of the 91st Bomb Group after making a belly-landing at her Bassingbourn base.

ing up and down, and I moved my piece of armor plating across the radio room to the chaff chute. We were carrying seven cartons of chaff bundles, which were held together by paper strips until they were pushed through the chute and hit the slip stream. Our group would create thousands of false blips on the enemy's radar screens to help the groups behind us. On the right side of the ship, I built up a flak shack of chaff cartons on my armor plating. Webb was too large to wear his flak helmet in the ball turret, so he loaned it to me. I pulled my own helmet down over my eyes, placed Webb's over my reproductive organs, and started throwing chaff.

"Suddenly the radio room lit up bright red, and the Plexiglas roof window blew inward in a thousand pieces with a number of shell fragments. Then another shell exploded just above the nose. We went into a dive, leveled out, and eased back into the formation. What had happened was that a piece of flak had come through the windshield and struck John on the right shoulder of his flak suit, turning him in a clockwise direction and making him chop all four engines with his right hand, which was holding the throttles. Randy had pushed the throttles forward and flown us back into position.

"Hilmer Beicker came out of the top turret and saw John struggling to turn himself forward. His seat belt was so tight, he was having a tough time, so Beicker went to help him. At that moment, Randy reached for his flak helmet and was just putting it on when another piece of flak came through the window and struck him on the head. Beicker stopped him from falling on the yoke, and grabbed the first aid kit. Randy came to and shook his head as Beicker was wiping the blood out of his eyes. It turned out that the flak had only grazed his forehead.

"Beicker took a look at the instruments, looked around the flight deck, and went back to the top turret. There was a hole in the Plexiglas and a chunk out of the housing; otherwise the turret was in good shape.

"I was just throwing a bundle of chaff out when another close burst, which I heard, sent three pieces through the skin of the plane four or five inches from my head. If I had been reaching for another bundle, my head would have taken all three fragments. The holes peeled outward, so the fragments had come right through the ship. I looked around: the right side of my liaison set had a hole the size of your fist in it.

"Another burst hit us, and a piece of flak struck my left glove, ripping the leather open from my left wrist to the end of my thumb. I felt the blood get warm on my hand, and visualized the thumb—shot off inside the glove. I didn't want to take the glove off, but I knew I had to because of the bleeding. I was relieved when I saw that the thumb was still attached to my hand. I dumped some sulfa out of the first aid kit on two cuts and put a bandage on. This had kind of held my attention and I realized that John had been calling on the intercom: 'Pilot to radio, pilot to radio . . .'

"I answered: 'Radio to pilot.'

"'Pilot to radio—Azevedo is down in the waist. See what's wrong.'

"I grabbed my walk-around oxygen bottle and took off for the waist. Azevedo was lying on his back. I saw him blink, so I knew he was alive. When I squatted down beside him, it was obvious he had been hit in the right thigh. Having checked that his mask was securely connected to the right waist oxygen supply, I disconnected my walk around bottle and plugged into the left waist hose. I took my Boy Scout knife and cut the leg of his pants open. The hole was the size of a silver dollar. It was bleeding but not pumping blood, so I assumed the fragment had missed the femoral artery.

"When I took my gloves off, my fingers stiffened up so they wouldn't function properly. I had to keep putting the gloves on to warm up. It got so bad I called the pilot and told him I needed help. By this time I was feeling a little drunk and I kind of plopped down beside Azevedo on my behind. He kept pointing at the ceiling, and I looked up and saw that the oxygen line I was plugged into had been sliced in two. I thought, although the flak had eased off, they were still trying to get

The crew of *Jersey Jinx* on their return from striking a German target in 1943; right: A The hospital on an 8AF base in WW2 England.

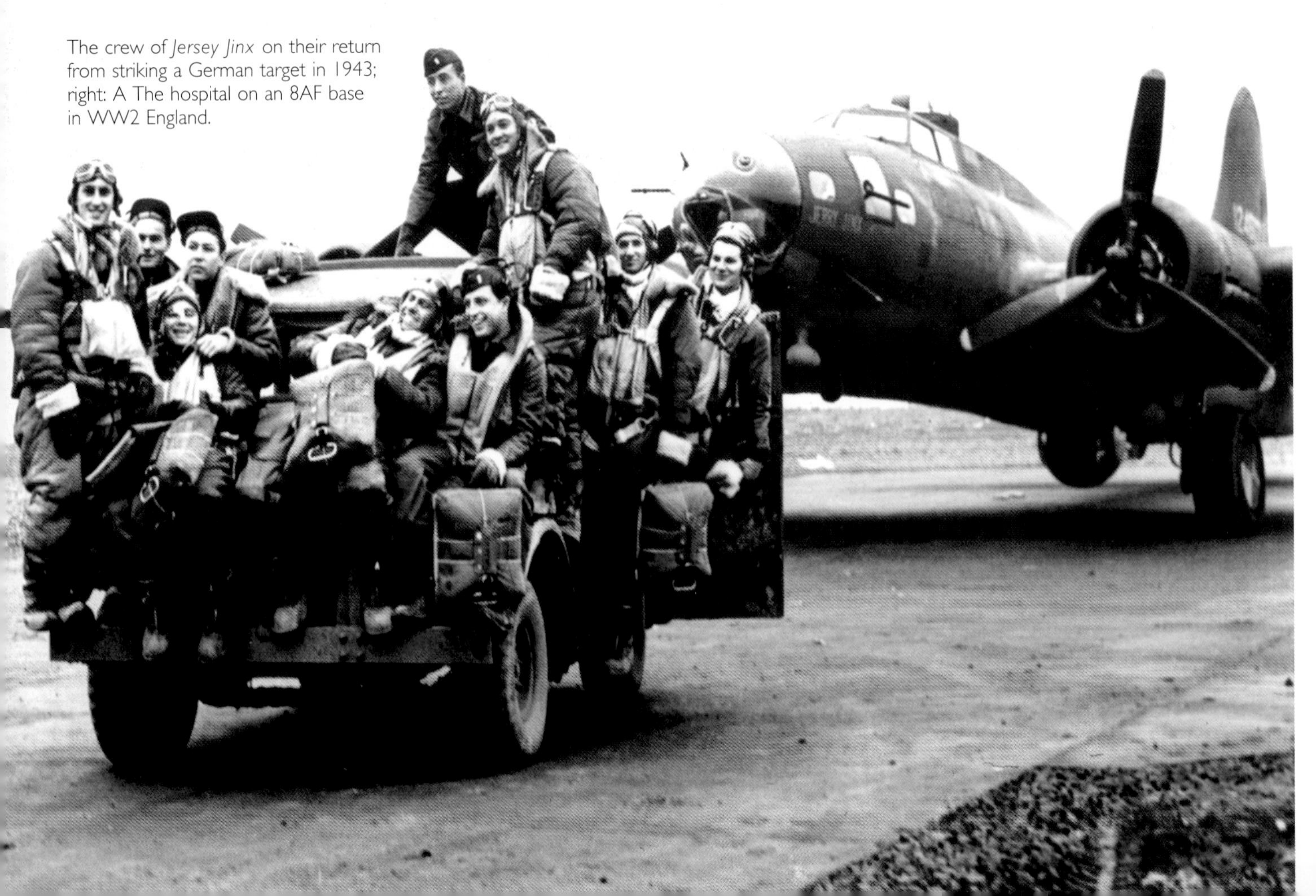
JERSEY JINX

me, one way or another. I plugged back in to the walk-around bottle and after a few deep breaths of pure oxygen I felt normal. It wasn't as good as feeling half-drunk.

"Beicker arrived to help, and between the two of us we got a pressure bandage on Azevedo's wound, but the temperature at our altitude did more to stop the bleeding. The co-pilot called for an oxygen check, and the first on his list didn't answer, so I crawled on back to the tail, lugging the walk-around bottle. I got to Loyless on my hands and knees. His eyes were as big as saucers and he was holding the cord to his mike which a piece of flak had cut in two, three or four inches from his throat. I plugged into his jack box and told Randy what had happened.

"Back at the waist, Beicker had found that the piece of flak had come out at the back of Azevedo's thigh. We started all over stopping the blood at that point and putting sulfa on the wound. Then we bandaged him up and put a couple of blankets round his legs. To talk to Beicker I had to take my mask off, yell in his ear, and put the mask back on quick. I yelled, 'Maybe we should give him a shot of morphine—he could be going into shock.'

"Beicker held his cupped hand behind my ear: 'I think we should. You give it to him.' My medical knowledge was confined to what I had picked up in the Boy Scouts, *Reader's Digest*, and a Red Cross class at Creighton University in the Aviation Cadet program. I yelled back, 'I've never given a shot before. Maybe you should do it: you know all about engines and stuff like that.' Beicker's eyes looked kind of funny. 'So what? You know all about radios. And you showed me a Red Cross card one time where it said you had qualified for first aid.'

"Azevedo was lying there and he

could hear my side of the conversation in his headset. He kept trying to get our attention, and finally he said, 'You guys aren't giving me any dope.' I said, 'Look, Azzie, you haven't got much say in this matter.'

"He said, 'Neither one of you guys knows anything about medicine. And when we got our shots at Sioux City, Beicker fainted when the first needle went into his arm.'

"That was true; they gave him three more shots while he was on the floor. Anyway, I was about to lose my voice from yelling. I took the morphine out of the first aid kit. It looked like a small tube of toothpaste with a needle in the end. I warmed it under my heated suit and aimed the needle at the muscle a few inches from the front hole in his thigh. At first I pushed real easy and it didn't go in. I looked up at Beicker. He

looked away. I shoved hard and it slid into the thigh. I squeezed the tube, and in a few minutes Azevedo had drifted off to sleep.

"I looked out of the window and saw we were still in flak. The plane shook and a burst over the nose knocked the bombardier off his seat. Later, I saw the dent in his helmet, and a lump on his head to match. He crawled back to the bombsight and I heard him say, 'Bomb bay doors are opening, follow the PDI.' That was the pilot direction indicator on the instrument panel.

"The group's bombs were dropped from 27,000 feet at 0928. The clouds had cleared and we were able to see our bombs striking the marshalling yards. John had feathered the numbers one and three engines while we were working on Azevedo. Other planes

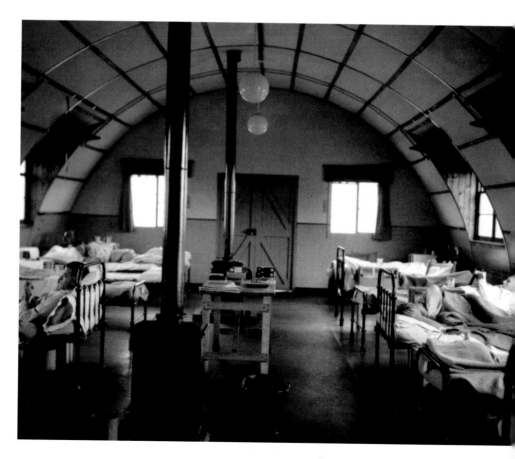

Coffee and doughnuts dispensed by the American Red Cross from a mobile van to airmen returning from a bombing mission.

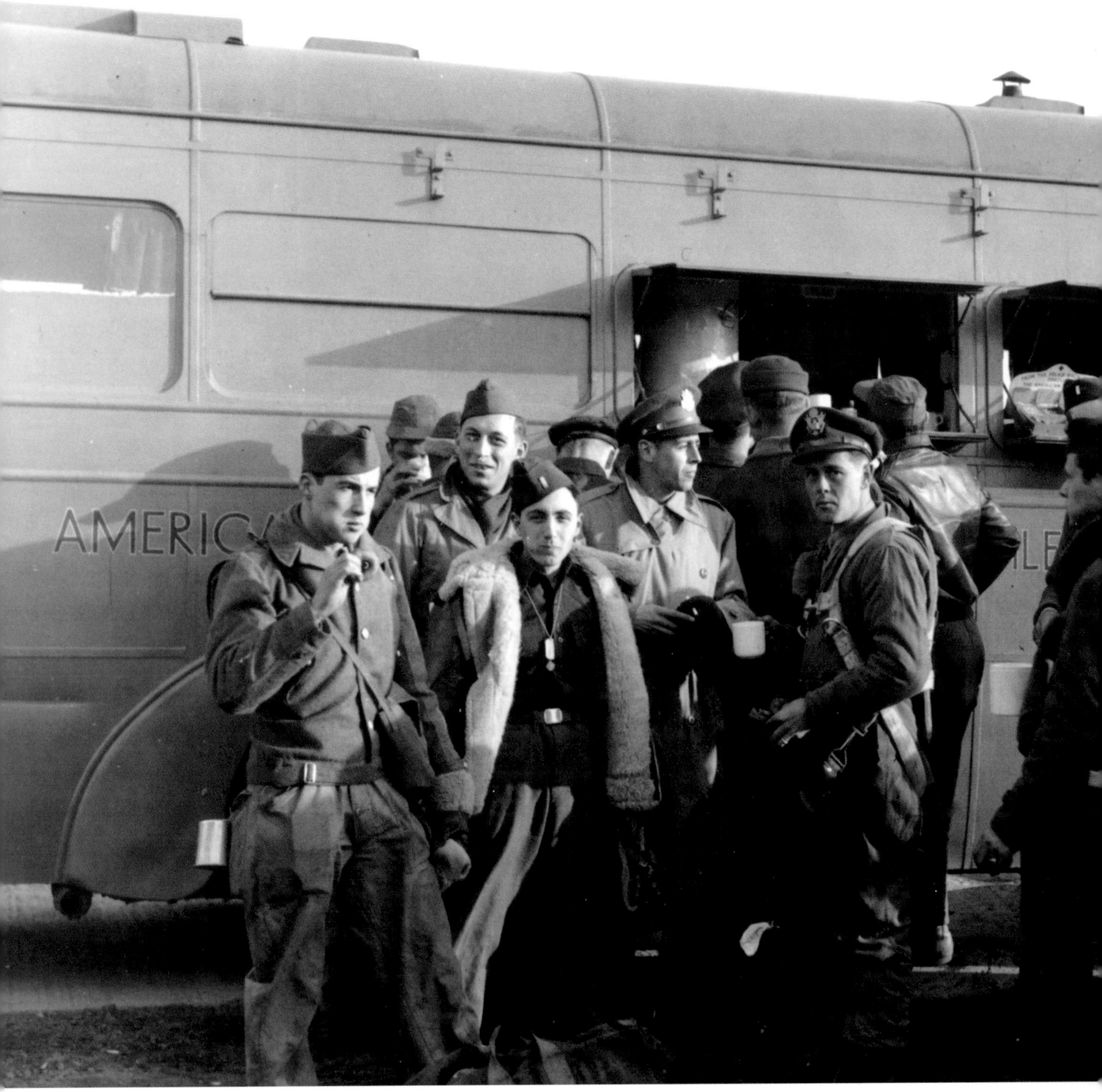
AMERIC

near us also had engines feathered. John got number one engine started again and we were able to stay with the formation. Several bombers from the lead and low squadrons were straggling behind. On the fighter channel, I heard the lead ship ask for 'little friends' to assist the damaged planes.

"There was cloud at our altitude when we reached the Channel, and the group let down to get under it. This helped the stragglers to keep up with the formation. The fighter protection was excellent. At 1143 we crossed the English coast at Clacton, and the wing broke up with each group heading back to its own base, pretty well strung out and flying loose.

"I went back every ten minutes to see if Azevedo was okay. I took his pulse to see if maybe he had died, but his heart was beating and his skin was warm. I took his mask off when we were at low altitude. John called me to the flight deck as we approached Bassingbourn and asked me to load the Very pistol with red / red flares to show he had injuries aboard. Looking out through the broken window I saw a number of planes also flying flares. On the final approach, the tail and ball gunners took their positions in the radio room, and the navigator and bombardier came out of the nose.

"The ambulances were lined up on the left of runway 25. As we touched down, one raced along the grass beside the runway, and when we turned off and stopped near the tower the medics were ready to come aboard and remove Azevedo. Instead of taking him to the base hospital they took him to Wimpole Hall, which was set up to treat the more serious injuries. I was kind of glad they took him there. It had been the home of Rudyard Kipling, who was a favorite in my family. My father used to quote Kipling's poems in his sermons at Sioux Falls.

"We left the *Qualified Quail* by the tower with a number of other badly damaged B-17s, and a truck took us to the interrogation building. We were escorted to a table where the S-2 officer poured double shots of scotch into coffee cups. He wanted to know what we all saw on the mission and asked about our injuries.

"Randy was sitting next to me; he had pulled up his jacket sleeve and was pushing at something just under the skin of his arm. It was a metal splinter about four inches long. He had worked it almost out when the S-2 asked what he was doing. Randy said, 'I felt my arm itch. I just found piece of flak in it.' He pulled it out all the way and put it in his pocket. The S-2 saw the nicks on his forehead and asked if he wanted to see the flight surgeon. Randy said no, he had a date. I did too. I said I had treated my cut hand in the plane. John didn't mention the bruise on his shoulder; he told me later it was sore for three weeks.

"After interrogation we took a look at the *Qualified Quail*. After finding two hundred holes we got tired of counting. John, Beicker, and the crew chief were looking at something under the right wing. As I walked up, John said, 'Our main spar was almost shot in two. If I had known about it, I wouldn't have banked so steep, and I would have taken it easier coming in for landing.' It turned out that, of thirty-six B-17s of the 91st Bomb Group, sixteen sustained minor damage and twenty had major damage.

"We had an excellent lunch of steak and potatoes, with ice cream for dessert. I took a shower and went into Royston where I met my date. We did some pub-crawling, and next morning I slept in as we didn't fly a mission. Two days later, they sent us back to Cologne."

GAME CHANGER

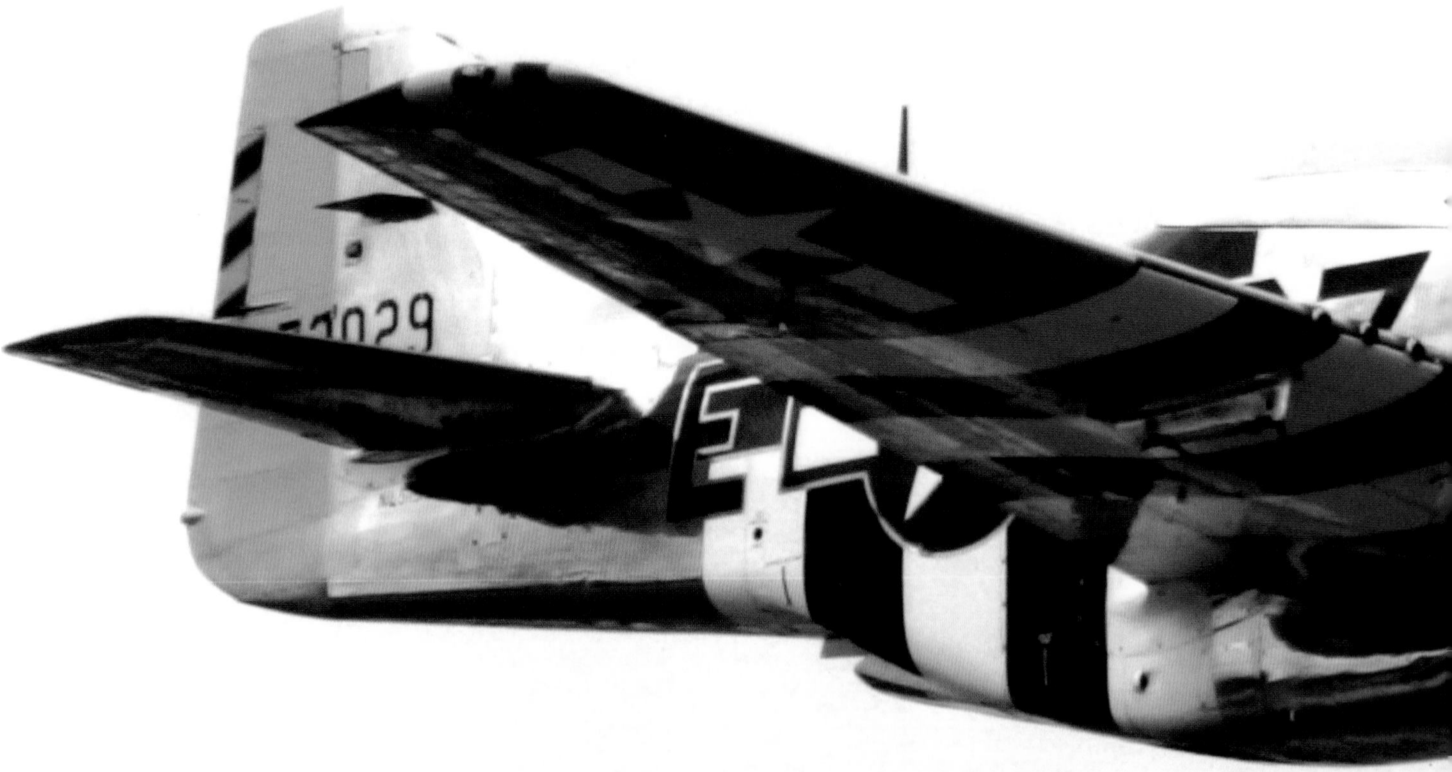

E

Good and potentially great was the opinion of
Rolls-Royce test pilot Ronnie Harker after
flying the North American P-51 Mustang. His
idea was to replace the plane's Allison engine
with a R-R Merlin. That changed everything for
the Eighth Air Force and the war.

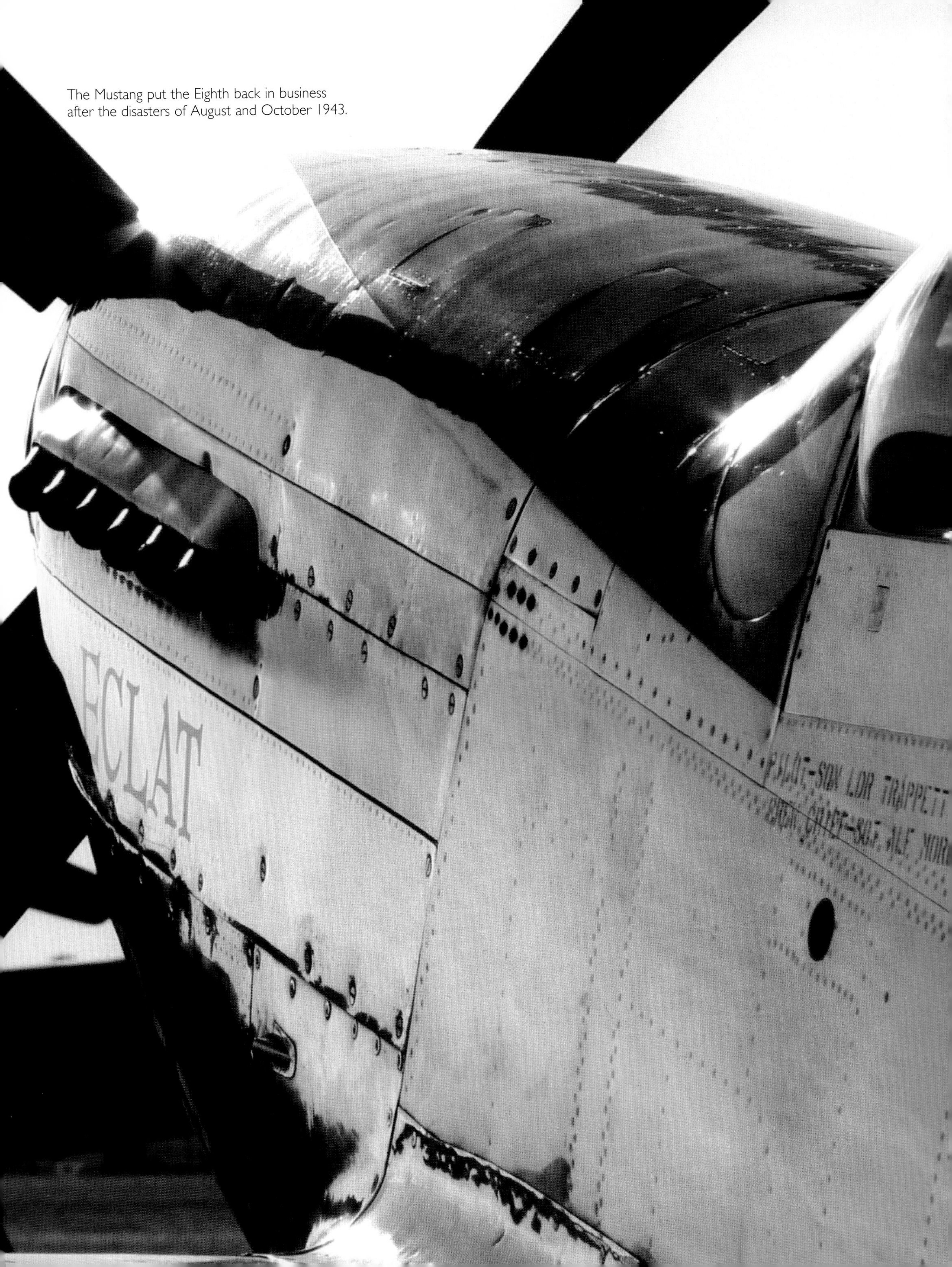
ECLAT
PILOT-SQN LDR TRAPPETT

The Mustang put the Eighth back in business after the disasters of August and October 1943.

BEFORE the Second World War broke out in September 1939, the planners in the British Air Ministry, knowing that such a shattering event was almost certainly in the offing, assumed they would be able to sustain the Royal Air Force requirement for the air defense of Great Britain with their two best front-line fighters, the Rolls-Royce Merlin-engined Hawker Hurricane and Vickers-Supermarine Spitfire. In the misguided belief that with these fighters the RAF could field an unbeatable deadly force in both numbers and performance to fend off whatever the enemy might bring to bear, they looked no further to augment their capability. Had they felt a need then to improve and increase that capability, they showed little sign of it, and they expressed no interest whatever in any American-made fighter type of the day. If they had, there was no existing U.S.-built type that might have been a match for the speed, firepower, and maneuverability of their own Spitfire, which, as good as it was, was rather short on range, or the solid, reliable gun-platform that was the Hurricane, also lacking in range. Both had been designed as purely defensive fighters with range a lower priority consideration.

But these British-designed-and-manufactured types were simply not available in the quantities the Air Ministry finally realized it needed by the fifth month of the war, as the Italians posed a genuine threat to Egypt and the Japanese to Singapore. The AM staff suddenly found themselves approximately 1,000 fighters short and they needed delivery of that quantity in 1941. With little on offer in fighter possibilities, the Air Ministry took a flyer and ordered the American Brewster Buffalo only to be told that the Brewster company could deliver no more than 170 such aircraft in 1941, forcing the AM buyers to look for another type.

France too was in desperate need of fighter aircraft in late 1939. It went shopping for them at the Curtiss Company in New York and signed a purchase order for 420 H75A Hawks and 259 H81A types (an export version of the P-40). Additionally, the French were anticipating that, by 1941, the U.S. Army would permit them to buy Lockheed P-38 Lightning and Bell Aircraft P-39 fighters. A joint Anglo-French Purchasing Commission was soon created which entered into conversations with American airplane makers including Republic, Lockheed, and Bell as well as Curtiss. After much

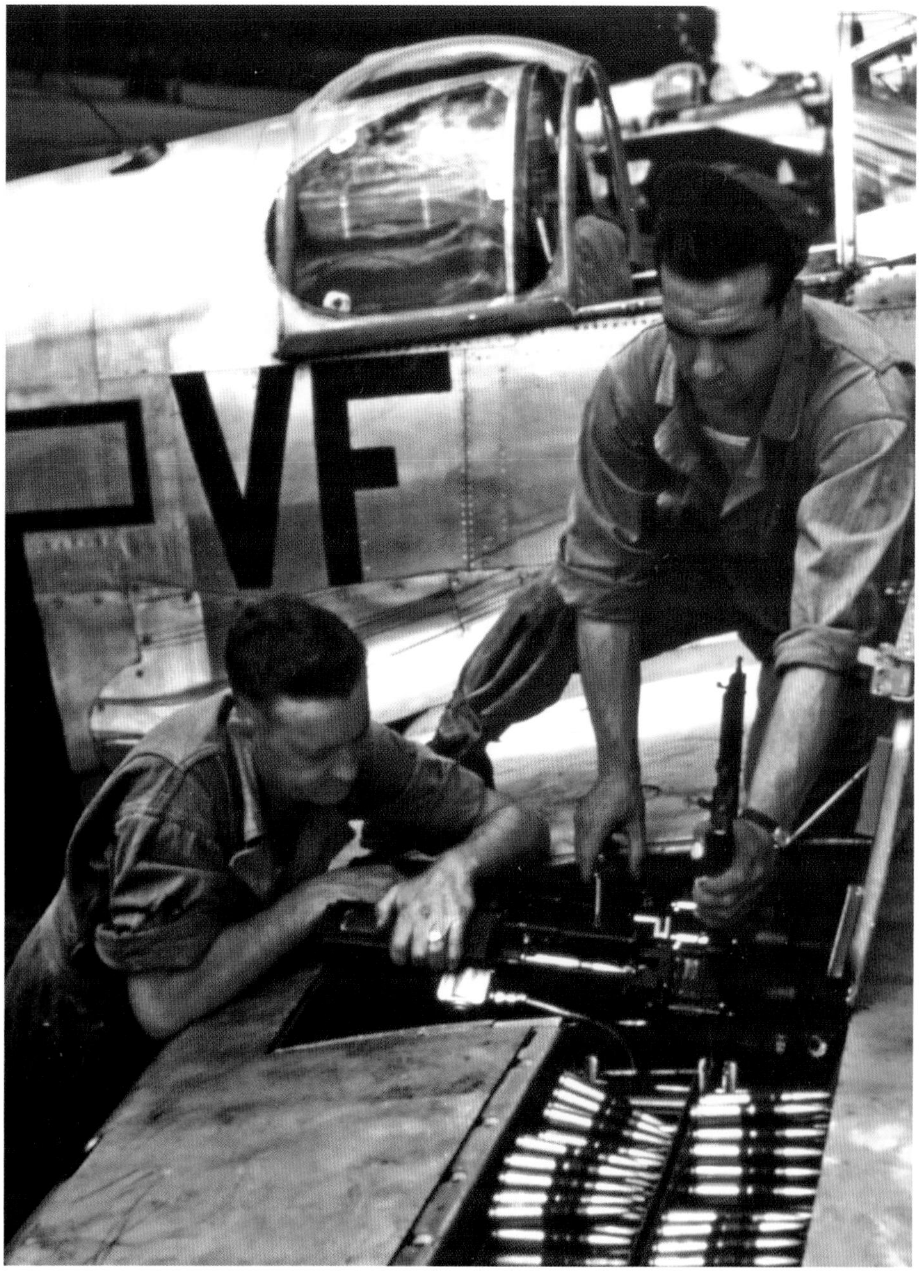
VF

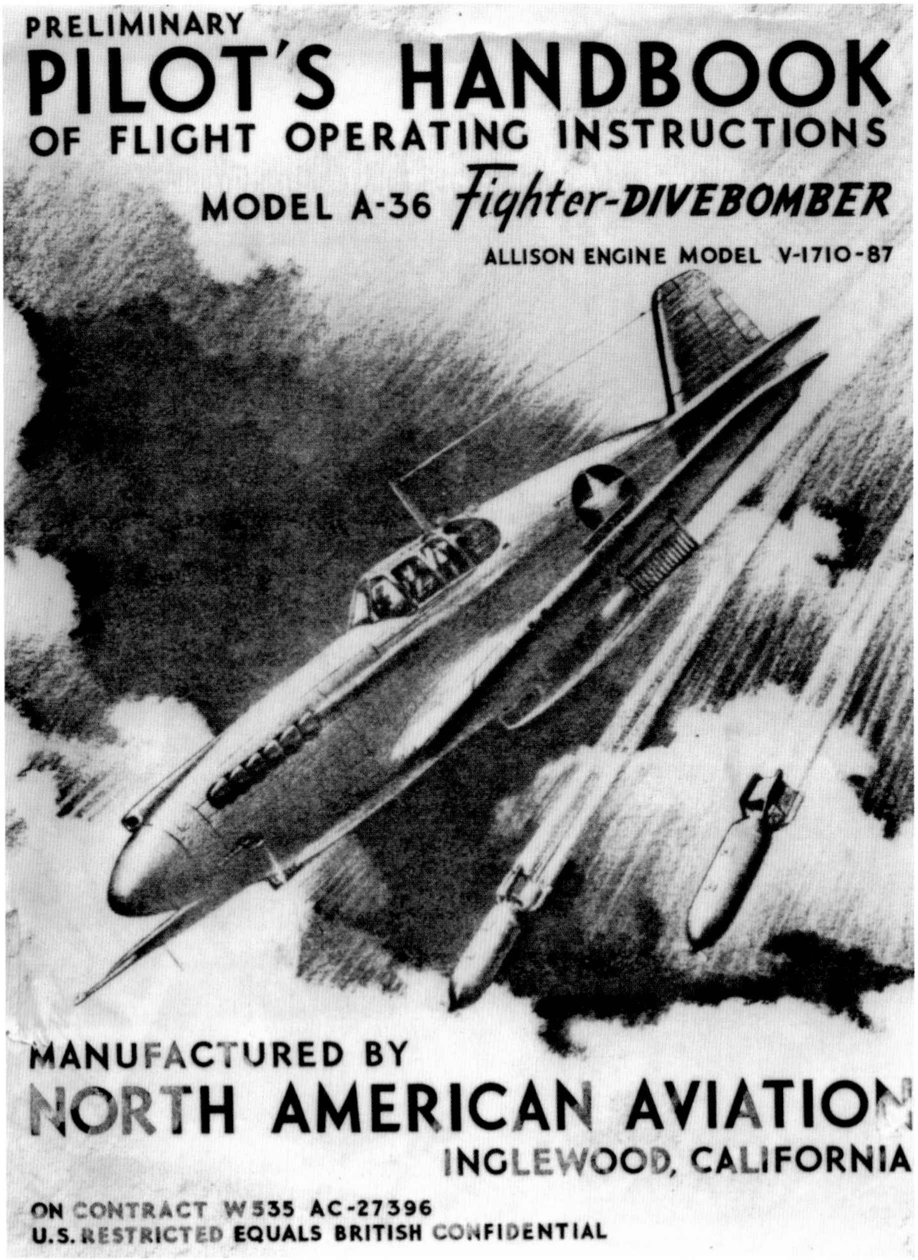
PRELIMINARY
PILOT'S HANDBOOK
OF FLIGHT OPERATING INSTRUCTIONS
MODEL A-36 Fighter-DIVEBOMBER
ALLISON ENGINE MODEL V-1710-87
MANUFACTURED BY
NORTH AMERICAN AVIATION
INGLEWOOD, CALIFORNIA
ON CONTRACT W535 AC-27396
U.S. RESTRICTED EQUALS BRITISH CONFIDENTIAL

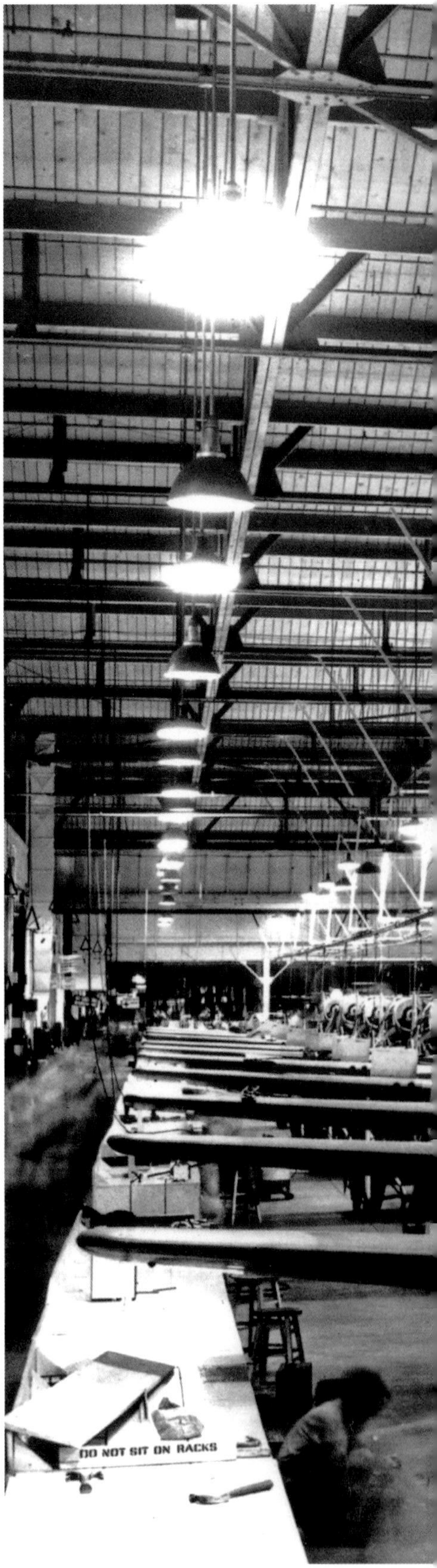
DO NOT SIT ON RACKS

deliberation the commission decided it would place an order with Lockheed for 667 Model 322 fighters, a P-38 variant, an order which could not begin to be delivered in quantity until the end of 1941.

Ultimately, the Royal Air Force was to inherit the Curtiss aircraft that the French had ordered. France

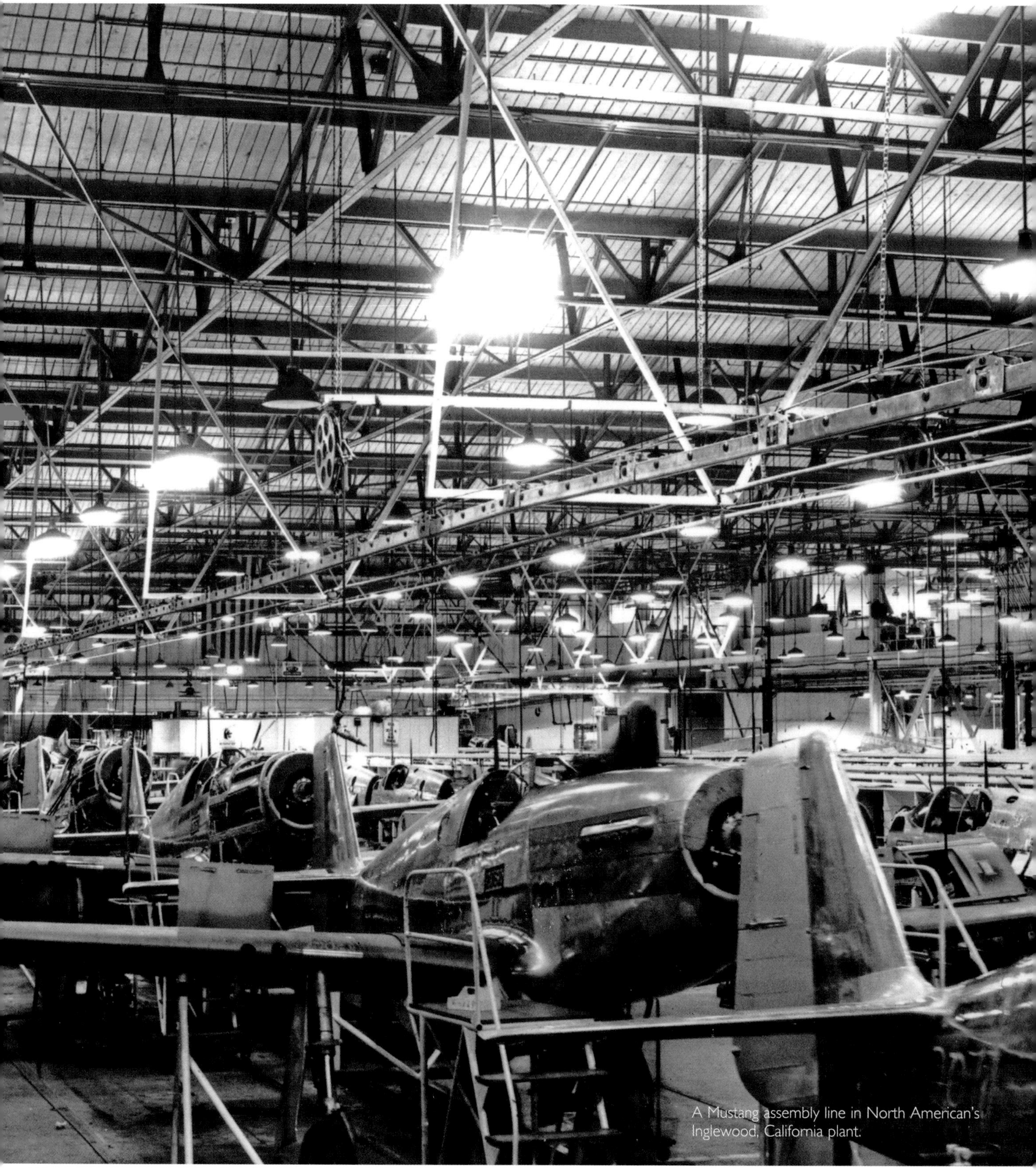

A Mustang assembly line in North American's Inglewood, California plant.

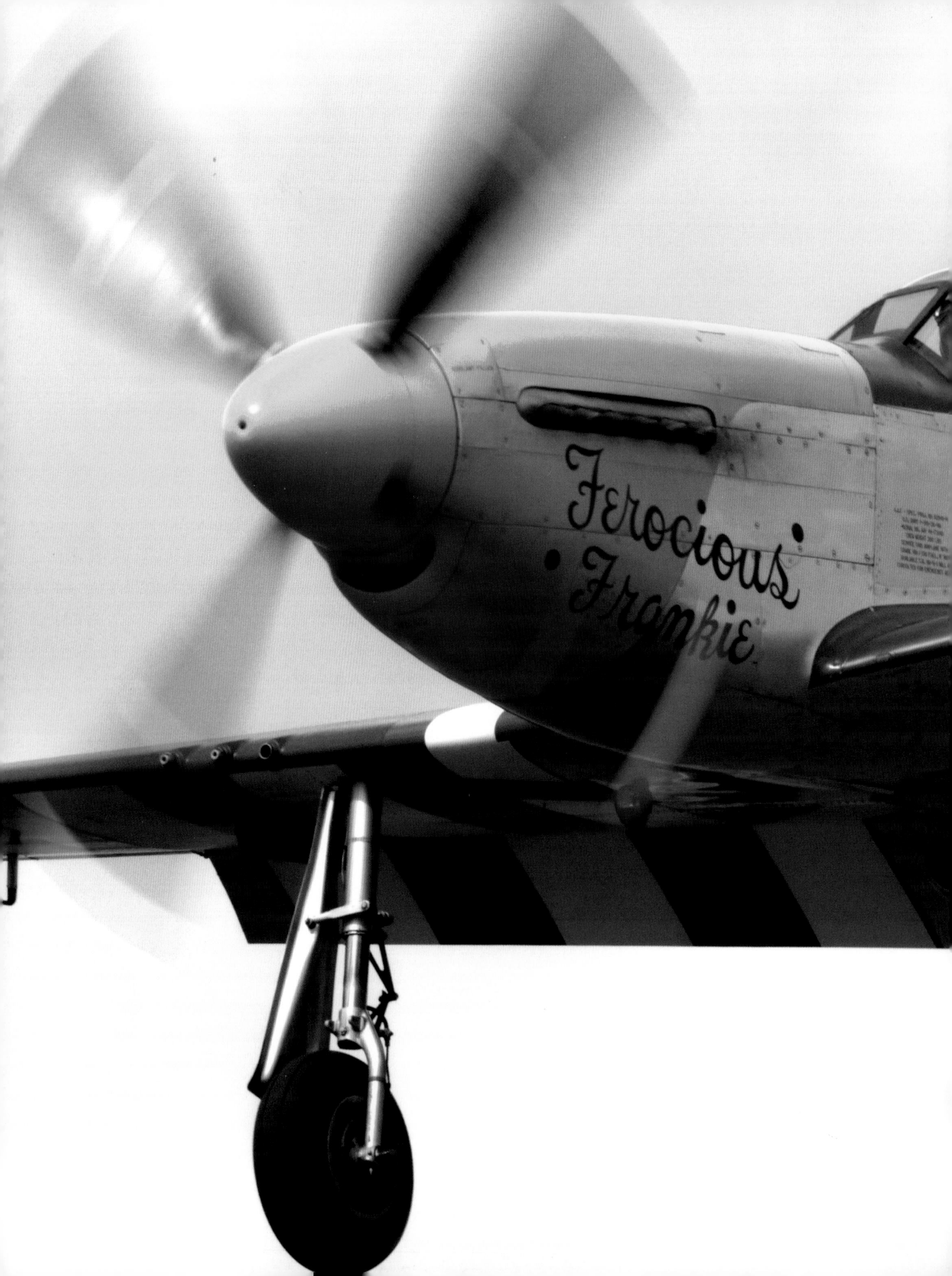
Ferocious
Frankie

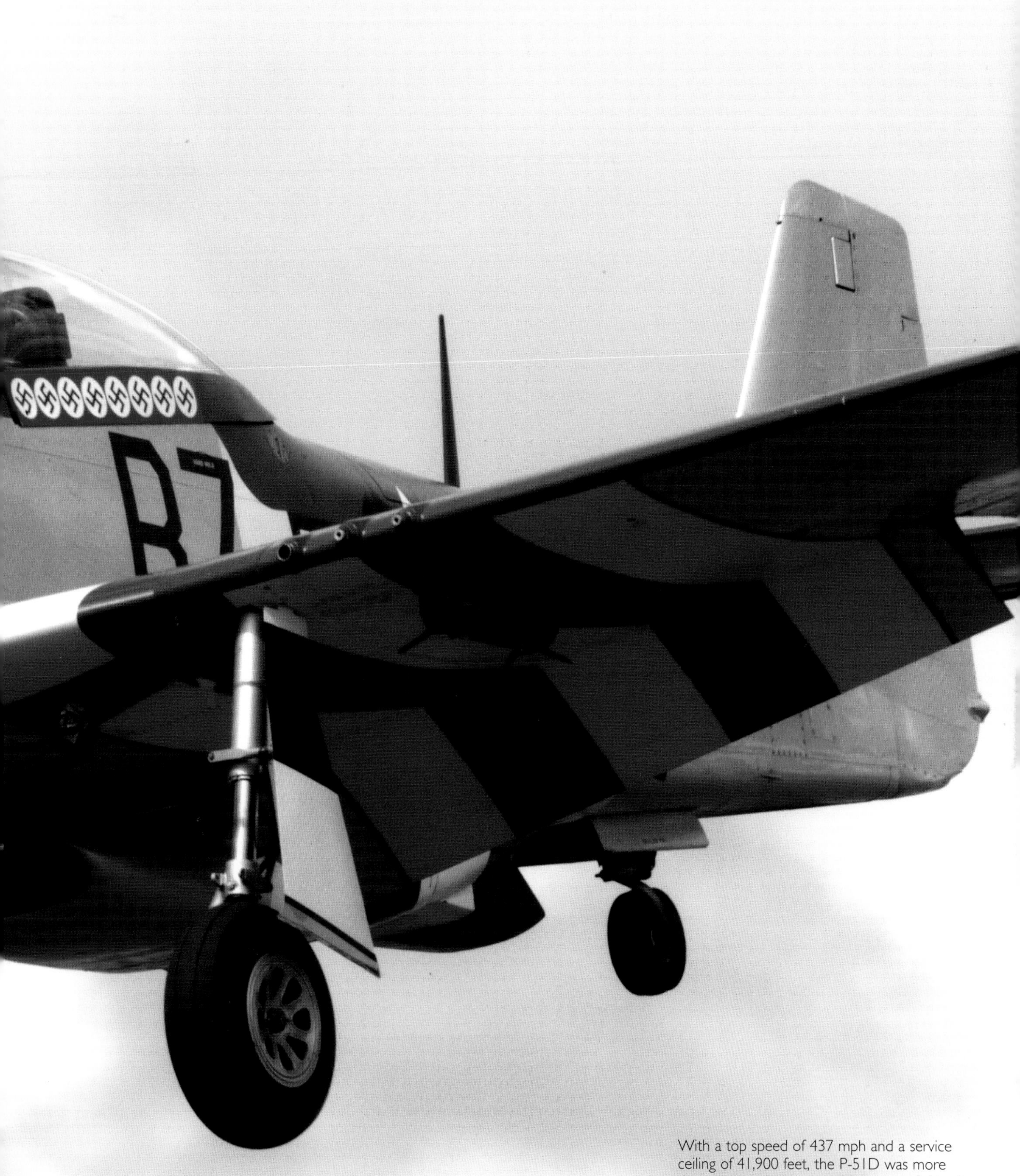

With a top speed of 437 mph and a service ceiling of 41,900 feet, the P-51D was more than a match for any propeller-driven fighter in the Second World War.

fell to the Germans in June 1940 and the RAF was soon regretting the AFPC commitment to purchase the Lockheed 322s. Everything had changed again in late May when the Curtiss Company altered its production plans and offered instead to build the P-40D for the AFPC, an airplane that both the RAF and the U.S. Army Air Force believed to be better than any other type then available—and it would have an earlier delivery date. The RAF jumped at the chance and ordered 471 of a version it named the Tomahawk and 560 of a version it called Kittyhawk. But the British were not out of the woods yet. They now needed more fighters than Curtiss alone could provide and, even before the Kittyhawk production line was established, they went out looking for another source of P-40 production. Their search took them to Los Angeles, where they met with James H. "Dutch" Kindelberger, president of North American Aviation, to ask him to consider building the Curtiss P-40 for them. Rumors then began circulating in the North American plant that the British wanted the company to build P-40s for them.

Edgar Schmued, a forty-year-old German aircraft designer who had emigrated to Brazil and then to the United States in 1930, was Kindelberger's chief designer. Friendly, quiet and methodical, Schmued was known among his fellow designers at North American to have an intense desire to create the best fighter plane in the world. Using a small engineering handbook he had brought with him from Germany, together with his own notebook of technical formulae and design ideas, he was ready for the challenge when Kindelberger entered his office and asked: "Ed, do we want to build P-40s here?"

Schmued: "Well, Dutch, don't let us build an obsolete airplane. Let's build a new one. We can design and build a better one." Kindelberger: "Ed, I'm going to England in about two weeks and I need an inboard profile, a three-view drawing, a performance estimate, a weight estimate, specifications and some detail drawings on the gun installations to take along. Then I would like to sell that new model airplane that you develop. Make it the fastest plane you can and build it around a man that is five feet ten inches tall and weighs 140 pounds. It should have two 20mm cannon in each wing and should meet all design requirements of the U.S. Army Air Corps." A company specification was issued, NAA SC1050, and work on the new fighter began.

With Ed Schmued's paperwork in hand, Kindelberger soon left for Britain. Ed and his design team then went to work building a paper and plaster of Paris mock-up of the new plane. In less than a month, the director of the AFPC, Sir Henry Self, had signed a letter of intent to purchase 400 of the North American Model NA-50B, and the greatest all-round fighter of the war had been launched.

One condition of the purchase was that North American agree to hold the cost of producing the new plane to a minimum. The Lend-Lease program had not yet gone into effect and the British needed to control their spending. The new fighter was to be powered by an Allison engine and the agreed unit price of the plane was not to exceed $40,000. North American also agreed to deliver 320 of the planes between January and the end of September 1941, and fifty a month thereafter. An estimate then established the actual unit cost to Britain would be $37,590.

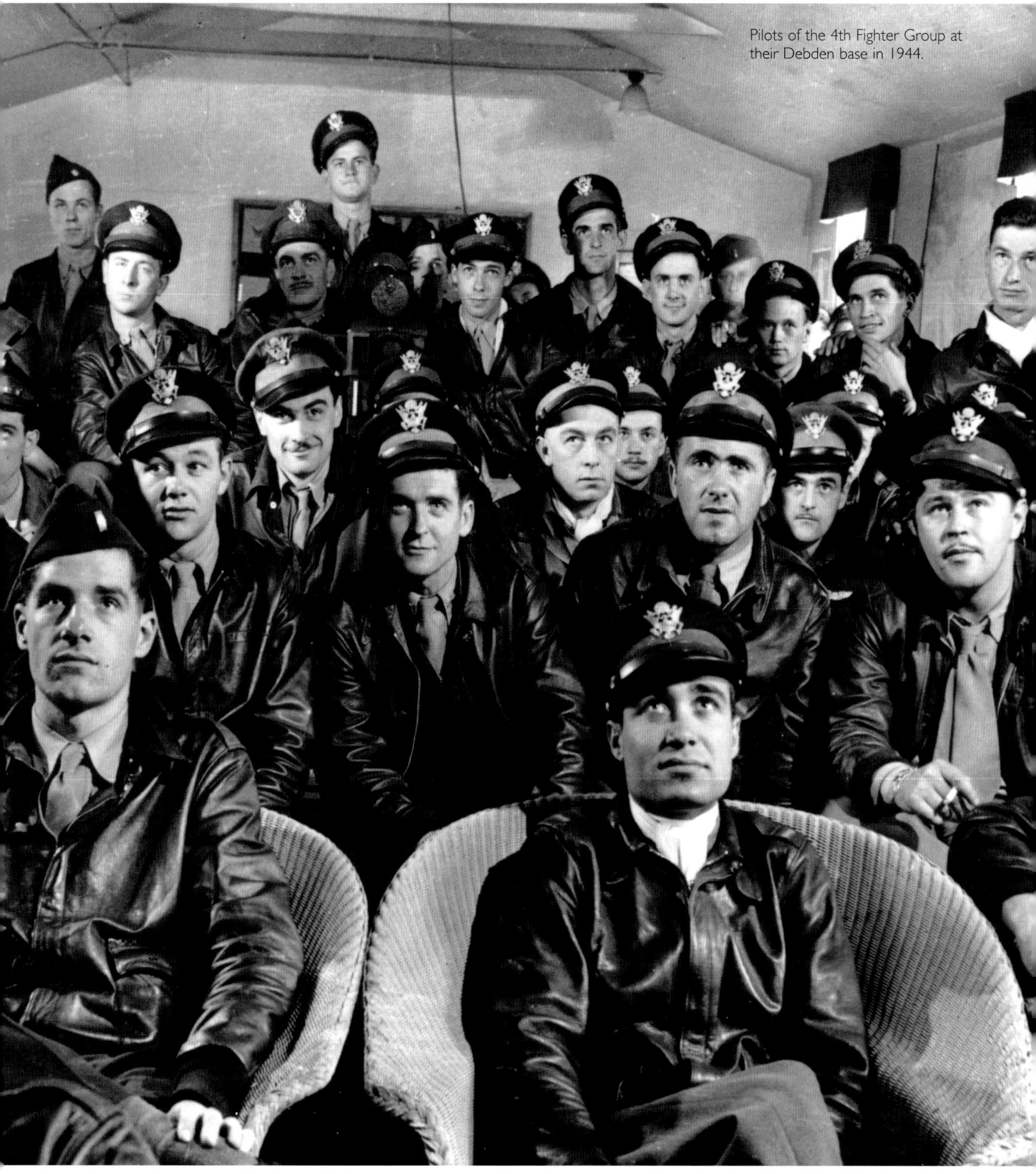

Pilots of the 4th Fighter Group at their Debden base in 1944.

To arrive at the airplane design that Ed Schmued had in mind for his amazing new fighter, he blended his existing fighter design concepts with a new, laminar-flow airfoil, leading to the Model NA-73 and an RAF contract for 320 of the evolved-design aircraft, with final British approval given on 20th July, after the fall of France and the beginning of the Battle of Britain.

One hundred days was Schmued's estimate of how long it would take him and the specialized groups under his supervision to build the first experimental example of the new airplane. A key aspect of the purchase agreement was the British requirement that North American have the plane flight-tested, debugged, and in production within one year. Internally at North American, many engineers were concerned about the anticipated performance of the new laminar-flow wing. But considerable testing had proven the viability of the wing and hopes were high for actual results.

In addition to Ed Schmued's other gifts, his exceptional scheduling and project co-ordination ability enabled the company to complete work on that first example of the new plane, by both engineering and the shop, in 102 days, almost exactly as predicted and promised. Forty-four years later Schmued would comment: "We could never build another plane today in a hundred days as we did then. Today they just don't have what it takes. There are too many levels of authority within the building companies. They have a president, a vice-president, another vice-president and many other levels. We had formed an exceptional group of engineers. There was an enthusiasm in this group that was unequalled anywhere. We worked every day until midnight. On Sundays we quit at six p.m., so we knew we had a weekend."

The disappointment came when the Allison Engine plant in Indianapolis failed to deliver the aero engine for that first new fighter within that one hundred days. The engine delivery took a further eighteen days. With the engine installed in the airframe, the North American Flight Test Division got the instrumentation ready and initial engine run-up tests began on 11th October 1940.

On 26th October, the first flight testing of the airplane began and continued until 20th November. That flight ended prematurely when the test pilot neglected to switch the fuel valve to reserve and the plane ran out of gas after just fifteen minutes of flight. The pilot was forced to put the only existing flying example of the world's most promising new fighter plane down on a freshly-plowed field. The wheels dug into the soft earth and the fighter flipped onto its back. The hapless pilot was not injured, but NA-73X was significantly damaged and needed a lengthy rebuild. To overcome this enormous setback, Ed Schmued elected to have the second airplane on the assembly line—actually the first production airplane—prepared for flight test so as not to delay the gathering of critical test data and to keep production of the new plane on schedule.

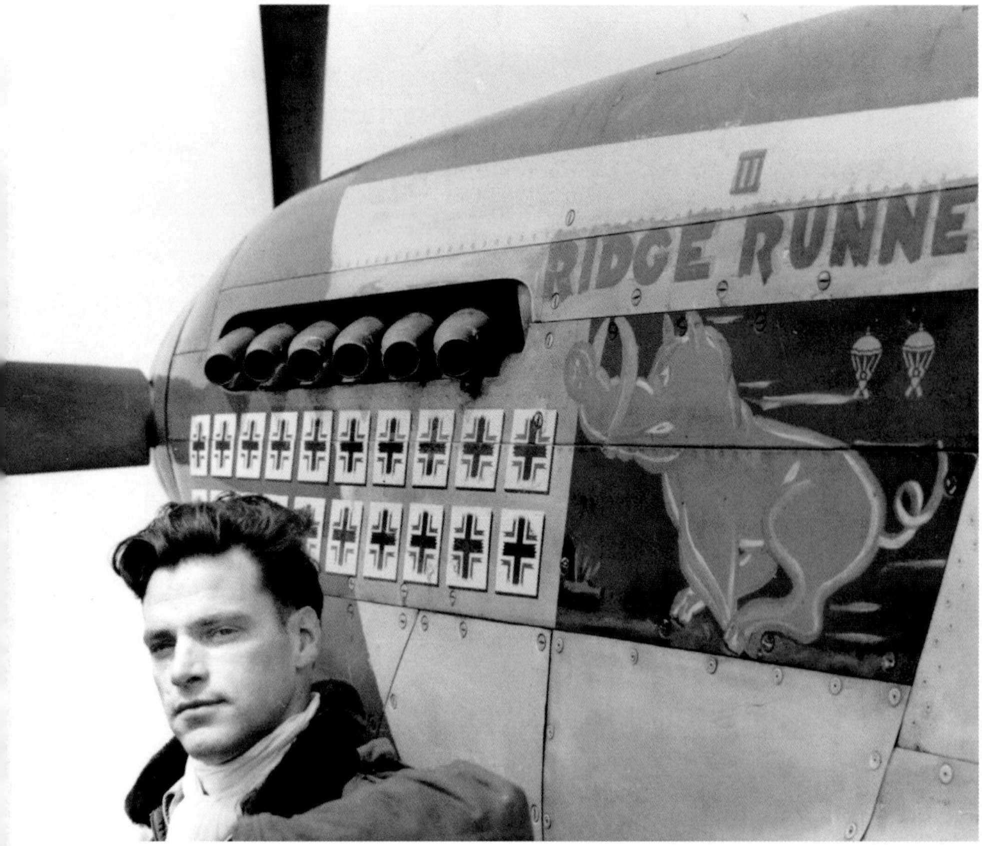
RIDGE RUNNE

Even before NA-73X had flown for the first time, the British had ordered an additional 300 of the planes. And, in a letter to North American Aviation dated 9th December 1940, the British Purchasing Authority for the first time referred to the new fighter as the Mustang, its official name. By August 1941 the first production example of the the Mustang I was crated and shipped via the Panama Canal from California to England and by November it had been assembled and test-flown. During that same period, several of the new fighters had been accepted by the U.S. Army, designated XP-51 and flown to Wright Field, Ohio, for testing and evaluation. The entire RAF order of 620 of the new planes was delivered by July 1942 and by December many of them were flying with fifteen RAF Army Co-operation Squadrons. They mostly flew reconnaissance and low-level cross-Channel sweeps to shoot up enemy barges, trains, and troop concentrations. The Royal Air Force pilots of these Mustang Is were impressed by them, referring to them as "easily the best American fighters to have reached Britain." It was shown that the airplane was faster than the Spitfire VB and faster up to 25,000 feet and had twice the range of the Spitfire. The Spit, however, could go much higher, had a better overall rate of climb and a better turn rate. Very importantly, the Spitfire's general high-altitude performance was attributable to its excellent Rolls-Royce Merlin engine.

Ronald Harker was a test pilot with Rolls-Royce and was invited to RAF Duxford in Cambridgeshire on 30th April 1942 to fly and evaluate the Mustang I. Harker thought highly of the American fighter and was highly impressed by its handling, its performance, and its fuel capacity. He liked the positioning of the plane's guns too. In the report he wrote for the RAF Air Fighting Development Unit he commented positively on the general performance of the airplane, but suggested that a really special fighter might result if the exceptional North American airframe were to be combined with the proven, fuel-efficient Rolls-Royce Merlin engine. Harker's report and the subsequent lobbying he did with R-R company executives and Air Ministry officials raised little enthusiasm initially among the majority who still wanted nothing to do

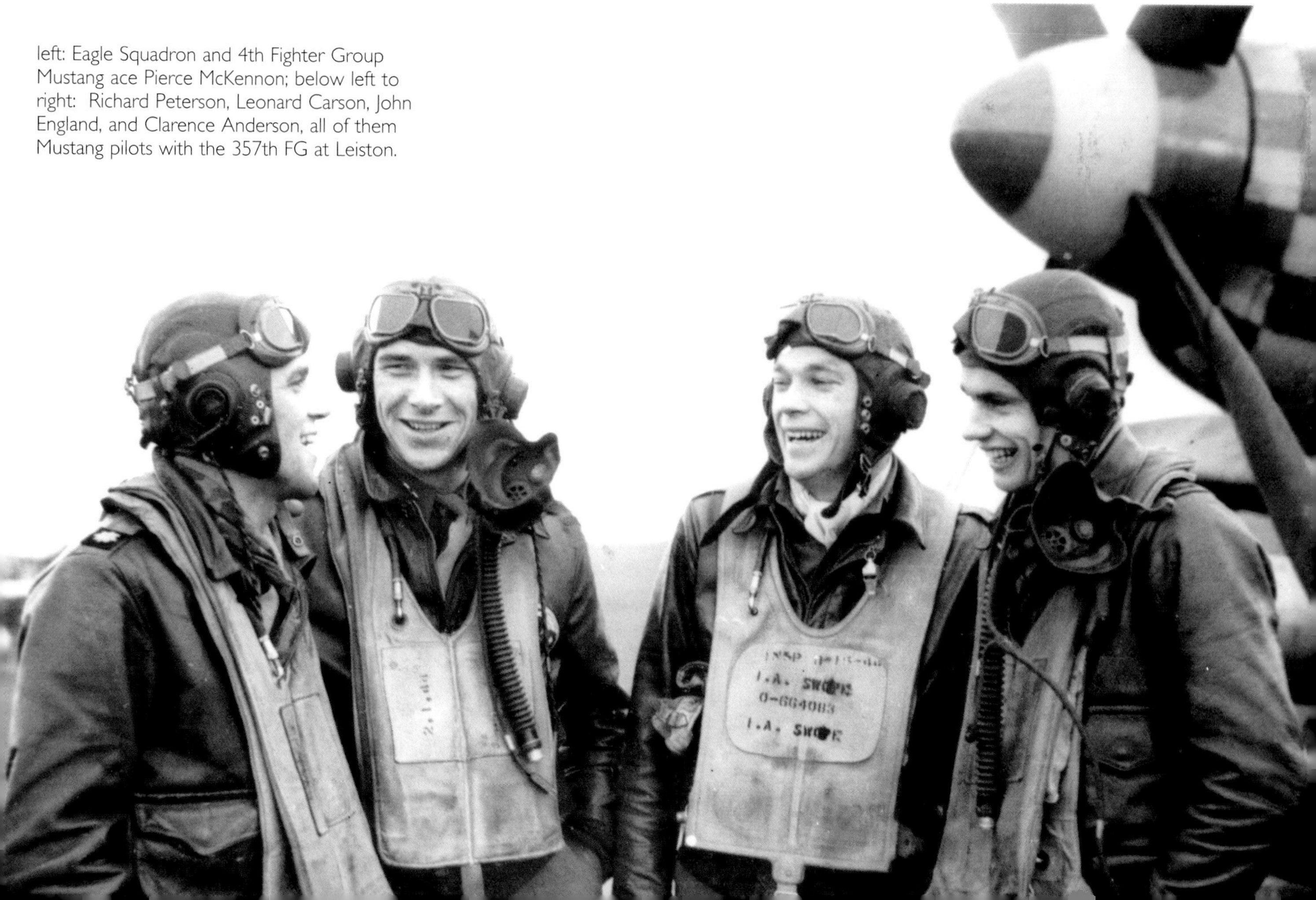

left: Eagle Squadron and 4th Fighter Group Mustang ace Pierce McKennon; below left to right: Richard Peterson, Leonard Carson, John England, and Clarence Anderson, all of them Mustang pilots with the 357th FG at Leiston.

with any American aircraft. Eventually, though, the test pilot did persuade some senior people at Rolls of two tempting points: that mating the Merlin to the Mustang airframe was highly likely to result in an extraordinary new weapon to use against the Nazis; and that it would certainly generate a great amount of new aero engine business for Rolls-Royce.

The company leaders then convinced the RAF to provide three Mustangs for Merlin installation at the Rolls Hucknall factory, where redesign of the cowling and cooling system as well as other modifications, conversions, and changes finally led to a Merlin 65-powered airplane given the RAF designation Mustang Mk X, an extremely successful realization of Ronnie Harker's inspired idea.

The evolution of the great new fighter continued when Rolls-Royce sent factory installation and performance data on the Merlin Mustang to the design staff of North American in Los Angeles, who were soon at work incorporating the Merlin engine into the airplanes on their production line near what today is Los Angeles International Airport. Arrangements were then made with the Packard Motor Car Company and Continental Motors in the U.S. for the mass production of the thousands of Merlins that would soon be needed—many thousands more than Rolls-Royce facilities in the UK could produce. Soon

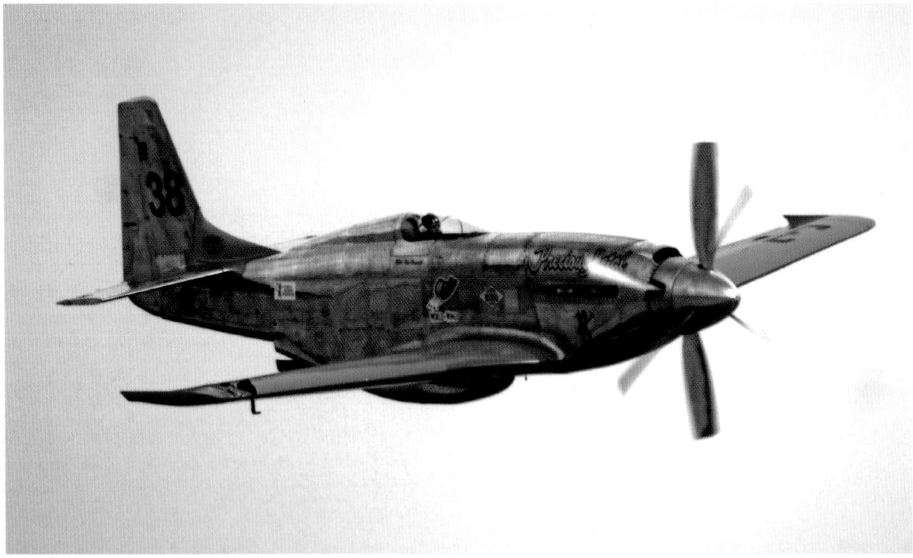
38

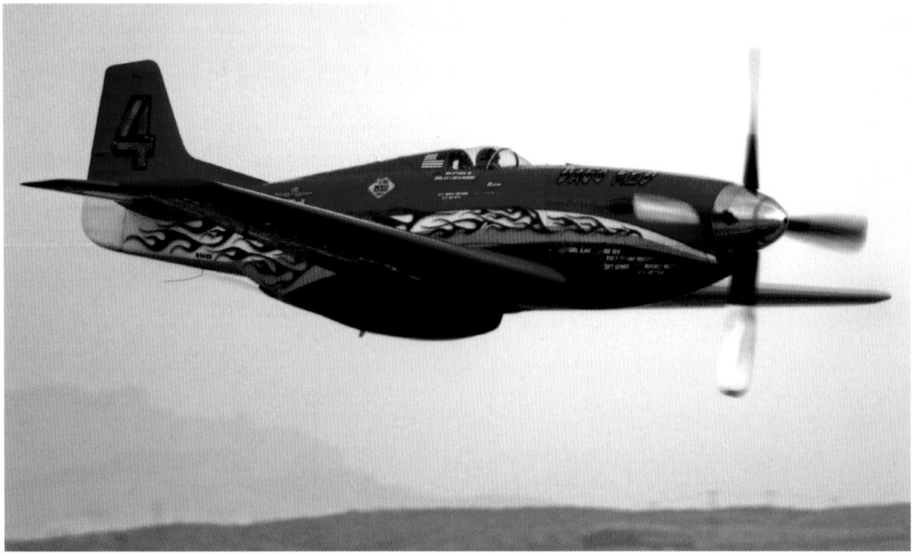
4

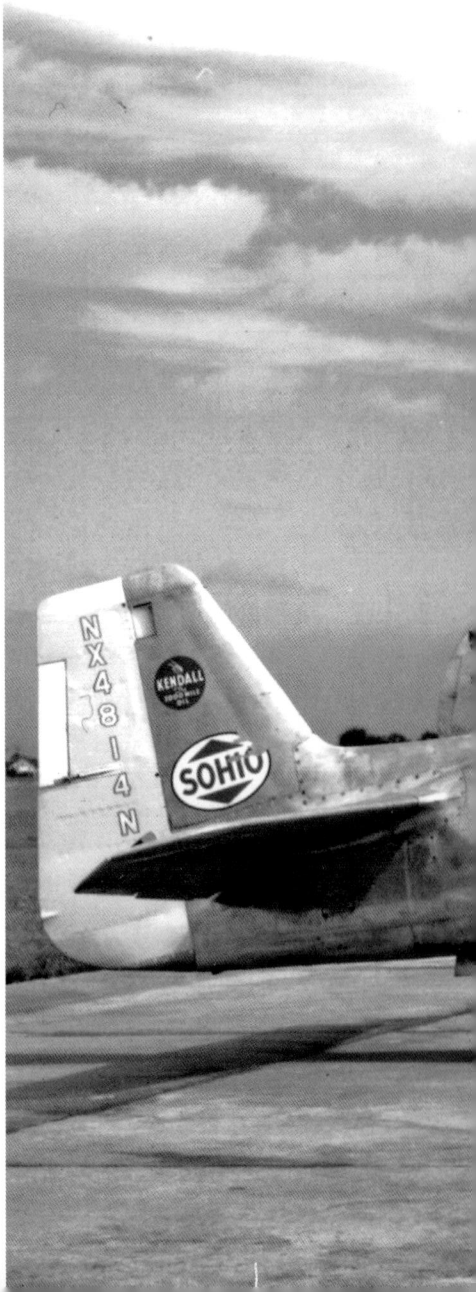
NX4814N
KENDALL
SOHIO

some of those American-built Merlins would be powering RAF Lancaster bombers and other Merlin-equipped British aircraft, in addition to the thousands of Mustangs about to be produced. Many changes were needed to shoehorn the mighty Merlin into the production Mustang, and the Packard and Continental-built Merlins were to be fitted with four-bladed, eleven-foot-two-inch Hamilton Standard Hydromatic propellers.

Late in November 1942, the results of the brilliant marriage of Merlin and Mustang had made such an impression on U.S. Army Air Corps General Henry H. "Hap" Arnold, that he had his branch order more than 2,200 of the new planes. But North American was by then swamped with orders for its AT-6 Texan / Harvard trainer, and B-25 Mitchell medium bomber, as well as the Mustang, now designated P-51B, that the company had to construct expanded manufacturing facilities at Inglewood and build new production facilities in Dallas, Texas, and near Tulsa, Oklahoma.

Production activity at the North American facilities took off (pun intended) smoothly once initial engine delivery delays from Packard were overcome and the performance testing soon proved the brilliance of Ronald Harker's notion. The Merlin-powered Mustang had a top speed of 441 mph, more than fifty mph faster than the Allison-powered version had produced. In virtually all areas it was

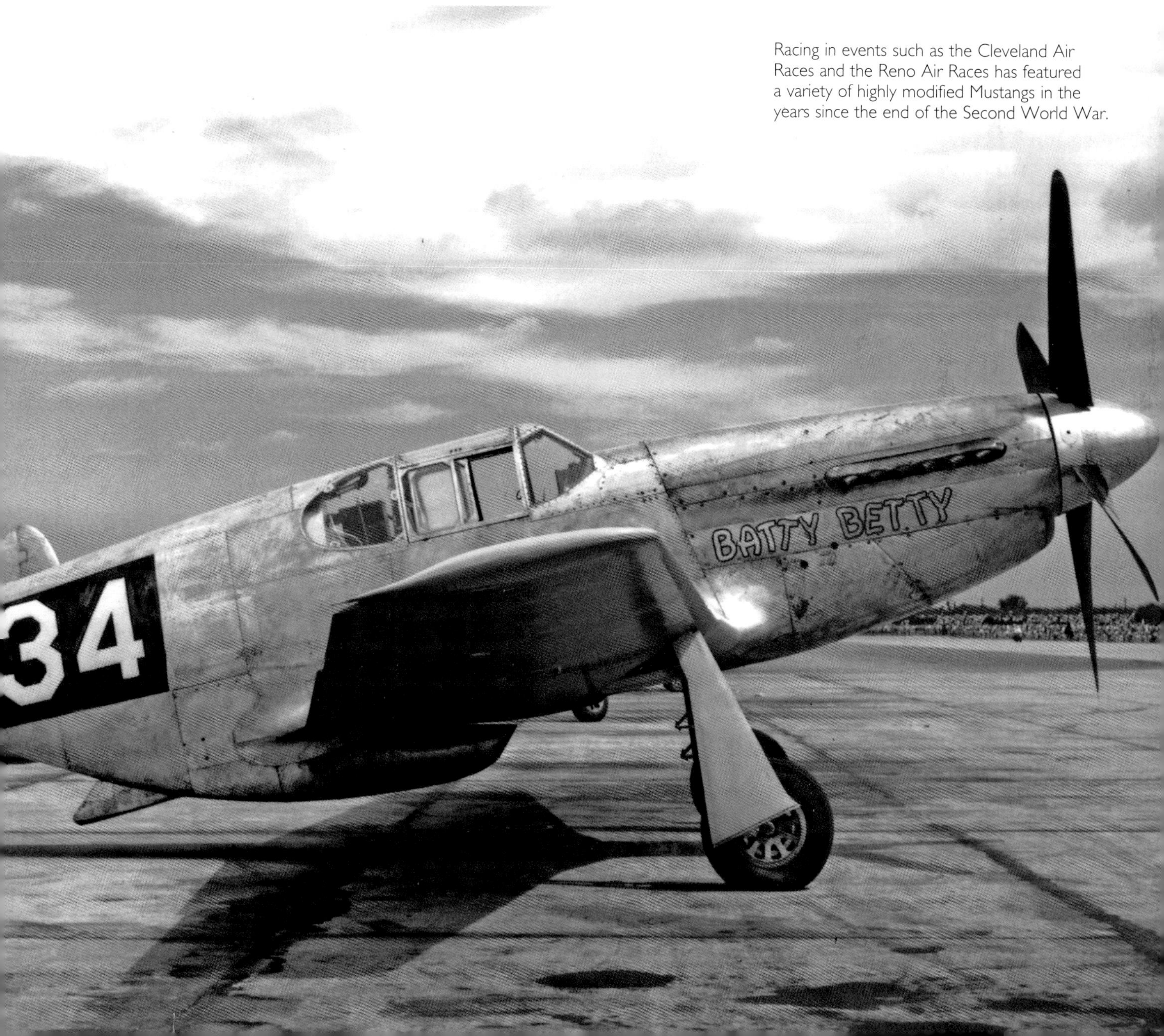
BATTY BETTY
34

Racing in events such as the Cleveland Air Races and the Reno Air Races has featured a variety of highly modified Mustangs in the years since the end of the Second World War.

greatly improved and its enormous range would secure its reputation as one of the greatest aircraft in history. Its ability to escort the heavy bombers of the Eighth Air Force all the way to their targets deep in Germany and back to England finally made it possible for the American bomber crews to fly their grueling missions with a reasonable chance of survival, dramatically reducing the U.S. aircraft losses in encounters with German fighters.

To ready the new Mustangs for combat in the European Theatre of Operations, the newly arrived fighters had to undergo vital field modifications at the hands of their ground crews starting at Boxted, home to the 354th Fighter Group, 8AF, the first American operational unit to be equipped with the P-51Bs. Though administratively a part of the American Ninth Air Force, the 354th operated their Mustangs with the 8AF on the initial Mustang escort missions protecting the bombers of the Eighth. The early Mustang escort missions, including those of the Debden-based 4th Fighter Group, identified a variety of "teething" troubles that needed the attention of both the ground crews and North American Aviation factory representatives sent to England. The prolonged high-altitude operation on the bomber escort missions underscored problems ranging from the freezing of oils and lubricants, to oxygen starvation, the build-up of ice on windscreens, coolant loss and the resultant engine overheating, fouled spark plugs, and jammed ammunition belts during high-G manuvers. Other field modifications included the addition of external fuel capacity in the form of droppable aluminum or pressed paper fuel tanks and an eighty-five U.S. gallon fuel tank right behind the pilot's seat. The information about all such modifications was passed either by the ground crew chiefs or the North American representatives to the company in Los Angeles where the modifications were incorporated into the production line airplanes.

Early in January 1944, USAAF General Jimmy Doolittle arrived in England to take command of the Eighth Air Force. As the new Mustangs were by then arriving in sufficient quantity, Doolittle decided to release some of the pilots from their full-time commitment to escorting the bomber missions and, for the first time, give them freedom to attack and destroy German fighters both before and after the Germans attacked the American bombers. The move allowed the Mustang to really come into its own, just as more and more American fighter groups were being equipped with the new fighter. As many more of them appeared in the skies to shepherd the B-17s and B-24s, the bomber crews realized that at last the Eighth Air Force had the long-range fighter it needed to defeat the German Air Force.

But North American wasn't content with the superb air weapon it had created; it continued to develop the Mustang into an even better and more impressive performer. A new version, the P-51D, began arriving in England, offering greatly improved visibility with the addition of a teardrop or bubble canopy. The new model had a strengthened airframe, a slightly modified cowling, the eighty-five U.S. gallon behind-the-seat fuel tank as standard, a modified landing gear, standardized six .50 caliber Browning machine-guns in the wings, and a V-1650-7 Packard or Continental Merlin engine of 1,695 hp.

As the new D model Mustangs came into the England-based squadrons of the Eighth and Ninth Air Forces in large numbers, General Doolittle wasted no time in releasing many of them from direct bomber escort to attacking German aircraft that were still parked on their airfields, striking at the enemy hangars, runways, and other airfield facilities to make them unserviceable. They also went after other important ground targets and were highly successful in this new effort, but their results did not come cheap. Many Mustangs were lost in this ground attack role, brought down by the hundreds of German guns employed in the defense of their airfields; many more of the new American fighters fell in these attacks than in air-to-air combat action. The German ground defense gunners were extremely efficient and the Mustangs

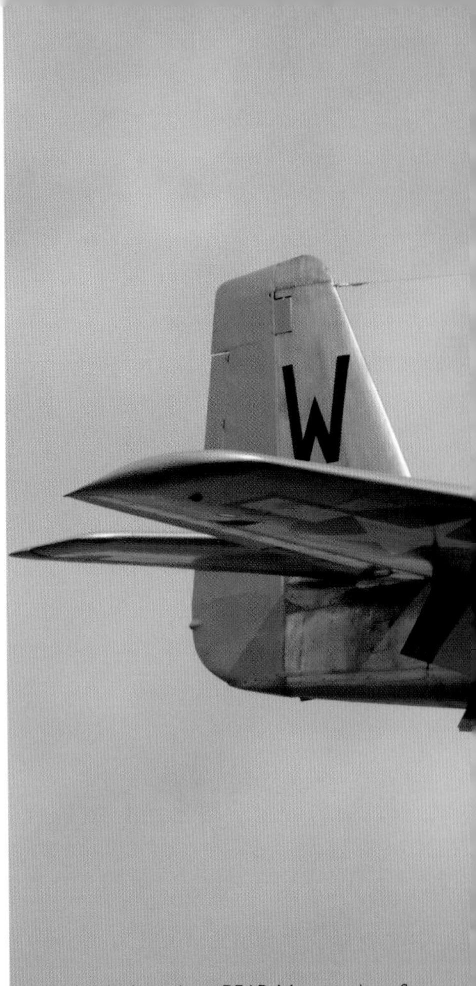
W
A North American P51B Mustang in a fine image by aviation photographer Stephen Fox.

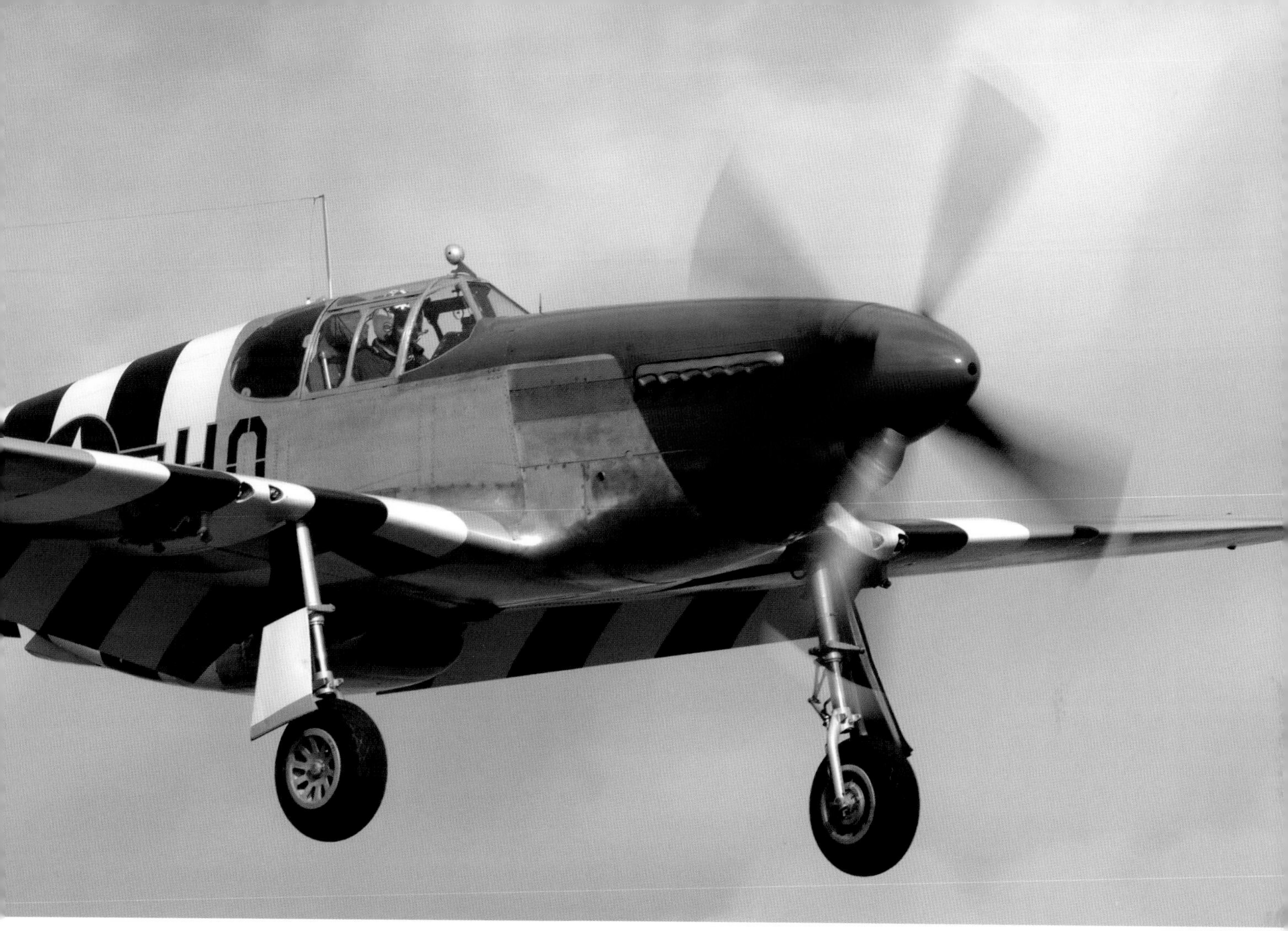

proved more vulnerable than some of the other Allied fighters owing to hits in the P-51 radiators and cooling tubes.

Just as the engineers and technicians of North American Aviation were making continuing progress in their development and refinement of the Mustang, so too were those in the German aircraft industry over the course of the war years. Just as the pilots of the P-51s were dominating their opposite numbers in the Luftwaffe over Germany in the summer of 1944, the German fighter pilots upped the game again introducing the jet and rocket-propelled fighters, the Me 262 and 163 respectively. As competent and effective as the Mustangs were against the fighter mainstays of the enemy, the Me 109 and Fw 190, they were no match for the much faster German jet and rocket planes which were slicing through the American daylight bomber streams with near impunity, often bringing down two or three of the heavies in a single devastating pass. Their menace and effectivity was, however, minimized by their limited numbers. Had they been available to the Luftwaffe earlier and in far greater numbers, the outcome of the air war might have been quite different.

On the other side of the world, in the Pacific war theatre, another new American plane was making its combat debut. The big Boeing B-29 Superfortress, four-engined successor to the B-17 Flying Fortress, was about to embark on a long-range bombing campaign against the home islands of Japan. All is, supposedly, fair in love and war, and the Americans brought some tricks that they and the British had learned in the European air campaign, to the raids they would fly to Japan. The majority of the buildings in Tokyo and the other Japanese cities were of wood and paper construction and the Allied bomber crews had certainly learned how to start big fires. The B-29s would exploit the incendiary bombing of the sixty key target cities of the enemy in a series of unprecedented attacks and the

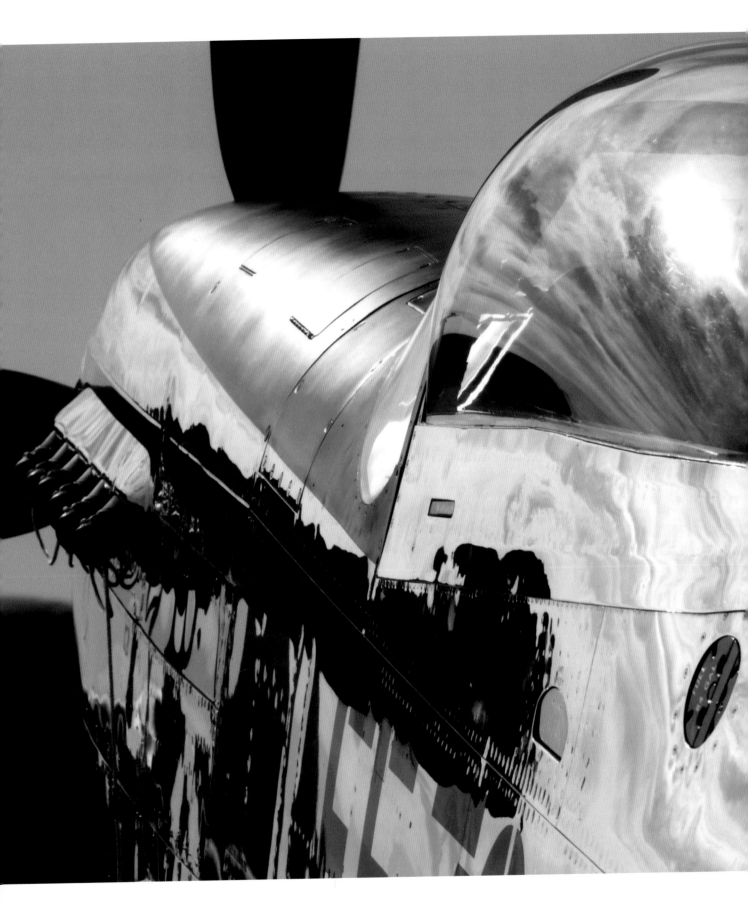

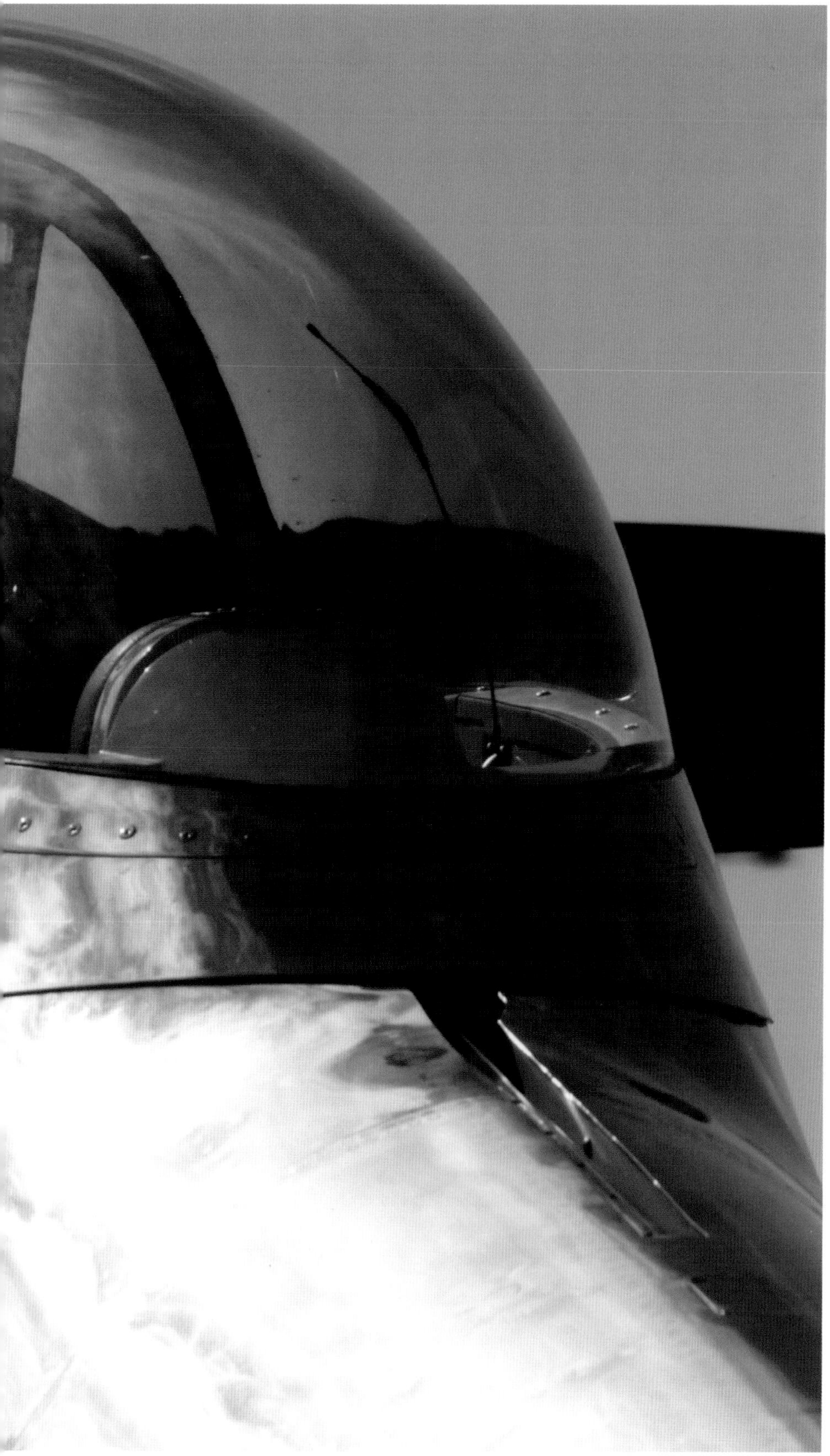

single-engined Mustangs would play a vital role shepherding the Superforts on these lengthy over-ocean missions. Frequently they were escorting bombers crippled by attacking enemy aircraft or mechanical failure. For a while those early 29s were prone to developing engine fires and soon acquired a reference to that tendency: three turning, one burning. Such problems added to the burden of the Mustang pilots who then had to fend off Japanese fighters who were on the lookout for crippled enemy bombers, easy pickings. The Mustangs operated on the long-haul fire-bombing raids from a new base, a SeeBee-built airfield on the tiny island of Iwo Jima. Those punishing raids would continue until August 1945 when the Japanese finally surrendered after the delivery of atomic bombs over the cities of Hiroshima and Nagasaki by two B-29s from North Field, the huge American air base on the island of Tinian in the Marianas.

Seventy years after the end of that war, more than two hundred P-51 Mustangs are still airworthy, most of them flown frequently; careful, beautiful restorations, the pride of enthusiasts who appreciate the character, performance, and history of that wonderful plane.

When eighty-five-year-old Ed Schmued, the quiet, modest, brilliant designer of the Mustang, died in June of 1985, his body was cremated and at the request of his widow, his ashes were flown from Los Angeles International Airport out to sea and released. His last flight was in a Mustang.

OPERATIONAL SUMMARY OF THE
EIGHTH AIR FORCE IN WWII
INFORMATION PROVIDED BY
LT. GENERAL JAMES H. DOOLITTLE,
COMMANDER 8USAAF, 1944-1945

The Eighth Air Force was activated at Savannah, Georgia, on 28th January 1942. In February a small detachment of officers arrived in England to make initial arrangements for the housing and basing of groups to follow, and by June, 1942, aircraft, crews, and ground personnel had begun to arrive in the UK. On 17th August 1942, the first operational mission in its own aircraft was carried out by the Eighth Air Force . . . the first of 459 days on which its heavy bombers struck at enemy targets.

In World War Two the Eighth Air Force was commanded by a total of five officers from the date of its activation. They were Brigadier General (then Colonel) Asa M. Duncan from 28th January 1942 to 4th May 1942; General (then Major General) Carl A. Spaatz from 5th May 1942 to 30th November 1942; Lieutenant General Ira C. Eaker from 1st December 1942 to 5th January 1944; Lieutenant General James H. Doolittle from 6th January 1944 to 9th May 1945; Major General W.E. Kepner from 10th May 1945.

At peak personnel strength, the Eighth Air Force numbered more than two hundred thousand officers and men. At peak operating strength, it numbered forty and one-half Heavy Bomb Groups, fifteen Fighter Groups, and two Photo Reconnaissance Groups operating from bases in the UK. At this strength a typical mission consisted of 1,400 heavy bombers escorted by 800 fighters, consuming 3,500,000 gallons of aviation gasoline, expending 250,000 rounds of .50 caliber ammunition, destroying twenty-five German aircraft in the air and on the ground for

the loss of four U.S. fighters and five bombers, and dropping 3,300 tons of bombs on enemy targets of which on visual missions, forty percent fell within one thousand feet of assigned MPIs and seventy-five percent within two thousand feet. A typical damage assessment report from photographs taken by Eighth Air Force photo aircraft after the attack reads as follows: "Very severe damage is seen in both the North and East Marshalling Yards. In the N/MY, both semi-round houses are severely damaged, one turntable is wrecked, many tracks are obliterated in the center of the yard, all through-running lines cut, the large transshipment shed burning, large numbers of locomotives, wagons and cars derailed, damaged and destroyed. In the E, M/Y, the locomotive depot is severely damaged, all through-lines cut, and all sidings unserviceable. The passenger stations in both Marshalling Yards are severely damaged." (from K Report covering attack on Falkenburg M/Y, 19th April 1945.)

This partial statistical record of the 459 days when bombing operations were carried out (with related fighter, photo and special operations) represents only a collection of facts and figures on effort, consumption, strength, and costs. No attempt has been made—or can be made—to properly reflect in statistics the devotion to duty, heroism, and sacrifices made by personnel of the Command to accomplish the mission of the Eighth Air Force. Behind the figures on these pages are the combat crews and fighter pilots who fought in the skies— 46,456 of whom became casualties; the maintenance / ground personnel who kept the airplanes flying, repaired 59,644 battle-damaged aircraft, loaded the 732,231 tons of bombs expended, and linked and loaded the 99,256,341 rounds of ammunition; and the planners who directed the missions.

HIGHLIGHTS
1942
28th January: Eighth Air Force activated at Savannah, Georgia.
20th February: First detachment of Eighth Air Force officers arrived in UK.
4th July: Six Eighth Air Force crews in RAF Bostons participated in mission to DeKooy airfield.
17th August: First mission flown in Eighth Air Force aircraft. Twelve B-17s bombed Rouen, France.
9th October: B-24s joined the air assault. First mission of more than one hundred bombers. 108 attacked airfields in France.
November / December: Four Eighth Air Force Fighter Groups and two Heavy Bomb Groups transferred to Mediterranean Theatre of Operations for "Torch" Project.
1943
3rd January: First use of "formation" instead of individual precision bombing.
27th January: First mission to Germany; ninety-one bombers dispatched to Wilhelmshaven and Emden.
January: Forty-eight percent of all bombers crossing enemy coast received battle damage.
18th March: First use of automatic flight control linked with bombsights.
13th May: 3rd Division became operational Air Force with twelve heavy bomb groups.
14th May: First mission using more than two hundred bombers; eleven B-26s joined heavies in attacks on Kiel, Antwerp, Courtrai, and Ijmuiden. Ten B-26s were missing in action.
May: P-47s began regular escort up to 200 mile range.
24th July: Longest bomber mission to date and first mission to Norway.
28th July: P-47s equipped with auxiliary fuel tanks escorted bombers across German border for first time.
1st August: B-24s of 2nd Air Division on detached service to MTO joined

with Ninth Air Force to attack Ploesti oil fields. Of 102 Eighth Air Force B-24s dispatched, thirty were shot down.

17th August: First shuttle mission to North Africa bases after attack on Regensburg. Sixty bombers lost in attacks on Schweinfurt and Regensburg. 319 enemy aircraft destroyed by heavy bombers.

27th September: First use of radar instruments to bomb through cloud. Used over Emden.

September: P-47s range increased to 325 miles. Air Force dropped over 5,000 tons of bombs in one month.

7th October: First night propaganda leaflet mission.

15th October: VIII Air Support Command Medium Bomb Groups transferred to Ninth Air Force.

October: 214 bombers were lost; 9.2 percent of aircraft entering enemy territory.

3rd November: First mission using over five hundred bombers; 574 dispatched to Wilhelmshaven.

25th November: First fighter-bomber mission carried out.

1944

January: Eighth Air Force dropped over 10,000 tons of bombs.

11th February: P-51s joined Eighth Air Force fighters.

20th-25th February: Four devastating attacks on German aircraft plants and assembly factories crippled German aircraft production.

25th February: First fighter low-level strafing attack.

6th March: First major attack on Berlin; sixty-nine bombers MIA in this attack; largest number MIA in one day.

March: First month more than 20,000 tons of bombs dropped.

7th May: First mission of over 1,000 bombers.

6th June: D-Day; forty and one-half heavy bomb groups were operational;

2,698 bombers dropped 4,478 tons of bombs on two missions; 1,966 fighters provided escort and cover.

21st June: First shuttle mission to bases in Russia.

22nd June: German Air Force destroyed forty-seven U.S. aircraft on the ground at Eastern bases.

June: 25,402 fighters were sortied; greatest number in any single month.

28th July: First German Air Force jet / rocket enemy aircraft used; operationally encountered by U.S. fighters.

13th August: Fighters dropped 334 tons of bombs on fighter-bomber attack; largest tonnage for one mission.

16th August: First jet aircraft destroyed by fighters.

29th August: Trucking operations to ground troops commenced.

18th September: Bombers dropped supplies to beleaguered Warsaw.

27th November: Fighters encountered 747 enemy aircraft; greatest number sighted in one day; 102 enemy aircraft destroyed.

November: Fighter effective strength averaged 1,031; largest of any month.

24th December: Largest bomber mission to date; 2,055 in the air at one time to attack targets in the "Ardennes Bulge" sector; 4,302 tons of bombs dropped in one operation.

1945

14th January: Fighters destroyed 161 enemy aircraft in the air; largest fighter air claims in one day.

January: An average of 2,799 heavy bombers and 1,484 fighters were assigned; greatest aircraft strength of the Air Force; fighters destroyed 319 locomotives, 657 goods wagons and 58 tank cars in strafing attacks.

February: Highly successful attacks on Marshalling Yards in Berlin, Dresden, and Nuremberg carried out on six days.

28th March: Last mission to Berlin; the most heavily bombed U.S. target; 27,985 tons of bombs dropped on

Greater Berlin.

March: Greatest bomber effort for any month; 31,297 bombers were sortied; 73,878 tons of bombs dropped; 74,009,324 gallons of gasoline were consumed in 395,829 flying hours; 92.3 percent of bombers sortied were effective; enemy jet aircraft shot down twenty-four bombers.

16th April: 752 enemy aircraft destroyed in one operation by fighters; thirty-four U.S. fighters MIA in strafing attacks.

25th April: Last bombing operation carried out.

April: Bombing accuracy on visual operations best of any month; 59 percent within one thousand feet; 85 percent within two thousand feet; over two thousand enemy aircraft destroyed in air and on ground.

1st May: First "Chow Hound" operation carried out to Holland.

8th May: V-E Day.

HEAVY BOMBARDMENT EFFORT 17TH AUGUST 1942 TO 8TH MAY 1945

Total sorties: 330,523
Sorties less spares: 318,450
Credit sorties: 293,599
Effective sorties: 266,565
Tons on targets-Bombs: 686,406
Tons on targets-Leaflets: 2,807
Tons on targets-Gas and Supplies: 6,184
Enemy aircraft claims-Destroyed in air: 6,236
Enemy aircraft claims-Probably destroyed in air: 1,826
Enemy aircraft claims-Damaged in air: 3,198
Enemy aircraft claims-Destroyed on ground: 3,079
Operational losses-Aircraft MIA: 4,137
Operational losses-Category E: 1,556
Operational losses-Missing: 162
Personnel casualties-MIA: 39,007
Personnel casualties-KIA: 2,818

Personnel casualties-Wounded Ser:
1,933
Personnel casualties-Wounded SI:
3.015

AMMUNITION EXPENDITURE
Bombers-.50 caliber: 72,339,729
Bombers-.30 caliber: 31,300
Fighters-.50 caliber: 26,623,123
Fighters-20 millimeter: 262,189

ENEMY AIRCRAFT CLAIMS BY
BOMBERS IN THE AIR
DESTROYED
FW190: 3,107
FW189: 1
FW290: 2
ME109: 1,955
ME110: 449
ME210: 182
ME410: 81
JU87: 5
JU88: 299
DO217: 7
HE111K: 1
AR240: 1
ME163: 2
ME262: 57
OTHER AND UNKNOWN: 110

PROBABLY DESTROYED
FW190: 880
ME109: 459
ME110: 151
ME210: 63
ME410: 43
JU87: 1
JU88: 94
DO217: 2
HE113: 1
ME163: 3
ME262: 43
OTHER AND UNKNOWN: 93

DAMAGED
FW190: 1,356
FW189: 1
ME109: 1,022
ME110: 310

ME210: 140
ME410: 69
JU86: 1
JU87: 1
JU88: 164
DO217: 2
ME163: 3
ME262: 54
OTHER AND UNKNOWN: 87

ENEMY AIRCRAFT CLAIMS BY
FIGHTERS IN THE AIR
DESTROYED
FW190: 1,948
ME109: 2,535
ME110: 185
ME210: 40
ME410: 74
FW200: 8
JU88: 82
JU188: 2
JU290: 1
HE111: 22
HE177: 6
DO217: 26
ME163: 4
AR234: 12
ME262: 130

PROBABLY DESTROYED
FW190: 137
ME109: 159
ME110: 13
ME210: 4
ME410: 4
JU88: 7
HE111: 2
DO217: 1
ME163: 2
ME262: 9
OTHER AND UNKNOWN: 146

DAMAGED
FW190: 584
ME109: 639
ME110: 80
ME210: 20
ME410: 22
HE111: 10

HE177: 2
DO217: 7
ME163: 1
AR234: 4
ME262: 44

ENEMY AIRCRAFT CLAIMS BY
FIGHTERS ON THE GROUND
DESTROYED
FW190: 664
ME109: 509
ME110: 185
ME210: 49
ME410: 192
FW200: 8
JU88: 637
JU188: 15
HE111: 293
HE177: 216
DO217: 178
JU52: 89
ME163: 3
AR234: 14
ME262: 100
HE280: 3
OTHER AND UNKNOWN: 1,094

PROBABLY DESTROYED
FW190: 5
ME210: 2
JU88: 11
DO217: 1
OTHER AND UNKNOWN: 4

DAMAGED
FW190: 340
ME109: 307
ME110: 130
ME210: 39
ME410: 120
FW200: 13
JU88: 427
JU188: 9
HE111: 198
HE177: 104
DO217: 131
JU52: 54
ME163: 7
AR234: 2

ME262: 55
OTHER AND UNKNOWN: 949

FIGHTER GROUND CLAIMS
FEBRUARY 1944 TO APRIL 1945
Locomotives destroyed: 4,660
Locomotives damaged: 2,791
Oil tank cars destroyed: 1,500
Oil tank cars damaged: 1,422
Trains destroyed: 20
Trains damaged: 226
Goods wagons and other RR cars
destroyed: 6,069
Goods wagons and other RR cars damaged: 23,929
Armored vehicles and tanks destroyed:
178
Armored vehicles and tanks damaged:
253
Flak towers and gun positions
destroyed: 270
Flak towers and gun positions damaged:
557
Motor trucks destroyed: 3,858
Motor trucks damaged: 3,091
Other vehicles destroyed: 1,021
Other vehicles damaged: 720
Tug boats, barges, and freighters
destroyed: 129
Tug boats, barges, and freighters damaged: 853
RR stations and facilities destroyed: 51
RR stations and facilities damaged: 234
Radio and power stations destroyed:
102
Radio and power stations damaged:
294
Oil storage tanks destroyed: 73
Oil storage tanks damaged: 127
Hangars and misc. buildings destroyed:
234
Hangars and misc. buildings damaged:
600

AIR-SEA RESCUES: PERSONNEL
SAVED JANUARY 1943 TO MAY
1945
B-17 CREWMEN
Men who ditched or bailed out over

water: 3,336
Men rescued: 1,266
Percent rescued: 37.9
B-24 CREWMEN
Men who ditched or bailed out over
water: 1,025
Men rescued: 272
Percent rescued: 26.5
P-47 PILOTS
Men who ditched or bailed out over
water: 69
Men rescued: 27
Percent rescued: 39.1
P-38 PILOTS
Men who ditched or bailed out over
water: 27
Men rescued: 12
Percent rescued: 44.4
P51 PILOTS
Men who ditched or bailed out over
water: 131
Men rescued: 56
Percent rescued: 42.7

AIRCRAFT ATTRITION AUGUST
1942 TO MAY 1945
B-17
Missing in action: 3,093
Category E: 1,025
Missing: 126
War weary: 180
Non-op salvage: 386
Gains from previous losses: 56
Net inventory losses: 4,754
U.E. end of month: 27,624
Attrition as percentage of U.E.: 16.6
B-24
Missing in action: 1,099
Category E: 551
Missing: 36
War weary: 213
Non-op salvage: 221
Gains from previous losses: 8
Net inventory losses: 2,112
U.E. end of month: 12,720
Attrition as percentage of U.E.: 16.6
P-47
Missing in action: 529
Category E: 176

Missing: 44
War weary: 176
Non-op salvage: 131
Gains from previous losses: 13
Net inventory losses: 1,043
U.E. end of month: 7,950
Attrition as percentage of U.E.: 13.1
P-38
Missing in action: 266
Category E: 84
Missing: 2
War weary: 29
Non-op salvage: 74
Gains from previous losses: 4
Net inventory losses: 451
U.E. end of month: 1,800
Attrition as percentage of U.E.: 25.1
P-51
Missing in action: 1,235
Category E: 514
Missing: 132
War weary: 168
Net inventory losses: 2,201
U.E. end of month: 12,375
Attrition as percentage of U.E.: 17.8

FLYING TIME COMPUTED TO
NEAREST HOUR AUGUST 1942 TO
MAY 1945
Operational flying time: 3,192,081
Non-operational flying time: 1,398,310

GASOLINE CONSUMPTION
AUGUST 1942 TO MAY 1945
Grade 100 / 150: 53,321,258
Grade 100 / 130: 811,466,295

DEFINITIONS: Extracts from U.S.
Strategic Air Forces in Europe, Regs
80-6, 8 May 1944, 80-6A, 16 January
1945, 80-6B, 20 January 1945, and
Eighth Air Force Memoranda 15-15, 18
April 1945, 15-7, 14 December 1944
and 15-6, 10 December 1944.

OPERATIONAL DEFINITIONS
SORTIE: A "sortie" is an aircraft airborne on a mission against the enemy;
synonymous with terms: aircraft dis-

patched, aircraft airborne, and aircraft taking off.

A/C CREDIT SORTIE: An "aircraft credit sortie" is deemed to have taken place when an airplane, ordered on an operational mission and in the performance of that mission, has entered an area where enemy anti-aircraft fire may be effective or where usual enemy fighter patrols occur; or when the airplane is in any way subjected to enemy attack.

EFFECTIVE SORTIE: An "effective sortie" is a sortie which carries out the purpose of the mission. An aircraft, when loaded with bombs or markers, is considered an effective sortie when it has released one or more armed bombs or markers, either by individually sighting or upon that of the formation leader, such sighting being made with the use of sighting or radar equipment, in a deliberate attempt to destroy or mark a target. Aircraft not loaded with bombs or markers are considered effective sorties if they carry out the purpose of the mission, e.g. drop leaflets, drop chaff, carry out weather flights, take photos, provide escort, carry out diversion as ordered, etc. Lost aircraft, unless definitely known to have been lost before reaching the target, are to be considered as effective sorties.

NON-EFFECTIVE SORTIE: A "non-effective sortie" is a sortie which for any reason fails to carry out the purpose of the mission.

JETTISONED: Bombs are considered to have been jettisoned: a) when they are dropped anywhere in safe condition, b) when they are released either armed or safe, in the interest of the safety of the aircraft or its crew rather than in an effort to destroy a target, or c) when dropped on operations without attempting to destroy or mark a target, d) when dropped either safe or armed by any other non-effective sortie.

OUR PERSONNEL CASUALTIES
MISSING: If personnel have not returned.
WOUNDED: (i.e. due to enemy action) qualified by such words as "slightly" or "seriously."
KILLED: (or FATALITIES when pertaining to aircraft accident deaths).
INJURED: (i.e. not due to enemy action) qualified by such words as "slightly" and "seriously."
ENEMY AIRPLANE LOSSES
DESTROYED: A. An enemy aircraft in flight shall be considered "destroyed" when: 1) seen to crash, 2) seen to disintegrate in the air or to be enveloped in flames, 3) seen to descend on friendly territory and be captured, or 4) pilot and entire crew seen to bail out. B. Enemy aircraft not in flight shall be considered "destroyed" when: 1) seen by photograph to have been blown apart or burned out, 2) seen by strike photo to have been within unobstructed lethal radius of a fragmentation bomb, 3) seen to sink in deep water, or 4) known to have been aboard carrier or other ship at time of confirmed sinking.
PROBABLY DESTROYED: Aircraft shall be considered "probably destroyed" when: 1) while in flight the enemy airplane is seen to break off combat under circumstances which lead to the conclusion that it must be a loss, although it is not seen to crash, 2) so damaged by bombing or strafing as to have less than an even chance of being repaired.
DAMAGED: Enemy aircraft shall be considered "damaged" when: while in flight it is so damaged as to require repair before beginning another mission, but has better than an even chance of continuing its flight, or 2) so damaged by bombing or strafing as to require repair before becoming operational.
OUR AIRCRAFT LOSSES
OPERATIONAL LOSSES
MISSING IN ACTION: Airplanes which

are known to be lost in enemy territory or at sea.
CATEGORY E (SALVAGE): An airplane damaged beyond economical repair while engaged in or in performance of an operational mission.
MISSING (UNKNOWN): An airplane reported as believed to have landed in friendly territory or on the Continent, unlocated and / or unheard of during the month of loss or thirty days thereafter. (applies only to operations after D-Day)
NON-OPERATIONAL LOSSES
WAR WEARY: Tactical aircraft which because of age, obsolescence, excessive repair requirements, or other reasons are classified as permanently unfit for combat.
NON-OP SALVAGE: An aircraft damaged beyond economical repair while not in performance of an operational mission (accidents not due to enemy action, training flights, etc.).

OTHER DEFINITIONS
MISSION: Any ordered flight.
SERVICE MISSION: A mission such as ferrying personnel, material, or aircraft within or between theatres of operations when no enemy opposition is expected. ("Trucking" was a service mission.)
TRAINING MISSION: A mission for training purposes.
OPERATIONAL MISSION (COMBAT OPERATIONAL MISSION OR COMBAT MISSION): An ordered flight with the designed purpose of operating against the enemy.
ENCOUNTER: An encounter is deemed to have taken place whenever unfriendly airplanes meet, whether a combat ensues or not.
COMBAT: Combat is deemed to have taken place whenever contact is made with opposing forces and fire is exchanged or developed by one side of the other.

DIVERSION: A diversion may be a real mission, and it is a movement regardless of size or composition to draw the enemy defenses away from the main effort.

DIVERSIONARY ATTACK: An action wherein a force actually attacks a target, other than the main target, for the purpose of drawing enemy defenses away from the area of the main effort.

MEAN POINT OF IMPACT (MPI): Assigned point on the earth's surface on which a formation of aircraft, bombing as a unit, is ordered to place the center of its bomb pattern.

LEAFLET DROPPING: The dropping of leaflets over enemy-held territory as part of the psychological warfare effort. (The British term for leaflets is "nickels.")

AWARDS AND DECORATIONS 17 AUGUST 1942 TO 15 MAY 1945

Medal of Honor: 14
Distinguished Service Cross: 220
Oak Leaf Cluster to DSC: 6
Distinguished Service Medal: 11
Oak Leaf Cluster to DSM: 1
Legion of Merit: 207
Oak Leaf Cluster to L of M: 2
Silver Star: 817
Oak Leaf Cluster to SS: 47
Distinguished Flying Cross: 41,497
Oak Leaf Cluster to DFC: 4,480
Soldier's Medal: 478
Oak Leaf Cluster to SM: 2
Purple Heart: 6,845
Oak Leaf Cluster to PH: 188
Air Medal: 122,705
Oak Leaf Cluster to AM: 319,595
Bronze Star: 2,972
Oak Leaf Cluster to BS: 12
Unit Citation: 27
Meritorious Service Unit Plaque: 19

PER · ARDUA · AD · ASTRA
McM
WAR SAVINGS CAMPAIGN 1943
PRESENTED BY THE AIR MINISTRY
IN RECOGNITION OF
SUCCESSFUL ACHIEVEMENT IN
WINGS FOR VICTORY WEEK

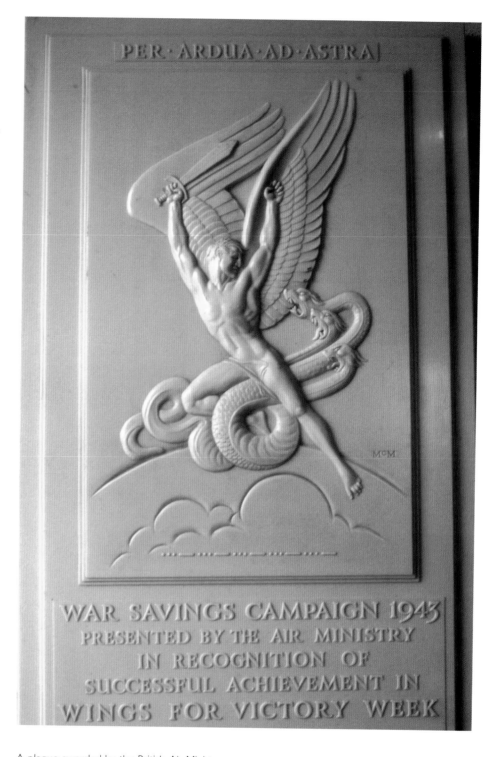

A plaque awarded by the British Air Ministry to towns, villages and counties in Britain in recognition of having raised money toward the purchase of an aircraft during the WW2 Wings For Victory Week Savings Campaign in 1943. It depicts the Archangel Michael as leader of the Celestial Armies fighting the rebel Angels led by Lucifer who is represented by the serpent.

PICTURE CREDITS

Photographs from the collection of the author are credited AC; photos by the author are credited PK; photos from the U.S. National Archives and Records Administration are credited NARA; photos from the Imperial War Museum are credited IWM; photos from the United States Air Force are credited USAF; photos from the U.S. Air Force Academy are credited USAF Academy; photos by Toni Frissell-The Library of Congress are credited Toni Frissell.

P2 PK; P3 top USAF, bottom both PK; P5 PK; P6 Toni Frissell; P7 AC; PP8-9 USAF; PP10-11 AC; P12 AC; P13 PK; P14 AC; P15 USAF Academy; PP16-17 NARA; PP18-19 AC; PP20-21 AC; PP22-23 AC; PP24-25 Charles E. Brown; PP26-27 courtesy Jonathan Falconer; P28 IWM; P29 USAF Academy; PP30-31 AC; PP32-22 AC; P35 NARA; PP36-37 all AC; PP38-39 AC; PP40-41 PK; P42 NARA; P43 top courtesy John Pawsey, bottom PK; P44 USAF; P45 AC; PP46-47 all AC; PP48-49 all PK; P50 top AC, bottom both PK; P51 AC; PP52-53 PK; PP54-55 USAF; P56 top AC, bottom PK; P57 PK; PP58-59 PK; PP60-61 PK; PP62-63 Toni Frissell; PP64-65 all AC; PP66-67 AC; PP68-69 San Diego Aerospace Museum; PP70-71 Mike Durning; PP72-73 AC; PP74-75 AC; PP76-77 AC; PP78-79 USAF; PP80-81 Michael Brazier; PP82-83 PK; PP84-85 NARA; P86 AC; PP88-89 courtesy Oscar Boesch; P90 courtesy Bill Sharpe; P91 both PK; PP92-93 NARA; PP94-95 USAF; PP96-97 AC; PP98-99 Zdenek Ondracek; PP100-101 USAF; P102 USAF; P105 NARA; P106 IWM; P107 AC; PP108-109 USAF; PP110-111 AC; P113 Toni Frissell; PP114-115 USAF; PP116-117 Simon Thomas; PP118-119 USAF; PP120-121 courtesy Andy Saunders; P122 AC; PP124-125 courtesy Jay and Bob Godfrey; PP126-127 courtesy Quentin Bland; P128 top AC, bottom Simon Thomas; P129 all AC; PP130-131 Toni Frissell; PP132-133 all Mark Brown USAAF; PP134-135 AC; PP136-137 AC; P138 Bundesarchiv; P139 Mark Brown USAAF; PP140-141 AC; P142 PK; PP144-145 USAF; P146 both AC; P149 USAF; PP150-151 AC; P152 20th Century Fox; P154 20th Century Fox; P155 AC; P156 both 20th Century Fox; P158 20th Century Fox; P159 20th Century Fox; P160 20th Century Fox; P161 20th Century Fox; P162 left Metro-Goldwyn-Mayer, right Warner Brothers; PP164-165 20th Century Fox; P166 AC; P167 Toni Frissell; P168 top USAF, bottom AC; P169 NARA; P171 NARA; P172 Toni Frissell; P174 Toni Frissell; P176 AC; PP178-179 all PK-courtesy Dave Hill; PP180-181 courtesy Merle Olmsted; PP182-183 courtesy Merle Olmsted; P184 AC; P185 Willem Honders; PP186-187 USAF; P188 both PK; P189 AC; P190 courtesy Merle Olmsted; P191 AC; PP192-193 courtesy Merle Olmsted; PP194-195 USAF; P197 courtesy Robert F. Cooper; P198 USAF; PP200-201 USAF; PP202-203 USAF; P205 PK; P207 AC; PP208-209 USAF; P210 AC; PP212-213 PK; P214r USAF; P215 left NARA, right PK; P216 USAF; P217 USAF; PP218-219 PK; PP220-221 AC; PP222-223 all USAAF; PP224-225 NARA; P226 Toni Frissell; PP228-229 USAF; PP230-231 USAF; P232 AC; PP234-235 AC; P237 courtesy of Albert Tyler; PP238-239 NARA; P240 USAF; P241 AC; PP242-243 NARA; P244 AC; P245 courtesy John Hurd; P246 AC; P247 courtesy of Roger Armstrong; PP248-249 USAF; P251 courtesy of Roger Armstrong; P252 AC; PP254-255 USAF; P256 AC; P257 AC; PP258-259 USAF; PP260-261 G. Phelps; P262 Phil Vabre; P263 AC; P264 AC; PP264-265 San Diego Aerospace Museum; PP266-267 Stephen Fox; PP268-269 DeGolyer Library-Southern Methodist University; P270 DeGolyer Library-Southern Methodist University; P271 courtesy Merle Olmsted; P272 both Tony Zeljeznjak; P273 San Diego Aerospace Museum; P275 Willem Honders; PP276-277 Mike Durning; P283 AC.

ACKNOWLEDGMENTS

To Margaret Mayhew, novelist, my wife and best friend, for all you are and all you do.

Grateful acknowledgment is made to the following for the use of their previously published material. All reasonable efforts have been made to contact the copyright holders.

James H. Doolittle, excerpts from *Statistical Summary of Eighth Air Force Operations European Theatre 1942-1945*.

Abbeville Press, excerpts from *One Last Look* by Philip Kaplan and Rex Alan Smith.

W.W. Norton, excerpts from *Serenade to the Big Bird* by Bert Stiles.

Algonquin Books, excerpts from *Screaming Eagle* by Major General Dale O. Smith.

Dutton and The estate of Martin Caidin, excerpts from *Black Thursday* by Martin Caidin.

The PutnamGroup, excerpts from *The Fall of Fortresses* by Elmer Bendiner.

Alfred A. Knopf / Random House, excerpts from *The War Lover* by John Hersey.

Random House, excerpts from *The Look of Eagles* by John Godfrey.

Viking Adult, excerpts from *Yesterday's Gone* by N.J. Crisp.

East Anglian Magazine and Watermill Books, excerpt from *Suffolk Summer* by John Appleby.

Ballantine Books, excerpts from *Twelve O'Clock High* by Beirne Lay Jr. and Sy Bartlett.

Tab Books, excerpts from *Celluloid Wings* by James Farmer.

Phalanx Publishing, excerpts from *The 357th Over Europe* by Merle Olmsted.

Eagle Editions Ltd, excerpts from *To War with The Yoxford Boys* by Merle Olmsted.

Leo Cooper, excerpts from *Combat Crew* by J John Comer.

20th Century Fox, excerpts from the screenplay of *Twelve O'Clock High*.

Quail House, excerpts from *U.S.A. The Hard Way* by Roger A. Armstrong.

The author is grateful to the many Eighth Air Force veterans whose enthusiastic participation in its research has made this book possible. Thanks too to the English farmers, landowners, and caretakers for permitting access to their properties for photography and exploration of the disused airfields of the Eighth Air Force. Particular thanks to the following whose contributions and assistance in the areas of book and article reference materials, additional photographs, interviews, the loan of personal memorabilia and ephemera, research, and other forms of assistance have aided enormously in the preparation of this book: Robert E. Abrams, Beth and David Alston, Joseph Anastasia, John T. Appleby, John Archer, Malcolm Bates, Charles Bednarik, Dana Bell, Mike Benarcik, Elmer Bendiner, Ceceilia Bessette, Robert Best, Tony Bianchi, Larry Bird, Quentin Bland, Oscar Boesch, Charles Bosshardt, Sam Burchell, Piers Burnett, Richard Bye, The estate of Martin Caidin, The Chicago Tribune Syndicate, Paul Connolly, Robert F. Cooper, Jack Currie, Harry Crosby, John Curtiss, James Dacey, Clayton David, James H. Doolittle, Lawrence Drew, Ira Eakin, Jacob Elias, Gary Eastman, Jonathan Falconer, Gilly Fielder, Lou Christian Wilson Fleming, W.W. Ford, Roger Freeman, Royal Frey, Adolf Galland, Ernest K. Gann, Bill Ganz, Jon Goldenbaum, James Goodson, Sol Greenberg, Stephen Grey, Bill Harvey, Harold Haft, Alan Healy, John Hersey, Bill Hess, Dave Hill, John Hurd, Jack Ilfrey, Randolf Jacobs, Richard Johnston, Robert S. Johnson, Claire L. Kaplan, Joseph J. Kaplan, Neal B. Kaplan, Myron Kielman, John Kirkland, Cleon T. Knapp, Walter Konantz, Curtis E. LeMay, Robert Loomis, Will Lundy, David C. Lustig, Walter Lybeck, William McCarran, Donald Maffett, Walker M. Mahurin, Bob Mallick, Mike Mathews, Glen R. Matson, A.D. McAllister, Jr., Carroll McColpin, John A. Miller, Len Morgan, Jim Murrey, Robert Mygatt, Keith Newhouse, Frank W. Nelson, Michael O'Leary, Merle Olmsted, Bill Overstreet, David Parry, John Pawsey, Horst Petzschler, Max Pinkerton, Douglas Radcliffe, Sidney Rapaport, Walton Rawls, Jack Raphael, Lynn Ray, Duane Reed, Alan Reeves, Paige Rense, Peter Rix, Andy Rooney, Andy Saunders, Neil Shakery, Dave Shelhamer, Susan Simpson, Paul Sink, Norman Smart, Dale O. Smith, Wanda Smith, Mark Stannard, Bert Stiles, Ken Stone, Lloyd Stovall, Robert C. Strobell, Calvin Swaffer, John B. Thomas Jr., David Wade, Diana Barnato-

Walker, Tim Wells, Robert White, Ray Wild, Ray Wild Jr., Ruth Wild, Raymond Wilson, Dennis Wrynn, Sam Young, Hub Zemke.

BIBLIOGRAPHY

Armstrong, Roger W., *USA The Hard Way*, Quail House, 1991

Becker, Cajus, *The Luftwaffe War Diaries*, Doubleday, 1968

Bendiner, Elmer, *The Fall of Fortresses*, G.P. Putnam's Sons, 1980

Bennett, John M., *Letters From England*, 1945

Birch, David, *Rolls-Royce and the Mustang*, Rolls-Royce Heritage Trust, 1987

Birdsall, Steve, *Log of the Liberators*, Doubleday & Co., 1973

Blue, Allan G., *B-24 Liberator*, Charles Scribner's Sons, 1977

Bowman, Martin, *Fields of Little America*, Wensum Books, 1977

Brown, Eric, *Wings of the Luftwaffe*, Airlife Publishing Ltd., 1993

Butcher, Geoffrey, *Next to a Letter from Home*, Sphere Books, 1987

Caidin, Martin, *Black Thursday*, E.P. Dutton, 1960

Coffey, Thomas, *Iron Eagle*, Crown, 1986

Costello, John, *Love, Sex and War 1939-45*, Pan Books, 1985

Craven, Wesley and Cate, James L., *The Army Air Forces in World War II*, The University of Chicago Press, 1948

Crisp, N.J., *Yesterday's Gone*, Viking Penguin, 1983

Crosby, Harry, *A Wing and A Prayer*, Harper Collins, 1983

Davis, Kenneth S., *Experience of War*, Doubleday & Co., 1965

Deighton, Len, *Bomber*, Harper & Row, 1970

Dunmore, Spencer, *Bomb Run*, Pan Books, 1971

Falconer, Jonathan, *The Bomber Command Handbook 1939-1945*, Sutton, 1998

Farmer, James, *Celluloid Wings*, Tab Books, 1984

Fletcher, Eugene, *Fletcher's Gang*, University of Washington Press, 1988

Francillion, Rene J., *USAAF Fighter Units Europe 1942-45*, Sky Books Press, 1970

Frankland, Noble, *The Bombing Offensive Against Germany*, Faber & Faber, 1965

Freeman, Roger A., *Airfields of the Eighth*, Battle of Britain Prints International, 1978

Freeman, Roger A., *The Mighty Eighth*, Macdonald, 1970

Freeman, Roger A., *The Mighty Eighth War Diary*, Jane's, 1981

Freeman, Roger A., *Mighty Eighth War Manual*, Jane's, 1984

Galland, Adolf, *The First and the Last*, Ballantine Books, 1954

Godfrey, John *The Look of Eagles*, Random House, 1958

Goodson, James, *Tumult in the Clouds*, St Martin's Press, 1983

Green, William, *Famous Bombers of the Second World War*, Macdonald, 1959

Hall, Grover C., *1,000 Destroyed*, Aero Publishers, Inc., 1978

Harris, Sir Arthur, *Bomber Offensive*, Collins, 1947

Hastings, Max, *Bomber Command*, Michael Joseph, 1979

Healy, Allan, *The 467th Bombardment Group*, privately printed, 1947

Hersey, John, *The War Lover*, Alfred A. Knopf, 1959

Hess, William, *P-47 Thunderbolt at War*, Doubleday & Co., 1976

Hutton, Bud, and Rooney, Andy, *Air Gunner*, Farrar & Rinehart, 1944

Ilfrey, Jack, *Happy Jack's Go-Buggy*, Exposition Press

Jablonski, Edward, *Flying Fortress*, Doubleday, 1965

Jablonski, Edward, *Air War*, Doubleday & Co., 1971

Johnson, Robert S., with Caidin, Martin, *Thunderbolt*, Ballantine Books, 1958

Kantor, Mackinlay, *Mission With LeMay*, Doubleday, 1965

Kaplan, Philip and Currie, Jack, *Round The Clock*, Random House, 1993

Koger, Fred, *Countdown*, Algonquin Books, 1990

Lay, Beirne, Jr. and Bartlett, Sy, *Twelve O'Clock High*, Bantam Books, 1950

Littlefield, Robert M., *Double Nickel—Double Trouble*, R.M. Littlefield, 1993

Lloyd, Ian, *Rolls-Royce, The Merlin at War*, Macmillan Press Ltd., 1978

Longmate, Norman, *The Bombers*, Arrow Books, 1988

Loomis, Robert D., *Great American Fighter Pilots of World War II*, Random House, 1961

Lyall, Gavin, *The War in the Air*, William Morrow, 1968

McCrary, John and Scherman, David, *First of the Many*, Simon and Schuster, 1944

Merrick, Ken, *By Day and By Night*, Ian Allan

Merrill, Sandra, *Donald's Story*, Tebidine, 1996

Mitchie, Allan A., *The Air Offensive Against Germany*, Henry Holt, 1943

Nelson, Derek and Parsons, Dave, *Hell-Bent for Leather: The Saga of the A2 and G1 Flight Jackets*, Motorbooks, 1990

O'Leary, Michael, *Mustang A Living Legend*, Osprey, 1987

Olmsted, Merle, *The Yoxford Boys*, Aero Publishers, Inc., 1971

Olmsted, Merle, *The 357th Over Europe*, Phalanx, 1994

Overy, R.J., *The Air War 1939-1945*, Stein & Day, 1980

Peaslee, Budd, *Heritage of Valor*, J.B. Lippincott, 1964

Robertson, Bruce, *U.S. Army and Air Force Fighters 1916-61*, Harleyford Pub. Ltd., 1961

Saward, Dudley, *'Bomber Harris'*, Cassell, 1984

Scutts, Jerry, *Lion in the Sky*, Patrick Stephens, 1987

Scutts, Jerry, *USAAF Heavy Bomber Units ETO and MYO 1942-45*, Sky Books Press, 1977

Shepard, Jim, *Paper Doll*, Dell, 1986

Shirer, William L., *The Rise and Fall of the Third Reich*, Simon and Schuster, 1960

Simmons, Kenneth W., *Kriegie*, Thomas Nelson & Sons, 1960

Slater, Harry F., *The Big Square A—A History of the 94th Bomb Group (H) 1942-1945*, 1980

Sloan, John, *The Route as Briefed*, Argus Press, 1946

Smith, Dale O., *Screaming Eagle*, Algonquin Books, 1990

Speer, Albert, *Inside the Third Reich*, The Macmillan Co., 1970

Speer, Frank, *Wingman*, Frank Speer, 1993

Steinbeck, John, *Once There Was a War*, Viking, 1958

Steinhoff, Johannes, *The Final Hours*, The N.A. Pub. Co., 1985

Stiles, Bert, *Serenade to the Big Bird*, W.W. Norton, 1947

Sunderman, James F., *World War II in the Air*, Franklin Watts, 1963

Sweetman, John, *Schweinfurt: Disaster in the Skies*, Ballantine Books, 1971

352nd Fighter Group Association, *The Blue-Nosed Bastards of Bodney*, 1990

Toliver, Raymond and Constable, Trevor, *Fighter Aces*, The Macmillan Co., 1965

Turner, Richard E., *Big Friend, Little Friend*, Doubleday & Co., 1969

Turner, Richard, *Mustang Pilot*, New English Library, 1975

USAF Historical Studies No. 156, *Development of the Long-Range Escort Fighter*, MA / AH Publishing

Varian, Horace L., *The Bloody Hundredth: Missions and Memories of a World War II Bomb Group*

Verrier, Anthony, *The Bomber Offensive*, B.T. Batsford, 1968

Vietor, John, *Time Out*, Richard R. Smith, 1951

Wagner, Ray, *Mustang Designer*, Orion Books, 1990

Washington Infantry Journal Press, *The 56th Fighter Group in World War II*, Infantry Journal Press, 1948

Watry, Charles, and Hall, Duane, *Aerial Gunners: The Unknown Aces of World War II*, California Aero Press, 1986

Woolnough, John, *Stories of the Eighth*, The Eighth Air Force News, 1983

Yeager, Chuck and Janos, Leo, *Yeager*, Bantam Books, 1985

Zemke, Hub with Freeman, Roger A., *Zemke's Wolf Pack*, Orion Books, 1988

INDEX